Contents

GLOBAL JOURNALISM

INTERNATIONAL COMMUNICATION

THIRD EDITION

JOHN C. MERRILL

EDITOR

University of Missouri

Longman *Publishers USA*

Global Journalism: Survey of International Communication, Third Edition

Copyright © 1995, 1991, 1983 by Longman Publishers USA.

Longman, 10 Bank Street, White Plains, N.Y. 10606

Associated companies:
Longman Group Ltd., London
Longman Cheshire Pty., Melbourne
Longman Paul Pty., Auckland
Copp Clark Longman Ltd., Toronto

Executive editor: Pamela Gordon
Assistant editor: Hillary B. Henderson
Production editor: Electronic Publishing Services Inc./Linda Moser
Cover design: Ed Smith Design
Production supervisor: Richard Bretan

Library of Congress Cataloging-in-Publication Data
Global journalism : survey of international communication / John C.
    Merrill, editor.—3rd ed.
        p.   cm.
    Includes bibliographical references and index.
        ISBN 0-8013-1438-0
        1. Journalism.   I. Merrill, John Calhoun, 1924–.
    PN4775.G56   1994
    070.4—dc20   94-22482
                                                            CIP

345678910 CRS 0807060504030201

Preface

Again, with this third edition of *Global Journalism: Survey of International Communication,* we are trying to provide a survey of the issues facing world journalism and to describe the broad dimensions of international mass media. Thus, it is a two-pronged book that introduces students to global controversies and perplexing questions while providing them with a substantive framework of the physical aspects of international journalism.

The scope of this edition, however, is significantly broader than that of the earlier editions. In both parts of this book, new chapters and sections have been added. For example, in Part I, "The Global Perspective," the student will now find these new chapters: "Barriers to Media Development," "Freedom of the Press Around the World," "International Journalism Ethics," and "Global Advertising and Public Relations." Part I now has eight chapters instead of four as in earlier editions.

In Part II, "The World's Regions," the chapters have been expanded from six to seven. The old chapter on Europe is now two chapters, "Western Europe" and "East Central and Southeastern Europe/Russia, and the Newly Independent States." Another change is that Chapter 12, "Sub-Saharan Africa," has been divided into three main parts—East Africa, West Africa, and Southern Africa—each addressed by a different contributor.

This enlargement of the book means that additional contributors, writing on their areas of expertise, have been included. New contributors are Edmund Lambeth and Tim Gallimore of the University of Missouri; Kuldip R. Rampal of Central Missouri State University; Robert Stevenson of the University of North Carolina; Dean Kruckeberg of the University of Northern Iowa; Douglas Ann Newsom of Texas Christian University; Bob Carrell of the University of Oklahoma; Paul Grosswiler of the University of Maine; M. Kent Sidel and Aralynn Abare McMane of the University of South Carolina; Owen V. Johnson of Indiana University; Arnold S. de Beer, Francis P. Kasoma, Eronini Megwa, and Elanie Steyn from three regions of sub-Saharan Africa.

Other new contributors are Gonzalo Soruco and Leonardo Ferreira of the University of Miami (Florida), Herbert Strentz of Drake University, and Vernon Keel of Wichita State University. Remaining from the second edition are these contributors: Lowndes (Rick) F. Stephens of the University of South Carolina, Christine Ogan of Indiana University, Anne Cooper Chen of Ohio University, and Anju Grover Chaudhary of Howard University.

A book such as this is needed today more than ever before. Although books on media systems of various countries and regions of the world have been proliferating, and numerous tomes discuss such topics as news flow, third-world concerns, global propaganda, press freedom, news agencies, international broadcasting, and individual newspapers, there is a place for a single survey book that attempts to pull together the highlights of all this material and to summarize it for the uninitiated student. This is the purpose of *Global Journalism: Survey of International Communication,* third edition.

Certainly, this book does not pretend to be exhaustive or to probe the depths of issues of media systems. It is designed to give an overview, a survey of global journalism. It should serve well in a course dealing with comparative world journalism or international communication or as a supplemental text for a basic journalism or social science course.

All journalism students need at least an introduction to the world's media so that they may better appreciate and evaluate the media systems of their own countries. Such an introduction should go a long way in helping students shed their provincialism and begin thinking of their own press system in an international context. Since the 1960s, the study of global communication has been growing rapidly in schools and departments of journalism or communication. Courses in this broad area have become important fixtures in most curricula, a far cry from the 1950s, when only a handful of universities offered just a single course in the area.

Courses in global communication are now generally recognized to be as important for a journalism major as, for example, courses in world history would be for a student majoring in history. This volume is presented as such an introduction to the world's journalism and, if used intelligently and creatively with collateral readings, guest lectures, and the like, should provide insights into the scope and issues of global journalism. In addition, it should give the student an overview of the outlines and dimensions of various press systems of the world.

Global Journalism should, of course, be used in concert with the professor's fresh lectures, with classroom visits by resource persons from other countries with information from embassies and consulates, and with special oral reports on aspects of a country's journalism by various members of the class. None of this, however, will diminish the fact that the very nature of a book such as this makes some content somewhat dated even on the day it is published. But the editor and contributors have tried to keep it as contemporary as possible and hope that both professors and students will update it as they use it.

Because this is an attempt to give a panoramic view of journalism around the world, we purposely use rather broad strokes to paint our picture. Also we eschew minor qualifiers and footnotes to move readers forward rapidly and to acquaint them briskly with some of the generally agreed-on ideas and data relative to international journalism. We don't consider this volume a reference work as much as an overview and an introduction to communication problems and issues.

Quotations and statistical data, of course, are important. Although we do include a few such references, they have been kept to a minimum. Readers desiring to compensate for what they may see as statistical or evidential deficiencies are encouraged to consult reference works in international communication or more topical books listed in the bibliography for each chapter.

Information for this book has been obtained from innumerable sources—analyses of foreign publications, lectures, scholarly papers, articles, books, government pamphlets, interviews, embassy materials, journals and magazines of all types, and newspapers. It also should be noted that the editor and the contributors to this book have all had occasion to see press systems firsthand and have had numerous interviews and conversations with leading journalistic figures in the media and in academia the world over.

I am grateful to the following reviewers who read the manuscript and provided helpful suggestions:

Huber Ellingsworth, University of Tulsa

Festus Eribo, East Carolina State University

MacDonald Kalé, California State University

Casmus Nwokeafor, George Mason University

Kenneth Starck, University of Iowa

Chris Ulasi, University of Texas at Austin

One final note: In a very real sense, all the contributors to this work are coauthors; the chapters were all designed and written especially for *Global Journalism* and are not reprints from other publications. As editor, I would like to express my deep appreciation to, and admiration of, the contributors who have worked so diligently with me to bring out this third edition.

John C. Merrill

Introduction

International and intercultural communication courses have burst forth in recent years as popular courses in colleges and universities, not only in the United States, but also in many other countries of the world. This book is designed primarily for journalism and communications courses in this broad area of concern, for professors and students who are interested in an introductory and general survey of global media concerns and comparative communication systems.

Part I introduces the student to basic global communications theories, problems, and controversies. It provides a wide perspective on international issues such as press freedom, developmental barriers, the flow of information, journalistic ethics, and trends in global journalism. In addition, attention is given to international advertising and public relations, something new in this edition.

After Part I sets the global stage, the various regional press systems are introduced in Part II. Part II presents a substantive, descriptive overview of the dimensions of journalism in the main regions of the world. Thus, this is a survey book, which in its broad reaches is designed as a descriptive and comparative textbook.

The media systems described in Part II, as well as the more theoretical and controversial concerns dealt with in Part I, combine to provide a general picture of the physical and ideational dimensions of the world's journalism that will remain useful even as the student's knowledge grows. I believe that basic tendencies, paradigm ideologies of press systems, and underlying issues in global journalism change rather slowly—although events since about 1990 might refute that belief. Even the physical dimension (leading newspapers, news agencies, structure of broadcasting, etc.) in the various world regions tends to evolve extremely slowly. The student can glean useful concepts and patterns of world journalism from this book, even though year by year various media units (newspapers, magazines, and so on) continue to appear and disappear.

GLOBAL MEDIA PROBLEMS

Let us focus on some basic communication problems that global journalists face as they go about their work of spreading news and news-related information. Psychological and physical barriers exist in all countries; these are reinforced by a host of problems, such as cultural differences, languages, definitions of journalistic concepts, educational and economic deficiencies, control mechanisms, and propaganda proclivities. Such communication barriers constantly block global journalistic progress and frustrate international understanding.

In spite of improved international relations, distrust and misunderstanding among people are commonplace; it is problematic whether such global communications networks as CNN and Star TV are improving or harming the world's psychic nerves, creating global harmony or stimulating international friction. There is no doubt that the world's masses are being increasingly exposed to global communication. All who are in a position to think about such things are aware that the world is still in crisis and that one hasty or irresponsible action (or message) might plunge the world into a disastrous, even catastrophic, war. Although the cold war is over, the planet is plagued with warring factions, and human suffering appears to be on the increase.

Representatives of nations meet constantly to discuss world problems, design plans, try to negotiate peaceful solutions, attempt to allay fears, gain global justice, and improve world understanding through better communication. But seated with these men and women at United Nations' and other forums are deep-rooted prejudices and suspicions, strong national feelings, and vested interests; beneath the smooth patina of the words are long-simmering antagonisms, traditional power politics, and fundamental misunderstandings. And all the while, the media of mass communication are pouring a glut of messages over vast audiences. The global press—the giant organism holding together cultural and nationalistic groups—is busy "reporting" and "interpreting" the constant succession of world crises and conferences dealing with them.

The global media wield tremendous power as purveyors of vital information. They have the potential to erase erroneous impressions and stereotypes and to ease tensions; they can shake people from complacency or lull them into an unthinking and dangerous sleep. With psychological warfare raging fiercely, the media find themselves in a position of tremendous responsibility today. Modern technology has made the world become a small house in which human beings are locked together, with everyone forced to share the consequences of one another's actions.

Physical means of communicating news and disseminating it throughout the world are well developed and capable of providing the quantity of messages needed for proper understanding among peoples. But as messages flow more rapidly and in greater quantity than ever before, questions of quality, impact, significance, balance, truth, and motive come to the forefront. Although on the surface adequate information appears to be moving through most parts of the world, government pressures, secrecy, censorship, and propaganda impede the free flow of news.

As some governments get larger and more complex in bureaucratic structure, the problems of media access to basic and relevant information become more difficult. And as other governments, new and struggling to get some kind of viability, creep toward modernity often under defensive, secretive, and authoritarian leaders, media hardly exist, and the news flow is anything but free flowing. At the same time, sincere and normally cooperative government representatives find that with more exposure to the mass media, they are misrepresented—their statements are twisted and their meaning is distorted, all of which can lead toward a climate of suspicion and mistrust on the part of public officials and, in turn, to a reluctance on their part to say very much for public consumption. As governments become more sensitive and cautious when confronted by the media, the universe of frank and open news reporting is restricted, and honest and thoroughgoing dialogue becomes more difficult.

A BASIC CONCERN: FREEDOM

On the world scene, as on the national scene, truthful and unfettered media can best serve the people. Such media freedom can go far to mend differences among nationalities, classes, and groups; it can frustrate the plans of war-hungry leaders and rulers. The realization of these possibilities is a prodigious task for the media, one that requires the acceptance and application of the free-press theory; for only with a free press can people have more than a foggy or lopsided picture of what is happening around them.

Throughout the world, freedom of communication is an ideal; no country has actually achieved a pure version of it. This ideal is simply on a continuum somewhere between absolute control and complete freedom. Recent surveys and studies tend to indicate that in many ways freedom of communication is not firmly entrenched globally. Restrictive laws are proliferating, sanctions of many kinds are hindering the free workings of the media, and authoritarian persons and groups are moving in to guide media activities.

The so-called "post–cold war world" is full of would-be media controllers as new nations try to get a footing and political stability. Government leaders desire political and social viability and realize that too much communication freedom endangers national stability and the status quo. Hence it is quite understandable that the natural national tendency is toward more media regulation. Control, then, is the common—not the exceptional—state of things in the world, and relatively free media today may be highly restricted tomorrow.

Even the casual observer will note world journalism today is subjecting people's minds to a ceaseless bombardment of messages calculated to influence and control. Internally, a nation's media try to mold the state into a consolidated, smooth-running machine ready to repel any outside danger, and externally, they direct their broadsides at real or potential enemies. This may be a practical course in times of danger, but it does not make for objective, information-oriented communication within or among countries.

Perhaps the media have come in for too great a share of blame for this situation. Responsibility to all people of all nations is a fine concept, but responsible media in an irresponsible social or government context are hardly to be hoped for except by those too uninformed or too idealistic to know better. And the individual citizen may be to blame for the bias and government propaganda that permeate large segments of world journalism today.

Many critics say that the media are actually hindering world understanding and cooperation and that they are stretching animosities among nations to dangerous dimensions and thereby worsening the international psychic crisis. This does not seem an unlikely thesis. It implies that exceptional incidents are disseminated as important news; it further implies that eccentric and dangerous people are the subject of much of the news. In short, it implies that unreal and alarmist news dominates newspaper columns and television screens.

MEDIA AS AGITATORS

When we examine the world media today, we get the feeling that the jangled nerves of the world's populations can hardly be eased by the newspapers—and certainly not by TV. On the contrary, anxieties are created, magnified, and perpetuated; religion is set against religion, social class against social class, race against race, and nationality against nationality. Instead of being conveyors of enlightenment and harmony, the national media systems tend too often to be mere extensions of factional and party differences and animosities, thus doing a good job of increasing irritations and suspicions among groups and governments and giving distorted pictures of various nations.

Very few observers would deny that the news media are involved largely in creating and destroying images. Certainly, the world's communication channels have been all but choked in recent years by inflammatory and slanted messages concerning explosive situations in the Balkans, the Middle East, the states of the former Soviet Union, the struggling nations of Africa, and parts of Asia and Latin America. Readers, listeners, and viewers searching for the "real story" are often left bewildered. Contradictions in the news, discrepancies among world news agencies, and opinions creeping more and more into news columns and network newscasts puzzle them and frustrate their quest for truth.

All indications are that the world's consumers of news and views are in for a long siege of ideological messages. There have been few truces in global psychological warfare. As technology pushes mass messages into the more remote regions and saturates ever-growing populations, the world's psychosis is bound to worsen. Truth in the messages is no assurance of enlightenment or emotional stabilization; recent history has shown clearly that even the most truthful statement can boomerang, that it can appear as something quite different when viewed from the perspective of a particular audience's traditional beliefs, desires, and expectations.

The mass media should not be looked on as a panacea for the world's problems. The most powerful radio transmitters and the most enterprising and honest newspapers and magazines will not be able to substitute for international cooperation and progress on the diplomatic level. Mass communication is obviously no substitute for direct involvement of persons and their technologies in the world crisis; international action certainly speaks louder than mass-oriented words.

Worldwide envy, resentment, suspicion, and hatred build emotional walls against the most objective and well-intentioned printed word and erect mental jamming stations against the most honest broadcast. When one considers that in every nation the government uses news as a weapon, with no sustained attempts at honesty or objectivity, the task of the mass media in the fight for peace and understanding takes on a dismal cast.

SIGNS FOR A BETTER FUTURE?

Communication specialists look with some hope to the future. This slight optimism seems to be based mainly on technological advances. Many believe that the growth of satellite communication to all parts of the globe, plus a plethora of new interactive and computer-based systems and cheaper hardware, will stimulate world communication and potentially bring us all into McLuhan's global village.

We are well into the final decade of the twentieth century. Europe's hard-line communist regimes are evaporating, but authoritarian forces of other kinds are rearing their heads. Especially daunting are the aspirations for national identity of various peoples of the world; communications media are increasingly looked on as political and ideological instruments for increasing certain power bases rather than for harmonizing various factions. Instantaneous messages precipitate immediate crises around the world, giving little time for calm and rational consideration of events and inflammatory statements.

One might feel that with the changes in the former Soviet Union and the seeming discrediting of authoritarian Communism in Europe, things are getting better. But there are still plenty of trouble spots around the globe—especially in China, North Korea, the Balkans, parts of Africa, and the Middle East. And the world's media give increasing attention to stories of terrorism, factional fighting, coups and rumors of coups, and assorted details of increasing worldwide criminal activities. So the overall picture remains rather dismal.

*   *   *

With this introductory discussion of general global journalism problems behind us, we are ready to head into the main body of this book—a volume that has been almost entirely rewritten and expanded from the second edition. Part I will bring to the forefront some important contemporary issues and problems in international journalism and major aspects of of communication developments in a worldwide context. Part II will discuss the more specific and substantive matters of global journalism (e.g., leading media, government–press relations, journalism education, and media economics) in even more detail than in earlier editions. In part II, the descriptive and comparative dimensions of the book will be found. It is hoped that the student will get a good introduction to (1) the broad problem areas of global journalism and the international communication controversies and (2) the basic components of the media systems of countries in the world's main regions.

part **I**

The Global Perspective

News Agencies ?

0

chapter **1**

Global Media Philosophies

Edmund B. Lambeth

The late Wernher von Braun, the German rocket scientist recruited by the Americans after World War II, once speculated that the chief influence of the space program would be its unifying impact on humans exposed repeatedly to satellite pictures of the planet taken from Earth orbit. He believed that the planet itself would eventually replace the nation-state as the primary unit of reference and analysis. The late Marshall McLuhan's vision of a "global village"—in which media foster a common consciousness—is an even more advanced version of von Braun's forecast.

It is easy for a casual student of mass media, circa the 1990s, to be persuaded by von Braun's prediction and McLuhan's metaphor. With computers and satellites, corporate communication conglomerates—mostly based in Western democracies—now reach around the globe. They dispense a steady stream of news, talk, music, sports, drama, and advertising. Moreover, with the collapse of the Cold War and the demise of totalitarianism within the former Soviet bloc nations, democratic political systems have begun to emerge—albeit at times uncertainly—in Central and Eastern Europe as well as in Latin America and parts of Asia. Some are tempted to conclude that it is only a matter of time before democracy and democratic mass media systems will become the norm throughout the planet.

Were this, in fact, the case, there would be little more than historical reasons to examine the philosophies underlying media systems around the globe. But any expectation that a worldwide global news system would evolve quickly to serve increasingly homogeneous democratic nation-states has been shown to be unrealistic.

As succeeding chapters of this book will document, there are major socioeconomic, political, and cultural differences within and between national and regional media. New media technologies are not uniformly available. Indeed, many nations across the planet are without access to contemporary media. Dictatorial regimes predominate in Africa; the governmental initiators of China's new "socialist market economy" still permit little of what the older democracies would regard as genuine press freedom. And the news media of newly liberated states in Eastern and Central Europe are far from free of the debilitating tendencies of a half century and more of totalitarian political rule. Moreover, these nations have quite distinctive historical and cultural backgrounds—differences that are beginning to be expressed assertively in the post-1989 environment.

No citizen of the planet who hopes to be well-informed about mass media can fail to take these countervailing factors into account. They qualify and place into context the recent socioeconomic, political, and cultural changes in Eastern and Central Europe, Latin America, and Asia. And they show that there have been limits to the impact of recent political changes and to the globalizing reach of new media technology. Nor, in the hands of transnational media corporations, has such technology been shown to be inherently democratic.

Moreover, the post–Cold War era is proving to be more dynamic and less predictable than previously expected. In short, the news media and the philosophical systems underlying them are in flux. Calipers are needed to take their measure.

THE USES OF PHILOSOPHY

In this intellectual enterprise, philosophy—derived from the Greek *philia* (love) and *sophia* (wisdom)—can be a major resource in at least four ways. First, philosophy can help us describe and distinguish the major values that inform and influence the operation of national and regional media systems. Second, knowing the philosophical orientations within news media systems can help us understand the way those systems define their attitudes toward and stake in the emerging global communication networks. Third, philosophy can provide a conceptual framework for critically evaluating news media performance, whatever the nature of the political system in which a nation's media operate. Finally, philosophy can give us the means to compare news media systems.

It was with some of these uses in mind that in 1956 communication scholars Fred Siebert, Theodore Peterson, and Wilbur Schramm articulated what they termed *Four Theories of the Press*. Their typology, illustrated in Table 1.1, consisted of the authoritarian, libertarian, social responsibility, and Soviet Communist concepts of the press. Several generations of aspiring journalists and educators were influenced by their approach to media philosophy.

Now, four decades later, it is clear the approach fails to fully match reality. The Soviet bloc is no more. Libertarianism is more an ideal and stringent construal of standards of freedom of speech and of the press than a description of any particular existing state's system. The post-colonial era produced new perspectives on the media not represented in the *Four Theories* typology. Some nations, especially in Europe, are continuing to evolve a system that does not fit well under any of the four older classifications. But the social responsibility theory, first fully articulated in 1947 by a private commission headed by University of Chicago President Robert Maynard Hutchins, remains influential today, even as it is under revision.

TABLE 1.1 Siebert–Peterson–Schramm typology

Authoritarian	Libertarian	Communist	Social Responsibility
Developed in sixteenth- and seventeenth-century Europe	Arose in England in the late seventeenth century; spread to America and the European Continent	Arose in the early twentieth-century USSR	Arose in the mid-twentieth-century United States out of the libertarian tradition
Stemmed from the absolute power of the monarch	Stemmed from Enlightenment thought and natural rights	Stemmed from Marx and Lenin	Stemmed from the writings of the Commission on Freedom of the Press and other critics of the libertarian press
Purpose: To support state and leadership	Purpose: To help find truth, inform, interpret, entertain	Purpose: To support the Marxist system, to serve the people	Purpose: Mainly to inform and educate, to help social progress
Licensing, censorship, autocratic power, laws	Editorial self-determination; separation of state and press	Theoretically, the people own the press and can use it	Press should be open to anyone with something to say
No criticism or threat to the power structure is permitted	Media controlled by owners in a free market of ideas and by courts	Media controlled by the Communist Party government apparatus	Social responsibility of the press is more important than its freedom
Owned by ruler, party, or private persons	Nothing forbidden from publication prior to publication	Media cannot criticize Party objectives	Controlled by community opinion and consumer action and by codes of ethics, press councils, etc.
Forerunners: Hobbes, Hegel, Machiavelli	Private ownership	Owned "by the people"	No publishing of socially harmful information or invasion of private rights
Examples today: Iran, Paraguay, Nigeria	Forerunners: Locke, Milton, Mill, Adam Smith	Developers: Marx, Lenin, Stalin, Mao, Castro, Gorbachev	Private ownership, but threat of government interference to assure public service
	Examples today: United States, Japan, Germany	Examples today: China, Cuba, North Korea	Examples today: none; several countries tending, including the United States

SOURCE: Adapted from Fred S. Siebert, Theodore Peterson, and Wilbur Schramm, *Four Theories of the Press* (Urbana: University of Illinois Press, 1956).

However inadequate the *Four Theories* approach is as contemporary description, its concepts are still useful in constructing a historical sketch of the evolution of social and political philosophies and of the ideological orientations of media systems that arose with them. Moreover, the media systems of many nations combine elements of the four theories in ways that make the four theories analytically useful. However, the *Four Theories* approach needs to be supplemented by the reflections of contemporary scholarship.

John Merrill, in *The Imperative of Freedom* (1974; 1990), introduces a schematic that illustrates the dynamics of philosophical ideas as they are applied to press and state relationships. (See Figure 1.1.) Arguing for the centrality of freedom, Merrill shows that it can be lost in either collectivist or capitalistic societies and has unique features in societies that fall between those poles. He also includes important forms not identified within the *Four Theories* typology.

Authoritarianism

The political ideas that gave the twentieth-century dictators such as Adolf Hitler of Germany, Francisco Franco of Spain, Benito Mussolini of Italy, Idi Amin of Uganda, and Juan Perón of Argentina had ancient origins. They can be as primitive as the human lust to seize power and as synthetic as the rationales advanced to ensconce and preserve the power of kings, colonels, and tribal chiefs. Because in authoritarian cultures the state is the ultimate end rather than the individuals within it, the news media in the authoritarian regime must serve the state.

Protection of individuals is ancillary to preservation of the state; hence laws serve the head of state, who is the ultimate interpreter of law, either directly or through designees. Obligation is thus to the state and its leader, who often presents himself or herself as the source of superior knowledge, wisdom, and power. Whatever degree of news media independence can survive in an authoritarian state is usually exercised over the narrowest of ranges. Because laws provide no ultimate protection for the press, sources of internal media opposition to the regime are often either few or weak.

Dictators or their intellectual courtiers often have turned to the books of Plato (427-347 B.C.)—*The Republic, Statesman*, and *Laws*—for a justification of their authoritarian regimes. Most of their reconstructions of his views have ignored the humane elements in Plato, such as his ideal of public service, and have drawn instead on the Platonic argument for the superiority of a philosopher-king to perpetuate authoritarian rule.

Of much more direct use to aspiring autocrats have been the manipulative strategies of Niccolò Machiavelli (1469-1527), the Florentine diplomat. His Renaissance era classic, *The Prince*, advised rulers to keep power by behaving like both the fox and the lion. It likewise could be read as a model for politicians, bureaucrats, and press secretaries who would rely on artifice in coping with news media.

Much more straightforward, Thomas Hobbes (1588-1679), in *The Leviathan*, propounded a sovereign to rescue humankind from a life that is "solitary, poor, nasty, brutish and short." The sovereign was to rule not by divine right but under a sophisticated contract that required total obedience in return for total security. Historians have

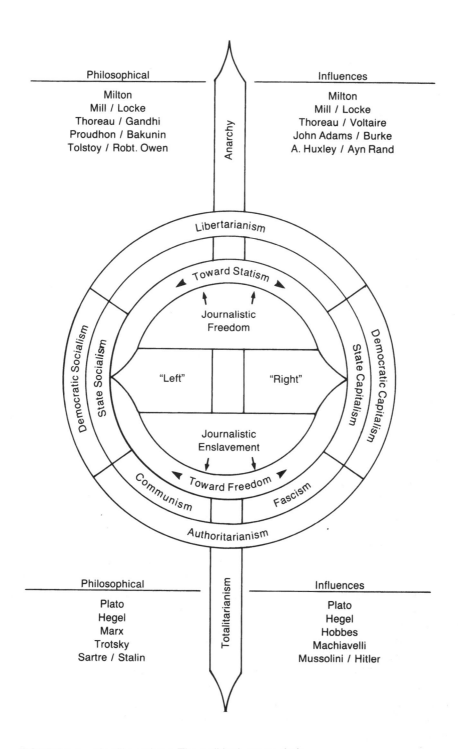

FIGURE 1.1 Merrill typology: The political–press circle

SOURCE: John C. Merrill, *The Imperative of Freedom* (New York: Hastings House, 1974), p. 42.

noted that dictators often have risen to power in societies whose democratically in-clined elites, including journalists, have not read deeply enough in these classics—either figuratively or literally—to forewarn themselves of either their fallacies or their persuasive power.

Once established, a state seeking to preserve itself could have few philosopher friends as steadfast and serviceable as G. W. F. Hegel (1770-1831), an admirer of Napoleon and of Prussian authoritarianism. Hegel openly rejected the Judeo-Christian idea that God, reason, nature, and spirit are prior to and superior to the state. Like-wise, by his lights genuine freedom could only be derived from subordinating oneself to the wishes of the state, which he defined as "the march of God through the world." Hegel, through his principal books—*Philosophy of Law* and *Philosophy of History*—helped create what political theorist William Ebenstein calls "the cult of the state." As fascist apostles of that cult, Hitler and Mussolini would enroll journalists as state prop-agandists. Authoritarians of every stripe aspire to destroy the independence of the press and recruit the news media to their own service.

Libertarianism

No philosopher is more closely associated with the intellectual structure of the liber-tarian tradition than John Locke (1632-1704), Oxford tutor, physician, civil servant, and fellow of the Royal Society. His *Two Treatises of Government* and *Essay Con-cerning Human Understanding* are said to have founded, respectively, both classical liberalism and empiricism.

Two Treatises of Government articulates ideas which, although modified in ap-plication, provide a foundation for free government and free press: (1) government by consent of the governed; (2) equal protection of the laws administered by an inde-pendent judiciary; (3) separation of legislative and administrative authority; (4) pro-tection of life, liberty, and property, all of which are inalienable rights that precede and are not derived from government; and (5) the right of the people to revolt and dis-card governments that attempt to trample liberty. Little wonder that Locke was em-braced and echoed so faithfully by American revolutionaries such as Thomas Jeffer-son, Thomas Paine, and Benjamin Franklin, all of whom used the press to propagate the application of Lockean ideas to citizens of the then-unfolding American continent. They also drew upon Locke in designing the U.S. Constitution, the First Amendment of which protects speech, press, religion, petition, and assembly, all of them vital to free journalism.

Locke's affirmation of private poverty grew by the next century into the sturdy oak of laissez-faire capitalism advocated and elaborated in *The Wealth of Nations* by Adam Smith (1723-1790). In its shade, captains of manufacturing—including fledgling newspaper moguls—accumulated the wealth that financed the modern industrial state. Excesses of capitalism—poor working conditions, child labor, festering indus-trial slums—emerged so dramatically early in the nineteenth century that Lockean and laissez-faire liberals were forced to rethink the doctrine.

In the 1830s, a French aristocrat had reminded thinkers and citizens alike that democracy could develop a form of tyranny more fatal than a king's edicts—the tyranny of a majority capable of inhibiting the expression of dissent, such as against unbridled capitalism. Alexis de Tocqueville (1805–1859), the French aristocrat turned democratic champion, struck this latter theme in his *Democracy in America*, published in 1830 and 1835. He wrote:

> The authority of a king is purely physical, and it controls the actions of the subject without subduing his private will; but the majority possesses a power which is physical and moral at the same time; it acts upon the will as well as upon the actions of men, and it represses not only all contest, but all controversy.

Tocqueville's warning about striking a proper balance between individualism and democratic equality influenced the contents of the historic treatise *On Liberty*, by John Stuart Mill (1806–1873). Mill, smitten with Tocqueville's argument, went on himself to craft a thesis on free expression that many regard as the strongest defense available to a free society as well as a free press. Especially powerful is a passage from *On Liberty* in which Mill identifies four reasons why society should not suppress the assertion of controversial facts and opinions.

First, such opinions may be true. To think otherwise presumes one's own infallibility. Second, they may be partly true—and contain that very portion of the truth needed for the emergence of the whole truth. Third, suppression of contrary viewpoints is tantamount to holding one's own opinions as though they were prejudices. And, finally, to hold one's opinions as prejudices is to risk losing their effect on our conduct and character.

In Tocqueville and in Mill we see a new emphasis on the need to protect freedom by assuring the social health of the body politic. In their view, merely preventing government from interfering with free expression is not enough. Societies can be truly free—and "liberal"—only by building intellectual integrity and moral character within individuals as well as social institutions. Only then will democracies have the wisdom to steer clear of the eddies and undertows that lead to the slow decline into tyranny.

Tocqueville and Mill kept alive a debate on the nature and definition of permissible limits of free expression that is reflected in contemporary press debates on libel, privacy, confidentiality of sources, and the public's right to know. Their essays still are relevant to the contemporary debates on freedom and responsibility in journalism and mass communication and also to the continuing debate over a New World Information and Communication Order.

Social Responsibility

The strand of Western social philosophy that emphasized the centrality of "community" or "public" can be traced to locales as different as Athens, Jerusalem, Geneva, Paris, London, and Plymouth Rock, Massachusetts. It runs like a thread—sometimes thin, sometimes thick—through the written works of Aristotle, Rousseau, Bentham, and Mill. In contemporary letters, Robert Bellah and his colleagues refreshed its meaning in their book, *Habits of the Heart: Individualism and Commitment in American Life* (1986).

However, the document that most fully embodies the philosophy of public service journalism is the 1947 Hutchins Commission report, *A Free and Responsible Press*. Its authors gave their most cogent definition of journalism's role when they set forth the "requirements" of a free and responsible press. They argued that the press should provide:

1. A truthful, comprehensive, and intelligent account of the day's events in a context which gives them meaning.
2. A forum for the exchange of comment and criticism.
3. Coverage of the opinions, attitudes, and conditions of the constituent groups of society.
4. Vigorous editorial leadership, by presenting and clarifying the goals and values of society.
5. Full access to the day's intelligence.

Were these five desiderata viewed as goals, there would appear to be little in them to which a conscientious journalist could object. What ignited the ire of media leaders, however, was the apparent commission sentiment that government should be the "residuary legatee of responsibility for an adequate press performance," in the words of William Ernest Hocking, author of an accompanying report, *Freedom of the Press: A Framework of Principle* (1947, p. 182). In short, the Hutchins Commission aroused fear by media executives that instead of pursuing its legitimate role in restraining interference with free press and speech, government would actively seek to define and promote conditions of free expression.

In 1980 William L. Rivers, Wilbur Schramm, and Clifford Christians wrote *Responsibility in Mass Communication*—a sequel to *Four Theories of the Press*. In it they agreed with Hocking that the government should serve as "residuary legatee" for press responsibility. However, they added:

> . . . government inherits such responsibility as is not adequately borne by the media themselves or by the public. But of the three instruments which can promote change—government, the media, and the public—government should be the third. (p. 271)

Rivers, Schramm, and Christians applauded the Hutchins Commission for providing a moral foundation for social responsibility. But they argued for the continued evolution of journalistic standards of professionalism; vigorous stimulation of the public's awareness of its own potential for influencing media content; encouragement of new forms of media criticism; and government alertness to public policies that impede fair competition between media or slow the benefits of new media technology. These correctives, they thought, were needed to counter the "superficial collectivism" of the Hutchins report.

In 1993, Christians and colleagues John P. Ferre and Mark Fackler wrote *Good News: Social Ethics and the Press*, a seminal contribution to the development of a communitarian ethic for contemporary journalism. They sought to build upon the

Hutchins Commission by articulating a view of the press's mission "not as civic intelligence but transformation." They would replace the classical liberalism bequeathed by the Enlightenment with a social ethics of the press emphasizing persons as interdependent and in need of mutuality. "The telos of communitarian journalism," they contend, "has distinctive features: justice, covenant and empowerment." In short, write the authors:

> Operating within a communitarian world view itself, the news media seek to engender a like-minded philosophy among the public. A revitalized citizenship shaped by community norms becomes the press's aim—not merely readers and audiences provided with data, but morally literate persons. (p. 89)

As the twentieth century edged to a close, major circles within North American journalism began debating whether they are using the First Amendment wisely or vigorously enough to keep alive a civic ethic strong enough to cope with the demands of the twenty-first century. They are in quest of a new civic journalism that seeks to invigorate the democratic purposes of their craft/profession and freshen its connections with a thinking public. In a genuine sense, their effort is a philosophical descendant of the Hutchins Commission. But, unlike Hutchins, it was born to achieve— and its worth will be tested by—more pragmatic results within the practice of both journalism and public policy-making.

Thirty or more North American newspapers are experimenting with new methods of reporting, editing, and presenting public policy issues. They are even collaborating with radio and TV in news coverage explicitly designed to revive civic life and public dialogue. Typically, these news-media-generated civic initiatives include (1) public opinion polling or systematic focus group consultations to define public needs or priorities; (2) extended commitments to in-depth coverage; (3) continuous feedback mechanisms to express and display public reaction; (4) opportunities for competing policy perspectives to court public favor; (5) timely identification of sources available to citizens to deepen their understanding of issues and, especially, participate in the formation of policy affecting their lives; and (6) an attempt to both broaden and lengthen the effective attention span of media consumers to public issues. Civic journalism also continues to emphasize watchdog journalism that serves the public interest by exposing governmental and societal wrongdoing.

Among media active in this movement are the Wichita, Kansas, *Eagle*; the Charlotte, North Carolina, *Observer*; the Norfolk *Virginian-Pilot*; the Dayton *Daily News*; the Miami *Herald*; the Minneapolis *Star Tribune*; and, among smaller media, the Bremerton, Washington, *Sun*, and the Columbia, Missouri, *Missourian*. A number of these actively cooperate with radio and TV newsrooms in their systematic coverage not only of elections but of key public policy issues such as crime, education, local jobs and the economy, and the care of children.

These initiatives may be the most significant attempt by news media themselves to give voice, life, and body to the philosophy of a socially responsible press. To assist the leaders of the movement, the Knight Foundation has funded and the Kettering Foundation has participated in a new Project on Public Life and the Press. It is directed by Jay Rosen, coauthor with Paul Taylor of *The New News v. The Old News* (1992). Likewise, the Pew Charitable Trusts have created the Center on Civic Journalism to support innovative experiments to empower citizens. Another major player in this effort is New Directions for News, a newspaper think tank, whose supporters include the Robert R. McCormick Tribune Foundation. Parallel to the work of these media is the work of political scientist James Fishkin, author of *Democracy and Deliberation: New Directions for Democratic Reform* (1992). In the spirit of his book, Fishkin and his colleagues began testing, with the cooperation of media in England, a synchronized use of public polling and policy discussions to improve civic judgment.

Marxism and Leninism

Born in Trier, Germany, a region receptive to the revolutionary democratic ideas of the French Revolution, Karl Marx (1818–1883) came to maturity when the excesses of the Industrial Revolution were highly visible. He was angered at an early age by the exploitation of workers, the irresponsibility of the ownership class, and the residual filth that manufacturers left behind as they enriched themselves. As a journalist and militant intellectual, Marx, at the age of 25, wrote a searing article denouncing Prussian censorship and exalting the efficacy of free expression. As a young revolutionary, he participated in the revolts by workers in Germany and France in 1848—the year in which he and Friedrich Engels published the *Communist Manifesto*. Expelled by the Prussian government in 1849, Marx went to England, where five years earlier Engels had written *Conditions of the Working Class in England*.

Marx's most important work, *Das Kapital* (1867), became the foundational document on political economy for many socialists and communists in the nineteenth and twentieth centuries. The Bolsheviks in Russia embraced Marx, but doctrinal additions by Vladimir Ilyich Lenin gave Communists a rationale for enlisting the press as an instrument of totalitarianism in Russia, much of Eastern and Central Europe, and China.

Disputes exist to this day over the precise interpretation of Marx's writings. But the essential ideas of Marx and his key followers are clear. They took Hegel's abstracted idea of a dynamic, dialectical process and applied it to the economic struggle they beheld in the material world. They vivified history and concluded that feudalistic economic relationships (thesis) had led inexorably to capitalism (antithesis) and would thence give birth to communism (synthesis). The capitalistic bourgeois class would be overthrown by a dictatorship of the proletariat, which would eventually evolve into a classless society in which each citizen would give according to ability and receive according to need.

That this primitive economic prediction within early communism did not follow its historical script was less important in discrediting contemporary communism than the totalitarian dictatorships that accompanied the actual Communist governments. The Communist party maintained a police system to suppress dissent, a justice system to enforce its will, and a press system fully integrated with and in service to the state. The "socialist criticism" it permitted under Lenin and Stalin in Russia was in matters of procedure and execution of already settled policy, never a challenge to state judgment.

State ownership of the press also set Communist totalitarianism apart and gave it distinctive features. Earlier authoritarian regimes allowed private ownership of the press and thus kept alive at least a kind of separateness from governing authority. They prohibited deviations from the ruling policies. But Communist regimes expected the press to perform a wide variety of functions for the state—education, propaganda, indoctrination, surveillance, and assistance in the execution of policy. The key remaining Communist nations with such systems intact are the People's Republic of China, North Korea, and Cuba.

It is popular in some quarters to attribute the demise of communism in the former Soviet Union to the failure of the economy and the government to finance the enormous expense of an arms race in the Cold War with Western nations. However, no such single causation can suffice as an explanation. Whatever else historians discover in their analysis of why communism crumbled, they will certainly count as an important factor the steadily increasing awareness in the Soviet Union of the ideas, practices, and conditions of life under Western democracies. In the development of this awareness during the 40 years of the Cold War, the free press of the Western democracies played a major role.

Democratic Socialism

Robert Picard's scholarship on the Scandinavian press has brought to the fore a new consciousness of the merits of the region's press systems. In *The Ravens of Odin: The Press in the Nordic Nations* (1988) and in *The Press and the Decline of Democracy* (1985), Picard argued persuasively for its unique contributions. Through his work and related scholarship, press practices in Scandinavia—and similar features adopted in parts of Western Europe—are seen by Picard and others as reflecting virtually a separate span in the spectrum of media philosophies. Although Scandinavia and kindred nations in Europe have legal or constitutional guarantees against prior censorship, they have a "proactive" stance toward the press. It is based on the assumption that governments have a responsibility to actively promote not only press freedom but citizen access and diversity of political expression.

Until the 1980s, the Scandinavian and, to a lesser extent, the Western European media were commonly regarded as embracing merely variants of socially responsible press theory. Picard and other scholars argue that such an interpretation ignores the substantive initiatives taken in these regions to assure the public benefits of a free press specified by democratic philosophy. By contrast, the United States—despite postal subsidies, antitrust exemptions, and other supports—has embraced a philosophy much more reliant on private market mechanisms and only limited intervention by government. That posture reflects a deeper fear of governmental manipulation of the public and a North American culture resistant to governmental intrusions into civic and political life.

By contrast, in Scandinavia and sectors of Western Europe, the practice of state intervention is common. This takes the form of preferential tax, postal, telecommunication, and transportation rates; subsidies, loans, and loan guarantees to privately owned media; and direct operation of state broadcasting properties. Democratic socialist philosophy and the government subsidies it espouses both lost some ground amid the sweep of conservative and promarket opinion in the 1980s and early 1990s. But democratic socialism is not likely to disappear soon from Europe or elsewhere. It likely will be a strong influence on the press systems of countries in Africa, Latin America, and some of the nations in Eastern and Central Europe liberated from Soviet domination after 1989. Of major importance in the 1990s will be how these nations cope with competing pressures for free market economies and older traditions of governmental support for public media.

An original Swedish contribution to the critical tradition in journalism is the self-regulatory device of the press council. It hears complaints against the press by citizens, mediates disputes, conducts investigative hearings, and issues findings to be published in the press. Sweden first established a press council in 1916; Finland and Norway did so in the 1920s. Denmark started a weaker version of the press council in 1964. A unique Swedish institution—transplanted outside Scandinavia but in less authoritative roles—is the ombudsman, a public representative and advocate who intercedes for the citizen not only with the press but with government bureaucracy and abusive business monopolies.

Democratic socialist press systems usually can be described by policies that outlaw prior censorship, provide direct and indirect economic support to achieve diversity of expression and broader distribution of civic information, give legal backing to citizen access, and offer active mediation of civic disputes arising from the practice of journalism. Many who favor such press systems are influenced by a nonauthoritarian or cultural interpretation of the writings of Karl Marx.

"Advancing" or "Developmental" Press Philosophy

Although philosophy has important uses to the student or practitioner of global journalism, the complexity of its application increases when one confronts the rich variety of contexts posed by developing societies. *Four Theories* and its several mutations grew from values represented by a common religious, cultural, political, and socioeconomic heritage. Parts of these traditions were carried by the colonial Western powers to the continents of Africa, Asia, and Latin America. Indigenous traditions, while equally as vital there, have nonetheless imported some of the vocabulary of modernism and development.

Some nations—Taiwan, South Korea, Costa Rica, and India—have achieved "developed" or "advancing" status with widely varying press systems. Economic high performers such as Taiwan and South Korea, ruled by dictatorships for decades, now are beginning to develop truly representative governments. And their rambunctious news media are being urged to develop a professional ethic to match the democratic aspirations of their countries. India, often beset by communal, economic, and political strife, nonetheless boasts an intrepid democratic press admired around the world. Tiny, and democratic, Costa Rica, although not yet where it wishes to be economically, has steadily improved the educational level and professional quality of its journalists. For many in Central America, Costa Rica's press system represents a model toward which to strive.

As the twentieth century draws to a close, dozens of developing nations in Africa, Latin America, and Asia can find reason for both hope and discouragement in the experiences of these four states. However, barring an unforeseen change in trends, most are likely to follow traditions described as "developmental" in the five-concept typology of William Hachten's *The World News Prism* (1981, 1987, 1992). A developmental press is most likely controlled by government or a political party. Its stated policies are most often aimed at development of the nation's economic infrastructure, internal political unification, and the alleviation of hunger, illiteracy, and ill health. Like others, Hachten finds these circumstances prevailing in the nonindustrialized and non-Communist nations of the Third World.

By contrast, Hachten reserves the description "revolutionary press" for those that may be illegal, subversive, or unsubdued by the prevailing authorities. They operate underground, sometimes from a neighboring country, and aim to overthrow an existing regime. Examples include Lenin's revolutionary journalism preceding the 1917 Bolshevik revolution, the French resistance press during the Nazi occupation of the early 1940s, the anticolonialist revolutionary journalism in Africa and Asia following World War II, and the Peruvian revolutionaries of the 1980s.

Their techniques are abetted by modern technology, as when Ayatollah Khomeini smuggled his revolutionary speeches into Iran by audiocasette and photocopying. Likewise, underground opponents of the Soviet bloc advanced their revolution through the *samizdat*—articles, pamphlets, and booklets which were typed or mimeographed and distributed hand-to-hand.

Important as the revolutionary press was and is, its existence is usually a transitional phase. Because it manifests a variety of political and philosophical orientations, it is not easily classified as representing a separate press type.

J. Herbert Altschull, in his *Agents of Power* (1984), uses chiefly economic descriptors to organize the fundamental beliefs or "articles of faith" of the world's press systems. His descriptors set forth the ideology and, by implication, the associated behavior of press systems. (See Table 1.2.) He prefers the phrase "advancing" press to describe the press in developing societies, partly from the belief that the label "developmental" can be construed as pejorative.

Leaders of the nonaligned nations—those usually classified as "advancing" under Altschull's typology—were champions of the New World Information and Communication Order so widely debated in the late 1970s and early 1980s. NWICO—outlined in the famous report authored by Sean MacBride, *Many Voices, One World* (1980)—aimed chiefly at strengthening the internal media systems of Third World nations and reducing their information dependence on the developed world. Concern about restrictions NWICO might place on the free flow of information across national boundaries led the United States to withdraw from UNESCO. The drive for a sequel to NWICO is kept alive by Third World leaders and a network of political economists and communication policy specialists operating as the "MacBride Roundtable."

TABLE 1.2   Altschull typology

Market (First World)	Marxist (Second World)	Advancing (Third World)
Journalists seek truth.	Journalists seek truth.	Journalists serve truth.
Journalists are socially responsible.	Journalists are socially responsible	Journalists are socially responsible.
Journalists inform in a nonpolitical way.	Journalists educate in a political way.	Journalists educate in a political way.
Journalists serve the people impartially and support capitalism.	Journalists serve the people by demanding support for socialism.	Journalists serve the people and government by seeking change.
Journalists serve as watchdogs of government.	Journalists mold views and change behavior.	Journalists serve as instruments of peace.
The press is free from outside interference.	The press teaches workers class consciousness.	The press unifies; it does not divide.
The press serves the public's right to know.	The press serves the needs of the people.	The press works for social change.
The press seeks to learn and present the truth.	The press facilitates effective change.	The press is an instrument of social justice.
The press reports fairly and objectively.	The press reports objectively about reality.	The press is a vehicle for two-way exchanges.
A free press means that journalists are free of all outside controls.	A free press reports all opinion, not only that of the rich.	A free press means freedom of conscience for journalists.
A free press is not servile to power or manipulated by power.	A free press is required to counter oppression.	Press freedom is less important than the visibility of the nation.
A free press does not need a national press policy to remain free.	A free press requires a national press policy in order to be correct.	A national press policy is needed to safeguard freedom.

SOURCE: Adapted from J. Herbert Altschull, *Agents of Power* (White Plains, N.Y.: Longman, 1984).

A POSSIBLE FUTURE FOR MEDIA PHILOSOPHY, ETHICS, AND CRITICISM

The discerning student of global journalism will either know or soon notice that, at their best, typologies are verbal depictions of existing media systems and the beliefs that underlie them. They attempt to describe macro orientations of media, and as political systems of the planet change, so do the typologies. The nomenclature of social philosophy has been summarized and used in this chapter to describe the larger features of functioning media systems.

It also was intended as an invitation to students of media systems to pursue the perennial and larger questions of the philosopher's craft/profession. First, how accurate are the existing descriptions of journalistic and social experience, society by society? Second, what should be the norms by which journalistic and civic behavior can be judged? Third, how can journalists and citizens of the nations of the planet establish clear meanings of the terms of political discourse—truth, justice, freedom, independence, fairness, goodness, and the like? Fourth, whither are the media systems of the planet tending, and how, if those trajectories collide or run akimbo, can they be righted? And what does it mean to "right" them?

These questions are more than academic quizzes. Whether, how, and how well they are answered will shape an important part of the future of our planet. Whichever path or paths a student of media philosophy travels, the succeeding chapters will furnish insights and systematic observations for the journey. Books referenced for this chapter also will be helpful companions, especially for extended travelers.

BIBLIOGRAPHY

Altschull, J. Herbert. *Agents of Power*. White Plains, N.Y.: Longman, 1984.

———. *From Milton to McLuhan: The Ideas Behind American Journalism*. New York and London: Longman, 1990.

Bellah, Robert, Richard Madsen, William Sullivan, Ann Swidler, and Steven M. Tipton. *Habits of the Heart: Individualism and Commitment in American Life*. New York: Harper & Row, 1986.

Christians, Clifford G., John P. Ferre, and P. Mark Fackler. *Good News: Social Ethics and the Press*. New York and Oxford: Oxford University Press, 1993.

Commission on Freedom of the Press. *A Free and Responsibilities Press*. Chicago and London: University of Chicago Press, 1947.

Dahlgren, Peter, and Colin Sparks. *Communication and Citizenship: Journalism and the Public Sphere in the New Media Age*. London and New York: Routledge, 1992.

Ebenstein, William. *Great Political Thinkers, Plato to the Present*, 4th Edition. New York: Holt, Rinehart & Winston, 1969.

Fishkin, James. *Democracy and Deliberation: New Directions for Democratic Reform*. New Haven, Conn.: Yale University Press, 1992.

Friedland, Lewis A. *Covering the World: International Television News Services*. New York: 20th Century Fund, 1992.

Gerbner, George, Hamid Mowlana, and Kaarle Nordenstreng. *The Global Media Debate: Its Rise, Fall and Renewal*. Norwood, N.J.: Ablex, 1993.

Hachten, William A. *The Growth of Media in the Third World, African Failures, Asian Successes*. Ames: Iowa State University Press, 1993.

———. *The World News Prism: Changing Media of International Communication*. Ames: Iowa State University Press, 1981, 1987, 1992.

Hardt, Hanno. *Critical Communication Studies, Communication, History and Theory in America*. London and New York: Routledge, 1992.

Hocking, William Ernest. *Freedom of the Press: A Framework of Principle*. Chicago: University of Chicago Press, 1947.

Lambeth, Edmund B. *Committed Journalism*, 2nd Edition. Bloomington: Indiana University Press, 1992.

Langan, Thomas. *Tradition and Authenticity in the Search for Ecumenic Wisdom*. Columbia, Mo., and London: University of Missouri Press, 1992.

MacBride, Sean. *Many Voices, One World*. Paris: United Nations Educational, Scientific and Cultural Organization, 1980.

Merrill, John. *The Imperative of Freedom: A Philosophy of Journalistic Autonomy*. New York: Hastings House, 1974; Freedom House, 1990.

Mowlana, Hamid. "A Paradigm for Comparative Mass Media Analysis," in *International and Intercultural Communication*. New York: Hastings House, 1976, pp. 474–484.

Picard, Robert G. *The Press and the Decline of Democracy: Democratic Socialist Response in Public Policy*. Westport, Conn.: Greenwood Press, 1985.

———. *The Ravens of Odin: The Press in the Nordic Nations*. Ames: Iowa State University Press, 1988.

Rivers, William L., Wilbur Schramm, and Clifford Christians. *Responsibility in Mass Communication*, 3rd Edition. New York: Harper & Row, 1980.

Rosen, Jay, and Paul Taylor. *The New News v. The Old News*. New York: Twentieth Century Fund, 1992.

Sabine, George H. *A History of Political Theory*, 3rd Edition. New York: Holt, Rinehart & Winston, 1961.

Siebert, Fred S., Theodore Peterson, and Wilbur Schramm. *Four Theories of the Press*. Urbana: University of Illinois Press, 1956.

chapter **2**

Media Systems: Overview

Lowndes F. Stephens

> *. . . In a global village, to deny people human rights or democratic freedoms is not to deny them an abstraction they have never experienced but to deny the established customs of the village. It hardly matters that only a minority of the world's people enjoy such freedoms or the prosperity that goes with them: Once people are convinced that these things are possible in the village, an enormous burden of proof falls on those who would deny them.*
>
> —*Walter B. Wriston, former Chairman/CEO, Citicorp*
> *"The Inevitable Global Conversation,"*
> Media Studies Journal *8:1 (Winter 1994): pp. 20–21*

The significance of knowing more about global media systems is that people's political rights and civil liberties and their economic well-being are linked to press freedom and media availability, though there is some debate about whether prosperity follows freedom or is even possible without it.

The press system or media philosophy models discussed in the first chapter show that media systems reflect the political and economic values of the nation-states they serve. The authoritarian, Western, communist, revolutionary, and developmental philosophies of the press accord different weights to the importance of individual freedoms versus persistence of the collective will, as represented by the ruling regime governing nation-states.

The most important development in the final decade of the twentieth century affecting global media systems is that information technologies are expanding access to information and entertainment to people all over the world, and nation-states can do little to prevent transnational information/entertainment news flows. So while governments operating under various press systems try to control the kinds of messages people get, their borders are porous. Fax machines, cassettes, computer links to on-line databases, satellite dishes, and direct broadcast satellites (DBS's), and broadcasts from other lands know no geographic boundaries.

As Walter Wriston, former chairman/CEO of Citicorp, notes in his book *The Twilight of Sovereignty: How the Information Revolution Is Transforming Our World* (1992), the revolution in information technology is threatening the sovereignty of nation-states. The global economy is an information economy in which information is the most important factor of production of goods and services. Intellectual capital (knowledge and information) is the new source of wealth for nations (not manufactured goods or agricultural products, but information). In another context Wriston says, "Intellectual capital will go where it is wanted and stay where it is well treated" (Wriston 1994, p. 24).

The intellectual capital has come largely from the market economies of the West, from Western Europe and Japan but increasingly may come from developing nations that are moving to market economies. Jeffrey Garten, U.S. undersecretary of commerce for international trade, who once wrote a book about the tripolar global economic battles among the United States, Germany, and Japan, now says 75 percent of the world's trade growth for years to come will involve 10 quite different places, all of them large developing countries trying to expand free-market systems. These 10 emerging markets are: Argentina, Brazil, Mexico, Poland, South Africa, India, Turkey, South Korea, Indonesia, and the economic zone of China, Hong Kong, and Taiwan. Most have great geographical size and populations, free-market reforms and high growth rates. By year 2010, they'll double their share of global output, and their merchandise imports by then will be $1 trillion higher than in 1990 (plus services). That's triple the combined increase expected for Japan, Europe, North America, and the world's 120 other developing nations. Thailand and Vietnam might be in this group too (Keatley 11 February 1994, p. A10).

This overview of global media systems will (1) examine the relationship among and the extent of individual freedoms, press freedom, media availability and economic prosperity around the world, (2) summarize trends in economic concentration in media industries, and (3) identify some of the global information organizations. Other chapters of this book examine many of these concepts in more detail and within a specific geographic context. In this chapter the author is trying to explain why a study of global journalism is significant. It is because press freedom is associated with individual freedoms, information has become the most significant form of capital in the global economy, and the economic well-being of us all is associated with access to freedom and to information.

POLITICAL RIGHTS, CIVIL LIBERTIES, AND PRESS FREEDOM AROUND THE WORLD

Pro-democracy movements in Eastern Europe and China and elsewhere around the world in the late 1980s and early 1990s represented peaks, not valleys, in the proportion of the world's people who are "free." Freedom House says the proportion of the world's people living in freedom has been declining since 1991, from 39.23 percent (2,088.2 million) in 1991 to 19.00 percent in 1993 (1,046.2 million). Likewise, the numbers of people living in "not free" nations has increased from 32.86 percent (1,748.7 million) in 1991 to 40.59 percent in 1993 (2,234.6 million). The world's population was 5,322.6 million in 1991 and 5,505.2 million in 1993.[1] The 20 worst-rated countries are Afghanistan, Angola, Bhutan, Burma (Myanmar), Burundi, China, Cuba, Equatorial Guinea, Haiti, Iraq, North Korea, Libya, Saudi Arabia, Somalia, Sudan, Syria, Tajikistan, Turkmenistan, Uzbekistan, and Vietnam. Each of these countries also receives the worst rating on press freedom.

The best-rated countries are Australia, Austria, Barbados, Belize, Canada, the Greek side of Cyprus, Denmark, Finland, Gambia, Iceland, Kiribati, Liechtenstein, Luxembourg, Malta, Marshall Islands, Micronesia, Netherlands, New Zealand, Norway, Portugal, San Marino, St. Kitts and Nevis, St. Vincent and the Grenadines, Sweden, Switzerland, Trinidad and Tobago, and the United States. Each of these countries receives the best rating for press freedom. All the countries rated "free" by Freedom House are democracies. While the proportion of the world's people who are living "free" has declined, the number of democracies increased from 99 in 1992 to 107 in 1993.

Many factors may explain the decline of freedom: movements of rage in multi-ethnic states (growing Islamic fundamentalism); feeble international response to turmoil in Bosnia, Somalia, and Haiti, which may encourage other tyrants to ignore international law; unsuccessful economic shock therapy in new democracies; too little resolve to empower citizens in these new democracies with the information necessary to build citizenship skills and respect for democratic norms; an isolationist foreign policy orientation on the part of many advanced industrial societies worried about economic growth at home.

Freedom House fears a new post–Cold War polarization between a group of "free" states on the one hand and an increasingly repressive group of "not free" states on the other, led by China and Iran, countries with growing economic resources.

FREEDOM AND ECONOMIC PROSPERITY

Some economists have cautioned that the United States and other advanced industrial societies should not push human rights and democratic reform as cornerstones of foreign policies designed to increase international trade. Harvard economist Robert Barro says pushing democracy is no key to prosperity. With secondary data for 1960s, 1970s, and 1990—subjective measures of political democracy (0 = pure dictatorship

---

[1] 190 sovereign states are ranked in 1993 according to political rights and civil liberties by Freedom House, a New York-based organization interested in strengthening democratic institutions. Freedom House has conducted an annual Comparative Freedom Survey since 1972. Ratings for political rights and civil liberties are combined into a rating ranging from 2 (most free) to 14 (least free). Freedom House also makes an assessment of press freedom, rating press systems as "free" (+1), "partly free" (0), or "not free" (–1). See Adrian Karatnycky, "Freedom in Retreat," *Freedom Review* 25:1 (January–February 1994), pp. 4–9.

to 100 = total democracy) and empirical measures of economic growth (growth rate of real GDP [Gross Domestic Product] per capita, 1965–90, and real GDP per capita in 1990, based on 1985 dollars)—Barro shows in a sample of 101 countries that there is little relation between democracy and growth. The average level of political democracy was 67 in the early 1960s, 47 in the mid 1970s, and 59 in 1991. Average growth rates of real per-capita GDP was 1.6 percent per year from 1965 to 1990. Real GDP per capita averaged $5,120 in 1990. He did find, however, that political democracy and economic growth were correlated in the case of the 22 European or European-origin countries in his sample. In these countries political democracy ratings increased from 91 in the 1960s to 100 in 1991, economic growth rates increased annually by 2.5 percent from 1965 to 1990 and real GDP per capita averaged $13,210 in 1990. He thinks the democracies have a poor track record of economic growth because they pursue Robin Hood-style policies that extract unfair rents (taxes) from citizens. Wealth is redistributed from rich to poor, stifling economic growth. He also believes that public and private interest groups demand too much of government, taking money away from investments that might spur economic growth (Barro 1993, p. A14; 1991, p. 407).

Autocratic centralized governments such as South Korea, Singapore, and Chile (under Pinochet) and federalist unions like China (People's Republic) have sustained economic growth. Economist John F. Helliwell at the University of British Columbia has compared economic growth rates from 1960 to 1985 in 100 countries and concludes that authoritarian regimes and non-democracies have slightly better growth rates in the short run, if they respect individual "economic rights" such as the protection of private property, but that economic growth ultimately leads to democracy (Pennar, Smith, et al. 1993, pp. 84–88). Freedom House argues that neither democracy nor authoritarianism guarantees growth and prosperity, but democracies are more successful in the long run in achieving and sustaining economic growth and prosperity. One resident scholar at Freedom House notes that several authoritarian Asian states have thriving business sectors, but are profoundly antidemocratic, so prosperity comes at an unacceptable price (loss of political and civil rights) (Ryan 1994, p. A13).

This author has analyzed measures of purchasing power in the countries rated by Freedom House in 1993, and there is a strong positive association between high levels of purchasing power and freedom. For example, the median purchasing power per capita of citizens living in the 71 countries with free press systems is $6,116 compared to $1,215 for citizens living in countries (55) with no press freedom and $2,622 for citizens of countries (62) with some press freedom.[2] In 1990 the differences were less pronounced: median purchasing power of $4,948 in countries with free press systems, $794 in countries with no press freedoms and $2,618 in countries with some press freedoms. In the countries with the most overall freedom in 1993 (political rights and civil liberties), the median purchasing power was $15,695 per capita ($12,524 in 1990) but only $1,608 ($750 in 1990) in those countries rated least free.

---

[2] The median is that measure of statistical average (central tendency) that splits the values measured in half, so one half the citizens are above and half below the median.

FREEDOM, ECONOMIC PROSPERITY, AND MEDIA USE AND AVAILABILITY

Comparative measures of these concepts for 1989–1993 have been correlated by this author to determine the relationships among freedom, economic prosperity, and media use and availability. Two graphs show the relationships. In Figure 2.1, Freedom House's measure of overall freedom ("most free" = 2 to "least free" = 14) is shown on the horizontal axis. On the left vertical axis is the measure of economic well-being (per capita purchasing power parities). The dark square boxes connected by lines show the purchasing power parities for the countries with various freedom ratings. The curve is downward-sloping to the right, and it shows that countries with freedom ratings of 4 or lower have much higher per capita purchasing power parities than do countries with ratings above 4.

The media use and availability indicators are shown on a logarithmic scale, the right vertical axis. The newspaper circulation per thousand population measure ranges from a high of 671 per thousand in Georgia to 1 per thousand in Zaire, Niger, and Ethiopia. The other indicators are measures of media availability: persons per television, radio, and telephone sets. These data are taken from *The World Almanac and Book of Facts 1994*. There is considerable variability in the availability of telephone and television sets around the world; radio sets are readily available everywhere. Television set diffusion ranges from 1.20 persons per set in Latvia to 1,707 per set in Zaire.

FIGURE 2.1 Freedom, prosperity, and media use in 190 countries, 1993 median

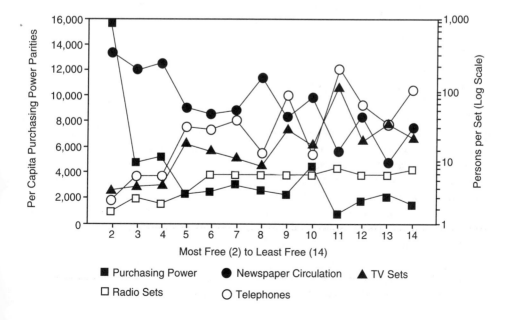

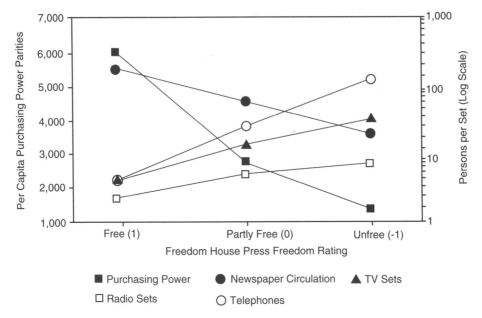

FIGURE 2.2   Freedom, prosperity, and media use in 190 countries, 1993 median

Radio set diffusion is highest in the United States (.50 persons per set) and lowest in Bhutan with 64 persons per radio set. In Liechtenstein there are enough telephones for every citizen (highest diffusion rate) but only 1 set for every 3,300 people living in Cambodia (lowest rate). Because of these enormous variations we transformed the actual values in the graph to logarithmic values. The graph shows that citizens living in the most free nations are much more likely to have newspapers to read than are those people living in partially free, or nonfree countries. These citizens also have more television sets, radio sets, and telephones available to them.

Figure 2.2 plots purchasing power parities, media use, and availability against Freedom House's ratings of press freedom. Here the relationships are easier to see because the graph is less cluttered. Purchasing power parities are substantially higher in free press states, and higher in partly free nations than in countries with no press freedoms. Newspaper circulation is also substantially higher in free press countries, and higher in partly free nations than in countries with no press freedoms. The upward-sloping lines for television, radio, and telephone sets indicate that there are more of these sets available to citizens in free press countries.

Multiple regression analysis was used to sort out the relationships among these variables and measures of them for 1989, 1990, and 1993. One analysis sought to explain variation in 1993 purchasing power parities per capita. Three independent variables in a robust regression with 90 countries remaining in the analysis accounted for 77 percent of the variation (adjusted R-square) in purchasing power (F = 99.87, with

3,86 df, p = .000). The most significant predictor was 1990 freedom ratings (the more freedom in 1990 associated with higher purchasing power in 1993). Newspaper circulation in 1990 was the second most important variable, followed by newspaper circulation in 1993. Higher newspaper circulation is associated with higher levels of purchasing power parities. Literacy, population size, availability of telephones, televisions, and radio sets were insignificant in explaining variation in purchasing power.

A second regression analysis sought to explain variation in 1993 overall freedom ratings by Freedom House. Four independent variables in a robust regression with 91 countries remaining in the analysis accounted for 55 percent of the variation (adjusted R-square) in overall freedom ratings in 1993 (F = 28.42, with 4,86 df, p = .000). The most significant predictor was 1993 literacy levels (higher literacy levels are associated with higher freedom ratings). Purchasing power parities in 1993 are the second most significant predictor of 1993 overall freedom ratings (positive correlation). Radio set availability in 1993 is the third most significant variable in the equation (positive correlation), followed by population size in 1989 (negative correlation). Availability of telephones and televisions and newspaper circulation were insignificant in explaining variation in 1993 freedom ratings. These analyses do not explain whether freedom follows economic growth or vice versa, but our measure of economic well-being, purchasing power parities, is strongly related to the freedom measures used by Freedom House. These data do make clear that people living in countries that respect political rights and civil liberties are heavily plugged into the information society in that they have far better access to the media of mass communications.

In this global information economy, news and popular culture are commodities for export and import. The advanced industrial societies are especially big players in the global information economy, and companies in these countries are either buying or being bought by other firms.

TRENDS IN ECONOMIC CONCENTRATION AND PROFITABILITY IN THE GLOBAL MEDIA INDUSTRIES

Some of the largest mergers and acquisitions in the last decade have involved media companies. What was to become the largest corporate merger ever, proposed in October 1993 and involving Bell Atlantic's $33 billion takeover of Tele-Communications, Inc. (TCI) and Liberty Media, was called off in February 1994.

What was the promise? That one conglomerate would provide wire and wireless service, video-on-demand, and interactive media. TCI would provide TV programming and high-capacity networks capable of carrying dozens, even hundreds, of program channels. Liberty Media controls major interests in cable programming companies. Bell Atlantic (BEL) was to provide switching technologies that would allow two-way communications on the interactive TV networks of the near future. In 1991 BEL won the right to provide electronic services rather than just carry those created by others, and the company gained federal court approval in 1993 to provide TV programming in Virginia.

The merger fell through because the CEOs of the companies involved came from different corporate cultures and because BEL saw the price of its stock decline. It had planned to use its stock to make the purchase. Moreover, in the week the merger was canceled, the FCC mandated a rollback in cable TV monthly customer rates, and that was perceived by BEL to have a negative future effect on TCI's earnings.

On the other hand, Viacom's $10 billion bid to purchase Paramount was consummated in February 1994 after a five-month bid–counterbid battle with QVC, the home shopping network. Viacom owns controlling interest in a number of cable TV networks, including Nickelodeon and MTV, with more than 260 million viewers worldwide. Viacom believes the fact that many countries in Europe are privatizing their broadcast operations is going to create demand for television programming. Paramount is a huge "electronic publishing house" with the programming might to meet that demand. Since 1912, Paramount has been making movies and today it has a library of 900 films and 600 hours of TV programs.

Young and Rubicam's 1994 European marketing and media survey shows state TV monopolies depress not only advertising rates but also total ad spending for other media in the same markets. Until 1988 only four European countries had private national TV—Italy, France, Germany, and the United Kingdom. Today, only four countries have state monopolies—Switzerland, Finland, Ireland, and Austria. Total ad spending over the last seven to eight years has been flat in Switzerland and Finland, and it has doubled over the last 10 years in Italy and almost doubled in Germany (Bannon 1994, p. A5C). Viacom hopes more private TV markets emerge in Europe.

Blockbuster Video joined Viacom in its bid to buy Paramount because it can take advantage of Paramount's huge library and recycle movies in video form for rent or sale. Today, about two-thirds of the gross receipts for children's movies and about half the adult movie receipts come from video sales and rentals.[3] Paramount derives 40 percent of its operating income from book publishing (Simon & Schuster, Prentice Hall), so Viacom also sees opportunities in the multimedia educational textbook market.

Other large mergers and acquisitions include Time's purchase of Warner Communications in 1989 for $13.9 billion; AT&T's acquisition of McCaw Cellular in 1993 for $12.6 billion; Sony's purchase of Columbia Pictures for $3.4 billion in 1989; and Capital Cities' purchase of ABC Broadcasting for $3.5 billion in 1985.

More than $75 billion has changed hands in 160 recent multimedia deals, according to Janice Hughes, a London-based telecomm consultant. The players are phone and cable companies, which own the delivery systems; electronics producers, which sell VCRs, TVs, and stereos; studios; and publishers.

The 15 corporations best positioned to survive in the emerging multimedia industry, those that can operate along several parts of what Hughes calls the "media value chain," include eight American firms (AT&T, Bell Atlantic, TCI, Microsoft, Time-Warner, US West, QVC, and Viacom); four Japanese companies (Matsushita, Sony, Nintendo, and Sega); two European companies (British Telecom and Philips); and one Australian company (News Corp.). Smaller production, broadcasting, and publishing houses that fail to recognize the potential value of their software (content) could be subject to takeovers or may simply fail to grow with the market (Hughes 1994, pp. 53–59).

---

[3] For a thorough discussion of the economics of this business see Bruce M. Owen and Steven S. Wildman, *Video Economics* (Cambridge, Mass.: Harvard University Press, 1992).

Table 2.1 Total return on stockholders' equity and projected growth rates of selected communication companies

Company	Percent Total Return in 1993	Total Return Rank	Percent Projected 5-Year EPS Growth Rate
Philips NV	91.8	1	12
CBS	54.1	2	11
Time Warner	52.3	3	12
Sony Corp	47.3	4	9
Matsushita	46.2	5	0
TCI	42.3	6	11
Dow Jones & Co.	35.4	7	12
News Corp LTD	29.9	8	14
Reuters Hldgs	25.7	9	13
U.S. West	25.1	10	6
Capital Cities/ABC	22.0	11	12
Bell Atlantic	20.8	12	6
British Telecomm	20.0	13	9
Gannett	15.4	14	11
Omnicom Group	15.1	15	11
McGraw-Hill	13.9	16	9
Viacom	11.1	17	28
Times Mirror	10.2	18	12
Standard & Poor 500	10.1	Benchmark	
AT&T	5.5	19	10
Knight-Ridder	5.4	20	10
New York Times	1.7	21	17
QVC Network	1.0	22	22
Microsoft	−5.6	23	24
Saatchi/Saatchi	−16.1	24	15
WPP Group	−23.5	25	0

SOURCE: Standard & Poor Corporation.

Enormous amounts of capital are going into media companies because investors apparently agree with Wriston that the global economy is an information-driven one. The fifth-best performing stock in the Dow Jones World Stock Index in 1993 was Oriental Press Group in Hong Kong (newspaper publishing). Publicly traded communications companies in the United States broadly outperformed benchmark stock market averages in 1993. For example, the Dow Jones Equity Market Index was up 6.99 percent but media company stock prices increased on average 18.88 percent in 1993. Table 2.1 shows the 1993 total return for stockholders in selected companies and the projected average 5-Year Earnings Per Share (EPS) Growth Rates for these companies. Total return reflects price appreciation in the stock, dividends, and capital gains. Earnings per share reflects net income on a per-share basis.

The concerns about the quality of transnational news and entertainment flows, cultural imperialism, broadcasting in the public interest, and other issues are addressed in other chapters of this book. One case, recently described by *The Economist*, will illustrate the fact that lots of people are displeased with the quality of the global media system.

The Economist laments the folly of the European Union's continued attempts to limit importation of American programming. In October 1991 the European Commission directed member states to reserve "where practicable" a majority of their TV transmission time to European programming. France has decided 60 percent will be European programming and 66 percent of that programming will be of French origin. In December 1993 the French parliament said the eight national FM radio networks must within two years raise French-language content of music they play to 40 percent. But *The Economist* notes the impact of technology allowing for transborder transmissions. Satellite TV means that the English-language programs of America's CNN and NBC Super Channel, as well as Britain's BSkyB and the BBC, are all available to any European with a receiving dish and decoder (a modest investment). In Belgium of the 4 million households with TV sets, 3.5 million are connected to cable systems with the BBC and CNN. These same cable systems connect TV viewers in Portugal, Italy, France, Germany, Holland, and Spain, so it makes little sense to "persevere with doomed attempts to defend native-language television," says *The Economist*. Nevertheless, in February 1994 the state-owned broadcasting authorities of France, Spain, Italy, and Switzerland are likely to inject new capital to keep a loss-making, multilingual company called Euronews TV on air for 20 hours a day. It is continental Europe's "little-watched antidote to CNN," says the magazine, published out of London. The trouble with Euronews is production values aren't very good, because you can watch it (44 million households can receive Euronews in English, French, Spanish, Italian, German, and Arabic) in so many languages. *The Economist* explains: "Each language is meant to give a European perspective to television footage. Unfortunately, that means there can be no on-camera reporters or presenters, just disembodied voices. No wonder viewers are not switching on in droves." CNN has 61.5 million subscribers in Europe, while BBC's "World Service Television" has 1.8 million householder subscribers (Economist 1994, pp. 52–53). So EuroDisney is not the only American thing upsetting the French!

GLOBAL MEDIA ORGANIZATIONS

The reader's attention is drawn to two excellent sources of information on global communication satellites and the international news system. Raymond Akwule's *Global Telecommunications: The Technology, Administration, and Policies* (1992) is a comprehensive treatment of telecommunications systems and how they are managed. He explains the role of the International Telecommunication Union (ITU), UNESCO, and the World Bank in administering global telecommunications. More than 166 nations coordinate their telecommunications traffic through the United Nations agency known as ITU. Global satellite communication traffic is largely managed through INTELSAT, a not-for-profit cooperative of 119 member countries, with headquarters in Washington, D.C. Almost all transoceanic television broadcasts and more than half of all international telephone calls are carried by INTELSAT. The demands of international financial networks, multinational corporations, and international news services resulted in a doubling of the international traffic carried by INTELSAT from 1981 to 1988. Seven INTELSAT satellites have been launched since 1965 (the last, INTELSAT VII, in 1992). INTELSAT membership is open to all nations that are members of the ITU. In 1994 the Pentagon will launch the most sophisticated communication satellite ever built, MIL-STAR. Milstar can transmit up to 50,000 one-page letters an hour and serve thousands of users at one time.

The third edition of William A. Hachten's *The World News Prism: Changing Media of International Communication* (1992) provides a comprehensive review of the international news system, including news agencies and communication satellites. He discusses as well the importance of personal media as a tool of freedom for journalists and citizens. While Voice of America provided an alternative source of information to 100 million Chinese during the Tiananmen Square crackdown in 1989, CompuServe and Internet link people in Russia to citizens of the United States, via personal computers and a phone modem. The Center for Foreign Journalists in Reston, Virginia, and its Clearinghouse on the Central and East European Press also maintain "E-mail" bulletin board systems using Internet, the largest network of computer-based communications in the world.[4] Graduate students in Russia can complete a degree at an American university through distance education without ever leaving Moscow (He and Zhu 1994, pp. 1–45; Szymczak 1993, pp. 46–48; Gransden 1994, pp. A41–A42).

In this chapter the significance of knowing more about global media systems has been stressed by demonstrating that people's political rights and civil liberties, and their economic well-being, are linked to press freedom and media availability. We live in an age when information is the lifeblood of a global economy. Technological developments enable communicators to leapfrog political, economic, and geographic boundaries. You, the communication workers and managers of the twenty-first century, will decide what the software (content) will be.

BIBLIOGRAPHY

Akwule, Raymond. *Global Telecommunications: The Technology, Administration, and Policies.* Boston: Focal Press, 1992.

Associated Press. "Dissidents Say Western Acts Forced China to Free Them." *The State (Columbia, SC)*, 28 January 1994, 4A.

Avery, Robert K., Editor. *Public Service Broadcasting in a Multichannel Environment.* New York: Longman, 1993.

Bannon, Lisa. "State-TV Monopolies Stunt Ad Growth as Well as Rates in Europe, Y&R Says." *The Wall Street Journal*, 11 February 1994, A5C.

Barro, Robert J. "Economic Growth in a Cross-Section of Countries." *The Quarterly Journal of Economics* 106, no. 2 (1 May 1991): 407.

———. "Pushing Democracy Is No Key to Prosperity." *The Wall Street Journal*, 14 December 1993, A14.

---

[4] The Center for Foreign Journalists Internet address is "EDITOR@CFJ.ORG." Write CFJ Clearinghouse, 11690-A Sunrise Valley Drive, Reston, VA 22091.

Beck, Ernest. "Assets of Radio Free Europe Sought by Soros." *The New York Times*, 10 February 1994, A5.

Binder, David. "Senators Battle over Foreign Broadcast Cuts." *The New York Times*, 31 October 1993, 16.

Bloomberg Business News. "Westwood Buys Network." *The New York Times*, 7 February 1994, C3.

Bollen, Kenneth A. "Political Democracy: Conceptual and Measurement Traps." *Studies in Comparative International Development* 25, no. 1 (Spring 1990): 7.

Bollen, Kenneth A., and Stephen J. Appold. "National Industrial Structure and the Global System." *American Sociological Review* 58, no. 2 (1 April 1993): 283.

Braman, Sandra. "Harmonization of Systems: The Third Stage of the Information Society." *Journal of Communication* 43, no. 3 (Summer 1993): 133–141.

Brezis, Elise S., Paul R. Krugman, and Daniel Tsiddon. "Leapfrogging in International Competition: A Theory of Cycles in National Technological Leadership." *The American Economic Review* 83, no. 5 (December 1993): 1211–1220.

Carmody, Deirdre. "For People Magazine, a New Charity Program May Be Good Business, Too." *The New York Times*, 14 February 1994, C6.

———. "Times Mirror Widens Environmental Push." *The New York Times*, 14 February 1994, C6.

Cmiel, Kenneth. *Democratic Eloquence: The Fight over Regular Speech in Nineteenth Century America*. Berkeley: University of California Press, 1990.

Cox, Meg. "How Do You Tame a Global Company? Murdoch Does It Alone." *The Wall Street Journal*, 14 February 1994, A1.

Economist. "Cultural Protectionism: Television of Babel." *The Economist*, 5 February 1994, 52–53.

Elliott, Stuart. "French Merger Aims to Lift New York Shop." *The New York Times*, 10 February 1994, C5.

Fabrikant, Geraldine. "Merger Talks Halt on $33 Billion Deal in Communications." *The New York Times*, 24 February 1994, A1.

Famighetti, Robert, Editor. *The World Almanac and Book of Facts 1994*. Mahwah, N.J.: Funk & Wagnalls, 1993.

Farnsworth, Clyde H. "Book Deal Rouses Ire in Canada." *The New York Times*, 22 February 1994, C6.

Feder, Barnaby J. "Motorola, Long a Proponent of Sanctions Against Japan." *The New York Times*, 15 February 1994, C2.

Fischer, Stanley. "Socialist Economy Reform: Lessons of the First Three Years." *American Economic Review 83*, no. 2 (May 1993): 390–396. *Papers and Proceedings of the 105th Meeting of the American Economic Association*, vol. 83, edited by J. David Baldwin and Ronald L. Oaxaca. Anaheim, Ca.: American Economic Association.

Freedom House. "1994 Freedom Around the World." *Freedom Review* 25, no. 1 (January–February 1994).

Gaunt, Philip, Editor. *Beyond Agendas: New Directions in Communication Research*. Westport, Conn.: Greenwood Press, 1993.

Glaberson, William. "As a Family Business, the San Francisco Chronicle Is Finding That Pain Accompanies Change." *The New York Times*, 14 February 1994, C6.

Graham-Yooll, Andrew. "New Dawn for Press Freedom? A Personal and Prejudiced Opinion." *Media Studies Journal* 7, no. 4 (Fall 1993): 21–29. *Global News After the Cold War*, vol. 7. New York: The Freedom Forum Media Studies Center.

Gransden, Gregory. "Distance Education in Russia: Students in a Pilot Program Earn Degrees from State U. of New York." *The Chronicle of Higher Education*, 14 January 1994, A41–A42.

Grunwald, Henry. "Opening Up 'Valleys of the Uninformed.' " *Media Studies Journal* 7, no. 4 (Fall 1993): 29-33. *Global News After the Cold War*, vol. 7. New York: The Freedom Forum Media Studies Center.

Hachten, William A. *The World News Prism: Changing Media of International Communication*. 3rd Edition. Ames: Iowa State University Press, 1992.

———. *The Growth of Media in the Third World: African Failures, Asian Successes*. Ames: Iowa State University Press, 1993.

He, Zhou, and Jianhua Zhu. "The 'Voice of America' and China: Zeroing in on Tiananmen Square." *Journalism Monographs*, no. 143 (February 1994): 1-45. Columbia, S.C.: Association for Education in Journalism and Mass Communication.

Hudson, Richard L., and S. Karene Witcher. "Murdoch's British Satellite-TV Venture, Long a Loser, Posts Huge Jump in Profit." *The Wall Street Journal*, 4 February 1994, A4.

Hughes, Janice. "The Changing Multimedia Landscape." *Media Studies Journal* 8, no. 1 (Winter 1994): 53-59. *The Race for Content*, vol. 8. New York: The Freedom Forum Media Studies Center.

Inglehart, Ronald. *Culture Shift in Advanced Industrial Society*. Princeton, N.J.: Princeton University Press, 1990.

Iyer, Pico. "The Global Village Finally Arrives." *Time* 142, no. 21 (Special Issue) (Fall 1993): 86-87.

Karatnycky, Adrian. "Freedom in Retreat." *Freedom Review* 25, no. 1 (February 1994): 4-9.

Katz, Elihu, and George Wedell. *Broadcasting in the Third World: Promise and Performance*. Cambridge, Mass.: Harvard University Press, 1977.

Keane, John. *The Media and Democracy*. Cambridge, Mass.: Polity Press, 1991.

Keatley, Robert. "South Korea Loses Ground in Asia's Race." *The Wall Street Journal*, 25 February 1994, A9.

———. "Commerce Department Changes Tune, Trumpets Investing in 'Top 10' Nations." *The Wall Street Journal*, 11 February 1994, A10.

Kennedy, Paul. *Preparing for the Twenty-First Century*. New York: Random House, 1993.

Kotkin, Joel. "Commuting via Information Superhighway." *The Wall Street Journal*, 27 January 1994, A28.

Kwiatkowski, Leonard. "Why the Military Needs Milstar Satellites." Letter to the Editor. *The New York Times*, 7 February 1994, A10.

Lehman, H. Jane. "A Global Perspective: U.S. Well Housed, but Other Nations Hold Lessons." *The Chicago Tribune*, 19 December 1993, 4F.

Levine, Ross, and Sara J. Zervos. "What We Have Learned About Policy and Growth from Cross-Country Regressions?" *American Economic Review* 83, no. 2 (May 1993): 426-431. *Papers and Proceedings of the 105th Meeting of the American Economic Association*, vol. 83, edited by J. David Baldwin and Ronald L. Oaxaca. Anaheim, Ca.: American Economic Association.

McColm, R. Bruce, Survey Coordinator. *Freedom in the World: The Annual Survey of Political Rights and Civil Liberties, 1992-93*. New York: Freedom House, 1993.

Merrill, John C. *The Dialectic in Journalism: Toward a Responsible Use of Press Freedom*. Baton Rouge: Louisiana State University Press, 1989.

Meyrowitz, Joshua. *No Sense of Place: The Impact of Electronic Media on Social Behavior*. New York: Oxford University Press, 1985.

Mills, Joshua. "Satellite Service Will Extend the Reach of Bloomberg Radio." *The New York Times*, 21 February 1994, C3.

———. "Bloomberg Plans Television Service." *The New York Times*, 10 February 1994, C5.

Mowlana, Hamid, and Laurie J. Wilson. "Communication Technology and Development." In *Report No. 101: Reports and Papers on Mass Communication*. Paris: UNESCO, 1988.

Noam, Eli. *Television in Europe*. New York: Oxford University Press, 1991.

Owen, Bruce M., and Steven S. Wildman. *Video Economics*. Cambridge, Mass.: Harvard University Press, 1992.

Owens, Cynthia. "The Developing Leap: Many Emerging Nations Are Moving Directly into the New Age, Bypassing the Wired Stage." *The Wall Street Journal*, 11 February 1994, R15.

Parenti, Michael. *Make-Believe Media: the Politics of Entertainment*. New York: St. Martin's Press, 1992.

Pennar, Karen, Geri Smith, Rose Brady, Dave Lindorff, and John Rossant. "Is Democracy Bad for Growth?" *Business Week*, 7 June 1993, 84–88.

Perley, Jane. "A Key Czech Learns to Speak Politics." *The New York Times*, 25 February 1994, A4.

Picard, Robert G. *The Press and the Decline of Democracy*. Westport, Conn.: Greenwood Press, 1985.

Popowitz, Rick, Publisher. "It's Less Than Seven Years to the Year 2000." *TAIPAN*, Fall 1993, 7–8. 824 E. Baltimore St., Baltimore, MD 21202.

Redburn, Tom. "An Evolution in an Economy: Jobs in Thinking, Not Making." *The New York Times*, 18 February 1994, A1.

Rigdon, Joan E. "Technological Gains Are Cutting Costs, and Jobs, in Services." *The Wall Street Journal*, 24 February 1994, A1.

Rogers, Everett. *Communication Technology: The New Media in Society*. New York: The Free Press, 1986.

Romer, Paul M. "Two Strategies for Economic Development: Using Ideas and Producing Ideas." In *Proceedings of the World Bank Annual Conference on Development Economics*, edited by Lawrence H. Summers and Shekhar Shah, 63–93. Washington, D.C.: The World Bank, 1992.

Ryan, Joseph E. Letter to the Editor. *The Wall Street Journal*, 24 January 1994, A13.

Saint-Paul, Gilles, and Thierry Verdier. "Education, Democracy and Growth." *Journal of Development Economics* 42, no. 2 (1 December 1993): 399–407.

Scherer, Frederic M. *International High-Technology Competition*. Cambridge, Mass.: Harvard University Press, 1992.

Schiller, Herbert I. *Information and the Crisis Economy*. New York: Oxford University Press, 1986.

Schlesinger, Jacob M., and Yumiko Ono. "Japan's Appetite for U.S. Shows Grows." *The Wall Street Journal*, 22 June 1992, B1.

Severin, Werner J., and James W. Tankard, Jr. *Communication Theories: Origins, Methods, and Uses in the Mass Media*. 3rd Edition. New York: Longman, 1992.

Shenon, Philip. "Detained Burmese Laureate Speaks Out to U.S. Visitors." *The New York Times*, 15 February 1994, A1.

Shoemaker, Pamela J., and Stephen D. Reese. *Mediating the Message: Theories of Influences on Mass Media Content*. New York: Longman, 1991.

Stevenson, Robert L. *Communication, Development, and the Third World*. New York: Longman, 1988.

Stevenson, Robert L., and Donald L. Shaw. *Foreign News and the New World Information Order*. Ames: Iowa State University Press, 1984.

Szymczak, Pat Davis. "The Newest Soviet Unions." *Compuserve Magazine*, September 1993, 46–48.

Toffler, Alvin, and Heidi Toffler. "Avoiding Global Future Shock." *World Monitor: The Christian Science Monitor Monthly*, October 1988, 48–52.

Trachtenberg, Jeffrey A. "Record Industry Revenue Climbed 11% Last Year, but Gain Slowed from 1992." *The Wall Street Journal*, 25 February 1994, B8A.

Tyler, Patrick E. "Prominent Dissident Says Beijing Has Warned Him Not to Publish." *The New York Times*, 12 December 1993, Y14.

UNESCO. *A Documentary History of a New World Information and Communication Order Seen as an Evolving and Continuous Process, 1975–1986*. In *Communication and Society No. 19*. Paris: UNESCO, Undated.

Wriston, Walter B. *The Twilight of Sovereignty: How the Information Revolution Is Transforming Our World*. New York: Charles Scribner's Sons, 1992.

———. "The Inevitable Global Conversation." *Media Studies Journal* 8, no. 1 (Winter 1994): 17–27.

———. *The Race for Content*. Vol. 8. New York: The Freedom Forum Media Studies Center.

chapter **3**

The Collection and Flow of World News

Kuldip R. Rampal

The collection of news around the world has come a long way since James Gordon Bennett, founder of the *New York Herald* in May 1835, retained Daniel Craig's carrier pigeon service to fly in news reports from distant points. Although faster than any other mode of news collection used earlier, this service was not always reliable, even though Bennett provided his own pigeons to Craig. The aggressive penny newspapers of the 1830s, each wanting to be the first in providing news and more of it, turned to pony express runs to transport news stories between cities. By 1836, the express pony service provided by the postal authorities could transport important news stories between New York and New Orleans in less than seven days. Today, news agencies using state-of-the-art telecommunications facilities—telephone, computer, cable, radio, mobile antennas, and satellite circuits—can transmit up to 12,000 words per minute between any two points on the globe. On a typical day, the Associated Press (AP), for example, is said to deliver 20 million words and hundreds of photos and graphics.

The dissemination of such a heavy volume of news and information with an incredible speed might suggest that all parts of the world are well represented in the flow of news, but that is not the reality, as this chapter will explain. An ongoing debate since the early 1970s has revolved around complaints of developing countries that there is an inequity in the quantity and quality of news flowing between the North (the rich, industrialized, developed countries) and the South (the poor, developing countries). Studies have also found that even among the advanced industrialized countries of the world, some receive more attention on a consistent basis than others in the coverage of news. Systematic investigation of the patterns of news flow around the world and factors that influence them has received much scholarly attention for several years.

Before addressing the issues related to the flow of news, this chapter will focus on the big players in the area of news collection and the emergence of regional news agencies around the world. First the need for news agencies is briefly discussed and the origins of the major international news agencies are traced to understand the circumstances and forces that have shaped their contemporary operations.

NEED FOR NEWS AGENCIES

Something of a revolution in journalism occurred when inexpensive newspapers made their appearance on both sides of the Atlantic in the first half of the nineteenth century, starting with the penny press of New York City in the 1830s. The French saw their own versions of the so-called "cheap press" in 1836, and 19 years later, following the final abolition of the newspaper stamp tax, British publishers ushered in the penny press era. Until the introduction of the penny press, newspapers had been concerned more with principles and polemics out of loyalties to political parties or special interests than with "news" for its own sake.

The market for "news," however, was ripe by the 1830s. In America, it was attributed to the emergence of what sociologist Michael Schudson (1978) calls a "democratic market society." More Americans were interested in business and politics than ever before. In business, this movement was expressed in the growth of a capitalistic middle class; in politics, it was known as the Jacksonian or "mass" democracy. The penny press in America, Schudson argued, was the product of this new spirit of individualism in business enterprise and independence in politics. In France, the growing middle class began to resent the fact that only 200,000 people could vote under the limited monarchy of Louis Philippe. Newspapers became a vehicle to push the public's demand for more democracy. In Britain, lowered newspaper production costs, as a result of the removal of the stamp tax, enabled the penny press to emerge in the 1850s to cater to a large, urban middle class.

As demand for news grew, it became clear to newspaper publishers in America and Europe that no publication in any country had the financial and technical means to gather, transmit, and ensure the rapid reception of all the news demanded by its readers, whose curiosity was expanding with their education. Thus, the birth of the mass-oriented penny press was a very important factor in the development of news agencies. By selling their product to an increasing number of newspapers, news agencies could supply a large amount of news at less expense than a newspaper would have to incur if it were to gather such an amount of news on its own. News agencies also had better financial resources to invest in technical facilities, such as the telegraph, than an average newspaper did to transmit the news as quickly as possible.

News agencies have evolved rapidly since their introduction just over 140 years ago, a process that has been greatly facilitated by the phenomenal improvement and general spread of telecommunications. Today, no news organization that aims to inform its consumers about world events can afford to be without the services of at least one major news agency. Even for domestic news, a news organization could not ensure that it has access to all the important news, regardless of the number of its own correspondents, unless it subscribed to at least one news agency. Most news organizations, especially those aimed at people in large, urban areas, typically subscribe to more than one news agency.

When it comes to "foreign" news, only the great international news agencies have the financial and technical resources to establish the necessary infrastructure for gathering and transmitting all the essential news of the world in the shortest possible time. Indeed, in view of the prohibitive costs involved in maintaining correspondents abroad, it is difficult even for large news organizations, such as the *New York Times*, to be totally self-reliant in covering international news. And the greatly increased number of news centers throughout the world does not make matters easier. News agencies, therefore, have become indispensable for any news organization wanting to inform its consumers of all the key developments at home and abroad.

DEVELOPMENT OF NEWS AGENCIES

Five news agencies—AP, United Press International (UPI), Reuters, Agence France-Presse (AFP), and TASS—have been the major world agencies, although the status of UPI is increasingly in doubt, and TASS has lost its former status when it was a global news outlet of the Soviet Union. According to UNESCO, a truly international news agency maintains a network of correspondents to collect news in a great number of countries and a headquarters staff that edits these news items, as well as domestic news, and dispatches them to subscribers as quickly as possible. Such agencies use extensive telecommunications facilities to receive and transmit their services. The development of the international agencies is discussed next in the order of their creation.

Agence France-Presse

The origin of news agencies goes back to 1835. In that year, a young Frenchman, Charles-Louis Havas, created the Havas Agency in Paris, predecessor to the current AFP. Havas had organized a news distribution service 10 years earlier, which was used mostly by merchants and government officials. His success in getting newspapers to subscribe to the Havas Agency is attributed to the emergence of "cheap press" in France, with *La Presse* in 1836. The demand for news was up, and Havas moved to satisfy it. He increased the number of his correspondents, provided a speedy translation of foreign newspapers, and most of all, improved his communications by using the newly invented telegraph. By 1860, he had expanded his news network all over Europe and concluded agreements with the English Reuter agency and the German Wolff agency for cooperative news exchange. Speed of communications was one of the major factors that persuaded newspapers in most parts of Europe to subscribe to the Havas Agency.

In 1879, Havas Agency became a joint stock company, with separate news and advertising branches. The introduction of the advertising branch was a business strategy by Havas, who bartered his news service for free space from newspapers that could not afford to subscribe to the agency. He would sell this free space, in turn, to advertising clients.

Faced with Nazi aggression, the French government purchased the agency's news branch in 1940 to set up a propaganda office at Vichy. When the Germans came, they took over the agency and turned it into a part of the official Nazi news agency, DNB. In 1944, following liberation from occupying Nazi forces, the Havas Agency was given its present name of Agence France-Presse. In 1957, the French parliament passed legislation guaranteeing independence to the AFP.

The Associated Press

The AP grew out of the Harbor News Association formed by six New York City newspapers in 1848 to share the cost of collecting news by means of "news boats," which met incoming ships from Europe. Thus, the Harbor News Association was essentially a news-gathering cooperative, which continues to be the operational policy of today's AP. Following merger with another news agency, the Harbor News Association became the New York Associated Press in 1857. This news cooperative never had more than seven members, all of them New York City newspapers.

To cut telegraphic costs, the New York AP formed news exchange agreements with groups of newspapers in other parts of the country. It distributed the most important news to them, including news from Washington, D.C., and overseas. To this, each group added regional coverage. One such group, the Western Associated Press, withdrew from the cooperative in 1885 and went on to form the AP, incorporated in Illinois, in 1892. The New York AP, which had fought this reorganization, lost and went out of business the same year. The AP expanded rapidly, with 700 newspapers subscribing to its service by the mid-1890s. In 1900, the AP was reorganized and incorporated in New York, where its headquarters have been ever since.

Two changes have taken place in the AP organization since 1945. In a historic decision that year, the U.S. Supreme Court held illegal a clause in the AP bylaws under which members could block the effort of a competitor in the same city to obtain the AP news service through election to membership. As a result of the court ruling, the AP membership was opened to all qualified U.S. newspapers. In 1946, radio stations for the first time were granted associate membership of the AP, which allowed them to subscribe to its regular service. Previously, radio stations could subscribe only to a subsidiary service designed exclusively for them.

Reuters

Reuters's founder, Paul Julius Reuter, was a German immigrant to Britain who set up his telegraphic agency in London in 1851. From a two-room office just outside London Stock Exchange, he began his telegraphic transmission of stock market quotations between London and Paris using the first undersea cable. This followed the success of his pigeon post in delivering stock prices on the Continent.

Reuter soon extended his service to other European countries, expanding its content to include general and economic news. At first serving only financial institutions, Reuter was by 1859 supplying all leading British and many Continental European newspapers with general news. The early Reuter business quickly spread. Branch offices sprang up throughout Europe and beyond as the international telegraph network developed. By 1861, Reuter agents were located in Asia, South Africa, and Australia. By 1872, Reuter had established a presence in Japan.

A family concern until 1915, the agency became a private company later that year with its current name of Reuters Limited. In 1941, following acquisition of a substantial amount of the Reuters stock by British press associations, the agency became cooperative property of the British press. In 1947, the Australian Associated Press and the New Zealand Press Association became partners in Reuters. Reuters share ownership is now spread around the world, with the most significant holdings in Britain and the United States. A 15-member Reuters board of directors oversees the agency's operations.

TASS

Shortly after the Bolshevik revolution of 1917, a news agency, ROSTA, was created to distribute official communiqués and news items, as well as send out propaganda material to the press in areas under Bolshevik control. The Telegrafnoie Agenstvo Sovietskavo Soiuza (TASS), with its headquarters in Moscow, replaced ROSTA on July 10, 1925. Under the Soviet media structure, TASS provided federal, state, and foreign news to national media and to each Soviet state's local news agency. Ever since its founding, TASS has been a government-controlled and financed news agency, although its status has changed with the fall of communism and disintegration of the Soviet Union.

After the breakup of the Soviet Union in the last days of 1991 and the forming of the Commonwealth of Independent States (CIS), TASS lost its affiliate news agencies in the ex-Soviet republics, which became independent agencies. In December 1991, the Russian Supreme Soviet adopted the "Law of the Press," which abolished censorship for the first time in Russian history and gave people the right to read any publications they desired. A number of media organizations, however, were classified as "official," to be financed by the state budget. TASS was identified as one such "official" organization, although its director-general, appointed by President Boris Yeltsin, expects it to operate in an objective and professional manner. In February 1992, the agency's name was changed to ITAR-TASS following its merger with the Russian Informational Telegraph Agency.

UPI

Edward Wyllis Scripps, who owned a chain of afternoon newspapers and could not gain membership in the AP, started his own news service in 1907 called the United Press Association (UP). Unlike the AP, the UP was started as a profit-making agency, so it began to compete fiercely with the AP and developed its foreign news service. In 1958, it merged with William Randolph Hearst's International News Service to become the UPI, which has been the AP's main U.S. rival.

As a result of huge losses, the UPI has changed hands several times since the early 1980s. It was sold to Media News Corporation, a group of American newspaper and television executives, in June 1982. Key news operations were shifted at that time from New York to Washington. The agency, however, continued to lose money and in 1985 filed for bankruptcy. In 1986, the agency was purchased by a Mexican publisher, Mario Vazquez Rana. Vazquez turned over control in early 1988 to an investor group, Infotechnology, Inc., which also controlled Financial News Network. All three firms were plagued by insufficient cash flow. As a result of its 1991 declaration of bankruptcy, UPI was purchased by owners in Saudi Arabia in 1992.

RISE AND DEMISE OF NEWS CARTEL

An interesting phenomenon occurred in the collection of news in 1869, when Havas, Reuters, and the German Wolff news agencies signed a "Treaty of Alliance" to carve up the world into news zones, in each of which one of the three agencies had an exclusive right to gather and distribute news. They also agreed to exchange their services. The alliance was forced by the need to cover the greatest possible number of countries, which no single news agency could do at the time because of limited financial resources. Under the agreement, Reuters was assigned the nations in the British empire as well as those in the Far East; Havas, the French, Spanish, Italian, and Portuguese empires; and Wolff, the holdings of Germany, Austria, the Netherlands, Scandinavia, and Russia. As a result of this agreement, Havas ultimately assumed a dominant role throughout Latin America.

In 1893, the AP agreed to join the European cartel, thus receiving the right to distribute the dispatches of Reuters, Havas, and Wolff in the United States. The agreement prohibited the AP from selling its service outside the United States and restricted its news gathering operations outside the United States to Canada, Mexico, Central America, and the Antilles. The first challenge to the cartel came from the United Press, which soon after its establishment in 1907 moved independently to sell its service abroad, first to Britain and then to Japan. At the outbreak of World War I, its service also came in demand in South America. Not wanting to be left behind, the AP signed an agreement with Havas in late 1918 to sell its service in South America. In 1926, the AP concluded a similar agreement with Reuters to allow it to operate in Japan and China, although both agreements came after considerable resistance from Havas and Reuters. The Wolff agency ceased to exist in 1933. The closure of Wolff and operational disagreements among the remaining three members led to the formal breakup of the cartel in 1934.

The demise of the cartel has meant that in the new competitive environment only the fittest can survive. The competition has resulted in a greater choice of news stories on a given issue and a more comprehensive coverage of the world. It has also forced the news agencies to be innovative in providing news-related and specialized services, as may be seen from a review of the contemporary operations of the international news agencies.

INTERNATIONAL NEWS AGENCIES TODAY

AP

The AP continues to be a nonprofit news cooperative, owned by its 1,551 member daily newspapers and about 6,000 member broadcast outlets throughout the United States as of November 1993. The AP says it serves 98.8 percent of daily newspapers in the United States, representing 99 percent of the newspaper circulation. In addition, 230 nondaily newspapers subscribe to the agency. According to the AP, 1 billion people hear or read its news every day.

Member papers send copies of their stories to the AP, generally by computer; the AP rewrites many of these stories and transmits them to its members (and to subscriber news organizations abroad), along with stories and photos provided by the AP's own staff in the United States and abroad. The agency's photo service, offered since 1935, has been expanded to include a graphics service providing maps, illustrations, and charts related to breaking news stories. Its PhotoStream system links up with "electronic darkrooms" at many papers. This digital process enables newspaper editors to edit photos—adjust size, shape, contrast, and color—on a computer screen before sending them on to production.

The AP has offered a separate sports wire since 1946. A domestic business news wire provides specialized coverage of business, labor, economics, and finance. Supplementing this is AP-DJ, a specialized financial and economic news service distributed abroad by a partnership of AP and Dow Jones & Co. Press Association, an AP subsidiary, provides the AP news to more than 1,000 private subscribers. Another subsidiary, Wide World, makes the AP's photo library and specialized photo services available to nonmember publications and clients.

The AP has 143 domestic and 91 international news bureaus in 71 countries and translates its service into five languages. It has a total of 8,500 foreign subscribers in 112 countries. Its total number of employees is 3,157, with 2,411 in the United States (including 160 in Washington, D.C.) and 746 overseas. In 1993, the agency had a budget of $372.8 million. The AP membership elects its board of directors, which serves as the governing body of the company and oversees its budget.

UPI

Although the UPI has not turned a profit since 1963, it began to experience serious financial difficulties starting in the late 1970s. Owner Scripps Howard sold the agency to a group of American media executives in June 1982 and, as noted earlier, it has changed hands several times since then. Its current owner is a London-based media company, the Middle East Broadcasting Center (MBC), controlled by interests in Saudi Arabia. Although the UPI's Saudi owners have promised to rebuild it, the succession of owners over the past 12 years has resulted in a deterioration of the agency in terms of the size of its business, staff, and reputation.

Staff layoffs began in late 1987, with 350 positions cut by the end of 1988. In late 1991, the UPI drafted a business plan that called for a 51 percent further cut in staff and the paring down of domestic news coverage to 16 states. In August 1993, the agency offered a voluntary employee buyout plan to 200 employees as it reported losses of as much as $1 million a month. At the same time, the UPI placed help-wanted advertisements in several American newspapers seeking stringers for its new regional setup.

All the cutbacks and turmoil at the UPI have resulted in a steady loss of clients. When Scripps sold the agency in 1982, it served some 960 newspapers and 3,700 broadcasting stations in the United States. It also served approximately 2,200 media in 90 countries. In late 1990, the UPI was down to fewer than 400 newspaper clients in the United States, although the total number of media, business, and government subscribers was put at 3,000. By June 1992, the agency had only 2,000 clients around the world. No figures on the scope of its operations and the number of its clients were available from the UPI at the time of this writing in early 1994 because of "proprietary reasons." It should also be noted that the AP, Reuters, and Agence France-Presse no longer consider the UPI to be a major competitor.

Reuters

Unlike other major international news agencies, Reuters dedicates the bulk of its resources to serving banks, brokers, and other organizations involved in financial markets, although it is also heavily involved in supplying news services to the world's media. Reuters gathers information from around 180 exchanges and over-the-counter markets, from some 4,000 customers who contribute data directly to Reuters, and from a network of about 1,200 journalists, photographers, and cameramen. Most of the Reuters staff of 10,426 are employed in the financial and information products divisions.

As of June 1993, Reuters had 123 news bureaus in 75 countries, including 18 in the United States. Reuters has a greater presence in the United States now because it must gather its own news and photos after ending a long-standing cooperative agreement with the UPI, which has lost a number of clients because of operational difficulties. Reuters has customers in more than 130 countries; most are business clients receiving screen-based services. The total number of subscribers is 29,297.

The agency's news service, known as the Reuters World Service, is primarily an English-language service for newspapers, broadcasters, and nonmedia organizations throughout the world. In some countries, Reuters provides this service to national news agencies, which translate its contents into other languages for further distribution. Produced by editing desks in New York, London, Hong Kong, and Nicosia, the World Service contains international stories as well as regional and domestic news. About half of the 150,000 daily word count is filed to all customers, while the balance differs according to the news requirements of each region. Regional services are offered in French, German, Spanish, and Arabic. Reuters's other media services include news graphics, news pictures, and television news.

Because three-fourths of Reuters's revenue comes from services provided to financial markets, it has invested heavily in the development of computer technology and softwares to provide such services to traders, brokers, dealers, analysts, and investors. The systems in use include the Reuter Monitor Service, bringing computerized information to the foreign exchange markets; the Reuter Monitor Dealing Service, bringing transactions to the screen; Dealing 2000, personal computer-based "intelligent" work stations available to foreign exchange dealers; Instinet, offering screen-based transaction facilities to equities dealers; and GLOBEX and the second phase of Dealing 2000, introduced in 1992, offering international computerized matching systems for futures, options, and foreign exchange.

Agence France-Presse

The AFP continues to be a big player in international news dissemination. It provides news in English, French, German, Spanish, Portuguese, and Arabic. It has five news wires in English, targeted to different regions of the world, with each carrying 60,000–90,000 words daily. Five of the six French news wires are targeted similarly, ranging from 50,000 to 120,000 words daily. The agency also provides 250 photos, six news graphics in four languages, 15 audio spots in French, and a variety of special services on a daily basis.

The AFP says it has 12,500 subscribers worldwide, including 1,146 media clients, as of early 1994. The media clients are broken down as 650 newspaper and periodical publishers, 400 broadcasting stations, and 96 national news agencies. Financial institutions, governments, and public and private organizations form the rest of the subscribers. The agency's regional headquarters in Paris, Washington, Hong Kong, and Nicosia supervise news operations in Europe, the Americas, Asia, and the Middle East, respectively. It has 1,100 staff correspondents and photographers, and 2,000 stringers provide news from bureaus in 129 countries.

The AFP has built a unique niche among the international news agencies for its photo service, which is recognized in the industry for its unique angle on sports and general and international news. It claims to be the first such agency to design and install a complete system of digital photo transmission, which delivers the photo five times faster than with analog systems. The agency transmits 50,000 photos a year, all in color, to subscribers around the world by satellite. Major American media organizations subscribe to the AFP's photo services. The agency says that it reaches some 22 million people in the United States daily through its photos alone.

The AFP's special services include the AFP-ECO news wire, which carries 50,000 words daily of economic news from around the world. AFP-FINANCE news wire carries 15,000 words daily on international share prices, trends, and exchange rates. AFX, a joint venture between the AFP and Extel News Limited of London, provides economic and financial news in English. A separate sports news service provides 25,000 words of coverage of the French and international sports scene.

ITAR-TASS

Ever since its founding, TASS was considered a key arm of the Soviet propaganda machine, always portraying national and international developments from the Marxist-Leninist perspective. Speed, timeliness, and objectivity were not critical criteria in news coverage, as they were to its Western counterparts. Often, it "sold" its service free of charge to media in developing countries that had socialistic political systems or were possible candidates for conversion to such a political philosophy. Author Theodore Kruglak (1962) wrote that a number of TASS correspondents overseas worked as intelligence operatives on behalf of the Soviet intelligence agency, the KGB.

The collapse of communism and the Soviet empire, and the emergence of democracy in Russia, should have given ITAR-TASS the necessary freedom to operate as an independent, reliable news gathering service, but that has not been the case so far. It continues to be classified as an "official" organization by the Russian government, receiving most of its finances from the state. ITAR-TASS's Director-General, Vitali Ignatenko, appointed by President Boris Yeltsin, said in an interview with the London-based International Press Institute in 1993 that Yeltsin did not make any "visible effort" to censor any of its material. Ignatenko also complained, however, that despite the abolition of censorship and other official restraints over the media in Russia, there was still a political desire to make use of the media because "[t]he feeling remains very strong that those who control the media control the country." Ignatenko noted that the new Russia does not need a news agency like the old TASS, adding, however, that "bad habits die hard" (International Press Institute 1993, p. 50).

Ignatenko wants ITAR-TASS to inform people of all important events in a professional manner and to exclude any manipulation of opinion. The agency has the necessary potential to compete with other wire services with its 1,300 reporters, editors, and photographers in 113 countries, 1,200 foreign subscribers, and an annual budget of $160 million. It remains to be seen whether it will live up to Ignatenko's expectations.

Meanwhile, ITAR-TASS has faced stiff competition from two agencies, Interfax and Postfactum, formed in late 1989. Interfax established its credibility during the attempted coup in August 1991, when it became a major source of accurate and reliable information to subscribers via FAX machines. The leadership of TASS, on the other hand, was said to have willingly cooperated with the plotters of the coup in carrying out their orders.

SUPPLEMENTAL NEWS AGENCIES

Supplemental wire services have fulfilled a need in American journalism normally not met by the conventional news agencies such as the AP and the UPI, and have been excellent in providing spot news. David Shaw (1988) of the *Los Angeles Times*, who has been covering the American media for years, says that reporters who like to write investigative stories or other stories that challenge the establishment generally complain the most about traditional wire services such as the AP or UPI. One reason these agencies do not encourage controversial stories, especially investigative stories, is that they serve customers with so many political perspectives. Newspapers needing more specialized fare—such as hard news exclusives, investigative reporting, political commentary, and concentrated business coverage—turn to supplemental wire services.

The major supplemental services in the United States are the New York Times

News Service, the Los Angeles Times–Washington Post News Service, and Dow Jones News Service. Founded in 1917, the New York Times News Service has more than 500 subscribers in 54 countries. Most of the copy for this service is provided by the *New York Times*'s 30 foreign correspondents, 40 Washington bureau staffers, and the city room. The Los Angeles Times–Washington Post News Service, which began in 1962, has more than 600 clients in 56 countries and is served by 65 foreign correspondents of the *Times* and the *Post*, their Washington bureaus and local staffs, their other U.S. bureaus, and the news services of the AFP and the *Guardian* of London.

Introduced in the 1890s, the Dow Jones News Service continues to be recognized as the premier business and financial news wire for brokerage firms, banks, investment companies, and other businesses. AP-Dow Jones, a joint venture with the AP that provides international economic, business, and financial news, distributes its services to more than 26,000 terminals in 63 countries. Other important supplementals include Copley News Service, Cox News Service, Gannett News Service, Scripps-Howard News Service, Knight News Tribune, Field News Service, and Newhouse News Service.

VIDEO AND AUDIO NEWS SERVICES

Visnews and World Television News (WTN) have been the key players in the international television news agency business, although there are several others suppliers of footage to end-users. Visnews was established in 1957 with the aim of providing independent news coverage to television broadcasters worldwide. Acquired outright by Reuters in 1992, Visnews claims to be the largest television news agency in the world. Its daily coverage, provided by more than 500 staff members, is estimated to reach some half-billion households worldwide, via more than 650 broadcasters in over 80 countries. News coverage is sent to subscribers by a series of daily satellite news feeds. In Europe, Reuters Television operates the only news-dedicated satellite service that delivers to broadcasters regular news feeds and news flashes throughout the day, often live from the story.

WTN is 80 percent owned by Capital Cities/ABC, with 10 percent belonging to Britain's Independent Television News, and the remaining 10 percent to Channel 9 in Australia. WTN serves as the video wire service for over 1,000 clients worldwide. CBS operates a profitable foreign operation called Newsnet, which is classified as a news agency by the European Broadcasting Union. By mid-1993, Newsnet had established business relations with some 30 European broadcasters and several others around the world. Cable News Network (CNN) and the British Broadcasting Corporation (BBC) also sell news footage to clients in many countries. Television news is also supplied by National Broadcasting Company (NBC), American Broadcasting Company (ABC), and the Japanese and German news agencies. The AP had plans to offer a separately staffed video news agency before the end of 1994. The UPI was considering a joint venture with its parent company, Middle East Broadcasting Co., which produces and supplies general television entertainment and news programming targeted to Arab populations in Europe, the Middle East, and Africa.

In radio, the AP operates the AP Network News, the largest single radio network in the United States. This audio service, which provides voice feeds and actualities to supplement the broadcast wire, was created in 1974 and reaches nearly 1,000 AP broadcast members. As of early 1994, the UPI was also continuing to provide voice feeds and actualities in addition to its broadcast wire, but the number of subscribers was not available. Dow Jones's two radio networks offer "The Wall Street Journal Report," sold primarily to AM stations, and "The Dow Jones Report," heard primarily on FM stations. Together, these programs are carried on more than 160 stations for a combined coverage of nearly 90 percent of the United States, including all of the top 50 markets. "The Enterprising Manager," a new series of three weekly programs designed to assist small-business owners, is now heard on more than 40 stations.

INTERNATIONAL NEWSPAPERS, MAGAZINES, AND BROADCASTERS

Besides news agencies, several international newspapers, magazines, and broadcasting organizations play an important role as purveyors of news globally. Three newspapers that are believed to be especially important among opinion leaders around the world are the *New York Times*, the *Times* of London, and the *Guardian*, also from England. *The International Herald Tribune*, based in Paris, is printed simultaneously via satellite at ten locations worldwide and distributed globally. It had a circulation of 178,002 in 1993. Much of its copy comes from the *New York Times* and the *Washington Post*, which, along with Whitney Communications, own this newspaper. *The Wall Street Journal*, the flagship publication of Dow Jones and Company, is the global business daily. With the *Wall Street Journal Europe*, published in Brussels, and the *Asian Wall Street Journal*, published in Hong Kong, worldwide circulation is more than 1.9 million. Another prestigious global business newspaper is the *Financial Times* of London, which also publishes a North American edition via satellite. In 1993, it had a total circulation of 248,015. A *USA Today*-style newspaper, established in 1990 in London for readers across Europe, is the *European*. It had a weekly circulation of 151,270 in 1993.

Among newsmagazines, three stand out for their global reach—*Time, Newsweek,* and Britain's *Economist. Time*, with its 1993 circulation of 4.25 million in the United States alone, sold an additional million-plus copies to readers overseas. It publishes editions for Canada, Europe, the Middle East, Asia, Africa, and Latin America. *Newsweek*, whose 1993 U.S. circulation was just over 3 million, sold about a million copies internationally through its editions for Europe, Japan, Latin America, the Pacific, and Southeast Asia. *The Economist*, reputed for its comprehensive coverage of global issues and good writing, is increasingly becoming an important newsmagazine in the United States, where it sold 142,000 copies in 1993. It had a total circulation of 450,737.

In international television news broadcasting, CNN has been a major player, particularly in view of the credibility it established in covering Iraq's invasion of Kuwait in August 1990 and the resulting Gulf War. Launched in 1980, CNN provides news coverage 24 hours a day to 136 million viewers in the United States via satellite and cable distribution. In 1985, owner Ted Turner launched CNN International, which in 1993 served 70 million homes outside the United States. Faced with criticism that CNN International had too much emphasis on U.S. news, it is taking steps to provide greater regionalized coverage of world events. In 1991, the venerable BBC, which has operated a highly credible international radio service for over six decades, launched a 24-hour international television news service, which is increasingly seen as a competitor to CNN International. Called BBC World Service Television, it was available to more than 17 million homes in Asia, the Middle East, Africa, Europe, and Canada as of mid-1993. The Japanese are also eyeing the international news market, having already established "Japan Business Today," a half-hour, English-language business news program. It is seen widely in the Asia-Pacific countries. As more countries take advantage of the satellite communication technology, additional sources of television news will be available for international audiences. For example, in late 1993 China began a daily 18-hour transmission of news and entertainment programming to the United States via satellite. The three television networks in Taiwan have also been sending their news programming via satellite to American viewers. Special-interest channels, such as Scola in the United States, are offering a replay of news programs broadcast from various countries.

Flow of news internationally through radio has been a reality for several decades, although it has generally been viewed as propaganda because international radio broadcasting has been done primarily by government-run stations. Two government-sponsored stations, however, have established their credibility as reliable sources of news to listeners worldwide. They are the BBC World Service and the Voice of America. The BBC, which went on the air in 1932, broadcasts to an international audience of 130 million in 36 languages for 768 hours weekly. Studies have shown that in several countries, BBC news is held in greater credibility than the native radio newscasts. The Voice of America, established as the international broadcasting service of the U.S. government in 1942, reaches 127 million listeners worldwide. The Voice of America broadcasts for 1,050 hours on a weekly basis in 44 languages. It has some 17 million listeners in China alone, but during the 1989 Tiananmen prodemocracy movement, its audience shot up to an estimated 100 million because of its extensive and reliable coverage of the movement. Other major international broadcasters include Radio Moscow, Radio Beijing, German radio Deutsche Welle, Radio France International, Radio Nederland, and Radio Cairo.

PROBLEMS AND PATTERNS IN THE FLOW OF NEWS

The dominance of news collection and dissemination by Western news agencies and other media organizations has caused quite a friction between developed and developing countries since the 1970s. Four areas have been of special concern to developing countries. First, several studies since the 1960s have shown that more than 75 percent of the nonlocal news contents in developing countries' media comes from Western news agencies. Developing countries say that they, therefore, are forced to see practically all issues, including themselves, through Western eyes. Second, the Western information monopoly has resulted in a heavy imbalance in the flow of news, with information moving predominantly from advanced Western countries to developing countries. Third, what little coverage developing countries do receive in the Western media is often tainted by stereotypical portrayals of such nations, with a focus on violence, pestilence, murders, and other catastrophes. The fourth area of concern is that the West continues to maintain "cultural imperialism" through its dominant position as supplier of news, information, and cultural fare to the developing world.

Several studies cited by Mowlana (1986) support developing countries' claim of an imbalanced news flow. Three of the conclusions of the studies are important to note here. First, the majority of international news flows vertically from the developed to the developing nations by way of the dominant Western news agencies. Second, the United States and Western Europe receive the greater amount of coverage in the media while the socialist countries and the developing nations receive the least. Third, although horizontal news flows do exist within the developing as well as the developed world, this type of flow constitutes a substantially smaller portion of the overall coverage than does vertical flow.

Several news flow studies have also lent validity to developing countries' concern that they are often portrayed in a stereotypical manner. The studies indicate that the quality of international flow of news remains poor, with intensifying focus on third-world violent conflict and crisis. For example, a content analysis study of U.S. wire service coverage by Giffard (1982) found that developing countries are depicted as relatively more prone to internal conflicts and crisis; more likely to be the setting of armed conflict; more frequently the recipients of disaster relief or economic and military aid; and more often the location of criminal activities.

In an attempt to address these problems, developing countries pushed for a New World Information Order (NWIO) in the late 1970s through UNESCO. Among a variety of actions proposed to address problems associated with international news flow, one called for regulating collection, processing, and transmission of news and data across national frontiers. Western countries strongly rejected such a move. The proposed NWIO was extensively discussed by a 16-member commission appointed by UNESCO, known as the MacBride Commission, whose members came from all ideologies and parts of the world. The commission's report, *Many Voices One World*, published in 1980, acknowledged developing countries' concerns about international information flow but rejected their proposal to regulate free flow of news.

The MacBride Commission encouraged developing countries to lessen their dependence on Western news agencies by developing their own strong national and regional news agencies to cover international news. The developing countries, to the extent that it was feasible given their inadequate financial resources, had already begun moving in that direction. The nonaligned countries, for example, had established the Non-Aligned News Agencies Pool in 1976 under the aegis of Tanjug, the Yugoslav news agency. Its aims were to promote mutual understanding among the developing countries and to reduce dependence on the Western news agencies for international news. It languished, however, because much of its material was colored by ideological rhetoric. A more successful third-world news agency has been the Inter Press Service, which was founded in 1964 by a group of Latin American and European journalists to provide news supporting political and social reform in Latin America. In the 1970s, it abandoned its political activism in favor of focusing on development-oriented issues in developing countries at large. It has since extended its operations to Africa, Asia, and Europe. A U.S.-based Interlink Press Service uses Inter Press Service information for distribution in the United States. Other regional news agencies established by developing countries include DEPTH, operated by the Manila-based Press Foundation of Asia; the Latin American News Agency; Egypt's Middle East News Agency; Pan-African News Agency, developed by the Organization of African Unity; and the Caribbean News Agency, developed by the region's 13 English-speaking countries.

The imbalance of news flow is not just a developed–developing countries phenomenon, however. Studies have shown that such an imbalance exists even among the developed countries of the West. Semmel (1976) found that Scandinavian countries, as well as developing regions of the world, were mostly ignored in the American media. Larson (1984) also found Scandinavia to be among the least covered nations on U.S. network television news. A 1993 study by Professor Lianne Fridriksson of coverage of Scandinavia in the elite American media supports the earlier findings. In this comprehensive content analysis study of the *New York Times, Washington Post,* the three major newsmagazines, and the commercial network news, Fridriksson found that Scandinavian coverage was mostly crisis oriented, "enough so as to conclude that the Third World has no exclusive right to complaints that the U.S. media largely overlook developmental stories in favor of spot crisis-oriented news." The study also found that were it not for the reporting of various, isolated crises, overall coverage of Scandinavia in the American media would be so scant as to be practically nonexistent.

The news flow studies on developing countries and Scandinavia indicate that the quantity or quality of international news flow is not necessarily correlated with the economic level of a nation or a region, because Scandinavia has been a part of the developed first world for many years. Several studies have been done to determine factors that influence the flow of news globally. Galtung (1971) hypothesized that there is a "center–periphery" pattern in the flow of international news. News, he noted, flows mostly from the "center," or dominant countries, to the "periphery," or dependent areas. A study by Kariel and Rosenvall (1984) supported this hypothesis by finding that the "eliteness" of a nation as a news source was the most important criterion for news selection. Hester (1973) said that at any given time, the nations of the world have designated places in an international pecking order. Perceptions of positions in that order partially determine the flow, direction, and volume of information. Hester also hypothesized that strong economic relations or cultural affinities will increase the flow of news among nations, as will the perception of threat between any two nations.

THE OUTLOOK

Political, economic, and technological progress in several parts of the world appear to bode well for the collection and free flow of news. The rise of democracy in Eastern Europe and Russia, as well as in a number of developing countries, has considerably lessened, if not eliminated, the obstacles encountered by news agencies and foreign correspondents in covering news. Totalitarian holdovers and authoritarian governments in many countries, however, will continue to create several obstacles in the coverage of news, including restricted access, explicit or implicit censorship, and pressure against correspondents, extending as far as expulsion.

Restricted access results in incomplete and unreliable information because information must be obtained from radio broadcasts and visitors. Explicit censorship results in deletions or refusal to transmit correspondents' copy. Implicit censorship is less obvious but nearly as inhibiting to balanced news coverage. An example is the inaccessibility in some countries of key government officials. Often the most difficult official sources for the foreign correspondent to reach are those who can best explain the story of their countries to the world. Also, when the local press is restricted to publication of only government-approved news, foreign correspondents' access to balanced local information suffers. This makes more difficult the foreign correspondents' efforts to understand and explain the country to readers in distant places. Direct action against foreign correspondents is the most extreme and dangerous obstacle to free news coverage. Wire services correspondents are often expelled by various countries because the government involved objected to the reporting of specific news. It is hoped that the trend against such restrictions will continue to grow.

Economic growth in many developing countries is allowing them to expand their news gathering and news dissemination operations, which should increasingly reduce their dependence on the services of Western news agencies. The Malaysian news agency, Bernama, for example, has expanded its reach into the member countries of the Association of Southeast Asian Nations. India, China, Indonesia, Mexico, and countries in the Arab League already have their own communication satellite systems in place, which are bound to improve their abilities to both collect and disseminate news globally. This prospect also looks good in view of the fact that developing countries are increasingly stationing their own correspondents in the Western news capitals and elsewhere in the world. Many other developing countries in the world, especially in Africa, are likely to take longer to break out of the media dependency situation because of lack of financial resources to develop their media infrastructures.

In the advanced, technologically sophisticated countries of the world, news flow will increasingly acquire new dimensions. On-line interactive news services, such as the ones provided by Nexus, VU/TEXT, Data Times, Dow Jones, NewsNet, and DIALOG in the United States, are likely to be in increasing demand as countries build and expand their information superhighways. Such services allow comprehensive, retrospective searches for newspaper and news agency coverage. Dow Jones News/Retrieval, for example, is already widely recognized as the nation's leading on-line supplier of business and financial news and information. As of early 1993, the service provided 68 data bases drawn from more than 1,300 sources—including the full text of 37 of the top 50 U.S. newspapers—to subscribers.

Another group of on-line services that gives access to news, specifically news wire stories, also promises to be in increasing demand. These consumer- or business-oriented systems include CompuServe, Delphi, DIALCOM, GEnie, and Prodigy. News coverage on these systems ranges from an edited version of today's news only to one or two weeks' transmission from the AP, the UPI, Reuters, and the Business Wire. The Australian-born media baron, Rupert Murdoch, who acquired Delphi in 1993, is planning to offer an electronic newspaper on this on-line service.

Thus, the prospects for news collection and flow look better than ever before as the twentieth century draws to a close. The confluence of an increasingly open political climate, growing economies in many developing countries, and the marvels of technology points to a free flow of information at a greater scale than the world has experienced until recent years.

BIBLIOGRAPHY

Agence France-Presse. Material and information supplied by Sarah Jackson of the AFP, December 1993.

The Associated Press: Origin, History and Development. Typed monograph and information supplied by Susan Clark of the Associated Press, December 1993.

Barker, Greg, and Eileen Mahoney. "A New Soviet Source." *Columbia Journalism Review* 29 (March 1991): 11.

Chang, C. J. Section Chief, Department of Radio and Television Affairs, Government Information Office, Taipei, Taiwan. 14 January 1994. Interview. Much of the perspective on the services of the four Western news agencies was gained by the author in his capacity as an assistant news editor at the *Straits Times*, Singapore, during 1992-1993.

Dow Jones Annual Report. New York: Dow Jones & Co., Inc.

Editor & Publisher International Yearbook 1993. New York: Editor & Publisher.

Emery, Michael, and Edwin Emery. *The Press and America*. Englewood Cliffs, N.J.: Prentice Hall, 1992.

Fenby, Jonathan. *The International News Services*. New York: Shocken Press, 1986.

Fridriksson, Lianne. "Coverage of Scandinavia in U.S. News Media." Paper presented at the Association for Education in Journalism and Mass Communication annual conference. Kansas City, Mo. August 1993.

Galtung, Johan. "A Structural Theory of Imperialism." *Journal of Peace Research* 8, no. 2 (1971): 81-117.

Giffard, C. Anthony. "Coverage of Developed and Developing Nations in American Wire Services to Asia." Paper presented at the Association for Education in Journalism annual convention, Athens, Ohio, August 1982.

Gordon, Gregory, and Ronald E. Cohen. *Down to the Wire: UPI's Fight for Survival*. New York: McGraw-Hill, 1990.

Hester, Al. "Theoretical Considerations in Predicting Volume and Direction of Information Flow." *Gazette* 19 (1973): 238-247.

International Press Institute. "Vitali Ignatenko, Director-General of ITAR-TASS News Agency." *IPI Report* 42 (June/July 1993): 50.

Kariel, Herbert G., and Lynn A. Rosenvall. "Factors Influencing International News Flow." *Journalism Quarterly* 61 (Autumn 1984): 509-516.

Kruglak, Theodore E. *The Two Faces of TASS*. Minneapolis: University of Minnesota Press, 1962.

Larson, James F. *Television's Window on the World: International Affairs Coverage on the U.S. Networks*. Norwood, N.J.: Ablex Publishing Co., 1984.

MacBride Commission. *Many Voices, One World*. London: Kogan Page, 1980.

McClellan, Steve. "The Growing Focus on Global News." *Broadcasting and Cable* 123 (31 May 1993): 40-41.

Mowlana, Hamid. *Global Information and World Communication*. New York: Longman, 1986.

Olson, Kenneth E. *The History Makers*. Baton Rouge: Louisiana State University Press, 1966.

Rampal, Kuldip R., and W. Clifton Adams. "Credibility of the Asian News Broadcasts of the Voice of America and the British Broadcasting Corporation." *Gazette* 46 (1990): 93–111.

Schudson, Michael. *Discovering the News: A Social History of American Newspaper*. New York: Basic Books, 1978.

Semmel, Andrew K. "Foreign News in Four U.S. Elite Dailies: Some Comparisons." *Journalism Quarterly* 53, no. 4 (1976): 732–736.

Shaw, David. "The AP: It's Everywhere and Powerful." Reprinted from the *Los Angeles Times*. *The L.A. Times Monograph* (3 April 1988): 1–11.

This Is Reuters. Material and information supplied by Dorothy Delman, assistant manager, Reuters, December 1993.

Ulrich's International Periodicals Directory 1992–93. New Providence, N.J.: R.R. Bowker, 1992.

UNESCO. *News Agencies: Their Structure and Operation*. Paris: UNESCO, 1953.

"UPI Sold to Arab Firm." *Editor & Publisher* 125, no. 26 (27 June 1992): 9.

chapter **4**

Barriers to Media Development

Tim Gallimore

INTRODUCTION

Before discussing barriers to media development, it is necessary to define what is meant by the words *media* and *development. Media* can be defined as the means of communication. But media comprise the technology for sending and receiving messages and the organizations for gathering, processing, and transmitting news and information to a mass audience. The wire services, newspapers, magazines, broadcast stations, and satellite networks around the world are most easily and commonly identified as the media. However, the means of communication also include books, pamphlets, billboards, and computer bulletin boards. These individual entities together form an institution that provides for the informational needs of a society.

Important in this process is the ability of the media to identify, create, manipulate, and spread public opinion. The media is the institution in society that not only informs the public but also helps to move the masses in collective, purposeful, and productive action.

Development may be defined as increasing the quantity and improving the quality of the available means or media of communication. Development of the media is an improvement in the availability and diversity of news and other information to meet the needs of the audience. Development also includes improved individual access to the channels of communication for the purposes of sending and receiving messages from the mass audience. In short, media development is facilitating the flow of information among and between individuals and institutions in any given community or society.

There are at least four categories into which barriers to media development may be placed. There are physical, social/psychological, political/legal, and economic barriers to media development. These barriers often account for differences in the level of development or sophistication that we observe among the media systems in the

53

world. There is no media system or society that can accurately claim to be without any of these barriers that hinder the ideal conditions for communication.

PHYSICAL BARRIERS

The first and foremost physical barriers to media development include the Earth's topography. Physical features or natural obstructions often prevent the installation, deployment, or efficient operation of communication equipment and hinder the dissemination of information via mass media channels. In many parts of the world, mountainous and other inhospitable terrain block the installation of telephone lines and even the reach of broadcast signals.

Geography is sometimes a physical barrier to communication. The vast distances between population centers, or audiences, and the location of media organizations make communication difficult or impossible. This is often the case in Russia with its land mass that spans 11 time zones. In India and on the island nation of Indonesia, rivers and the ocean present physical barriers to communication and the development of certain forms of media. However, satellites and repeater stations have provided the solution to bridging some of these distances, waterways, and obstructing terrains.

Other physical barriers include the unavailability of basic infrastructure such as roads for the transportation of printed communication and the equipment for broadcasting. In the West African nation of Mauritania, for example, the quickest way to travel from the capital of Nouakchott to the northern part of the country is to drive along the beach at low tide. It's an overnight trip by truck or four-wheel drive vehicle to reach the nearest population center, if the tide is just right.

The scarcity of electricity, gasoline, spare parts, and other necessities of transportation hinder not only development of the media but all other activities in many parts of the world. The scarcity of available electromagnetic frequencies for broadcasting and of geosynchronous orbital slots for satellites are physical barriers to developing the mass media and telecommunications systems in many countries. Although the telecommunication scarcities appear to be physical barriers, they have more to do with unequal allocation of the celestial pie in an international order where the technologically capable have more than what might be considered their fair share. A lack of access to frequencies and orbital slots are more accurately described as political/legal barriers to media development.

The scarce supply of newsprint and printing technology is another formidable barrier to media development. Most newsprint is produced in North America and Europe and is then exported to the rest of the world. Because of climatic and soil conditions, some nations, like those in sub-Saharan Africa, are incapable of growing the trees necessary for producing their own newsprint. Therefore, this physical barrier hampers the development of their domestic print media and keeps them in a constant state of dependency on imported newsprint.

At times, governments create an artificial scarcity of imported newsprint and other necessary production supplies by controlling access to and distribution of the commodities to punish or reward individual media outlets.

Many nations do not have the presses and other technology for printing mass copies of publications. They also often lack the equipment for printing in color, for photographic reproduction, and for other advanced production processes that add to the quantity and quality of printed materials.

SOCIAL/PSYCHOLOGICAL BARRIERS

The social and psychological barriers to media development are perhaps the most difficult to overcome because the solutions often involve a change in the individual's attitude and deep-seated beliefs about very important matters. The most common of these barriers are illiteracy and ignorance. Nearly 70 percent of the world's population is illiterate according to some estimates. The 1990 United Nations (UN) statistics show the rate of illiteracy ranging from 5 percent in the United States to 91 percent in the West African nation of Bukina Faso. According to UN figures, 28.6 percent of the population in China and 59.2 percent of the population in India is illiterate.

The inability to read and write limits the individual's capacity to communicate, but more importantly, it also limits the ability to learn and grow. Lack of enlightenment and knowledge of the world profoundly influences attitudes and beliefs, often in a negative manner. Literacy opens up the world to the individual and drives the desire for more and better communication content. Enlightened and literate individuals are much more likely to make demands of the media that will force them to a higher level of development. The printed media can flourish only to the degree that a domestic population is literate.

Multilingualism in a nation and the logistics of serving the information needs of audiences from different cultural and ethnic groups can be barriers to media development. In most African nations, three or four languages are used for daily communication. The mass media are therefore faced with the challenge of providing content in each of these languages to meet the needs of the entire population. This is particularly true where the media are owned by the government and operate on a fixed budget that does not allow expansion of service for all those who need it.

In nations with commercial, privately owned media, specialization and market segmentation usually ensure that this content is available as competitors scramble to supply a demand and make a handsome profit. Under these circumstances, it is common for individual media outlets to focus on the information needs of a single segment of the audience, whether that segment is defined by its language, culture, or other unique interests. Where there are not enough media organizations to meet the needs by catering to specific language or cultural groups, many go without. Lack of capital is often the reason why media operators do not step forward to fill the information void.

The reliance on interpersonal communication and public opinion leadership in some societies sometimes hinders the development of the mass media. Where the population is removed from the institutions of formal government and lacks contact with the larger community or society, mass media have little or no effect on the daily life of the ordinary citizen. Local authority figures, like the elders, the skilled, the physically powerful, and the wealthy tend to dominate communication and control public opinion in such situations. What these opinion leaders and their circle of associates have to say is what matters in the absence of mass media and the diversity of views they tend to contribute. These information elites have little or no incentive to foster development of the mass media that normally will usurp their power and diminish their status.

The social hierarchy and community decision-making practices in some nations, particularly the Islamic nations, serve as a barrier to development of the mass media. Again, in societies like these, there tends to be a stronger reliance on interpersonal and group communication than on the channels of mass media. Therefore, there is not as much incentive or need to develop the institutional mass media to a high degree.

Religious beliefs and cultural practices often result in diminished reliance on mass media and less desire to improve it. Even in American society, there are religious groups like the Amish, fundamentalists, and Evangelicals, who shun or disapprove of their members using the mass media, particularly television, because they consider the media to have corrupting or immoral influences on the audience.

The fear of negative influences from media content is by no means confined to any individual country or region of the world. This concern was part of the call for a new information order to end what is called *cultural imperialism*. Third-world nations argued that communication content imported from Western countries would decimate the indigenous culture and replace domestic attitudes and practices with those embedded in the foreign materials.

These nations erected barriers against imported media content and the "dangerous" ideas contained therein. Western entertainment products are often the target for exclusion because of the products, services, and practices they promote—many of them anathema to the cultural norms of non-Western societies. The use of alcoholic beverages, cigarettes and tobacco products, condoms, and other birth control devices depicted in entertainment programs or in advertisements is often found objectionable or even offensive in some societies. The depiction of violence, nudity, and sexual content also prevents materials from being disseminated via the domestic media in some countries. It is interesting to note that some Western European nations are now making the same cultural imperialism argument that the third world did and are also taking steps to limit or exclude American and other foreign-produced content from their domestic media.

The lack of training and professionalization of journalists is perhaps the greatest barrier to media development in most nations. Formal journalism education is embryonic or nonexistent in many of the newly independent nations and in most of the third-world countries. On-the-job training is the norm for journalists in these countries. Most of this training is being done by practitioners with little or no formal training themselves.

For journalists in the former communist nations, retraining was needed before they could work in the media with a new philosophical and ideological approach. Those who could not be retrained were purged to improve the credibility of the "new" media in the eyes of the public. A shortage of journalists resulted, and with the end of communism, the field was—in theory—suddenly open to anyone who wanted to have a go at it. A good number of these journalists found themselves in the media as a consequence of having to pursue a new occupation or as a part-time avocation while holding down another job.

The experience of press freedom for the first time, or liberation after an era of suppression, often leads to an immediate surge in the number and variety of media outlets. Experience in Eastern Europe and elsewhere has proved that the newness wears off quickly. New and inexperienced journalists then turn their attention to partisan reporting with the new-found tool of a potentially powerful press.

The content of the news organs at this point is nothing more than party polemics of politically aligned media constantly carping on the regime or party in power but offering no new objective information, solutions, or direction to the population. They usually are quickly dismissed by the public for not meeting its expectation. This is a common complaint about the media in nations as varied as Mauritania and Slovakia.

This lack of training and professionalism in reporting feeds the low status of journalists in society and the lack of power and prestige ascribed to the media in general. Accuracy and fairness are measures of professionalism that can add to the quality of the news media coverage and can generate credibility and trust in the eyes of the public. However, these elements are not found in media systems that practice partisan or advocacy journalism.

POLITICAL/LEGAL BARRIERS

The tyranny and dictatorship associated with the authoritarian operation of the press, which was discussed in earlier chapters, also hinder the development of the media. Herbert Altschull's thesis that the media serve as agents of power to maintain and perpetuate the sovereign is worthy of consideration (Altschull 1984). But to maintain political power, the sovereign often finds it effective to suppress, stunt, and otherwise stifle the means of communication for fear that they would be used to usurp him.

In such instances, the sovereign resorts to making the mass communication media part of his dominion. Government ownership of the media greatly hinders its development. And where government does not own the means of communication, it sets up other barriers to control the private or independent press. Censorship, licensing, and restriction of the media are common practices engaged in by despots around the world who fear the rising voices of dissidents who, with the potential of free expression in an open media system, could galvanize public opinion and create popular support for collective action to overthrow the regime.

Because of this potential that the media have for promoting or instigating political change, journalists are often jailed, beaten, or killed by political leaders attempting to control communication and hold on to power. Organizations such as Freedom House, Amnesty International, the Committee to Protect Journalists, and other international organizations regularly document and publicize the human rights abuses, media suppression, and the killing of journalists around the world.

Threats to life and limb are serious political barriers to media development. But so too is the self-censorship that often results from these threats. Journalists in Central and South America have been under the greatest pressure of practicing quality journalism at their peril. The media personnel in Peru and Colombia have suffered particularly great losses because recently they have been hit hard on both sides by repressive regimes, would-be leaders in guerrilla movements, and by crime groups organized to carry out a lucrative trade in illegal drugs. The Shining Path guerrillas and the Medellin drug cartel are well-known groups that have carried out bombings on newspaper offices and other deadly attacks on journalists.

Although media self-censorship is psychological in nature, the very real consequences of being victimized by political violence is the source of this significant barrier to media development. However, not all self-censorship is the result of political repression of journalists. The co-optation and corruption of the media also produce a fair amount of self-censorship that robs the public of necessary information that any well-developed media system should provide. Journalists and media organizations do support regimes, even despotic and abusive regimes, by remaining silent at times and serving as the mouthpiece of government at other times.

Political leaders may also disenfranchise groups to maintain power and privilege. The outlawing of opposition parties and suppression of minority groups are other political barriers to developing diversity of views and information in a society. These political and legal measures amount to barriers to media development because political parties and ethnic or minority populations often sponsor or operate organs of communication that significantly augment and enrich the flow of information in any media system.

At times these suppressed groups provide the only means of mass communication for a significant portion of the population in some countries. Radio broadcasting plays an important role in South Africa, with its multitude of languages and high rate of illiteracy. But the formerly apartheid government of South Africa has only recently started to allow private ownership and operation of radio stations that broadcast in indigenous languages to the various ethnic groups in the country. The printed media were available for the most part only to whites and to blacks who were privileged to gain literacy under the now-fading regime of systematic disenfranchisement and suppression of the majority population.

Similarly, the Palestinians living in the Israeli-occupied territories of the West Bank and Gaza have been prevented by Israel for decades from establishing their own media. Palestinians have been relying on the media in neighboring Jordan and on sparse programming in Arabic from the Israeli media, which caters mostly to Palestinians in Israel. With Israel and the Palestine Liberation Organization (PLO) formally recognizing each other in 1993, the PLO quickly moved to begin the development of a media system operated by Palestinians to meet the information and entertainment needs of Palestinians.

In a broad sense, the legal barriers to media development stem from the general lack of respect for human rights around the world and the lack of legal protection for journalists as they perform their news gathering and dissemination functions. As a practical matter, guaranteeing human rights, including the right to communicate, is more a moral function than the result of lax enforcement of any law. Where human rights are elevated, liberty and creativity of the human spirit abounds and so too does the need and desire for well-developed channels of communication.

An essential component of the ideal media environment is a legal right for the public and the media to have access to documents and information held by the government. Those nations that have laws guaranteeing access to public records and public meetings where the people's business is conducted provide a great advantage for their media to develop and thrive. In the United States, the First Amendment, the federal Freedom of Information Act, and similar state open meetings and open records laws, called state "Sunshine" laws, provide public access. The media in nations without such laws are usually devoid of the rich and important content that characterizes a quality information system.

In addition to mandating access to information, open records and open meeting laws also create a climate that generally facilitates news gathering. Government officials and bureaucrats are more likely to cooperate with journalists when there is a presumption of openness and the right of the public to information. In many countries, journalists face a significant barrier in gathering the news because government sources refuse to talk to them and to explain public policy.

Some of these sources are uncooperative because of instructions from their superiors. Independent journalists in Mauritania have found this an insurmountable barrier in their attempt to inform the public. The journalists reported that government ministers and low-level bureaucrats have been dismissed because they granted interviews or provided public documents to the press. Party officials from the former Soviet Union have demanded payment from Western journalists before consenting to interviews. While no single law, or collection of laws, could possibly end all these types of abuses, the presumption of access and openness in a society can greatly facilitate the flow of information. Increased access to government documents and sources can also help to end the journalism polemics and improve the quality of media content in nations that are starting out on the road of independent journalism.

The lack of a right of individual access to the channels of mass communication is a great failing in the legal and media systems of most nations, even those with the most highly developed and functional media. In the United States, for example, the First Amendment to the Constitution, which is the highest law in the land, has been interpreted as preventing individuals from mandating access to newspapers for expressing their views (*Miami Herald v. Tornillo* 1974). And only in limited circumstances do the broadcast media in the United States have a legal obligation to give political candidates access to the electronic channels of mass communication.

Another significant legal barrier to media development is the lack of individual access to the mass media. Only 12 nations, including Costa Rica and Sweden, even come close to granting anything like a legal right for individuals to access the mass media to express opinions and set the record straight in instances of inaccurate reporting or claims of libel.

Under the 1989 Constitutional Jurisdiction Law, individuals in Costa Rica have a legal right to reply when they believe inaccurate news reporting impugned their honor or harmed their reputation. The law allows a maximum of 11 days for the injured party to get redress from the media even when the offending publication does not amount to libel. The law also applies to personal attacks made in paid political advertisements.

Right-to-reply laws are the exception, and even they do not provide adequate individual access to the mass media. In government-controlled press systems, access is nonexistent. In commercial, privately owned systems, with the exception of the right to reply, granting access is completely voluntary on the part of the media. In an attempt to be socially responsible, media organizations will sometimes take other steps to recognize public criticism and to deflect general access.

For example, the association of journalists, or Colegio, in Costa Rica investigates complaints against the media and may issue reports to the public in response. The Swedish press council and media ombudsmen work to increase public input into the operation of the media and to ensure responsible behavior on the part of journalists as they inform the society. These activities are all voluntary and may be suspended by the media at any time.

The lack of a general right of access is a barrier because it is often difficult, if not impossible, for the lone individual to have an impact on the all-important public opinion mechanism and the process for peaceful democratic-style social change unless that individual has prominence or some other newsworthy quality that may command access to the mass media. However, legally guaranteed access to the court of public opinion is a great indicator of individual freedom and empowerment as well as a criterion for a highly developed media system that meets the informational needs of the society or sovereign it serves.

International regulations against operating an unlicensed or pirate broadcast station may be considered legal barriers to media development. The licensing of newspapers by governments and the denial of licenses to operate broadcast stations are other legal barriers to media development.

The banning of objectionable content, especially programs imported from the West, and the total prohibition of advertising may also be viewed as legal barriers to media development in that they diminish the quantity, if not the quality, of information available to individuals through the mass media.

In some respects, copyright law also inhibits the availability and flow of information. Broadcasters in many nations that are media content-poor have resorted to pirating programs by illegally capturing and redistributing the signals from orbiting communications satellites. World broadcaster Cable News Network (CNN) tried unsuccessfully to prevent this widespread theft of its newscasts by labeling a conspicuous portion of the video with its name and a message about its ownership. Enterprising and ingenious broadcasters blanked out the CNN message and are now selling the space to domestic advertisers while they continue to pirate the signal.

ECONOMIC BARRIERS

On a macrolevel, world geopolitics and the accompanying economic order have tremendous impact on the world's media. Unequal economic and trade relations hinder the development, or at least the equal development, of the media in many nations. In some countries, political and economic instability retard development of the media by preventing the enticement of much-needed foreign capital.

Therefore, poverty and inequality in the allocation of the world's resources play a major part in blocking the development of the media in many countries. This, of course, assumes that the media are privately owned rather than government owned.

Private or commercially owned media have an economic incentive to improve and develop to capture the largest possible audience. Competition between media outlets is thought to have an overall positive effect on the quality and sophistication of the media in the area or market that they serve.

Despite the advantages of an independently owned and competitive media system, the cost of national telecommunication systems and of communication satellites puts a well-developed media system out of reach for all but the most wealthy nations. Only a handful of the world's nations have the money and technical capability to build, buy, or launch their own communication satellites. These satellites have proven to be tremendous enablers of national broadcast networks; of remote printing for newspapers; and of individual communication via telephone, telefax, and personal computers.

Limited economic resources prevent countries from deploying any or as many satellites as they wish to meet the information and communication needs of their citizens. Through the cooperative Intelsat organization, most of the world's nations gain access to satellite communication by leasing transponders and accompanying frequencies on orbiting satellites. Without the resources to purchase and operate their own full-time satellites, these nations operate on whatever time and services they can lease.

Those nations with satellite technology can earn additional money to further develop their capabilities and thus keep outdistancing the poor nations with increasingly sophisticated means of communication. The United States's space program is a prime example of this in operation. Just a few nations have the economic and technical ability to launch satellites, but the United States is the only one with the ability to maintain them once they are in orbit. Specifically, the success of the NASA space shuttle's "search and repair" missions will help the United States to maintain leadership in the world information economy for a long time. Even the other technologically capable nations will have to depend on the NASA shuttle program to help them maintain and improve the high-tech media systems that they have developed. Fortunately for them, they have the money to pay for the expensive maintenance.

For third-world nations, the cost of building major infrastructure to enable communication and significant development of national media is indeed a formidable barrier, even after the decades of debates, diatribe, and development projects aimed at changing the old information order. When technology was transferred from the media-rich nations to the third world, that transfer usually amounted to the dumping of old and outdated equipment on the poor nations. Although this practice did help the recipient nations in some measure, for the most part it served to delay and retard the development of the recipients' own infrastructure or production facilities. Moreover, if we consider the speed at which even state-of-the-art communication equipment becomes obsolete, the technological gap between rich and poor nations is increasing dramatically. There are obvious disadvantages, if not dangers, in this growing disparity, but it takes money to close the gap.

Competition from imported programming and the increased availability of international broadcast media content are major barriers to development of the indigenous media in many parts of the world. Because of economies of scales, efficiency, and expertise in production and marketing, Western nations can provide almost unlimited quantities of high-quality media content at a lower cost than producers in most nations. Therefore, third-world nations are finding it economically difficult to develop indigenous entertainment programs by local production companies that can supply the constantly increasing need. The inability to produce local programming in this competitive situation quickly gives way to charges of cultural imperialism against the West, but this barrier has its roots firmly in the economic arena.

The emerging trend toward globalization of the world's media under the ownership and control of a few multinational corporations indicates that new and perhaps insurmountable barriers to media development are on the horizon. This trend offers reasons for legitimate concern if we consider the criteria of individual freedom to communicate and gain access to communication channels that were mentioned in our beginning definition of media development.

As William Hachten outlines in *World News Prism* (1992), globalization of the media has helped to bring communication infrastructure and investment capital for private ownership of the media to many of the former communist countries of Eastern Europe. But the influx of capital and investors has meant giving up ownership and control of these domestic media outlets to media barons and corporations in distant and foreign lands.

Control over the content of communication also goes along with ownership of media channels, and absentee owners are less likely to sacrifice economic profits to support the social good derived from a well-developed and civic-conscious media system that does not serve their personal needs. It is possible to consider this emerging trend in international financing and ownership of the media as a barrier to the potential of these and other nations in developing their own domestic media systems to serve the needs of their citizens.

On a smaller scale, the cost of starting a media operation or purchasing an existing one is prohibitively high for individuals in any nation—more so for those in poor nations. The cost of radio and television sets also limits individual access to receive communication. Even the cost of a subscription or a single issue of a publication puts mass media out of reach for many people in the poorer nations.

It does not matter whether a country is rich or poor; there are always barriers that prevent the optimal development of the media in that country. Not all nations present the same barriers or challenges for the media, but they exist nonetheless. Experience also indicates that the physical barriers are easiest to overcome, whereas the barriers erected by human attitudes and actions remain steadfast and immovable fixtures on the horizon of the information highway.

BIBLIOGRAPHY

Altschull, J. Herbert. *Agents of Power*. New York: Longman, 1984.
Hachten, William. *The World News Prism*. 3rd Edition. Ames: Iowa State University Press, 1992.
Miami Herald v. Tornillo. 418 U.S. 241 (1974).

chapter 5

Freedom of the Press Around the World

Robert L. Stevenson

INTRODUCTION

Everyone is in favor of freedom of the press. The problem is a lack of agreement on what it is and who has it. By the definition used in this chapter, press freedom is still a rare commodity in the world and an elusive goal in most of the countries that rushed to Western market-based democracy after the collapse of communism.

HISTORY

Western democracy, including the key element of freedom of speech and press, is a product of the revolution set off by the invention of printing with movable type in the late 1400s. The explosion of knowledge that followed led to modern European languages, literacy, popular government, and newspapers. As governments and media developed the symbiotic relationship that continues today, governments tried to maintain control over information about their activities. Newspapers—and usually the public—wanted to know what governments were doing. The struggle between the two forces continues today.

The history of that struggle includes several important milestones. Certainly the most famous—and possibly the most influential—was the inclusion of a strong statement of press freedom in the U.S. Constitution, the famous First Amendment that states flatly "Congress shall make no law . . . abridging the freedom of speech, or of the press." In a skeptical assessment of the hyperbole surrounding the First Amendment, J. Herbert Altschull (1984, p. 26) nevertheless acknowledges its continuing influence:

No doctrine announced by the new republic has been more widely cheered around the world than the declaration of free expression. The declaration has fueled the fires of every revolutionary movement for two centuries.

Virtually every national constitution now contains some reference to press freedom, even though, as we shall see, the principle of free expression is often honored more in the breach than in the observance. Around the world, there is no agreement on what press freedom means or on the relative importance of this right compared to other freedoms.

Even in most Western democracies, the collective good of the nation can take precedence over the rights of the individual. Some would argue that political and civil rights of individuals that are enumerated in the Bill of Rights are only part of an expanded set of individual and collective "rights" appropriate for the twenty-first century. A United Nations (UN) commission in the 1970s affirmed this position when it argued that the American and French revolutions established individual political rights. It then argued that the Bolshevik revolution in Russia established a second generation of individual economic rights such as work and housing, followed by a third generation of collective or national rights. These included a national right to communicate that included elements of a collective press freedom. Efforts to implement this new-found collective press freedom were part of a broader call to restructure global communication that was known as a New World Information and Communication Order (NWICO).

However, efforts to define a new level of press freedom appropriate for a NWICO largely disappeared with communism's claim as a legitimate political ideology and with the NWICO debate itself. Now after more than 200 years, the simple and uncompromising formulation of the First Amendment remains a model for the world. But what does it mean?

DEFINITIONS

Even cursory attention to international media reveals a surprising variety of form, content, and purpose despite nearly universal homage to freedom of the press. The first effort to make sense of this diversity a generation ago identified four distinct "theories" of the press. Recently, William A. Hachten (1992) modified the four theories into five "concepts." Altschull concluded that global media comprised a three-part "symphony." In all classification schemes, press freedom is a key variable, a reminder of the lack of a single definition of press freedom and even greater differences in practice. To highlight differences and similarities in the world's diverse media, this chapter will consider a three-part classification, using Altschull's (1984) terms of *market, Marxist*, and *advancing* media systems.

Market

Even among the Western democracies, there is no agreement about the fine points of press freedom. And to the American observer, our fellow democrats accept restrictions on free expression that are both surprising and disconcerting. However, a reasonably general definition common to market-based media systems (i.e., Western democracies) might go something like this:

> Freedom of the press is the right to speak, broadcast, or publish without prior restraint by or permission of the government, but with limited legal accountability after publication for violations of law. It may also encompass legal guarantees of (1) reasonable access to information about government, businesses, and people; (2) a right of reply or correction; (3) a limited right of access to the media; and (4) some special protections for journalists.

The use of words such as *limited, reasonable*, and *some* is a reminder of the differences within even the Western democracies. In all countries, press freedom is balanced against other social values, such as the citizen's right to privacy and justice and the nation's security.

If press freedom is defined simply as freedom from government control, the United States has the freest system in the world, but even there, the right is not absolute. It stops at the law. In the name of press freedom, you cannot break a law, criminal or civil. Lawyers and journalists argue endlessly about where the fine line between free press and permissible restriction is—or should be—but most agree that it exists. The First Amendment does not allow you to destroy a person's reputation, sell pornography, or give away the nation's defense secrets.

Outside the United States, the first principle of absence of prior restraint or censorship gets less attention, while the ancillary aspects get more. Most democratic governments can, in fact, prevent publication and do so routinely. It is done in the name of national security, protection of privacy, or maintenance of social order. But these same governments also frequently protect reporters from testifying in court or identifying sources. A few countries, notably in Scandinavia, guarantee reporters unusual access to government offices and documents.

On the other hand, libel and privacy laws are stronger than in the United States. Penalties are often modest, a symbolic slap on the wrist for the journalist and return of the victim's good name. The principle of emphasis on the public good is extended to government power to withhold information and to stop publication of embarrassing revelations. In most Western countries, this is accepted as essential to cultural survival and good order. Even where the laws give special protection to journalists, investigative reporting of the kind we expect from "60 Minutes" and the *Washington Post* is rare. Some things, it is argued—sometimes even by journalists—are better left unreported.

Whatever the differences among the Western nations' theory and practice of press freedom, they are shades of gray compared to the black and white differences between the Western or "market" theory and its main twentieth century competitor for the hearts and minds of journalists, Communism.

Marxist

For most of the twentieth century, journalists from East and West talked past each other about what press freedom was and why the other side's definition was spurious. Karl

Marx produced the intellectual framework for Communism but wrote relatively little about journalism itself or press freedom. His occasional impassioned defenses of freedom, which were written in response to suppression of his radical newspaper by German authorities, must be juxtaposed against his intolerance of press dissent or even open discussion during his later tenure as head of the Communist International and part-time journalist in London.

The real "Marxist" definition of press freedom belongs to Vladimir I. Lenin, who compared the press to the scaffolding used in construction of a building. He extended the analogy to the construction of the socialist state. His statement of the press's function as collective agitator, propagandist, and organizer is well known. A Leninist definition of press freedom is more difficult to piece together, but he clearly rejected the market media definition as "freedom for the rich, systematically, unremittingly, daily, in millions of copies, to deceive, corrupt and fool the exploited and oppressed mass of the people, the poor." Instead, he called for state control of the press—including advertising, newsprint, and printing facilities—which would increase access to the press by various citizens' groups (*Lenin About the Press* 1972, p. 187):

> Yet if large *Soviet* newspapers were to be published, with all advertisements, it would be perfectly feasible to guarantee the expression of their opinion to a much greater number of citizens—say, to every group having collected a certain number of signatures. Freedom of the press would *in practice* become much more democratic, would become incomparably more complete as a result.

Instead, Lenin and those who carried forward the banner of Communism emphasized freedom of the press as the right of access to the media. Soviet newspapers developed a reputation for encouraging readers' letters and using the media as a watchdog on local government bureaucrats and party leaders, but within narrow limits, of course. Until Mikhail S. Gorbachev introduced the policy of *glasnost* ("openness") to support economic restructuring (*perestroika*), the government and party maintained the right to a monopoly of information. The only media permitted by law were those authorized by the government or party.

Authors of unauthorized media that challenged the unitary official view—the *samizdat* ("self-publishing") periodicals and later audio and videotapes—were vigorously persecuted and prosecuted, although never with complete success. Unwanted radio voices from the outside were jammed—also with limited effectiveness—and the Soviet government at one time claimed the right to destroy any satellite that could broadcast uninvited television signals to Soviet TV sets.

Of course, communist regimes maintained the same centralized monopoly on information that Lenin decried in the capitalist press. Limited access to the media for the purpose of supporting the regime is not a satisfying definition of press freedom. Even during the cold war, Soviet journalists occasionally acknowledged their frustrations with jokes. In one, the Western journalist defends his or her right of press freedom with the statement, "I can stand in front of the White House and criticize the American president." To that, the Soviet journalist replies, "But I can also stand in front of the Kremlin . . . and criticize the American president." In another, the Soviet journalist explains the difference between Communism and the West: "In the Soviet Union, we have freedom of speech, too, but in the West, you have freedom *after* speech."

Even in the West, it is sometimes easy to forget that freedom is measured by the freedom given to the hated idea, not the popular one, just as justice is defined by the justice accorded the worst criminal, not the good citizen. The freedom to stand in front of the Kremlin (or White House) and praise the incumbent is not much of a freedom.

Advancing

The idea of advancing media embraces authoritarianism, included in both the original four theories and Hachten's separate concept of development media, which came to prominence in the 1970s. According to Fred S. Siebert (1963), one of the coauthors of the original "Four Theories" formulation, authoritarianism was the theory of journalism that evolved along with mass media. It is still the most common theory of journalism practiced in the world and embraces some countries we consider Western. In fact, most Western countries practice some of the elements of authoritarianism.

The key element of an authoritarian media system is that the media are allowed to flourish as long as they present no challenge to the government. This means that most authoritarian media are privately owned and are often rich and powerful. They tend to stay aloof from the affairs of government, sometimes because they are intimidated by the government, sometimes because they are part of the governing oligarchy.

The relationship between government and journalists is complex and varied. In some countries, government uses its considerable power openly to prevent critical reporting or embarrassing disclosures. In others, the threats to press freedom come from other powers that render governments themselves powerless. In almost all countries, journalists chafe under restrictions and constantly test and challenge the limits. In many authoritarian countries, journalism is a dangerous profession.

A good example of the first situation is Singapore, where, despite unparalleled economic growth and prosperity, the government is openly intolerant of critical reporting from either domestic or foreign media. It is probably the only country where a prohibition against private satellite dishes is enforced, and authorized cable carries only the domestic service and programs from neighboring Malaysia. Strangely enough, the British Broadcasting Corporation (BBC) World Service continues to broadcast on medium-wave FM, a holdover from colonial days. In recent years, foreign media, including the *Economist, Asian Wall Street Journal*, and *Far Eastern Economic Review*, have had circulation reduced or suspended, have been ordered to apologize or pay heavy fines, or were forced to close news bureaus over squabbles with the government about reporting of Singaporean events. The word from the government is straightforward: Enjoy the convenience and efficiency of a Singapore base, but don't do anything local media cannot do.

The local media do not do much, at least in criticizing the government. Domestic media are tame, but in late 1993, the government brought criminal charges under a British-inspired Official Secrets Act against two editors, two security analysts, and a government economist. The "crime" was premature publication of a government estimate of economic growth. The trial disclosed the Kafkaesque detail that the government did not warn the paper about publishing the statistic, because it did not want the journalists to know that it knew that they knew; whether the journalists knew that the information was considered "secret" was not clear. An estimate of economic growth is not the kind of information normally stamped *Secret*. After a trial that was reported with both ridicule and alarm in the West, all five defendants were found guilty but given small fines rather than prison sentences.

The other extreme of authoritarian media can be found in Colombia, where journalists are frequently targets of attacks that the government is powerless to prevent. Both government and journalists challenge the power of drug lords—and often pay a heavy price in blood. In 1992 alone, five journalists were killed there (following nine murders in 1991), but only one in 1993. Similar problems exist in other countries at war. Journalists were frequently targeted in Bosnia following the collapse of Yugoslavia (21 were killed in ex-Yugoslavia in 1991, 8 in 1992, 5 in 1993), and reporting is an especially hazardous occupation in places as disparate as Sri Lanka and Liberia, where long-running civil wars have engulfed both government and media.

The year 1992 was the worst since Freedom House began keeping records a decade earlier. Ninety-eight journalists in 27 countries were killed, up from a world total of 62 the previous year. In all, 1,222 cases of attack or harassment of journalists in 115 countries were recorded. The gloomy statistic increased steadily from 436 incidents in 57 countries in 1987. Figures from the Committee to Protect Journalists are somewhat smaller (49 killed in 1992, 66 in 1991) and showed a decline in 1993 to 43 killed.

In many cases, governments were unable to prevent attacks on journalists—or they got caught between opposing sides in a war. However, sometimes the linkages between the shadowy forces threatening press freedom and governments were closer if still shadowy. During the harsh military dictatorship in Argentina between 1976 and 1983, more than 100 journalists were assassinated or simply disappeared. The experience there and in other Latin American countries introduced to English the use of *disappear* as a transitive verb, as in "they disappeared him." While most of the disappearances were never resolved, the assumption—and existing evidence—was that they were carried out by government forces or private thugs operating with the implicit sanction of the government. Most journalists would argue that this kind of threat has a more chilling effect on press freedom than an open authoritarian system, because the rules of permissible reporting are undefined and journalists are denied the protection of even a harsh or flawed judicial system.

During the 1970s, the authoritarian principle that journalism should not challenge governments was expanded to include mass media as an active tool of government. Hachten (1992) defined it as a separate media system, the development concept of the press. The idea was not new, of course. It was—and is—a key element of Marxist-Leninist press theory, but the development concept of the press also borrowed from Western experience. The United States especially had a history of incorporating mass media into programs of rural development. They included the federal agricultural extension service and educational radio and television that evolved into public broadcasting.

From the widespread use of mass communication in social third-world development programs, it was a small leap to redefine development goals in political terms. That gave journalists the new responsibility of actively supporting the nation or, more commonly, the regime in power. Altschull (1984) acknowledges the importance of subordination of press freedom to interests of the nation (or regime in power) in advancing countries with these three summary statements of press freedom: "A free press means freedom of conscience for journalists; press freedom is less important than the viability of the nation; a national press policy is needed to provide legal safeguards for freedom" (p. 294).

"Advancing" media—whether called that or by the more familiar terms of *authoritarian* or *development*—are still the most common. In the old communist countries of Central and Eastern Europe, media tended to evolve from the communist concept to authoritarianism rather than to Western. Even as the NWICO lost its legitimacy, third-world media tended to reflect old-fashioned authoritarian control rather than Western independence. Were "advancing" media en route to the Western model or stuck in permanent authoritarianism? The 1990s are a prelude to the next century, when we'll find out.

FREEDOM TODAY

The early years of the 1990s were a triumph for market-based Western democracy and for the principles of journalism associated with it. The most dramatic event, of course, was the collapse of Communism in the Soviet Union and Central Europe and the loss of legitimacy in the few remaining outposts of Marxism. Independent, critical journalism from both inside and outside was given part of the credit. The triumph of independent (i.e., Western) journalism is one of the global trends of communication in the 1990s.

While most attention was fixed on the extraordinary events taking place from Berlin to Moscow, something similar to *glasnost* was taking root in most other parts of the world. Latin American countries, which traditionally swung from fragile democracy to military dictatorship, moved almost uniformly toward democracy. Even Mexico, where corruption and control of the press were part of a long authoritarian tradition, moved toward critical reporting.

In Africa, too, multiparty democracy, which goes hand in hand with Western-style journalism, gained a small foothold. The Pan-African News Agency (PANA), which had been built on the principles of the NWICO and development journalism, announced a change to independent reporting. In several African countries, independent papers—economically weak, politically insecure—began to challenge government authority.

A curious exception to the wave of democracy sweeping the "advancing" world was parts of Asia. The extraordinary economic success of the "four tigers" (Singapore, South Korea, Hong Kong, and Taiwan) and a second tier of little tigers right behind them (Indonesia, Thailand, Malaysia, and maybe the Philippines) ought to have been preceded by or led to a flourishing of Western freedoms. As we have seen in the example of Singapore, it did not.

The juxtaposition of Asia against Central and Eastern Europe raises the interesting and long-debated question whether press freedom is a force promoting economic development or whether it is a product of it. In the lexicon of the 1990s, the question is which comes first: *glasnost* or *perestroika?* The global test currently underway favors the development-first-then-freedom side advanced by many governments in the old third world, but a single pattern equally applicable to the cultural diversity and histories of the world's nearly 200 countries may not exist. At best, we can look at the experiences of individual countries as a global laboratory and hope that they can learn from one another while moving collectively toward a common goal of press freedom. The recent record is hopeful.

RECENT CHANGES

A study of human rights in 104 countries in 1991 that incorporated several measures of press freedom into a larger composite 0–100 index of human rights noted a five-year improvement "unparalleled in history." Humana (1992, p. xi) concluded that the world's composite human rights rating rose from 55 percent in 1986 to 62 percent in 1991. In human terms, the proportion of the world population living in multiparty democracies rose from 40 to 48 percent, while the proportion under one-party or one-person rule dropped from 51 to 44 percent. The remainder—9 percent in 1986, 8 percent in 1991—were under military rule. The report noted that if three countries in Asia—China, Vietnam, and Indonesia—adopted multiparty rule, the proportion of world population living in democracy would increase from 62 to 75 percent.

Similar progress was reported by Freedom House (1993) in its annual assessment of civil and political rights and by the UN, which incorporates civil and political rights into a new "Human Development Index."

Freedom House collapses 7-point scales of political and civil rights into three categories of "free," "partly free," and "not free." As of January 1993, it found that 25 percent of the world's population was "free," a decline from 38 percent five years earlier. However, the proportion living in "partly free" countries increased from 24 to 44 percent, while the population "not free" declined from 38 to 31 percent. The report concluded:

> Although the world is freer than at any time in history, there are new manifestations of nationalism and brutal civil wars that threaten the progress of the past decade and augur a new cycle of authoritarianism if the community of democracies does not respond adequately to the challenge. (McColm 1993, p. 3)

The report described "a world that has undergone a political transformation of biblical proportions but one fraught with Old Testament sins." A separate analysis of press freedom classified 67 of 177 countries as "free press," while 60 countries were "partly free," and 50 were "not free" (Table 5.1). The number of countries improving

TABLE 5.1   Press freedom in 1992

Free Press in 67 Countries

Antigua and Barbuda, Argentina, Australia, Austria, Bahamas, Barbados, Belgium, Belize, Bolivia, Botswana, Brazil, Canada, Cape Verde (↑), Chile, Costa Rica, Cyprus (Greek), Cyprus (Turkish), Czechoslovakia, Denmark, Dominica, Dominican Republic, Ecuador, Finland, France, Gambia, Germany, Greece, Grenada, Honduras, Hungary, Iceland, India, Ireland, Israel, Italy, Jamaica, Japan, Korea (South), Luxembourg, Malta, Mauritius, Mongolia (↑), Namibia, Nauru, Nepal (↑), Nether- lands, New Zealand, Norway, Panama, Papua New Guinea, Poland, Portugal, Romania (↑), St. Kitts- Nevis, St. Lucia, St. Vincent, Spain, Sweden, Switzerland, Thailand, Trinidad and Tobago, United Kingdom, United States, Uruguay, Vanuatu, Venezuela, Zambia (↑)

Partly Free Press in 60 Countries

Albania (↑), Armenia, Bangladesh (↑), Belarus, Benin, Bulgaria, Burkina Faso, Colombia, Congo (↑), Egypt, El Salvador, Estonia, Fiji, Gabon, Georgia, Ghana (↑), Guatemala, Guinea (↑), Guinea– Bissau (↑), Guyana (↑), Indonesia (↑), Jordan (↑), Kazakhstan, Kenya (↑), Kyrgyzstan, Latvia, Lebanon (↑), Lesotho (↑), Lithuania, Macedonia, Madagascar, Malaysia, Mali (↑), Mexico, Moldova, Morocco, Mozambique (↑), Nicaragua, Nigeria, Pakistan, Paraguay, Peru, Philippines, Russia, São Tomé and Principe (↑), Senegal, Seychelles (↑), Singapore, Slovenia, South Africa, Sri Lanka, Suriname, Swaziland (↑), Taiwan, Tanzania (↑), Tonga, Tunisia, Turkey, Ukraine, Zimbabwe

Not Free Press in 50 Countries

Afghanistan, Algeria (↓), Angola, Azerbaijan, Bahrain, Bhutan, Bosnia-Herzegovina, Brunei, Burma, Burundi, Cambodia, Cameron, Central African Republic, Chad, China, Croatia, Cuba, Equatorial Guinea, Ethiopia, Haiti, Iran, Iraq, Ivory Coast (↓), Korea (North), Kuwait, Laos, Liberia, Libya, Malawi, Maldives, Mauritania, Niger, Oman, Qatar, Rwanda, Saudi Arabia, Sierre Leone (↓), Somalia, Sudan, Syria, Tajikistan, Togo, Turkmenistan, Uganda, United Arab Emirates, Uzbekistan, Vietnam, Yemen, Yugoslavia (↓), Zaire

↑ = improvement over previous year; ↓ = decline over previous year.
SOURCE: Leonard R. Sussman, "New Seeds of Press Freedom," Freedom Review (January–February 1993), 63–67.

press freedom outnumbered those with declining freedom 23 to 4. As the end of history arrived, was global press freedom triumphant?

CHALLENGES TODAY

Even in the democratic West, press freedom is under one kind of threat or another. This is nothing new. Democracy is a constant battle among competing forces, most of which demand freedom for themselves but lose some of their enthusiasm for it when they are in power and facing challenges from the political and journalistic opposition. The skirmish lines in Western countries are important because they collectively define the limits of press freedom to which the rest of the world aspires. A few examples from the early 1990s suggest how the general principles of the Western concept are being defined—and redefined—as the end of the century approaches.

Great Britain

Americans are often surprised to find that Britain, from which the U.S. legal tradition derives, has a number of restrictions on reporting that would be unthinkable at home. They result from a lack of a written constitution to define press freedom and an independent judicial process to measure government actions against it. The result is strong inhibitions on investigative reporting, particularly where the courts themselves or the national security apparatus are concerned.

In 1988, Parliament passed a law prohibiting the broadcast of voices of members of a number of groups associated with the independence movement in Northern Ireland. The intent, according to Prime Minister Thatcher, was to deny terrorists "the oxygen of publicity." Most admittedly were terrorists, but the banned list included local elected officials and one man who had been elected to Parliament but never took his seat. The law allowed exceptions for campaigns and constituency affairs.

British broadcasters found they could skirt the law by having an actor repeat the words of a banned individual or by using subtitles without sound. The chilling effect—if any—on debate over policies in Northern Ireland was unclear. At the end of 1993, the British government announced that it had no plans to relax the ban, even though the loophole allowing broadcasters to substitute actors' voices rendered it ineffective and made the government look foolish. The government looked even more foolish when journalists revealed that the British government had maintained long-standing contact with some of the same organizations it had tried to keep off the airwaves. The Irish government, trying to encourage the Irish Republican Army (IRA) to switch from bombs to the ballot box, dropped its even more severe broadcast ban of any appearance of any member of Sinn Fein. The 20-year-old ban led, among other things, to cutting off a caller to a call-in gardening program and elimination of an interview with an eyewitness to a fire. The British government dropped its ban in 1994 after the IRA agreed to a cease-fire and promised to end violence.

Germany

In Germany, a schoolgirl set off an uproar when she began investigating what happened in her Bavarian hometown of Passau during World War II (Atkinson 1993). Her own story was the basis of the movie *The Nasty Girl*. A second book accused a local doctor of complicity in forced abortions of East European laborers during the war. The doctor had died, but his widow and children brought suit under a German law that forbids defaming the dead. A judge ruled that a newspaper interview included charges the author could not prove and threatened imprisonment or a fine if she repeated them.

Germany, along with most European countries, bans symbols and paraphernalia from the Nazi era and has moved—albeit cautiously—against extremist groups that use these icons to enflame social tensions today. The general view is that groups or individuals promoting hate, divisiveness, or extremist views are outside the limits of free expression and should be silenced in the name of the common good. A German court also ordered removal of audiotapes and CDs that contained the line, "I want to have sex with Steffi Graf," after she complained.

European Union

The argument that "commercial speech" such as advertising should enjoy the protections associated with freedom of the press meets with skepticism in most Western countries. The tradition of public service broadcasting committed to education and culture (and often the political fortunes of the incumbent government) and financed by taxes and license fees rather than advertising makes possible a range of controls.

In 1989, two officials from J. Walter Thompson described the problem of promoting a theoretical low-fat diet candy bar, "Jupiter" (Mayer 1991, p. 204). A commercial designed for TV use across Europe would emphasize three points: "Your waistline will like it, and you get a free tape measure to prove it"; "It's an after-school treat that won't spoil your evening meal"; and "When your doctor says cut down, reach for Jupiter, with one-third of the calories of other chocolate bars." Here are some of the obstacles the campaign would encounter:

> In Belgium, commercials may not refer to dieting. In France, premiums can't be worth more than one percent of the sale price, which rules out the tape measure, and children can't give endorsements, which means no child eating a Jupiter after school. In West Germany, any comparisons with another candy bar would be illegal; in Denmark, ads can't make nutritional claims; in Britain, candy must be presented as only an occasional snack—and no doctors in the commercial. (Mayer 1991, p. 204)

Some of these commercial restrictions may be codified into rules for all members of the European Union (EU, formerly, the European Community or Common Market). Eurocrats of the EU, usually in the name of protection of individual rights or protection of cultural identity, established quotas for imported TV programs and proposed rules that would severely restrict public opinion surveys. France, of course, nearly sabotaged ten years of global trade negotiations to maintain various restrictions and taxes on U.S. audiovisual materials, then passed a law requiring radio stations to play 40 percent domestic music.

The kinds of controls that France and its EU partners enacted or promoted resonated in other parts of the world. In some countries, it was a real or imagined threat from U.S. dominance in all areas of information that produced sympathy and imitation. In others, the real or imagined threat was to shaky governments that wanted to avoid the glare of publicity. In many Western democracies, the tradition of press freedom clashed with the equally strong tradition of multiparty elections. At issue was the ubiquitous phenomenon of twentieth-century democratic life, the public opinion survey.

Opinion Polling

An informal global survey by the World Association for Public Opinion Research (WAPOR) in 1992 found restrictions on the reporting of pre-election (and sometimes other) surveys in many Western democracies. Various proposals to restrict the use of scientific sample surveys to predict the outcome of elections before the votes were counted or even cast were also floated in the United States, but the nearly absolute guarantee of the First Amendment precluded most legal restrictions. Not so in other countries.

Five of the 12 EU countries, along with many other democratic or semi-democratic nations, had moratoriums on the reporting of pre-election polls. The period during which poll results were banned ranged from one day to six weeks before the election. The reasoning behind the restrictions is curious. It assumes that a vote made in isolation and ignorance is more democratic than one made with some knowledge of the likely outcome and dynamics of the campaign. Because restrictions apply to publication, not systematic collection of information, which would be impossible, the effect tends to be not more democracy but a two-tier information system. Insiders such as politicians, journalists, and business people still have access to the results. In 1985, late poll information sold to brokers had a substantial effect on stock prices in Belgium.

Moratoriums also turn the traditional argument for restricting information on its head. Contrary to the legal principle still operable in some countries that information can be banned if it is false, poll restrictions essentially apply to information that is true. The restrictions do not seem to apply to casual man-on-the-street polls and other traditional reportage that is unlikely to predict or influence the outcome.

Other EU proposals, mostly in the name of protection of privacy and maintenance of social order, would restrict collection of data of a sensitive personal nature and attitudes toward sensitive topics. In other countries, particularly authoritarian regimes, all public opinion polling is proscribed or limited. Typically, questions about royalty, high government officials, or sensitive domestic issues are off-limits, and polling on them can be dangerous. As late as 1990 in Indonesia, a journalist was imprisoned after a casual newspaper poll put President Suharto well down on a list of public figures whose popularity the poll tried to assess. Another journalist in that Muslim-dominated country ran into legal trouble with a popularity poll that included the Prophet Mohammed in a list of public figures.

Despite current restrictions, the global trend is toward more democracy and more polling. As a Soviet pollster put it shortly before the collapse of his country, "In the old regime, there was only one opinion, and you didn't need a poll to find out what it was." Now even in the shaky semidemocracies, there are multiple opinions and inevitably polls to measure them.

Democracy is a messy way to run a country—the worst form of government, as Winston Churchill noted, except for all the others. Despite the setbacks and disappointments that followed the euphoria of the late 1980s, global press freedom in the 1990s is neither secure in the countries that now enjoy it nor inevitable in the countries that want it.

OUTLOOK

The rapid political change engulfing most of the world in the 1990s is reflected in the Freedom House surveys. In 1989—the year of the great revolutions in Europe and, of course, the attack on Tiananmen Square—27 nations changed their ratings. In 1991, 58 changed, and in 1992, 73 did. Of those, 39 improved in human rights, while 31 (twice the number of 1991) declined. In the remaining three, improvements in one measure were offset by a decline in the other. Preliminary assessments of 1993 suggested a similar pattern of movement away from both "free" and "not free" toward the "partly free" category, although a retreat from the democratic gains in Central and Eastern Europe made 1993 overall a losing year for democracy.

"Partly free" usually means authoritarianism, which, in turn, usually means significant limits to press freedom. Jeane J. Kirkpatrick, President Reagan's UN ambassador, caused a considerable controversy when she recommended a distinction in U.S. foreign policy between authoritarian and totalitarian regimes. She proposed cooperation with authoritarian regimes, which could reform themselves into democracies, but opposition to totalitarian regimes, which could not. The trend away from totalitarianism toward authoritarianism—not directly to Western democracy—seems likely to continue into the twenty-first century.

For most of the twentieth century, communists argued that Marx and Lenin had provided a guidebook for the inevitable transformation of capitalist society into socialism. With Communism discarded in most countries where it had been tried and discredited in the others, many countries are looking for a new guidebook to lead them to the economic wealth and political stability found in the West. Freedom of the press is no magic bullet to speed that process and no guarantee of success. But if the long and often painful experience of the West is a useful guidebook to the two-thirds of the human population that still aspires to freedom—and it is the only case study to date—press freedom is both a product of social change and a tool to speed the process.

BIBLIOGRAPHY

Altschull, J. Herbert. *Agents of Power: the Role of the News Media in Human Affairs*. New York: Longman, 1984.

Article 19 Freedom of Expression Manual: International and Comparative Law, Standards and Procedures. London: Article 19, 1993.

Atkinson, Rick. "German Muckraker Sets Off an Uproar." *International Herald Tribune*, 9 November 1993, 2. From the *Washington Post*.

Coliver, Sandra, Editor. *Striking a Balance: Hate Speech, Freedom of Expression and Non-Discrimination*. London: Article 19, 1992.

Evans, Harold. "The Norman Conquests: Freedom of the Press in Britain and America." In *The Media and Foreign Policy*, edited by Simon Serfaty. New York: St. Martin's Press, 1991.

Hachten, William A. *The World News Prism*. 3rd Edition. Ames: Iowa State University Press, 1992.

Humana, Charles, Editor. *World Human Rights Guide*. 3rd Edition. New York: Oxford University Press, 1992.

International Commission for the Study of Communication Problems (MacBride Commission). *Many Voices, One World*. Paris: UNESCO, 1980.

Lahav, Pnina, Editor. *Press Law in Modern Democracies: A Comparative Study*. New York: Longman, 1984.

Lenin About the Press. Prague: International Organization of Journalists, 1972.

Mayer, Martin. *Whatever Happened to Madison Avenue? Advertising in the '90s*. Boston: Little, Brown, 1991.

McColm, R. Bruce. "The Comparative Survey of Freedom, 1992–1993: Our Crowded Hour." In *Freedom of the World: The Annual Survey of Political Rights and Civil Liberties, 1992–1993*. New York: Freedom House, 1993.

Nimmo, Dan, and Michael W. Mansfield, *Government and the News Media: Comparative Dimensions*. Waco, Tex.: Baylor University Press, 1982.

Press Law and Practice: A Comparative Study of Press Freedom in European and Other Democracies. London: Article 19, 1993.

Restricted Subjects; Freedom of Expression in the United Kingdom. New York: Human Rights Watch, 1991.

Siebert, Fred S., Theodore Peterson, and Wilbur Schramm. *Four Theories of the Press*. Urbana, Ill.: University of Illinois Press, 1963.

Stevenson, Robert L. *Global Communication in the 21st Century*. New York: Longman, 1994.

chapter 6

International Journalism Ethics

Dean Kruckeberg

On the eve of the twenty-first century, discourse about journalism ethics on a global scale requires primary consideration of the ramifications of communication technology. A host of questions must be examined and satisfactorily resolved:

- As in centuries past, when emerging Protestant religions declared that everyone could become his own priest and now could read his own Gutenberg Bible, is today's communication "revolution" more accurately a "reformation" in which each person can be his own journalist within a global milieu of interactive multimedia?

- Will "professional" journalism—undoubtedly always having been ill-defined— exist in the future other than as a handy descriptor for a type of research and its accompanying methodologies? In the future, will this possibly "deprofessional- ized" craft of journalism be best prepared for vocationally through course work in library science with technical education in computer-based information retrieval—addended perhaps with some practice in mining information from primary personal sources and in writing according to formula? Moreover, will "professional" journalism schools and the "professional" practices they espouse become passé?

- For that matter, will the concept of "news"—and any sense of news "values"— still have operational meaning in an era when readily available computerized information overwhelmingly will exceed its reasonable and useful consumption?

- Will the agenda-setting role of the traditional mass media worldwide be continually eroded because of the surfeit of ungraded "news" and information selected from myriad electronic channels—with no one to suggest collectively to consumers what is and what is not "news"?

- Relatedly, will the pervasive, increasingly consolidated and seemingly all-powerful *mass media*—while perhaps destined to increase in global economic power—diminish politically in their importance as news gatherers and providers and as influencers of public opinion? That is, will a diffusion of concentrated power and influence result from a predicted future era of cacophonous 500-channel "narrowcasting"? Will a loss of power and influence among the mass media result from the fiber-optic information superhighway whose global trunk lines are fast extending their tentacles to access anyone and everyone worldwide sharing in this technology?

- And, if such will be the case, who will buy all these people their telecomputers, and what will third world peasants—with unfulfilled needs for food and fiber—have to say to one another electronically? Andrew Belsey and Ruth Chadwick (1992) note that one-fifth of the world's population—one billion people—is in a state of dire physical need. One might assume that their immediate and primary concerns will transcend sustained deliberation about the relative merits of microcomputer software.

- As unseen engineers working for market-driven computer and telecommunication companies contribute to what James W. Carey (1989) calls a "high communications policy," that is, a policy aimed solely at spreading messages further in space and at reducing their cost of transmission, will a new age of "communitarianism" result?

- Or, will there be only increasing alienation and anomie—both for those availing themselves of communication technology and for a global underclass of people who cannot or will not accept telecomputers, powerbooks, electronic note pads, digital computer-linked cameras, portable faxes, cellular telephones, and satellite uplinks?

- Finally, will the tiresome platitudes about the "Global Village" indeed prove accurately prophetic in an imploded, McLuhan-esque world of "Mechanical Brides"?

Such are indeed weighty questions, and ones for which precise definitions of concepts and constructs are required.

WHAT IS *JOURNALISM*?

Any cogent discussion of journalism ethics requires an operational definition of *journalism*. At one level—and particularly so from a global perspective—we can be no more precise than to argue that "'journalism' is what 'journalists' do."

News reporters in the "free press" of the Western media—both for print and for broadcast—rightly call themselves "journalists." However, many of the most commonly cited gross delineations that are designed to provide exclusionary distinctions do *not* define journalism sufficiently well for any precise and meaningful discussion about journalism ethics. For example:

- What form of fish or fowl is the plenitude of advice columnists and similar information-providers who fill a substantial amount of the newshole of contemporary media, that is, those whom Nigel G. E. Harris (1992) calls "expert" contributors; what—if not journalists—are those reporting for televised tabloid news/feature programs and those interviewing guests on the plethora of talk shows?
- Are those reporting and ideologically interpreting "news" in "propagandistic" media owned or sanctioned by authoritarian government regimes not to be considered journalists?
- Finally what about those using "controlled" media within countries having "free" press systems, such as public relations practitioners and marketing communicators and ideologues producing sundry journalistic-appearing messages in media owned and controlled by their respective organizations? Can these special interest mass communicators likewise be called journalists, even though they may disavow themselves or their media of any pretense to objectivity or impartiality? Are such media to be considered part of a nation's "press system"?

SCHOLARS TYPECAST SYSTEMS, NOT JOURNALISTS

Western mass communication scholars readily designate a place in their typologies for journalists in authoritarian press systems, although it must be emphasized these scholars are typecasting respective systems rather than journalists serving them.

Fred Siebert, Theodore Peterson, and Wilbur Schramm's venerable 1956 volume, *Four Theories of the Press*, included the authoritarian, libertarian, Soviet communist, and social responsibility theories.

Ralph Lowenstein (Merrill and Lowenstein 1971; Mundt 1991) modified this typology, identifying ownership types as well as proffering a somewhat different five-categoried typology of press philosophies—with the former category including private, multiparty, and government ownership.

John C. Merrill (1974) proposed a relatively complex, but highly functional, political–press circle to distinguish the different press systems, and other scholars have developed additional typologies.

Confusion sometimes results about which media and messages are to be included as part of a nation's press system, particularly when considering special interest messages and media in nations whose institutionalized free press systems claim objectivity and fairness in their news coverage. Helpful is the identification of a predominant *general* news orientation of qualifying media as a uniform and consistent threshold criterion. Public affairs reportage about journalists' respective governments likewise is a strong definitional component of such journalism as it is practiced in the general news media.

Special interest periodicals and media controlled by public relations practitioners, marketing communicators, and the like—even if appearing as news in media formats that appear to be news-oriented—by and large should *not* be considered journalism.

Such a distinction, although perhaps not entirely defensible, is ultimately correct and appropriate. Public relations practitioners and marketing communicators—as well as a range of other purposive mass communicators using controlled media to report specialized information in a country otherwise having a commercial press that claims objective and fair news coverage in a free press system—cannot reasonably be considered journalists in any rigorous context relating to journalism ethics.

Rather, these special interest mass communicators have their own unique ethical concerns and professional identities that are substantively different from those of journalists. Likewise, their concerns and deliberations predominantly are those that journalists in free press systems by and large need not consider.

As noted, however, such a distinction is not entirely defensible. Differences between such purposive mass communicators and journalists often can be blurred, most particularly when such purposive communicators in free press systems are compared to journalists working for propagandistic media in authoritarian press systems. This sometimes can even be the case when they are compared to bona fide journalists in their own free press systems.

Although the jobs of such purposive mass communicators require the considerable application of journalistic knowledge and skills, they nevertheless are not practicing journalism per se as the role is being considered here, that is, as an occupational specialization of those who gather and report on general interest news in the *general* news media and/or those who editorially comment on such news appearing in these media.

Lest this point appears to be belabored, the warning nevertheless must be emphasized that distinctions between journalists and a range of nonjournalistic purposive mass communicators often are anything but clearcut—especially when purposive mass communicators are compared to their journalistic counterparts in authoritarian, state-owned, or state-sanctioned press systems having strong ideological and propagandistic components.

These blurred lines become important to stress at this time, not only because of the increasing and confusing proliferation of "infotainment" and "infomercials" on television channels and of the growth of substantial desktop publishing enterprises by sundry special-interest groups.

Rather, these questionable distinctions are particularly important to note because of the increasing inclusion into the global mass communication milieu of overwhelming amounts of computer-accessible "news" and information from a myriad range of perhaps questionable—frequently highly biased—sources. Emerging use of telecomputer technology as a "news" medium will significantly add to the confusion, not only about what constitutes news, but about who reasonably may be considered a bona fide and credible journalist.

THE ROLE OF THE JOURNALIST IS NOT IN JEOPARDY

Despite significant changes brought about by increasingly sophisticated communication technology, and despite oft-heard prognoses to the contrary, the role of the professional journalist will be secure in the future; also, despite the certainty of massive innovations in media technology, neither will the press be in any appreciable jeopardy as an institution.

This specialized occupation, as well as its sponsoring institution, the press, will not be substantively threatened—and most likely will be further entrenched as a highly needed professional occupation—in the milieu of the new global communication technology.

However, this role may well be ensured because of journalists' ability to digest, that is, to condense and to grade, overwhelming amounts of information that already may be computer-accessible to consumers in raw form. The journalist's function may decrease in its need to present substantial amounts of new information otherwise unavailable to consumers of news and information. Of course, news gathering of primary sources will remain, but—in an increasingly technological world—the exercise of news gathering may not be as dependent on "personal" sources as historically has been the case.

Just as the Reformation's emerging "priesthood of believers" and Gutenberg's inexpensively reproduced Bible did not threaten the need for an organized church as an institution, extensive and immediate computerized information entry and retrieval in an information society will not threaten journalism as an occupational specialization nor the press as an institution.

Such technology, however, may well threaten journalists' individual well-being as well as that of their sponsoring media organizations within their press systems. Both the role of the journalist and that of the press as an institution are destined to be changed in significant ways, with accompanying ethical ramifications.

As diffusion literature readily affirms, it seems almost certain that an overwhelming majority of people will continue to rely on journalists as experts and on news media (perhaps in the future only in telecomputed, rather than in newsprint, form) to gather and to report the news. This majority will depend on the gatekeepers of an established press to set news agendas, to grade news, and to provide informed comment about current events.

It seems reasonable to expect that even the most ardent technophiles and the most prodigious "channel surfers" will continue to rely on journalists, that is, those mainstream, well-established professionals proven to be credible and perceived to be fair and objective occupational specialists who are highly capable in gathering and reporting, as well as interpreting and commenting on, general-interest news in recognized and well-respected news media.

Highly busy people who are feeling overwhelmed by information overload, as well as those who perhaps are not so busy but who are not confident of their own abilities to become aware of and to interpret their environment, will continue to seek out experts, those trained as news gatherers and reporters as well as those skilled as gatekeepers, who can set the news agendas and digest and grade the news accordingly.

The educational requirements of such experts as liberally educated professionals likewise cannot decrease, but by necessity will have to increase—and truly as professionals as opposed to technicians. (The term *professional* is used here not in its strictest sociological sense, but in the sense of an occupational specialist who enjoys substantial amounts of power and freedom in performing a socially necessary job that has a substantial amount of status.)

People will rely increasingly on journalists to make sense of the overwhelming amount of information available to them. News, as gathered and reported by such professionals, will continue to be a valued commodity, either to be sold and consumed as such, as is common in the market-driven free press, or to be presented to support ideology, as in authoritarian press systems.

JOURNALISTS WILL LOSE THEIR MONOPOLY OF KNOWLEDGE

The most significant change to be wrought by the new global communication technology will be the invariable loss of the monopoly of knowledge on the part of journalists and the press in all types of press systems.

Carey (1989) has noted that the concept of the free press had consolidated the position of mass media's monopoly of knowledge. He argues that, through newspapers' dependence on both advertising and news, the free press was instrumental in spreading the values of commercialism and industrialism.

Of course, authoritarian types of press systems historically have relied on this monopoly to preserve the status quo by attempting to limit the agendas both about what people knew and—by extension—about what they thought.

However, John O'Neill (1992) argues this is even true in a free market press. Such a press will tend to work against the idea of an informed and critical citizenry, he says, simply because it cannot afford to confront its consumers with information, beliefs, and knowledge that do not conform to their preexisting preferences.

John C. Merrill, Carter R. Bryan, and Marvin Alisky (1970) remind us that each nation's press system and philosophy are usually very closely in step with that nation's basic political and social system and ideology. Thus, they conclude, each country's press system is usually truly a branch of the government—or at the least a cooperating part of the total national establishment.

However, new global communication technology at the least will ensure the *potential*—and arguably will encourage the *likelihood*—of massive fragmentation of communication audiences because of audience members' ample, indeed virtually unlimited, opportunities to use alternate journalistic news and information sources. The only defense that established mainstream journalists and their media organizations can have will be to strive for a comparatively higher quality product, that is, their commodity of news.

For the commercially dependent free press, competition will be intense among competing professional journalists and their media organizations for a significant and financially viable share of the consumer market for news and information. The same competition will exist within authoritarian-type press systems that previously by and large were accustomed to a controlled monopoly of news.

Simply put, those consumers dissatisfied with the perceived quality of a media organization's news and information commodity will have ample opportunities to access other media news and information. Most likely, little effective recourse will be available to prohibit consumers from such choice in news and information access.

With intense competition both for subscribers of the news as well as for an advertising base in a free-market economy, the economic challenges resulting from such audience fragmentation may be financially devastating to at least some of those media organizations in free press systems. Such fragmentation is already being bemoaned by Western advertising agencies that are having increasing difficulty reaching their markets via the mass media. Indeed, some media organizations may be driven out of business.

PRESS SYSTEMS WILL LOSE AGENDA-SETTING ABILITIES

Although such economic concerns may not be considered of paramount importance for the state-owned or sanctioned press of authoritarian governments, such press systems will to a great extent lose their exclusive agenda-setting abilities and their abilities to singularly dictate media content.

For example, at least one Middle Eastern Islamic country has begun to recognize the threat of the latest television technology, such as commercially available sets having unobtrusive built-in satellite dishes that can bring fare—perhaps as culturally void as *Baywatch*, Western daytime talk shows, and ancient sitcom reruns or as insidious as hard-core pornography—that is inconsistent with state-sanctioned Moslem religious values.

Charges of cultural imperialism and of propaganda in its most pejorative sense will continue to be forthcoming, only with heightened concern and accompanying hysteria. Many charges will have considerable validity. Conversely, however, this same global communication technology will allow those seeing themselves as part of the new world information order to have ample opportunities to attempt to compete head-on with first-world news media.

LOSS OF MONOPOLY WILL HAVE AN IMPACT ON ETHICS

This loss of monopoly by the press in all types of press systems will have a tremendous and highly paradoxical impact on any sense of journalism ethics on a global scale.

Bernard Rubin (1978) reminds us that no ethical standards are built into the mass media. Those who are associated with free press systems—with their traditional and much-revered news values, including their ideal of objectivity, a sense of fairness in presenting all sides of a story, value placed on attribution, as well as their vehement appreciation of First Amendment-type rights—often lose sight of this fact.

With the potential for virtually infinite numbers of accessible channels within the worldwide mass communication media milieu, tensions will increase between commercially driven free-market journalists and their media organizations within free press systems, not only competitively among themselves, but also with the counterbalancing efforts of those considering themselves to be part of the new world information order as well as those presuming to be part of any remaining vestige of the press of the second world.

Tensions likewise will increase in Western-styled free press systems as demarcations become blurred between journalists and such purposive mass communicators as public relations practitioners, marketing communicators, and advertisers as well as a range of ideologues—because, paradoxically, a free press system allows the freedom to have a controlled press as a subsystem.

DEMANDS WILL BE MADE FOR "ETHICS" IN JOURNALISM

What people and their respective governments can't meaningfully and effectively legislate and prohibit as illegal, they will quickly pronounce as unethical. A renewed and revigorated cry will burst forth for "ethics" in journalism by those who feel they, their cultures, their values, and their beliefs are being wronged! And John C. Merrill's advocacy for *Existential Journalism* (1977) and its *Imperative of Freedom* (1974) may prove victorious in the ensuing melee.

Merrill, who eschews journalism professionalism and decries journalism schools' increasing concern with standardized mechanisms, methods, forms, and techniques, argues that the struggle for autonomy, freedom, and authenticity in journalism is a personal struggle.

Relatedly, he submits that press responsibility is in the eye of the beholder. He makes compelling arguments against any responsibility of the press as it is described in the social responsibility theory of Fred Siebert, Theodore Peterson, and Wilbur Schramm and as it was championed in the 1947 report of the Commission on Freedom of the Press headed by Robert M. Hutchins, entitled *A Free and Responsible Press*. Merrill observes in his book, *The Imperative of Freedom: A Philosophy of Journalistic Autonomy*:

> Increasingly one hears reference to the responsibility of the press and less and less about its freedom to react independently in a democratic society. Not only has the concept permeated the authoritarian countries, where it is an expected development, but in recent years it has made notable incursions into the press philosophy of the United States and other Western libertarian countries. (1974, p. 88)

In the emerging mass communication milieu, with its potential for virtually infinite numbers of communication channels throughout the world, professional journalists within their respective press systems—as well those uncounted numbers within an emerging "priesthood of journalists" participating in a communication "reformation"—will by and large be part of a highly libertarian, or free press system, which will be virtually impossible to regulate. In a future era of electronically inexpensive and pervasive media on a global scale, pluralism will be ensured—and undoubtedly so will a massive diffusion of power in controlling news and information.

Professional journalists and their media organizations—as well as a highly diverse priesthood of journalists in the communication reformation—will be as ethical as they want to be according to what *they* perceive to be ethics and ethical conduct.

BIBLIOGRAPHY

Arthur, Robin. *Advertising & Marketing in the United Arab Emirates*. Dubai, United Arab Emirates: Galadari Printing & Publishing Establishment, 1991.

Barney, Ralph D. "The Journalist and a Pluralistic Society: An Ethical Approach." In *Responsible Journalism*, edited by Deni Elliott. Beverly Hills, Calif.: Sage Publications, 1986.

Belsey, Andrew, and Ruth Chadwick. "Ethics and Politics of the Media: The Quest for Quality." In *Ethical Issues in Journalism and the Media*, edited by Andrew Belsey and Ruth Chadwick. London: Routledge, 1992.

Boorstin, Daniel J. *The Americans: The Democratic Experience*. New York: Vintage Books, 1974.

Brody, E.W. *Communication Tomorrow: New Audiences, New Technologies, New Media*. New York: Praeger, 1990.

Carey, James W. "Space, Time, and Communications: A Tribute to Harold Innis." In *Communication as Culture: Essays on Media and Society*, edited by James W. Carey. Boston: Unwin Hyman, 1989.

———. "Technology and Ideology: The Case of the Telegraph." In *Communication as Culture: Essays on Media and Society*, edited by James W. Carey. Boston: Unwin Hyman, 1989.

Carey, James W., with John J. Quirk. "The History of the Future." In *Communication as Culture: Essays on Media and Society*, edited by James W. Carey. Boston: Unwin Hyman, 1989.

———. "The Mythos of the Electronic Revolution." In *Communication as Culture: Essays on Media and Society*, edited by James W. Carey. Boston: Unwin Hyman, 1989.

Christians, Clifford G. "Ethical Theory in a Global Setting." In *Communication Ethics and Global Change*, edited by Thomas W. Cooper, Clifford G. Christians, Frances Forde Plude, and Robert A. White. White Plains, N.Y.: Longman Inc., 1989.

———. "Reporting and the Oppressed." In *Responsible Journalism*, edited by Deni Elliott. Beverly Hills, Calif.: Sage Publications, 1986.

Christians, Clifford G., John P. Ferré, and P. Mark Fackler. *Good News: Social Ethics and the Press*. New York: Oxford University Press, 1993.

Commission on Freedom of the Press. *A Free and Responsible Press; A General Report on Mass Communication: Newspapers, Radio, Motion Pictures, Magazines and Books*. Chicago: University of Chicago Press, 1947.

Cooper, Thomas W. "Global Universals: In Search of Common Ground." In *Communication Ethics and Global Change*, edited by Thomas W. Cooper, Clifford G. Christians, Frances Forde Plude, and Robert A. White. White Plains, N.Y.: Longman Inc., 1989.

———. "Methodological Challenges: Comparison of Codes and Countries." In *Communication Ethics and Global Change*, edited by Thomas W. Cooper, Clifford G. Christians, Frances Forde Plude and Robert A. White. White Plains, N.Y.: Longman Inc., 1989.

Dennis, Everette E. "Social Responsibility, Representation, and Reality." In *Responsible Journalism*, edited by Deni Elliott. Beverly Hills, Calif.: Sage Publications, 1986.

Dicken-Garcia, Hazel. *Journalistic Standards in Nineteenth-Century America*. Madison: University of Wisconsin Press, 1989.

Edgar, Andrew. "Objectivity, Bias and Truth." In *Ethical Issues in Journalism and the Media*, edited by Andrew Belsey and Ruth Chadwick. London: Routledge, 1992.

Elliott, Deni. "Foundations for News Media Responsibility." In *Responsible Journalism*, edited by Deni Elliott. Beverly Hills, Calif.: Sage Publications, 1986.

Emery, Michael, and Edwin Emery. *The Press and America: An Interpretive History of the Mass Media*. Englewood Cliffs, N.J.: Prentice Hall, 1988.

Gilder, George. *Life after Television*. New York: W.W. Norton & Company, 1992.

Glasser, Theodore L. "Press Responsibility and First Amendment Values." In *Responsible Journalism*, edited by Deni Elliott. Beverly Hills, Calif.: Sage Publications, 1986.

Goodwin, H. Eugene. *Groping for Ethics in Journalism*. Ames: Iowa State University Press, 1987.

Grunig, James E., and Larissa A. Grunig. "Models of Public Relations and Communication." In *Excellence in Public Relations and Communication Management*, edited by James E. Grunig. Hillsdale, N.J.: Lawrence Erlbaum Associates, 1992.

Grunig, James E., and Jon White. "The Effect of Worldviews on Public Relations Theory and Practice." In *Excellence in Public Relations and Communication Management*, edited by James E. Grunig. Hillsdale, N.J.: Lawrence Erlbaum Associates, 1992.

Hardt, Hanno. *Social Theories of the Press: Early German & American Perspectives*. Beverly Hills, Calif.: Sage Publications, 1979.

Harris, Nigel G. E. "Codes of Conduct for Journalists." In *Ethical Issues in Journalism and the Media*, edited by Andrew Belsey and Ruth Chadwick. London: Routledge, 1992.

Hauss, Deborah. "Global Communications Come of Age." *Public Relations Journal* 49, no. 8 (1993): 22-26.

Hester, Al. "The Collection and Flow of World News." In *Global Journalism*, edited by John C. Merrill. New York: Longman, 1991.

Hodges, Louis W. "Defining Press Responsibility: A Functional Approach." In *Responsible Journalism*, edited by Deni Elliott. Beverly Hills, Calif.: Sage Publications, 1986.

Innis, Harold A. *The Bias of Communication*. Toronto: University of Toronto Press, 1973.

Jones, J. Clement. *Mass Media Codes of Ethics and Councils: A Comparative International Study on Professional Standards*. Paris: UNESCO Press, 1980.

Kruckeberg, Dean. "Ethical Decision Making in Public Relations." *International Public Relations Review* 15, no. 4 (1992): 32-37.

Kruckeberg, Dean, and Kenneth Starck. *Public Relations and Community: A Reconstructed Theory*. New York: Praeger, 1988.

Lambeth, Edmund B. *Committed Journalism: An Ethic for the Profession*. Bloomington: Indiana University Press, 1992.

McElreath, Mark P. *Managing Systematic and Ethical Public Relations*. Madison, Wis.: Brown & Benchmark, 1993.

McLuhan, Marshall. *The Gutenberg Galaxy*. New York: Mentor, 1969.

——. *The Mechanical Bride: Folklore of Industrial Man*. Boston: Beacon Press, 1967.

——. *Understanding Media: The Extensions of Man*. New York: McGraw-Hill, 1964.

Merrill, John C. "Global Commonalties for Journalistic Ethics: Idle Dream or Realistic Goal?" In *Communication Ethics and Global Change*, edited by Thomas W. Cooper, Clifford G. Christians, Frances Forde Plude, and Robert A. White. White Plains, N.Y.: Longman Inc., 1989.

——. "Ethics and Journalism." In *Ethics and the Press: Readings in Mass Media Morality*, edited by John C. Merrill and Ralph D. Barney. New York: Hastings House, 1975.

——. *Existential Journalism*. New York: Hastings House, 1977.

——. *The Imperative of Freedom: A Philosophy of Journalistic Autonomy*. New York: Hastings House, 1974.

——. "The Professionalization of Journalism." In *Ethical Issues in Professional Life*, edited by Joan C. Callahan. New York: Oxford University Press, 1988.

——. "Three Theories of Press Responsibility and the Advantages of Pluralistic Individualism." In *Responsible Journalism*, edited by Deni Elliott. Beverly Hills, Calif.: Sage Publications, 1986.

Merrill, John C., Carter R. Bryan, and Marvin Alisky. *The Foreign Press: A Survey of the World's Journalism*. Baton Rouge: Louisiana State University Press, 1970.

Merrill, John C., and Ralph L. Lowenstein. *Media, Messages, and Men: New Perspectives in Communication*. New York: David McKay Company, 1971.

Mowlana, Hamid. *Global Information and World Communication: New Frontiers in International Relations*. New York: Longman, 1986.

Mundt, Whitney R. "Global Media Philosophies." In *Global Journalism*, edited by John C. Merrill, New York: Longman, 1991.

Ogbondah, Chris W. *Military Regimes and the Press in Nigeria, 1966-1993*. Lanham, Md.: University Press of America, 1994.

Olen, Jeffrey. *Ethics in Journalism*. Englewood Cliffs, N.J.: Prentice Hall, 1988.

O'Neill, John. "Journalism in the Market Place." In *Ethical Issues in Journalism and the Media*, edited by Andrew Belsey and Ruth Chadwick. London: Routledge, 1992.

"Organizations Want Diversity: A Culture Change Job for PR." *PR Reporter* 37, no. 4 (1994): 1-2.

Picard, Robert G. "Global Communications Controversies." In *Global Journalism*, edited by John C. Merrill. New York: Longman, 1991.

Rivers, William L., and Cleve Mathews. *Ethics for the Media*. Englewood Cliffs, N.J.: Prentice Hall, 1988.

Rubin, Bernard. "The Search for Media Ethics." In *Questioning Media Ethics*, edited by Bernard Rubin. New York: Praeger, 1978.

Schudson, Michael. *Discovering the News: A Social History of American Newspapers*. New York: Basic Books, Inc., 1978.

Siebert, Fred, Theodore Peterson, and Wilbur Schramm. *Four Theories of the Press*. Urbana: University of Illinois Press, 1956.

Sriramesh, K., and Jon White. "Societal Culture and Public Relations." In *Excellence in Public Relations and Communication Management*, edited by James E. Grunig. Hillsdale, N.J.: Lawrence Erlbaum Associates, 1992.

Stephens, Lowndes F. "The World's Media Systems: An Overview." In *Global Journalism*, edited by John C. Merrill. New York: Longman, 1991.

White, Robert A. "Social and Political Factors in the Development of Communication Ethics." In *Communication Ethics and Global Change*, edited by Thomas W. Cooper, Clifford G. Christians, Frances Forde Plude, and Robert A. White. White Plains, N.Y.: Longman Inc., 1989.

Wiebe, Robert H. *The Search for Order: 1877-1920*. New York: Hill & Wang, 1967.

chapter 7

Global Advertising and Public Relations

Douglas Ann Newsom and Bob J. Carrell

Technology places organizations and governments all over the planet, even if they don't intend to be there. Satellite, computer, and fax communication systems connect the world so it's no longer possible to think in terms of restricting most messages— commercial or otherwise—to particular audiences. This global access to messages is occurring at a time when most organizations are looking at a more direct targeting of their messages. The focus is usually short-ranged and sharp, but the effect is likely to be broad and diffused. Messages get through the clutter of competing media or in-effective delivery systems only through individual choice.

The recipients of mass media messages are volunteer readers, listeners, or view-ers. If something gets their attention, they may opt to receive the message. The prob-lem is that what is received may not be a message intended for them, such as com-mercials and ads that come with imported media when the products are not available in that market. Or recipients' cultural experience may not give them the same frame of reference for the message, such as the romance that surrounds much media con-tent, especially advertising.

The effects of either are usually negative. There is frustration when products are not available or are too costly, perhaps because of import duties. There is bewilder-ment at not understanding the context of messages or themes for both editorial and

Contributors' note: An exhaustive and exhausting literature review left many information gaps, especially in materials of recent origins. In an effort to get up-to-date information on advertising and public relations as practiced and taught around the world, the authors sent questionnaires to members of the Inter-national Public Relations Society of America (IPRSA) and selected personal contacts. Respondents provided not only answers to the survey questions but in most cases sent the requested additional materials such as published articles (some from IPRSA's magazine, the *International Public Relations Review*) and sometimes even books. These provided critical information, and the authors are grateful to their colleagues for their help.

advertising content. Appreciation of foreign mass media content is often limited to cultural elites. This is not something peculiar to other than so-called "first-world" cultures.

Advertising and public relations efforts rely on carefully crafted messages and graphics designed for specific audiences to persuade them to accept a product or service or to support an idea. The haphazard mass media delivery system of a global marketplace considerably complicates such communication. It can even create problems for the most conscientious efforts.

Thus, most so-called "global" campaigns are not exactly that. They are concepts that are adapted to the media and the cultures where the communication effort is being made. What public relations and advertising practitioners have relied on for years is a local contact, someone to guide the communication effort safely through the culture, which often includes religious and legal traps for the unwary.

Connections with individuals and agencies or firms have often led a multinational advertising and public relations organization to found a branch in the city where the contact was established. More recently, areas identified as potentially critical combination points have become the site of the newest office. Global recession in the late 1980s and early 1990s caused the closing of many of these new offices, but the pattern has been established. What often occurred is that a local advertising or public relations facility grew up in its place.

As these local practices matured, they have taken on characteristics particular to their social, economic, and political environments. Generalizations are risky, but in many countries the communication function seems to have developed with a public relations emphasis in government and nongovernment organizations (NGOs) that have social missions. The communication function takes on a marketing emphasis when focused on an industrial or commercial enterprise. In some, though, perhaps because of media structures, the lines between advertising and public relations have blurred into a general communication function. This began in government-directed social campaigns, which have used all media and a mix of advertising, publicity, and promotion. Because some advertising agencies have been involved in these, many have developed a public relations segment. The size of some of these accounts has attracted transnational and multinational advertising and/or public relations groups that have opened offices abroad to service these accounts. These new offices then attracted other clients from the commercial part of the economy.

The proliferation of advertising and public relations people employed around the world has had another impact on education. Whereas previously most universities outside of the United States preferred the European model of teaching disciplines, not professions, many have now added courses and even majors in public relations and/or advertising. In nations where a tradition of teaching journalism already existed, such as India, the addition of public relations and advertising seemed to come easily. Giving support to these fledgling academic endeavors have been the resident professionals, who have also encouraged continuing education courses, seminars, and workshops.

The question used to be, Where was such growth in the practice and the education occurring? Now the question is, Where is it not? Even governments that used to look at their development communication as a journalistic or information campaign are not recognizing what is readily identified by most public relations practitioners as a public affairs effort—a campaign by government to change the behavior of a specific group of citizens.

Looking at the world in sections, as this book does, makes it easy to identify major trends, although some specific countries may exhibit more profound change than others. These observations have been drawn from public relations and advertising practitioners living and working abroad, most of them nationals (see authors' note).

ASIA AND THE PACIFIC

The maturity of advertising and public relations practice in Australia and New Zealand provides a sharp contrast to the developing status in China, which has Hong Kong as a sophisticated neighbor. Other areas with considerable experience are Japan, Singapore, Korea, and Taiwan. Malaysia and Indonesia are growing and paying a great deal of attention to education for practitioners. The Philippines, like Hong Kong, is experienced, but government difficulties over the years have interrupted a steady development.

A distaste for confrontation and braggadocio make some Western-styled approaches out of place in Japan, which depends more on respect for the messenger and the depth of trust established through long-term relationships, most particularly with media and government. Although public relations and Western-styled advertising were introduced to Japan after World War II, the acculturation process has changed the practice considerably. Advertising is much more subtle, and news is disseminated through the press clubs, some of which are industry related. Some are government oriented, and a couple of them are for political parties. Establishing relationships with the press clubs is the only way to get information in the news media, which are not competitive and tend to share information. The news is also presented the way it is announced by the authorities, releasing it rather than presenting it in an objective or investigative way.

China's potential as a market has been a temptation for traders for centuries, and no less so now, but the cultural and political land mines require a good guide. The media system also offers a challenge, because it involves waiting for weeks or months to be able to buy advertising space and buying the services of journalists through the China News and Culture Promotion Committee to get publicity.

Nevertheless, public relations is being taught in China, with its first program having opened in 1985 at Shenzhen University, the area just north of Hong Kong, where the practice of public relations began in 1981. Public relations is now being taught in more than 100 universities, which use a nationally approved text.

In "the other China," or Taiwan, public relations and advertising have been developing steadily since the 1950s. In 1990 a Foundation for Research and Education in Public Relations was established in Taipei, which has about seven universities offering public relations courses. Most of the books used are Western, and the practices have a strong Western influence.

The Western influence is also strong in Singapore, which is the focus for high-tech multinational companies. Hong Kong remains, for now, the world's marketplace for consumer goods, and the practice of advertising and public relations in these areas is strongly affected by their economic thrust.

The Philippines, because of the islands' strong ties to the United States, may lay claim to the Pacific birthplace for public relations and a climate where advertising has always played an important role. The Philippines dates its "beginnings" for public relations practice to the 1940s, and by 1955 it had a national public relations association. Constraints on corporate speech during the period of martial law were a setback, but by 1977 the government authorized a bachelor of science degree in public relations. Universities that could support the degree were allowed to offer it. Also in 1977, an institute was formed to serve as a liaison between education and practice.

In Australia public relations education began about the same time as in the Philippines, 1970, and the first associations in Australia were established in 1949 and 1952. Now, the Public Relations Institute of Australia has taken the leadership in looking at the educational programs offered throughout the country and setting standards for the both education and practice. Doctoral degrees in public relations are now being offered in Australia.

New Zealand has experienced similar influences as Australia, just as the market center of Korea has been influenced by its position and its neighbors. Neighbors Indonesia and Malaysia, on the other hand, seem to be developing somewhat differently, which is perhaps due to their different government structures, but both are aggressively seeking assistance in developing communication strategies for government and commerce. Thailand, always a market center too, but one of a different kind, has seen a growth of trade-related professional activity. Government changes have been somewhat of a constraint on the growth of advertising and public relations activity, but tourism is a major activity. The practice of public relations in Korea, Indonesia, Malaysia, and Thailand is more structured and centralized than in the more Western-like Philippines, Australia, and New Zealand.

LATIN AMERICA AND THE CARIBBEAN

Mexico would seem to be a natural setting for advertising and public relations in this area, and actually such activities have a long history with professional ties, especially to the United States, going back to the early 1940s. However, formalization of practices is fairly recent, with the Mexican Academy of Public Relations only being formed in 1993. Nevertheless, Mexico has shown a strong parallel development of commercial and government communication that involves both advertising and public relations.

Mexico City has been home to international public relations and advertising agencies for more than 30 years and has had its own agencies and firms for at least 25 years. Mexico City was host to the first Inter-American Conference on Public Relations in 1960, and that provided a framework for the Inter-American Federation. The Federation, now headquartered in Caracas, Venezuela, includes Mexico as well as Argentina, Bolivia, Brazil, Chile, Colombia, Costa Rica, Dutch Antilles, Ecuador, Panama, Paraguay, Peru, Uruguay, and Canada. It is the Federation that provides some of the framework for research on the growth of public relations activities in the area.

One of the first universities to offer public relations courses was the Pontifical Catholic University in Peru, but public relations courses are also taught now at universities in Argentina, Brazil, Ecuador, and Mexico. Brazil claims the most published authors of public relations materials and was the first country to license or regulate the practice of public relations (1967). Other countries where the practice is regulated include Panama and Peru. In some of these, regulation has been an occasion for abuse when governments changed, but these nations, like others in the area, have seen dramatic changes in the past few years.

Many countries have democratized or moved in that direction. They have privatized previously government-owned segments of the economy and have seen their economies become more stable. This has set the style for communicators as strategic planners and policy advisers, rather than as communication tacticians. The growth of the economic sector has brought in foreign companies from all over the world and, with them, more advertising and public relations activities for locals and for international practitioners. Financial public relations (investor relations) is growing, and the importance of media relations is increasing as the world becomes smaller and the changes in these nations put them in the international spotlight more frequently.

Sometimes, the spotlight has turned on them as a result of political problems such as allegations of corruption in government and scandal, but many watchers of the area see these as less disruptive than in the past. The Southern Cone Common Market (Mercosur), which includes Argentina, Brazil, Paraguay, and Uruguay, is an integral part of the free-trade pact, the North American Free Trade Agreement that went into effect January 1, 1994, although economic differences between Argentina and Brazil are seen as potential hindrances.

Trade is almost always a fertile field for the growth and development of advertising and public relations, and other countries in this area should not be overlooked. The Bahamas' free zone of Freeport is attracting high-tech companies, and the country is expanding its role as an international financial market. Privatization continues apace in the Dominican Republic, which seems to be maintaining its equilibrium despite the difficulties of its neighbor Haiti. The problems in that country, like continuing difficulties in El Salvador and some tension still between Belize and Guatemala, have economic consequences. However, places like Guyana, with a new gold mine and a forgiveness of its debt by Great Britain, seem to be working though difficulties like territorial disputes with Venezuela. One Caribbean public relations practitioner, based in the Bahamas and trying to deal with the Haiti refugee problem, called it a time of special challenges and opportunities.

The image of the carefree Caribbean is not quite that, as public relations and advertising activities accelerate there, primarily as a result of government campaigns to improve social conditions and attract investment, as well as tourists, which remain a major economic factor. A significant development is the Caribbean Community and Common Market, or Caricom, which has agreed to increase its economic ties to Cuba. Changes in Cuba itself have left many watchers waiting for the other shoe to drop.

SUB-SAHARAN AFRICA

Most of the public relations practice in sub-Saharan Africa is in government, and there is increasing demand for more accountability on the part of the government, thus broadening the need for public relations people. At the same time, increased literacy and a growth in democracy have made the demand even more compelling.

Most of the public relations people learned "on the job," and there is still only limited opportunity for public relations education. This is a serious problem for continuing education and educating new practitioners. University-level public relations courses do exist Africa, though, and the Enugu State University in Lagos has a master's degree. In South Africa, the Public Relations Institute of South Africa is very involved in continuing education, and the *technikons* offer practical training to prepare students for careers in public relations. After three years, *technikon* students can graduate with a national diploma in public relations. These studies can be continued at a higher national diploma level and master's level as well as laureatus level.

The private sector has the more professionally trained (usually abroad) public relations people, who are the counselors and managers, and it is they who are able to work across the cultures of this vast continent and cope with the increasing technology employed in communication. Technology is pulling the various African nations closer together, but cultural misunderstandings and ethical challenges provide some critical barriers to professional performance.

An encouraging development was the 1992 All Africa International Public Relations Conference that brought together the French- and English-speaking parts of the continent for the first time. The English-speaking section has been the more active, but the history of public relations in Africa is not new. The convener of the 1992 meeting was the more than 20-year-old Federation of African Public Relations Associations.

The oldest and most sophisticated public relations organization is the Public Relations Institute of South Africa (PRISA), which began in 1952. There is a rich media mix in South Africa that stimulates the practice of both advertising and public relations. PRISA established an accreditation and ethics council in 1986 and has begun two certificate programs, one for public relations practice and the other for public relations management. PRISA is also the national external examiner for those who study for a diploma in public relations through distance learning, a three-year diploma effort.

Zimbabwe's Institute of Public Relations is 27 years old, and its major focus has been on continuing education for its members. Fortunately, this is not as difficult as it might seem, because most of them work in Harare, the capital, but there is also a branch in the second-largest city of Bulawayo. Most of the institute's members work in the commercial and industrial sectors. The greatest area of growth for the nation is commercial, because it now has a free-market economy for the first time in history. The institute offers accreditation, holds development lectures and workshops, and offers a one-year diploma course. This nation, in the heart of Africa, is a bellwether of the growth the rest of the continent is experiencing to catch up with South Africa and North Africa.

MIDDLE EAST AND NORTH AFRICA

Nigeria is developing a strong educational public relations program, with a master's degree at the University of Nigeria Enugu campus. The degree there, like the one at Enugu State University of Science and Technology in Hiberia, is a public relations program in the marketing department. The public affairs segment of public relations practice also is strong, and the Nigerian Institute of Public Relations Code of Ethics was incorporated into the country's laws.

Egypt is the founding place of the Arab Public Relations Society, which was begun in 1966 by Dr. Mahmoud El Gohary, who also founded its Institute. Because most of Egypt's business was in the hands of the government until the early 1970s, the public affairs aspects of public relations flourished. In the 1970s, the commercial aspects of public relations began to grow, as well as efforts to educate students for careers in communication.

In the nearby United Arab Emirates, public relations courses are taught at the university, which is moving toward establishing a major. Practitioners are in the government, nonprofit or service sector, in companies, and in agencies or firms.

In Israel, public relations as a discipline is still relatively new, as is education for the field, so much so that it can be found only in one university. However, seminars and workshops are held for Israeli practitioners, most of whom came to public relations from careers in the news media. While most of the public relations practitioners there work as staff or employees of companies, some have worked for the public relations departments of advertising agencies, and some independent public relations firms have developed.

A country that has a long history of public relations activity is India. There the discipline is taught in marketing and journalism departments of colleges and universities and in various workshops and seminars, many sponsored by the Foundation for Public Relations Education and Research, founded in 1989 by the Public Relations Society of India.

Some areas still are just developing, though. For example, the first meeting of university public relations officers was held as late as 1988, and many public relations people in government are not educated in public relations. However, most of the senior practitioners weren't either but have learned on the job so that their proficiency is at the level of any top-notch international public relations person.

The foundation has begun producing professional papers and monographs on different aspects of public relations practice. The society itself hosts conferences where papers are presented and proceedings published. All of these contribute to the nation's body of knowledge, which is also being enlarged by books on public relations by national authors. The society has developed a diploma examination and gives these examinations in different cities to meet the needs of students all over the country. Currently, it is also collaborating with the University Grants Commission to introduce a graduate public relations program in major Indian universities.

EASTERN EUROPE AND CIS

Public relations practice is just getting started in Russia. It might be said to have emerged from having Gennadi Gerasimov as a government spokesman, first for then-USSR Foreign Minister Eduard Shevardnadze and later for then-USSR President Mikhail Gorbachev. Moving from editor-in-chief of *Moscow News*, an English-language weekly, to the nation's first public affairs officer was a rather dramatic job change, since Gerasimov was the *only* public affairs officer in the nation at the time. Now that the USSR is divided, many of the new nations are developing their own public affairs officers. Russia, however, remains the focal point, because many commercial enterprises have begun, and some public relations books and courses have appeared there. Some Russian students have attended student public relations meetings in the United States, and some are studying public relations abroad to take their new skills back to their homeland.

All of the other nations emerging from the Communist system are learning about commercial enterprises as privatization occurs. Bulgaria, Romania, and Slovenia are among those emerging countries looking at public relations and public affairs to build their economies and their governments. Public relations in Turkey is much older and more sophisticated, but the political tensions there have caused some disruptions. The separation of what used to be Czechoslovakia into Czech and the Slovak Republic has disrupted a fledgling public relations activity that probably will settle down into a practice much like what is found in Europe.

The Croatian practice of public relations is very much like the European model, but the entire region of what used to be Yugoslavia is still in the process of sorting out and settling down. The Croatian practice includes nongovernment agencies, government, and commercial enterprises, especially those recently privatized.

WESTERN EUROPE

The European Community is the biggest single factor in the growth of public relations activity in this part of the world, and the focus is Brussels. But a community does not mean homogeneity by any means. In fact, the single biggest problem in conducting pan-European campaigns is the cost, because it must be done according to culture, language, media, and national laws. The solution has been to choose the most effective agency or firm in each region (not necessarily country), but the costs are causing clients to look at the single firm with the best connections.

In each of these countries, public affairs still dominate public relations activities, and privatization is important even in some highly developed countries that had, nevertheless, centralized many significant functions that are being sprung loose from the government. Second in concentration of public relations activity is business-to-business relations, which are easier and less expensive than consumer contact operations.

Public relations is closely related to advertising and marketing in many of these countries, and it is more likely to be publicity and media relations rather than strategic management in a number of others. Where public relations is being understood as a management tool rather than merely a marketing function, organizations are using public relations to improve employee relations in a recessionary economic climate. Companies are also using public relations to improve their relationships with related industries and governments outside their own. In short, they see the value of public relations in building and maintaining a reputation in a global society. Environmental issues are important in all of these countries and command much public relations attention, as does issue and crisis management.

Education for the field varies dramatically by country, but most offers some sort of continuing education for public relations, usually through professional organizations. Most European universities remain dedicated to the traditional liberal arts, but some have put in public relations courses, most notably in England, Germany, and Finland, which offers a doctorate.

Finland has one of the oldest (dating from the 1970s) and largest individual membership public relations organizations. (In Europe members may belong as individuals to professional associations or may participate in trade associations to which the major agencies belong.) Expenditures for advertising and public relations activities in this media-rich country are high. Germany's reunification has been a special challenge for public relations practitioners, as a whole other part of the country has been opened to new enterprises. A different approach is required in this new part of Germany, but the demand for information is high, and public relations strategies are being called on to help work through the problems of reassembling a nation. Germany's focus in the European Community as a financial power base heightens the significance of advertising and public relations practices there.

Germany and France began public relations associations about the same time, in 1958, and France has always practiced a more unified communication management style. It is also less structured and less controlled, yielding to enthusiasms that have earned it some criticism in other countries. The nation's mixed economy means a good bit of activity is focused within the government. Italy is another European country where this is the case, and for its companies, the personality of the owners is usually a part of the culture that is manifest in its public relations and advertising, Benetton being perhaps the most extreme example.

Spain shares this to some extent, but the public relations practice is more likely to be subsumed under the marketing function there, and publicity would describe most of the activities. Although public relations practitioners there are university educated, they come from marketing, commerce, or journalism and learned their craft on the job. In Norway, a specialized public relations curriculum has just developed, although public relations courses at the university level were first taught in the Norwegian School of Marketing in 1982. Most public relations practitioners are trained in marketing or other fields such as journalism or business.

The opposite is true for public relations practitioners in the Netherlands, which has a highly developed system for education in public relations at practical and theoretical levels. The practice there also focuses on skills in the area in which the public relations person would be working, such as health care. As in most of the European countries, command of several languages is necessary.

Austria also stresses use of the public relations function at the management level, and this may derive from an educational system that encourages such an orientation. In this sense, it is more like the U.S. system, as is Portugal's. That country was strongly influenced by a multinational, Mobil, which had a public relations department there in 1959. Portugal also had close ties to Britain as one of the founding members of the 1958 European Free Trade Association.

Britain's system is the one most like that in the United States, and yet it differs. The biggest difference is between educational systems, where vocational training has been strictly separated from university education. After 1992 however, the only way to qualify for membership in the Institute of Public Relations in that country is through examination, which must be passed to receive the industry-controlled and regulated Diploma in Public Relations. The training is offered through distance learning produced by the Open University for the Public Relations Education Trust. Additionally, university-level courses began to be offered at Stirling in 1987, thanks to Sam Black, whose IPRA Gold Paper has been a model for his country and others. Now Britain has public relations courses at the undergraduate and graduate levels at several institutions.

In summary, although it is almost impossible to talk about an internationally definable practice of public relations, it is even more difficult to talk about a Western European model. However, the ingredients seem to exist in most countries for an identifiable practice called public relations, and it is clearly glued to advertising and marketing, most inseparably in countries that have long been involved in a competitive market economy. Individual practitioners may belong to the Confédération Européenne des Relations Publiques, if they live in the following countries: Austria, Belgium, Cyprus, Denmark, Finland, France, Germany, Greece, Great Britain, Ireland, Iceland, Italy, Luxembourg, Netherlands, Norway, Portugal, Sweden, Switzerland, and Turkey. Eastern European members include the Czech Republic, Hungary, Poland, Russia, and Slovakia. Agencies and consultancies belong to the International Committee of Public Relations Consultancies Associations Ltd.

NORTH AMERICA: THE UNITED STATES AND CANADA

More education for and experience in the global practice of advertising and public relations have characterized the major change in North America, which includes Canada and the United States. The diversity of the populations in both nations has given them a particular affinity for global interaction, and both have a long history of trade with other countries and with each other. Approval of the North American Free Trade Agreement seems likely to encourage more interaction between the two nations, stimulating additional business and communication activity.

Education in the international aspects of advertising and public relations began to appear in North American colleges and universities in the late 1980s and grew dramatically in the early 1990s, largely in response to the growing reality of the practice. The reality of the practice is that the advertising and public relations functions, always complementary, have begun to be more blurred, especially because the differences between the two are less distinct in some other countries.

The expense of going global has meant that more people in advertising and public relations have had to learn to be better managers of people and funds. When this is not the case, they are relegated to the role of technicians, and the communications "boss" is someone from the business who happens to be a good communicator or is someone from marketing who is accustomed to offering proof of cost-effectiveness and being accountable for results.

Another demand of the global marketplace is the knowledge of other languages and other cultures. Land mass has created a limited familiarity with other languages for most natives of North America, although many people in Canada speak French as well as English, and many people in the United States speak Spanish as well as English. Developing liaisons with practitioners in other countries has been the standard practice, but more advertising and public relations practitioners are getting experience abroad to give depth to the planning and counseling they need just to function at home.

RESULTS OF THE SURVEY

Because the number of usable cases from our survey was small, results must be considered general rather than specific about particular parts of the world. About 60 percent of the respondents said their entire professional activities are in public relations. The other 40 percent focus on advertising or about equally on advertising and public relations. Their activities spread over four major areas: client services, 14.3 percent; strategic planning, 32.1 percent; management, 39.3 percent; and 14.3 percent in tactical execution. None focused primarily on research or evaluation. Better than 75 percent have been in the communication business 20 years or more. Half have been with their present organizations 11 years or more. Also, 55 percent of them have been in their current positions for seven years or more. These characteristics suggest respondents who are quite senior and have the benefit of a broad range of global experiences.

That is reinforced by the fact that respondents collectively have been directly involved in the development of communication strategic plans or the execution of them in 34 countries around the world. These countries include Australia, Argentina, Bahrain, Belgium, Canada, Cyprus, Denmark, Finland, Greece, Hong Kong, Hungary, Great Britain, Indonesia, India, Israel, Kuwait, Netherlands, New Zealand, Norway, Oman, Philippines, Portugal, Qatar, Saudi Arabia, Singapore, Slovenia, Slovakia, Spain, Sweden, Switzerland, Turkey, United Arab Emirates, Venezuela, and Zimbabwe.

The Preferred Strategic Model

A critical decision for any global organization is which strategic planning model it will use to guide its communication programs. There are three basic types. One is a *standardized* strategic model. Strategy is formed at global headquarters and implemented in all operating areas. Another is known as the *adaptive* strategic model. A basic strategy is developed, but it is adapted appropriately to the environments of the host countries in which it will be implemented. The third model is the *country-specific* model. As its name implies, strategic planning is shaped to fit the uniqueness of a host country.

Fewer than a tenth of the respondents said their current organizations use the standardized model. Nearly 55 percent said their organizations use the country-specific model. Better than 90 percent of them said that an adaptive or country-specific strategy is much better at promoting good analyses of internal and external environments affecting clients. They also said that adaptive or country-specific strategic approaches help more in defining missions, setting objectives and goals, and formulating better strategies. Respondents unanimously favor adaptive or country-specific models for tactical planning and execution. In fact, 70 percent prefer the country-specific model for tactical applications.

Potential Problem Areas

Respondents see rigid organizational policies as interfering with good communication tactics. This results in too much reliance on communication campaign plans books and manuals. Respondents also seem to think that growth through mergers and acquisitions tends to increase the distance between those who plan campaigns and those who execute them. A companion belief is that centralized planning tends to take initiative from the people on the firing line, who are in the best position to know what needs to be done. The result is that many decisions are made by poorly informed people. Better than 90 percent of the respondents agree that if too many decision makers are involved in strategic planning, effective communication strategy may be diluted.

Indigenous Personnel

Fewer than half of the respondents say that well-qualified indigenous personnel are readily available in the countries where they work. Still fewer believe that well-qualified indigenous managers are readily available. This may be due to the poor state of educational programs and opportunities available in some countries, although that can't be demonstrated from the survey. Respondents also noted that most indigenous personnel seem to come from fields not directly related to advertising or public relations.

Indigenous men are usually paid more than indigenous women with the same credentials for doing the same work. Women also are not as common as men in the communication industries. Respondents seemed to think that salaries for indigenous communication personnel are not as good as they are in other professional fields. Respondents also strongly believe that most of what indigenous personnel know about the communication business is learned on the job.

The Media

In the countries where they work, respondents perceive the mass media as politically very powerful. And almost half of them say that buying influence is a common practice. More than half of the respondents say that it is difficult to get unpaid editorial coverage and support in the mass media. And most of them seem to think that the mass media are effective ways of reaching target audiences with paid messages. But more than half of the respondents say that a majority of their budgets go for costs other than paid space or time in mass or specialized media.

Mass media are generally accessible to the average person in countries where respondents work. The level of literacy usually is not seen as a handicap.

Law and Ethics

More than half of the respondents say that laws and regulations governing communication practices are not overly restrictive. At the same time, respondents say that in the countries where they work, fewer than half of practitioners are greatly concerned with ethical issues. But more than half say that ethical issues are of great concern in those countries. When asked about their own clients, more than 90 percent said that their clients were greatly concerned with ethical practices. These observations seem to suggest that some practitioners are out of touch with the standards of their clients and cultural environments.

Status, Strategies, and Clients

Respondents generally believe that the status of the communication business in their countries is not very high. At the same time, only a little more than a third of them believe that nation building is an implicit part of most communication activities. Better than 70 percent say that strategic decisions are mostly client driven, but nearly half see communication strategies as being driven by audience needs.

This seeming conflict is not unusual, because organizations generally will spend resources only to meet their own agendas. It is only when an organization recognizes that its own success is tied inextricably to meeting audience needs that it can be successful in the long term. In this context, the most fruitful policy is one in which strategic planners work until they find a match between their organization's needs and the needs of target audiences.

Even so, respondents were realistic enough also to say that most communication programs are market driven. Successful organizations know that they must respond with alacrity to economic, political, or social challenges, or else their futures are uncertain.

Type of Work

About three-quarters report that they never or infrequently do pro bono work for clients. More than half of them never or infrequently work for nonprofit clients. More than half also do work very frequently or frequently for government agencies, but they rarely serve clients such as physicians, engineers, politicians, or political parties. About 85 percent of the respondents indicate that advising and counseling clients best characterizes the work they produce for clients.

CONCLUSIONS

There is no single, universal model of the professional practice of advertising and public relations. The Western model seems to be dominant in much of the world, but it is clear that as advertising and public relations practices develop and mature in many areas, their character is directly influenced by local economic, political, and social structures. Advertising practices seem to have been adopted earlier than public relations in many countries and seem to be a little more mature. However, the growth and development of public relations practices throughout much of the world now seems to be unusually rapid.

Moves to open free trade among countries is accelerating the growth of both advertising and public relations. Democratizing and privatizing also are adding considerable weight to this movement. Indigenous personnel are not readily available to fill this need. Most personnel come from fields other than advertising and public relations and learn on the job. However, formal educational programs are developing at universities around the world. Professional associations are trying hard to support professional development through workshops, seminars, and certification programs.

chapter 8

Continuing Media Controversies

Paul Grosswiler

THREE RECURRENT THEMES IN CONTEXT

Negative media content, monopoly control of the technologies of communication, and an imbalanced information current have been three continuing controversial issues in international communication, beginning with the creation of the European telegraph system in the mid-1800s through the conclusion of the General Agreement on Tariffs and Trade in late 1993, which restricts U.S. movie imports in the European Community, and the inauguration of a U.S. administration plan to propose legislation for a national "information superhighway" in 1994. The nations, the organizations, and the media have changed, but these three themes have persisted in various incarnations and developments throughout this century and a half of international mass communication.

Often, the attempt to change the existing information order is exclusively associated with a highly charged and polarized debate in the United Nations Educational, Scientific and Cultural Organization (UNESCO) in the late 1970s and early 1980s over the merits of a "new international information order," also known as the New World Information Order (NWIO) and the New World Information and Communication Order (NWICO). Both proponents of the NWIO in UNESCO—mostly from newly liberated countries in the third world, socialist countries, and Western media critics—and NWIO's opponents—including mostly Western nations and their media—considered this to be a "new" and unique attempt. The U.S. media and, to a lesser degree, the U.S. government categorically attacked any attempt to change the structure of the Western-dominated global media system.

Often, all attempts to change the information order are declared dead, having died when the United States withdrew from UNESCO and the new information order debate in 1985. This misunderstanding, however, ignores the continuing struggle to negotiate the structures and content of international communication that predates the UNESCO debate by more than a century and succeeds it by almost a decade. While the players have shifted, even reversing roles, as the Associated Press (AP) and the United States have done, the issues largely remain intact and unresolved.

BEFORE AND SINCE THE NEW INTERNATIONAL INFORMATION ORDER DEBATE

Long before the new world information order debate, the invention of the telegraph led to the European-based International Telegraph Union in the 1860s, which was transformed into the International Telecommunication Union (ITU) in the 1930s. After World War I, the League of Nations called on the press and radio to help preserve world peace. Between the wars, the United States' strongest news service, the AP, complained about the negative effects of global news flow controlled by the European news cartel of three news agencies, Germany's Wolff, France's Havas, and Britain's Reuters. The United Nations (UN), newly created after World War II, developed a series of resolutions calling for freedom of communication as a human right, culminating in the Declaration of Human Rights in 1948. Also in the 1940s, a nongovernmental U.S. group, the Commission on Freedom of the Press, known as the Hutchins Commission, advocated changes in the media to make them more responsible. And the U.S. Commission on Civil Disorders, or the Kerner Commission, noted the failure of American media to cover minorities in the United States in the 1960s.

Since the United States withdrew from UNESCO and the polarized new world information order debate subsided, the UN has continued to address some of the same issues between the rich industrial countries of the northern hemisphere and the poor countries of the southern hemisphere. Scholars have studied the aftermath of the debate, finding both biased U.S. media coverage of the debate (Giffard 1989) and distorted information presented in communication textbooks in the United States (Roach 1993). It appeared in early 1994 that the United States would rejoin UNESCO in 1995.

Much of the debate over international content, control, and current, however, has shifted to concerns about the cultural impact of American media and transnational media corporation programming on other industrialized countries in North America and Europe, especially as public media in those countries are commercialized and privatized. The recently concluded General Agreement on Tariffs and Trade (GATT) included provisions by the French, for example, to protect their movie industry. Other Western countries have initiated domestic programming quotas. The U.S. government proposal for an information superhighway, unveiled in 1993, had within a few months given rise to concern among groups such as the MacBride Round Table, a nongovernmental body meeting annually since 1989 to carry on the work of UNESCO's MacBride Commission and its seminal work on global communication, *Many Voices, One World*

(MacBride et al. 1980). The 1995 round table will focus on the global effects and im-plications of the information superhighway.

NEGOTIATING INTERNATIONAL TELEGRAPH COMMUNICATION IN THE 1800s

With the growth of a viable international communication system beginning with the telegraph in 1837, underwater cable in 1866, the telephone in 1876, the wireless in 1897, and radio in 1907—which were all used in the formation of the global European empires—the problem of negotiating telegraph content, control, and current began in the mid-1800s. The initial nations involved were Western European governments that formed the International Telegraph Union in 1865. This group set technical in-terconnection standards among national telegraph services, set mechanisms for tariffs and sharing revenue across borders, and ensured privacy of messages. An international working group on radiotelegraph issues formed in 1903, which merged with the highly active Telegraph Union in 1932 to form the International Telecommunication Union. The 1903 conferences dealt with monopolization. The sinking of the *Titanic* in 1912 led to the first international agreement requiring ships to carry wireless technology able to communicate with any ship, regardless of the manufacturer of the wireless equipment (Fortner 1993, pp. 11-12).

The process of establishing this international communication system revolved around two conflicts, according to Robert Fortner. This process involved the struggle between governments and private businesses for control over the system, as well as the struggle between competing private interests. Governments tried to protect their domestic private firms because the governments depended on them. To illustrate the struggle between private interests, newspapers sided with governments against mo-nopoly of the international telegraph cable system because rates charged to customers, like newspapers, were too high (Fortner 1993, pp. 78-79).

As the telecommunication system developed, it traced the economic and politi-cal points of the European empires, connecting European capitals to colonial capitals and trading centers. The telegraph lines followed the railroads, which were set up to extract commodities from colonies, not to communicate indigenously. As a result, ge-ographic points on the system without geopolitical clout were bypassed in a way that presages complaints a century later from the third world. In the 1800s, however, the information flow bypassed Ireland and Canada as the transAtlantic cable linked New York and London. The cable went through Canada first, but Canada had to send and receive all cables through New York (Fortner 1993, p. 88).

The imperial governments in Europe sought rapid communication with colonies to manage them internally, but the cables also tied empires together as channels of busi-ness, diplomacy, and the military. The private interests operating the system also strug-gled for monopoly control, working with governments to help achieve colonial sta-bility, receiving government subsidies, and making demands of government (Fortner 1993, pp. 76-77). This early international system, forged from these battling private and government interests to control international communication, laid the roots for the controversies debated in the 1990s.

THE EUROPEAN CARTEL'S "NEWS IMPERIALISM"

The rise of the three European news agencies, Havas, Wolff, and Reuters, and of the United States' AP between 1835 and 1850 led to agreements among the three European agencies from 1856 to 1914 that led to a European cartel. Disputes arising among the three were resolved by the agreements, which carved up areas of monopoly control. In 1859, the "Ring Combination" agreement gave Reuters the British colonial empire, North America, China, Japan, and most of Asia and the Pacific. Havas controlled the French empire, southern Europe, South America, and parts of Africa. Wolff was granted Prussia, the rest of Europe, the Slavic countries, and Scandinavia, according to Howard Frederick (1993, pp. 38, 39).

The AP was let into the cartel in 1887 but was confined to North America. The United States experienced during the cartel's long existence a form of "cultural imperialism" that the third world would later object to in the 1970s and 1980s (Frederick 1993, p. 39). In the words of AP's former general manager, Kent Cooper, who fought to dismantle the cartel:

> When Reuter, Havas and Wolff pooled their resources, established complete news agency control of international news and allotted to themselves the news agency exploitation in all countries of the world, they brought under their control the power to decide what the people of each nation would be allowed to know of the people of other nations and in what shade of meaning the news was to be presented. . . . International attitudes have developed from the impressions and prejudices aroused by what the news agencies reported. Monopoly made the system of deception work. The mighty foreign propaganda carried on through these channels in the last hundred years has been one of the causes of wars that has never been uncovered. (Cooper 1942, p. 8)

According to Cooper, because the AP agreed to bar itself from sending news about the United States beyond its borders, agreeing that only Reuters could send U.S. news abroad, stereotypes and inaccuracies resulted:

> So Reuters decided what news was to be sent from America. It told the world about Indians on the war path in the West, lynchings in the South, and bizarre crimes in the North. The charge for decades was that nothing credible to America was ever sent. American businessmen criticized the Associated Press for permitting Reuters to belittle America abroad. (1942, p. 12)

Cooper complained that Reuters and Havas kept out AP competition, presented "disparaging" U.S. news or none at all to Americans and "glorified" news of their own countries (1942, p. 43). He charged that "the big three collectively and individually exercised a dictatorship over their weaker colleagues in the smaller countries" (p. 36). These ideas are echoed in the 1970s call for a new information order, although the AP is on the other side of the latter contest.

The critics of the Western press in the 1920s and 1930s, Stuart Bullion (1982) notes in tracing back the information order debates, proposed media, and audience responsibilities to correct the imbalances. Calls ranged from self-censorship to better journalistic and reader training.

For its part, the AP left the cartel in 1919, signing 25 newspapers in Central America. It began service to Japan in 1930 and signed a contract with Reuters to exchange news in 1934 (Fortner 1993, p. 116). The AP was partially inspired by two newer U.S. news agencies, United Press Association and International News Service, which were not part of the cartel and ignored the cartel's regions of influence. But it was World War II that destroyed the European cartel. The Nazis turned Wolff into a propaganda agency in the 1930s, causing Reuters and Havas to end their contracts. The Nazis closed Havas after Germany occupied France, and Reuters received a British government subsidy during the war to offer a second news service.

THE LEAGUE OF NATIONS

Between the two major European wars, the League of Nations in 1925 addressed the role of the press in preserving world peace, and in 1936 set forth obligations of radio. Calling the press an effective means of leading the public toward "moral disarmament," the League in 1925 asked for a panel of experts to outline the role of the press in maintaining world peace and reducing international risks, using rapid and cheap transmission of news (Fortner 1993, pp. 116-17). In 1927, the League adopted resolutions concerning the working conditions of journalists and press freedoms (Galtung and Vincent 1992, p. 112). The League's final report stressed the need to protect the sending of news from reporters to parent companies and the need to eliminate censorship in peacetime and propaganda (Bullion 1982, p. 162). In 1936, the League asked for states to regulate broadcasts harmful to international understanding, including those that incite social unrest. The convention also sought prohibition of broadcasting falsehoods that harm international understanding and messages that incite war (Mehra 1986, p. 104). Nongovernmental bodies also discussed international media issues in the 1920s and 1930s, including the Press Congress of the World, which heard a Latin American concerned about imperialism of the U.S. and British press, as well as concerns about news coverage of emerging societies. The group in 1926 called for worldwide codes of journalism ethics and standards of conduct (Bullion 1982, p. 163).

The League-sponsored meetings all reflected broad participation of countries in addition to the Western powers (Bullion 1982, p. 163), although the concerns of the 1920s centered on European powers and excluded the two-thirds of the world colonized by Europe. Only after the colonial empires were shaken by World War II and the wave of national liberation movements in the 1950s through the 1970s emerged could the third world voice its concerns about international communication issues. Before that time, however, the League of Nations collapsed in the late 1930s, and its work in international communications was lost in the wake of World War II, when the UN was formed.

THE UNITED NATIONS AND UNESCO UP TO 1970

The League's successor, the UN, after witnessing the crucial role of the media during World War II as a force for great good or evil, created a series of resolutions concerning international communication leading to and stemming from its Declaration of Human Rights adopted in 1948. The 50 countries then existing in the world soon divided between the camps of the United States and the Soviet Union over the desirability of a "free flow of information." The United States, supporting free flow of information and in a powerful global position after World War II, helped the AP establish its dominance in international news, as other U.S. media, including television and film, spread their products globally in the postwar decades.

According to critical media scholar Herbert Schiller, the U.S. media and government built a U.S.-dominated information order between 1945 and 1960. Under U.S. guidance, the UN and UNESCO collaborated in building that system, as U.S. capital became the dominant force in war-ravaged Europe and many former colonial areas. In addition to the AP and United Press dislodging European news agencies, the following changes occurred by 1960: Hollywood movies saturated the globe's movie screens; U.S. television programs became the dominant fare; and U.S. tourism, advertising, popular music, and print media, as well as the English language, filled international commercial culture (Schiller 1989, pp. 141–143). The UN and UNESCO interpreted these events as progress as the media modernized third-world nations, leading them to adopt the features of private economy and a consumer society. UNESCO itself endorsed the free flow of information doctrine at the urging of the United States. The doctrine, Schiller argues, permitted the global penetration of U.S. media industries that created the U.S.-dominated information order.

Cees Hamelink remarks that the tension in the process of communication between synchronization, consensus, and centralization, on the one hand, and diversity, independence, and decentralization, on the other, has shaped the UN and UNESCO from the beginning (1983, p. 56). Howard Frederick identifies the former as the "free-flow" advocates and the latter as the "balanced flow" advocates (1993, pp. 128–29), but the United States has advocated both sides of the tension. For example, the U.S. Commission for UNESCO recommended in 1947 that obstacles to the free flow of information should be removed but that UNESCO should also look at the quality of international communication and identify ways that the media can positively and creatively serve international understanding (Hamelink 1983, pp. 56–57). As Kaarle Nordenstreng notes, the United States stressed the importance of the media in serving understanding and promoting security (1986, p. 11).

Other early examples illustrate the tension Hamelink identified. The first session of the UN General Assembly requested a conference on the "rights, obligations and practices" to be included in the "freedom of information." UNESCO's constitution in 1945 accepted the principle of a free flow of ideas but stressed the need to use the media for mutual understanding (Hamelink 1983, pp. 56-7). The United States had pushed for the inclusion of the "free-flow" language in UNESCO's constitution but failed in an attempt to get the idea of free flow in the UN Charter in 1945 (Frederick 1993, p. 128). The UN in 1945 supported free access to information; it accepted communication as a basic human right in its first general session in 1946; and it declared in Article 19 of the 1948 Universal Declaration of Human Rights that

> Everyone has the right to freedom of opinion and expression; this right includes freedom to hold opinions without interference and to seek, receive and impart information and ideas through any media and regardless of frontiers. (Nordenstreng, Manet, and Kleinwachter 1986, p. 123)

Article 28, by contrast, calls for an international order in which the rights of the individual can be fully realized (Hamelink 1983, p. 57).

The UN's early action on three communication issues includes the passing of Resolution 59, calling freedom of information a basic human right; Resolution 110, condemning all forms of propaganda designed to threaten peace or promote war; and Resolution 127, calling for increased diffusion of information to strengthen understanding and combat false or distorted news. These all occurred in a General Assembly dominated by the United States, Europe, and the Soviet Union, in which there was much consensus in the late 1940s (Frederick 1993, p. 164).

Free expression is also included in the International Covenant on Civil and Political Rights, adopted in 1966, while the same article adds that the right carries "special duties and responsibilities" and may be subject to restrictions (Hamelink 1983, p. 57). Free expression is also cited in the Western European Convention for the Protection of Human Rights and Fundamental Freedoms in 1950; the American Convention on Human Rights in 1969; the African Charter on Human and People's Rights in 1981; and the well-known Helsinki Accords, adopted by the Conference on Security and Cooperation in Europe in 1975 (Fortner 1993, p. 40).

UNESCO first became involved with information issues in the 1950s through early studies of one-way information flow between the North and the South. In 1951, the Economic and Social Council called for protections for journalists in gathering and sending news. The UN's news studies in the 1950s reviewed news in major dailies and the role of foreign correspondents. In the 1950s and 1960s, several conferences examined imbalances and inequities that were seen as obstacles to the free flow of information. Although concerns were raised as late as 1969, the conferences took no action to restrict the flow of information (Galtung and Vincent 1992, pp. 72-73).

The UN in 1957 began issuing almost annual calls for aid in developing media in the third world, with resolutions passed in 1958, 1959, 1961, and 1968, with repeated requests again in 1973 and 1976. Little, however, was done in response to these resolutions in a UN dominated by the West, advocating "free flow," and the Soviet sphere, advocating "balanced flow" (Mehra 1986, p. 38). The third world had not yet emerged in the 1950s and 1960s to formulate a unified response to the information order debate.

Throughout the 1960s, developing countries had sought technical aid from the UN, the International Monetary Fund, the World Bank, and the ITU to build media systems to address the imbalance in information flow. The U.S.-inspired free flow of information doctrine was questioned, and a new model that became known as "development journalism" was proposed. But the global media system continued to serve the developed world, linking Europe, North America, and other first-world countries. The rich northern countries dominated radio, recordings, film, television, and data flow, while the Big Four news agencies dominated international news flow. The developing countries emerging from colonial rule outnumbered the industrialized Western countries by 1970, but they were unable to gain access to the international communication system and were ill-equipped to develop their own systems. It was not until then that the call intensified for full equality in global communication (Fortner 1993, pp. 177–78).

THE HUTCHINS AND KERNER COMMISSIONS

Before the emergence of the third world, the content, control, and currents of international communication were addressed by groups that were not international, yet were significant critics of the media system that addressed international or intercultural issues. A group formed by U.S. media owner Henry Luce, the Commission on the Freedom of the Press, proposed a number of changes in international communication structures and content in the 1940s. Known as the Hutchins Commission, this group sought to persuade the media to be more responsible and fair in carrying out their obligations to society, including the preservation of world peace.

Another U.S. commission, the National Advisory Commission on Civil Disorders, appointed by President Lyndon Johnson to examine the causes of racial unrest in U.S. cities in the 1960s, also commented on the performance of the media. Although studying a domestic issue, the Kerner Commission found the media had not complied with the Hutchins Commission or the United Nations. Moreover, it found racial minority bias in U.S. media reporting, which reflects on international communication between dominant European-American racial groups and less powerful third-world countries comprising people of color.

Although mostly concerned with mass media within the United States, the Hutchins Commission also considered problems of international communication, calling for improved communication structures, fewer political and economic obstructions, and more accurate, representative, and higher quality reports and images in global information (Mehra 1986, p. 99). Critical of the commercial press interests in marketability for inhibiting balanced and comprehensive information, the Hutchins Commission members called for a government and media committee to fill in the void where commercial media interests fail. A public service function of private industry was suggested, with a government undertaking as a last resort (Mehra 1986, p. 100). The Hutchins authors also called for creation of a foreign reporters' organization with binding ethical codes and the authority to arbitrate complaints. They also suggested creation of an independent unit within UNESCO to monitor abuses.

In its seminal work, *A Free and Responsible Press,* the Hutchins Commission (1947) thought the mass media to be a powerful force to either promote civilization or to "thwart," "debase," and "vulgarize" civilization and endanger world peace. With increasing scope and power, the mass media can spread lies with speed not imagined by the framers of the U.S. Constitution (p. 3). If it is "irresponsible," the press would contribute to "universal catastrophe"; or the press would fulfill its "duty" in a "new world struggling to be born," according to the commission (p. 4). Fearing the threats from both totalitarian governments and concentration of economic powers, the authors placed their faith in the free press and free expression as the key to a free society (pp. 5-6). They thought mass communication was most complete in the United States, with mass communication elsewhere suffering in countries as a result of poverty, censorship, and poor physical facilities (p. 67).

Among the five basic responsibilities of the media in a free society, two are particularly focused on international—and intercultural—communication. First, the Hutchins Commission called special attention to the need to report the "truth about the facts" in international news (p. 22), and second, it saw the need to project a representative picture of different cultures and nations without stereotyping (pp. 26-27).

Regarding the U.S. role in international mass communication, the Hutchins group (1947) suggested action by the government, the media, and the public. First, the U.S. government should use its own media as a substitute to inform the public of U.S. policies where private media are unwilling to supply U.S. information abroad (pp. 88-90). Second, arguing that the mass media should remain a private industry with a public interest, the commission urged the media to elevate rather than degrade public wants and to accept responsibilities of common carriers of information and discussion (pp. 92-93). Third, the public needed to recognize the crucial role of the media in world crisis (p. 96). With a "world on the brink of suicide" after World War II, adults must "learn how to live together in peace," the commission said (p. 99). The public was urged to develop nonprofit institutions to ensure that the public receives the supply, variety, quality, and quantity of media services that it requires (p. 97). The public also could establish an independent agency outside of government to report annually on media performance, including minority access and international cooperation regarding the picture of life presented by the U.S. media (pp. 100-102).

The international aspects of the Hutchins Commission's work are generally not considered in treatment of these persisting communication controversies, although scholars Kaarle Nordenstreng and Mercedes Lynn de Uriarte (1992) have in different contexts argued for its incorporation while addressing international and multicultural media issues in the 1990s. Uriarte also draws on the Kerner Commission's work as an important thread running from the UN and the Hutchins Commission. The Kerner Commission itself mentioned the Hutchins Commission and the UN, saying that the U.S. media had not complied with their recommendations or resolutions in reporting race relations in the United States. The Kerner Commission criticized the media for reporting race relations from the perspective of white, upper-middle-class men with news values that support elite individuals and institutions, Uriarte notes. By failing to portray blacks regularly and in the context of U.S. society, the news media contributed to racial disorder. Minorities are not covered except in times of crisis and are associated with problems of crime, drugs, and school dropouts.

NWIO IN UNESCO IN THE 1970s AND 1980s

Finding that political independence from European colonizers had not resulted in eco-nomic independence, a call from the highly diverse global minorities in the third world for a "new international economic order" was followed in the mid-1970s by a call for a "new international information order" to correct information imbalance, neg-ative content, and monopoly control between the rich Northern countries and the poor Southern countries. Several key UNESCO documents from the new international in-formation order movement, including the 1978 Mass Media Declaration and the 1980 MacBride Commission Report, led to a highly polarized and irrational debate in UNESCO in the early 1980s, with the U.S. media and other Western media categori-cally opposed to any changes in the global media system. The United States, citing in-formation issues and and claiming an anti-Western bias in UNESCO, withdrew from the organization January 1, 1985, followed by Britain and Singapore, effectively cutting off the debate.

The third-world countries first took issue with the international economic order in the early 1970s and then included cultural and communication issues. These ob-jections to the state of the economic and information systems remained consistent as they were expressed primarily in UNESCO, but also in the United Nations, at the ITU, and at Non-Aligned Movement meetings. Evidence of the lopsided distribution of com-munications technology in the North, from mail services to telephones and books, in addition to the media, showed that the third-world countries had reason to be con-cerned with the imbalanced flow of media messages and the inability to stem the flow of television, film, news, and recordings from the West. In the face of this dominance, third-world countries responded by setting up alternative news agencies, mostly be-gun after the NWIO debate started in the early 1970s, but the impact of these regional or Southern news services remained negligible through the early 1990s.

The Western countries and media that defended the existing information order generally did not deny the existence of an imbalance in global information flow or a technological gap between the North and South. But, for the most part, the West fo-cused on technical aid, through INTELSAT, the World Bank, and the ITU, to close the technological and information flow gap, while maintaining the essential role of the free flow of information (Fortner 1993, pp. 195–198). At the start of the NWIO movement, third-world countries found supporters in socialist countries that wanted to control the flow of information across borders, but for different reasons. The socialist world, at philosophical odds with the West over the notion of free flow of information, ar-gued that its media were free from private control, which prevented the Western me-dia from being objective. As the embodiment of the people, the state-owned press was freer than the capitalist-owned press of the West.

Fortner (1993, pp. 195–198) analyzes the debate by saying that the Western media, divided over the issue of communication control, argued that state control of informa-tion was anathema, while the socialist world and the third world argued that Western-dominated media did not provide free flow but provided information that was by and for Western media and audiences. At heart, the West saw information as a commodity; the socialist world and the third world saw information as a social good. As a commodity, information flow prevents third-world countries from attaining political and economic independence. To balance the flow, suggestions ranged from alternative news systems, to reserving satellite slots for future use, and even to licensing journalists.

The first objections by the third world were made at UNESCO's general conference in 1970, when a two-way information flow was called for, as was the need for third-world countries to preserve their cultures and the need for third-world national communication policies. UNESCO responded by initiating research on news flow, on obstacles to a free flow, cultural autonomy, and on problems with isolationism. Following this meeting, a panel of UNESCO experts identified problems of "cultural neo-colonialism" caused by new communications technologies. The 1970 meeting has been recognized as the starting point for the UNESCO Mass Media Declaration, which was published in 1978 (Galtung and Vincent 1992, p. 74). In 1970, therefore, UNESCO shifted its approach to media problems from asking for technical aid to exploring social and political questions about the media (Mehra 1986, pp. 38–39).

The UN began responding to direct broadcast satellite transmissions, when the Soviet Union called for approval of principles in 1972. A resolution was adopted 102–1, with the United States alone in opposition, as it would be in many later General Assembly votes on communication issues, to endorse prior consent for DBS broadcasts (Galtung and Vincent 1992, p. 74). The Soviets backed another measure to establish principles governing the media, but the United States opposed this, as the other, because it would restrict the free flow of information (Galtung and Vincent 1992, p. 75).

Some media scholars have designated the birthplace of NWIO as the 1973 Algiers meeting of the Non-Aligned Movement. That group, which started in the mid-1950s, comprises third-world leaders representing more than 100 third-world countries— more than two-thirds of the world's people but little of its wealth (Galtung and Vincent 1992, p. 82). That 1973 meeting led to the establishment of a third-world news agency, the Non-Aligned News Agencies Pool. At UNESCO-sanctioned meetings around the world, by 1976 the group had articulated the need to change the global communication system to decolonize information and create a new international information order.

A Soviet-sponsored resolution in UNESCO in 1974 asked states to make sure their media were not used for war and racial propaganda and asked for a "more balanced flow of communication." A Swedish consultant's report became the pattern for a 1974 UNESCO draft declaration for "balance" between "freedom of information" and "responsibility to prevent abuses." The draft, which formed the first effort to form what would become the Mass Media Declaration adopted in 1978, caused a debate in 1974 in which Western countries protested that it would muzzle the free press. In 1974, UNESCO did call for a "two-way flow" of information and for a "free and balanced flow." The draft declaration on the media was made the topic at a 1976 conference, at which UNESCO called for "liberating the developing countries from the state of dependence" (Mehra 1986, pp. 39–42).

In 1978, UNESCO unanimously adopted, with the support also of the United States, a modification of the draft, which became known as the Mass Media Declaration. This document set the agenda for the global communication debate. It affirmed freedom of expression and information, called for access and protection of journalists, and asked the media to help give a voice to the third world. It asked the media to report about all cultures and peoples, exposing the problems that affect them, such as hunger, poverty, and disease. It asked the media to include the opinions of those who find the media prejudiced against them, and it sought correction of the imbalance in global news flow. The declaration also asked media professionals to include its ideas in their codes of ethics and asked countries to help develop media systems in the third world. UNESCO sought to promote "a free flow and a wider and better balanced exchange of information between the different regions of the world." In 1980, a resolution was adopted to implement the declaration, and a global congress was set for 1983.

Also in 1980 was the culmination of another effort set in motion by UNESCO in 1976, when a 16-member commission was set up to review the problems of communication in today's world. The MacBride Commission, headed by Irish politician Sean MacBride, was asked to look most closely at problems relating to the free and balanced flow of information and the needs of third-world countries. The task put the NWIO in the perspective of the new world economic order. Following an interim report that met with Western opposition to government intervention, involving the licensing of journalists, the MacBride Commission issued its toned-down report, called *Many Voices, One World* (MacBride et al. 1980), containing 82 recommendations, of which 72 were unanimous. The remaining ones were opposed, with the West against anticommercial media suggestions, the Soviet bloc opposed to the abolition of government controls, and third-world countries seeking more balanced flow. UNESCO did not formally adopt or follow up the MacBride report, saying that some recommendations could be implemented, while others required more study. Instead, UNESCO in 1980 created the International Program for Development Communication (IPDC) to help develop media systems in the third world.

The result of compromise, nonetheless, the MacBride report called for "a free flow and a wider and better balanced dissemination of information," not a "free and balanced flow." It also called for a "new, more just and more effective world information and communication order" (Galtung and Vincent 1992, p. 87). With recommendations on media economics, administration, technological uses, training and research, the report also dealt with journalistic standards but rejected the idea of licensing. It called for U.S. journalists abroad to receive language and culture training and for gatekeepers in the West to be familiar with cultures in the third world.

Among its other recommendations, the MacBride report condemned censorship as well as the use of journalists for spying. It supported the need for national communication policies as a vital social resource. Emphasizing the media's role in helping oppressed peoples gain independence and the right to expression and information, the report called for reducing commercialism in the media. The report encouraged UNESCO to take a crucial role in carrying out the recommendations and suggested taxing profits on raw materials, the use of the radio spectrum, and the profits of international media corporations (Frederick 1993, p. 168–169).

One supporter arguing for the adoption of the NWIO has been Mustapha Masmoudi (1984), the former Tunisian secretary of information and ambassador to UNESCO. Masmoudi outlines the problem as centering on one-way, imbalanced information flows between the North and South managed by unequal information resources dominated by the Big Four news agencies. In television, the first-world controls the spectrum and the programming, so that the third world becomes consumers of information. The lack of information about the third world other than coups and earthquakes perpetuates the colonial era bias and cultural imperialism. Masmoudi argues that the third world needs national communication policies, horizontal exchanges of information, and media personnel training. The third world also should alert the first world to the imbalance and work to democratize information structures by developing national news agencies and curtailing the Big Four monopoly. The first world, Masmoudi urges, should call public attention to the problem and, with an objective approach, help balance the information flow with more third-world news, cultural exchange, and respect for the laws of third-world nations.

WESTERN OPPOSITION TO NWIO

By the late 1970s, Western media and their owners had united to lobby against NWIO by associating it with government control of media. The World Press Freedom Committee was formed before the 1976 meeting on the Mass Media Declaration to disrupt its progress (Frederick 1993, p. 171). The Inter-American Press Association, a group of media owners in the Western Hemisphere, called its own meeting in 1976 to oppose a UNESCO-sponsored session on Latin American communication policies. The UNESCO meeting was postponed.

Opposition to the NWIO movement intensified after the MacBride report with the gathering of more than 50 representatives of private media from 20 countries in Talloires, France, in 1981 (Hachten 1987, pp. 139–140). The private gathering, arranged by the World Press Freedom Committee and the law school at Tufts University, formulated a declaration that called press freedom a "basic right" and urged UNESCO to drop attempts to restrict the press in violation of the Declaration of Human Rights and other international covenants. The group opposed plans to license journalists, and it opposed an international code of ethics. The group also reiterated the MacBride report's call for the end of censorship and the journalists' right of access to all news sources.

The response to the Talloires Declaration was nearly unanimous in the United States, with the *New York Times, Newsweek,* and the major U.S. media solidly opposed to the NWIO. The conservative Heritage Foundation claimed the U.S. withdrawal from UNESCO in 1985 was its doing, but the government's change was stark with the Reagan administration's shift away from the flexible, accommodating policies of President Jimmy Carter in the late 1970s that led to the creation of the IPDC in the United Nations. The ultraconservative Reagan policy attacked the UN system itself, making UNESCO what one official called "the Grenada of the UN" (Frederick 1993, pp. 171–73).

In general, Western opposition to NWIO centered on seeing the problem as the need for improving third-world media systems and providing a greater variety of news outlets, while UNESCO focused in the early 1980s on media projects and technical training for journalists through the IPDC. Despite this change in UNESCO, the United States announced in late 1983 that it would withdraw from UNESCO in 1985 because the

Reagan administration felt UNESCO was politicized, with an anti-U.S. bias. The U.S. withdrawal silenced the debate about the NWIO (Hachten 1987, p. 143).

According to NWIO supporters, the increasing attack after 1980 was led by a U.S.-dominated coalition including the private media group, the World Press Freedom Committee, and the U.S. State Department, which together accused UNESCO of using NWIO to promote "government-controlled media" and backing attempts to thwart press freedom (Traber and Nordenstreng 1992, pp. 5–6). Despite UNESCO's reminders that the MacBride report endorsed press freedom, the criticism continued. UNESCO, in several ways, still supported NWIO, including meetings in 1983 that pursued the problem of building communication systems in the third world, and it adopted an international code of ethics for journalists. The United States responded with its withdrawal from UNESCO, although some scholars debate whether NWIO was part of the larger issue of multilaterilism to which the United States was opposed. But NWIO supporters and critics alike agree that the U.S. action silenced the debate in UNESCO. In 1986, the Round Table on the NWIO discussed the need to correct imbalances while maintaining media freedom.

THE NWIO DEBATE SINCE 1985

Although these issues of content, control, and current continued to be addressed in the UN and UNESCO after 1985, UNESCO altered its focus away from more controversial elements of the debate by reaffirming Western values of free flow. Efforts have continued quietly within both the UN and UNESCO, as well as in other intergovernmental bodies, such as the ITU, and in nongovernmental organizations, such as the World Association for Christian Communication, and other professional groups, such as the MacBride Round Table, which has met annually since 1989 to assess issues and suggest action revolving around the MacBride report, *Many Voices, One World* (MacBride et al. 1980).

Since the 1980s, however, the more forceful debate has shifted back to the context of the industrialized Western nations with advanced communication systems. With concerns about new telecommunications technologies, limits on foreign entertainment programming and concerns about cultural imperialism are stirring in Western Europe and Canada in reaction against U.S. media dominance that sound similar to issues raised by third world countries. Within GATT trade talks, the cultural industry issues were a primary concern, with, for example, the French film industry successfully gaining from the United States a concession to limit importation of U.S. films into France. With the breakup of the Soviet bloc and then the Soviet Union itself between 1989 and 1991, followed by breakout of war in the former Yugoslavia, a significant realm of global media is in flux that must lead to negotiation of the shape of the new media. Within the United States itself, concern about the effects of violent media programming have led to a discussion in Congress to control television content and to calls for self-regulation of the television networks and companies. Finally, the emergence of a government plan in 1994 for a U.S. information superhighway has brought with it the same questions and concerns raised by the introduction of the telegraph more than 150 years ago, with the prospect of a global information highway on the horizon.

After 1985, UNESCO redirected its energies to avoid the politically sensitive issue of communication by taking a more moderate stance. UNESCO has reaffirmed its commitment to the freedom of the press and is focusing on activities to build media systems in the third world through infrastructures, training, and education. The goal of these technical programs is a balanced flow of information that attains a free flow of information (Galtung and Vincent 1992, pp. 99–100). In early 1994, the possibility that the United States would rejoin UNESCO in 1995 increased, but supporters of the NWIO did not feel the issue would be revived.

Although fading in UNESCO, the debate resurfaced in the mid-1980s in the ITU, which in 1985 issued the Maitland Report, or the *Missing Link,* which framed the ITU's task as political and declared that the gap between the developed and third world should be closed. Radically departing from its previous role as a technical, engineering group, the ITU became a more activist organization calling for a New World Telecommunications Order (Frederick 1993, pp. 176–77). The Non-Aligned Movement continued to support the outlines of NWIO in 1989 and into the 1990s, but the influence of the Non-Aligned Movement also is thought to be reduced since the end of the cold war. Still other examples of NWIO remaining on the agenda of southern countries includes the 1990 World Conference on Islamic Thought in Iran and the UN's annual Non-Governmental Organization's Conference in New York in 1991 (Traber and Nordenstreng 1992, pp. 16–17). Also, the South Commission of former Tanzanian President Julius Nyerere in 1990 called on the South to reduce information dependency on the North and to build media ties between countries in the South (Frederick 1993, p. 177).

The debate also has shifted to other organizations, mostly nongovernmental and professional ones, such as a 1989 meeting of the Union for Democratic Communications and the National Lawyers Guild on the media and international law (Galtung and Vincent 1992, pp. 101–102). Also in 1989, the World Association for Christian Communication adopted a declaration focusing on communication as an individual right. The first MacBride Round Table was held that year, sponsored by the International Organization of Journalists, the Media Foundation of the Non-Aligned, and the Federation of Southern African Journalists. It was the first of six annual meetings of the MacBride Round Table, including the most recent in early 1994. In 1989, the Round Table found that NWIO topics were more relevant, including concern over expanding technologies, and the statement called for a free and responsible press, echoing the Hutchins Commission. At its meeting in 1991 in Turkey following the Persian Gulf War, the MacBride Round Table called for new coalitions of media professionals, activists, consumer groups, women, minorities, and labor and environmental groups to regain participation in cultural policy for peace and security.

Other groups meeting with NWIO as a central topic include an Institute for Latin America and World Association for Christian Communication seminar in 1990, an Intercontinental Journalists Conference in 1990, a Gannett Foundation Media Center conference in 1991, and an International Press Service Council on Information and Communications meeting in 1991. In the scholarly research community, The International

Association for Mass Communication Research has provided strong support for NWIO since the mid-1970s. Another research group, The International Communication Association, held panels on NWIO at its 1991 meeting.

Aside from the shift to professional organizations, the issues of content, control, and current have primarily shifted to disputes among Western countries themselves. The Conference on Security and Cooperation in Europe, known as the Helsinki process, has drawn together more than 40 European countries, the United States, and Canada to discuss communication and the changing nature of Europe, including the breakup of the Soviet Union, democratization, and the redrawing of borders in Eastern Europe. Two themes of this conference in 1989 were human rights and information issues as important to international cooperation (Frederick 1993, p. 176).

"Cultural imperialism" increasingly in the 1980s and 1990s has not been a phenomenon reserved for third-world countries, but felt by Canada, France, and the European Community, which have expressed concern about the effect of foreign media. Some of their governments have adopted policies to reduce foreign media and advertising. In Canada, 98 percent of all drama on English-language television is imported, and 90 percent of all drama on French-language television is imported. Only 28 percent of all Canadian television programming is Canadian (Frederick 1993, pp. 135–36). Canada has responded with program quotas and subsidies for Canadian content in prime-time television, but the regulations have affected only the margins of viewing patterns, Canada also has program and employment guidelines to better reflect Canada's cultural diversity. In 1991, Canada also required the Canadian Broadcasting Corporation to foster an image consistent with Canada's multiculturalism. Private broadcast media have followed with codes to avoid minority stereotyping and increase hiring of minorities (Ferguson 1993). The U.S.–Canada free trade agreement exempts cultural industries, giving evidence of the resentment of U.S. media influence.

In Western Europe in 1989, the European Community urged an increase in European television production through government support and a limit on imported U.S. television programs, among foreign imports, to less than 50 percent (Stevenson 1994, pp. 113, 146, 169). France, along with Italy, in the early 1990s was calling for quotas on foreign broadcasting imports to reduce "cultural contamination." These calls led to a standoff over the latest GATT talks, at which, as mentioned, the French won concessions from the United States to put trade restrictions on U.S.-produced movies and television programs in the European Community. These restrictions are similar to those that Canada negotiated with the United States in their 1989 trade agreement.

Closely related to the concept of communication sovereignty in the developed world is transborder data flow, which involves the collection and dissemination of electronic data across national borders. These data include insurance, banking, and credit information. Western European nations and Canada have complained that transborder data flows disregard national security and privacy. Some European countries have sought to restrict this flow, with Sweden in 1973 making it illegal to set up data records without government approval. Japan, Canada, and France have set up policies to protect their local computer and information processing businesses, while many privacy or data protection laws have been enacted. Sweden and others also have expressed concern about U.S. data banks containing information about their citizens (Frederick 1993, p. 122).

With Western European countries and Canada more open to regulating the content, control, and current of international communication, even as they undergo the process of commercialization and privatization of their broadcast media, the U.S. media and government are more isolated as proponents of the free flow of information doctrine. But technological developments within the United States appear to be generating forces that could engage the government and media in the kinds of discussions that they have resisted since World War II in opposing government-controlled media. The National Information Infrastructure, which has been dubbed the "information superhighway," has become an initiative of the Clinton administration, involving the public in the creation of the new, multimedia, computerized, data base-centered, media environment of the future. The White House in late 1993 released its "agenda for action" to begin shaping the information superhighway, with its promise of telecommuting and tele-educating within the United States. Vice President Al Gore proposed the national information network in early 1994, bringing up questions of government regulation, competition among communications companies, right to privacy, and public access to information.

The Clinton administration agenda for the information highway is seeking to define the government's role in complementing the private communication industry to ensure that the information infrastructure has universal public access and is affordable. The Clinton administration's goal is to develop the U.S. information highway policy with business, labor, academia, the public, Congress, and state and local government to provide universal service, technological innovations and applications; seamless operation of the network of networks; information security and reliability; and of import in international communication, coordination with other nations to avoid obstacles and to prevent unfair policies that would hinder U.S. private industry and public access to government information.

Information superhighways are also being developed in Australia and elsewhere. In Australia, for example, a media journal in early 1994 began seeking critical analyses of these proposals, which will provide new entertainment, communications, education, and information services, and their social, economic, and political impact. Areas of special concern in cross-national analyses of the superhighways include political and economic motivations, emerging information industries and new power roles, notions of universal service, the roles of regulators and consumer interest groups, privacy and surveillance, public policy for principles of common carriers, and public access.

As these new media are developed, issues of international communication content, control, and current will most certainly be sources of conflict and negotiations. Fortner (1993) suggests that societies set up and sustain monopolies of knowledge to provide a centralized means of social control. Historically, Western states have controlled other countries' policies and their media systems, with the Soviet Union also gaining, then losing, influence and more recently Japan and Germany increasing their influence. However, the inability to achieve equity and access within the international communication system remains an issue, as it has for the 150 years since electronic communication created a meaningful international system.

BIBLIOGRAPHY

Bullion, Stuart J. "The New World Information Order Debate: How New?" *Gazette* 30 (1982): 155-65.

Cooper, Kent. *Barriers Down.* New York: Farrar & Rinehart, 1942.

Ferguson, Marjorie. "Invisible Divides: Communication and Identity in Canada and the U.S." *Journal of Communication* (Spring 1993): 42-57.

Fortner, Robert S. *International Communication: History, Conflict, and Control of the Global Metropolis.* (Belmont, Calif.: Wadsworth, 1993).

Frederick, Howard H. *Global Communication and International Relations.* Belmont, Calif.: Wadsworth, 1993.

Galtung, Johan, and Richard C. Vincent. *Global Glasnost.* Cresskill, N.J.: Hampton Press, 1992.

Gerbner, George, Hamid Mowlana, and Kaarle Nordenstreng. *The Global Media Debate: Its Rise, Fall and Renewal.* Norwood, N.J.: Ablex. 1993.

Giffard, C. Anthony. *UNESCO and the Media.* New York: Longman, 1989.

Hachten, William A. *The World News Prism.* 2nd Edition. Ames: Iowa State University Press, 1987.

Hamelink, Cees J. *Cultural Autonomy in Global Communication.* New York: Longman, 1983.

Hutchins, Robert, and the Commission on the Freedom of the Press. *A Free and Responsible Press.* Chicago: University of Chicago Press. 1947.

Kerner, Otto, et al. *Report of the National Advisory Commission on Civil Disorders.* New York: Bantam. 1968.

MacBride, Sean, et al. *Many Voices, One World.* New York: Unipub, 1980.

Masmoudi, Mustapha. "The New World Information Order." In *World Communications: A Handbook,* edited by George Gerbner and Marsha Siefert. New York: Longman, 1984.

Mehra, Achal. *Free Flow of Information: A New Paradigm.* New York: Greenwood, 1986.

Nordenstreng, Kaarle, Enrique Gonzalez Manet, and Wolfgang Kleinwachter. *New International Information and Communication Order Sourcebook.* Prague: International Organization of Journalists, 1986.

Roach, Colleen. "American Textbooks vs. NWICO History." In George Gerbner et al., *Global Media Debate: Its Rise, Fall and Renewal.* Norwood, N.J.: Ablex, 1993.

Schiller, Herbert I. *Culture Inc.: The Corporate Takeover of Public Expression.* New York: Oxford University Press, 1989.

————. "Breaking the West's Media Monopoly." *The Nation,* 21 September 1985, 248-251.

————. *Communication and Cultural Domination.* New York: International Arts and Science Press, 1976.

Stevenson, Robert L. *Global Communication in the 21st Century.* New York: Longman, 1994.

Traber, Michael, and Kaarle Nordenstreng. *Few Voices, Many Worlds: Towards a Media Reform Movement.* London: World Association for Christian Communication, 1992.

Uriarte, Mercedes Lynn de. "Educators Do Little to Prepare Students for Multiculturalism." *Quill* (April 1992): 12-14.

part

The World's Regions

chapter 9

Western Europe

M. Kent Sidel and Aralynn Abare McMane

Western Europe today is undergoing one of its most exciting periods of economic activity since the rush to rebuild following World War II. The joining of the continent as a fully integrated Economic Union (formerly the European Community) and a frontier-free single market has provided 320 million people with a freedom of movement for themselves, goods, and services never before possible (Figure 9.1). In a way, since 1993, people can act as radio waves have in the past—unencumbered by the political divisions of nation-states. They are free to reside, work, and shop where they choose. Much of this same sense of freedom is affecting the growing communications industries. This chapter highlights the direction of mass communications in the New Europe and what the realities of unification are bringing to the continent.

Not all the developments are positive. Newspaper growth is flat. The concept of public service broadcasting is being reevaluated in light of increased competition with more popular advertiser-supported programming. Questions continue to be raised about the cultural impact of imported television and radio programming. On the other hand, magazines are flourishing. Community radio is continuing to develop and enfranchise more listeners with a media voice. Television is expanding and finding its voice in the media mix. Technology is providing access to programming never before possible. And probably most far-reaching is the merger of communications with telecommunications. Information empowerment could be the reality of the next century.

HISTORICAL HIGHLIGHTS

The written dissemination of news existed in Western Europe well before newspapers arrived. By 60 BC, Rome saw hand-copied *acta diurna* for elite customers, listing official announcements, court news, births, deaths, marriages, ceremonies, and building projects.

FIGURE 9.1 Western Europe

Movable type was developed in Germany between 1438 and 1454, long after such type had existed in China and Korea, and allowed a faster if less well-produced copy of a page. The initial use was for theological works, such as the famed Gutenberg Bibles, but eventually, the technology could be applied to less heavenly projects, and the printing press became more cost-effective. By the end of the sixteenth century, even before regular, printed periodicals emerged, sensationalism was present in what Linton and Boston describe as "a veritable flood of crudely printed publications dealing most pruriently with such topics as rape, abortions, devilish conflagrations, bloody robberies involving torture—and mermaids" (1987, p. x).

Earliest periodical print media concentrated on foreign news and were often foreign owned. It was an Amsterdam printer in 1620 who provided England with its earliest English-language single-page periodical *coranto,* which carried foreign news. About the same time, newspapers in the form of weekly publications with a variety of stories first appeared in the Netherlands and Germany. By the end of the seventeenth century, most countries had government-sanctioned newspapers. By the eighteenth

century, daily papers had emerged, as well as a revolutionary press. The early nineteenth century saw the emergence of a "penny press" in Europe at about the same time
it began in the United States. By the end of the century, Europe, like the United States
was peppered with mass-circulation popular dailies. The wars of the twentieth century hurt or helped newspapers depending on the locale. For example, the German
press was restructured by victorious allies after World War II, with the West German
press becoming relatively rich. In France, meanwhile, the postwar press had a brief
flourishing but soon began suffering a slow but steady decline.

Broadcasting developed throughout most of Europe in the 1920s as an extension
of the communicative mission of the post office (which had also taken charge of the
telegraph and telephone services). Governments not only controlled the radio transmitters but also developed a philosophy of programming called public service broadcasting, which stressed the use of the media for higher societal rather than purely entertainment goals. The systems were generally financed from either a direct government
subsidy or from license fees charged owners of receiving sets.

Television, generally introduced following World War II, followed much the same
programming and financing path as radio. In Britain an independent commercial television service financed from advertising was begun in the early 1950s, but for the most
part television remained state-run into the 1980s. In the last decade or so, most countries adopted some form of advertiser-supported television, but probably more importantly, the programming tended to move toward entertainment with less concentration on public service.

The development of new delivery systems such as cable and direct broadcast satellites dramatically altered not only the number of channels available to homes but the
regulatory thinking of most media managers. The physics of broadcasting, and the
numerous nations crowded together on the continent, forced most countries to restrict
over-the-air broadcast to a very few television channels. But satellites and, more importantly, cable removed the need for spectrum-bound delivery. It became immediately
feasible to provide multiple new program sources and to open the way for eventual
interactive capability in every home. It is the integration of mass communications and
telecommunications that holds the most promise for high-level information exchange
in the future (Table 9.1).

PRINT MEDIA

Compared to the rest of the world, Western Europe remains a region of newspaper
and magazine readers. UNESCO (1993) estimated that the world average for newspaper circulation per 1,000 population was at 111, about one copy for every 10 people. Only two Western European countries have routinely fallen below that figure: Spain
and Portugal. Readership generally increases as one moves north, with Scandinavian
countries regularly topping worldwide lists of per capita circulation. Norway led in
1992 with about six copies for every ten people, followed by Sweden, Finland, Germany, and Switzerland (Fédération Internationale des Editeurs de Journaux 1993). Further, at least one consumer magazine reached at least half of the adult population in

TABLE 9.1 Top ten European media groups

Rank	Firm	Media Revenue (U.S. $ Millions)	Total Revenue (U.S. $ Millions)
1.	Fininvest (Italy)	2,665.9	6,310.7
2.	Reed International (Great Britain)	2,183.6	2,822.2
3.	Bertelsmann (Germany)	1,918.3	8,891.0
4.	Hachette (France)	1,874.1	5,518.4
5.	Axel Springer (Germany)	1,814.1	5,518.4
6.	RCS Editori (Italy)	1,576.1	2,003.2
7.	Hersant (France)	1,561.1	1,561.1
8.	Heinrich Bauer (Germany)	1,465.8	1,547.0
9.	RTVE (Spain)	1,424.8	1,455.0
10.	United Newspapers (Great Britain)	1,372.8	1,480.7

SOURCE: Based on figures for 1991. Zenith Media Worldwide, 1992.

13 of the 16 Western European countries assessed in a 1991 study, with nine countries at the three-quarters level (Carat 1992).

UNESCO figures also indicated that a majority of Western European countries saw increased readership between 1975 and 1990 even as the number of daily newspapers in the region declined. Of the 17 Western European countries studied, nine had a higher per capita newspaper circulation at the end of the period, six had a lower level, and one remained about the same. Meanwhile, all but three countries, the Netherlands, Norway, and Greece, showed fewer newspapers in 1990 than in 1975.

Europe has three main kinds of print journalism: pan-European, multinational, and uninational.

The most widespread of Europe's print media come in the form of single-language pan-European publications, such as the American-owned daily newspaper the *International Herald Tribune,* that sell one product in one language to audiences in all Western European countries. The most successful of these publications are in English. The growing number of multinational publications are either the product of one company's subsidiaries in another country or simply a translation of a publication. For example, German-owned Prisma Press produces several magazines in France that may or may not have counterparts in Germany. Prisma's *Geo* travel magazine has a German twin while *Femme Actuelle* does not. Uninational media, which include most magazines and newspapers, target readers in only one country.

A hybrid of the pan-European and multinational publication is *Reader's Digest,* a general interest American magazine that publishes worldwide, in languages besides English and using some local content. Since 1950, Western European editions have come in ten other languages, with content mostly from the parent publication edited in the United States. The Paris staff, for example, writes only three to five of that edition's 25 stories. The German edition ranked eleventh in circulation for all Western European magazines in 1991 with nearly 2 million sold. The English version ranked nineteenth in Europe with 1.5 million circulation. In other languages, *Reader's Digest* beats locally produced monthly magazines in many countries, including France, where circulation goes just over a million. In all, the magazine sells 6.4 million copies in Western Europe.

No other pan-European publication was selling more than a million copies in the region in 1992. Other leading English-language pan-European magazines include three U.S. publications: the general interest *National Geographic* magazine, with a Western European circulation of about 725,000, followed by international editions of the weekly newsmagazines *Time* and *Newsweek,* and the British newsmagazine *The Economist.* A weekly newspaper begun by Robert Maxwell in London in 1990 had about 140,000 circulation in Western Europe by 1992.

Pan-European daily newspapers tend to target the well-off business executives, depend on a variety of sales techniques, and use satellite technology to transmit pages to printing sites in several countries. *The Financial Times,* founded in 1888 and based in London, led these papers in 1991 with a 250,000 circulation. It goes to Western Europeans who are typical of people who read the leading pan-European dailies: mostly men between 35 and 54 years old, and earning an average $109,000 a year. *The International Herald Tribune,* owned by the *New York Times* and the *Washington Post,* ranks second among pan-European papers, with about 160,000 circulation in the region. In 1983, the *Wall Street Journal* began publishing a separate edition out of Brussels, and *USA Today* began editing an international edition from its U.S. headquarters in 1984. By 1992, those papers were selling about 50,000 copies each in Western Europe. Sales to airlines and hotels for free distribution to their customers account for an important part of total circulation. For example, these sales make up about a quarter of the *International Herald Tribune*'s circulation.

Within many countries, the leading magazine has highly local content but follows a widespread editorial formula and has another medium to thank for its success: television. Nine of the ten top-selling consumer magazines in 1991 were television listings magazines with circulations ranging from 1.8 million to 3.3 million. Five of the top 16 television guides were German. France and the United Kingdom had four each, with Austria and Italy at one each. The second most-read kind of magazine within most countries targets women.

The leader for newspaper circulation within a country has long been the United Kingdom, followed by Germany. The United Kingdom had six of Western Europe's top ten daily papers in 1991 and nine of the top ten Sunday papers. Germany had three dailies in the top ten and France had one. The other top Sunday paper was German. The highest-selling newspapers in both the United Kingdom and Germany are sensational papers characterized by splashy design often in tabloid format; extensive coverage of sports, crime, and sex scandals; gratuitous female nudity; and a right-of-center political tendency. Leaders in Europe are Germany's daily *Bild Zeitung* and the United Kingdom's daily *Sun* and, on Sundays, *News of the World.*

Several quality dailies call Western Europe home. These papers have smaller circulations than the sensational papers but considerably more prestige. They tend to have a more staid appearance and can also be tabloid size; emphasize thorough, serious coverage of international news and politics; and tend to have a centrist or left-of-center political tendency. These include *La Repubblica* of Italy, *El Pais* of Spain, *Le Monde* of France, *Frankfurter Allegemeine Zeitung* of Germany, and several British papers.

In a major 1993 study of leading daily newspapers in the five most populous Western European countries, researchers concluded that while national differences dominated, the papers shared some trends. Papers from the United Kingdom, Italy, Spain, Germany, and France shared a move from regular to more occasional readership by their audiences, difficulty in attracting female readers away from magazines, and difficulty in luring new readers at all (Rieffel et al. 1993).

The relative financial health of the print journalistic media varies within countries, but figures do allow some generalizations. In 10 of 16 countries studied by Carat International, print media got more than half of total advertising revenues. With the exception of France, Greece, Italy, and Portugal, newspapers generally had higher advertising revenues than magazines in 1991 (Carat 1992). Not surprisingly, highest print media percentages went to countries with the smallest number of commercial television stations: Scandinavia, the Netherlands, and Switzerland. In its 1993 report, the International Federation of Newspaper Editors (FIEJ), based in Paris, found that revenue shifts since 1989 had generally benefited television most. The United Kingdom emerged as an exception in which lost print advertising went to other media, such as direct mail.

The next section will briefly describe the magazine and daily newspaper press in specific countries. It starts with the most populous countries in alphabetical order: France, Germany, Italy, Spain, and the United Kingdom. Scandinavian countries make up the next grouping, again in alphabetical order: Denmark, Finland, Norway, and Sweden. The last group includes smaller countries outside Scandinavia, those with populations of under 16 million: Austria, Belgium, Greece, Ireland, Luxembourg, the Netherlands, Portugal, and Switzerland. Unless otherwise noted, all circulation figures are from 1991.

The Big Five

Western Europe's five most populous countries illustrate the cultural patchwork that makes up the region:

France. France possesses one of the region's weaker newspaper markets even as it has one of the world's elite newspapers, *Le Monde*. It is the fourth most populous country, but its per-capita readership ranks thirteenth. Its truly "national" press numbers few, and it is a regional paper, *Ouest-France,* based in Rennes, which sells more copies than any other French daily. Its 775,000 circulation is much higher than that of the next largest, the national *Le Figaro* of Paris at 391,000. *Le Monde* sells about 323,000 copies, placing it seventh among French papers. Other national dailies include *Libération,* which was started in 1973 by student activists and sells 167,000 copies, and *L'Equipe,* a sports daily that sells 274,000 copies. Other much smaller national papers, such as the communist *Humanité* (71,000 circulation) and the Catholic *La Croix* (102,000), cater to a specific audience and rely heavily on support other than advertising. France has an important weekly satirical newspaper, *Le Canard Enchaine.* Founded in 1916, it has often broken investigative stories before the mainstream press. *Le Parisien,* ranking third in circulation with 380,000 copies, concentrates on the capital and its suburbs, as does *Le Figaro*'s sister evening paper, *France Soir.*

Paris newspapers have long been considered the prestigious and somewhat aloof press of opinion, with regional newspapers—which often have a monopoly in an area—taking primarily an information role, with closer relations with readers. Recent developments indicate that this paradigm may be changing. For example, the newest Paris paper, *Infomatin,* announced at its 1994 debut that it wanted to "painlessly inform" and carefully labeled its commentary, and that same year *Libération* featured labeled commentary as part of its redesign.

Of the top eight weekly magazines, all with circulations over 1 million, five cover television. Two, *Femme Actuelle* and *Prima,* target women readers. *Notre Temps,* aimed at older readers, ranks eighth. France's leading newsmagazines have seen change in recent years. *Paris Match,* a photojournalism magazine, has turned increasingly to gossip. It ranked ninth in 1991, selling about 650,000 copies weekly. The leading newsmagazine, *L'Express,* with about 430,000 circulation, bought the much smaller *Le Point* in 1993.

Germany. Reunification in October 1990 brought a period of some turbulence for print media. In West Germany, the newspaper press had been characterized since soon after World War II by large regional papers based in Frankfurt, Munich, and Hamburg, where the country's largest paper, the sensational daily *Bild Zeitung,* originated. West Germany's postwar press system had emerged from revamping under mostly British and American influence with much more limited influence of the French. Magazines had blossomed since the 1980s with a net gain of at least 500 titles in that decade. Former East Germany, whose postwar press had emerged under Soviet-Communist influence, had few magazines and newspapers but avid readers, with one out of two people getting a paper each day. Before reunification, UNESCO counted about 300 daily newspapers in former West Germany and about 40 in former East Germany.

West Germany rushed a presence into the *Lander* of former East Germany even before the two became one country. In the summer just before reunification, a special edition of West Germany's circulation leader, *Bild Zeitung,* was selling a million copies in the East. A year later, sales were less than half that figure (LeMoine 1992). In Berlin, no fewer than six dailies started and closed between 1990 and early 1993, including a sensational daily from the press baron Rupert Murdoch. The *Freie Press* of Chimintz in former East Germany ranked in 1991 as united Germany's third-largest daily, with 522,000 copies sold. New magazines appeared at a faster rate, with net gain of more than 700 titles for Germany between 1991 and 1993. Three titles joined a crowded field of television magazines in 1992, increasing the total to 16 publications with a total circulation of more than 30 million. In 1993, the Burma group launched a new newsmagazine, *Focus,* which one observer called a "perky child of the television age." It had much shorter stories and more visual elements than its older counterparts and within a year was selling more than 400,000.

In the first few years after reunification, some dominant elements of the former West German press remained relatively stable. The sensational national daily *Bild Zeitung* still had Germany's highest circulation, more than 4.5 million readers three years after unification. Germany's periodical press continued to do well, giving the country 13 of Western Europe's 25 top-selling magazines in 1991. Despite some loss of readers to the new *Focus* magazine, the internationally known weekly news-magazines *Der Spiegel* (focusing on business) and *Stern,* which all date to just after World War II, maintained circulations of more than a million copies each. Selling 2.6 million copies each week, *Bella* led magazines targeting women. *Tina* and *Brigitte* each sold more than a million copies.

Italy. North and central Italy account for about 80 percent of newspaper sales, with the largest dailies in Milan and Rome. Rome's highly respected daily, *La Repubblica,* made its debut in 1976 as a novelty to the Italian press world: a serious, independent, tabloid-sized paper without much commentary or sports. It has become a major newspaper of record and, in 1991, led Italy's dailies with a circulation of about 677,000. Behind that year by 4,000 copies, and more often ahead, was Milan's *Il Corriere della Sera,* founded in 1876.

Milan also provides Italy's third-largest paper, *La Gazette dello Sport.* This sports daily was founded in 1896 and on Mondays outsells any other newspaper, more than 700,000 copies. Italy has two other similar but much smaller papers, *Il Corriere dello Sport* and *Tuttosport.* Sensational papers, however, have had little success.

While Italy, second in population, ranks low in level of newspaper readership, fourteenth, nearly three-quarters of adults there see some magazine regularly (Carat 1992). The television guide *Sorrisi e Canzoni TV* ranked among Western Europe's 25 highest-selling titles in 1991 (Carat 1992). The church-oriented *Famiglia Cristiana,* at a million copies, ranked second.

Spain. The Spanish press blossomed after the death of General Francisco Franco in 1975, which marked the end of 40 years of censorship, frequent seizures of offending publications, and prosecutions of journalists. Overall readership of dailies has remained low since—better only than Portugal—but dozens of magazines and new newspapers cater to younger, well-educated readers. The success of such newspapers, led by *El Pais,* an internationally respected independent Madrid paper founded in 1976, made Spain one of the few countries to see an increase during the 1980s in the proportion of advertising going to daily newspapers. *El Pais* sells about 395,000 copies daily. Older papers also flourished after the Franco regime ended. *ABC,* a Madrid paper founded in 1903, has Spain's second largest circulation with 292,000 copies, and *La Vanguardia,* a Barcelona paper founded in 1881 and for decades the most read, ranks third at 259,000. The newspaper boom had calmed by the early 1990s. In 1992 alone, three of the new Madrid dailies, *El Sol, El Independiente,* and *Claro,* closed. Spain has four major sports dailies, two of which—*As* and *Marca* in Madrid—rank in the top five for circulation. Spain's regions, which differ markedly in character and economy, have produced an active regional press: Four regional dailies rank among the country's top ten in circulation, with Catalonia alone accounting for a third of the regional press circulation.

The television guides, *Teleindiscreta* and the French-owned *Teleprogramma,* have Spain's highest circulations for weekly magazines, selling about a million copies each. Two gossip magazines, *Pronto* and *Hola!,* rank next (815,000 and 640,000). Grupo Zeta, Spain's largest magazine publisher, produces the leading newsmagazines, *Tiempo* and *Interviu.*

United Kingdom. The United Kingdom offers two major types of national daily newspapers, populars and qualities. The London popular press provides many of Western Europe's highest circulation daily and Sunday papers. *The Sun, The Daily Mirror, The Daily Mail,* and *The Daily Express* all sell more than a million copies. The *Sunday News of the World* sells nearly 5 million copies, more than any other Western European paper, Sunday or daily. These papers share a tabloid-sized format and a stress on sensation, sports, and crime.

The city's quality dailies have smaller circulations, with only the Canadian-owned *Daily Telegraph* attracting more than a million sales and the rest at between 200,000 and 425,000. *The Times* is the oldest, founded in 1785 and now owned by Australian Rupert Murdoch. The newest is the *Independent,* founded in 1986, followed by *The Guardian,* owned by Guardian newspapers of Manchester and founded in 1976. These newspapers share several traits: a larger size known as broadsheet and a more serious approach to news. The *Independent,* however, broke with some traditions when it stayed away from off-the-record government background sessions, turned down all free trips from business and government, and declined to endorse political candidates or parties.

Unlike the national dailies, which tend to be morning papers, most regional dailies appear in the afternoon, including the main dailies of Wales, Scotland, and Northern Ireland.

The United Kingdom saw the number of magazines double during the 1980s but also an advertising drop in that market by the early 1990s. Fatalities included *Punch,* the country's oldest satirical magazine, which closed in 1992 after 150 years. Three television guides, two weekly women's magazines, *Bella* and *Take a Break,* and the British edition of *Reader's Digest* had top circulations in the United Kingdom for 1991, all selling more than a million copies.

London is also home to two of the major pan-European publications, *The Financial Times* newspaper and *The Economist.*

Scandinavia

As we shall see later, Western Europe's Nordic countries share similar approaches to governing mass media but, as is shown here, also exhibit differences in the nature of their most-read publications.

Denmark. Copenhagen accounts for a fifth of Denmark's dailies and about half the total circulation. The two leading papers, *Ekstra Bladet* and *BT,* are both sensational tabloids selling about 200,000 copies daily. Regional daily papers have seen a decline in what was known as the four-paper system, in which each of the major political parties had its own local newspaper. Very few openly partisan papers have survived, although the bulk of newspapers tend to be right of center politically. Aimed at women, *Familie Journalen* leads Danish magazines with a 320,000 circulation. The general-interest *Se og Har* and the *Seg Og Hor* television guide follow, with about 310,000 circulation each.

Finland. Finland's leading daily newspapers are *Helsingin Sanomat,* the newspaper of record, which has a front page of all ads with about a half million circulation, and the more sensational *Ilta-Sanomat,* which sells about 200,000 copies. Finland has an unusual magazine landscape. Consumer cooperatives use their periodicals as information media for both members and customers. *Pirkka,* a free monthly for customers of retail stores, has the country's highest circulation: 1.7 million. Others of this genre send out 300,000–700,000 copies. Finland's limited television offerings help keep its leading television guide to only 70,000 copies. Among magazines targeting women, *Kotivinkki* leads with a 200,000 circulation. About 20 percent of magazines are in Swedish, Finland's second language.

Norway. Norwegians are Europe's most loyal readers, holding the world's highest per-capita newspaper readership and spending a very high proportion of advertising money (86 percent) on print media. Norway is also among the most generous in direct government subsidies to weaker papers, providing $45 million in 1992.

Oslo has the country's three leading dailies. The somewhat sensationalist *VG,* or *Verdens Gang,* has been the country's largest daily since 1981 and was selling more than 350,000 copies in 1991. *Aftenposten,* owned by the same company and considered a prestigious paper, ranks second. Founded in 1860, it had been the largest paper for most of the twentieth century. *Dagbladet,* a sensationalist tabloid, ranks third.

As in other Scandinavian countries, general interest magazines lead in circulation, with seven selling more than 100,000 copies. The low circulation of the main television guide, under 50,000 copies, reflects the past lack of diversity in television programming.

Sweden. Regional and local newspapers bought by subscription have traditionally dominated the Swedish press. Exceptions include two Stockholm tabloids sold on the street, *Expressen* with a half million copies and *Aftonbladet* with about 300,000 circulation and the more serious morning *Dagens Nyhter,* with about 380,000 circulation.

The Swedish government spent $89 million, more than any Western European country, subsidizing its low-circulation papers in 1992. Funds included a three-year-old program designed to foster competition by helping low-circulation papers and those that participate in joint-distribution programs.

Magazines focusing on the home do best in Sweden, with the top two, *Vi i Villa* and *Vårt Hus,* selling nearly two million copies each. A third home magazine, *Vår Bostad,* sells about 800,000 copies, as does the automotive magazine *Ratten.* As in other Nordic countries, television guides rank relatively low, with at most about 80,000 - circulation.

The Smaller Countries

Western Europe's smaller countries, all with populations of no more than 15 million, exhibit a wide array of settings and situations for magazines and newspapers.

Austria.   One of six Austrians reads the country's largest daily paper, the *Neue Kronen Zeitung,* a splashy tabloid published in Vienna. The past few years have seen two new dailies serving very different audiences. In 1988, *Der Staandard,* a liberal, independent paper, began, providing political, cultural, and business news with little emphasis on sports or police news. The German group Springer has half ownership. Four years later came *Taeglich Alles,* an inexpensive, full-color paper specializing in sports, police news, and television. By 1994, each had at least 100,000 readers.

Most other Austrian papers have a political affiliation, although the most partisan dailies have declined in recent years. To try to help newspapers survive without resorting to concentrated ownership, the government began a system of subsidies and special grants in 1975.

Belgium.   The Belgian press reflects the country: multicultural and relatively small. About two-thirds of Belgians live in the northern Flemish region where Dutch is mainly spoken, with most of the remaining third in the southern French-speaking area, along with a few German speakers.

Brussels is home to the largest dailies in both French and Dutch. The largest, *De Standaard* of Brussels, is in Dutch and acts as a newspaper of record for both internal politics and international affairs. It supports autonomy for Flanders. The largest French-language paper, *Le Soir,* is also in Brussels.

The Flemish weekly *Kerk & Leven* leads magazines with more than twice the circulation of the top television guide. In addition, the country imports fully a third of all the newspapers and magazines that neighboring France exports.

Greece.   A sensational rightist Athens daily, *Eleftheros Typos* and the centrist *Ta Nea,* sell the most copies in Greece, about 150,000 each. The respected quality paper *Kathimerini* is one of the rare morning papers and sells only 31,000 copies daily. Television guides far outsell other magazines in Greece with three titles at more than 160,000 circulation.

The leading general interest magazine, *Klik,* sells about 75,000 copies with the leading magazines for women, *Kai, Genika,* and *Praktiki,* all at about 60,000.

Ireland.   Ireland's newspapers tend to be politically conservative and face competion from British national dailies, especially the more sensational ones, which are less expensive. This partly explains why statistics that measure per capita readership of just Irish newspapers put Ireland fairly low (sixteenth among 18 countries measured in 1991), while those that measure the proportion of the adult population that reads any newspaper rank Ireland much higher (ninth of 16 countries measured another way in 1991).

Dublin has six of the country's eight daily papers and all five of its Sunday papers. The city's three largest daily papers are Irish owned, with the remaining three partly owned by foreigners. The *Irish Independent* is the country's largest daily with a circulation of about 150,000. The same company owns the second-largest paper, the *Evening Herald.* The Irish magazine world is dominated by titles imported from the United Kingdom. Ireland's television guide sells about 150,000 copies, the highest circulation within the country. *Woman's Way* and the *Farm Journal* follow with about 70,000 circulation each.

Luxembourg. This tiny country's largest daily, the 86,000-circulation *Luxemburger Wort/La Voix de Luxembourg,* belongs to the Catholic bishop of Luxembourg, is linked to the main political party, and has three times the circulation of the second-largest paper. That group also owns the country's leading magazine, the weekly *Télécran.*

Netherlands. The century-old Amsterdam daily *Der Telegraaf* has by far the highest circulation in the Netherlands. Its three-quarters of a million copies place it twelfth among all dailies in Western Europe. It has always been right of center and was banned for five years after World War II under charges of Nazi collaboration. The next-highest paper sells only about 400,000 copies. The Netherlands lacks a highly visible sensationalist press, and the country's only Sunday paper closed in 1992 after 18 months.

By far the most successful Dutch magazine is *Kampioen,* edited for family reading by the Dutch Touring Club and selling 2.5 million copies a month. VNU is the leading Dutch publisher, with control of nearly half of the magazine market. Its properties include most weekly magazines targeting women, including the top-selling, 790,000-copy *Libelle,* and the million-copy television guide *Veronica.*

Portugal. Portugal ranks last among Western European countries for readership of daily newspapers. Fewer than 4 in 100 people buy a newspaper on any given day, and no paper attracts more than about 80,000 readers. Portugal's newest daily, founded in 1990, is partly owned (16.5 percent each) by Spain's *El Pais* and Italy's *La Repubblica.* That paper, *Publico,* is based in Oporto and has at times overtaken the traditional circulation leader, *Jornal de Noticas,* a more than century-old paper in the same city. Lisbon's somewhat sensational *Correio da Manha,* founded in 1979, usually ranks third in circulation.

The respected newsmagazine *Expresso* was founded in 1973 and attracts about 90,000 readers. The country's other major newsmagazine, *Tiempo,* closed in 1990 after 15 years.

Switzerland. The Swiss press is highly fragmented in a country of two main languages, French and German. Of the top eight papers, only two are not in German. Of the 103 newspapers in 1991, only 12 had circulations of over 50,000. The country's highest-selling daily, the sensationalist *Blick* at nearly 400,000 circulation, represents the only paper launched after World War II that has survived. *Blick* and the *Tages Anzeiger,* at about 270,000, rank far ahead of other daily papers by at least 100,000 copies.

Among magazines, French-language publications fare better, having both the leading magazine targeting women, *Femina,* that sells about 240,000 copies, and the top general interest magazine, *Trente Jours,* which goes free to about 400,000 people. However, German titles otherwise dominate, led by a television guide that ranks highest, selling nearly 800,000 copies. *Neue Zuercher Zeitung* of Zurich is the country's best daily and one of the best in Europe.

ELECTRONIC MEDIA

Europe has traditionally been a very settled continent for electronic media. However, changes in ownership and financing patterns, plus the emergence of new program delivery systems, have changed the continent's media dynamic. Commercially funded broadcast organizations have taken their place beside state-run media enterprises in virtually every country. Direct-broadcast satellites, home video recorders, and cable systems have changed the traditional terrestrial broadcasting paradigm. Established patterns of operation are being reexamined on many levels. In some cases regulations are lagging behind innovative media practices. In other cases traditional groupings such as radio with television are open to a new look. In still others, local and regional programming are more prominent, and few observers are certain where digital technology will take production and distribution. The key word in the new media world of Europe is *integration*—routing information to the consumer by new methods and through new structures.

One of the foundational changes that has facilitated the integration of media in Europe is the demise of the government broadcasting monopoly and the mindset that went with it. Throughout much of this century, and only until fairly recently in many cases, broadcasting in most countries was regulated as if it were a public service such as the post office. Broadcasting was considered by some governments as little more than a multiparty telephone conversation; it was something a nation did "for" its citizens and was financed by a tax collected on receiver sales. As a result, nation-states were exceedingly reluctant to relinquish control over access to media systems. In the few cases where private broadcasting was permitted, legislation many times limited cross-media shareholding to avoid too much private governance. Countries feared the kind of control that print media publishers such as Springer and Bertelsmann exercised in Germany.

A philosophy called public service broadcasting grew up around providing high-quality programming in state-financed systems. A key to the ethos of public service broadcasting is to serve the entire populace of a nation balanced and diversified programming. This is in direct contrast to the primarily mass-only appeal of commercially oriented broadcasting systems. Generally, public service broadcasting had at its core accountability to the public through other than market forces, close regulation of content, public financing, and broad-based geographical service protected from competition. Such a system certainly had its critics, who cited inefficiencies, too many programming obligations, and political interference. By the mid-1990s public monopolies of ten years ago have been replaced by dual or mixed systems, which allow some advertising support for programs. Public service broadcasting's new role remains an active issue in the rechartering of the British Broadcasting Corporation (BBC) in 1996.

The new broadcast financing systems value elements of a commercial aesthetic and base decisions on economic analyses of the marketplace. This mindset (combined with changes in distribution technology) has helped shift television in Europe from its old role as a public good, paid for only indirectly, to a private good with buyers and sellers (Noam 1991). This approach has been adopted in varying degrees by countries. Austria, Italy, Luxembourg, Portugal, and Switzerland are viewed by the Euromedia

Research Group (1992) as having moved the least along the continuum from public monopoly to completely commercially funded. The Scandinavian countries, the Netherlands, and Greece are leaning more toward private than public financing. Still more progress toward a commercial system has been seen in Belgium, Spain, France, Germany, Ireland, and the United Kingdom.

Some critics decry moves away from the public service ethos. In reality it is very unlikely Europe will evolve into a mostly market-driven broadcasting system such as that of the United States for several reasons. The most important is that public service broadcasting has served the continent very well overall, and Europeans, given their appreciation of the impact of broadcasting on the social fabric, may be reluctant to completely unchain free-market commercialism. But there is little question that Europe has moved from social and political policy to economic policy as the driving force behind the expansion of broadcast offerings. It is also apparent the underlying funding mechanism for commercial broadcasting has grown beyond advertisers' willingness to pay for commercial time and has moved to the media consumer's willingness to pay for specific programs. Relying on viewers to fund the system encourages additional program suppliers to market their products and does not force the broadcast media to depend on an ever more thinly sliced pie of advertiser budgets. Thus, the limiting factor in financing new broadcast programming is the ability to deliver to consumers ever more available channels.

This market-driven approach necessitates changes in traditional signal delivery systems. These traditional systems are limited by the physics of radio transmission. The resulting restrictions are not as acute in the newer delivery technologies of direct broadcast satellites, home video playback, and cable. In over-the-air terrestrial broadcasting, the speaker is linked with the listener by way of a single communication channel. This has been the case throughout this century in both radio and television. Whether the radio signal was modulated on long wave (LW), medium wave (AM), or VHF (FM) or the television signal on UHF or VHF, the delivery system required at least one, or at times many more, transmitter and antenna for each program to be distributed. This electronic reality with its attendant costs (at times combined with a political desire to limit information) and the philosophical foundation of public service broadcasting resulted in entire countries being limited to fewer than half a dozen radio or television program choices.

Two other technical considerations limited European access to terrestrial broadcasting signals. The first is electromagnetic spectrum space. The radio spectrum is a limited natural resource. Carefully managed, there could be some use of it by all of the independent nation-states given rights to access it. With the relatively small size of some countries, this equates to rather limited numbers of frequencies in any given broadcast service for each country. And with the tendency of radio signals not to respect international borders, signal spillover is inevitable. Whether the signal happened to be in a language understood by the population of neighboring countries could make the issue problematic.

The second issue involves differing television video standards. The 1960s fight over which type of picture transmission method each country would adopt (and thereby require its citizens to buy) has been most appropriately labeled Technological Nationalism by Eli Noam (1991). Most of Europe adopted the PAL system, with the notable exception of France, which opted for SECAM. Today, televisions are available that receive both standards. The 1980s version of the technical standards struggle involved a system called MAC and was an attempt at an all-Europe television system. This debate currently centers on high-definition television and direct-satellite broadcasting.

Most such technical matters are resolved by consensus in organizations such as the International Telecommunication Union (ITU) and the European Broadcasting Union (EBU). The ITU is a United Nations (UN) unit that handles the registration of worldwide radio frequencies and coordinates wired and wireless communication system specifications. The EBU, formed in 1950, serves to coordinate technical standards among national public service broadcasters and to assist in program exchange (principally sports and some news) through a satellite distribution system called Eurovision. Commercial broadcasters formed the Association of Commercial Television (ACT) in 1989 to compete with EBU in bidding for broadcast rights for special events. As satellite distribution became more sophisticated and cable television increased, Eurovision has a become less significant player in trans-Europe program exchange.

Direct-broadcast satellites, cable distribution systems, and home video players have also dramatically expanded European viewer and listener options. Videotape dramatically decreased the time to get news to viewers, helped reduce production costs, and has become a strong contender as a preferred programming medium. But probably the VCR's most important impact is that it gives consumers control over their viewing. At a time when program choices were limited, this was an empowering message for viewers. VCR penetration in Europe approaches 50 percent in many countries, although it is significantly lower in Italy with its large number of commercial over-the-air channels.

Direct-broadcasting satellites grew from cold-war technology and once were considered so threatening to the Soviet empire that Russia publicly threatened to blow such propaganda platforms from orbit. The Soviets, who learned to live with foreign international radio signals invading their airspace, could not live with the idea that pictures might be beamed to their citizens behind the old Iron Curtain. Direct-broadcast satellites had advantages over terrestrial broadcasters. Satellites could cover a European-sized area, were not restricted by antenna height, and could send a Europe-wide color television standard to all receiving dishes. But the technology is expensive and far from foolproof.

Governments have launched several direct-broadcast satellite systems (French/German TDF/TV, British Marco Polo, and Swedish Tele-X), but the most aggressive direct-broadcast satellite operation is Rupert Murdoch's BSkyB system, serving 1.25 million British households. However, even with receiver dish size and costs shrinking, enabling medium-power distribution satellites (i.e., Astra or Eutelsat) to be received by modest home units, some critics wonder if satellites would not be more efficiently used to distribute additional program services to established cable systems and from there to viewers' televisions.

It is broadband cable that is breaking the technological bottleneck of spectrum scarcity in Europe and opening up many new opportunities to news and entertainment programmers and viewers. An early 1990s pan-Europe survey showed that 106 television channels were available in eleven Western European countries. Of these 106

TABLE 9.2 European media distribution

Country	1991 Population in Millions (Rank)	Copies in Thousands* (Rank)	% TV Households with Cable‡
Austria	7.7 (11)	409 (5)	23.7
Belgium	9.9 (9)	173 (12)	88.9
Denmark	5.1 (13)	340 (7)	61.9
Finland	5.0 (14)	521 (3)	42.3
France	56.7 (4)	157† (13)	1.5
Germany	79.5 (1)	335 (8)	32.3
Greece	10.1 (8)	83 (15)	Very small
Ireland	3.5 (16)	177 (11)	30.9
Italy	57.7 (2)	115 (14)	0.4
Luxembourg	0.4 (17)	333 (9)	64.3
Netherlands	15.0 (6)	317 (10)	79.5
Norway	4.3 (14)	619 (1)	31.8
Portugal	10.4 (7)	39 (17)	Very small
Spain	39.0 (5)	81 (16)	3.0
Sweden	8.6 (10)	522 (2)	52.3
Switzerland	6.8 (12)	415 (4)	72.0
United Kingdom (Great Britain and Northern Ireland)	57.6 (3)	362 (6)	1.9

*Ratio between average daily newspaper circulaion and population for 1992. World Press Trends, 1993.
†1991 figure for France.
‡Figures from 1990 (OECD, 1993).
SOURCES: OECD, *Competition Policy and a Changing Broadcast Industry* (Paris: OECD, 1993); Fédération Internationale des Editeurs de Journaux (FIEJ), *World Press Trends* (Paris: FIEJ, 1993).

channels, 46 were delivered by satellite. In 24 million cable households there was a dramatic increase in the audience share watching commercial satellite television (to 39 percent) and a decline in viewership of terrestrial broadcast channels (to 60 percent) (Euromedia Research Group, 1992).

Cable penetration figures by country show exceptional variation (see Table 9.2) (OECD 1993). The highest penetration is found in Belgium (89 percent cable households of TV households), Netherlands (80 percent), Luxembourg (64 percent) and Switzerland (72 percent). Each of these countries developed their involvement in cable for indigenous reasons, many of which had little to do with regulatory policy planning. For example, in the Netherlands there was a concern about too many outside antennas, and in Belgium the lack of a structured regulatory framework (with its inherent restrictions), combined with an inherent openness to adjacent nations, facilitated heavy development. Britain's cable development (1.9 percent) was partially hindered by the government's decision not to involve the state telephone company in the construction of the actual network (as was the case in Germany and France) (Noam 1991).

For cable to develop its full potential as an information highway to the home, it must go beyond simply providing television signals to viewers. It will be necessary to converge mass communication (one-to-many) with telecommunication (one-to-one) technologies. There have been several attempts to integrate technologies and move beyond the first-generation delivery systems to converge technologies and regulation. The European Community (EC) plan to encourage investments in and use of an updated telephone/telecommunications systems is the integrated services digital network (ISDN). The EC's Television Without Frontiers Directive and the Council of Europe's Transfrontier Broadcasting Convention were designed to encourage transmission and distribution of electronic signals, specifically to eliminate obstacles to broadcasting television programs throughout Europe.

Western Europe has been a leader in both interactive and one-way systems that deliver text to television screens or computer terminals in the home or office. The BBC had one-way systems as early as 1974 that sent pages of brief news stories, along with sports, finance, weather, travel, and cultural information, to an audience with specially equipped televisions. The cost to users ended once they bought the set. Most European countries now have some form of this "teletext" system. Some countries also have interactive "videotex" services that involve the national phone companies and charge users by the minute or by subscription. France has clearly been the world leader in this field since it began its Teletel system in 1983. Nine years later, it had more than 6 million Minitel terminals in use that provided access to more than 20,000 different services through the nationwide system. France Telecom expected to have spent $9 billion by the year 2000, breaking even by 1998. News organizations had early and lucrative involvement in this kind of system, acting for the first nine years as sole providers of interactive services. The success of the system lay in the telephone company making the process as simple as possible. It gave subscribers the computer terminal for the first decade of operation and handled all the billing for everyone who provided a service. In 1992, revenues reached about $1 billion (5.8 billion francs), with about 40 percent going to service providers. Newspapers and other periodicals made money less on the news they provided than from their games and horoscopes and the mechanism they provided for people who wanted to write messages (often erotic) to each other. Telephone companies in Belgium, Germany, Greece, Ireland, Italy, Luxembourg, the Netherlands, Spain, and Switzerland are at varying levels of success in efforts to have similar service, and none begin to approach the French level.

Scandinavia

Denmark exemplifies a country committed to opening up its media system. From a typically highly restricted centralized system ten years ago, Denmark currently has about 350 local radio and 50 local television license holders in addition to the two national television services (Danmarks Radio and TV2 Danmark) and three national radio services. Each of the national services maintains regional services.[1] Danmarks Radio does not carry advertising, but TV2 Danmark gets most of its funding from ads (no more than 12 minutes per hour placed in distinctive blocks). Programming over TV2 Danmark must be at least half Danish or Nordic. The extensive cable networks carry local

[1] Much of the broadcasting information was originally compiled by OECD.

and national Danish programs, foreign broadcast, or satellite services (40 television and 10 radio), and some cable-only broadcasters. Print media publishers are not allowed to own a majority in private radio or television operations.

Finland's location straddling northern Europe and linking it with the former Soviet Union, as well as its language isolation, has provided it with opportunities to be creative with its media structure. Oy Ylesradio Ab (Finnish Broadcast Company, YLE) is owned by the government and has the official state monopoly for nationwide radio and television broadcasting, including transmission facilities. However, YLE leases 20 percent of its airtime to MTV, a commercial broadcasting company. Between the two organizations, Finns receive a variety of public service and commercial fare (including some U.S. imports). YLE receives most of its operating budget from license fees but also gets almost two-thirds of MTV's gross advertising revenue as payment for leasing it facilities. A third television program (noncommercial) has been authorized. About 70 local commercial radio licenses have been issued, many to newspaper publishers. Cable companies are owned by both the government and private companies.

Norway's Broadcasting Corporation (Norsk Rikskringkasting, NRK) maintains an exceptionally strong commitment to local broadcasting. Over 100 licenses have been granted for private local television and about 400 for private local radio (Naerradio). Advertising is permitted, but funds are also raised from radio bingo and donations. The local character of the stations is ensured by regulations, which require that 75 percent of the radio programs be locally produced and feature indigenous material, and 50 percent of the TV programs must be edited locally. Advertising is limited to one minute in ten of total daily transmission time and no more than 15 percent of this total in any hour. The goal of the radio service is to increase social and cultural identity in small communities. Also, in a striking attempt to free NRK from possible state influence, it was made a foundation in 1988.

Sweden has remained a bastion of public service broadcasting into this decade. The national broadcasting company Sveriges Radio AB (SR) will have its two television services supplemented by TV 4, a private concern headed by Nordisk Television AB. TV 4 will be allowed to advertise up to 10 percent of its daily transmission time; SR had not allowed advertising. SR also supplies four channels of radio service, and there is a very active local radio system which has issued 2,500 licenses. Scandinavia satellite program services are based in Sweden and include two film subscription services. A majority of the extensive cable market, which includes 30 satellite services (most in English), is owned by Swedish Telecom (Televerket). Plans are underway to upgrade the entire cable system to 30 channels.

Benelux

Belgium is a two-language country—Flemish-speaking Flanders in the north and French-speaking Wallonia next to France. Neighboring Luxembourg also targets Belgium with its French broadcasts. The public broadcasters (French language RTVF and Flemish language VTM) also share their audiences with an exceptionally developed cable industry where penetration approaches 90 percent of TV households. Public broadcasters began accepting commercials in the late 1980s.

Luxembourg has managed to exploit its location as a small nation in the heart of Europe throughout its broadcasting history. Unlike its neighbors, Radio Television Luxembourgeois (RTL) has been openly commercial from its inception. Millions of aging Europeans grew up listening to the pop music and commercials that poured from the powerful RTL radio transmitters. RTL also led the way into commercial television in Europe and more recently has exploited its entitlement to satellite frequencies with its commercially successful Astra systems, covering Western Europe. RTL's parent company is also involved in commercial television in Germany, France, and the Netherlands.

The very tidy Dutch system of pillarized broadcasting (granting proportional air time to established public interest groups) is trying to regroup following the injection of commercial television by RTL-4 from Luxembourg. RTL-4's signal is delivered by the Astra satellite into the extensive Dutch cable system. It based its entry on EC regulations, which promoted cross-border program exchange. The Netherlands was left playing legislative catch-up, trying to amend its established broadcasting act to account for commercial influences, while maintaining and strengthening its solid broadcasting system. The system allots broadcasting time to political and religious organizations based on their membership figures—more members, a bigger share of the radio/television airtime. NOS (the Netherlands Broadcasting Corporation) serves as an umbrella programming entity providing basic news, culture, and sports programming and the organizational framework. The eight broadcasting organizations then use the NOS system to carry their programs. The new law prohibits commercial terrestrial broadcasting and restricts such commercial programs to cable, which is extensive, covering 80 percent of the households.

Islands

Ireland has established the structure for commercial broadcasting but seems to be having problems getting the system off the ground. A private television station was authorized in the early 1990s under a communications act rewritten to permit such service. The Radio and Television Act also placed limits on the amount of advertising profit the state-operated television service could make. This was done to equalize the competitive advertising environment for the new private station. Unfortunately, the private service never began broadcasting, and the license was withdrawn (although the licensing authority was later found to have acted improperly in rescinding the permit). A national private radio service was active briefly but stopped operation because of financial difficulties. However, over 20 private local radio services have begun. This is in addition to three national public radio channels and two national television channels operated by Radio Telefis Ireann (RTE). Many Irish can receive broadcasts from the United Kingdom, and about a third of the households subscribe to cable service.

The United Kingdom has recently been fine-tuning its well-established commercial electronic media system. The names of some of the players have changed, but the framework remains essentially the same—a duopoly of terrestrial television services with ancillary radio, direct broadcast, and cable operations. The foundation for these changes is the Broadcasting Act 1990. The Independent Television Commission (ITC) regulates commercial television (including cable) but has no involvement in programming. The new Channel 3 remains a regionally based operation, and commercial Channel 4 is responsible for selling it own advertising time under the new broadcasting act. The act also establishes commercial Channel 5, which should be on the air in the mid-1990s with a terrestrial signal that reaches 70 percent of the population. Radio is now administered by the Radio Authority; radio services should expand to include over 200 new radio stations and three national licensees in the next decade. Britain is closer than many countries to integrating its communication services. Under new regulations, cable operators will be able to provide telephone services, and eventually telecommunications companies will enter the entertainment field. As mentioned, the charter for the BBC (which continues to operate two public service television channels and an extensive radio network) comes up for renewal in 1996.

The British government is coming under increasing pressure to withdraw its controversial 1988 ban on broadcasting direct interviews with 11 Irish organizations considered to be politically violent. The issue involves the continuing struggle in Northern Ireland. Recent 1993 Index on Censorship articles by a BBC News official, as well as a respected academic, call for the removal of the broadcasting ban, saying it hampers reasonable journalistic coverage of the issues in the conflict.

Central

France's outspoken protectionist stance in communication and other international matters continues to attract world attention. France and the United States agreed to disagree on the issue of motion picture import/export quotas at the final round of negotiations for the General Agreement on Tariffs and Trade (GATT). France refuses to give up its protectionist stance on film importation quotas, fearing the loss of indigenous French culture through American media imperialism. This comes at a time when the largest independent French producer, Hamster, is partially owned by CapCities/ABC; the second largest producer, Tele-Images, works with NBC and Group W; and a third producer is partially owned by Hearst newspapers in the United States. The demise of the Le Cinq television network has reduced offerings to three public and one private network and the Canal Plus pay-TV operation. The government continues to promote French culture and the French communications industry. In radio, up to 1,800 local stations have been authorized.

Germany continues to sort out the impact on the communications industry of reunifying East and West. The five new states (or *Lander*) have established their own broadcasting organizations, and these are melding into the established ARD coordinating association responsible for First German Television and Second German Television (ZDF). Audience research figures from the former East Germany showed a tenfold increase in newscast viewing after the fall of the wall and before the old system was folded into the West German organizations. Actual viewing time is significantly higher in the old East Germany, and there is a very strong desire for light entertainment programming. In the reunified Germany, each state (or *Lander*) continues to be responsible for broadcast legislation rather than the national government. The *Landers* do coordinate their efforts on some communications matters. Cable penetration is over 40 percent in the former West Germany but only 8 percent in the former East Germany.

Four major private television program services continue to challenge ARD and ZDF for viewers and advertising.

Alpine

Austria is making plans to relinquish what has been one of the strongest monopoly grips on broadcasting control remaining on the European continent. Regional and local private radio broadcasting is expected in 1994. Up to this point, public broadcaster ORF maintained the only authority to originate broadcast programs within the country. ORF did not give up its control willingly; it took a court challenge to get the new broadcast law on the books. The court case was alleging violation of the European Convention on Human Rights because the country had no licensing provision for private radio and television. Austrian cable systems do carry a number of private, advertiser-supported programs, most of which are German.

Switzerland faces an interesting broadcasting problem for such a small country. It must service its population in four national languages (Romansch, 1 percent; Italian, 5 percent; French, 20 percent; and German, 73 percent). It does this through the Société Suisse de Radiodiffusion et Télévision (SSR), which is a classic public service broadcaster. It is given monopoly national broadcaster status and license fees and advertising income in exchange for providing programming to the entire country in the three major languages. SSR is supplemented by over 50 advertiser-supported local radio and television stations. Cable penetration is understandably high (given the mountainous terrain) at about 70 percent. Several satellite programs service the country.

Iberia

Portugal has authorized two private television channels to complement the two public service stations RTP-1 and RTP-2. The RTP channels receive about half their income from advertising; the new stations will be completely funded by advertising. Local production is supplemented by programming imported from Brazil. Cable and satellite reception are permitted, but neither is well developed, and 315 local commercial radio stations have been authorized.

Spain is unusual in that its two public service broadcast channels (Television Espanola, RTE) were financed from advertising revenues rather than household license fees. Profits were used to help finance the public radio service. However, with the competition from three nationwide commercial channels, there is growing concern that programming standards are being sacrificed in the name of audience ratings. Several viewer groups and the Catholic Church have announced their opposition to programs that stress sex, violence, or obscene language. Almost 600 private radio stations have been authorized. This follows a period of intense pirate activity during and after the Franco years.

Mediterranean

In Greece, confrontational politics and broadcast policy have been closely linked, but the results have not always been satisfying. Radio is experiencing the results of a legislated but unregulated attempt at providing alternative voices to established public service broadcasters. What began as several conservative majors challenging the socialist government by setting up very successful municipal radio stations in the late 1980s has led through a period of legalization to the chaos of an unenforced and unenforceable cacophony. The situation is out of control as stations of all types (municipal, political, purely commercial, industry-linked, nonprofit amateur, and provincial) all compete for listeners, air space, and funding. The television situation is less complicated in terms of players but appears equally unworkable.

Italy has tried to legislatively control what began in the 1970s as a flood of private broadcasting activity following a high court decision effectively voiding Radio-televisione Italiano's (RAI) established state monopoly over broadcasting. It took 16 years for new legislation to be enacted (1990), and it effectively codified the results of a dynamically competitive struggle that effectively left the Fininvest Group of Silvio Berlusconi as the dominant private player in a state/private broadcasting duopoly. With the terrestrial broadcasting situation settled on paper, there may be more development of cable and satellite-delivered programming.

Europe is also home to some of the world's most respected international short-wave broadcasters. Almost every country maintains some form of long-distance radio (and increasingly television) facility to communicate with its far-flung nationals or put its particular twist on world events.

WIRE SERVICES

Western Europe acts as home to two of the world's major wire services: Agence France-Presse (AFP) of France and Reuters of the United Kingdom. Each relies on hundreds of full-time correspondents and even more part-time stringers to provide primarily news from other countries. Each offers stories in several languages to subscribers that include newspapers, radio and television stations, government agencies, businesses, and individuals. Both agencies offer both written and broadcast news and pictures. AFP began an informational graphics service in 1988. Reuters became owner of the Visnews video news agency in 1993 and renamed it Reuters Television.

AFP emerged after World War II from the Havas news service founded in 1835. The agency has been by statute independent of the French government since 1957, but remains highly dependent on it. Press representatives hold a majority on the 15-member board of directors, but government subscriptions account for more than half of revenues, and issues involving its influence occasionally arise.

Paul Julius Reuter, a German employee of the French Havas news agency, founded his namesake service in London in 1851. The service began with stock information, adding general news six years later, and a worldwide news exchange in 1870. In recent years, the company has increasingly emphasized financial services. In 1992, three-fourths of its revenues came from stock and money market and other financial information it provided to clients, mostly on special terminals. Another 18 percent came from its communications service for international financial traders. Only 7 percent of its revenues came from subscriptions to its news service.

Most Western European countries have a main national wire service and many also have other specialized agencies. For example, along with its national Deutsche Presse-Agentur (DPA), Germany has dozens of other agencies, including services that specialize in news of Protestant and Catholic churches, in sports, and in finance. Other nations' principal agencies include Spain's Agencia Efe; Italy's Agenzia Nationale Stampa Associata and, in the Vatican, Agence Fideles; Sweden's Internationella Presse-byran; and Greece's Agence d'Athènes. One of the few countries without its own wire service is Ireland, which relies on a cooperative with the principal British dailies outside London.

GOVERNMENT–MEDIA RELATIONS

Although all Western European countries have press freedom as a basic tenet of their constitutions, all governments have put some form of restriction on their mass media or its practitioners.

Scandinavian countries rank among the world's most free, and yet governments still set key rules. The Swedish government gives journalists and other citizens wide access to official documents but also determines which kinds of documents would remain secret. Swedish law not only forbids government officials from asking a journalist to reveal the identity of an anonymous source but also prohibits the journalist from revealing an anonymous source without that source's permission. Most Nordic governments, like those in some other Western European countries, fix responsibility for everything in a newspaper on one person at that newspaper. Further, they, like all countries in the region, have laws about defamation, violation of national security, and obscenity.

That said, Scandinavia is the birthplace of two institutions that help avoid the push for further government restriction: the press council and the ombudsman. In response to government criticism, Swedish newspaper executives set up a press council to voluntarily regulate themselves in 1916. Finland and Norway followed suit in the 1920s and Denmark in 1964. Councils hear complaints and offer judgments that carry varying degrees of weight within the press industry. In 1953 the United Kingdom set up its Press Council, which became the Press Complaints Commission in 1991. Few other Western European countries have press councils.

The ombudsman idea, which first emerged in Sweden in the 1960s, provided for a person to help ease the workload of the council by mediating many complaints. The position changed as it moved to the United States, with individual newspapers designating someone as the ombudsman representing reader interests.

Western Europe has a wide range of libel and privacy laws. In France, such laws are very complex and strict with, for example, all information about a person's activities during World War II "amnestied" and therefore off-limits. Nordic countries have strong protections against libel, but cases are more often handled by press councils or the parties involved than by the courts.

The most radical changes in government–media relations have been in the evolving status of broadcasting from a highly controlled medium aligned with the state in varying degrees to a player more closely aligned with newspapers in its independence. As the issue of spectrum scarcity evaporated with the coming new technologies such as cable, so did the underlying rationale for subjecting it to such tight state control. Broadcasting freedom is now specifically included within the European Convention on Human Rights.

Efforts at pan-European press legislation have met with little success. One controversial set of recommendations emerged in 1993 that offered guidelines for laws concerning journalistic conduct. By early 1994, several press organizations had come out against the guidelines.

Governments help support mass media financially. Newspapers in all countries get some form of government financial breaks, ranging from cheaper postal rates or value-added taxes in most countries to direct subsidies in Austria, Belgium, Finland, France, Italy, Luxembourg, Norway, Portugal, Spain, and Sweden. In addition to providing other direct subsidies, France allows journalists to reduce their taxable income by 30 percent. German political dailies pay half the normal value-added tax. The Danish press benefits from cheaper postal rates and exemption from sales tax. In Greece, publishers can exempt up to 4 percent of their gross revenues from taxes. Ireland gives some money to Irish-language papers. The Swiss press gets postal breaks, and the press in the United Kingdom a sales tax reduction.

CONCEPTS OF MEDIA FREEDOM

The foundations of modern democratic concepts have their roots in European philosophy from Greece and Italy to England, France, and Germany. The development of printing helped disseminate additional interpretations of the Bible (Calvin and Luther) as well as spread awareness of new scientific theories (Copernicus, Galileo, and Newton). Mass communication by printed word involved ordinary people in the political thinking of Machiavelli, More, and Hobbes. The English Enlightenment challenged the past (Milton, Hobbes, Locke, and Hume), and the French pursued the Age of Enlightenment (Montesquieu, Voltaire, and Rousseau). Hegel's discussions of Kant and the former's effect on Marx were felt throughout Europe until the fall of the Berlin Wall in 1989 (Altschull 1990).

The essence of freedom of the press is a historic balance between two competing protections. The press is protected from state interference in the forms of censorship or restrictive licensing. At the same time, the right of each individual to his or her personal reputation is protected from violation by a vengeful press. Thus, the press ideally respects the rights of individuals to their earned reputations, and the state respects the rights of the press to objectively report and comment on the day's events. However, the economic and political clout of large press organizations sometimes tempts them to exercise their powers in less than judicious ways. In such situations, nation-states are faced with the tricky problem of trying to regulate an errant press without violating the perceived and public proscriptions from interfering with press operations. Usually, nations are reduced to using monopoly law to limit press power or to shoring up opposition press entities with state subsidies. The general feeling has been that the market will keep an irresponsible press in check. Thus, there has been very little need, from the state's point of view, to reform press law as newspapers expanded internationally as well as into radio and television investments (Hoffmann-Riem 1992).

Broadcasting is viewed in the European Union context as an economic matter and, as such, is protected under regulations that provide market freedom. Interestingly, these marketing protections are only for international broadcasts, not those originating within member states. As such, national legislatures have the right to reorganize their broadcasting entities completely along noncommercial lines, should they wish to so subject their broadcasting industry to almost certain death in terms of audience appeal.

MEDIA ECONOMICS

An often-stated goal of the European Union is that of a "United Europe." The point has been to reduce centuries of insularity that groups and nation-states have erected to protect themselves from neighbors, often thought to be too close or too different. Such enforced provincialism seemed entirely suitable for a relatively small continent packed with heterogeneous populations. But the realities of world trade have changed these old rules. No longer can any nation stand alone if it is to be competitive in the world's new global marketplace. Alliances have replaced animosities as the way by which societies can survive, grow, and prosper in the twenty-first century. Businesses, both corporations and individual entrepreneurs, accept these concepts as the new paradigm for survival and are trying to realize as much economic advantage as possible. It is in this context that a discussion of global media concentration begins.

Communication businesses understand they must diversify if they are to successfully weather the vacillations of advertising-driven incomes. They also understand it is simply good business practice to control as many elements of any industry as possible. It is always better to pay oneself rather than pay someone else for goods or services. This can be especially important in the communications business, with its myriad elements of production. It makes perfect business sense to create television programs or print publications using wholly owned or at least controlled talent, equipment, and other facilities.

Two competing philosophies are at work as Europe deals with media economics in the 1990s. On the one hand, the basic purpose of uniting Europe in a common market is to promote broader free trade. The European Union has drafted policies that specifically prohibit restraints on competition. This opens up the broadcasting market, one that has traditionally been closed to private business because the field was controlled by government. On the other hand, there are regulations that restrict cartels so they do not stifle competition by creating monopolies (Negrine and Papathanassopoulos 1990). The unfortunate reality is that parochialisms still exist. Governments may be willing to open up their media to increased privatization, but they may become concerned when foreign businesses target their national media for takeovers. The issues have yet to be resolved. In the meantime, Silvio Berlusconi of Italy continues his expansions into Eastern Europe and elsewhere. Rupert Murdoch's holdings go well beyond his control of *The Times* and BSkyB in England to Fox Television

Network, 20th Century Fox studios, and CBS/Fox Home Video in the United States to over 100 newspapers and magazines worldwide. Other exceptionally powerful media conglomerates are controlled by Bertelsmann, the Axel Springer group, and Leo Kirch in Germany, and Hachette, Havas, and Robert Hersant in France.

JOURNALISM EDUCATION AND TRAINING

The number of options available to a person seeking to enter the journalism field in Europe is quite large by American standards, but some may also view the situation as quite restrictive, given the relatively few number of available jobs and the extraordinarily competitive entrance requirements. Journalism education in Europe can best be visualized as a continuum. At one extreme is on-the-job training for those with a high school education or less (practiced to some extent in the United Kingdom, France, Germany, Austria, Ireland, and Greece). Students become apprentices in actual newsrooms and learn by doing, under the guidance of seasoned professionals. Employment after the apprenticeship is built into the system.

Some large newspapers and broadcasters operate very highly competitive private schools of journalism for college graduates based on the apprentice concept (Springer-Verlag in Berlin and Hamburg School of Journalism funded by Gruner & Jahr). At the other extreme is the highly theoretical communication science program at an established university with little practical training but that culminates after approximately four years with a bachelor's degree (Belgium). Employment may be problematic, and students may or may not plan on staying in the communications field. Those who do may pursue doctoral study in communication research.

Less extreme on the continuum are highly practical courses at well-established journalism institutes, funded by local media, primarily newspapers (United Kingdom, Sweden, Norway, Italy, Austria). Students, who may be required to enter with a high school degree or undergraduate diploma, may receive a certificate, diploma, or even a graduate degree. A job is virtually ensured. Next on the continuum toward the theoretical is what the Germans call "integrated study courses." Here are the university degree programs in media studies and communications (Universities of Berlin, Bochum, Göttingen, Mainz, Munich, Münster, Erlangen/Nuremburg). Many accredited American state university journalism/mass communication programs resemble such integrated courses. These programs lack the full range of technical facilities to be considered fully vocational programs, but students undertake a specialized academic curriculum in social sciences. Journalistic skills are gained in student practicum newsrooms and in required internships in local professional media. In highly developed countries, many of these schemes are in operation.

With the communications field rapidly expanding beyond the traditional fields of print and broadcast journalism, there is an increasing need for educated workers in public relations, advertising, and media consulting. In Italy, such people are called "pubblicisti" and outnumber journalists well over two to one. The field is growing rapidly and is attracting many more women than men. In many small European countries, however, the national economies cannot support such extensive media networks. Here there are fewer annual job openings. The result can be frustration for young graduates from ever more popular communication programs. The University of Vienna in Austria has 5,000 communication students; the University of Salzburg has 1,000. This represents a sixfold increase since the early 1970s (Gaunt 1992).

Another interesting trend developed in Spain and Portugal, both of which experienced a resurgence of democracy in the mid-1970s. During the days of tight government control, journalists were trained in government supervised schools or on the job. With a return to democracy, both countries opted for more theoretical education programs, because they felt a democratic society required students more able to critically analyze events rather than those trained in mere professional and technical skills.

The European Journalism Training Association (EJTA) is attempting to evaluate journalism programs in Western Europe and has opened a new European Journalism Centre in Maastricht, Holland, to bring together practitioners from across the continent for discussions on topics related to the field. It will also provide continuing training for professionals and management seminars for those journalists promoted to management positions. The EJTA hopes to increase pan-European awareness among journalism students through a series of school linkage projects.

FUTURE PROSPECTS

The early years of a unified Western European market indicate that regional harmonization of approaches to complex issues such as ownership concentration will remain slow in coming and that national differences will remain the norm.

Western European publishers will continue to concern themselves simply with surviving because penetration and proportion of total advertising revenues continue to fall and, as elsewhere, young people show no signs of turning back to newspapers for their news, if they seek it at all. Magazines, especially inexpensive quick reads, show signs of continuing growth. In both kinds of publishing, foreign participation in ownership, especially by entities in other parts of Europe, shows signs of increasing in importance.

Broadcasting in Western Europe has been freed of the public service requirement and has leaped into the advertising-based world of mass entertainment. This will probably lead to more media assuming more of the same look. But with the new face for the broadcast media, the question remains whether either the public or the state will tire of television's new face and reinstitute some form of obligatory public service programming commitment. This may be a place for a revised version of the traditional press council—a new-style ombudsman with the portfolio to examine the societal impact of the broadcast media. Suggested corrective actions may provide creative avenues to better examine the new role of a less constrained visual medium.

Will the tube become a mere video jukebox à la MTV, or will we undertake the self-discipline necessary to protect its standing with regulatory authorities and the public? One would hope that Western Europe could forge a concept of responsible broadcast media that will create a new paradigm for the European Union and the transitional media of the democratizing eastern portion of the continent.

BIBLIOGRAPHY

Albert, Pierre, *Histoire de la Presse.* Paris: Presses Universitaires de France, 1993.

Altschull, J. Herbert. *From Milton to McLuhan.* White Plains, N.Y.: Longman, 1990.

Blumler, Jay G., Editor. *Television and the Public Interest.* London: Sage, 1991.

Blumler, Jay G., and T. J. Nossiter, Editors. *Broadcasting Finance in Transition.* New York: Oxford, 1991.

Browne, Donald R. *Comparing Broadcast Systems.* Ames: Iowa State, 1989.

Carat International. *The European Newspaper and Magazine Minibook.* Oxfordshire: Carat, 1992.

Charon, Jean-Marie. "Decline of a Polemical Press: The Case of France." *Gannett Center Journal* 4 (Fall 1990): 103–110.

———. *L'état des Médias.* Paris: La Découverte/CFPJ/Mediaspouvoirs, 1991.

Congdon, Tim, Brian Sturgess, National Economic Research Associates, William B. Shew, Andrew Graham, and Gavyn Davies. *Paying for Broadcasting: The Handbook.* London: Routledge, 1992.

Dyson, Kenneth, and Peter Humphreys, Editors. *The Political Economy of Communications: International and European Dimensions.* London: Routledge, 1990.

Euromedia Research Group. *The Media in Western Europe.* London: Sage, 1992.

Fédération Internationale des Editeurs de Journaux (FIEJ). *World Press Trends.* Paris: FIEJ, 1993.

Feron, François, and Armelle Thoraval, Editors. *L'Etat de l'Europe.* Paris: La Découverte, 1992.

Gaunt, Philip. *Making the Newsmakers: International on Journalism Training.* Westport, Conn.: Greenwood, 1992.

Guerin, Serge, and Jean-Luc Pouthier. *La Presse Ecrite, 1992-1993.* Paris: CFPJ, 1993.

Hoffmann-Riem, Wolfgang. "Trends in the Development of Broadcasting Law in Western Europe." *European Journal of Communication* 7 (1992): 147–171.

Kist, Joost. *Electronic Publishing.* New York: Croom Helm, 1987.

LeMoine, Jean François. *L'Europe de la Presse Quotidienne.* Paris: Syndicat de la Presse Puotidienne Regionale, 1992.

Linton, David, and Ray Boston. *The Newspaper Press in Britain.* London: Mansell, 1987.

McMane, Aralynn Abare. "La presse quotidienne Americaine en France." In *Les Médias Américains en France: Influence et Penetration,* edited by Claude-Jean Bertrand and Francis Bordat, 27–34. Paris: Belin, 1989.

McQuail, Denis. *Media Performance: Mass Communication and the Public Interest.* London: Sage, 1992.

Negrine, Ralph, and Stylianos Papathanassopoulos. *The Internationalisation of Television.* London: Pinter, 1990.

Noam, Eli. *Television in Europe.* New York: Oxford, 1991.

OECD. *Competition Policy and a Changing Broadcast Industry.* Paris: OECD, 1993.

———. *New Telecommunications Services: Videotex Development Strategies.* Paris: OECD, 1988.

Palmer, Michael, and Jeremy Tunstall. *Liberating Communications: Policy-Making in France and Britain.* Oxford: Basil Blackwell, 1990.

Picard, Robert G. *The Ravens of Odin: The Press in the Nordic Nations.* Iowa State University Press, 1988.

Pilati, Antonio. *Media Industry in Europe.* London: John Libbey, 1993.

Porter, Vincent, and Suzanne Hasselbach. *Pluralism, Politics and the Marketplace.* London: Routledge, 1991.

Regourd, Serge. *La Télévision de l'Europe*. Paris: La Documentation Francaise, 1992.

Reus, Gunter, and Lee B. Becker. "The European Community and Professional Journalism Training." *Journalism Educator* (Winter 1993): 4–12.

Rieffel, Remy, Marie-Françoise Lafosse, Christine Leteinturier, and Jean-Pierre Marhuenda. *Analyse comparative de la Presse nationale en Europe*. Paris: Institut Francais de la Presse, 1993.

Sanchez-Tabernero. *Media Concentration in Europe: Commercial Enterprise and the Public Interest*. Manchester: European Institute of Communication, 1993.

Stephen Saxby, *The Age of Information*. London: Macmillan, 1990.

Silj, A. *The New Television in Europe*. London: John Libbey, 1992.

Suine, Karen, and Wolfgang Truetzschler for the Euromedia Research Group. *Dynamics of Media Politics: Broadcast and Electronic Media in Western Europe*. London: Sage, 1992.

Smith, Anthony. *The Newspaper: An International History*. London: Thames and Hudson, 1979.

UNESCO, *Statistical Yearbook 1993*. Paris: UNESCO, 1993.

Weaver, David H. *Videotex Journalism: Teletext, Viewdata and the News*. Hillsdale, N.J.: Lawrence Earlbaum, 1983.

Zaharopoulos, Thimios, and Manny E. Paraschos. *Mass Media in Greece*. Westport, Conn.: Praeger, 1993.

chapter **10**

East Central and Southeastern Europe, Russia, and the Newly Independent States

Owen V. Johnson

Under communist rule, the Russian and East European mass media were supposed to be instruments of mobilization and propaganda. Communist party authorities sought to use the media to deliver ideologically correct messages. They exerted control through the management of equipment, personnel, and censorship.

Today, the key to understanding the mass media in East Central and Southeastern Europe and in Russia and the Newly Independent States is change. No longer are the mass media centrally managed as the servant of the Communist party and the government. No longer do they always disparage the free market. In fact, in the East Central European countries, they were the pioneering institution of the free market (Figure 10.1).

Several main themes are useful for understanding today's mass media in the formerly communist states. One is the change in their economics. In the more western countries of this region, very little remains in the way of government subsidies, except for cultural, scientific, and scholarly periodicals, but in the east and south, most mass media would perish without government support. In some countries, banks and large companies underwrite media institutions.

The second major theme is a new media relationship with politics. Some media continue to serve the state, while others serve political parties. Some are committed to, but independent of, political points of view. A small number strive to be politically independent and objective. A few papers, especially the tabloids, ignore politics and concentrate on making money.

The third theme is a search for a new role for the mass media in society. Many journalists and editors believe their newspapers should express a clear political point of view, while others think independence is the highest value. Still others believe their mission is to relate the official version of events. Readers and viewers are concerned about their jobs, their income, and the rising cost of living, and say they have lost

FIGURE 10.1 Eastern Europe

interest in politics. A severely complicating factor is that many of these societies have not yet determined what kinds of governing systems they want or will have. Governments, particularly those further east and south, tend to argue that freedom of the press is a luxury they cannot afford.

There are many different kinds of democracies; the most effective media system for each one is different. In many of these countries, people increasingly distrust the media. A rapid increase in the price of newspapers has sent circulations plunging in many countries, particularly those of the former Soviet Union, making radio and television the only media with which many people have daily contact.

For nearly half a century, the similarities of the media in different communist countries were much greater than their differences. That is no longer true. This chapter divides treatment of the media into three different areas: East Central Europe, consisting of the Czech Republic, Hungary, Poland and Slovakia; Southeastern Europe, consisting of Albania, Bulgaria, Romania, and the successor states of the former Socialist Republic of Yugoslavia; and the newly independent states, consisting of Russia and the other 14 countries that emerged from the breakup of the Soviet Union (Figure 10.2).

The divisions are somewhat arbitrary. The Baltic republics of Estonia, Latvia, and Lithuania, for instance, have as much in common with the East Central European countries as they do with their former neighbors in the Soviet Union. Slovenia is as much a part of East Central Europe as it is of Southeastern Europe. The Central Asian countries have media today that are most similar to those of the old Soviet Union, while in many of its cities Russia has vibrant and very democratic media.

The greatest similarities among the groups remain in broadcasting. In most of the countries, television is still owned and operated by the state, although that has begun to change, with private television stations already on the air in Poland and the Czech Republic, and other neighboring countries soon to follow suit. Private ownership has made much greater progress in radio, but almost all of the stations must continue to rent time on transmitters owned by the state.

East Central Europe

Four countries—the Czech Republic, Hungary, Poland, and Slovakia—constitute this area. They are the heirs to the pluralist press system that flourished in the Habsburg Empire before 1918. All of them were independent countries between World War I and World War II, although the Czech Republic and Slovakia at that time constituted a single country, Czechoslovakia.

HISTORICAL HIGHLIGHTS

The first Polish newspaper, *Merkuriusz Polski Ordynaryjny,* appeared in 1661, first in Krakow and then in Warsaw. Hungary's first paper, published in Latin, was *Mercurius Hungaricus,* begun in 1705. The first regularly published Czech paper was *Cesky postylion nebolizto noviny Ceske* (1719). The first Slovak paper was *Prespurske noviny,* published in the years 1783–1787. Until the twentieth century, however, newspapers did not thrive in an area that except for the Czech Lands was primarily rural and agrarian.

Both the Czechs and Slovaks were ruled by the multinational Habsburg Empire. From the mid-nineteenth to the early twentieth century, the Czech and Slovak press helped create a sense of Czech and Slovak national identity, even as some of the newspapers became increasingly politicized. There was little of the objective, fact-based, middle-class form of the press common in Western Europe. The first commitment of

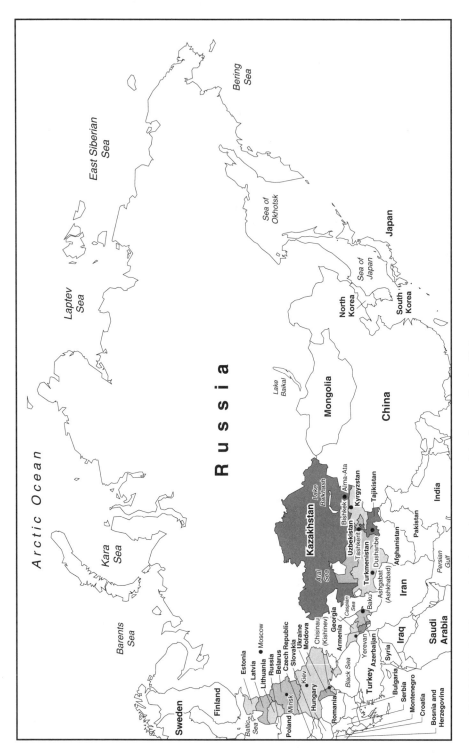

FIGURE 10.2 The newly independent states of the former Soviet Union

almost every newspaper was to the political party that sponsored it. Beginning around the turn of the century, some of the parties began to support urban, sensationalist, non-political dailies. Not only did these newspapers attract large numbers of readers to newspapers, but they helped finance the more limited-circulation political papers. *Lidove noviny,* founded in Brno, became the most important Czech paper, and while not completely nonpartisan, it did develop into a very influential paper of the elite during the interwar period.

Hungarian domination until 1918 made life difficult for the Slovak press, which lacked an economic base. The only Slovak daily paper in the Hungarian kingdom before 1918 was *Slovensky dennik,* based in Budapest. There were no Slovak dailies in what is today Slovakia, although there were six Slovak daily newspapers in the United States!

The nineteenth-century Polish press became an important national institution during the partitions of Polish territory among the empires of Austria, Russia, and Prussia. It was an institution providing employment for national elites, especially the gentry. Only the church was more important than the press in preserving Polish identity. The Polish press could serve as a preserver of language and a source of employment for members of the elite. The Polish press, in contrast to the Czech, developed a greater sense of opposition to the regime. At the same time, the Polish press was even more political than the Czech or Slovak. It was impossible to start a Polish political party without first starting a newspaper.

PRINT MEDIA

People in East Central Europe used to be among the world's leading consumers of newspapers. Not any more. The prices of periodicals are constantly on the rise as the price of newsprint, printing, and delivery increase. People also have less time to read in the once-again competitive, capitalist world.

The most widely read Czech newspapers are the tabloid *Blesk* (founded in 1992 and a box office success with nearly 300,000 copies printed daily), the partially French Hersant-owned *Mlada fronta Dnes* (340,000), and the once communist *Rude pravo* (308,000). Other important papers are *Zemedelske noviny* (202,000), *Svobodne slovo* (178,000), *Hospodarske noviny* (163,000), and *Lidove noviny* (95,000, but it is read by 33 percent of people in top management positions). There are at least a dozen daily newspapers in Prague.

About 800,000 copies of daily newspapers are published in Slovakia. The most widely read newspaper is the tabloid *Novy cas,* looked at daily by almost a third of the population in the country. It is followed closely by the leftist *Pravda* and by *Praca,* once the communist trade-union paper.

There are more than 2,500 newspapers and periodicals in Poland, including 11 nationwide dailies addressing general topics and 10 specialist dailies. There are also 62 regional dailies. *Gazeta Wyborcza* has the largest print run (approximately 500,000), followed by *Rzeczpospolita.* Forty percent of Polish readers read regional newspapers more or less regularly, while little more than 20 percent are regular readers of nationwide newspapers. Perhaps as many as half of Poland's publications are of a religious or denominational nature. There are also 45 women's magazines, about 40 business publications, and 40 or 50 political magazines, led by *Polityka* and *Wprost.*

Hungary has 33 daily newspapers, 12 of which are located in Budapest. The leading paper is the formerly communist *Nepszabadsag,* with a circulation of 360,000. Also respected is *Magyar Hirlap,* which prints 60,000 copies. Other important dailies include *Mai Nap, Nepszava, Esti Hirlap, Magyar Nemzet,* and *Nemzeti Sport.* Several of the Budapest dailies are in financial trouble.

ELECTRONIC MEDIA

The first statewide private television station in the region is the Czech Nova, which went on the air February 4, 1994, opening its prime time schedule with *Ghostbusters,* dubbed into Czech. Three-quarters of the capital for the venture comes from the North American partner, Central European Development Co., whose investors include two former U.S. ambassadors. The other one quarter ownership is held by the Czech Savings Bank. By May, Nova was claiming that it had won over the majority of viewers ages 15 to 49. Nova was not the first private station in the Czech Republic, however. Premiera, with 55 percent ownership by the Prague Investment Bank, but with strong Italian participation, had hit the screen in the Prague region the previous summer.

The public Czech Television is limited by law to broadcasting advertising on no more than 1 percent of its time on its first channel and 7 percent on the second channel. Further funding comes from a tax of about $18 a year on all households owning television sets.

Fourteen competitors sought the first Slovak statewide private television license, scheduled to go on the air in 1994 or 1995. The Radio and Television Council first selected CTV, based in the eastern Slovak city of Kosice, as the winner, but the decision was rejected by parliament, leaving the outcome up in the air. Meanwhile, 5 million Slovak viewers watch the two state television channels, with about two out of every three people watching the first channel.

The most popular radio station in the Czech Republic is the state-owned Cesky Rozhlas. Another state station, Praha, is close behind. But private local stations are rapidly gaining ground in the cities. The station Country Radio is listened to regularly by 12.4 percent of the population in Prague, for instance, where there are more than 40 stations.

The three most listened to Slovak radio stations are government owned. Nearly three-quarters of the population listens to Slovensko 1 every day. Second is Rock FM, followed by Slovensko 3 and Fun Radio. Local private radio stations are popping up all over Slovakia. By early 1994, there were 17 private stations, and the number was expanding rapidly.

For 93 percent of Poles, radio and television are the main sources of information. The number of stations they can watch is rapidly increasing. A new Broadcasting Act went into effect in 1993 that makes the National Broadcasting Council (appointed by both Houses of Parliament and the President) responsible for supervising programming, allocating broadcasting frequencies and licenses, and apportioning radio and TV fees paid by owners of receivers. The NBC also awards licenses to private broadcasters. It quickly awarded the one available national commercial television channel to PolSat, a satellite service already on the air ten hours daily and serving 4.5 million Poles. PolSat is scheduled to extend this to 14 hours when it adds nationwide over-the-air broadcasting at the beginning of 1995, with plans to expand to around-the-clock broadcasting. It is already broadcasting over the air in some of Poland's larger cities. Half of PolSat's broadcast schedule is films; news and current affairs account for 9 percent of its broadcast time. The Council also awarded a special license for broadcasts on low power transmitters to Canal Plus, a joint Polish–French venture.

Telewizji Polskiej broadcasts 22 hours daily on each of its two channels. It has also operated 12 regional stations. One of Poland's most popular programs on public television, watched by 70 percent of the audience, is *Kolo Fortuny,* the Polish version of Wheel of Fortune. Viewers are also fond of other quiz shows, as well as soap operas. The newly reorganized public television promises that it will increase the amount of information and culture available on the tube.

The NBC has created 19 new broadcasting organizations, including one national TV company, one national radio company, and 17 local radio companies. Each has a five-member executive board and a nine-member supervisory council.

More than 3 million Poles are receiving Western satellite stations broadcast via cable. There are an estimated 1.2 million satellite dishes, located in more than 10 percent of Poland's 10.5 million television homes. The rapid growth in receivers was sparked in the mid-1980s by Western satellite channels. Cable and satellite television is also undergoing rapid growth in the Czech Republic, Hungary, and Slovakia. The Czech Kabel Plus already has linked together more than a quarter million households and offers CNN, SkyNews, MTV, Eurosport, TV 5 Europe, and 16 other television and 10 radio channels. In Bratislava, Slovakia, 62,000 households are on cable, where they can choose from 35 channels.

Poland's broadcasting council issued two licenses for nationwide radio broadcasting to Radio Zet of Warsaw and RMF of Krakow. The Catholic-run Radio Maryja, which broadcasts primarily religious programs, has a virtual network because it broadcasts from 38 local frequencies. Meantime, there are four state radio networks.

Hungarian State Television has two channels and regional stations in Szeged, Pecs, and Budapest. In mid-1994 there were still no licensed independent statewide television stations, but some production companies, such as NAP TV, contribute programs to the state system. The government has also launched a satellite TV system, Duna TV, to broadcast Hungarian programs abroad.

The Hungarian Ministry of Culture has begun to grant local private TV licenses, which could lead to the launch of up to 80 new stations. Foreign ownership in the stations is limited to 49 percent. HBO, meanwhile, has started a pay-television service in Hungary and invested in that country's 300 or more cable systems.

Hungarian Radio produces programs on four channels and operates seven regional stations. It also operates two commercial stations.

Radio Free Europe, which for more than 40 years broadcast to this region, will drastically cut back its activity both because of budget cuts by the U.S. Congress and the relative success of the domestic media. The budget for Radio Free Europe and Radio Liberty is to be cut by nearly two-thirds to $75 million in fiscal year 1996. Czech and Polish services of Radio Free Europe no longer broadcast from Munich. Remaining operations will move to Prague in 1995.

NEWS SERVICES

News agencies continue to have great influence among the media because many newspapers and radio stations rely on them heavily for economic reasons. If they appear somewhat to favor the government, it is because they see one of their major roles as informing the public what the government is doing.

The Czech Press Agency (CTK), formerly a government agency, is now a public corporation, partly dependent on state subsidies. In 1992, before Slovakia's independence, TASR, the Slovak press agency, was founded under close government control. The old state agencies also continue to function in Hungary and Poland.

A Television Information Agency (TAI), created in 1992, produces newscasts for Polish TV, as well as selling actualities and services to outside users, including commercial broadcasters and foreign news organizations.

GOVERNMENT–MEDIA RELATIONS

In principle, government–media relations in these countries are civilized, although the governments think the media should engage in more self-control, given the fragile quality of their democracies. The Czech Republic was the first newly noncommunist country to pass a broadcast law. The most difficult situations existed during the more nationalist governments in Hungary (1990–1994) and Slovakia (1992–1994).

While Prime Minister Vaclav Klaus has occasionally complained about lack of coverage in the mass media, relations between the government and the mass media in the Czech Republic are comparable to those of a modern Western state. Proof of this was given in April 1994, when the Constitutional Court, at the request of President Vaclav Havel, declared unconstitutional a legal provision that made much criticism of the parliament, government, and the court libelous.

In Poland, serious postcommunist journalism began even before the demise of communism in the widely circulated underground press (*drugi obieg*) of the 1970s and 1980s. Today, much daily journalism is very respectable, but President Lech Walesa prefers a media, especially television, subservient to his wishes. When he was dissatisfied with the decisions of the NBC, for example, he dismissed the head of the council from the chairmanship. Relations between the printed press and the government are generally good.

In Hungary, the right-of-center government that ruled from 1990 to 1994 was almost universally editorially opposed by the media, despite the government's efforts to somehow create some print friends. In broadcasting, relations were so bad for a while that the term "media war" came to be used. The heads of Hungarian radio and television who promoted what they termed objectivity and fairness in the broadcast media were seen by the government as simply being critical. Finally, the heads resigned, but the president of Hungary refused to accept their resignations. Nonetheless, the prime minister appointed people to take their places, people who followed his will and made state broadcasting into an institution promoting the government's interests. In March 1994, just two months before nationwide elections, the Hungarian radio head fired more than 100 journalists for not meeting standards. Tens of thousands of people poured into the streets to protest what they saw as a simple case of politics. Four months later, a new radio head promised to rehire the journalists.

Vladimir Meciar, Slovak prime minister in his newly independent state, had a stormy relationship with the media and applied various kinds of pressure, such as controlling access to information, or delaying foreign investment, to try to tame the press. But the part of the media opposed to Meciar stood its ground, and the result was lively political debate. Meciar's government intervened most directly in the media through appointments in the state broadcasting.

CONCEPTS OF MEDIA FREEDOM

Journalists and government leaders in these countries share a commitment to freedom of speech and press, but only for responsible people, especially themselves. Many government and political leaders do not think that a free and open press can be tolerated when the democracies and economies of their countries are still so fragile.

In each country, there have been laws on the books that specifically limit the mass media. For instance, when Poland passed a new broadcasting law in 1993, it included a passage requiring broadcasters to "uphold Christian values." No one has been able to define precisely what that means (does it mean no shows or programs about abortion?); as a result, it has not limited journalistic freedom. The Hungarian government supervises broadcasting on the basis of a 1974 decree that has been declared unconstitutional but remains in effect because there is nothing to take its place.

In Hungary, the Openness Club and the National Federation of Hungarian Journalists defend journalists and freedom of press as a force serving the public by promoting good government. They are opposed by the Hungarian Journalists' Community, formed in 1992 in support of the then-rightist government, who do not favor free speech.

One of the most difficult issues that arose in Czechoslovakia (and in neighboring eastern Germany) was what to do with the lists of names of people who had allegedly collaborated with the old communist governments. The lists were notoriously inaccurate: they contained not only the names of some dead people, they also included names of people the police had tried to attract, such as Vaclav Havel, now the president of the Czech Republic. People in favor of publication argued that publication of names was absolutely necessary because they opposed government limitations on publication and because they said they believed that people whose names were wrongly on the list would be able to clear themselves. The issue was further complicated because some politicians' positions had nothing to do with issues of freedom of the press, but with their own personal political gain.

Legally, these countries are still usually governed by press legislation from the communist period. The difficulty of putting together government coalitions, the apparent priorities of economic reform, the division of the country in the case of the former Czechoslovakia, and a debate about how specific press legislation should be written have prevented in most cases the adoption of new press laws.

MEDIA ECONOMICS AND SPECIAL PROBLEMS

Widespread Western investment makes possible the economic independence of the print media in these countries. Nearly 80 percent of Hungarian newspapers are owned by Western investors, a development that happened so quickly in 1990 that some neighboring countries moved to place limits on the extent of foreign investment. In Poland, half of the national circulation dailies have foreign ownership. But Western investment is not necessarily the key to success. *Gazeta Wyborcza* has only 12.5 percent ownership from the Cox Company of Atlanta, but it is the dominant presence in the Polish media market. The Frenchman Robert Hersant has bought up eight Polish dailies and almost half of the shares of *Rzeczpospolita.* German publishers such as Bertelsmann, Burda, and Bauer have especially bought into Polish women's and teenagers' magazines and entertainment periodicals. German investors have been rapidly buying up the Czech regional press, although they have been much more tentative with central newspapers. The French-based Hersant owns a significant share of the Czech *Mlada fronta Dnes,* while a subsidiary of the Swiss Ringier owns a majority interest of the once-liberal *Lidove noviny,* which it hopes to recast into an important financial daily. Ringier owns 17 publications in the Czech Republic, making up 16 percent of all copies of publications printed in that country, including many of the most popular. Sixteen of the 25 most widely read Czech dailies are at least partially owned by foreign investors, with at least a 40 percent holding in 14 of them. German publishers own 46 of the 75 provincial newspapers in Bohemia. The formerly communist *Rude pravo* appears to be making a profit without any apparent Western investment.

The only U.S. company besides Cox and the *Wall Street Journal* (which publishes a Polish edition tucked inside *Gazeta Wyborcza*) that has plunged into East Central Europe is Gannett, which has purchased a 50 percent stake in four business weekly newspapers, including one each in Poland and Hungary.

Press distribution in these countries is still largely controlled by old state companies that once held monopolies in this field. In Poland there are 40 private distribution agencies, but they account for less than 10 percent of deliveries.

Although the economies of these countries are beginning to recover from the decline that followed the end of communist rule, only limited resources are available from advertising. It is estimated, for instance, that only $60 million was spent on advertising in Slovakia in 1993, or $11.40 per person. But growth is rapid. In Poland, only $6 million was spent on television advertising in 1990, but by 1995, the amount is expected to exceed $400 million.

JOURNALISM EDUCATION AND TRAINING

Except in Hungary, journalism education under communist rule was primarily vested in journalism departments or schools in the leading university of each country. Their curriculum and teaching were strongly influenced by the communist party. Today, journalism education is in transition: Although it has been depoliticized, it still has more of an academic than a practical focus. The departments cannot come close to meeting student demand. For instance, there were more than 15 applicants for every opening in the class beginning journalism study at Charles University in the fall of 1994. At Comenius University in Bratislava, there were five or six applicants for every available spot. Warsaw University remains the center of journalism education in Poland, although journalism study is also available at the Jagiellonian University in Krakow, and at smaller programs in Poznan, Lublin, and Katowice. Hungary never had undergraduate study in journalism, but a program was started at Lorand Eotvos University in Budapest in 1992. Some journalism courses are given at provincial universities in Pecs and Szeged.

Although the curricula vary from country to country, they usually include some general liberal arts education; some theoretical, philosophical, and historical courses; and some practical work. Because of tight government budgets, most of the journalism departments do not have enough modern equipment to support top-quality journalism technology. It is also difficult to attract today's outstanding journalists into teaching because of the low salaries.

Independent journalism education initiatives, primarily funded by Western sources, have been set up in each of the countries to assist both journalism professionals and journalism students in strengthening skills. They have few faculty of their own, but rely on lecturers from abroad who visit for anywhere from a few days to a full year. They are well equipped with new technology and facilities. Increasingly, some critics believe these initiatives may insufficiently take into account the specific needs of the media systems of each of the countries. Their future may well depend on their ability to continue to attract external funding. The best run of these institutes is the Center for Independent Journalism in Prague.

PROSPECTS FOR THE FUTURE

In the Czech Republic, the most stable of the once-communist countries, journalists rose from sixteenth to eleventh in surveys conducted in 1990 and 1992 of the prestige of various professions. It is an indicator of a system rapidly adjusting to a more open media. A similar process is underway in Poland. In Hungary and Slovakia, the situation will remain contentious until democracy is more firmly established, although in Slovakia, only a small minority (less than 10 percent) of the population does not trust the media.

The key value underlying the media in East Central Europe in the mid-1990s is freedom. Despite the fact that the governments in this region have criticized the press and sometimes interfered with privatization, they have had almost no impact on the content of the press. Even efforts to retain control of broadcasting are slowly failing. It is now governments and parliaments who feel they are being denied access to the media, a distinct contrast to the old communist days. Also left out of the new media systems have been the dreams of the anticommunist dissidents who wanted to create a media democracy, with equal access for all.

The continuing economic changes will contribute to a reduction in the number of publications in coming years, but the further development of a market economic system will provide the wherewithal for a media system more independent of political pressure. Radio will diminish in importance as more and more local radio stations are created. Television will increasingly slip out of the hands of the government through the pressures of commercialization and alternative channels available by satellite or cable.

By the time these countries are serious candidates for the European Union in the next decade, their media systems will be virtually indistinguishable from those of today's Western Europe.

Southeastern Europe

This area consists of Albania, Bulgaria, Romania, and the successor countries of the former Socialist Republic of Yugoslavia, including Slovenia, Croatia, Yugoslavia, and Macedonia. The centuries-long presence of the Ottoman Empire has left its mark on this ethnically mixed area. The economies are generally more backward than their northern neighbors. A democratic political culture is generally less developed. Tiny Slovenia, which gained its independence in 1991, is most like neighboring Austria and other Central European states.

HISTORICAL HIGHLIGHTS

The political and economic backwardness of this area delayed the development of the press. The appearance of the first newspapers and magazines was not just significant from an informational standpoint but also because their mere existence gave evidence of a developing national consciousness and served to help further develop that consciousness. The first periodical publication in any of the South Slav languages, *Slaveno-Serbski Magazin,* first appeared in Venice in 1768. The first newspaper in the territory of the former Yugoslavia (and the first Slovenian newspaper), *Ljubljanske Novice,* was not founded until 1797. The Croatian press dates effectively from 1835 (*Narodna Novine,* published in Zagreb). The domestic Serbian press began with *Novine Serbske* in 1834. The first Bulgarian and Romanian language papers appeared in the mid-nineteenth century. The first newspaper to appear in a Romanian territory was the German-language *Temesvarer Nachrichten,* which began publication in April 1771. More than 50 years later came the first Romanian language newspaper, *Curierul Romanesc,* published in Bucharest.

In Albania it was not until about 1910 that the first domestically produced newspaper was published, just two years before the country gained its independence. In the 1930s there were only three papers in Tirana, the Albanian capital, the most important of which had a circulation of only 2,800. Before World War I, a circulation of 10,000 copies for a Belgrade daily was unique, not surprising when the population was 70 percent illiterate and 85 percent rural. Communist rule introduced the mass circulation press to Southeastern Europe.

The media in Southeastern Europe had widely varying functions under communist rule. The media in Yugoslavia were among the freest in the communist bloc, and the Yugoslav News Agency Tanjug was a highly respected independent agency serving an international audience. After the death of longtime leader Josip Broz Tito, however, the Yugoslav media increasingly were called into the service of national interests. Albania, in contrast, was the most tightly controlled media system in the communist bloc, where even television did not appear until the 1970s. Romania featured a press whose main task was to worship party and state leader Nicolae Ceausescu.

PRINT MEDIA

Most of the newspapers in Southeastern Europe have been privatized. That means they can no longer depend on money from the government and have to make their own way in the market. Hundreds of titles have gone out of business. Circulation of the remaining titles has plunged dramatically. Advertising income is limited because of the slow development of the private economy. Some political parties still provide subsidies.

Although nearly 250 publications are registered in Albania, at most, only about 60, 40 of them in Tirana, are actually published, which is due to extremely bad economic conditions. The only daily is *Zeri i Popullit,* representing the opposition socialists. Other important papers include *Rilindja Demokratike,* the ruling democratic party's paper, which appears four days a week, *Alternativa SD,* and *Republika.* All papers except *Koha Jone* and *Gazeta Shqipetare* are affiliated with political parties.

In Bulgaria, there are more than 1,000 publications, many of them provincial newspapers. It is typical for a large city to have five dailies and weeklies, while Sofia alone has 60. Former communists have founded and edited some successful newspapers, perhaps using money the party had once squirreled away somewhere. The most widely circulated paper since 1992 has been the tabloid *24 Chasa* (24 hours), selling most of its copies on the street. It mixes sin and sex with in-depth political commentary, as does its sister weekly, *168 Chasa.* Although nominally independent, the paper was most successful (up to 300,000 copies) when it was attacking the Union of Democratic Forces government. *24 Chasa* was so popular for a while that it had to raise advertising prices substantially to control the demand of advertisers. The voices of the political parties, such as *Duma* (Socialist Party), *Demokratsiia* (Union of Democratic Forces), and *Svoboden Narod* (Liberal Democratic Party) have seen their circulations shrink drastically to well under 100,000 so that now they serve little more than the party faithful. Only Sofia newspapers and one published in Plovdiv (*Denyat*) circulate nationwide. The Turkish minority, perhaps as large as a million, is served by the weekly *Prava i Svobodi* in both Bulgarian and Turkish language editions. There is also a weekly, *Tsiganite,* for the country's nearly 300,000 Romany.

Readers can find almost anything in the press in Romania. Its best-selling daily (700,000 copies), *Evenimentul Zilei,* offers a combination of sex, politics, investigative reporting, and strong antigovernment comment. In that kind of climate, serious, objective, fact-based newspapers can hardly be heard. The main independents are *Adevarul* (87,000 copies) and *Romania Libera* (148,000). Party newspapers have limited circulation.

There are six daily newspapers in Slovenia, *Delo, Slovenske Novice, Dnevnik, Republika, Vecer,* and *Slovenec.* The first two are put out by the same company and produced by the same journalists, but one is a serious paper and the other tabloid in style. Five of the newspapers are published in Ljubljana, with only *Vecer* published in Maribor. All are independent, though state-owned and subsidized, with the exception of *Slovenec,* owned by the Christian Democratic party, and the private *Primorski Dnevnik.* Together, the six papers produce about 250,000 copies for a population of 2 million, with *Vecerno Delo* leading the way with 90,000 copies.

Croatia has three main daily newspapers, along with several regional ones and 30 local newspapers. The tabloid *Vecerniji List* in Zagreb has had a press run as high as 250,000. *Novi Vjesnik,* the country's most serious daily, probably sells no more than 30,000 copies. For a time, *Slobodna Dalmacija* achieved fame as an opposition paper, but it has been taken over by the government.

Supply shortages produced by the economic blockade of Serbia drastically reduced the circulation of newspapers there. *Vecernje Novosti,* a tabloid, saw its circulation slashed by 80 percent to 70,000 copies in the second half of 1993. The independent-minded *Borba* also fell by 80 percent to 7,500. Also important is *Politika,* once a model for independence, but today a loyal servant of the government in Belgrade. Two printed publications regularly criticize the Serbian government. One is the longtime Belgrade daily, *Borba,* and the other is the weekly *Vreme.* The Serbian government closed down all Albanian media in the province of Kosovo in 1990, so that the overwhelmingly Albanian population there has had hardly any media of its own.

In Macedonia there are two dailies, *Vecer* (20,000 copies) and *Nova Makedonija* (16,000). The former is a local Skopje paper with a tabloid orientation, while the latter, with a strong news orientation, serves the whole country. There are also thrice-weekly papers in Albanian (*Flaka e Vlazerimit*) and Turkish (*Birlik*).

Only one newspaper, *Oslobodenje,* has continued to publish during the fighting in Bosnia-Herzegovina. Its 5,000 daily copies do not circulate much beyond Sarajevo.

ELECTRONIC MEDIA

The difficult economic and material condition of the Southeastern European countries means that radio and TV are the chief sources of news, education, and entertainment.

The Romanian revolution of 1989 that overthrew communist dictator Nicolae Ceausescu was said to have been decided in the battle for the television studio. In the flush of victory, the newscasters apologized for having lied for 40 years and said they wouldn't do it again. But in Romania and most of the Southeastern European countries, TV has been usually speaking the government's truth. Private radio stations in many cases have broken the state monopoly on broadcasting, but most pay little attention to news. Unusual is the Romanian public radio whose credibility is consistently higher than television and newspapers.

Albanian Radio Television is a state institution controlled by parliament through a board of specialists. There is one television channel broadcasting 12 hours a day. There is no private television for both legal and economic reasons. Some people watch Italian television broadcasting across the Adriatic. There are two domestic state radio stations, one broadcasting 19 hours a day, the other 6. There is no private radio.

Television is still primarily state owned and run in Bulgaria. The first private TV station, Nova Televiziya, began test broadcasts in July 1994. There are two state-owned channels. They are separate organizations so that there is a small element of competition. The first private regional station, Rodopi, went on the air in early 1994 with two hours of programming daily. The state owns two channels of national radio. The country already has several dozen private radio stations. All the private media must compete for advertising if they are to survive.

In Romania, there are two public television channels and three public radio stations. Several companies hold private broadcasting licenses. The first two channels are both part of Televisiunea Romana. The first channel reaches 98 percent of the country, while the second reaches only 30 percent. The private commercial channels in Bucharest are TV Sigma and Amerom, RTI, CMC, and Antena 1; other channels, such as TV Intact, Soti, and Teleuniversitea broadcast on the same channel as Antena 1. There are 82 licensed private radio stations and 50 private, local television stations. Cable television is most developed in western Romania. Nearly 200 cable TV license have been issued in the country, but not all of them are operational.

Slovenia's media-rich environment features 20 radio stations and 4 national television channels, 2 of which are government owned. Six privately owned regional TV channels could go on the air as early as the end of 1994.

There are two national television channels in Croatia under the control of state-owned Hrvatska Radiotelevizija, along with several independent local television stations. They are joined in broadcasting by 3 state-run national radio channels and 30 local radio stations.

The most watched TV station in Serbia, Belgrade Television, and its supervising organ, Radiotelevizija Srbije, are controlled by the government. That is important when nearly two of every three Serbs say they depend on television for news, compared to 12 percent for radio and 11 percent for newspapers, even when a third of the population says it distrusts TV news. This was a result of the government's replacing most of the main editorial personnel when it seized control of the state broadcasting system in July 1991. In addition to four state-controlled TV stations in Serbia and Montenegro, there are several smaller independent stations.

Two thorns in the side of Serb leader Slobodan Milosevic in Serbia have been Radio B-92 and Television Studio B. The stations promote political dialogue, the protection of minorities, and antiwar demonstrations, all while lacking an official broadcast license. Their signals cannot be received much beyond Belgrade, however, so authorities seem not to mind that they continue broadcasting. In Bosnia-Herzegovina, radio was far and away the most important medium during the fighting. With distribution and supply routes blocked for newspapers, and electricity lacking for television broadcasting and reception, radio proved itself the most vital medium.

Macedonian broadcasting is almost all in the hands of the state. Makedonska Televizija offers three TV channels, and Makedonska Radio provides three radio programs. There are a few local TV stations which broadcast mostly films, and two private radio stations. Native-language programming is provided regularly for Macedonia's large minorities, including Albanians, Turks, Romany, and Vlachs. There are at least a dozen small private radio stations, but equipment is limited.

There is some limited cable broadcasting in all of the Southeastern European countries.

NEWS SERVICES

In almost all of Southeastern Europe, government press agencies operate, often with the same names they had under communist rule. Some of them, however, such as the Bulgarian Telegraph Agency (BTA), have adopted a somewhat nonpartisan and analytical style of reporting to make their product attractive to media institutions of all political persuasions. Among the agencies are ATA in Albania and Rompress in Romania. Each of the republics of the former Yugoslavia has a news agency, for example, HINA in Croatia. Some Croatian journalists founded a small independent news agency, AIM. Tanjug, once a widely respected news agency, is today notable for its pro-Serbia reporting and commentary. Romania has at least six private agencies, the most important of which are A. M. Press, Mediafax, and R. Press.

GOVERNMENT–MEDIA RELATIONS

In none of the Southeastern European countries can press–government relations be considered good. Most of the governments make use of a combination of political, economic, and legal pressures to try to muzzle the press, with varying success. The governments exercise control in particular over broadcasting, with broadcasting chiefs and regulatory boards appointed by some combination of president, government, and parliament.

In Albania, the government forced through a law that makes the printing of false information a crime, with fines of up to $8,000 if an individual is convicted. Another clause in the law makes it a crime to reveal state secrets. The government quickly employed the law to arrest a journalist from *Koha Jone* and sentence him and his editor to prison, only to release them on International Press Day in 1994.

In Bulgaria, government actions threatened the media economically and politically. Most Bulgarian newspaper journalists went on strike for four days at the end of March 1994 to protest a value-added tax of 18 percent that applied to newspapers, the highest rate in East Central and Southeastern Europe. The tax posed a direct economic threat to the newspapers' survival. The strikers were joined by their colleagues in private radio. Bulgarian TV fired its leading investigative reporter at the end of 1993 after she made too many enemies in government and parliament by her reports of corruption. She joined the directors of the two television news programs on the sidelines. The government has also placed police and security officials in the Radio-TV building in Sofia.

In most of former Yugoslavia, the government maintains strict control of most of the media. Slovenia is something of an exception, where younger journalists, strongly influenced by their Western European neighbors, have resisted affiliation with political parties and, therefore, pressure from the government. The government also has resisted the temptation of greater media control for fear of jeopardizing its chances of becoming part of the greater part of Europe. That many journalists in Slovenia have pulled their punches has made the government less likely to intervene, too.

No such fears have affected the Croatian government of Frano Tudjman, which has used administrative means to crack down on critical voices in the press. When some outspoken newspapers were transferred from government to private ownership, it made sure that boards of directors of the winning bids for ownership shared the views of the government. In the case of the satirical *Feral Tribune,* it declared the publication pornographic and thus subject to a 50 percent tax. The state holds virtual monopolies on printing and distribution.

The Serbian government holds a dominant position in the new shrunken Yugoslavia. Independent sources can reach only limited audiences but are harassed nonetheless. Independent newspapers, such as the daily *Borba* and the weeklies *Vreme* and *NIN,* however, have been able to maintain a degree of independence. The Serbian government chose a more creative route to attack *Borba* when it froze the price of the paper at the same time that the rate of inflation was 20 percent daily!

More than 40 journalists have been killed covering the fighting in the former Yugoslavia. Another 20 or so are missing.

CONCEPTS OF MEDIA FREEDOM

Some observers argue that the media in the former Yugoslavia played a major role in the outbreak of fighting. At best, that is a vast oversimplification; at worst, it is wrong. Almost all of the media in the former Yugoslavia were based in and circulated or broadcast to the individual republics into which the country was divided. The media reflected rather than caused the deep divisions that led to the breakup of the country and the fighting that subsequently developed. The majority of journalists placed patriotic loyalty to their country higher than commitment to balanced presentation of the news. Some journalists and media institutions objected, but they were slowly subjected to both public and state pressure. Censorship and other wartime conditions have only exacerbated the situation. Despite all of these difficulties, more than two of every three Croatians say domestic media coverage of their country is good.

Many of the Balkan countries have taken passages from existing Western European media legislation and adopted them for their own. The problem is that some elements of these laws, very restrictive of the media, are no longer used in Western Europe even if they remain on the books. In Albania, for instance, the media law provides for jail terms measured in years for journalists who criticize the president, the parliament, or visiting representatives of foreign countries. In Romania, it is illegal to insult, slander, or threaten the president or other government officials, including the police and the military. Romanian journalists have no juridical protection and they are not guaranteed access to information.

In the spring of 1994, the Serbian government banned both Cable News Network (CNN) and the Agence France-Press from the country. It also ousted some foreign correspondents, charging them with distorting news about the Serb role in the Yugoslav wars.

What continues to dominate in Southeastern Europe is opinion-oriented journalism. This is true to such an extent that party political newspapers often carry more information than so-called independent newspapers. Most of these countries do not have stable political situations, and new groupings appear regularly, demanding publicity. Under these conditions, media autonomy is difficult.

MEDIA ECONOMICS AND SPECIAL PROBLEMS

The state is still the dominant player in Southeastern Europe when it comes to supplying newsprint and distributing printed copies. In many cases it also controls prices of such necessities as electric power and heat. That means the economic well-being of the media often depends on the state's good will. The dependence is heightened by the lack of advertising in most Southeastern European countries. Struggling businesses of every size do not find it financially worthwhile to advertise. Some newly founded private businesses do not advertise because they are not legally registered and paying taxes and do not want authorities to notice.

Inflation (which reached 50,000 percent a month in Serbia) and the lack of capital for investment only magnify the problems. More and more citizens in Southeastern Europe cannot afford to buy newspapers. Recently, for instance, a citizen in Macedonia had to pay the equivalent of 25 cents for a newspaper at a time when the average monthly salary was only 78 dollars. In Croatia, even in the best of times, only one in ten households buys a newspaper. In Bulgaria, the only media that do not have to worry about the market are owned by banks and industries.

JOURNALISM EDUCATION AND TRAINING

A wide variety of approaches to journalism education is seen in Southeastern Europe. They include large programs at leading universities, developing programs at regional universities, and several private institutions, including one founded on a U.S. model.

Most journalists in Albania have not studied journalism, because under communism, journalism education was only offered in the years 1968–1974. A journalism program was established at Tirana University in 1992, but only one of its five professors has any journalism experience.

Bulgaria has two programs, a large journalism and mass communication program at Sofia University, founded in 1952, and a newly founded journalism major at the American

University of Bulgaria in Blagoevgrad. The New Bulgarian University has also begun to organize a program. The AUBG program, which will graduate its first class in 1995, admits about 25 students a year. It is a U.S.-type program, organized by the University of Missouri. The Sofia program is more academic in nature, with 800 regular undergraduate students.

Romanian journalism education is dominated by the School of Journalism and Mass Communication Science at the University of Bucharest, with more than 300 students. Some 500 other students are enrolled in journalism programs or courses in six state and private universities and three other nonuniversity institutions. Joining Bucharest with full-fledged programs are universities in Timisoara and Sibiu.

Slovenia averages about 100 students a year in the Department of Communication of the School of Social Sciences at the University of Ljubljana, which features a Western European type of journalism education. In Croatia there is a single program, located in the School of Political Science, enrolling about 100 students a year.

PROSPECTS FOR THE FUTURE

Southeastern Europe is characterized primarily by a mixed system of freedom, where most newspapers are now in private hands and committed to making a profit, and authoritarianism, where the government still has the power, through legal, economic, and political means, of intervening in the operations of the media and has particular influence in over-the-air broadcasting. Greater independence of the media from state control will require economic growth throughout society. That's most likely to happen in Slovenia, where the media will look more and more like the East Central European media, and least likely to take place in mountainous, poverty-stricken Albania. The other countries fall somewhere in between. Readers and viewers have tired of the political fusillades and prefer media that offer sensationalism and entertainment. They have limited trust in their media. It will be decades before there is substantial improvement.

A special situation exists in the war-torn countries of Serbia, Croatia, and Bosnia-Herzegovina. In the first two cases, independent-minded journalists struggle with restrictions on many media institutions and have continued to support a few opposition newspapers. In both Serbia and Croatia, the media will benefit as the economy rebounds and governments concentrate more on economic issues. But the experience of the war will remain a part of journalists' outlook far into the future, casting much of the political content of the media in national terms.

Russia and the Newly Independent States

The media in the countries that used to be part of the Soviet Union face a three-fold challenge. First, they are changing from control by a totalitarian power to some kind of different political arrangement, usually more democratic than in the past. Second, they must address their economic fate. In the past, the media and the communist party financially supported each other. Now they face a more market-based system. Third, they face transformation from a centrally controlled imperial power whose lingua franca was Russian and whose most important media were in Russian to one of national independence where there are competing pulls of professionalism and nationalism. Even in Russia media exist for the first time in a national state.

The results in the different parts of the former Soviet Union have been dramatically different. The Baltic media of Estonia, Latvia, and Lithuania have begun to look most like Western European media. The Ukrainian media have been afflicted with the same economic and national problems that entire country has undergone. Three Central Asian countries (Tajikistan, Uzbekistan, and Turkmenistan) have retained strong elements of authoritarian control, while in Kazakhstan and Kyrgyzstan the media are not as tightly controlled. Fighting has wracked the Transcaucasian republics of Azerbaijan, Armenia, and Georgia, leaving little room for autonomous action on the part of the media. The republics of Belarus and Moldova have been split between Russian or Russian-speaking populations who do not want to be split off from Russia and the Belarusian and Moldovan titular nationalities.

HISTORICAL HIGHLIGHTS

The precommunist history of the press of Russia and the newly independent states is one of development limited by authoritarianism or foreign control. As part of Peter the Great's effort to have the state take a more active role in Russian life, he created *Vedomosti* (1702–1727). Long celebrated as the first Russian newspaper, *Vedomosti* was, in the words of Gary Marker, "more a perpetual celebration of governmental authority and military glory than a newspaper in any modern sense." (1985, p. 27). Russian newspapers did not begin to become influential until the "Great Reforms" of Alexander II, who became tsar in 1855. Especially important was a significant easing of censorship in 1865. Still, when the tsar was assassinated in 1881, only about 23,000 single issues of various periodicals were sold on Russian streets daily.

During the last three decades of rule by the Romanovs, the printed word in Russia exploded, driven by rapid urbanization, improvements in education, and an increasingly pluralist society. Journalists for the mass circulation press sought to find out and publish facts, to develop codes of ethics, form a union, and organize schools of journalism. *Gazeta kopeika*, which promised the world each day for a kopeck, was a St. Petersburg tabloid aimed at the city's newly literate lower class. Founded in 1908, its circulation had reached 250,000 by the following year. Ivan Sytin, an entrepreneur as successful as Joseph Pulitzer or William Randolph Hearst, piloted *Russkoe slovo* to the million mark in circulation by 1917. While the communists would later glorify the prerevolutionary impact of such political newspapers as *Pravda* and *Iskra,* they were in fact as insignificant at the time as hundreds of other small political newspapers.

Early Baltic newspapers appeared under the strong influence of their German, Swedish, and Polish overlords. The history of Estonian and Latvian journalism until 1850 was closely connected with the development of the Baltic German community. Latvian press historians disagree whether the first paper in present-day Latvia was *Rigische*

Novellen (1681) or *Rigische Montags (Donnerstags) Ordinari Post Zeitung* (1680). The first regular newspaper in Estonia was *Revalsche Post-Zeitung* (1689-1710). Latvian and Estonian language papers came later, owing to the delayed development of a native-language intelligentsia. The first Estonian publication was *Tarto maa-rahwa Naddali-Leht,* founded in 1806. The first Latvian-language paper was *Latviesu Avizes,* published in Jelgava beginning in 1822. The first newspaper in Lithuania was the Polish-language *Kurier Litewski* (1760-1763). Then came newspapers in French, German, Russian, and Yiddish. Apparently, the first regularly published Lithuanian weekly in Lithuania was *Lietuviskas Prietelis,* founded in 1849. Rising nationalism and renewed political activity released in the Baltics in the 1870s as part of Alexander II's reforms contributed to the growth of the native-language press. During the interwar period of Baltic independence, a party-oriented press thrived.

Because the Russian rulers disparaged a separate Ukrainian identity, it was difficult for Ukrainian media to develop under the tsars. Greater progress was made in Galicia under Habsburg rule. In Central Asia and Belarus, there was little significant media activity until the twentieth century. Russia introduced print technology to central Asia. Newspapers founded by the Jadid reform movement first appeared in Turkestan in 1905; the first newspaper in a central Asian language was printed under Russian control. The Jadid papers all had died by 1908 because of government interference, financial problems, and illiteracy. The Kazakhs were more successful, with several periodicals appearing after 1905, with one reaching a circulation of 8,000.

When the Bolsheviks came to power in 1917, the overwhelming majority of the people that came to be included in the Soviet Union were out of reach of the mass media. Many were illiterate. Poorly developed infrastructure meant that distribution of newspapers was difficult. What became the Soviet Union at the beginning was a primarily rural society whose peasants saw little need for the media. Radio was the first medium to gain an important role throughout society. It was not until the 1960s and 1970s that the printed Soviet word began to reach the broad range of people. The Soviet journalists who wrote for these publications had multiple roles: ideological warrior, literary craftsman, publicist, investigative reporter, citizen's friend, and member of the collective. The most important newspapers were the all-Union papers, such as *Pravda* and *Izvestiya,* whose circulations climbed past 10 million. Journalism was designed to serve the party through a complex system of appointments, rewards, party control, and censorship.

When *glasnost* came in 1985, only a few Soviet media institutions responded at first. Eventually, though, journalism helped to open up Soviet society under Mikhail Gorbachev by rewriting history, exposing corruption and inefficiency, and promoting debate and discussion. *Glasnost* meant more timeliness, an expansion in the news agenda, more factual information, more human interest, and more "moderately negative" stories. Outside Moscow and in the non-Russian republics, the extent of openness in the press depended on the local party and government leadership. The Baltic republics used the opportunities to promote national patriotism. Central Asian leaders saw *glasnost* as an attack from outside, a threat to their power, although they grudgingly allowed some domestic openness. The tension was exemplified by a 1990 article in a Moscow newspaper showing the high rate of infant mortality in Turkmenistan.

The head of the Turkmen Young Communists demanded the newspaper's office in Turkmenistan be closed and asked readers to cancel the subscriptions. The Union of Journalists supported the action.

PRINT MEDIA

There are five types of national newspapers in Russia. Fewest in number are the independent papers, such as *Moscow News, Nezavisimaia gazeta,* and *Segodnia.* Also relatively few in number are the commercial newspapers, such as *Kommersant* and *Delovoi Mir.* Most prominent are the progovernment newspapers, including *Komsomolskaya pravda,* the country's most widely circulated newspaper (2.6 million subscribers), *Trud* (2,386,000), and *Izvestiya* (750,000), the last-named having become the closest thing to a newspaper-of-record. *Izvestiya* has launched weekly supplements devoted to financial news and television. A separate category of newspapers is made up of government newspapers, such as *Rossiiskaya gazeta* (1,067,000) and *Rossiiskiie vesti* (524,000). There are also opposition newspapers, most prominently *Pravda* (218,000), *Sovetskaia Rossiia* (110,000), and *Iuridicheskaia gazeta.* It doesn't take much imagination to figure out what another popular publication, *Skandali,* publishes. Local newspapers are increasingly important. The best example is *Moskovskii komsomolets,* whose Moscow circulation exceeds all other local dailies combined. Two-fifths of Moscow's inhabitants say they read it for its detailed reporting of the economic, political, and social life of the Moscow region. Women and older people tend to support the established press, while younger readers gravitate toward the new and more liberal papers. One of every seven Muscovites reads every issue of *SPID-Info,* a weekly whose title suggests a commitment to providing information about AIDS. In St. Petersburg, the former communist youth newspaper *Smena* has the largest circulation, 300,000.

A survey of Moscow political elite showed that *Izvestia* was the most widely read paper, being read regularly by 35 percent of the respondents. Other top papers were *Nezavisimaya gazeta* (30 percent), *Kommersant-Daily* (28 percent), *Moskovskii komsomolets* (25 percent), *Pravda* (22 percent), and *Rossiiskaya Gazeta* (21 percent).

The Estonian mass media are among the most vibrant in all of the former Soviet Union. There are 7 national daily newspapers, along with 16 local papers published two to five times a week, with an average circulation of 11,200. The largest daily is *Postimees* (74,000) of Tartu, the only national newspaper not published in the capital of Tallinn. *Rahva Haal* claimed a circulation of 64,000 in 1993, but the following year was racked by a struggle for control, with the result long uncertain. Another important paper is *Paevaleht.*

Latvia has six national and five local daily newspapers. The most important are *Diena* (81,000 copies in Latvian and 18,000 in Russian), *Neatkariga Cina* (90,000 Latvian), *SM-Segodnia* (65,000 Russian) and *Rigas Balss* (36,000 Latvian and 19,000 Russian). There are four main dailies in Lithuania: *Lietuvas Rytas* (118,000, and read by 38 percent of the population at least once a week), *Respubliks* (85,000), *Lietuvas Aidas* (60,000), and *Tiesa.*

In 1994, *Silski Visti,* a paper for farmers, had more subscriptions (312,000) than any other Ukrainian newspaper, but a tiny figure compared to the country's population of more than 50 million. It was followed by *Holos Ukrayiny* (250,000), *Uryadovyy Kuryer* (182,000), *Kiyevskiye Vedomosti* (150,000), *Ukrayina Moloda* (81,000), *Pravda Ukrayiny* (79,000), *Molod Ukrayiny* (70,000), and *Nezavisimost* (55,000). In the past, Russian newspapers were widely read, especially in eastern Ukraine, but the perilous Ukrainian financial situation means many readers can no longer afford to subscribe to such publications as *Argumenty i fakty, Komsomolskaya pravda,* and *Trud.* In 1993, only 9.8 percent of Ukrainian readers subscribed to Russian newspapers, compared to 30.4 percent for central Ukrainian newspapers and 59.8 percent for Ukrainian local publications.

The Republic of Belarus owns nine major newspapers accounting for 80 percent (1.5 million copies) of press circulation. The largest circulation newspaper is *Narodnaya Hazeta* (600,000), published in both Russian and Belarusian. *Sovetskaya Belorussia,* a Russian language paper whose name carries old-time symbolism, now prints 305,000 copies. Because most people prefer to read in Russian, rather than the previously restricted Belarusian, Belarusian newspapers have fewer readers. In 1992, Russian newspapers outsold Belarusian papers by more than ten to one. The most successful Belarusian paper is *Zvyazda* (220,000). *Vecherny Minsk* has wide appeal in the capital city. The literary weekly *Literatura i Mastaztva* reaches 14,000 subscribers. The independent opposition paper *Svaboda* publishes only 20,000 copies weekly in Belarusian. Several newspapers from Russia are still widely read in Belarus, including *Argumenty i fakty* and *Izvestiya.*

Economic crisis has gripped the media of the last western republic, Moldova. Circulation dropped by a factor of ten between 1990 and 1992. It continued to fall in 1993. Some daily newspapers only appear three, four, or five times a week. *Sfatul Tarii,* the most professional and widely circulated of the country's papers (circulation 60,000 in 1992) has occasionally gone weeks without publishing. The second most important Moldovan paper is *Moldova Suverana* (30,000 in 1992). The leading state-owned Russian-language paper is *Nezavisimaya Moldova.* There is also a tabloid daily *Vechernii Kishinev,* most of whose copies are in Russian, and a city daily, *Dnestrovskaya pravda* in Tiraspol. New Russian papers include several business weeklies.

Monitoring the press of Transcaucasia and Central Asia is difficult because travel there is limited and very few copies of local papers are exported. In late 1992, Armenia, whose economy has been devastated by war with Azerbaijan, had almost 60 newspapers, most of them belonging to opposition parties who had external resources to provide newsprint and printing presses. There are several dozen unofficial newspapers in Azerbaijan representing a broad range of political points of view, but only 20 of 600 registered papers were publishing in early 1994. The 20 included the government newspapers *Azerbaijan, SES, Meydan,* and *Ekran-Efir.* There are two Turkish papers, including a daily *Zaman,* in special editions in the capital of Baku. It is difficult to tell whether the Russian-language *Bakinsky rabochii* or the opposition *Azadlyg* are still publishing. A special challenge in Azerbaijan is the decision to switch from the Cyrillic to the Latin alphabet. Georgian papers are mostly supporting the government of Eduard Shevardnadze, the former Soviet foreign minister. Principal Georgian newspapers are *Akhalgazrda Iverieli, Eri, Iberia Spectrum, Respublika, Sakartvelos Respublika, Tavisupali Sakartvelo,* and *Vestnik Gruzii.*

One survey of media in Turkmenistan reported there were 70 newspapers, virtually all controlled by official organizations of the ruling Democratic party, the successor to the Communist party. No specific information is available. Officially, Uzbekistan in 1990 reported 279 newspapers. Many no longer publish, including the opposition *Birlik* of the Birlik Popular movement. The most important paper is *Ozbekistan Avazi,* representing the ruling party. *Pravda vostoka,* the main Russian language daily during the communist period, is apparently still publishing by avoiding attacks on the government. Uzbekistan also has papers in Greek, Ukrainian, Tajik, and Karakalpak. Data for 1990 reported 74 newspapers in Tajikistan. Civil war in 1991–1992 clouded the picture.

The freest press in central Asia is in Kazakhstan, with an especially wide range of publications in the capital city of Almaty. The two most respected newspapers in the country are the Russian language *Kazakhstanskaya pravda* and its Kazakh-language equivalent *Egemen Qazakstan.* Also popular are two papers of the country's parliament, *Sovety Kazakhstana* in Russian and *Halyk Kenesi* in Kazakh. There are also many independent publications reflecting a broad political spectrum as well as special interest publications, especially in business.

Nearly as free has been the Kyrgyz press. The most prominent papers are *Slovo Kyrgyzstana* in Russian and *Kyrgyz Tuusu* in Kyrgyz. Other prominent titles are *Svobodnie Gory, Bishkek Shamy,* and *Vechernii Bishkek.* The Kyrgyz language daily with the largest circulation is *Aalam* (20,000 copies).

ELECTRONIC MEDIA

Television is particularly important in Russia, a country whose size makes distribution of a national newspaper difficult. Only 50 percent of Muscovites, and 36 percent of people in European Russia outside Moscow read newspapers daily, making radio and television increasingly important in the media mix. Two state-owned stations dominate Russian television. One is Russian TV, essentially a state network. The other is Ostankino TV, formerly Soviet TV. Neither one could raise the more than $100 million a year it would require to be independent. Together they broadcast on four channels, including one educational program. In mid-1994, Ostankino reduced its broadcast day as an economy measure. St. Petersburg has its own channel, broadcast in some other parts of Russia, including Moscow. Moscow has a channel, too. TV-6, a joint U.S.–Russian project, offers still another channel. An independent television station called NTV, and featuring some of Russia's most respected journalists, began broadcasting on the fourth channel of Russian television in January 1994, featuring entertainment, game shows, cartoons, and foreign films.

To some degree, the cultural uplift of broadcasting is a thing of the past. Soap operas, especially from third-world countries, are the most popular programs on Russian television. But two of the most-watched programs are "Vesti" and "Novosti," the main evening news programs of the two networks.

Radio broadcasting in Moscow is dominated by rock-oriented stations. There are no ratings services to measure radio listenership, so it's impossible to know how many people are listening to each station. Many Moscow residents think the best of the bunch is Ekho Moskvy, which first gained widespread public attention for its coverage of the attempted Soviet crackdown in the Baltic republics in January 1991 and of the failed coup attempt seven months later.

Estonia boasts 16 local radio stations, 8 of which are privately owned. Four of the radio programs come from official Estonian Radio. The most popular private radio stations are Radio Kuku and Radio Tallinn. Similarly, half of the eight television stations are in private hands. Estonians can also watch Finnish TV, because their languages are similar. ETV is the state television service. Most of its broadcasting is in Estonian, with 2.5 percent of the broadcast time given over to Russian. RTV, originally a commercial agency, broadcasts five hours each Saturday and Sunday. Since August 1993, EVTV has been on the air 28 hours a week, with entertainment shows and CNN broadcasts. The newest entry is Kanal Kaks, a joint U.S.–Estonian undertaking that has visions of expanding its service to Helsinki, St. Petersburg, and Latvia.

Latvia's national TV is state-owned, but there are private regional stations dependent on advertising. The country has two state radio stations and five or six private FM stations. The second state radio station broadcasts in Russian to the country's Russian inhabitants and also carries various foreign services, including Voice of America, Radio Free Europe, Radio Sweden, and Deutsche Welle. Latvian television includes a two-channel state broadcaster and 36 commercial stations. The state service is hampered by serious financial problems. The largest independent station is NTV-5, which broadcasts to a 40-mile radius from Riga.

Lithuania has 30 television stations, 29 of which, mostly regional, are private. Tele-3 is a nationwide private station that mostly rebroadcasts foreign satellite channels whose presence is not liked by the state network. Lithuanian radio also competes against private stations, three of which broadcast nationwide. Surveys report that two of the private stations, Radiocentras and M-1, attract more listeners than does the state service. Radio Vilnius broadcasts in Lithuanian, Russian, Polish, English, Yiddish, Belarusian, and Ukrainian.

Ukrainian television includes two national channels with separate studios in 23 districts. About a thousand companies have been registered to produce TV programs, but most are not on the air. There are about 200 local commercial TV stations on the air, with as many as five local stations in some cities. Some of them have formed small networks, such as Unika and Tonis. The higher professional quality of Russian TV means it still has many viewers in Ukraine, especially among the dominant Russian population in eastern Ukraine. There are four national radio stations.

The National State TV-Radio Company of Belarus attracts only a small number of viewers because many of them prefer the more professional Russian-language broadcasts from Russia. The Belarusian State Television and Radio Company owns one TV channel and four national and seven regional TV stations. There are ten or so small independent TV stations, but they reach only a few villages or groups of high-rise apartment buildings. MM 4, an independent TV company, used to broadcast to the 2 million residents of its capital Minsk, but it no longer has access to state transmitters. There are at least 200,000 cable and 100,000 satellite TV subscribers in Minsk.

The state Moldovan Television broadcasts mostly in Romanian but also has some programs in Russian. It also broadcasts weekly programs in Ukrainian, Bulgarian, and Gagauz/Turkish, for citizens who speak those languages. Two other channels broadcast programs from Moscow or Bucharest. The breakaway Transdniestr and Gagauz republics have their own channels. The state radio has separate frequencies for Romanian- and Russian-language programs. The first nonstate local radio station in Moldova went on the air in Chisinau in mid-1993, but its signal has limited reach.

Radio and television are state owned in Armenia. Their broadcasting is severely restricted by energy shortages to only a few hours a day. The TV broadcasts in both Armenian and Russian, and the radio in Armenian, Russian, and Kurdish. Azerbaijani radio and television, state owned and run, broadcast in Azerbaijani and Russian. The radio also carries programming in Arabic, Persian, and Turkish. Georgian TV and radio broadcast in Georgian and Russian, with the radio adding programming also in Armenian, Azerbaijani, Abkhazian, and Ossetian.

In Central Asia, state-owned broadcast media retain their monopolies. The Television and Radio Company of Turkmenistan broadcasts 7.5 hours of television and 16 hours of radio daily. Uzteleradio supervises radio and television in Uzbekistan, but hours of broadcast are limited. The State Radio and Television Company of Tajikistan broadcasts four channels of television in Tajik, Russian, and Uzbek to 60 percent of the population. Tajik Radio broadcasts in those languages. While the Islamic nationalist party was in control in 1990, Iranian television's evening news was available.

In Kazakhstan, the radio and television remain in state hands, managed by the Teleradio Company of Kazakhstan. It broadcasts on two TV channels. At least four private television stations are on the air in the capital: Asia TV broadcasts Turkish films and musical dramas, A/O KTK TV broadcasts mostly foreign films as well as two TV programs, TAN + TV deals with the Turks, and Tvin TV has mostly music videos and news inserts. KTK and the also available Ostankino from Moscow are the two most popular channels. Mayak (from Moscow) is the most popular radio station in Almaty (49 percent of audience), followed by Radio Max, operated by Tvin TV (43.5 percent), and Kazakh Radio's First Program (39.9 percent).

Kyrgyz TV broadcasts on only one channel for three hours a day. Two Russian channels, the Russian TV and Ostankino, are also available, and a Turkish-language TV station operates in the capital of Bishkek. Kyrgyz GYR, a video production company, buys some time over the state TV network. There are five channels of radio. Private broadcasting is limited to stations in the capital. Radio Pyramid and Radio Almas share one channel, each broadcasting four to seven hours daily in Russian.

Turkish TV is available several hours a day in most of Central Asia. Many people also watch Ostankino TV from Moscow, although some Central Asian governments, especially Uzbekistan, have clashed with Moscow over the content and the cost.

NEWS SERVICES

President Boris Yeltsin issued a decree in December 1993 turning the ITAR-TASS news agency back into a government agency after less than two years of independence. But even after it declared itself independent in the late summer of 1991, it behaved as if it were a government agency. Yeltsin has also brought another news agency, RIA-Novosti, back under government control. The first private news agencies, such as Postfactum and Interfax, founded in 1989, have continued to function. There are also several minor private news agencies, especially in the Urals and southern Russia.

Even under communist rule, all Soviet republics except Russia had their own news agencies working alongside TASS. Many of these agencies still exist and play a dominant role in supplying news to their countries' newspapers.

A Baltic News Service serves all three Baltic countries. The Estonian News Agency is the official Estonian service. In Moldova, a private (and more professional) news agency, Basapress, began in early 1993 to compete with the official news agency Moldovapres. In Belarus, the official agency Belinform has to compete against at least 10 private agencies such as Belapan, RID, and Vybranetskiya Shykhty. The official Armenpress in Armenia shares facilities with the independent agencies of Snark and Noyan Tapan. In Azerbaijan, the state's Azertac has an advantage over the persecuted service, Turan. Kazakh press agencies include Asia-Press, Kazreview, and Dana-Press. The official Kyrgyz agency is Kyrgyzkabar.

GOVERNMENT–MEDIA RELATIONS

The post-Soviet governments continue to control many of the physical needs of the media, whether printing plants, distribution systems, or transmitters. As long as economic crisis hinders the growth of the market, even independent media will often find themselves dependent on the government for subsidies. A Law on the Press was put into effect in December 1991, very similar to the liberal Soviet Law on the Press of 1990. But the law mandated that the state control broadcast media, and it offered no enforcement powers for its right-to-know provisions.

When Russian president Boris Yeltsin used tanks to oust the parliament in October 1993, he also dispatched censors to all of Moscow's main printing houses. They were quickly withdrawn. Yeltsin also ordered more than a dozen newspapers, including *Pravda,* shut down. Most of them reopened within a few weeks. Yeltsin insisted that the television program, "600 Seconds," a hard-biting news program that was increasingly offering nationalist and rightist commentary by Alexander Nevzorov, be canceled. After elections in December 1993, he fired Vyacheslav Bragin, head of Russian television, for giving too much airtime to Yeltsin opponent Vladimir Zhirinovsky during the election campaign. Yeltsin also set up a new committee for the press, not to control what newspapers print but to work out their finances, and he set up a media-monitoring unit.

Sometimes there have been struggles between parts of the government for control of media institutions. In 1992 and 1993, the Russian parliament sought to seize control of *Izvestia* while the president disagreed. Later the conflict extended to television.

Governments in almost all of the newly independent states can intervene in the press of their countries through control of monopolistic printing and distribution services. In the Baltic countries and Ukraine, this is the primary way in which the governments have intervened in media operations from time to time. In Belarus, *Svaboda,* the only independent daily, was mysteriously prevented from publishing during the election campaign in summer 1994.

The Estonian Newspaper Association, uniting 40 newspapers from all over the country, condemned the Estonian government when it fired editor-in-chief Toomas Leito of *Rahva Haal* in April 1994. The entire staff left with Leito and began publishing *Eesti Sonumid.*

In the Transcaucasian and Central Asian countries, most of the governments have pulled no punches when it comes to controlling the press. In both Azerbaijan and Georgia that was literally true when prominent government officials beat up journalists who had offended them. In July 1992, the Azerbaijani parliament passed a law on the media guaranteeing free circulation of information, but the text of the law was not published until five months later!

The government of Turkmenistan took control of all the Communist party–owned media. It censors its own press and refuses to register any opposition press. One newspaper, *Today's Turkmenistan,* founded during the *glasnost* period, still survives. Restrictions on the press in Uzbekistan are just as severe. In fact, when the opposition Birlik movement attempted to print its newspaper *Nezavisimyi Ezhenedelnik* in Russia, Uzbek police went to Moscow to harass its editors. In December 1993, the Uzbek government required all publications to reregister: Not a single independent newspaper was accepted. The journalists who worked for them are all now dead, jailed, exiled, or have retreated to private life. The better Russian papers have been banned. In the second half of 1992, the Uzbek government moved to repress opposition media in response to events in Tajikistan where pro-Islamic politicians had come into the government. The conservative communist government initially supported the development of an opposition press in Tajikistan. The opposition seized power at the beginning of a civil war that was eventually won by the original government, which then declared it would not make the same mistake again. Journalists are now harassed, arrested, tortured, and even killed. At least 17 journalists died in the civil war.

Kazakhstan has the freest media in central Asia, but the government has limited reporting on ethnic relations, an action that has been supported by the Kazakh Union of Journalists. (Forty-four percent of the population is Kazakh, compared to 36 percent Russian.) The publication of the trade union *Birlesu* has been pressured because of its defense of its Russian membership. For a while, the Russian-language *Karavan* could not be published in Kazakhstan, so it was printed in Bishkek, Kyrgyzstan. All Kazakh presses remain in state hands, as is the case in Kyrgyzstan. The Kyrgyz reputation for openness was tarnished in July 1994 when the country's president charged that the press was behaving irresponsibly and should be subject to new controls.

Many of the Central Asian countries have legislated restrictions on the subjects on which media may report, including such topics as violence or ethnic conflict, religious intolerance, pornography, or false information.

CONCEPTS OF MEDIA FREEDOM

While press freedom in the United States is grounded in the First Amendment to the U.S. Constitution and an independent judiciary, this freedom in the former Soviet Union usually belongs to the state and is subject to the whims of presidents and prime ministers. Very few people in Russia today would agree to a First Amendment approach to the mass media. In January 1994, Russian President Boris Yeltsin issued decrees on freedom of information and on the judicial resolution of media disputes. The first decree stated that state agencies, organizations and enterprises, public associations, and officials must provide any information that is of public interest. But the decree provided for no independent powers of enforcement. The second decree set up a board to assist the president in guaranteeing the rights and freedoms of citizens. It meant that an institution of the state had been charged

> to ensure that reports are objective and accurate; to uphold the principle of equal rights in the news media; to ensure the protection of the moral interests of children and young people in the news media; to uphold the principle of pluralism in news and public affairs programs on radio and television; to correct factual errors in the news media reports that affect public interests; and to issue warnings to media outlets. ("On a Judicial Board" 1984, p. 25)

The most repressive measures have been taken against the media in Central Asia and the Caucasus, even when constitutions and press laws proclaim freedom of the press. Central Asian society has no historical experience of open debate in the press. Most of the leaders (and many of the people) prefer stability and order to a free press. In Tajikistan, for instance, the government closed all independent newspapers.

MEDIA ECONOMICS AND SPECIAL PROBLEMS

Inflation, the constantly rising price of paper, and the rising cost of printing services are putting newspapers, their journalists, and readers in very difficult circumstances. The poorly developed economy means media in the Russian provinces and in the non-Russian successor states of the Soviet Union are especially beholden to sponsors, either governmental or private. From 1992 to the first quarter of 1994, the Russian government provided various printed media with nearly 33 billion rubles in subsidies. Thirty percent of the sum went to four publications: *Komsomolskaya pravda, Trud, Argumenty i fakty,* and the journal *Ogonek.* An important exception is subsidy-free *Izvestiya,* which turned a small profit in 1993 and has a waiting line for advertisers.

The best Russian journalists are leaving journalism for richer pastures in public relations (including serving as political spokespersons). The best paid journalists work for publications sponsored by entrepreneurs, businesses, or banks.

In Ukraine, delivery of newspapers costs more than all other outlays for publishing combined. Subscriptions to newspapers and magazines in Ukraine dropped 75 percent from 1992 to 1993. In November 1993, advance subscriptions for 1994 amounted to only 3.7 percent of what they had been a year earlier. Households that used to subscribe to three or four periodicals now do not buy any at all. A study of the sources of funds for the Ukrainian press in spring 1994 showed that well over half of the support came from the Communist party, the state, and industrialists, especially those in the military-industrial sector. Two smaller slices were provided by local governments and commercial sponsors. Less than 5 percent came from foreign sponsors. The remaining 10 percent was earned by the mass media itself, from advertising and other income. Readership and advertising, then, account for a very small portion of the newspapers' income. There is no newsprint factory in Ukraine, despite its large population, meaning that all supplies must be imported from Russia.

According to a winter 1994 poll, Russians distrusted the mass media more than they trusted it. But only 1 of 12 institutions, the army, was more trusted than distrusted, and the mass media finished far ahead of the president, the government, parliament, and political parties. A mid-1993 survey showed only 27 percent of the population fully trusted the press, radio, and TV. Close to half of the population of Belarus does not trust its country's media, a feeling even more widespread among the elite.

Ethnic questions, related primarily to Russians, bedevil much of the mass media in the "near abroad," as Russians refer to the non-Russian countries that used to belong to the Soviet Union. In some of the countries, Russians dominated the cities while the local ethnic group lived in the countryside. This was true of Moldova, eastern Ukraine, northern Kazakhstan, and other places. What can happen is exemplified in Moldova, where many Moldovan journalists and writers favor unification with their Romanian-speaking compatriots in Romania. But the Moldovan papers are struggling in the Russian-dominated cities. While Moldovans are generally bilingual (Romanian and Russian), the Russian inhabitants speak only Russian, so read only the Russian press. The Russian-speaking urban population generally has more money and can more easily purchase the Russian-language press. It is also easier to distribute the press in the cities as compared to the more sparsely populated countryside. Private investors generally come from the cities, too, and when they choose to invest in the media, they invest in the Russian media. No newsprint is produced in Moldova, so it is all imported from Russia, with Russian newspapers sometimes getting more favorable prices.

In the Baltic countries of Estonia and Latvia, the Russian population is especially numerous. There have not been high-quality Russian-language papers, but that is beginning to change under the pressure of market forces.

In Tajikistan, the poorest of the former Soviet republics, there is a shortage of newsprint, too, so that many newspapers could only print once a week. Fuel shortages cut off most circulation of newspapers outside of Dushanbe. Kazakhstan has to import all of its newsprint, so that rising prices of newsprint imports have led to some reduction in frequency of publication and an increase in single-copy prices. Economic factors have been the major factor limiting press development in Kyrgyzstan. In June 1992, *Slovo Kyrgyzstana* announced it would serve only annual subscribers and only with the weekend edition.

JOURNALISM EDUCATION AND TRAINING

Nearly half of Russia's journalists were educated at Moscow State University (MGU). Many of them studied at the university's School of Journalism, which dominated journalism education in the old Soviet Union. According to a survey conducted by two MGU researchers in cooperation with Indiana University, nearly 60 percent of Russia's professional journalists are graduates of either the MGU journalism school or one of about fifteen other such schools in Russia. St. Petersburg University has the second most important program.

The Department of Journalism at the University of Tartu provides journalism education in Estonia. Blessed with one of the strongest research programs in the former Soviet Union, its faculty includes one professor who is a member of the Estonian government. Three of its graduates are also in the cabinet. In Latvia the only program is located in the Department of Communication and Journalism at the University of Latvia, while Lithuania's program is located in the Institute of Journalism of the School of Communication at the University of Vilnius.

Ukraine has two journalism programs, one at the Institute of Journalism in the Taras Shevchenko State University in Kiev and the other at the Department of Journalism in the Lviv University. The Belarusian State University has the only fully developed journalism program in Belarus, staffed primarily by people from the old communist days. A similar situation applies at the School of Journalism in the Moldovan State University in Chisinau, from which one third of Moldova's working journalists have graduated.

No information is available about journalism education programs in the Transcaucasus and Central Asia. Low-quality, underfunded programs did exist there under Soviet rule.

PROSPECTS FOR THE FUTURE

The news media of Russia and the newly independent states are primarily authoritarian, a function both of the political culture and the economic situation. Only a few newspapers and television stations are self-sufficient; most depend on subsidies. There was never much of a dissident movement under communism, so social democratic approaches to the media are virtually nonexistent.

Economic growth holds the key to the future of the mass media in Russia and the newly independent states. Media institutions that can provide an independent economic base for themselves, such as *Izvestiya,* have a promising future. That seems most likely to happen soonest in the Baltic States and parts of Russia. In other parts of the area, only government funding or subsidies will keep the media alive.

Even if economic security existed, media's role as communication for politics and government is not secure. The media of central Asia, for instance, are still strongly influenced by the communist view of the press as educator and social activist whose purpose is to disseminate correct views and promote official policies and values. Even where the government has tried to be more open, such as in Tajikistan, journalists have used the media as a weapon to help destroy their opponents. The media owned by political parties is especially susceptible to intolerance. Most politicians throughout the former Soviet Union believe the media is still an important propaganda tool.

The difficult economic circumstances of the print media have made broadcasting the dominant form of mass media in the newly independent states. Governments have been generally unwilling to yield much independence to radio and TV stations, so they generally are servants of the state rather than being responsive to public needs, a factor that further hinders the development of democracy.

The final problem for mass media in Central Eurasia is nationality and ethnicity. Not only are there substantial numbers of Russians in each of the republics, but there are numerous other minorities. The different national groupings do not share the same civic space, which helps foster civil discord. Russians, in particular, have not been willing to learn the languages of the countries in which they live, thereby exacerbating ethnic conflict. Furthermore, nationality is not so easily and closely related to language in Central Asia, particularly among the elite, many of whom are Russian-educated, and among urban residents. Many Kazakhs, for instance, read only Russian.

On the one hand, the situation of the news media in Russia and the newly independent states is a bleak one because of the economic, political, and national difficulties. On the other hand, there are some bright spots. As the transition from communism to an uncertain future continues, the media will participate in and be affected by the changes.

CONCLUSION

The last days of communism were glory days for journalism in the Russian and East European area. The Communist party had lost most of its influence on the media but still paid the bills. Journalists answered to no one. Today, the first priority of the mass media in East Central and Southeastern Europe and in Russia and the newly independent states is economic survival. He who pays the piper still calls the tune. The need to turn a profit, or at least break even, means the media have to pay attention to what people will buy. Even then, people may not be able to afford to buy the printed media. On some occasions the media must reflect the nationalist outlook pervasive in some countries. In some cases, such as Russia, where most of the press is still subsidized by the government, or where the government still holds a virtual monopoly over transmitters, printing plants, and distribution networks, the media cannot ignore the government's wishes. Many journalists know how to practice investigative journalism, or how to behave ethically, but they cannot afford to practice their beliefs. If the media must pay attention first to the financial or government master, they find it difficult to fulfill the democratic role of providing diverse, objective news reports designed to create an informed electorate.

In conditions of economic hardship, the broadcast media potentially play an extremely influential role because for many citizens that is the only source of news and information. It should not be surprising that governments do everything in their power to retain control of state broadcasting networks. But even governments have difficulty when they encounter alternative media resources, such as cable or satellite television.

In the modern media world, it takes vast financial resources to found a newspaper or a TV station and then to keep it going. In the formerly communist countries, these financial resources are limited, especially when economies in transition do not yet produce much interest in advertising. These financial limitations often can be overcome only with government assistance or tainted commercial profit. Until this economic question has been resolved in each of the countries discussed in this chapter, the media will continue to be at least partially in thrall to government.

BIBLIOGRAPHY

Albright, Madeleine K. *Poland: The Role of the Press in Political Change.* New York: Praeger, 1983.

Alexeyeva, Ludmilla. *U.S. Broadcasting to the Soviet Union.* New York: Helsinki Watch, 1986.

Barghoorn, Frederick. *Soviet Foreign Propaganda.* Princeton, N.J.: Princeton University Press, 1964.

Bassow, Whitman. *The Moscow Correspondents: From John Reed to Nicholas Daniloff.* New York: William Morrow, 1988.

Benn, David W. *From Glasnost to Freedom of Speech: Russian Openness and International Relations.* New York: Council on Foreign Relations Press, 1992.

———. *Persuasion and Soviet Politics.* New York: B. Blackwell, 1989.

Brooks, Jeffrey. *When Russia Learned to Read, 1861–1917.* Princeton, N.J.: Princeton University Press, 1985.

Buzek, Anthony. *How the Communist Press Works.* New York: Praeger, 1964.

Connor, Walter D., and Zvi Y. Gitelman, *Public Opinion in European Socialist Systems.* New York: Praeger, 1977.

Curry, Jane Leftwich. *Poland's Journalists: Professionalism and Politics.* New York: Cambridge University Press, 1990.

Goban-Klas, Tomasz. *The Orchestration of the Media: The Politics of Mass Communications in Communist Poland and the Aftermath.* Boulder, Colo.: Westview Press, 1994.

Hannah, Gayle Durham. *Soviet Information Networks.* Washington: Center for Strategic and International Studies, 1977.

Hanson, Philip. *Advertising and Socialism: The Nature and Extent of Consumer Advertising in the Soviet Union, Poland, Hungary and Yugoslavia.* White Plains N.Y.: International Arts and Sciences Press, 1974.

Hester Al, and Kristina White, Editors. *Creating a Free Press in Eastern Europe.* Athens: University of Georgia, 1993.

Hollander, Gayle D. *Soviet Political Indoctrination: Developments in Mass Media and Propaganda Since Stalin.* New York: Praeger, 1972.

Hopkins, Mark W. *Mass Media in the Soviet Union.* New York: Pegasus, 1970.

Horlanus, Sepp. *Mass Media in CMEA Countries.* Prague: International Organization of Journalists, 1976.

Hoyer, Svennik, Epp Lauk, and Peeter Vihalemm, Editors. *Towards a Civic Society: The Baltic Media's Long Road to Freedom.* Tartu, Estonia: Baltic Association for Media Research, 1993.

Inkeles, Alex. *Public Opinion in Soviet Russia: A Study in Mass Persuasion.* Cambridge: Harvard University Press, 1958.

Johnson, Owen V. "Bibliography of Russian and East European Journalism," *International Communication Bulletin* 24 nos. 1–2, (Spring 1989): 13–27.

———. "The Press of Change: Mass Communications in Late Communist and Post-Communist Societies," in *Adaptation and Transformation in Communist and Post-Communist Systems* edited by Sabrina P. Ramet. Boulder, Colo.: Westview Press, 1992.

Judy, Richard W. and Virginia L. Clough, *The Information Age and Soviet Society.* Indianapolis: Hudson Institute Press, 1989.

Kaplan, Frank L. *Winter into Spring: The Czechoslovak Press and the Reform Movement 1963-1968.* Boulder, Colo.: East European Quarterly, 1977.

Katz, Zev. *The Communications System in the USSR.* Cambridge, Mass.: MIT Press, 1977.

Kenez, Peter. *The Birth of the Propaganda State: Soviet Methods of Mass Mobilization, 1917-1929.* New York: Cambridge University Press, 1985.

Kruglak, Theodore H. *The Two Faces of TASS.* Minneapolis: University of Minnesota Press, 1962.

Lendvai, Paul D. *The Bureaucracy of Truth: How Communist Governments Manage the News.* Boulder, Colo.: Westview Press, 1981.

Lenin About the Press. Prague: International Organization of Journalists, 1972.

Marker, Gary J. *Publishing, Printing, and the Origins of the Intellectual Life in Russia, 1700-1800.* Princeton N.J.: Princeton University Press, 1985.

Marx, Karl. *On Freedom of the Press and Censorship.* New York: McGraw-Hill, 1974.

Mason, David S. *Public Opinion and Political Change in Poland 1980-1982.* New York: Cambridge University Press, 1985.

McNair, Brian. *Glasnost, Perestroika and the Soviet Media.* London: Routledge, 1991.

McReynolds, Louise. *The News under Russia's Old Regime.* Princeton, N.J.: Princeton University Press, 1991.

Mickelson, Sig. *America's Other Voice: The Story of Radio Free Europe.* New York: Praeger, 1983.

Mickiewicz, Ellen P. *Media and the Russian Public.* New York: Praeger, 1981.

———. *Split Signals: Television and Politics in the Soviet Union.* New York: Oxford University Press, 1988.

"On a Judicial Board for Media Disputes Under the President of the Russian Federation." *Current Digest of the Post-Soviet Press* 46, no. 2 (9 February 1994): 25. Translated from *Rossiiskaia gazeta* (10 January 1994): 4.

Rantanen Terhi, and Elena Vartanova, *From State Monopoly to Competition: The Changing Landscape of News Agencies in Russia.* Helsinki: University of Helsinki, 1993.

Remington, Thomas F. *The Truth of Authority: Ideology and Communication in the Soviet Union.* Pittsburgh: University of Pittsburgh Press, 1988.

Robinson, Gertrude J. *Tito's Maverick Media.* Urbana: University of Illinois Press, 1977.

Ruud, Charles A. *Fighting Words: Imperial Censorship and the Russian Press, 1804-1906.* Toronto: University of Toronto Press, 1982.

———. *Russian Entrepeneur: Publisher Ivan Sytin of Moscow, 1851-1934.* Montreal: McGill-Queen's University Press, 1990.

Shanor, Donald R. *Behind the Lines: The Private War Against Soviet Censorship.* New York: St. Martin's Press, 1985.

Shlapentokh, Vladimir. *Soviet Public Opinion and Ideology: Mythology and Pragmatism in Interaction.* New York: Praeger, 1986.

Siefert, Marsha, Editor. *Mass Culture and Perestroika in the Soviet Union.* New York: Oxford University Press, 1991.

Sola Pool, Ithiel de. *Soviet Audiences for Foreign Radio.* 1976.

Spechler, Dina R. *Permitted Dissent in the USSR: Novy Mir and the Soviet Regime.* New York: Praeger, 1982.

Splichal, Slavko. *Media Beyond Socialism: Theory and Practice in East-Central Europe.* Boulder, Colo.: Westview Press, 1994.

Splichal, Slavko, John Hochheimer, and Karol Jakubowicz, Editors. *Democratization and the Media: An East-West Dialogue.* Ljubljana, Slovenia: Communication and Culture Colloquia, 1990.

Taylor, Sally J. *Stalin's Apologist: Walter Duranty, the New York Times Man in Moscow.* New York: Oxford University Press, 1990.

Welsh, William A., Editor. *Survey Research and Public Attitudes in Eastern Europe and the Soviet Union.* Elmsford, N.Y.: Pergamon Press, 1981.

chapter **11**

The Middle East and North Africa

Christine Ogan

The 1991 Gulf War can be considered the single most important event affecting the course of communication in the Middle East and North Africa. It has caused media professionals and government leaders to give serious thought to the news and information available in this region and the mechanisms for its distribution. Policymakers and citizens in many countries were concerned when the only immediate and detailed coverage of the war came from Cable News Network (CNN) and other non–Middle Eastern sources. Consequently, the time since the war has witnessed tremendous growth in the launching of satellites and the proliferation of electronically delivered information and entertainment throughout the region. It has also fostered the satellite delivery of information that circulates in print format.

In some countries of the area, trends to privatization of electronic media breaking up former government monopolies of information have paralleled the growth of satellite channels. As in the rest of the world, the Middle Eastern and North African countries have discovered that it is impossible to control the flow of information within their borders, so most of these countries are taking a serious step in the direction of allowing greater free flow of ideas—although it may be against their will in certain countries.

Before discussing the media in the Middle East and North Africa, it is first necessary to define the geographical boundaries of the region (Figure 11.1). Because there is no consensus on which countries are included in this area, the arbitrary decisions on specific countries will be somewhat based on characteristics that link them.

Geographically, these countries span three continents—Africa, Asia, and Europe. The largest part of the region is in Africa and Asia, but a small part of Turkey is in Europe. Although the bulk of the residents are Muslim, the area is also home to large Christian and Jewish populations; and in the Sudan, indigenous beliefs are prevalent among some of the people. To define the citizens as Arab would exclude the Persians, Turks,

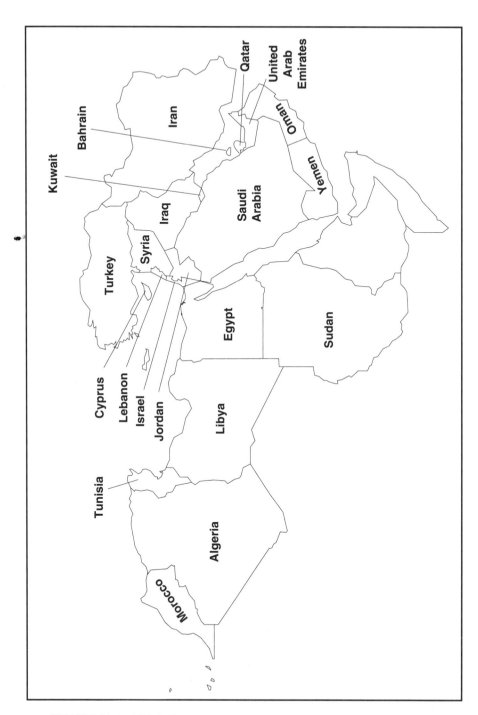

FIGURE 11.1 Middle East and North Africa

Kurds, Berbers, and non-Arab Semitic peoples. It also would exclude the Beja, Nubians, and black Africans from several ethnic groups in the Sudan. Linguistically, the citizens of the several countries are mainly Arabic speaking, but other prominent languages include Persian, Turkish, Hebrew, French, Italian, English, Kurdish, and some others. In this chapter, the discussion of the media will cover the following countries in the Middle East: Bahrain, Cyprus, Egypt, Iran, Iraq, Israel, Jordan, Kuwait, Lebanon, Oman, Qatar, Saudi Arabia, Syria, Turkey, the United Arab Emirates, and Yemen; and in North Africa: Algeria, Libya, Morocco, the Sudan, and Tunisia.

Economically, all of the countries are classified as low- or middle-income economies by the World Bank, with the exception of the oil-producing countries of Bahrain, Kuwait, Oman, Qatar, Saudi Arabia, and the United Arab Emirates. For the last year that statistics were available (1991), Sudan, Egypt, and Yemen had GNP per capita annual incomes of about $600 or less, putting them in the low-income category. The other non-oil-producing countries had 1991 per capita GNPs of between $1,000 for Morocco and $1,780 for Turkey. Qatar and the United Arab Emirates are the richest of the countries for which data were available, with per capita GNPs in excess of $12,000. Israel, classified by the United Nations (UN) as a developing country, had a 1991 GNP of nearly $12,000 (*World Development Report* 1993).

Income is one predictor of media development and penetration, but there are others. Educational level, journalistic traditions, and the nature of the political system within which the media operate are also correlated with media development.

HISTORICAL HIGHLIGHTS

Before the advent of the printing press, the bazaar, coffeehouse, and mosque served as the loci of news and information in much of the Middle East. And those places still function as important traditional communication centers alongside the modern mass media. Media scholar Majid Tehranian characterizes this as a dual system in Iran, but it works much the same way all over the Middle East (1982).

The history of the modern daily and nondaily press dates to the nineteenth century in a few countries of this region; others, such as the Gulf states, had no newspapers until the mid-1970s. In spite of the fact that all these countries (except Iran) lived under the domination of the Ottomans for more than 400 years and under the British and French following World War I, indigenous newspapers developed from an early date in several sites. The first Arab newspaper published by Arabs was the *Jurnal al-Iraq*, dating from 1816; the first Arab daily began in Beirut in 1873. And *Al-Ahram*, the influential Cairo daily that circulates nearly a million copies a day, began in the 1870s, established by two Syrian brothers. According to Turkish press scholar Hifzi Topuz (1973), the first Ottoman newspaper was the *Takvimi Vakayi*, a weekly published by Ottoman rulers in Istanbul from 1831 to 1876. The *Takvimi Vakayi* was published not only in Turkish but also in Arabic, Farsi, Armenian, and Greek. The early Arab press in the nineteenth century was primarily an official press, says William Rugh in his book *The Arab Press* (1987). That was also true of the Ottoman press of the time.

TABLE 11.1 Newspapers published in the Middle East and North Africa

Country	Population (in millions)	Literacy (%)	Dailies*	Weeklies*
Algeria	26.7	50	10	3
Bahrain	0.6	77	5	6
Cyprus	0.7[a]	95	11	NA
Egypt	56.4	48	17	30
Iran	61.2	54	11	15
Iraq	18.4	60	9	7
Israel	4.7[b]	92	26	22
Jordan	3.6	80	5	6
Kuwait	1.4	74	9	NA
Lebanon	3.4	74	39	28
Libya	4.5	64	1	5
Morocco	26.7	50	11	11
Oman	1.6	20	5	4
Qatar	0.5	76	4	6
Saudi Arabia	17.1	62	10	11
Sudan	28.3	27	2	1
Syria	13.7	64	10	10
Tunisia	8.4	65	4	15
Turkey	59.6	81	34	19
UAE	2.5[c]	68	10	6
Yemen	10.4	38	3	11

*The number of dailies and weeklies listed is approximate; latest available data were used to determine actual numbers.
NA = not available.
[a]Population is 78 percent Greek and 18 percent Turkish.
[b]Excludes population of the West bank, Gaza Strip, and East Jerusalem.
[c]Population is 19 percent Emirian, 23 percent other Arab, and about 50 percent South Asian. Other expatriates make up about 8 percent.
SOURCES: *1992 Statistical Year Book* (Paris: UNESCO, 1993); *CIA World Factbook 1992* (St. Paul, Minn.: Quanta Press, Inc., 1992); *Europa Year Book* (London: Europa Publications, 1992); *World Development Report* (New York: Oxford University Press, 1993); *The World Almanac and Book of Facts 1994* (Mahwah, N.J.: Funk & Wagnalls, 1994).

PRINT MEDIA

Generally, where literacy is high, print publication has also reached an advanced state (Table 11.1). At least 70 percent of the adult population is literate in Bahrain, Cyprus, Israel, Jordan, Kuwait, Lebanon, Qatar, and Turkey. These countries also have a relatively high level of newspaper penetration. By contrast, in the countries of North Africa, Yemen, and even in oil-rich Saudi Arabia and Oman, fewer newspapers circulate.

The exception to this generalization is Egypt, a country where less than half of the population is literate. Cairo is the largest publishing center in the Arab world and also in Africa. It is home to 17 dailies, 30 weeklies, and more than 30 other publications that publish less frequently. The environment for publishing in Egypt is quite competitive. Four major publishing houses are independent of one another and are commercial competitors.

Of course, Egypt is also a very populous nation, which partially accounts for the large number of publications. That is also true of Turkey, the largest country in the region. And Israel's very high literacy rate of 92 percent forms the audience for its 26 dailies and 22 weeklies. But tiny Lebanon, the site of a protracted civil war that lasted from 1975 to 1990, is hardly the place one would expect to find 39 dailies to serve its small population. Sources report that even when the internal strife was most fierce, about a dozen publications appeared regularly. Part of the explanation may be based on Lebanon's history as a home to the freest press in the Middle East. Though more government control has been exercised under the leadership of President Ilyas Hrawi, its tradition for strong independent journalism continues.

Partly arising from colonial tradition and partly because of the number of foreign workers in several of the oil-rich countries, the press in each of these countries includes foreign-language newspapers alongside those in the indigenous language. Israel has the widest range of foreign language publications because of the large immigrant population from Poland, the Soviet Union, Germany, Romania, and Hungary. Newspapers that are published daily, weekly, or biweekly appear in at least 11 languages in addition to Hebrew. In Arab countries with large expatriate communities and in those with strong colonial legacies, publications in English and French appear. Some of the widest circulating of these papers include the Tunisian *L'Action,* Saudi Arabia's *Arab News,* Morocco's *Le Matin du Sahara,* and Egypt's *Egyptian Gazette.*

The total number of dailies in the region ranges from 1 in Libya to 39 in Lebanon. The most influential dailies in the region are published in Turkey and Egypt, but new expatriate Saudi publications are changing the print press environment throughout the Arabic-speaking countries.

The new papers, among two dozen publications, which are rapidly gaining power and influence originate in London (Ibrahim 1992). Though the Saudi Arabian newspapers are not explicitly censored, the journalists self-censor any material critical of the Saudi government, its national friends, the Islamic religion, or that has sexual content. However, the Saudi-owned press in London writes critically about all Arab countries except Saudi Arabia and those in the Gulf. And because most Arab countries exercise some degree of control over domestic newspaper content, many readers are happy to get uncensored news in their own language. The two most influential in this group of about two dozen Saudi-owned newspapers belong to Saudi princes (Evans 1992). *Al-Hayat* is owned by His Royal Highness, Lt. General Prince Khalid bin Sultan, who is nephew to King Fahd. The other, *Ash-Sharq al Awsat* is owned by the king's brother, His Royal Highness Prince Salman. The owners deny that these papers are subsidized by the Saudi government, but rumors persist that this is so. For one thing, the resources of these newspapers are extensive, in spite of the reported losses they suffer. Editor-in-chief of *Ash-Sharq al-Awsat* is quoted as saying, "We have the biggest banks, the biggest pan-Arab trading companies, why not the biggest newspapers? Twenty years ago, we were run from Cairo radio and Mohammed Heikel of *Al-Ahram* [the most influential of Cairo's dailies]. Now it is our turn. It is our age, it is the Saudi trend." (Evans 1992, p. 16). The newspapers are based in London but printed in several international sites, including Saudi Arabia, Bahrain, Cairo, and Casablanca in the Middle East and North Africa, but also in Marseilles, New York, and Frankfurt.

The Saudis also own the United Press International (UPI) news agency, which they bought in June 1992 for $3.95 million. Though UPI was in a state of bankruptcy, the British company, Middle East Broadcasting Center, owned by another relative of King Fahd, his brother in-law, Walid al-Ibrahim, made the purchase to improve the news gathering resources of its satellite television channel.

At home, the Saudi press has shown the same restraint in covering controversial issues. In an analysis in the *Columbia Journalism Review,* Stephen Franklin (1991), a reporter for the *Chicago Tribune,* notes that the Saudi press was remarkably unchanged even by the events of the Gulf War. The news of the invasion itself was ignored for several days, and even then was described only as the "Iraqi aggression." Throughout the war, journalists followed their long-term policy of not reporting on sensitive affairs until the government has first formulated its policy regarding these affairs.

The politics of Saudi Arabia may be covered critically in the press of other Arab countries, but some writers are worried that the customary debate in the Middle East between the progressive Muslims and the Islamic clerics may be coming to an end, however, as attacks of violence have been made on writers in Egypt, Turkey, and Algeria in recent years. Concern over what the press can include and what ideas can be challenged has reached such a state that some writers have withdrawn into self-imposed exile.

Though the Arab press out of London has considerable influence in the region, several Arab dailies hold their own in domestic influence. Egypt's *Al-Ahram* and *Al-Akhbar,* with close to 1 million circulation each, continue to be counted among those papers. Though the Egyptian press is considered the most free of the Arab countries' newspapers, the government largely owns and controls all newspapers and magazines. The control by the Mubarak government has become more severe since his re-election in October 1993. In an effort to silence the voice of the Moslem Brotherhood opposition to Mubarek's rule, a new Press Syndicate law was passed in March 1993 that makes it more difficult for journalists who support the fundamentalist party to head the Syndicate. And another law proposed later in the year threatened to put the press under complete government control.

One challenge to the mainstream press in Egypt has come from a tabloid that began selling 800,000 copies a day just two months after its appearance in 1992. Though local intellectuals criticize the lurid headlines and stories of crime, gossip, and love, the paper has obviously caught on with a large number of Egyptians. The newspaper is also filled with colorful pictures but contains no details of sexual encounters. In that way it differs from tabloids common in the United States.

The other prominent press in the region has also fallen on hard times. Once the most flourishing press in the Arab World, the Lebanese press has suffered circulation declines and rising costs in the last few years (Abboud 1992). Since the civil war, the Lebanese people seem to be less interested in print publications. Some writers speculate that the problem stems from the loss of the younger audience. The average age of Beirut daily *An Nahar* readers has increased from 31 to 35 before the war to 48 to 50 following the war. But others say the purchase of a newspaper has to be weighed against the available resources a family has to spend for necessities. But competition with the increased numbers of private television and radio stations in the country is also a factor. Advertising has declined to about 20 percent of the space, insufficient for supporting a daily newspaper. The decline in readership has caused journalists to seek employment elsewhere.

In North Africa, the Algerian press has attracted a lot of attention that grew out of a democratic movement in the country beginning in 1990. More than 150 new dailies, weeklies, and magazines have come on the scene in the last four years, but the publications ran into hard times when political clashes between the Islamic fundamentalists and the more liberal government increased. In the last year and a half, the government has suspended papers more regularly for threatening the public order. Journalists in Algeria have viewed their own press as one that is more diverse and independent than that of either of their neighbors. Fouad Boughanim, editor-in-chief of *Le Soir,* an independent daily, put it this way in a December 1992 interview: "In Morocco, when the king says something, all the press sings the same tune, and in Tunisia it's pretty much the same thing, but that's still not the case here." (LaFranchi 1992, p. 14). Circulation of independently owned newspapers in Algeria has surged ahead of that of the government dailies. The most recent news about the state of the journalists working for the independent press in Algeria is less encouraging, however. Many of those journalists have been reportedly forced into exile or hiding by the Islamic fundamentalists as the conflict heats up in that country. One publisher, Omar Belhouchet of *Al Watan* newspaper, was shot at by Islamic militants and later arrested for several days.

Concern over the conservative control of the Arab press from the inside by strong fundamentalist movements and from the outside by the rich Saudi expatriate press was best expressed in a poem written by the popular Syrian poet Nizzar Kabbany,

> Long Life for you,
> You that buy women by the pound
> And buy pens by the pound.
> We don't want anything from you
> Sleep with your slave women as you please.
> Slaughter your dependents as you please.
> Blockade the nation with fire and steel.
> No one wants to take away your happy monarch.
> No one wants to steal your khalifa's headband.
> So drink the oil wine to its end,
> And leave culture to us
> *(quoted by Murphy 1994, p. 1)*

According to analysis of the problems of Arab journalists and other intellectuals in the region, the threat to democracy and to freedom of expression from conservative forces has evolved from three major events: the collapse of the Soviet Union, which had supported the more radical governments in Iraq, Libya, Syria, and Egypt; the internal conflict in the Arab countries over the Iraqi invasion of Kuwait; and the rapprochement between the Palestinians and Israel, which many Arabs do not support (Murphy 1994).

The same trend can be found in Turkey, a non-Arab country that shares the Muslim heritage with its Arab neighbors. Turkey has a thriving press with a long independent tradition, marked by intermittent clashes with government over what it might print and what was unacceptable. But the increased influence of Islamic fundamentalists can be seen in the press quite clearly of late. At the beginning of 1993, Turkey boasted 290 publishing houses and printing presses, 300 publications including four daily newspapers, about 100 unlicensed radio stations, and 30 unlicensed television stations (see broadcasting section for information on licensing changes) owned by Islamic fundamentalists (Rouleau 1993). These publications and broadcast stations' primary goal was to promote Islamic ideology.

The ongoing conflict in the southeastern part of Turkey with the Kurdish people is also reflected in activities of the press. In November 1993, all reporters from Turkish publications were ordered out of the region by the Kurdish military commander. He also banned distribution of Turkish newspapers in the area. The only newspaper to circulate in southeastern Turkey is a pro-Kurdish paper, *Özgur Gündem.*

Meanwhile, the three most widely circulating Turkish dailies, *Hurriyet, Milliyet,* and *Sabah* (each with close to half a million subscribers) are competing fiercely for circulation. Lotteries and other giveaways have led to widespread distribution of encyclopedias to Turkish homes since the start of the campaigns. Circulations of all three papers jumped to more than 700,000 following the encyclopedia giveaway. *Sabah* is said to have increased its circulation to 2 million overnight (Rugmain 1993). Its promotional scheme also includes gifts of cars and color television receivers. Expensive television commercials tout the advantages of one daily over another. Satellite delivery of these and other publications allows for localization of the papers to Turkish workers in Germany and expatriate Turks in the United States.

Of the smaller countries and territories in the Middle East and North Africa, two are interesting for their role in helping people hold onto their national identities. The Palestinian press has recently fallen on hard times with the closure after 22 years of publishing of *Al Fajr* (The Dawn) in the summer of 1993 for financial reasons, and the closure of *Al-Sha'ab* (The People) earlier in the year following the withdrawal of its subsidy from the Palestinian Liberation Organization (PLO). In spite of the loss of these important dailies, *Al Quds* (Jerusalem) continues to be a strong force, selling as many as 45,000 copies a day. Two other dailies circulate much smaller numbers of papers in the region—*Al Talia* and *Al-Nahar.* The Palestinian press has been described by Najjar (1994) as a tool for liberation, and it continues to play that role in spite of its reduced size.

ELECTRONIC MEDIA

The major changes in delivery and control of information have come through the electronic media. Though every country in this region has government-owned or controlled broadcasting systems, alternatives to state-run broadcasting are appearing in many countries. Some of these new stations are international channels, others are new domestic channels. Most of these new television stations are sent to the region by satel-

TABLE 11.2   Television receivers in the Middle East and North Africa

Country	Television Homes in 1993* (in millions)	Receivers per Person†
Algeria	1.6	1–15
Bahrain	0.2	1–2.3
Cyprus	0.2	1–3.4
Egypt	4.9	1–15
Iran	2.5	1–23
Iraq	0.6	1–18
Israel	0.7	1–4.1
Jordan	0.3	1–12
Kuwait	0.5	1–2.6
Lebanon	0.5	1–3.4
Libya	0.4	1–8
Morocco	1.7	1–21
Oman	0.3	1–1.4
Qatar	0.2	1–2.5
Saudi Arabia	4.8	1–3.5
Sudan	1.8	1–117
Syria	0.4	1–17
Tunisia	0.7	1–13
Turkey	7.2	1–5
United Arab Emirates	0.2	1–12
Yemen	NA	1–38

NA = not available.
SOURCES:
*"Growth Rate in TV Homes," *Screen Digest,* March 1993.
†*The World Almanac and Book of Facts 1994* (Mahwah, N.J.: Funk & Wagnalls, 1994).

lite. Proliferation of communication satellites has allowed information and entertainment to be delivered directly into people's homes despite regulations prohibiting such arrangements. Clever entrepreneurs have been able to bypass government authority and devise schemes for producing and disseminating content that consumers, hungry for alternatives to the limited choices previously available, are eagerly welcoming into their homes via satellite dish, master antenna, or direct microwave relay.

To be successful, satellite-delivered information needs to have a large percentage of television receivers in the target countries. As can be expected, a higher ratio of receivers per person can be found in the more affluent countries. Oman has one receiver for every 1.4 persons, while the poorest country in the region, the Sudan, has only one receiver for every 117 persons. Most countries fall in the range that might be considered one to a household or to two or three households (Table 11.2).

Despite the relatively small number of households in the region, the growth rate has kept pace with the diffusion of television receivers worldwide. The growth rate for the Middle East was 43.2 percent for the 1980–1990 decade and was projected to be 34.7 percent for the next ten years. The overall world growth rate in television households was 48.4 percent for the 1980s and is projected to be 31.7 percent for the 1990s ("World TV Households" 1993).

Aside from the government use of satellite services to receive international feeds for public broadcasting uses, no direct-to-home or cable-delivered channels existed before 1990. The launch of Arabsat 1C in February 1992 attracted many Arab clients. Observers believe that the Arab countries' view that satellite broadcasting can have a powerful effects caused 11 Arab state television channels to begin broadcast services via satellite. Several other clients, including Cable News Network International (CNNI) and Canal France International, also rent transponders on Arabsat.

The trend to Saudi domination in Arab-language publications distributed across the region can also be found in television broadcasting via satellite. The lone independent commercial satellite service in Arabic, Middle East Broadcasting Center (MBC), has been broadcasting since September 1991 and has plans for supplying the first encrypted pay channels to the region soon (Hicks 1993a). MBC is owned by two Saudis, Sheik Walid al-Ibrahim, King Fahd's brother-in-law, and Salah Kamal, a Saudi business man. Deputy chief executive Bob Kennedy claims the service reaches more than 100 million Arabic-speaking viewers (Hicks 1993b). The same concerns over the Saudi slant on news—of presenting a critical view of other Arab countries while soft peddling controversial information pertaining to Saudi Arabia—have been voiced. However, the U.S. government praised MBC coverage of the Israeli–Palestinian negotiations. MBC plans to put their new pay services on the next Arabsat satellite to be launched—a Ku band satellite that will either deliver direct to the home via dish or via microwave relay with decoder boxes in the home (MMDS). The new services are scheduled to be available beginning late 1994. Dishes can be found across the Arab world, despite laws prohibiting them in Syria, Qatar, Saudi Arabia, and some other countries.

The startup of a satellite channel to Turkey off the Eutelsat satellite from Germany by a Turkish company incorporated in Switzerland provided a direct challenge to the state-owned broadcast monopoly, the Turkish Radio and Television Corporation. Star 1, later renamed Interstar, was the first privately owned television station in Turkey with its 1990 launch. It was followed by several other private satellite services into Turkey on European satellites. At first delivered direct to homes or to master antenna systems, the channels were eventually rebroadcast terrestrially from several municipal systems. The de facto privatization of television in Turkey led to a constitutional challenge to the state broadcasting system's exclusive right to broadcasting in the country. The technological capability of circumventing the law by delivering domestic channels from an international base was impossible to prevent (Ogan 1992). As of July 1993, Turkey had no fewer than eight private channels, including a home shopping service. More channels have plans for opening, particularly after the launch of a domestic satellite. The general entertainment programming provided by these channels has made them popular in neighboring Jordan, too. Turkey is home to the most domestic privately owned channels in the region. Together with the five state-owned channels, 16 domestic broadcast choices were available at the beginning of 1994. Table 11.3 lists the satellite channels available in the Middle East and North Africa at the end of 1993.

The trend to privatization and the delivery of international channels from Europe and the United States seems to be in its early stages. What has happened in Turkey could spread rapidly to the Arab countries. The large market of Arabic-speaking consumers invites the entrepreneurial ventures of a number of broadcast

TABLE 11.3 Middle East and North African satellite channels

Channel	Startup Date	Language	Satellite	Ownership
ATV	June 1993	Turkish	Eutelsat II	Sabah Publishing Group
Dubai TV*	1992	Arabic	Arabsat 1C	UAE Government
Egyptian Satellite Channel (ESC)*	December 1992	Arabic	Eutelsat II Arabsat 1C	Egypt radio and TV Union
HBB	March 1992	Turkish	Eutelsat II	HAS Holding
Interstar	1990	Turkish	Eutelsat II	Interstar Group-Uzman Family
IRIB 1* IRIB 2*	1966	Farsi	Intelsat 602	Islamic Republic of Iran
Israel TV 1* Isreal TV 2* Israel TV 3*	NA NA NA	Hebrew Arabic	Intelsat 512	Israeli Broadcasting Corp.
Jordan Satellite Channel	NA	Arabic	Arabsat 1C	Jordanian Government
Kanal 6 Kanal Market Kanal D	March 1992 NA NA	Turkish	Eutelsat II	Plus Communications
Kuwait Space Channel*	1992	Arabic	Arabsat 1C	Kuwait Government
MBC	September 1991	Arabic	Eutelsat II	Sheik Walid al-Ibrahim
Oman TV*	1992	Arabic	Arabsat 1C	Oman Government
People's Revolution TV*	1992	Arabic	Arabsat 1C	Libyan Government
RIK*	November 1990	Greek	Eutelsat II	Cyprus Broadcasting
RTM-1*	February 1993	Arabic	Eutelsat II Arabsat 1C	RTV Marocaine
Saudi Arabia 1 Saudi Arabia 2	1992	Arabic	Arabsat 1C	Saudi Government
Show TV	March 1992	Turkish	Eutelsat II	AKSTV & Iktisat Broadcasting
Sudan TV*	1992	Arabic	Arabsat 1C	Sudan Government

(continued)

TABLE 11.3 (continued)

Channel	Startup Date	Language	Satellite	Ownership
Teleon	January 1992	Turkish	Eutelsat II	Interstar Group
TRT-TV1*	NA	Turkish	Intelsat 604	Turkish Radio-TV Corp.
TRT-TV2/TV Gap*				
TRT TV3*				
TRT TV4*				
TRT TV5 Int/Avrasya†			Eutelsat II	
TV 7	November 1992	Arabic	Eutelsat II	Radiodiffusion TV Tunisienne
UAE TV Abu Dhabi*	1992	Arabic	Arabsat 1C	UAE Government

*All state-owned channels. The rest are privately owned.
†State owned channel for broadcasting internationally.
SOURCE: "C-Band/S-Band Services Datafile," *Cable & Satellite Europe,* April 1993, 169–170.

services. Already an estimated 400,000–500,000 receiver dishes have been installed by viewers in Arab countries, and the reported growth rate is more than 10,000 per month. The Turks have also found the new markets in the Turkic republics of the former Soviet Union attractive for spreading their culture and information about their resources to 57 million new viewers in Turkmenistan, Uzbekistan, Azerbaijan, Kirghizia, and Kazakhstan. These links to Asia and others should grow as Turkey's own communication satellite was scheduled to finally get off the ground in summer 1994. The first launch attempt by the French company, Aerospatiale, failed in January 1994.

Broadcast news has certainly been affected by the internationalization of the television environment. The spread of CNNI to all of these countries has provided a model for television news format and style of delivery. During the Gulf War, viewers from throughout the region where CNNI was available tuned in for hour-by-hour coverage. In countries like Saudi Arabia, where the war was barely mentioned in the local press and on television, CNNI provided a service highly valued by Saudi viewers. In Turkey, the pressure to provide live coverage of the war was so great that the state broadcasting network gave over a channel to broadcast CNNI over the terrestrial network. Turkish Radio and Television (TRT) carried the CNNI signal live until the channel carried information and provided video footage of U.S. planes taking off from Incirlik Air Force Base in the south of Turkey on bombing missions into Iraq. Because the government had not wanted this information released, TRT soon cut off the live distribution of CNNI. Throughout the Middle East, viewers may have been surprised at the Israeli control of the stories about the war. A major issue in the war became the plight of the Palestinians when Saddam Hussein promised to withdraw from Kuwait if Israel would leave the West Bank and Gaza. Israel had set up press centers in Tel Aviv and Jerusalem and provided regular news conferences, issuing official statements to the more than

1,000 reporters who gathered there for any information they could get. Thus, control of the news from Israel came from the Israelis, and the Palestinian viewpoint was rarely aired.

The war had the most impact on Kuwait's broadcasting operation, however. Virtually all of the production equipment for radio and television were taken by Iraqi forces, leaving only the transmitters. Kuwait was therefore required to re-equip the country's broadcasting facilities. The reconstruction has allowed the government to evaluate the benefits of cable versus MMDS systems.

The war's impact could also be seen in the rapid move to deliver domestic broadcasting signals via satellite as soon as Arabsat II was launched. *Cable & Satellite Europe* reported that within six months of the launch in 1992, the Arabsat 1C was completely reserved (Hicks 1993). Eleven Arab state television channels were booked on that satellite. This was in contrast to the hesitation certain Arab countries had in renting transponders for broadcast use on Arabsat 1A and 1B. Originally, broadcasters of the Arab States' Broadcasting Union, the regional electronic news organization, expected that the convenience of having a local satellite would promote extensive news exchange. That never happened except on a limited basis. Disagreements over what was politically and culturally acceptable content for viewing in each country led to minimal use of the satellites for broadcasts. The Gulf War forced countries to rethink their use of Arabsat.

Despite the advanced technology and the increased number of privately owned domestic or international broadcast alternatives, government-owned or controlled broadcasting stations dominate every country of the region. The change in recent years is that many viewers now have other sources to check when attempting to get the truth about any given news event. But heavy-handed leaders continue to threaten control, despite the difficulty of enforcing it. In Lebanon, President Ilyas Hrawi, who claims the government has a monopoly over the ownership of television stations, has threatened to shut down all of the 45 private TV stations that operate in the face of the monopoly ("Lebanon's Lively Press" 1993).

NEWS SERVICES

All Middle East and North African countries have national news agencies. Most of them have a single official agency over which the government has full control. In some of these agencies, the government simply passes on bulletins from the various ministries to be carried directly by the wire service. At the very least, governments censor all information that is not flattering to the ruling parties in these countries. Exceptions to this rule are less common in these countries, and so more worth mentioning. Turkey's proliferation of news agencies reflects its economic growth of late. In addition to the semi-official Anatolian News Agencie, the country supports seven other agencies, several of which distribute economic and commercial news. The Hurriyet Haber Ajansi serves Hurriyet newspapers that are distributed widely in Germany and also in the United States. Ulusal Basin Ajansi also serves the Ulusal media properties in the country.

Israel has two agencies, the News Agency of the Associated Israel Press (ITIM), a cooperative; and the pro-PLO Palestine Press Service to serve the Occupied Territories. Palestinians outside the West Bank and Gaza make use of the PLO's Palestine News Agency (WAFA), which was located in Beirut until 1982, when it moved to Tunis. The agency is used to send bulletins in Arabic and English to newspapers, embassies and international offices of the PLO. Najjar (1994) notes that Palestinian reporters often work with the foreign press through the Palestinian Press Service. When they cannot publish the news they gather, for reasons of censorship, they will frequently leak that information to Israeli reporters. When the news is published in the Israeli press, the Palestinian reporters have the freedom to run the story as a translation from the Israeli press.

Most of the region's news agencies are relatively new, at least seven of them appearing after 1970. The impetus for the development of national news agencies in the 1970s and 1980s was the international discussion over a New World Information and Communication Order. One of the main purposes of the agencies is to present a positive picture of local events to the outside world. Most of the region's agencies serve to disseminate domestic and international news within the borders of their countries and to supply domestic news to the outside world through other domestic agencies or international agencies. Several of the national agencies are the sole suppliers of international news to domestic media, thereby having the capability to serve as editors and interpreters of certain unwanted international stories. Agencies in the Middle East that function as international agencies include Egypt's Middle East News Agency (MENA) and the Jewish Telegraphic Agency of Israel. MENA is the only Arab agency subscribed to by at least one news organization in every other Arab nation.

The major addition to the Middle Eastern-owned news agencies is the previously mentioned acquisition of the U.S.-based UPI agency by the MBC in June 1992. The Saudi Arabian company saved the agency from bankruptcy, but it was still not financially stable in late 1993 (Gersh 1993). Plans for restructuring international bureaus along with the addition of an Arabic service were announced in 1993.

GOVERNMENT–MEDIA RELATIONS AND CONCEPTS OF PRESS FREEDOM

Whether newspapers are government owned or private, they are subject to considerable influence, and even censorship, by authorities. This is also true of broadcasting, though more stations are government-owned or -controlled than private throughout the region.

Perhaps no country is more explicit in its censorship than Saudi Arabia. Despite reception of foreign satellite channels that do not follow these rules, the Saudi government forbids material that criticizes the domestic government, questions friendly nations, makes derogatory statements about Islam, or mentions sex (Boyd 1993; Franklin 1991). Women, especially Saudi or other women of the Muslim faith, are not to appear indecently dressed or in love or dance scenes, are not to be shown on television during the month of Ramadan, and are not to appear in athletic games or sports (Boyd 1993). The Saudi press's reaction to the Gulf War provides a good example of how it deals with controversial material. It avoids it. The war was not reported to the Saudi public until the third day. The press never dealt with the issue of why Saddam Hussein, who had received considerable financial assistance from the Saudi government over the years, had suddenly turned on his neighbors. Nor did the press describe the battle between religious extremists and Muslim moderates over the state of moral decay in the country. And the country's economic problems are also an off-limits subject for journalists. One high-ranking editor interviewed for a *Columbia Journalism Review* article went so far as to say that there were no journalists in the country, only messengers. "They go to the ministries, pick up the reports, and print what they are told," he said (Franklin 1991). Though the government can specifically delete references to objectionable material that enters the country in print form or in programs that are to be aired on Saudi television, it cannot control the reception of foreign satellite signals or short-wave radio reception in the country. Many of the people therefore are easily able to receive information with conflicting views. And articles of particular interest enter the country on fax machines and are copied for wide distribution.

Other countries also make serious attempts to control the output of the press. Egypt, which has long been considered a decided contrast to Saudi Arabia in providing a free environment for news gathering, has lately taken measures to keep the foreign correspondents in the country from covering events related to the activities of Islamic militants and other controversial subjects. Reporters have filed complaints related to telephone bugging, disconnection of international lines, denial of entry to trials of Islamic militants, and harassment by security officers. Anthropologist and journalist Barbara Nimri Aziz (1993) claims the difficulties experienced by foreign journalists in Egypt may be part of a larger problem for Arab journalists and writers—the silencing of the debate between progressive Muslims and the Islamic clerics. Aziz notes violent attacks on journalists in Egypt, Turkey, and Algeria. In trying to control the political activity of the fundamentalist movement in Egypt, President Hosni Mubarek may be attempting to control the media forum that journalists provide the activity.

Turkey has a similar problem with the war being waged by its Kurdish population in the southeast part of the country where between 10,000 and 20,000 people have been killed in the last nine years. The dead include least 14 journalists who have been assassinated. In 1993 alone six journalists and eight newspaper distributors were killed. The journalists have been referred to as terrorists by government officials. None of the crimes have been solved, and no one has been arrested. The government continues to harass the pro-Kurdish paper, *Özgur Gündem,* confiscating 80 issues of the paper since its launch in May 1992 ("More Troubles" 1993). Journalists are now forbidden entry to the war zone, and in Cizre, members of police special teams escorted foreign journalists out of town in early 1994. Earlier in 1993, two men, a British journalist and his Turkish companion, were arrested as they crossed the border to Silopi on their way back from Iraq.

One of Turkey's best known journalists and top investigative reporter for *Cumhuriyet* died when his car blew up outside his home in January 1992. Though the government claimed that Ugur Mumcu was killed by Iranian-based Hizbollah members, the case has never been solved. Mumcu was best known for the antifundamentalist stand he took in his column and was working on an investigative story related to the Kurdish uprising when he was killed.

Lebanon, another country in the region long known for its free press, has been subjected to severe control since the election of President Ilyas Hrawi. Acting on the premise that an unrestrained press can encourage renewed civil war in the country, Hrawi has closed three newspapers and shut down a television station. He has also threatened to enforce the state monopoly over television station ownership, though 45 private stations currently operate in Lebanon. In conjunction with the closings, Hrawi brought criminal charges against four journalists for violation of press regulations. The *Middle East Watch,* in a July 1993 publication on the crackdown, states that criticism of government policies was the real reason for the press censorship ("Lebanon's Lively Press" 1993). The organization's publication expresses its concern that the withdrawal of press freedom in Lebanon will have serious repercussions in Syria, Iraq, Saudi Arabia, Iran, Egypt, and Kuwait. These countries are reported to have feared the independence of the Lebanese press for a long time, pressuring Lebanon to control its journalists. The pressure has been applied through conditions on aid, political alliance, trade, and tourism to Lebanon. The Lebanese press reported that Hrawi, on a tour to raise money for Lebanon's reconstruction, had promised leaders in the Gulf and Saudi Arabia that he would silence journalists who wrote articles critical of those countries.

Israel applies most of its censorship authority to Palestinian publications. The media owners have to submit copy to the censors before publication. Anything considered a threat to Israeli national security is struck from the publication. Violations of the law are met with the withdrawal of press accreditation or the closing of newspapers. Foreign journalists are occasionally asked to leave the country for revealing information unfavorable to the Israeli government.

Journalists lead lives threatened by danger as well as censorship in many countries of North Africa and the Middle East. The Committee to Protect Journalists, in its annual report on violence against journalists in the world, announced that nine journalists in Algeria were killed in 1993. All of them were believed to be targets of militant Muslim factions in the country ("Journalism" 1994). These were the first attacks on journalists since the country won its independence from France in 1962.

JOURNALISM EDUCATION AND TRAINING

Journalism education is a relatively recent phenomenon in the Middle East. Most journalists learned as apprentices on the job, and if they had university degrees, they were educated in the liberal arts. With one of the most developed press systems in the region, Egypt was the first country to begin a degree program in a university—in fact, it began two of them. The American University in Cairo began a program in 1935 and was followed by Cairo University in 1939. However, these programs were mostly theoretical until the mid-1970s, when training in print and broadcast journalism was initiated. Since 1971, the American University has also offered a master's and doctorate in communications.

The next countries to launch university-level training in journalism were Turkey (1964), in the political science faculty of Ankara University, and Iraq (1964), with a department of journalism at Baghdad University. Today, Turkey offers degrees in print and broadcast communications at several more universities in Istanbul, Eskisehir, and Izmir and some form of training at eight institutions. Five schools offer master's degree programs, but only Istanbul University and Ankara University offer doctoral degrees.

Most programs in the region were not established until the 1970s, and today degree programs exist in Syria (since 1979, a two-year program); Saudi Arabia (at three different universities); Lebanon (at two schools); and Jordan (one degree program at Yarmouk University and a two-year program at the University of Jordan in Amman). Iran has probably continued its programs, but in 1980 all journalism schools were closed for Islamization and purification. During the Gulf War, Kuwait's universities were gutted, and most of the libraries and equipment were removed and taken back to Iraq. New programs were being established following the devastation.

In North Africa, Tunisia has the best-developed education system for journalism. The Institute of Press and Information Sciences at the University of Tunis has had a four-year program since 1967. Students can obtain state aid to train in journalism or in broadcasting. The University of Kar Yunis in Ben Ghazi also offers an undergraduate degree. Students studying in Tunis may also have access to publications from the Arab League Education, Cultural, and Scientific Organization (ALECSO). The Arab League's counterpart to UNESCO is based in Tunis and produces a journal, *Arab Communication.* Morocco. Sudan and Libya all have training programs.

Journalistic training is not necessarily sufficient. Algeria is the North African country with the oldest program, begun in 1965 at the Institute of Political Sciences and News in Algiers. But most of the journalists who obtained university training claimed it was unsatisfactory in a 1987 survey (Kirat 1993). Between 22 and 30 percent of the respondents in the study cited unnecessary courses, lack of practical training, lack of equipment and facilities, lack of internship programs, and a lack of qualified and experienced professors as problems with their education. Since the time of the study, Kirat has been working to improve that quality as a member of the faculty of the Institute of Information Sciences and Communication at the University of Algiers.

PROSPECTS FOR THE FUTURE

Countervailing trends in the region could send the media off in several directions. Though governments have tried hard to control them, the rapid technological developments have caused borders to be much more porous to international media than ever before. The international media has been mostly accessible by the affluent. But the fear in many of the more religiously conservative countries is that the increased exposure to foreign media content can lead to the corruption of traditional values. Governments are also concerned that their citizens will be able to access critical views of the political process in their countries. So governments will continue to try to seal the borders in whatever ways they can—by forbidding entry to particular journalists and publications, by banning the distribution of satellite dishes and controlling cable content, and by suspending licenses or shutting down stations or publications for distributing certain kinds of content. But in the long run, it will be extremely difficult for any government to keep the truth or controversial reports from the people. In Turkey, the onslaught from imported satellite signals led to a constitutional change to allow private broadcasters the same rights as the public company. But Turkey is a secular country with a greater openness to a full discussion of the issues. Countries such as Saudi Arabia, where the government is built on Muslim law, will have a much more difficult time allowing private media to circulate freely.

The trend to increased influence by Muslim fundamentalists can be found throughout the region. Religious groups have protested policies and political leaders in Egypt, Algeria, Turkey, and several other countries in the area. Should their power continue to grow, they will move to curb both domestic and international media content that they see as immoral and anti-Islam. That could lead to major clashes in the region.

The other cause for concern lies with the increased influence of the Saudi Arabian in Arabic-speaking countries. As more journalists are attracted to the high salaries and relative freedom of expression that the British-based publications and broadcast media offer, domestic media in several of these countries may suffer. The Gulf War stimulated interest in news and public affairs information throughout the region, but as the memory of that event fades, people may well be happy to return to their government-owned media and to supplement domestic news with imported entertainment.

BIBLIOGRAPHY

Abboud, Mounir B. "Lebanese Newspaper Industry in Decline." *Middle East News Network,* 10 May 1992.

Aziz, Barbara Nimri. "Assault on Muslim Writers." *The Christian Science Monitor,* 28 July 1993, 19.

Boyd, Douglas A. *Broadcasting in the Arab World: A Survey of Radio and Television in the Middle East.* Second Edition. Ames: Iowa State University Press, 1993.

Evans, Kathy. "Media: The Petro-Dollar Press." *The Guardian,* 30 November 1992, 16.

Franklin, Stephen. "The Kingdom and Its Messengers." *Columbia Journalism Review* (July/August 1991): 24.

Gersh, Debra. "UPI Buyouts." *Editor & Publisher,* 14 August 1993, 11.

Hicks, Bill. "Arabia Felix." *Cable & Satellite Europe,* May 1993a, 23–31.

——. "From Drought to Deluge." *Cable & Satellite Europe,* December 1993b, 20–21.

Ibrahim, Youssef M. "Saudis Pursue Media Acquisitions, Gaining Influence in the Arab World." *The New York Times,* 29 June 1992, D8.

"Journalism: Media Group Says 56 Reporters Killed in 1993." In Inter Press Service [on line], 24 January 1994. Available from the NEXIS Library; File: Allwld.

Kirat, Mohamed. *The Communicators.* Algiers, Algeria: Office des Publications Universitaires, Université D'Alger, 1993.

LaFranchi, Howard. "Algeria Flirts with a Free Press." *The Christian Science Monitor,* 1 December 1993, 14.

"Lebanon's Lively Press Faces Worst Crackdown Since 1976." *Middle East Watch* (July 1993).

"More Troubles and Trials for Turkish Paper." *IPI Report* (August 1993): 1, 3, 13.

Murphy, Kim. "Fighting to Keep Their Voice Alive." *Los Angeles Times,* 27 January 1994, 1.

Najjar, Orayb. "Palestine." In *Mass Media and the Middle East: A Comprehensive Handbook,* edited by Yahyakamalipour and Hamid Mowlana, 213-228. Westport, Conn.: Greenwood Press, 1994.

Ogan, Christine. "Communications Policy Options in an Era of Rapid Technological Change." *Telecommunications Policy* (September/October 1992): 565-575.

Rouleau, Eric. "The Challenges to Turkey." *Foreign Affairs* (November 1993): 110.

Rugh, William A. *The Arab Press.* 2nd Edition. Syracuse, N.Y.: Syracuse University Press, 1987.

Rugmain, Jonathan. "Foreign Fixations: Turks Stagger Under Weight of Too Much Knowledge." *The Guardian,* 26 December 1993, 9.

Tehranian, Majid. "Communications Dependency and Dualism in Iran." *Intermedia* 10, no. 3 (1982): 40-42.

Topuz, Hifzi. *Turk Basin Tarihi.* Istanbul: Gercek Yayinevi, 1973.

"Turkish Tragedy Continues." *IPI Report,* February 1993, 1, 4, 5.

World Bank. "Table 1. Basic Indicators." In *World Development Report 1993.* Oxford: Oxford University Press, 1993, 238-239.

"World TV Households: The Growth Continues." *Screen Digest* (March 1993): 61-64.

chapter 12

Sub-Saharan Africa

Arnold S. de Beer, Francis P. Kasoma,
Eronini R. Megwa, and Elanie Steyn

INTRODUCTION

In the eyes of much of the world, Africa[1] south of the Sahara has become a "basket case." As the *New York Times* stated, "Every bit of bad news—civil wars, military coups, refugees and displaced persons, drought and disease—has sadly reinforced a mood of fatalism or, still worse, callous unconcern" ("Editorial" 1994).

At the 1994 meeting of the International Press Institute in Cape Town, the despondent situation in Africa was summarized by a UNESCO official in the following way:

> Most African countries emerged from the struggle for political independence only to find themselves engaged in the struggle for food, water, shelter and clothing in the face of the ever-increasing population growth rate, of low life expectancy, high infant mortality, and continuous political and economic strife, resulting in millions of refugees. (Yushkiavitshus 1994, p. 1)

A total of 26 of the 34 least developed countries in the world are in Africa. It is home to about 11 percent of the world population, and more than 50 percent of its population is under 15 years old.

Africa's economic situation has declined significantly in the three decades of post-colonialism. This has further been exacerbated (Gurirab 1994, p. 9) by the lack of adequate health care systems, low literacy, high unemployment rates, and alarmingly high teenage pregnancies. According to a 1993 report by the Fellowship of Christian Communicators in South Africa (p. 1), AIDS is systematically wiping out a whole genera-

---

[1] In this chapter, Africa refers to the sub-Saharan countries (see Figure 12.1 for the grouping of countries according to East, West, and Southern Africa).

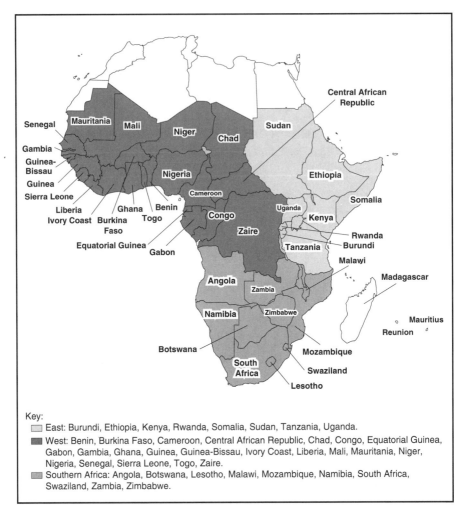

Key:
  East: Burundi, Ethiopia, Kenya, Rwanda, Somalia, Sudan, Tanzania, Uganda.
  West: Benin, Burkina Faso, Cameroon, Central African Republic, Chad, Congo, Equatorial Guinea, Gabon, Gambia, Ghana, Guinea, Guinea-Bissau, Ivory Coast, Liberia, Mali, Mauritania, Niger, Nigeria, Senegal, Sierra Leone, Togo, Zaire.
  Southern Africa: Angola, Botswana, Lesotho, Malawi, Mozambique, Namibia, South Africa, Swaziland, Zambia, Zimbabwe.

FIGURE 12.1   Sub-Saharan Africa: Grouping of countries according to east, west, and southern Africa

tion of young people in Africa. It is estimated that, by the end of this century, there will be more than 3 million AIDS orphans in sub-Saharan Africa. Compounding this problem is the emergence (Gurirab 1994, p. 9) of drug-trafficking, money-laundering and the proliferation of all types of weapons that have destabilizing and debilitating consequences in African states.

One of the results of this situation is that private investment flow to African countries has dropped from $10 billion to $4 billion in the early 1990s. Moreover, new loan commitments to this part of the world by the World Bank in 1993 fell by $1.2 billion (or 30 percent) as compared to an increase from $1.7 billion to $3.8 billion for Eastern Europe during the same period (Gurirab 1994, p. 10).

Lack of economic growth had a devastating effect on Africa. To mention but one example, the 1980s showed a dramatic reduction in educational development with expenditure per inhabitant being cut by half by the end of the decade compared to the late 1970s (Yushkiavitshus 1994, p. 4).

After some 30 years of independence, the peoples of Africa are actually worse off. "They have been neglected and impoverished by their own governments amidst an abundance of natural resources and wealth being siphoned off by their—in most cases—unelected leaders" (Gurirab 1994, p. 5).

But, Africa is not all gloom and doom: The 1990s saw important developments toward democracy and the strengthening of the media. As a United Nations (UN) observer remarked:

There is little doubt that, in the realm of politics, the most remarkable phenomenon in Africa in recent times has been the demise of authoritarian regimes and their replacement by democratic governments. [Southern African countries like Botswana, Lesotho, Namibia, Zambia and Zimbabwe held democratic elections in the last few years. Also, South Africans went to the polls in April 1994 for the first ever democratic elections in the country—Abiolo 1994, p. 1.] After years of autocratic or colonial rule, a number of countries have held multi-party competitive elections and several are in the process of organizing elections to be held in the near future. (King 1994, p. 1)

The one-party state, as a typical post-colonial African system with its adverse effect on media structures, was becoming in the mid-1990s:

a fallen standard, with hardly any defenders left. . . . As an instrument of political management, the one-party state has been a factor of retardation as far as economic growth is concerned and a dead hand on the flowering of personal liberty [as well as media freedom and journalistic enterprise]. (Anyaoku 1994, p. 3)

The movement toward democracy in the 1990s saw a number of independent publications—newspapers and magazines not owned and controlled by an often unpopular government—coming to the fore.

Consequently, there has been a wave of democratization activities across the African continent in the 1990s. Some African governments, under pressure from developed countries and internal opposition, have been forced to begin political changes.

In his address to the 1994 International Press Institute Meeting in Cape Town, Henrikas Yushkiavitshus, Assistant Director-General for Communication, Information and Informatics of UNESCO, stated the following on the matter:

The press has always been important in the political life of African countries, and so have been journalists. Such leaders as Kwame Nkrumah of Ghana, Nnamdi Azikiwe of Nigeria, Jomo Kenyatta of Kenya, Felix Houphoet-Boigny of Côte D'Ivoire and Leopold Senghor of Senegal were leading journalists who established or edited newspapers and other publications, criticized colonial policies and advocated political independence. They became political leaders, but as a rule they exercised excessive control over the media and did not make any modifications in the structure and orientation of the media to make them effective for development. (Yushkiavitshus 1994, pp 4–5)

It will take some time before Africa will be able to move away from both the stereotyped image and reality that it is the "media poorest" region in the world. Africa has fewer newspapers, radio and television sets, as well as any other form of communication technology at its disposal than any other continent (Faringer 1991, p. 1). Even so, the media in Africa have come a long way since the first newspaper was published in Sierra Leone in the latter part of the 18th century.

African news media practitioners and institutions, like their colonial predecessors, are, however, faced with two major threats: authoritarian governments still in power and economic constraints. Despite some African countries now having democratic governments, or moving in that direction, many African governments still control both the economy and the media. It also appears that where the media are economically viable in Africa, harassment of media practitioners by the government and other groups still seems to prevail. Countries such as Gambia, Cape Verde, the Ivory Coast, and Senegal can claim to have governments freely elected by the people, but many others are an amalgam of military dictatorships (Abiolo 1994).

While African countries slowly started concentrating on building media systems in the period after independence, the Western world had already entered the era of the electronic media (Cancel 1986, p. 60). By and large Africa did not actively become part of the newspaper reading world in the sense that one would find in Europe or the United States, but because of, among other things, illiteracy, radio became an important form of mass communication. Where newspapers were established, it was often done to promote the ideas and goals of its owners—the government, with the uneven development between the press in urban and rural areas being inevitable (Pratt and Manheim 1988, p. 85).

Still, the wind of democracy that has been blowing across the continent seems not to have brought sufficient levels of press freedom (Mandela 1991). Journalists are still losing their lives or are intimidated or victimized by their governments. Others are jailed or their families are threatened by governments and their agents. Yet others have their newspapers and magazines decreed out of existence, or they are denied access to import newsprints or even to distribute their products (e.g., see Qwelane 1994; Thloloe 1994 on the situation in South Africa, and Nation Printers and Publishers 1994 for the situation in Kenya). An example of extreme intimidation and physical violence used by the authorities to suppress the media was found in Rwanda in 1993. A number of editors have been jailed, while they also received death threats from government and security officials (*International Press Institute Report,* 1993, p. 51). Different forms of censorship were also used as a means of intimidation in 1993 in the Central African Republic (*International Press Institute Report* 1993, p. 15).

When it comes to media coverage, Africa is still too often regarded as "a black hole." On the continent only Libya and South Africa are generally considered as newsworthy countries by the international media (Ferdon & Harle 1989, pp. 220–226; Fitzgerald 1987, p. 24). Western media tend to ignore events on the continent, or focus only on the disaster-striken events in Africa (Martin 1992, p. 332, Paterson 1991, p. 133). Subsequently Africa is often depicted in the Western media as an economic and environmental disaster, a continent of instability and dictatorships (Anyaoku 1994, p. 2; Roser & Brown 1986, p. 118).

In this chapter attention will be given to, *inter alia,* the colonial past of countries in Africa and the influence thereof on the media, the relationship between the media and the government, international media coverage of Africa, as well as the role the media has to play in future.

THE COLONIAL HERITAGE

Colonialism had a decisive, adverse, and enduring impact on the African continent. Africa lost political power during the more than 70 years of colonialism, blunting its ability as an economic unit to bargain with other nations, and crippling its ability to survive as a physical and cultural entity. To appreciate the development of mass media in Africa, an understanding of contemporary mass communication philosophies of African countries is necessary. These mass media policies, to a large extent, are predicated on colonial experience, and African legends, myths, and traditions (Ziegler & Asante 1992). In addition, these media philosophies are shaped by the efforts of African governments to repudiate their colonial inheritance. This is done through seeking new ways to imbue their social institutions and people with both new meanings and new self-identities.

The idea of mass media did not develop in Africa. Not only technology, but also the practices, norms, and ethical standards were brought from North America and Europe to Africa (Hachten 1993, p. 14). According to Hachten (1993, p. 106), it is difficult to imagine what the press in Africa would be like without the Western influence.

The mass media in most African countries during the colonial era were used by settlers to promote their ideals. The media mostly ignored the local population, and mainly focused on events happening in the settler community (Hachten 1993, p. 17; Martin 1991, p. 159).

Press coverage in the early colonial period mainly focused on "home news" and news about the social affairs of whites (Martin 1991, p. 159; Ziegler & Asante 1992, p. 23). As Ziegler and Asante also put it: "One way to overcome the enormous loneliness of Africa was for them to read about what the latest developments in politics or fashion in clothing were in London or Paris" (1992, p. 24).

Early colonial West African newspapers were government owned. They reflected mainly the values and interests of colonial authorities and European business people while unpretentiously disregarding the needs, interests, and values of Africans.

Europeans controlled the economy of colonial Africa, and by implication they had monopolized the media during this era because "few Africans could afford to import the necessary equipment for printing newspapers or setting up radio stations" (Ziegler and Asante 1992, p. 26). It was also deliberate colonial policy to allow Africans little access to the capital needed to get newspapers or establish radio stations. The colonials denied the African press rights because they believed that the press in the hands of Africans was a potentially powerful tool against colonial rule. Thus, colonial administration in Africa could be said to have bequeathed contemporary African governments with draconian press laws and a legacy of government monopoly of the media. Some of these colonial press laws, unfortunately, still exist in some African countries. In some instances, these press laws, designed to curtail press freedom, have been put in practice by authoritarian African governments and have assumed even more sinister dimensions.

Colonial rule in Africa was also a period of sustained negative media campaigns against the continent. This persistent media propaganda was consistent with colonial political ideology and policy of repudiating the existence of Africans and expanding and perpetuating European domination of the African. The media, during this era, were more often than not willing partners in the ideological campaign to denigrate Africa and Africans by presenting them as primitive and as culturally and mentally inferior. The media of colonial Africa were used, among other reasons, to foster loyalty and conformity with the colonial system and to counter anticolonial and nationalist activities.

Still, the press, during this period, served as a critical force in mobilizing the indigenous population against colonial rule. African soldiers who had fought on the side of the Allies during World War II returned to Africa. Having been exposed to other cultures, they became aware of the inferior standard of living they were subjected to at home and began to question the idea of European superiority. Thus, the tradition of vociferous dissent emerged. Some editors and publishers started using their newspapers as a revolutionary tool in the liberation struggle. Many of them, notably Kwame Nkrumah of Ghana and Nnamdi Azikiwe of Nigeria, later became presidents of their countries, while others, like Percy Qoboza in South Africa, become internationally famous.

As Africans evolved to political independence, they battled with their material environment and created forms of government, social relations, systems of belief, and patterns of behavior that were different from those of especially Western societies. Often, these systems were intertwined and affected each other. Music, dance, and art, for example, as forms of communication, played key roles in the religion and politics of precolonial Africa.

Family and kinship were the predominant principles of social relations in precolonial Africa and still are crucial in the daily existence of the African. In precolonial Africa, age played an important role in determining an individual's rights and obligations in the community. For example, oldest members of the community and people in authority were central to the effective functioning of society and enjoyed the respect of other members of society. It was difficult for younger members to criticize them. Similar tendencies seem to predominate even in postindependence Africa. Still, that is not to say that criticism of authority figures and elders did not take place at all in precolonial Africa. For example, professional minstrels and historians enjoyed special rights and privileges of freely criticizing without fear of reprisal from those in authority or from elders.

Although colonialism is considered a deterrent to socioeconomic progress in Africa (Dodson 1987, p. 100), Hachten (1993, p. 106) feels that the United States and Europe should be held less responsible for not developing the press in Africa. Local governments and political leaders in Africa itself should also take some blame for not helping their countries on the way to development (*The Citizen* 1993).

The colonial press in Africa did, however, bring the tradition of newspapers to Africa and taught the people of Africa the values of press freedom (Keane, 1991). African journalists further also used the print media to "speed and ease the historic process of decolonization" (Hachten 1993, p. 20).

Religion, in particular Christianity, has played a very big role in the development of the media in Africa. As time passed, missionaries and church-related organizations focused their attention on the local population. In many countries, people first learned to read the Bible and later the newspaper. To bring Christianity to Africans, missionaries strove to turn oral communication into written communication. Mission newsletters and parish magazines containing church-related announcements have penetrated most rural and urban areas ever since missionaries first came to Africa in the second half of the nineteenth century (Martin 1991, p. 159). Missionaries collected stories, songs, and proverbs from the African community and translated and documented them (Abuoga & Mutere 1988, p. 4). Besides the educational role these people wanted to play, they also felt that the "colonial imbalance in the education to local Africans" should be redressed (Mytton 1983, p. 38). To do this, Attoh Ahuma and the Reverent Eggijir Assam, for instance, produced a series of articles on local African history. Newspapers sponsored by Catholic and Protestant churches have continued to be published, serving the purpose of being not only extensions of the pulpit but also news informers and opinion leaders. The Christian church newspapers in Uganda (*Munno*), Zambia (*National Mirror* and *Icengelo*), and Zimbabwe (*Motto*) are but a few outstanding examples.

When Africans started to print their own newspapers, however, confrontation between colonial authority and the press became inevitable. As early as 1855, a dispute between the weekly *New Era* and the governor of Sierra Leone ensued (Faringer 1991, p. 9). This was only the start of the control African governments had, and still have sometimes, over the press on the continent.

DEVELOPMENT OF THE PRESS

The press in Africa is far older than is generally accepted, with modern press activities in Africa beginning in the late eighteenth century, when Napoleon occupied Egypt. In Sierra Leone, significant press activities were recorded in Freetown, where a European-type printing press was established in 1794 (Ziegler and Asante 1992). Immediately after the delivery of this printing press from London, a French raiding party landed on the coast and sacked the city, destroying the press, raping women, slaughtering livestock, and looting businesses (Mytton 1983, p. 38).

The historic development of the press in East, West, and Southern Africa will subsequently be discussed.

East Africa

As in the rest of Africa, the advent of plural politics in East Africa has had a democratizing effect on the press by making it more plural and independent. Multiparty Botswana, Kenya, Malawi, Tanzania, and Zambia have seen a proliferation of an independent and pluralistic press. Somewhat surprising has been Uganda, with no political parties and ruled by a liberation movement that has come out of the chaos of many years of civil war to possess a multiplicity of some of the most outspoken newspapers on the continent. If outspokenness against government is a measure of freedom of the press (e.g., Vosloo 1989), then the private newspapers of Botswana, Malawi, Tanzania, Uganda, and Zambia are among the freest in the world.

The independent countries first being under British rule (Ghana, Nigeria, and Kenya) have the best developed press systems on the continent of Africa, with government gazettes, missionary papers, privately owned papers as well as the underground political news sheets all being published in these countries (Faringer 1991, p. 3).

West Africa

Journalism in West Africa dates back to the first part of the eighteenth century (Faringer 1991, p. 2). Since the small number of readers in the region did not make the publication of popular newspapers worthwhile, colonizers only published official government gazettes. Also, British officials allowed the publication of criticism against colonial policies, something that was not allowed in East Africa (Faringer 1991, p. 2).

The first known newspaper in West Africa, the *Royal Gazette and Sierra Leone Advertiser,* was established in Freetown, Sierra Leone, in 1801. Although it published for a short while, it nevertheless stimulated newspaper activity in West Africa. In 1822, a semi-official hand-written newspaper, the *Royal Gold Coast Gazette and Commercial Intelligencer,* was established in Accra, in the then Gold Coast, now Ghana. It lasted for three years. In 1826, in Liberia, Charles Force, an African American, established a hand-operated printing press and founded the *Liberian Herald,* a four-page monthly. A few months later, the *Herald* ceased publication after the death of Force. However, in 1830, the paper was revived by another African American, James Russwurm.

During the early colonial period, few newspapers were founded by Europeans independently of the colonial authorities. In 1858, the first privately owned newspaper in the then Gold Coast was *Accra Herald,* published by Charles Bannerman, the son of James Bannerman, the lieutenant-governor of the Gold Coast in the 1850s. Two years later, Bannerman moved the *Herald* to Cape Coast and renamed it the *West African Herald.* In neighboring Nigeria, the Reverend Henry Townsend, a devout missionary, founded the first Nigerian newspaper, *Iwe Irohin,* in 1859. It was first published in Yoruba and later in English for the Christian Missionary society. *Iwe Irohin* is believed to be the first bilingual newspaper and the first African language newspaper to be published in Africa.

Nnamdi Azikiwe founded the *West African Pilot,* a hard-hitting daily, in 1937. It was a political newspaper and provided competition to the *Daily Times.* The latter was bought by the Lagos Chamber of Commerce less than a year after. The *Daily Times,* which had the largest circulation in black Africa, was owned by the Nigerian government and public enterprise. It was bought by Cecil King after World War II. Cecil King also owned the *London Daily Mirror.* In 1928 Herbert Macaulay and Dr. J.A. Caulcrick took over the *Lagos Daily News* from Victor Babunmi.

The French colonial policy of assimilation hindered newspaper growth and development in the former French West African colonies. Also hindering media development were low literacy levels arising from the French policy of selective education, the French requirement that prospective newspaper publishers be French citizens who were in good standing, harsh taxes on importation of newsprint into the colonies, strict press laws, and Paris as the hub of intellectual activity. The press, as a result, remained an appendage of France and did not actively seek or encourage African readers.

In 1948, Kwame Nkrumah founded the *Evening News* in the Gold Coast. When Ghana gained independence in 1957, the *Evening News* was taken over by the Guinea Press Limited, a government agency. It later became the *Ghanaian Times.* There was also the *Daily Graphic,* an opposition newspaper, founded in 1950 by the *London Mirror* Group. The *Daily Graphic* was technically more advanced than any other paper published in Ghana during this period and became the most widely read, even though its sponsorship was European. It outsold the *Evening News* and quickly gained acceptance as an African newspaper largely because it had an African staff and catered to the interests and tastes of Africans. The *Daily Graphic* was later bought by the government at a time when it was enjoying a leading position in advertising and circulation. The *Daily Graphic* and the *Ghanaian Times,* both now government-owned, appear on a daily basis in Ghana.

In Nigeria, the federal government, aside from owning the *Daily Times,* also owns the *New Nigerian* jointly with the Kaunda State government. Individual state governments also own daily and weekly newspapers (also see Oniororo 1994 on the press in Nigeria). More than ten daily newspapers are published by private enterprises. These include the *National Concord,* the *Guardian,* the *Nigerian Tribune* and the *Punch.* Most of the dailies have Sunday editions, for example, the *Sunday Times* owned by the government has a magazine insert, *Lagos Weekend, Sunday Punch, Sunday Sketch, Sunday Tribune,* and *Sunday Observer.* These Sunday editions are very popular and have high readership. There are also weekly periodicals. A majority of them are privately owned. Prominent among them is the *National Concord* (owned by Chief M.K. Abiola, who is widely believed to have won the June 1993 annulled presidential elections in Nigeria). The *National Concord* was banned by the military government soon after June 12, 1993. Other weekly newsmagazines are *Newswatch,* and *Tell,* a hard-hitting magazine.

In Senegal, nationalist Golandin Diouf published *La Bastille,* and Blaise Diagne founded *Le Periscope* and *L'Echo de Rufisdue.* During this period in Senegal, two newspapers, *Le Reveil du Senegalais* and *Le Petit Senegalais* were established in Dakar.

At the beginning of 1900, newspapers blossomed in the French West African colonies with Senegalese and Ivorian newspapers playing prominent and leading roles in nationalist agitation. In 1920 in the Cameroon *L'Eveil des Camerounais,* the forerunner of the current daily, *La Presse du Camaroon,* was established by de Breteuil in 1955. It was published specifically for French merchants and civil servants. The government shut it down in 1974 and established a daily, *Cameroon Tribune* in Yaounde, the capital. Today it publishes in French except on Wednesdays when it appears in English.

In Ivory Coast, de Breteuil set up *France Afrique*. It came to be known as *AbidianMatin* 16 years later and continued publishing under the same name even when de Breteuil went into partnership with the government of the Ivory Coast and SNEI. About the same time in Dahomey, now Benin, three newspapers, *Le Guide* (the first newspaper to be established in Dahomey), *La Voix du Dahomey, Le Cri Negre,* and *La Phare du Dahomey,* were published.

In Guinea, de Breteuil established *La Presse de Guinee* in Conakary in 1954, but it closed down four years later when Guinea gained independence. Today, in Burkina Faso, there are dailies, *Dumia, Notre Combat,* and *Sidwaya,* published by the government. Togo has two daily newspapers, *Journal Official de La Republique du Togo,* and *La Nouvelle Marche,* published by the Togolese government in French and Ewe.

In the Iberophone area of Africa, *Ebano* is published in the Equatorial-Guinean capital of Malabo, and *Poto Poto* is published in Bata. Guinea-Bissau publishes a daily newspaper, *Voz Da Guine,* in Portuguese.

Because of a shortage in newsprint and lack of transportation, the periodical press in Ghana is not regular. Government, private, and religious organizations publish weeklies and biweeklies from time to time. The *Daily Graphic* and the *Ghanaian Times* publish weekly supplements, *Mirror* and the *Spectator,* respectively. There are other weeklies, for example, the *Pioneer* and *Palaver-Tribune.*

The only magazines that circulate outside their country of origin in any quantity in West Africa are published in Senegal. *Bingo* is published by de Breteuil and appeared for the first time in 1952; it is a popular picture monthly aimed at youth. Its circulation is over 100,000 throughout Francophone Africa. The French-language *Africa International,* published ten times a year and sold throughout Francophone Africa, was founded in 1962 as a political and economic review of African Affairs. Ivory Coast publishes a quarterly magazine, *Entente Africaine.* It is published in French and English. In Nigeria, the *Drum* publications publishes *Trust,* a general-interest picture monthly for internal distribution. The *Daily Times* publications puts out a widely read monthly family magazine, *Spear.*

The earliest publication in the former Belgian Congo, now Zaire, was produced by colonialists for Belgian settlers. One of the earliest newspapers in the Belgian Congo, *Le Journal du Katanga* was published in 1911 and started as a weekly and later became a daily in 1919. In 1930, it was succeeded by *L'Echo du Katanga.* In the same year, *Courrier d'Afrique* was published by missionaries. They also founded *La Croix du Congo* in 1936. It was taken over by Africans in 1956 and renamed *Horizons.* It lasted a short time, having been closed down by the government because of its revolutionary tone. Two other dailies were published by Africans, *Nkumu* in 1972 and *Presence Congolaise* in 1957, renamed *Epanza* in 1972 when it became a weekly. In 1934, two daily newspapers, *Les Nouvelles* and *L'informateur,* were established.

In 1972, all Congolese papers were given African names. Today, in Zaire, all daily newspapers are published in French and operated by the government. They include *Salongo,* formerly *L'Avenir Colonial Belge.* In 1962 it was called *Le Progres.* About seven small daily newspapers as well as weeklies published by the government in Kinshasa have readership outside Zaire. In addition, there are four French weeklies in Kinshasa and other provinces.

Southern Africa

Botswana, a multiparty democracy of 1.3 million people, hosts only one government daily newspaper, the *Daily News,* and four private weeklies, the *Botswana Guardian,* the *Gazette, Mmegi wa Dikang,* and the *Midweek Sun.*

In Botswana, a comprehensive national media policy has only now started to emerge—almost two decades after the country gained independence (Zaffiro 1992, p. 126). Through the years, the media in Botswana were faced with similar problems as other African countries, namely (Zaffiro 1992, p. 126):

- Urban-based centralization of infrastructure, resources, and audiences
- Emphasis in media coverage of the actions and activities of political leaders, especially the President of the country
- Heavy demands on media institutions to contribute to national development, as well as education, information and entertainment
- A lack of diversity between national media organs
- Monopolization and political manipulation of communications flow from the top

The four private papers in the country are centered in the capital, Gaborone. Their reporting on national security, defense, and police matters has, according to Zaffiro (1992, p. 131) decreased over the last few years, with the emphasis being placed on development-orientated news.

Fortunately, because Botswana is a more pluralist democratic society than any other state in sub-Saharan Africa, the national media often have the uniquely powerful position to pressure the government to maintain an atmosphere of openness and media freedom in the country (Zaffiro 1992, p. 138).

The government has since 1985 also become less reluctant to allow press conferences, grant interviews, and provide media access to policymakers in the country. Before 1985, officials' speeches were reported unedited by the media (Zaffiro 1992, p. 133).

Zimbabwe's two daily newspapers the *Chronicle,* published in the southern town of Bulawayo, and the *Herald,* published in the capital city Harare in the early 1990s, belonged to Zimbabwe Newspapers (Zim Papers), whose largest shareholder (45 percent) was the Zimbabwe Mass Media Trust, a parastatal that was set up at independence in 1980 by a grant from the government of Nigeria to buy out the previous owners, the Argus Group of South Africa. The other Zim Papers were the *Sunday Mail,* the *Sunday News, Kwayedza,* and *Manica Post,* all weeklies. The only other weekly not owned by the group, an independent newspaper launched in 1991, was the *Sunday Times,* which at least in the early 1990s did not seem to be a serious critic of the government as were the other private newspapers the *Daily Gazette* and the *Weekly Gazette.*

Other notable publications in the country included *Motto* (Fire), the old Shona publication that gave rebel Premier Ian Smith a hard time for years during his unilateral declaration of independence until he banned it. It started publishing again at independence in 1980. *Parade,* one of the oldest monthly magazines in Southern Africa, was still very popular, while a new muckraker monthly called the *Inside,* started at the end of 1990, promised to make the government of President Robert Mugabe rather uncomfortable.

In Zimbabwe, as well as Uganda and Zambia, it was the Christian press that provided the alternative voice when the mainstream media were severely censored by the governments of the day. In a way it can be said that it was the Christian newspapers that kept the flame of freedom of the press burning instead of being totally extinguished by political highhandedness.

The advantage the Christian press has had in Southern Africa over the mainstream official media is that it has generally been seen as genuinely nonpartisan in terms of trying to promote other political cliques or parties. Moreover, the spread of Christianity in most of Southern Africa has been so effective in both urban and rural areas that the Christian press has always been in a position to easily mobilize public opinion against the authorities when it came to a crunch. Few leaders, one of them being Rhodesia (Zimbabwe's) rebel leader Ian Smith, have ever dared to ban a recalcitrant Christian newspaper in Southern Africa. If Zambia's *National Mirror* had not been a Christian newspaper, President Kenneth Kaunda at the height of his dictatorial power would have certainly banned it. Instead, he tried all methods of silencing the vociferous weekly, including intimidating the country's Christian church leaders, but to no avail.

In the past, the media in Malawi were frequently censored, and the government was free to ban any publication (Brice 1992, p. 51, Fitzgerald 1989, p. 60). Before a newspaper could be established, a business license had to be obtained, and the editorial staff had to be cleared by the police ("Malawi" 1993, p. 8). Newspapers in Malawi had to carry a picture of the Malawian president every day, preferably on the front page. Also, speeches by the head of the state were not allowed to be edited or cut (Martin 1991, p. 172).

The only media available to Malawians were semi-official newspapers, owned by the government, and the official Malawi Broadcasting Corporation, mainly broadcasting news on the government and the president and government propaganda.

The tradition of Malawi being a two-newspaper nation was suddenly broken in 1992–1993 when about half a dozen weekly, independent newspapers were started in the wake of the agitation to multiparty politics (International Centre against Censorship 1994, p. 2). Names like the *Revealer,* the *Challenger,* the *Watchers,* the *New Nation* and the *New Voice,* paint the picture of the current revolution in the Malawian press ("Malawi" 1993, p. 8). They also included the *Financial Gazette,* edited and owned by Al Osman, who, like several Malawian journalists, returned from self-imposed exile to keep away from Kamuzu Banda's dictatorship. Most of these newspapers were one-man or one-woman enterprises with shaky financial bases and were bound to collapse any time unless managed properly. They all had one denominator: to support the march toward plural politics and to end the three-decade iron-fist rule of Banda. They took advantage of a lull in Banda's autocracy after the small Southern African nation voted

overwhelmingly in a referendum in support of multiparty politics. Malawi's new independent press challenged the two long-time newspapers, both owned by the government, the *Daily Times* and *Malawi News,* which continued to feed Malawians with
government propaganda as they had done for nearly 30 years.

The independent press in Malawi is, however, not free from problems (International Centre against Censorship 1994, p. 3; Puri 1993). One of the major problems
is the inadequate training of journalists, and the subsequent large number of libel suits
as a result of false information published ("Malawi" 1993, p. 9). However, the editorial staff of these newspapers insist that the public has a right to know.

Angola, before gaining independence, had a daily newspaper, *A Provincia de
Angola,* established in 1923. It was nationalized and renamed *O Journal de Angola* in
1976. In addition, Angola has two evening newspapers, *ABC Diariode Angola* and
Diario de Luanda, which was renamed *Diario da Republica* and closed down by the
government and reopened as an official government paper.

War-torn Mozambique, like Malawi, has been a two-newspaper country ever since
the Portuguese left the east coast nation in a hurry in 1975 following their defeat by
the Front for the Liberation of Mozambique (Frelimo) in a war that lasted for ten years.
Almost immediately after independence, another bloody war followed in which the
Marxist Frelimo government was challenged by the National Revolution Movement
(Renamo). The only two daily newspapers based in Beira and Maputo are *Diario de
Mozambique* and *Noticias,* respectively. Both are government owned and controlled.

For the first century and a half after the founding of a settlement at the Cape in
1652, there were no local newspapers. On August 16, 1800, the first small bilingual
newspaper, the *Cape Town Gazette and African Advertiser/Kaapsche Stads Courant
en Afrikaansche Berigter,* was published. This was the only newspaper allowed, and
it was printed on a government-owned press, although the editors, Alexander Walker
and John Robertson, undertook to make it their particular and anxious study to collect the most "Authentic Materials, and lay before the public the Information thus
obtained, in the fair Simplicity of Truth" (Diederichs 1993, p. 73).

On October 10, 1880, the Government of the day announced that it was "improper
and irregular . . . to allow the Editing of a Public Newspaper from a press in the hand
of private individuals. . . ." (Diederichs 1993, p. 73). After a short spell under Batavian
rule the paper was published throughout the nineteenth century, mainly in English,
and formally became the government newspaper, *The Cape of Good Hope Government Gazette.* Up to the founding of *The South African Commercial Advertiser* in
1824, this was the only newspaper at the Cape. As the first bilingual weekly in the Cape,
it was of great significance to the history of the South African press. It set an example
that was followed throughout the country in later years. At first the paper was distributed as a bilingual weekly among Dutch readers. This situation lasted until the population grew to such an extent that it became impossible to publish separate newspapers for each language group.

The *South African Commercial Advertiser,* printed by George Greig and edited
by Thomas Pringle and John Fairbairn, appeared on January 7, 1824, as South Africa's
first privately owned and independent weekly newspaper. Although it was an English
newspaper, the *Commercial Advertiser* soon published news and advertisements in

Dutch to satisfy the needs of both Dutch readers and advertisers; and in the 1830s, news about the Great Trek was published in both languages.

On March 5, 1824, the first edition of the bilingual monthly *The South African Journal and Het Nederduitsch Zuid-Afrikaansch Tydschrift* was published by Pringle, Fairbairn, and Abraham Faure, a Cape minister.

The freedom of expression enjoyed by the early press was short lived. The governor of the Cape, Lord Charles Somerset, had the *Commercial Advertiser*'s eighteenth issue confiscated and ordered publication of the newspaper to cease as a result of a series of clashes between the governor, Thomas Pringle, and John Fairbairn about newspaper stories with political implications.

The first Afrikaans newspaper, *Di Patriot* (1876–1904), was the mouthpiece of the *Genootskap van Regte Afrikaners* and later of the Afrikanerbond in the Cape. Although Afrikaans was published only in extreme cases in Dutch newspapers, *Di Patriot* encouraged readers to write in their own language.

By the end of the nineteenth century, there was hardly a town of any size without its own newspaper, the proprietor and editor being one and the same person. A strong provincial and very independent press developed. This was largely because of the 1820 British Settlers who came to the eastern Cape and brought printing presses with them.

The first so-called black newspaper, *Imvo Zabantsundu,* was published in King William's Town in 1884. It was edited by the first black journalist in South Africa, John Tengo Jabavu. Other early black newspapers include *Ilanga Lasa Natal,* founded by John Dube and others in 1904. *African Political Organization* was founded by Abdullah Abdurahman, chairman of the African People's Organization, and *Indian Opinion* (1904) was founded by Mahatma Ghandi.

The English anti-apartheid liberal press has a long tradition of striving for human rights, the abolition of apartheid, and the development of a sound capitalist economy. These newspapers are owned by two groups, namely the Argus Company and Times Media Ltd. All these newspapers have adopted a strong stance against the National Party Government on many issues, but primarily on apartheid policies, state security, and the free flow of information. In the 1992 Referendum, they all called for a yes-vote in support of President de Klerk's reform initiatives.

Alternative newspaper groups in the country include the following (Diederichs 1993, pp. 84–85; also see Tomaselli and Louw 1989 for a discussion on the South African progressive press):

- *The left-wing alternative press:* Starting in the 1980s, these newspapers supported organizations like the United Democratic Front (UDF) and the African National Congress (ANC). These papers argued that they filled the newsgap which the mainstream press did not cover. Many of them were financed by European governments or local and overseas church and human rights organizations.

- *The progressive-alternative community press:* This category included papers like *Saamstaan, Grassroots, Ukusa,* and *The Eye,* and were the furthest to the left. Journalists working for these papers considered themselves activists against apartheid.

- *The left-commercial press:* journalists working for newspapers in this category operated more like ordinary journalists. They were mainly concerned with the reporting of news events. Newspapers included *South, New Nation,* and *UmAfrika.*

- *The social democrat press:* Newspapers included in this category were *The Weekly Mail, Vrye Weekblad,* and *Indicator.* Although they were sympathetic towards organizations like the ANC, they also considered themselves as independent newspapers and criticized the ANC whenever they thought necessary. *Vrye Weekblad* eventually closed down in 1994 after changing its format to that of a magazine in 1993.

- *The right-wing alternative press:* These newspapers were established because the right-wing felt that their concerns were not efficiently dealt with in the mainstream press. However, these papers do not have a high circulation figure, with *Die Afrikaner* only selling about 10,000 copies. Other newspapers in this category include *Die Stem* (now *Volkstem*) and *Patriot.*

During the 1980s, chain ownership of newspapers in South Africa became the rule rather than the exception because of ever-increasing production costs, growing competition from other media (specifically television), and the acquisition of management efficiency by combining resources to the benefit of all. Today, at the one end of the scale, there are four major publishing groups that control the publications with the highest circulation figures and, on the other, there are smaller publications run by small companies or even individuals to supply information, knowledge, and entertainment on virtually every topic.

The press groups in the country include (Diederichs 1993, pp. 78–82):

- *Argus:* the oldest of the four press groups, controlling newspapers like *The Star* (Johannesburg), *Argus* (Cape Town), *Pretoria News, Sowetan* (Johannesburg). *The Star* (circulation 205,000 in 1993) and the *Sowetan* (circulation 210,000 in 1993) are the biggest dailies in the country.

- *Times Media:* was founded in 1987. Currently the company owns among others the *Sunday Times,* the largest Sunday newspaper in the country with a circulation of 540,000 in 1993, the *Cape Times, Business Day,* and *Eastern Province Herald.*

- *Nasionale Pers:* this is the biggest Afrikaans Press group in the country, founded in 1915. Its first daily was *De Burger,* started in 1915. *Die Burger* (circulation of 90,000 in 1993), as the first Afrikaans daily, was instrumental in cultivating the Afrikaner nation's cultural consciousness. The group also owns *Die Volksblad* (28,000 in 1993), *Beeld* (115,000 in 1993) and the Sunday paper *City Press* (250,000 in 1993), aimed at the black market.

- *Perskor:* this company owns several magazines, as well as the following newspapers: *The Citizen* (circulation of 110,000 in 1993), *Tempo,* and 50% of the Afrikaans Sunday newspaper *Rapport* (400,000 in 1993).

These four major groups are responsible for at least 27 urban dailies and weeklies.

Also, there are about 450 local, or suburban and country newspapers in South Africa. Most of these are bilingual. Local newspapers were initiated to supply communities with information and create an advertising medium. People's need to know what is going on in their community and vicinity guarantees a niche for these papers. News on local taxing, schools, societies, churches, sport, and crime is the preferred diet of the local paper reader. The news value proximity becomes the most important criterion for the local paper, which can also be described as a very personal medium, perhaps the most personal of all types of mass media. It operates on the first level of mass communication: the local community. This means that it serves the needs and welfare of the local society—good or bad, ugly or beautiful—reporting on failure as well as success.

Two historical elements, language and race, have played an important role in the formation of the South African Press.

The development of the print media in South Africa is closely related to the development and impact of the official languages on the country, at first English and Dutch, with the latter being officially replaced by Afrikaans in 1925.

In the first decade or two of the twentieth century, a political and cultural power struggle took place between the British conquerors, their business interests, and their press on the one hand and the impoverished Afrikaner community, which struggled to survive as a group and to assert its own identity and language, on the other. This formed the basis for the historical division between the Afrikaans and English press (e.g., see Fair 1987; McClurgh, 1987; Muller 1984). Today, nearly a century later, this division has been largely bridged by the practice of professional journalism and the changing political climate.

DEVELOPMENT OF BROADCASTING

Electronic media were introduced in Africa during the colonial period. First, in the early 1920s, a radio broadcasting system was established in South Africa. In 1928, radio broadcasting was introduced in Kenya and in the 1930s in Sierra Leone, Gold Coast (now Ghana), and Nigeria. In the territories ruled by France, Belgium, and Portugal, radio broadcasting started much later, namely, in the 1940s and 1950s. In the 1960s, when African countries emerged from colonialism into political independence, all of them had radio broadcasting systems (Yushkiavitshus 1994).

Because of the perceived role of broadcasting as a tool for both national integration and national development, African countries tend to have more extensive broadcasting services, sometimes in a number of languages. These services are usually centralized. Today, in most African countries, broadcasting stations are exclusively owned by governments and some of them are structured after the British Broadcasting Corporation (BBC) (e.g., Nigeria and Ghana). Although a few countries such as Ghana have constitutional provisions allowing private ownership of broadcasting, there appears to be little interest shown in this form because of cost and government control. About 30 countries in Africa permit commercial advertising. Most governments provide direct subsidies and allow little commercial advertising on the government-owned broadcasting stations. Hence, commercial advertising accounts for a very small proportion of broadcasting revenues at these stations. In some countries there are license fees, but they are low and are difficult to collect because many radio sets in Africa are not registered.

In the following two sections, the development of radio and television will be discussed separately. In each of the sections, attention will also be given to regional development of radio and television in East, West, and Southern Africa.

RADIO

Radio was introduced to Africa in the 1920s. It was established primarily to provide information on government policies and activities and to entertain European settlers, colonial administrators, and a handful of educated Africans. It was used as a propaganda instrument to secure the loyalty and support of the colonies during World War II. During this period, radio became an important vehicle for providing information on the activities of African soldiers fighting on the side of the Allies. In the French colonies, radio was used by the colonial authorities to promote their policy of assimilation among educated and "assimilated" Africans.

East Africa

As in Kenya, radio broadcasting in Tanzania was carried out on three channels of the government-owned Radio Tanzania Dar es Salaam (RTD): the National Service, the Commercial Service, and the External Service. The External Service was entrusted with programs dealing with the liberation of Africa, good neighborliness, support of African unity, and the publicizing of Tanzania to the outside world. The Commercial Service, unlike commercial broadcasting elsewhere, had a complimentary function to the National Service by informing people of the various services and goods produced and available in the country and educating them on how to consume and get most of these goods (Moshiro 1990, p. 22). All broadcasts were carried out in Kiswahili, the national language, although some of the programs on the External Service were done in English. Mainland Tanzania had, by 1994, still no television, although Zanzibar had been running a television station for many years.

Founded in 1954, Radio Uganda broadcast in two channels. The Blue channel was for listeners who spoke the Bantu languages of the East, West, South, and central regions, while the Red channel broadcast in vernaculars of the north and northeast.

Also in Kenya, government ownership and direct control of the media is the rule. Political and government leaders feel it is not wise to allow radio and television companies in the hands of those who can challenge state policies, or have alternative perceptions on the situation in the country (Heath 1988). According to the government, their monopoly on the media in the country will ensure political stability, national unity, development, and unnoticeable foreign cultural influence. Since 1959, commercials in the Kenyan media have to be approved by the government on the basis of content, length, and timing. Subsequently, the revenue the media get from commercials is rather small (Abuoga and Mutere, 1988, p. 114; Heath 1988, p. 101).

Kenya has one state-owned radio broadcasting station, the Voice of Kenya, which broadcasts on three services: national (in Kiswahili), general (in English), and vernacular (in some of the 15 African languages as well as Hindustani).

West Africa

Radio appeared in Nigeria in 1932, Sierra Leone in 1934, and Ghana in 1935. In the Belgian Congo (Zaire), the Jesuit priests started a radio station in Kinshasa in 1937. After World War II, more than 15 African countries including Cameroon, Gambia, Mauritius, and Senegal were operating radio stations.

In Nigeria, most of the 30 states own and operate radio stations. The federal government owns and operates, through the Federal Radio Corporation of Nigeria (FRCN), formerly Nigerian Broadcasting Corporation (NBC), three national networks, and on external service, the Voice of Nigeria. It broadcasts to Africa, the Middle East, Europe, and the Americas. In Ghana, external service broadcasts in English, French, and Hausa. Its domestic service broadcasts in six local languages and English. It allows commercials only on the English broadcasts.

Private and religious organizations operate commercial radio stations in Liberia. In Liberia, Lanco and Bong Mining Company, both iron-ore mining companies, operate radio stations ELNR and ELCBR respectively for their employees. Station ELWA, a noncommercial radio station founded by United States church groups in 1954, is run by the Sudan Interior Mission. ELWA broadcasts on short- and medium wave bands to West, Central, and North Africa in 45 languages including English, French, and Arabic.

In Senegal, there are two networks with a major station in Dakar. There are regional stations in six local languages. The two networks simultaneously broadcast the news in French.

Zaire operates the Voice of Zaire on a 600-kilowatt transmitter, which can be picked up from most of the western area of Central Africa. It has a total of 13 radio stations, including two shortwave transmitters of 100 kilowatts each, covering all of Zaire, and a number of medium- and shortwave transmitters that cover major towns in West Africa and Europe. These stations broadcast in French and four local languages.

There are three networks in the Ivory Coast operating at national, regional and international levels. The national and internal networks broadcast mainly in French but have five daily English newscasts for neighboring countries. The regional network broadcasts in 13 local languages.

Cameroon also operates three networks—national, provincial, and international—in English, French, and local languages.

According to the *International Press Institute Report* (1993, p. 39), the independent press in Mauritania is generally permitted to report freely, but in contrast, broadcasting remains firmly in the hands of the state. This was especially true since 1992.

Southern Africa

The beginnings of radio broadcasting in Botswana can be traced to the dying years of the 1930s when the Protectorate operated a broadcasting station called ZNB at Mafeking. The program's broadcast on ZNB included a round-up of district news compiled from reports of District Commissioners, which was broadcast every Sunday. The Mafeking broadcasting station existed for 26 years when another station at Lobatse was launched in May 1962 to counter growing African nationalism in Botswana, then known as Bechuanaland. It was the Lobatse station which was later transferred to the new capital at Gaborone in 1965, where it remained until the early 1990s (Kasoma 1992b, pp. 51–52). Radio Botswana, as it became known, broadcast in three channels: one in English, another in Setswana, and the third as a commercial channel. The station devoted a lot of airtime to agricultural and school broadcasts for both primary and secondary schools, with the latter taking up as much as 20 hours of airtime a week.

Malawi Broadcasting Corporation (MBC) dates from the country's colonial times in the mid-1940s (International Centre against Censorship 1994, p. 4). By 1994 it was broadcasting on two channels, one in Chichewa and the other in English, for 19 hours and 17 minutes each day. As a government station, it had for a long time been used as the voice of the ruling Malawi Congress Party (MCP) and its leader Kamuzu Banda.

The radio broadcasting system that the Portuguese colonialists bequeathed to Mozambique was a decentralized system in which every province had its own radio broadcasting station. By 1994, nine such stations were still operational. The most well-known ones were the stations in the capital Maputo and at Beira. Radio Maputo, in addition to Portuguese, broadcasts in 13 local languages out of the possible 30 languages in the country.

Zambia National Broadcasting Corporation (ZNBC) was started by the British colonialists in 1941 and still remained a government organ even in a multiparty Zambia. The MMD government in 1994 merely opened broadcasting to private enterprise but would not let ZNBC go. At the time of writing this chapter in early 1994, the government had advertised to members of the general public who wished to start private radio and television stations to put in their applications. ZNBC broadcasts in four channels: Radio 1 in seven out of the 73 languages and dialects in the country, Radio 2 for English broadcasts, Radio 3 for the external service, and Radio 4 as a commercial English channel. There were two transmitting stations, the main one in Lusaka and the one in Kitwe in the heart of the Copperbelt. In principle the provincial stations at Chipata, Mansa, Solwezi, Mongu, and Livingstone also had the capacity to produce and transmit programs. They had, however, for logistical reasons not been commissioned to do so.

As far as the Zimbabwe Broadcasting Company (ZBC) is concerned, it is regarded as a "semi-governmental" organization. Although it is part of the Ministry of Information, the Corporation has to generate its own funds, with 60 percent of its total annual budget coming from advertising (Committee to Protect Journalists 1983, p. 93). ZBC had four channels and transmitted from three stations, two from Harare and the other from Bulawayo. It only used two local languages, apart from English, namely, Shona and Ndebele. The ZBC was one of the few stations in Africa that had discarded short-wave broadcasting nationwide in preference for FM with the result that reception was generally good throughout the country.

The first radio program in South Africa was broadcast from Johannesburg on December 18, 1923. This was a concert from the headquarters of the erstwhile South African Railways. Regular broadcasting began in earnest on July 1, 1924.

In 1934, the Prime Minister, General JBM Hertzog, invited the Director General of the BBC, Sir John Reigh, to South Africa to advise the government on the future of local broadcasting. He advised that a corporation similar to the BBC should be created in South Africa. This organization was to be autonomous and free from government and political intervention. The South African Broadcasting Corporation (SABC) came into being on August 1, 1936, replacing the old ABC. The structure of the SABC was designed as a service organization along the lines of the BBC (de Villiers 1993, p. 128).

Ostensibly, the SABC was to have been an independent organization, a status that was negated by the fact that the corporation had to present an annual report to the government (also see Burger 1987).

In 1952, the SABC instituted black broadcasting with a rediffusion service to the Witwatersrand township Orlando. The purpose of the black service was to educate and entertain, and educational programs enjoyed special prominence in the programming. This resulted in black resistance to the implicit patronizing, but there was little doubt that black broadcasting had gained a foothold in South Africa. The black service was extended to include Jabuva, Dube, and Mofolo, and by the end of 1955 more than 60,000 black listeners were tuning into radio.

On January 1, 1962, Sotho and Zulu programs were carried on FM for the first time, and from July 1 of that year, programs were presented in Northern Sotho and Tswana. The creation of the erstwhile Radio Bantu meant that 51 hours of programming per week were broadcast in black languages. On February 1, 1963, these services were extended by the addition of a service in Zulu from Natal, and on June 1 a Xhosa service from Grahamstown.

The first regional service, Radio Highveld (now Highveld Stereo), started its broadcasts from Johannesburg on September 1, 1964. This was closely followed by the inception of Radio Good Hope, which commenced broadcasting on July 1, 1965 from Cape Town, and Radio Port Natal, which commenced broadcasting from Durban on May 1, 1967. South West Africa, now Namibia, could receive FM programs for the first time on December 1, 1968, through programs relayed from Windhoek and Oshakati.

An external service was created by the SABC. This service went on the air on December 21, 1950. On May 1, 1966, it was replaced by Radio RSA, which broadcasts programs to Africa and the Indian Ocean Islands in a multitude of languages. Radio RSA, as is the case with the BBC's world service and the Voice of America, is funded by the Department of Foreign Affairs and is operated by the SABC on an agency basis. The multilingual services of Radio RSA reach approximately 70 million listeners worldwide (de Villiers 1993, p. 129).

Broadcasting is a powerful medium which reaches millions of people daily. In South Africa, 14 million people listen to radio services every day.

A total of 47 radio services operate in Southern Africa (23 in South Africa, 2 in the Transkei, 3 each in Bophuthatswana and Swaziland, and 1 each in Venda, Ciskei, Botswana, and Lesotho) (de Villiers 1993, p. 129).

The vast SABC radio service network dominates radio broadcasting in South Africa. These services comprise national services, regional services, and groups of services aimed at specific language groups. The latter comprise the Nguni and Sotho service groups, and these services are the biggest attractions in SABC radio.

The 23 SABC radio services use a network of approximately 500 FM transmitters and the services of an INTELSAT satellite.

Apart from the SABC, a number of other radio stations broadcast to specific regions or wider audiences. The most important independent stations with studios within the borders of South Africa are Radio 702 and Capital Radio 604.

TELEVISION

East Africa

Kenya has two television stations: Kenya Television, which was part of Kenya Broadcasting Corporation (KBC), owned by the government, and Kenya Television Network (KTN), a supposedly private cable network that was discovered in early 1994 to be owned by the ruling party KANU as part of the Kenya Times enterprise. In January 1994, the only other shareholder in KTN, Jered Kangwana, was forced to sell his shares to KANU, which became the sole owner of the station.

Tanzania in 1994 still had television only on the island states of Zanzibar and Pemba, which was established in 1973 as the first color TV station in black Africa. With its one transmitter in the city of Zanzibar and a booster station in the neighboring island of Pemba, it covered most of Zanzibar's population of about 600,000 people (Kasoma 1988, p. 28). Like Malawi, the decision not to have television in mainland Tanzania was a political decision that was maintained when the country was a one-party state and that was bound to change with the arrival of a multiparty state.

Uganda Television is state owned and was established in 1954. It had been used extensively to rally the people behind the MNR government in the war-torn country. It was also often used by Idi Amin to make his breathtaking announcements during the heydays of his dictatorship. There was only one channel with few local programs. Most programs were from the United States and the United Kingdom, consisting of mainly outdated soap operas.

West Africa

The first television service in sub-Saharan Africa was established in Western Nigeria in 1959. In 1963, Sierra Leone inaugurated television services. In the same year, in the Francophone region of West Africa, Congo, Gabon, Ivory Coast, and Burkina Faso established television stations. To operate television services requires the commitment of enormous resources—to procure transmitters, studio equipment, and tapes;

to train staff; maintain equipment; and produce programs—which are sometimes not available in African countries (Shamuyarira 1985, p. vii). This has inter alia discouraged some African countries from operating television services. Rather, they are forced to rely on neighboring countries for television services. However, during the last two decades, there has been a modest increase in the number of West African countries owning and operating television services. This slow growth is attributed mainly to economic problems arising from difficulties in securing foreign exchange needed to procure and maintain broadcast equipment. In 1982, about 29 African countries had television stations. Today, more than 35 African countries own and operate television services.

Governments provide direct subsidies to television stations in West African countries and exert control over these services. Generally, television is highly centralized and controlled by the state. Stations earn revenues from commercials and license fees, and like radio, these fees are difficult to collect.

In Nigeria, television is exclusively owned by government—federal and state governments. The Nigerian Television Authority (NTA) was established as a body responsible for television production and operates a federal network. It has stations in several of the 30 state capitals. Most of the state governments established their own television stations between 1979 and 1983 during the civilian administration, mainly for political reasons.

One also has to mention the Western Nigeria Television Service. It was not only the first television station in Nigeria but also the first television facility in tropical Africa (Egbon 1983, p. 329). Permission was denied for the opposition leader in the country to launch his opinions on national radio in 1956. The only way he saw to address this situation was to form his own regionally controlled form of mass communication. On October 31, 1959, the Western Nigeria Television Station was established (Egbon 1983, p. 330), aimed at informing, educating, and entertaining some 12 million people.

Cameroon began regular television transmission in December 1985 after nine months of experimental transmission.

Television transmissions started in Chad and Niger in 1987 and 1980, respectively. Gabon has a commercial television station, which began in 1988 and is independent of the national broadcasting organization.

Southern Africa

Botswana was one of the last countries in the region to get television. Since independence, the country has had no television. It only had television in 1993 under a special arrangement with M-Net, the South African cable television network.

By 1994, Malawi continued to have no television, which was due to a deliberate government policy. It was hoped, however, that the advent of a multiparty political system would bring television to Malawi for the first time in the country's history.

Television broadcasting in Mozambique was only launched in the last years of the 1980s. By 1994, the one-channel government-owned station broadcast only to the residents of Maputo. The programs, which were almost totally in Portuguese, were mainly from Portugal, the former colonial power.

Television Zambia started in 1961 in Kitwe as a private enterprise by Lonrho. Government bought the facility and opened another station in the capital city Lusaka in 1964. By 1994, the station was still a government facility with the two studios alternating in programming but with Lusaka taking the lion's share. Unlike many African countries, television reception in Zambia was very widely spread, reaching all the nine provincial centers in the country. The Lusaka studios were housed in a Japanese-sponsored ultramodern station, one of the finest in Africa.

Zimbabwe Television became a two-channel station in the closing years of the 1980s after the Commonwealth Heads of Government Meeting in 1991. The second channel, however, which was mainly an educational and entertainment one, did not cover the country beyond Harare and Bulawayo. The old channel, however, covered most of the main towns and their immediate surroundings. Programs on both channels were mainly in English and were foreign originated.

South Africa was the last Westernized country to introduce television. During the 1960s, the ruling National Party, more specifically, the erstwhile Minister of Posts and Telegraphs, Dr. Albert Hertzog, regarded television as a negative influence on society. It was felt that the South African way of life should be spared the evils of the box (Mersham 1993, p. 175). However, in 1971 the government constituted the Meyer Commission to report on the introduction of a television service. The commission found that in a multinational and multilingual country like South Africa, television should be used to advance the self-development of all its peoples and to foster their pride in their own identity and culture (Mersham 1993, p. 175).

The government accepted the recommendations of the Meyer Commission. On April 27, 1971, it was announced that a television service for South Africa was to be introduced and that the SABC would run the service under statutory control.

The first SABC television test transmissions began on May 5, 1975, and a regular service was officially inaugurated on January 5, 1976. This service started off by carrying 37 hours of programming on a single television channel in English and Afrikaans. Television advertisements began in 1978.

During the 1970s and 1980s, tight control by the government led to a lack of diversity in ownership and control of television in South Africa as opposed to Western countries, but by the early 1990s there were signs that this situation could change. Despite these factors, South Africa has seen the introduction of a limited number of television services; mostly open services relayed by terrestrial and satellite transmitter systems.

Those services in operation in mid-1992 were Bop TV (2 channels), M-Net, SABC TV1, SABC CCV-TV, SABC TSS, Trinity TV (Ciskei), and Trinity TV (Transkei).

The 1980s also saw the development of television in neighboring countries. By mid-1992, the following were operational: Lesotho Television Service, Namibian Broadcasting Corporation, Swaziland Broadcasting Corporation TV, Zambia National Broadcasting Corporation TV, and Zimbabwe Broadcasting Corporation TV.

After having started with one channel in 1975, the SABC television network expanded in 1982 to two national television channels when TV2 and TV3 were launched on an additional channel. TV1 broadcast in English and Afrikaans, TV2 in Nguni languages, and TV3 in the Sotho languages. On March 30, 1984, TV4 (with programs mostly in English) was inaugurated, mainly as an additional entertainment service on the SABC's second channel. In the latter part of the 1980s, simulcasts on television and radio were introduced.

By the late 1980s, the SABC was using 11 languages on radio and 6 on television to reach a combined audience of 50 million people. This constituted one of the most extensive broadcast language diversities in the world (Mersham 1993, p. 178).

During the early 1990s, the SABC broadcast in seven languages on three services: TV1, CCV (Contemporary Community Values Television) and TSS (since 1994, National Network Television, NNTV). TV1 broadcasts in English and Afrikaans and has a daily multilingual audience of just under 6 million adults. CCV, mainly an English-language channel was introduced in 1990 to replace TV2 and TV4, although certain programs are available in the Nguni and Sotho languages. The SABC is perhaps the only national broadcaster in Africa that broadcasts to its viewers in their home languages, as well as in the official languages of the country. TSS is an additional channel that broadcasts sports, educational, and public service programs. Claimed total daily viewership of the SABC is in excess of 8 million (Mersham 1993, p. 178). The SABC has an operating revenue of some $40 million per annum and assets to the value of $40 million. It is considered to be the technically most advanced broadcasting service in Africa, and on the technical level, it competes with the most modern facilities worldwide.

SABC Television news presents five bulletins daily, reaching over 5 million viewers. Since the introduction of television in 1976, the SABC has maintained a monopoly on television news. Effectively, this has been a continuation of its dominance in broadcast news since the introduction of the SABC radio services in the 1930s. During the political flux of 1990 there was a marked change in SABC programs such as "Agenda," and interviews were held with formerly banned and jailed members of organizations such as the African National Congress (ANC).

M-Net is South Africa's first subscription service television station, which began operating on October 1, 1986. It provides about 120 hours a week of films, entertainment, documentaries, series and miniseries, and since July 1991, news documentaries. It has grown rapidly, increasing the number of subscribers to some 700,000 by March 1992. M-Net covers all the major metropolitan areas of South Africa by means of microwave links and terrestrial transmitters. M-Net offers a service in Hindu and Tamil ("East-Net") on Sunday mornings in addition to a Portuguese-language service ("Canal Português") during the same morning.

Bophuthatswana launched the first television service in competition with the SABC on December 31, 1983. Using the SABC's distribution network subject to signal restrictions, it also broadcasts to certain areas within the Republic of South Africa.

The introduction of popular international programs, and a less biased news program, drew considerable viewers from SABC TV1. In reaction, the SABC blocked the signal from reaching the white areas of Johannesburg and beamed it only to Soweto. Further signal blocking occurred when it became apparent that Bop-TV was more popular than TV2/3 in Soweto. The result was that only 40 percent of Soweto could receive a clear picture without the aid of a roof aerial or booster. Claiming that it is severely impeded by the SABC's restraint on its signal, Bop-TV has fought a long campaign to be allowed to extend its transmission into larger areas of South Africa and to prevent the SABC from broadcasting in Bophuthatswana (Mersham 1993, pp. 182–183).

On December 3, 1986, a religious television broadcasting service, Trinity Broadcasting Network, was launched in Ciskei. In 1991 the SABC allowed spare capacity on its television service to be used for religious broadcasts by Good News Television and Christian Television.

There are increasing pressures for African countries to improve on the quality of their programs. One way of achieving this is through commercialization of broadcast stations in Africa. This will lead to self-sufficiency and perhaps loosen the iron-grip African governments, as exclusive owners and main sponsors of broadcast stations, have on the broadcast industry on the continent. It will take proper and careful financial planning, commitment of resources, and political will for this to happen.

THE RELATIONSHIP BETWEEN THE MEDIA AND THE GOVERNMENT

It is commonly assumed that press systems in Africa are not as free as those in advanced Western democracies. It is the exception rather than the rule that the press in Africa functions as a Fourth Estate (Youm 1992, p. 483). Consequently, Africa is often considered as a continent without press freedom. However, according to Udoakah (1984, p. 35), press freedom is not an idea that can be conceptualized in a vacuum. The specific circumstances in a given society must also be taken into account.

Freedom of the press does not only refer to the right of journalists to publish news and comment without any interference from outside influences. It also means the right of the people to express themselves in the media of public communication without being curtailed by those who yield political, religious, economic, and other powers. It means the availability of the press to the people to bring them news and information if and when they need it. It means that the people should be given free and unimpeded access to news and information in which their destiny is at stake. Finally, freedom of the press means the relative absence of governmental, religious, economic, and other controls in the operation of the press.

All African countries have one form of press control or another. Some of these controls are contained in press laws, some are inherited from colonial administrators and made to suit prevailing political conditions and objectives of the government. Others exist in the form of exclusive ownership of broadcast media and joint ownership of the print media. Control of the media in most African countries is also seen in newsprint restriction or denial of foreign exchange needed to import newsprints. Censorship exists—prepublication as well as postpublication. Control can also be exerted on the media through licensing and registration of journalists.

The development of the media in Africa also has been affected by the conflicting perceptions of the role of the mass media in national development as advocated by

African governments on one hand and African media practitioners on the other. African governments see the mass media as an indispensable tool in national development. Some African journalists, however, as critical observers, remain skeptical of their governments' state development goals. They argue that the prevailing pattern of exclusive ownership of the broadcast media by African governments undermines the professional integrity of journalists employed by these governments and does not allow the media to fully contribute to national development (de Beer and Steyn, 1993a).

Few newspapers in Africa are owned by Africans, speaking out for Africans, and free from government control (Hachten 1993, p. 7). Government control has resulted in dull, obeisant, and uninformative papers, doing a disservice to African journalism.

Most African states gained political power through the barrel of a gun (Momoh 1987, p. 10). Governments used the press to inform the masses about what they thought the masses should know and whom they should support. Mass communication in Africa has basically been used as a tool for political power and influence rather than for disseminating public information and opinion to enhance political choices and hence democracy for the people. This has resulted in governments, regardless of whether they operate in a one-party or multiparty situation, clinging to the ownership of the main mass media so that they can use it to their benefit.

The lack of political will has been the biggest impediment to the development of a pluralist and free press in Eastern Africa and in Africa as a whole. This is borne out by the fact that in those countries that have introduced multiparty politics there has been a sudden increase in the number of private and independent newspapers. It cannot be denied that newspapers in countries with plural politics, except perhaps those in Uganda, have been freer than those without multiparty political systems.

The media in most African countries became propaganda mouthpieces to an increasingly unpopular government (Hachten 1993, p. 8) and lost their ability to criticize the government (Momoh 1987, p. 13). Journalists are often regarded by politicians as naive small boys and girls ready to do one's bidding, provided their hands are oiled with some petty bribes. Their questions ought to be conveniently brushed aside if one wants to keep his or her job and reputation. Only those questions that do not incriminate one should be answered. This mentality on the role of the press clashes head on with that of journalists who clearly see their role as providing the people with all the news and views that are fit to print or broadcast, regardless of who such news and views please or displease. Despite the journalistic background of many political leaders in Africa, their reaction to the press changed dramatically once they became heads of state (Faringer 1991, p. 125).

After independence, African nationalists wanted to transform the Western image of African society and replace it with indigenous institutions. They envisioned that a truly national press system would be an effective tool not only for promoting literacy and mobilizing the rural population to fight poverty and disease but also for fostering national integration and encouraging political stability.

These new media systems, Faringer (1991) argues, were expected to reconcile a new national identity with new loyalties, self-identities, and economic structures. But these nationalists and their governments soon discovered that political change is not synonymous with development.

In the following three sections, attention will be given to the present and past situation in each region, namely East, West, and Southern Africa.

East Africa

Measured against press freedom, government and media relations in East Africa, as anywhere else in Africa, have been sour at any period in history. The main reason has been the insistence by governments to own and control the mainstream mass media of daily newspapers and broadcast stations. Journalists working for these media have been constantly forced to run them in a way favorable to those in power. Failing to do so, they have been harassed and persecuted. Of the countries covered in this chapter, the country with the highest number of suppressions of press freedom was Ethiopia, with 33 reported cases between September 1991 and June 1992, followed by Kenya and Sudan, with 18 and 15 cases, respectively. Tanzania and Uganda had four cases each, while Malawi and Zimbabwe had three each. Botswana, Mauritius, and Zambia had only one case each (Kasoma 1992b).

Postindependence African governments' media policies were based on the assumption that the media is an effective and integral part of the ammunition needed to fight illiteracy, foster national unity, and promote national development. However, most of these governments hid from their people the covert policy of using the mass media to achieve their political goals. It is this not-so manifest objective that has remained a dominant factor in the structure and ownership of the media in Africa. It has also significantly shaped and continues to shape government–media relations and the concept of press freedom in Africa.

The political climate in East Africa has not, until very recently in some of the countries, been conductive to the development of a pluralist and independent press. The presence of authoritarian governments for several decades has left its mark on the media, which, as a result of strict controls, have not developed as well as they should have both in terms of numbers and freedom of expression. Not only have journalists been subjected to various forms of censorship, but the media houses themselves have not been left to operate freely. There have been numerous restrictions and sanctions to check newspapers that have dared to step out of line.

In Burundi, the tide of democracy was halted by a military coup in 1993 (*International Press Institute Report* 1993, p. 12). After a bloody tribal uprising, in which an estimated 70,000 people were killed, civilian rule was reinstated. During the coup, the media were suppressed and unable to report on tribal massacres.

Newspaper sanctions in Tanzania included economic strangulation such as the denial of government advertising revenue to "naughty newspapers" as well as restrictions of trading and import licenses for newsprint, which, except in the case of Tanzania, has to be imported from abroad. Since April 1992, when the government voted in favor of multiparty politics, thus ending 27 years of one-party rule, the press in Tanzania has been more pluralist, more open, more critical of government, and generally much freer than ever before. It is true that Tanzania had in the past seen flashes of a free press, particularly and ironically, during the latter half of 1969 when President Julius Nyerere nationalized the Lonrho-owned *Tanzania Standard.* Soon after the takeover, the government-owned newspaper displayed more freedom in publishing news embarrassing to the government than it did when it was a private newspaper (Kasoma 1986, pp. 202–204). But such flashes of press freedom did not come close to that enjoyed by multiparty Tanzania in the 1990s.

In the early 1990s, Tanzania had about half a dozen very outspoken, independent newspapers, which included *Family Mirror, Business Times,* and the *Express.* The biweekly *Family Mirror,* the accolade of Tanzania's independent press, which was founded in 1988, never failed not only to play the catalyst to the coming of multipartyism to Tanzania but also to reveal scandals and corruption within government. A typical example of its muckraking was the highly incriminating story headlined "Bonn Embassy Turned into Family Business," which alleged that the Tanzanian Ambassador to Germany was involved in massive misappropriation of government funds, misuse of official cars, and shameful disregard of diplomatic etiquette (*Family Mirror* 1992a). Although the diplomat in question was later in a subsequent issue given chance for a lengthy reply, the harm had already been done (*Family Mirror* 1992b).

The government of Tanzania repeatedly charged that the independent press in the country was going too far in departing from journalistic norms and that there was a need to introduce legislation to curb the excesses of such newspapers. However, by early 1994, no such law had been passed. Instead, the Tanzanian government continued to tolerate the outspoken newspapers in the true spirit of democracy.

The country's two daily newspapers *Daily News* (the renamed *Tanzania Standard)* and the Kiswahili Uhuru, owned by the government and the ruling Chama Cha Mapinduzi party, respectively, have continued to be proestablishment, trying their best to remove some of the heat on the administration caused by the independent press.

A treatise of the independent press in Tanzania would be incomplete without the mention of *Radi,* the highly respected Kiswahili monthly. In the 1990s, this publication often came up with investigative stories uncovering issues that the administration would have liked to sweep under the carpet. It was clear by the mid-1990s that the press in Tanzania was well on the road to liberalization comparable to that taking place in the country's political system, which was bracing itself for the first multiparty elections for three decades in 1995.

As can be seen from the previous paragraphs, the Tanzanian press has entered a new era with the emergence of a vibrant private press system (Shelby 1993, p. 62). Some newspapers have even started to publish stories in which government mismanagement and corruption are exposed. However, by means of journalists having to register, the government found a way through which these accusations could be stopped. The government could therefore also ensure that any competition for government-owned papers is stopped (Shelby 1993, p. 62). Although foreign aid for these independent newspapers from the West may be on the way, these newspapers will still have to stand on their own feet and become more independent (Shelby 1993, p. 63).

The relationship between the Tanzanian private press and the government has not been cordial. The government has often accused the newspapers of going too far in using their press freedom and threatened to pass a law to make journalists more responsible. For its part, the private press has continued to hound the government when it feels those in power are misusing their authority.

Uganda in the early 1990s no doubt offered the most exciting example of a free press in East Africa for two reasons. First, the independent press emerged unexpectedly from a political situation where an armed movement had been ruling unchallenged for more than a decade after seizing power in a bloody and long war. In short, a free press emerged in the absence of a multiparty democratic setup. It is true that Uganda, like its two Eastern African neighbors, Kenya and Tanzania, had its own share of official newspapers owned and operated by the government, which orchestrated mainly the official position. Such newspapers were led by the *New Vision,* edited by William Pike, a one-time bush ally of President Yoweri Museveni.

However, the outspokenness of Uganda's independent press by far outmatched any eloquence from the establishment press to the extent that people accepted it as the alternative voice causing its circulation to constantly rise. The leading critics of the Museveni government were *Uganda Confidential,* a monthly with a circulation of about 10,000, and *Weekly Topic,* with a circulation of about 20,000.

Uganda Confidential repeatedly revealed some hair-raising malpractices from the inner circle of the Museveni government. In one such article, headed "President Yoweri Museveni: Problems of Obsolete Power," the monthly described President Museveni as a powerful ruler who had maintained his absolute power by surrounding himself with incompetent and weak people who would not dare challenge him on any topic. The lengthy feature concluded:

> But on the whole, President Yoweri Museveni is still in control and many Ugandans are not calling for the overthrow of the NRM, but rather, they would wish the NRM to clean itself of corruption, and steer them to promised economic prosperity. But as to whether Museveni will from now on attempt to bridge the gap between himself and his followers in order to consolidate his movement, or as to whether he will continue to rule, like Alex Mukulu's play, without ears, only time will tell. (*Uganda Confidential* 1992a, p. 14)

In an unprecedented move, Museveni wrote a lengthy reply to *Uganda Confidential,* which the editor published with a pertinent introductory note saying in a continent where presidents respond by swords President Museveni had set a rare and unprecedented challenge by writing back a lengthy feature to the newspaper. It said the paper was grateful to Museveni's democratic approach.

In his reply, Museveni took time off to rebut some of the earlier personal allegations of corruption by the newspaper. He then point by point refuted allegations raised by the article that he had gained absolute power by surrounding himself with sycophants (*Uganda Confidential* 1992b, p. 15).

The equally outspoken *Weekly Topic* was set up in a rather unique way by reporters from other newspapers who write for it as well as own it without necessarily resigning from their full-time work. By 1993, this publication was dubbed Uganda's fastest-selling newspaper with a circulation almost rivaling that of the government-sponsored *New Vision.*

Apart from *Uganda Confidential* and *Weekly Topic,* other private newspapers in Uganda included dailies, *Ngabo* (The Shield) and *The Star;* biweeklies, *Financial Times;*

and weeklies, the *Citizen,* the *Economy,* the *Guide, Mulengera,* the *Shariat,* and *Munno.* The last one is an old weekly published in Luganda by the Catholic Church. The *Exposure* was another monthly, which as the name suggests, was bent on rivaling the exposures by the *Uganda Confidential* of government corruption and mismanagement.

For a country with a record of disappearances of journalists, particularly under the Idi Amin regime, Uganda, apart from some cases of questioning or arresting of journalists, accounted itself rather well in the maintenance of press freedom in the second half of the 1980s and early 1990s. The atrocities of Amin on journalists were simply unmatched anywhere in the world. Journalists murdered by his regime included Father Clement Kiggundu—editor of *Munno,* who was burned alive in his car by security agents after he published a resolution by the Uganda Women's Council demanding that the government investigate the mysterious disappearances of people—and Nicholas Stroh, an American journalist from the *Washington Star.*

One of the most ridiculous cases of arrest by the Museveni government, however, was that of three reporters Alfred Okware, Festo Ebongu, and Abdi Hassan of the *Third World Media Services,* the *New Vision,* and the BBC, respectively, who were charged with defamation for asking Zambia's President Kaunda what the authorities thought were embarrassing questions at a press conference during Kaunda's state visit to Uganda in January 1990. Apart from this case, Maja-Pearce (1992, p. 43) lists 10 such arrests and detentions between 1986 and 1992, most of them centered around security, especially where the military is concerned.

The high rate of incidents of suppression of press freedom in Ethiopia and Sudan was, no doubt, due to the extremely volatile political situation in the two countries, which had resulted in fierce and prolonged wars. The warring sides obviously did not want journalists to reveal information they did not like the other side to know, hence the suppression.

The Kenya of the 1990s no longer could boast of a press that was totally owned by private enterprise. The record had been tainted by the *Kenya Times,* which was started by the Kenya African National Union (KANU), the ruling party. This newspaper, which often reflected official government policy, published a daily Kiswahili version called *Kenya Leo.* The two dailies have joined the long-established *Daily Nation* (which also publishes a Kiswahili version called *Taifa Leo*) and the *Standard,* owned by the Aga Khan and the London Rhodesia Company (Lonrho), respectively. The country has a host of other independent weekly newspapers, most of which started in the wake of multiparty politicking in the early 1990s. These included *Society, Finance, Economic Review, Weekly Review,* and the *People.* The last one was started and owned by one of the opposition party leaders. In addition, there was the famous *Nairobi Law Monthly,* edited and owned by Gitobu Imanyara, which spearheaded the march to multipartyism in 1991 and 1992.

Kenya increasingly used extralegal controls to curb press freedom (*Index on Censorship* 1992; *Index on Censorship* 1993; Okoth-Owiro 1990; Schipper 1992). The mainstream newspapers, however, continued to soldier on against the odds of official harassment.

The high incidence of press suppression in Kenya came as a surprise, bearing in mind that Kenya has all along been regarded by the democratic world as a kind of model for a free press in Africa. But events leading to the advent of multiparty politics in that country did a lot to tarnish that image. In the run up to the coming of plural politics, journalists who either supported the opposition or published news that painted the government in unfavorable light were often harassed, some of them like Gitobu Imanyara, editor-in-chief of the *Nairobi Law Monthly* being incarcerated for lengthy periods without trial. Journalists arrested in the early 1990s in Kenya included Dedan Mbugua, editor of *Beyond;* George Mbugguss, editor of the *Daily Nation;* and Francis Githui Muhindi and James Kimondo, managing editor and production editor, respectively, of *Sunday Standard.* Publications that were banned included *Beyond, Financial Review,* and *Development Agenda* (Maja-Pearce 1992, pp. 42–45). Kenya's record of a free press was only somehow salvaged after the multiparty elections in 1993 when a number of fairly outspoken private weeklies appeared.

West Africa

At the start of the 1980s, Nigeria had one of the freest press systems in Africa. The political situation then allowed a considerable amount of freedom of expression in the media. However, successive military coups and, particularly at the beginning of the 1990s, draconian press decrees and governmental actions intended to limit this freedom weakened the Nigerian media. In the Ivory Coast, Burkina Faso, Gabon, and Sierra Leone, the press is censored, and criticism of government and its policies are not permitted. In Ghana, Cameroon, Niger, Mali, and Zaire, the press is censored, and there is no legal recourse. In Angola, Benin, Equatorial-Guinea, Guinea, Guinea-Bissau, Togo, and Chad, there is strict censorship, and only government views are permitted in the media.

According to Momoh (1987, p. 55), the press in Nigeria has the role of monitoring the situation both inside and outside the Nigerian borders. He claims that the press in Nigeria can only play a vital role in the country when the focus of events covered by the press stays Nigerian. The press needs to work to strengthen the idea of national unity within the country, the people's faith in the survival of the country, and the need to again establish the economy in Nigeria (Momoh 1987, p. 56). The press also plays a vital role in informing local citizens about the policies and objectives of the government, and telling foreigners coming into the country about the different cultures and norms in society (Momoh 1987, p. 56).

In Liberia, the biggest stumbling block to press freedom in the country came on July 21, 1984, with the promulgation of Decree 88A by the then People's Redemption Council government. According to this Decree, security forces could

> arrest and detain any person found spreading rumors, lies and misinformation against any government official or individual either by word of mouth, writing or by public broadcast. (Smith 1987, p. 59)

Despite this, only one newspaper in the country (hosting 2.3 million people) is owned by the government; the other four are privately owned (Smith 1987, p. 60). The electronic media, however—the largest radio station, rural radio, as well as the only television station—are mostly controlled by the government (Smith 1987, p. 60).

The media in Liberia therefore—and because of low circulation figures—have to rely on advertising revenue to make its existence profitable (Smith 1987, p. 60).

In Ghana, the independent press is slowly starting to emerge from the "culture of silence" (Butscher 1994, p. 4) evident since 1982 when the People's National Defence Council came to power. Since 1982, a number of newspapers were closed down and journalists were arrested and placed under exile. Both journalists and newspapers have to be granted a license by the government before being permitted to start working. Independent papers like the *Independent* and the *Chronicle* are very popular with readers because of their critical analysis of government policies and state functionaries (Butscher 1994, p. 5).

It seems that the press freedom situation in Ghana is not a hopeless one. The newly elected president of the Ghana Journalists Association, Amihere Kabral, pledged to continue the struggle for press freedom in the country (Butscher 1994, p. 6).

Due to official repression, exacerbated by economic and technical factors, the independent press in the Ivory Coast is "finding it difficult to cope" (Butscher 1994, p. 3). In the past two years, many journalists were arrested, detained, harassed and, assaulted for "insulting the head of state" (Butscher 1994, p. 3). Because the press never published anything negative about the government for more than 30 years, independent newspapers being critical of the government pose a serious threat to, as Butscher (1994, p. 4) puts it, "a system which has become a traditional institution." Apart from this, publishers in the country also face another problem as far as their financial conditions are concerned. The Ivorian Printing Company (SII) is the only standard printer in the country, and Edipresse, the sole distribution company, claims 35 percent for each copy of a publication that is distributed. This has led to a situation where most of the independent publications in the country will probably disappear from the newsstands in the near future (Butscher 1994, p. 3).

Since April 1992, the independent press in Sierra Leone is suffering due to the introduction of Decree No. 6 of September 1992. This decree requires newspaper editors to submit documents, pictorial representations, and photographs to an official censor for approval before publication (Butscher 1994, p. 11). Also, in January 1993, new press guidelines were introduced in the country, which, according to the Secretary of State, Information, should help to improve journalism standards and curb irresponsible reporting (Butscher 1994, p. 11). According to Butscher, official repression of the press in Sierra Leone already started in 1980, when the APC government introduced the Newspaper Amendment Act. This was only the start of a tradition handicapping the independent press in the country. Since then, this trend is continuing.

Southern Africa

South Africa is on the one hand described as one of the worst offenders of the rights of journalists in Africa (Committee to Protect Journalists 1983; Ziegler and Asante 1992, p. 80), yet it is also considered by both Africans and the rest of the world as having the freest press in Africa (Martin 1991, p. 193).

Press control in South Africa started as early as the nineteenth century. After determined efforts during the 1880s, Thomas Pringle and John Fairbairn initially won the fight for press freedom, when they freed the press from government intervention. Still today, this victory (stipulated in Ordinance 60), is known as the "Magna Carta" of press freedom in South Africa (de Beer and Steyn, 1993b, p. 210).

Different forms of media censorship have existed in South Africa from the time the National Party came to power in 1948 (de Beer 1991) until President F.W. de Klerk took over in 1989. According to media lawyers Reynolds and Jenkins,

> [Over the years] journalists have been imprisoned, newspapers closed down, newspapers confiscated, prosecutions brought for publishing restricted matter and perhaps, worst of all, for a short time (during the State of Emergency 1986–1990), a total blackout enforced on news of detentions, police action in quelling unrest, and on boycotts, strikes, stayaways, gatherings and other protest action. (cited in De Beer 1991)

In his policy speech to Parliament on February 2, 1990, President F. W. de Klerk repealed some of the more severe restrictions (including the 1986 Emergency Rules) on the free flow of information, in what was described as a "giant step towards a society where individual rights are protected against excess of government" and

> where freedom of association and freedom of speech are again real and tangible concepts, with the unbanning of political organizations (including the African National Congress and the South African Communist Party), the prohibition on quoting banned persons falling away and the press now free to report and publish the views of even the most outspoken and vehement of the government's critics. (cited in De Beer 1991)

Although the situation has changed since the start of the 1990s, South Africa does have a rather dismal history as far as press freedom and media control are concerned. Especially during the early 1980s, it was common practice to detain individuals, although the government authorities maintained that they did not detain individuals "because of their journalistic activity" (Committee to Protect Journalists 1983, p. 21), but "to protect and consolidate the system of apartheid and white rule as a whole" (Ziegler and Asante 1992, p. 82). As the then Minister of Law and Order, Louis le Grange put it:

> In my time, I have never detained a journalist because he is a journalist or because he is involved in journalism. We are concerned only about security laws. We are not suppressing people because they ply a particular point of view. Some of them have been acted against (I can't think of anyone in particular), because they have been associated with security that warranted strict action, in the government view, not because they differed from the government or were critical. We have media in South Africa as critical as in the United States. It is not a question of differing views. (Committee to Protect Journalists 1983, p. 22)

Apart from the formal state censorship practiced in South Africa over the years, of which most laws have now been lifted, journalists, and media practitioners in South Africa are still faced with what de Beer defined as "the censorship of terror":

> Censorship of terror is a form of unlawful controlled and/or uncontrolled psychological and/or physical violence directed and used to its own advantage by a political group in an effort to manipulate the free flow of news and comment in the media (manipulation of news) and/or to prevent specific news and comment from appearing in the media (coercive news evasion). As such, censorship of terror as a form of political violence is dichotomous and incongruous to the spontaneous and voluntary news coverage of and comment on terrorism in the media. (de Beer 1991)

The censorship of terror can be found in different forms:

Journalists are forced to write news reports with a specific content and slant or alternatively they are not allowed to write about specific themes or events. They are pressured to write positive news about certain organizations and negative news about others. In this way, a number of journalists were killed and assaulted, and some were tried by so-called people's courts. It has almost become endemic for journalists to receive threats. At the International Press Institute's meeting in Cape Town in February 1994, it was reported how black journalists are threatened by the waving of pistols during soccer meetings and by the infamous late telephone call at night (de Beer 1994).

Although not specifically serious in a physical sense, there is also another kind of censorship of terror. This is when intimidation has become so grave that journalists start evading news as a form of forced self-censorship. The result is that journalists now often do not ask certain questions, neither do they investigate news reports that might be perceived as negative by certain political groups. This has reached the stage where friendly journalistic criticism can easily be conceived as being the acts of a traitor—with disastrous results for the journalist (de Beer 1994).

Traditionally, the Afrikaans media in South Africa—especially the Afrikaans press—were considered as the propaganda arm of the National Party (for a complete discussion on the relationship between the National Party and the media, see De Beer and Steyn 1993b). However, this situation has changed over the years, and editors of Afrikaans newspapers point out that newspapers took, in many instances, independent viewpoints from those of political leaders (de Beer and Steyn 1993b, p. 210). Afrikaans newspapers also joined their English language colleagues during the 1980s in protesting against P.W. Botha's States of Emergency, as well as other measures affecting the free flow of information in the country (de Beer and Steyn, 1993b, p. 212).

Because of the political crossroads South Africa faces at the moment, there will be major influences on the future and freedom of the media in the country.

Another Southern African country that is considered to have one of the freest media systems on the continent is Zimbabwe. In an 1982 IPI Report, the monthly publication of the International Press Institute, it was stated that "with the exception of Nigeria . . . Zimbabwe now has the best press in Independent Africa" (Committee to Protect Journalists 1983, p. 81). However, there is only a small number of newspapers in the country, and almost all are controlled, either directly or indirectly, by the Zimbabwean government through The Media Trust (Committee to Protect Journalists 1983, p. 81).

One of the exceptions to the rule of authoritarian clamp-down on the media after independence is Namibia. According to the International Press Institute (1993, p. 41), the main problem facing the press in Namibia is not the relationship with the government but financial curtailments; there is very little governmental interference in editorial freedom. One of the main problems of the Namibian press is that the economy is still basically run by white capital, which includes publishing the main newspapers. This is especially true of the publishing house, Die Republikein, which not only owns most of the country's newspapers, but who also owns the country's only two private printing works. Even so, the so-called underground or revolutionary press as well as the Namibia Press Agency (NPA) played an important role in the liberation struggle, which led to the general election in 1991. Editors and other journalists were very much involved in the process of mobilization and political education of the Namibian people (Heuva 1993, pp. 94–103).

Newspapers in Zimbabwe are allowed to publish articles and editorials that express criticism toward the government, although the country does not have an opposition press (e.g., Shamuyarira 1985, pp. ix–x). According to the report by the Committee to Protect Journalists (1983, p. 83), this lack of an opposition press can be attributed to three reasons:

- A lack of tradition of such publishing
- The dearth of capital, skills, and equipment necessary for such publishing
- Government control

In the 1980s, Zimbabwe's extralegal methods of controlling the press have included the "promotion" of an editor-in-chief, Geoff Nyarota of the *Bulawayo Chronicle,* whom the authorities detested. Nyarota was pushed a rank higher in the Zimbabwe Mass Media Trust, the government organization that owns the newspaper, after he published a series of stories revealing details of a scandal in car sales to government ministers at a local motor assembly plant called Willowvale. The embarrassing news, which first came out in 1988, was later vindicated in a commission of inquiry resulting in the death of one cabinet minister by suicide. Nyarota's promotion ended when he finally resigned from his public relations job with the trust. He became editor-in-chief of a private newspaper, the *Financial Gazette,* but even there, government pressure had a bearing on his eventual removal by the same person, Elias Rusike, now chief executive of Modus Publications, owners of the *Gazette,* who had promoted him as editor of the *Chronicle.*

Nyarota's experience with political interference in the press was not isolated. Other journalists who have been dismissed include Willie Musarurwa, editor of *Sunday Mail,* for a story he published of a financial scandal at Air Zimbabwe, and his successor, Henry Muradzikwa, who was fired for publishing a story that said that Cuba had deported Zimbabwean students because they were suffering from AIDS. Bill Saidi was demoted from the editorship of *Sunday News.*

During the 1992 elections in Angola, widespread government manipulation of the media was revealed (Gray 1994, p. 13). According to the report by the Media Institute for Southern Africa, it is "clear that in Angola both the press and the electronic media are effectively muzzled by the ruling party and the government" (Gray 1994, p. 13). The report also claims that in the run-up to the elections, the MPLA government had exploited the media to the extent that it had claimed 49 journalists killed by Unita. The government's influence on the media is evident in the government's control and ownership of the only printing press, the government's control of the allocation of newsprint, and the government's ownership of all banks, which meant private operations could not obtain credit to set up independent media (Gray 1994, p. 13).

Although the right to criticize one's government is commonly seen as one of the fundamental rights in a democratic society, all national papers and magazines in Zambia are owned by the government (Lungu 1986, p. 386). Despite this, the media in Zambia has, since 1973, adopted certain techniques by means of which they criticize either the government or specific politicians. One of these is called the praise–blame technique and is commonly used in editorials: Often the president is praised for something, but at the same time the government is criticized for their actions (Lungu 1986, p. 392). The *Times of Zambia* has endeavored in educating locals about government policies (Lungu 1986, p. 394), and also prompted the government to act to rectify problems in the country.

The advent of multipartyism, which led to the overthrow, through the ballot box, of the 27-year-old one-party dictatorship of Kenneth Kaunda, opened the floodgates to a vociferous independent press in Zambia at the beginning of the 1990s. The lone nonestablishment critical weekly, *National Mirror,* owned by a combined force of Catholic and Protestant churches through Multimedia Zambia, was joined by more than half a dozen other private weeklies. They included *Weekly Post,* the *Sun,* the *Weekly Standard, Weekly Express,* and the *Financial Gazette.*

The *National Mirror* continued the tradition started in 1972 of acting as a watchdog against the government. In one of its issues, it castigated the MMD government for its corruption and drug trafficking, saying its downfall was imminent (*National Mirror 1993*). In a subsequent issue, the newspaper in its lead story headed "Chiluba Cheated" literally calling the president a liar. In an accompanying editorial on the reshuffles done in the wake of the drug trafficking and corruption allegations in the cabinet, *The National Mirror* (1994) said:

> The so-called reshuffles were nothing but a sham. In our view the Ministers would have better been left in their positions rather than the President trying to throw people off the scent of drug trafficking and corruption by putting people in fields they least understand.

Weekly Post, the most vociferous, owned by Zambians across the political line and a Briton and started in 1990, became a biweekly at the close of 1993. The newspaper led the campaign against drug trafficking and corruption in the Chiluba government, culminating in the resignation of two ministers and the deputy speaker of the national assembly and the firing of two ministers by the President. The *Sun* was another weekly that was very critical of the government. Like the *Weekly Post,* it had been agitating for Chiluba to get rid of corruption and drug trafficking in his government. In an editorial headed "Chiluba, Where Is Thy Sting?" The *Sun* criticized Chiluba for leaving out the real culprits in his reshuffles (the *Sun* 1994).

Not all the private newspapers were critical of government. The *Weekly Standard,* owned by none other than President Chiluba's special assistant for the press, Richard Sakala, was, for obvious reasons, generally progovernment. The on–off *Weekly Express,* edited by a former director of Zambia Information Service, Daniel Kapaya, like the *Weekly Standard,* was also generally supportive of the Movement for Multi-party Democracy (MMD) government. The 12-page broadsheet that claimed in its masthead to be Zambia's first independent newspaper showed its independence by being consistently progovernment and belittling the opposition parties and the newspapers that supported them. Editorializing on a lead story in the *Weekly Post,* which quoted defense minister Ben Mwila as saying Zambia was vulnerable to a military coup, the *Weekly Express,* which published a lead story in which Mwila denied ever making the statement, chided the *Weekly Post* for not acting responsibly since military matters were sensitive as they hinged on the security of the country (*Weekly Express* 1994).

The long-established government dailies, the *Times of Zambia* and *Zambia Daily Mail,* with their sister Sunday versions, the *Sunday Times of Zambia* and the *Sunday Mail,* continued publishing as government newspapers in spite of pledges by MMD ministers of information to privatize some or all of them. Their editorial policies of generally supporting government had, not surprisingly, not changed much from the times they published under the Kaunda regime. Zambia's better known monthly magazine was *Icengelo* (light) published by the Franciscan Fathers of the Catholic diocese of Ndola. This magazine, published in Chibemba, took a central role in agitating for multiparty democracy in 1989 and 1990 to the disappointment of a then reluctant Kaunda.

Such frictions between the private press and the government exist even in countries with few reported suppressions of the press, like Zambia and Zimbabwe where, apart from outdated legal controls on the media, governments have tried to impose extralegal controls. In Zambia, with probably the most outspoken press against the government in the region, journalists have been threatened by those in power for doing their work in a way displeasing to them. But most of these threats, particularly those against journalists working for the private or church media, have fallen on deaf ears. The journalists merely expose the threats and go on reporting as if nothing had happened. In the only reported case, the managing director of the *Weekly Post,* Fred M'membe, was briefly detained by police for a story the newspaper published in 1993.

Botswana has had a free and independent press since its independence in 1966, most probably because it has always been a multiparty state. Except for the government-owned *Daily News,* which is more of a government information bulletin than a newspaper, all the country's newspapers (all weeklies) are privately owned. They include the *Gazette of Botswana,* the *Botswana Guardian, Midweek Sun,* and *Mmegi—The Reporter.* All these newspapers are fairly young, the first one, the

Botswana Guardian, having started in 1982, giving opposition parties in Botswana the same coverage as the government.

The editors of the private press in Botswana see their role in the traditional Fourth Estate watchdog function given to newspapers in the older democracies of Europe and America. They are supposed to be critical of government, pointing out wrongs, suggesting solutions to problems, and generally setting the agenda for the Botswana people regarding which issues they should pay attention to (Kasoma 1992b, p. 80).

All the weekly newspapers in Botswana are printed in Johannesburg, South Africa, a country with which their owners have links. The only newspaper that nearly broke this jinx was *Newslink Africa.* By far the most exciting tabloid Botswana has ever had, the 28-page *Newslink Africa,* published in full color, died suddenly in 1992 after publishing for only a couple of years following a revelation that it was being financed by the South African Military Intelligence. Unlike the other weeklies, *Newslink Africa,* which published in full color, had managed to set up a printing press in Gaborone, the country's capital (Kasoma 1992, p. 80).

The future of the press in Botswana is connected with the evolving nature of the state and the social system. Both sociopolitical and economic forces in the region will help in the restructuring of the media–government relationship in Botswana (Zaffiro 1988, p. 117; also see Zaffiro 1992, pp. 125–141, on media policy in Botswana).

Press freedom does not have a universal meaning, and there can be no legal guarantees for press freedom in countries in transition to democracy (Brice 1992, p. 50). In Africa, the goals of individual countries, as well as the aspirations of the continent as a whole, must be seen in context when judging the state of press freedom on the continent (Udoakah 1984, p. 35).

As can be seen from the preceding discussion, the relationship between the government and the media in various African countries is one of controversy and tension. Although African countries will never be able to match the communication developments in the Western world, Momoh (1987, p. 18) says that they can "at least do a lot to streamline their information systems, each time emphasizing the cultural realities of their particular systems." He also believes that media practitioners in Africa must be allowed the freedom to become masters of their own systems, support these systems, protect them, and use them as springboard for other systems (Momoh 1987, p. 18).

Governments in African states must take the press as partners in progress, since the press is "some of the most loyal, patriotic citizens" a country can produce (Momoh 1987, p. 19). Through this, the government will not only allow press freedom in each individual country but also promote it.

WESTERN MEDIA COVERAGE OF AFRICA

Although Africa, Asia, and South America are said to be host to some 90 percent of the world population, Africa is one of the most underreported regions in the world (Hachten and Beil 1985, p. 626; Martin 1992, p. 331). According to Fitzgerald (1989, p. 59), "Many African governments seem to have succeeded in making it almost impossible for foreign journalists to operate with any degree of independence. As a result, the media have lost interest" (also see Paterson 1992, p. 190). Therefore, African countries are the first ones where the staff structure is cut when editorial budgets are tightened. The print media subsequently rely more on the use of photographs to explain the situation to its readers (Palmer, 1987, p. 241). Therefore, the problem is rather "too little news" than "too much bad news" (Hachten and Beil 1985, p. 630).

Especially during the 1970s, the Western media were strongly criticized by African and other developing countries for the way in which news about Africa was portrayed on international newscasts and in the international media. Developing countries were misunderstood in both the developed world and other developing countries (Fiofori 1985, p. 110).

As a result of the unbalanced flow of news from developing countries to the developed world, the 1970s saw the suggestion of the New World Information Order (NWIO),

> a proposed state in which the flow of news between the Southern and Northern Hemispheres would be equalized . . . in which much more attention would be given by the media to development news rather than violence and conflict. (Roser and Brown 1986, p. 115)

However, there were many problems surrounding this NWIO, for instance, the argument that an African news agency is not necessary, because Africa already receives news from many other sources (Paterson 1992, p. 190; also see Mytton 1983, p. 142; de Beer and Steyn 1993a, on the arguments surrounding the NWIO).

One reason for this one-way flow of information was the fact that developing countries could not, and in some cases still cannot, afford to buy the expensive technological equipment used in developed countries (Fiofori 1985, p. 108; Hooyberg 1993).

The uneven reporting on the continent was neither fair to Africa nor to the rest of the world (Martin 1992, p. 334). Africans agreed that their countries deserve more than stereotyped images of war, famine, and corruption (Fair 1993) and that the world should see more of their developmental side (Giffard 1987, p. 61). As Imanyara put it: "Africa is not simply wild game . . . [and] disasters" (1990, p. 18). Africa must be shown to the rest of the world as it wishes to be seen (Paterson 1992, p. 190).

Television journalism has a responsibility toward its audience in this regard. Since television was responsible for bringing hunger and poverty into people's living rooms (Palmer 1987), it must also be responsible for the education and information of its audience about the situation in Africa, as well as promoting social progress in these countries (Hooyberg 1993, p. 46; Ochola 1983; Williams, 1987, p. 527). According to Palmer (1987), Western television has done almost nothing to enhance the understanding of Africa since the 1960s, and its aims were incompatible with the real situation in Africa.

Ironically, although editors in developed countries encourage their journalists to write about the chaos in Africa, Western readers do not care about the reports on disasters and coups (Fitzgerald 1989, p. 59). Many Western newspapers and news services have therefore recently decided that Africa is no longer politically fashionable or newsworthy (Fitzgerald 1987, p. 24).

One reason for this, among many, is the fact that Western reporters see the situations in developing countries from their own perspective, mostly based on inaccurate information obtained from books and other literature (Fiofori 1985, p. 110; Imanyara 1990, p. 17). As one Kenyan editor put it:

> If I could have a reporter in London or Washington, I would want him to be a Kenyan with a Kenyan perspective and aiming at a Kenyan audience. (Martin 1991, p. 197)

Because of the high rate of intimidation against journalists in most of these countries and the subsequent situation of self-censorship, it becomes a special responsibility of the foreign media to accurately report on the situation in Africa (Fitzgerald 1989, p. 61; also see de Beer 1993a regarding the intimidation of South African journalists).

Journalists in developed and developing countries also have different attitudes toward the role of the media. Western journalists tend to see news as an impartial report on an event, while, according to Giffard (1987, p. 64), journalists from the third world always saw news as any statement that could advance the objectives of the government.

A possible answer for the unbalanced and biased news flow from African countries to the rest of the world lies in the fact that African governments have to subscribe to the developmental theory of the media, with the emphasis on positive, process-oriented news (Pratt and Manheim 1988).

Journalists from developed countries sometimes tend to apply the same criteria for press freedom in developing countries as in their own countries. When they do not get the same results, Africa is often described as having no press freedom. Also, government control is only one form of control applied to the media. Press control can also be influenced by the political beliefs in the country.

The media in Africa must also move away from state control and government interference and start to be profitable. This is the only way the media in Africa can become independent from government (Hooyberg 1993).

The press in Africa has a responsibility toward the rest of the world to ensure a more balanced perspective of the continent. As Martin (1992, p. 340) put it:

> A vibrant African press can . . . have an impact on the quality of reporting from Africa by the Northern media . . . (enabling) the media to report on Africa's economic and social situation with greater understanding of the underlying issues, and hopefully with more sympathy for what Africans are seeking to achieve.

The Establishment of News Agencies

Economic constraints and political intervention, to a large extent, limit the size of newspapers and the number of broadcast services in Africa. Also, most African countries cannot afford the cost of maintaining a staff of correspondents around the world. These countries are therefore forced to buy news wire service from one of the major trans-national news agencies (TNNAs): Reuters, the Associated Press, United Press International, Agence France-Press, and TASS. Some of the countries monitor international services of the BBC, Voice of America (VOA), and Radio Moscow.

Most African countries are dissatisfied with international news coverage provided by the four TNNAs. They argue that TNNAs emphasize negative news (conflict and disaster) while ignoring positive news. This dissatisfaction led to the formation of the Non-Aligned News Agencies Pool, designed to provide news coverage from the perspective of the developing nation. In 1975, the Yugoslav news agency Tanjug started relaying news from the developing nations. In 1977 membership of this pool was 41. Each member is permitted to submit 500 words each day; Tanjug translates the words into French, English, and Spanish and puts them in its daily file.

East Africa. For decades, all the countries in East Africa have had national news agencies, which were started as departments of ministries of information. These news agencies have been the official clearing houses for both local and foreign news. They include Botswana Press Agency (BOPA), Kenya News Agency (KNA), Malawi News Agency (MANA), Agence Informacao Mozambique (AIM), SHIHATA for Tanzania, Uganda News Agency (UNA), Zambia News Agency (ZANA), and Zimbabwe Inter-Africa News Agency (ZIANA).

They are all fairly decentralized in all the districts from where they send official news for the mainstream media, including the private newspapers, which rarely have or send reporters outside the capital cities. The biggest consumers of news agency news are, no doubt, the government broadcast stations, which partly rely on them for compilations of official tours in the districts by government officials. The other suppliers of district news are information service reporters who also are widely and evenly distributed throughout their respective countries.

No news agency reporters are based outside their respective countries to report from there. For outside news, the national news agencies rely on the established international wire and telecast services such as Reuters, Agence France-Presse, the Associated Press, and CNN. For some of the news within the continent of Africa, the national news agencies of East Africa subscribe to the Pan-African News Agency (PANA), of which they are members.

International wire and telecast services rarely use copy from PANA, and the national news agencies claim, with some justification, that their news is tinged with officialdom. In fact, even PANA has problems accepting some of the news sent by these agencies, which is nearly always tinted with official angles. On the other hand, the local news agencies often doctor news from foreign wire and telecast services to make it "suitable for local consumption." To make this possible, the international wire services in most countries are routed through the national news agencies, who then re-distribute copy to other subscribers after editing it.

By the mid-1980s, the region was witnessing a new breed of privately owned news agencies such as Palesa News Agency in Zambia, which was founded by a veteran journalist, Abe Maine. In Zimbabwe, there was Africa Information Afrique (AIA), which aimed at distributing news and features about Southern Africa. To make money to survive, such news agencies engage in a variety of activities, which include supplying video footage to television stations both within and outside the countries, providing news pictures as well as features to newspapers, and publishing newsletters.

West Africa.   Some African countries, for political reasons, do not permit the four transnational news agencies to have bureaus in their countries. Also in some cases, for some reason, some of these agencies have decided not to establish bureaus in some African countries. In such a case, African countries have also resorted to setting up their own national news agencies to provide international news coverage and to monitor incoming as well as outgoing news.

Thirty-one African states have national news agencies. In West Africa, more than 15 countries have national news agencies owned and operated by the government. The first news agency in West Africa, Ghana News Agency, was established in Ghana in 1957 immediately after Ghana's independence. It had a number of bureaus in African countries and in London and New York. In 1967, the Union of African News Agencies, comprising about 20 African countries, at a conference in Addis Ababa agreed to form a pan-African news agency. Ten years later, a secretariat was set up for such an agency in Kampala, Uganda. Two years later, the Pan-African News Agency (PANA) was founded and based in Dakar, Senegal, with no funds. UNESCO came to the rescue and the Arab Gulf states promised to help. However, by 1985, the agency was plagued with financial and technical problems.

Southern Africa.   The South African Press Association (Sapa) is the national news agency in Southern Africa. It is an independent, cooperative, non-profit news-gathering and distributing organization which is operated in the interests of the public and its own members. It was formed in 1938 by newspaper owners and replaced the Reuter SA Press Agency. Sapa receives and distributes news in Southern Africa. It has its own correspondents and is supplied with news by members and foreign news agencies like Reuters, Associated Press, and others (Diederichs 1993, p. 96).

In January and February 1991, millions of people all over the world, including South Africans, were able to watch events in the Gulf War through the eyes of Cable News Network (CNN). CNN was founded in 1983 by Ted Turner, based on the principle of providing a 24-hour news channel. CNN's regular programs reach about 70 million people in more than 125 countries, including countries in Africa (Foote and Amin 1993, p. 153).

In 1989 Bop-TV allowed uninterrupted CNN-broadcasts of news programming. In the beginning of 1990 the SABC also signed a contract that allowed unlimited transmission of any hard news (Mersham 1993, pp. 193–195). In 1993, CNN's broadcasts could be seen on a 24-hour basis in South Africa. Also in 1993, SKY News started broadcasts in South Africa.

It is also planned that KU-beam satellite technology will be introduced in South Africa in 1995. This will enable international stations like HBO and MTV, as well as CNN and SKY who are already broadcasting in the country, to broadcast their products to South African audiences without control by the Independent Broadcasting Authority (IBA) (Gevisser 1993, p. 53).

JOURNALIST ORGANIZATIONS

In most of the countries, journalists' organizations were rather weak in terms of membership as well as frequency of meetings. This was mainly due to the dictatorial one-party political system, which rarely entertained journalists to have a voice on any matter. Their job was merely to promote the party objectives by taking instructions from the party leadership.

With the advent of multiparty politics, however, the role of journalists started changing to that of watchdog against misuse of authority by politicians, particularly those in the government. Consequently, journalists started grouping together in a more purposeful way to fight for their rights and defend press freedom. Thus, in most countries, the real, strong journalists' unions and press associations started taking root with the arrival of multiparty politics, although some of the organizations existed nominally before the coming of plural politics.

The Botswana Journalists' Association, perhaps because of the lack of serious challenges from the government, has never really been very active. It has few members who rarely meet.

In Kenya, the Kenya Union of Journalists has been a bit more active, especially in the face of serious challenges from the government during the campaigns for multiparty politics when membership increased drastically as the journalists rallied together to defend press freedom in the face of serious threats to it by the government.

Similarly, Malawi's journalists only came together when the tight grip on the country by President Kamuzu Banda waned in 1993.

Mozambique was one of the few exceptions where journalists had the government to reckon with. As a result of their strength, they managed to influence the government to include a clause in the national constitution protecting freedom of the press as a basic human right. Mozambique is one of the very few African countries to do so, after Namibia.

The Tanzania Association of Journalists (TAJ) has for a long time been a weak talking shop with few real actions taken by those who attend meetings. So has the Uganda Journalists Association, whose members, especially in the days of Idi Amin, preferred to remain relatively silent to safeguard their lives.

The Press Association of Zambia (PAZA) has been badly organized except briefly in 1992, when it suddenly came to life to seek a successful court injunction to temporarily remove from office the director of Zambia Broadcasting Services, Dr. Steven Moyo, and the managing editor of the *Times* of Zambia, Mr. Bwendo Mulengela, for being extremely biased against the opposition parties in their coverage of political issues during the campaigns before the multiparty elections. After this good showing, the association again went to sleep. Its sister organization, the Zambia Union of Journalists (ZW) was no more successful, having been greatly hampered by a requirement made mandatory by the Kaunda government of not allowing journalists belonging to the government media to join the union, because they were regarded as civil servants who were supposed to belong to the Civil Servants' Union of Zambia. The membership in both organizations has been abysmal and meetings rare.

More active has been the Journalists Union of Zimbabwe (JUZ), whose leadership would have captured the all-powerful presidency of the now nearly defunct International Organization of Journalists (IOJ), if it had not been for internal squabbles.

In South Africa the following journalist or media organizations are found:

- The Broadcast Monitoring Project (BMP): The BMP is an independent, nongovernmental media research organization, funded by the European Community for the purpose of monitoring SABC news and current affairs broadcasts in the run up to the 1994 elections (Broadcast Monitoring Project 1993, p. i). The main objectives of the BMP are to analyze the content, selection, and manner of presentation of news and news programs; to inform appropriate monitoring bodies, interested parties, and the public of the results of the analysis; and to educate the broadcasting authorities, political parties, and the public in basic aspects of human rights.
- The South African Union of Journalists (SAUJ).
- The Media Workers Association of South Africa (Mwasa).

AFRICAN MEDIA IN THE FUTURE

When one looks at the future of media systems in Africa, certain problems, prospects, and functions comes to light.

This section addresses the challenges facing the media in Africa on the way to transition toward democratic political systems in various countries. Specific attention will be given to the role of the media in training and nation building in various countries.

Challenges Facing the Media

Training. Although politicians use journalists and the media to prop up their political images, not much attention is paid to financing the media to enable them to operate smoothly. Journalists are among the most lowly paid people and use outdated and obsolete equipment. Transport to ferry journalists to assignments is nearly always in short supply.

The root cause has been the token funds African governments allocate to official media in their annual budgets. In one country, the money allocated to run the broadcasting house for the whole year was not even enough to buy one small transmitter, leave alone maintain existing ones, which were in very bad shape. Little wonder this particular country had to go off the air for lengthy periods during the year because the spares for the shortwave transmitters could not be purchased. The problem with many African governments is that they rely too much on foreign aid money to run their information departments, particularly broadcasting. When donor money is not forthcoming, the state of the government-owned media remains in shambles. In 1989, for example, the government of Zambia was negotiating for $32.5 million aid money from the Italian government through UNESCO to develop its broadcasting in line with the recommendations of the UNESCO-sponsored study (UNESCO 1989).

When looking at the current state of affairs as far as the training of journalists in Africa is concerned, it seems that this aspect desperately needs attention if African media are to become independent and to be judged according to the same standards as those in the rest of the world (Martin 1992, p. 337). However, it is not only African media that are having a hard time. According to Winship the press is under assault everywhere, although he admits that "no segment of the world press is under heavier siege, nor fighting back harder than our African colleagues" (1994, p. 6).

Regular schools in journalism training and education in Eastern Africa were by the mid-1990s present in Kenya, Mozambique, Tanzania, Uganda, Zambia, and Zimbabwe. There were no journalism training institutions in Botswana and Malawi. Kenya and Zambia had the highest number and variety of training programs that range from certificate to master's levels.

Kenya's programs include those at university level, namely, the postgraduate diploma in journalism at the University of Nairobi, and the religiously biased bachelors and master's degrees in mass communication at Daystar University in Nairobi. In addition, the American University in Nairobi offers restricted minors in mass communication to those studying for various degrees. Further training is offered at the Kenya Institute of Mass Communication (KIMC), whose courses are tailored to suit the needs of the industry. The All Africa Conference of Churches (AACC) also offered diploma training with a stress on broadcast journalism.

Zambia is equally endowed with a variety of journalism education and training schools. They include the University of Zambia, which offers master of mass communication and bachelor of mass communication degrees; Evelyn Hone College, which provides a diploma course in journalism; Africa Literature Center (ALC), the interdenominational-sponsored pan-African school, which offers a 1-year diploma in journalism; and the Zambia Institute of Mass Communication (ZAMCOM), which, like its Kenyan counterpart, offers upgrading courses tailored to suit the journalism industry. The University of Zambia's two degree programs and the 1-year diploma at ALC attracts foreign students, making Zambia a journalism training center in the region.

Mozambique became, by virtue of being the coordinator of the culture and information sector of the Southern African Development Community (SADC), a training ground for journalists. The Nordic-SADC Journalism Center in Maputo was commissioned in 1993 to provide further training for working journalists in the region (also see Svarre 1994). The center, sponsored by the Danish International Development Agency (DANIDA) on behalf of all the other Nordic countries, started providing training on the spot in the respective countries on request. In addition to this center, Mozambique has its own National Journalism School in Maputo, which offers a two-year journalism diploma training to Mozambiqueans.

Tanzania has two training schools: the Tanzania School of Journalism (TSJ) in Dar es Salaam and the Nyengezi Social Training Center in Mwanza on the shores of Lake Victoria. The TSJ is a government institution while the Mwanza program is run by the Catholic Church as part of a community development college.

Uganda has two institutions: Makerere University, which offers the Bachelor of Mass Communication degree, and the National Institute of Public Administration, which caters for diploma level training. Both programs are based in Kampala and are heavily biased toward print media journalism training.

Zimbabwe's journalism training programs include a postgraduate diploma at the University of Zimbabwe, which was introduced in 1993 with aid from the Norwegian Agency for Development (Norad) through the University of Oslo. There is also the Harare Polytechnic, which offers a two-year diploma in mass communication, and the Christian College in Southern Africa, which provided training for Christian-biased journalism. All the three training programs are based in Harare.

Most of the journalism/mass communication training is based on the American model as attested by the predominance of American textbooks as well as American-trained teachers (Nordenstreng and Boafo 1989, p. 10).

Apart from these regular courses, the region benefits greatly from journalism/mass communication training and education conducted by overseas institutions and sponsored mainly by foreign donor agencies. Leading institutions in this regard include Britain's Thomson Foundation, the Friedrich Nauman Foundation and the Friedrich Ebert Foundation both of Germany, Radio Netherlands Training Center, the British Broadcasting Corporation, the U.S. Information Service through USAID, and the Nordic journalists' associations and donor agencies. These conduct or sponsor courses within the region. Some of them, however, like the International Institute of Journalism in Berlin, brought course participants to their campuses in Europe where they conduct residential training. Most of this type of training is short-term, lasting for about eight weeks.

Most of the training and education in the institutions is concentrated on print media journalism, leaving a big gap in broadcast journalism to be tackled by foreign donors and training institutions through piecemeal courses. Training at the technical support level such as engineering and printing was almost totally absent at the formal level and was mainly being conducted at the on-the-job training and in-service levels.

Africa needs, as Martin (1992, p. 337) put it, more written and African-oriented teaching materials specifically focusing on the region (Ogboajah 1985), more effort to recruit women as students, more emphasis on professional ethics, and more attention paid to the rural areas and environmental issues.

The oldest training institutions for journalists in West Africa is the Ghana Institute of Journalism in Accra, Ghana. It was established by Kwame Nkrumah in 1957. It offers a three-year diploma course in journalism and a two-year specialist course in public relations.

Four years later, in neighboring Nigeria, the University of Nigeria, Nsukka, established a department of journalism patterned after journalism schools in the United States. It temporarily closed down during the Nigeria–Biafra war in 1967 and reopened in 1970 after the war. In 1966, the University of Lagos founded bachelor's and master's degree programs in mass communication. In addition, a number of Nigerian universities and polytechnics offer degree and diploma courses in journalism or mass communication. Journalism training is also available at the Nigeria Institute of Journalism and at the Nigerian Broadcasting Staff Training School of Lagos.

In the French-speaking region of West Africa, the University of Cameroon offers a journalism program at the Ecole Superieure International de Journalisme de

Yaounde. In Senegal, the Centre d'Etudes des Sciences et Techniques de L'Information (CESTI) was established in 1970 to offer a diploma in journalism. In Zaire, before independence, there was a certificate program in journalism at the former University of Lovanium in Kinshasa. In 1973, a regular department of journalism was set up at the National University of Zaire. It offers bachelor, master's, and doctoral degrees in both print and electronic journalism.

However, there is a need in Africa for media professionals: publishers, journalists, announcers, and so on (Hooyberg 1993; Mwakawago 1986, p. 88), in addition to well-trained media managers (Martin 1992, p. 337).

According to Martin (1992, p. 338), external governments can assist in the following:

- Creating new schools and departments of journalism and communication
- Expanding practical training
- Financing press feasibility studies
- Helping local banks by guaranteeing loans to newspapers
- Assisting in the formulation of legal structures and rules to permit the establishment of an independent press

When considering a career in media-related fields in South Africa, various institutions and organizations offer training opportunities.

Several universities in South Africa offer a three-year bachelor of arts (communication) degree in which journalism is included for at least a semester and sometimes longer. Universities that are known for education in journalism are Potchefstroom University, which offers a four-year bachelor degree, as well as a bachelor of communications degree with communication and business communication as majors; Rhodes University offers the only four-year bachelor of arts (journalism and media studies) degree in South Africa. A one-year bachelor of arts (Hons) in journalism is offered at Stellenbosch University (for a discussion of the university programs, see Roodt 1993, p. 374). The three departments mentioned, as well as some other communication departments, offer programs leading to master's and doctoral degrees.

Also, *technikons* in South Africa offer a three-year National Diploma in Journalism, and colleges provide shorter private courses in journalism. The Argus School of Journalism offers a six-month training course for prospective journalists who have completed a relevant degree or diploma (Roodt 1993 p. 375).

As far as training in the field of broadcasting is concerned, courses similar to that of journalism are provided by most universities, *technikons,* and colleges. Also, the SABC offers employees extensive in-service training in different aspects of mass communications and broadcasting (Roodt 1993 p. 379).

There are also a small number of research institutions in South Africa specializing in journalism and media studies, such as the Institute for Communication Research at Potchefstroom University (which publishes the South African research journal for Journalism, *Ecquid Novi*), and the Center for Cultural and Media Studies at the University of Natal, Durban.

Although traditional journalism schools at South African universities have rather a tough time obtaining foreign financial assistance, new training organizations such as the Institute for the Advancement of Journalism in Johannesburg, South Africa, have easier access to foreign funding. For instance, the last mentioned institute received three quarters of a million Dutch guilders, more than $420,000, over three years to provide short intensive seminar courses, mainly for black journalists, and to give specialist mid-career training to practicing journalists (Snijders 1994, p. 3).

African newspapers often send their staff to Europe or the United States for in-house training, *inter alia* to expose them to objectivity in news reporting (Fitzgerald 1987, p. 26).

The Christian churches in Eastern Africa can serve as an example of to what extent the community in Africa must become involved in journalism training. They have not only been involved in the local and national media but have also gone into regional media organizations and journalism training. The All Africa Conference of Churches (AACC), based in Nairobi, Kenya, has for some time now been running the Africa Press Service (APS), a kind of news and features pool for both Christian and secular media in Africa. The AACC also conducts journalism training in mainly electronic media in Nairobi. The other notable Christian journalism training institutions are the Africa Literature Center (ALC) in Kitwe, Zambia, and the Christian College of Southern Africa (CCOSA) in Harare, Zimbabwe.

Nation Building. Because the majority of African nations have only become independent in the last two decades, there is a need in these countries for national integration (Faringer 1991, p. 128). Therefore, nationhood must be built. It is not something which can be taken for granted (Mwakawago 1986, p. 83; also see de Beer 1992).

The press is seen as a double-edged sword that can build or destroy those in power. What the politicians who own the main media, presumably on behalf of the people, are interested in harnessing is the power of the press to build them. They want to see the press involved in what they call "nation building" through reportage of the positive sides of their actions or the lack of them. A critical press is seen as destructive to national goals and aspirations. With the coming of multiparty politics, a critical press is seen by the ruling party as being used by the opposition to try to dislodge the government. On the other hand, the opposition parties see a press critical to them as being bribed by the government to keep the ruling party in power.

Along with this, the media also have the task of increasing the living standards of the local populations. If the media focus the attention of local inhabitants in a society in transition on the new national symbols, they can succeed in creating a sense of belonging as well as participation in the goals of this newly formed state (Mwakawago 1986, p. 83).

In the process of nation building, radio can play an important role in four areas, namely information, the facilitation of decision making, education, and entertainment (Mwakawago 1986, p. 87; Rama and Louw 1993, p. 71). As far as information is concerned, radio can report on events, as well as informing its listeners at the same time. By clarifying issues in society and informing listeners about the current trends in a community, it also helps listeners to make decisions through interviews, discussion groups, and so on. When it is not possible to use face-to-face education in a classroom, radio can fulfill this role. Because African people are very musical and extroverted (Mwakawago 1986, p. 88), radio is also the ideal medium for entertainment. In this case, music, poetry, drama, storytelling, and sports are among the main genres included.

West Africa experienced tremendous growth in radio after independence, partly because African countries realized that radio was a good instrument not only for promoting national development and integration but also for supporting formal and informal education because of its ability to transcend linguistic barriers and to reach literate as well as illiterate people in both the urban and rural areas. They also were seen by political agitators as a powerful vehicle for political change and political agitation. Hence, today in most African countries, broadcast stations are closely guarded by soldiers and the police.

Most radio stations in West Africa allocate considerable airtime to educational programs. This is in keeping with the importance African governments attach to radio as a vehicle for national development. News and current affairs and educational programs constitute about 40 percent of total program time. Request programs, including farmers', children's, women's, and trader's programs, are popular.

A variety of factors, principal among which are inadequate resources, a multiplicity of languages, lack of qualified personnel, and centralized media ownership, hinder the development of radio in Africa. This has resulted in a general reduction of important development-oriented and current affairs programs on radio stations in most West African countries.

Generally, most West African countries have not achieved satisfactory radio coverage. Although some cities do have FM stereo radio services, most rely on shortwave service. This type of radio transmission is limited because of various forms of interference.

Radio also has the very important role in a newly developing society of broadening the horizons of local inhabitants, or as one African listener described it:

> The radio can take a man up to a hill higher than any we can see on the horizon and let him look beyond. (Mytton 1983, p. 33)

With developmental journalism, there must be a national press to promote national integration, development, and ideological mobilization and also to contribute to education on basic economic needs (Youm 1992, p. 483). However, developmental journalism must not be seen as a justification for government regulation of the press in developing countries.

As far as control of the media in building a nation is concerned, Mwakawago (1986, p. 85) indicates that the state or government should own the media to create a national consciousness through educational programs.

FUNCTIONS OF THE MEDIA

The media in Africa have a very important future role to play: They must be given the liberty to speak out against local conditions, as well as those in other countries, and also make citizens more conscious of their rights and obligations in society (Martin 1992, p. 334).

Also, the media have a responsibility toward the continent as a whole to change the negative image of Africa in foreign media. If the world sees that Africa itself has vibrant and developing media, there is a possibility that the image of the continent will be reflected more positively in the Western media (Martin 1992, p. 334). In this regard, especially, radio and rural newspapers are worth mentioning and will be discussed next.

Radio

Literacy in Africa has been increasing since most African countries gained independence. However, newspaper readership, particularly of African language newspapers, has not kept pace with this increase. This may have to do partly with the belief that the number of daily newspapers read in a country and per capita income are highly correlated.

Because of high illiteracy, lack of funds and technology, the low life expectancy, poverty, and disease in Africa, radio can play an important role in the education of people (Mwakawago 1986, p. 82). Radio also can reach a majority of the population in African countries without major cost (Cancel 1986, p. 60).

In this sense, radio in specific countries can serve as an agent for total regional development (Olusa 1986, p. 3). However, only if there is collaboration between all role players in a given society can this be successful. In this regard the media, and especially radio, can have a very positive impact on agriculture, the creation of jobs, linking rural and urban areas with each other, the integration of heterogeneous groups in the same country, cooperation between regions, as well as educating people in a community (Domatob 1987, p. 109; Mytton 1983, p. 29; Mwakawago 1986, p. 83; Ziegler and Asante 1992, p. 45). Radio and television broadcasts are therefore thoroughly used in both Lesotho (see Molapo and Ntsani 1986, pp. 192–197) and Swaziland (see Makama 1986, p. 210) with these areas of development in mind.

However, the mass media most affected by the multiplicity of languages are radio and television. Lucky are countries such as Botswana, Madagascar, Tanzania, and Zimbabwe, with only one or two languages that are used in broadcasting. For most African countries, there is a problem regarding which of the many languages should be given airtime. For instance, Mozambique, in addition to Portuguese, broadcasts in 13 languages: Shangana, Shitswa, Sena, Shimanyika, Yao, Nyanja, Mapode, Nyungwe, Makuwa, and Swahili. Zambia broadcasts in seven local languages, apart from English: Nyanja, Bemba, Tonga, Lozi, Kaonde, Luvale, and Lunda (Kasoma 1988, p. 22). In nearly all cases, the owners of the languages not chosen are constantly agitating to have their languages included on the list. But there is a limit to how many languages can be broadcast in one day by one station.

The issue of which languages are used in the media is closely connected with the issue of which cultures the media are promoting and safeguarding. This makes the people whose languages are not being used even more incensed by the fact that the culture of their tribes is being neglected by the state-owned media, which they partly support with tax money. If the media were private, perhaps the issue of favouring some languages and cultures over others would not arise, because the private sponsors would have the sole prerogative of choosing which language their medium should use.

It would then be up to entrepreneurs from other ethnic groups to start media in their languages to promote their own culture and ethnic identity.

Also, radio can serve to air the meanings of political groupings when they do not necessarily agree with the policies of the government. This is the case in Zimbabwe, where Radio Truth is campaigning against the government. Illegal radio stations are in this case the only answer for an alternative voice, because the government owns legal stations and therefore does not allow any ideas conflicting with its own (Dexter 1986, p. 84).

This is, however, common practice in Africa, because according to Dexter (1986, p. 85), Africa probably has more clandestine stations in operation now than anywhere else in the world, with the possible exception of Central America. The number of radio stations in a country can be seen as an indication of its political situation (see Downer 1993).

Also in South Africa, there is currently a debate between the government and alternative radio stations, especially the right-wing-controlled Radio Pretoria. Although the government has ordered the closing down of this "conservative" radio station on a number of occasions (Rademeyer 1994, p. 4), the voice of Radio Pretoria can still be heard on air, although a temporary license was suspended ("Danie Schutte" 1994).

Rural Newspapers

Africa is basically an oral society with a multiplicity of languages and dialects that have no written forms. Thus, interpersonal communication is still a predominant mode of communication among Africans. Many people may not be able to buy newspapers, which does not mean that they cannot read. In some other cases, where some people can afford to buy newspapers, they are unable to read because they are not literate in the language in which these newspapers are published (mainly English, French, and Portuguese). Others are literate in African languages (e.g., Kiswahili, Hausa, Yoruba, siSwati, Afrikaans, Xhosa) but cannot find newspapers published in these languages. In Africa, a good amount of information is passed on by word of mouth from people who can read newspapers to those who cannot read.

It is therefore misleading to use the number of newspapers and newspaper readership as the only criteria for measuring Africa's media development. Even more misleading is to compare Africa's media development with that of the developed world without taking into account the structure of social relations, cultural foundations, communication habits, and information networks in Africa.

Rural newspapers were also the start of community media in Africa. The earliest rural newspapers started in Liberia in 1963 and in Niger in 1964. They appeared in mimeographed forms in support of literacy. Their content and style were designed to appeal to the rural reader. In the past few years one or more rural newspapers have been set up in Burkina Faso, Ghana, Liberia, Mali, and Togo.

In Africa, the words *rural newspaper* mean exactly what they say: It is a newspaper found in a rural community, with content and style oriented to the information and learning needs of the specific rural community in which it operates (Ansah *et al.* 1981, p. 7). The content and information level of each newspaper is determined by the community it serves, and these newspapers are also increasingly used with specifically literacy education in mind.

The growth of this form of media has been slow, mainly because of economic problems, a multiplicity of languages, and unavailability of infrastructures (electricity, roads, etc.) in rural Africa.

Rural newspapers have been found also to be effective teaching tools in the rural areas. They perform the important role of informing the rural population of local, regional, and national events, providing readers with development-oriented information to enable them to take part in social and economic development.

In accordance with guidelines set up by UNESCO communication and development experts, Mali was the first African country to establish a rural newspaper, *Kibaru,* published in the Bambara language in 1972 with an initial circulation of 5,000. This figure increased to about 10,000 copies.

Mali's success encouraged other African countries to experiment. Today, about 16 African countries have rural newspapers. They are mainly government publications operated by the state or its appointed agents. In some countries, nongovernmental organizations such as UNESCO and missionaries also assist in publishing rural newspapers. Most of the rural newspapers are monthly or weekly publications. A good number of them appear less frequently because of financial constraints. Generally, circulation ranges from 100 to 50,000. Many of them are published in local languages such as Kiswahili and Hausa and do not have their own printing facilities but are mimeographed or printed on offset presses on contract.

The low literacy rate diminishes the number of readers in many countries, except for Tanzania, which has a rather high literacy rate of 85 percent. But even for Tanzania, the readership of newspapers is affected adversely by the fact that all the newspapers are concentrated in Dar es Salaam and do not reach many literate rural people. Zambia has the next highest literacy rate in the region, 54 percent, followed by Madagascar, 53 percent. Then come Uganda, 52 percent; Kenya and Zimbabwe, 50 percent each; Somalia, 40 percent; Botswana, 35 percent (English); Malawi, 25 percent; Sudan, 20 percent; Ethiopia, 18 percent; and Mozambique, 14 percent (*The World Almanac* 1990). Bearing in mind that these literacy rates are much lower in rural areas, where most of the people, except for Zambia, live and which are poorly served by the urban-based press, it is reasonable to speculate that the number of literate people who read newspapers is even much lower than the literacy figures suggest.

Literacy education is where rural newspapers originated. Most of the first rural newspapers were linked to a literacy program (Ansah *et al.* 1981, p. 7). However, as these newspapers developed, they also had the following objectives in mind (Ansah *et al.* 1981, p. 11):

- The continual education of the community
- The regular informing of the local population
- The improvement of health, economic, and social conditions in communities
- The improvement of newspaper reading
- The development of the local press, as well as to encourage locals to express their views in the local press

- The economic and social development in communities with the help of locals
- The facilitation of dialogue between the local government and the rural population

These newspapers, however, also face difficulties as far as the training of personnel, economic viability, and printing facilities are concerned. Generally, personnel are self-taught and self-trained, with little or no professional training (Ansah *et al.* 1981, p. 30). There is definitely a need for professional journalism schools to concentrate on rural newspapers, rather than only focusing on the urban-based press.

As far as economic viability is concerned, it is rather difficult for these papers to maintain a high circulation figure, which is due to the fact that communities often have a large number of languages in which these papers must be printed to reach all members of the community. Except for unilingual Botswana, Madagascar, and Tanzania, all the other countries have scores of other languages. Malawi has certainly more languages than the Chichewa, which has been imposed by Banda's regime as the official language. Mozambique has more than 30 languages, while Zambia has 73 languages and dialects.

Because there is often no need or funds for advertising, advertising also cannot be seen as a way to increase the circulation figure of these newspapers (Ansah *et al.* 1981, p. 12). Therefore, none are self-supporting; all owe their existence to government subsidies. Very few private newspapers operate at a profit or break even. Most run at a loss, and sometimes the losses are so big that they have to close down. The turnover of private newspapers, especially in East Africa, has therefore been very high.

Recognizing this problem, the UNESCO seminar on promoting an independent and pluralistic media held in Windhoek, Namibia, in 1991 recommended funding some of the private newspapers to encourage pluralism as well as independence (UNESCO 1991 p. 26). Among the initiatives the Windhoek seminar identified were the financing of a feasibility study for the establishment of an independent press aid foundation and research into identifying capital funds for the foundation, financing of a feasibility study for the creation of a central board for the purchase of newsprint and establishment of such a board, the financing of a study on the readership of independent newspapers to set groups of advertising agents, and the support and creation of regional press enterprises (UNESCO 1991, p. 29).

The media in Eastern Africa, like the media in the rest of the continent, continued to be urban-centered both in terms of circulation and content. This had been so despite efforts by the governments, with the help of outside agencies, to introduce rural newspapers to support what many of them called development journalism. Unfortunately to many of them, development journalism has meant government-say-so reportage, glorifying government activities and brushing failures under the carpet. The so-called development reportage was mainly carried out in the government-supported rural newspapers, many of which were rural only by name, because they were compiled and edited in the urban centers and contained mainly town-biased information (Mbindyo 1985).

Botswana does not have what one can call rural newspapers. It does have a Setswana version of daily news, which the government gives as handouts in the main centers. The news in this newspaper is not particularly rural.

In contrast, Kenya has had rural newspapers for a very long time, which were initiated by UNESCO. But these, as Mbindyo (1985) has observed, have not been doing too well. Mbindyo's survey yielded empirical evidence, which indicated that the major problems affecting the rural press in Kenya related to bureaucratic structures, lack of management skills, poor production and distribution system, and acute shortage of operating capital.

Malawi does not have a rural newspaper, although the government monthly publication *Boma Lathu* (Our Government) circulates freely and widely in rural areas. It carries various development messages, from the government's viewpoint, in health, social, and economic fields. The government also prints a number of agricultural handouts to farmers on an irregular basis.

Mozambique has for a long time been ravaged by civil war to the extent that no rural newspapers have been allowed to exist.

In Tanzania, the country's rural press, which was started in 1974 as an integral component of a literacy development program, faced such problems as

- Weak management and administration
- Delays in distribution that were due to transportation difficulties
- A poor and inefficient system of collecting sales
- Poor budgeting and accounting procedures

To these inhibiting factors were added the general lack of seriousness and commitment on the part of the governments to the whole issue of democratizing and decentralizing mass communication structures and establishing media facilities in local communities and the absence of policies to integrate the media in the overall development plans (Kasoma 1994, p. xiii). Writing about development journalism in Tanzania, Mwaffisi has said that, although Tanzania purports to practice development journalism, its journalists are ill-prepared for it, because most of them have only basic journalistic skills and knowledge but lack the "scientific outlook" (Mwaffisi 1991, p. 93).

In spite of these problems, however, Tanzania is credited with some of the most successful rural development campaigns in the third world, one of them being the acclaimed *Mtu ni afya* (man is health), which was conducted in 1973 partly through rural publications and partly through radio (Hall and Dodds 1977, pp. 260–299).

Zambia's so-called provincial newspapers have a long history of failures. Like their Kenyan counterparts, their biggest problem has been the fact that they are provincial or rural in name only. Neither their content nor their circulation reflects rurality. The six newspapers, published in the various vernaculars, are edited and printed in metropolitan Lusaka and then shipped to their respective provinces, where the people hardly read them. To make matters worse, during some years, particularly during the closing years of the 1980s, the newspapers were published intermittently, the government giving the lame excuse that it did not have enough funds to publish them regularly. The newspapers merely served as poor propaganda organs for the government in power.

The Zimbabwean story is somehow different. The rural newspapers in that country are more prosperous, having been recently endowed with UNESCO and other donor funds and equipment. They are also published in English, unlike the Zambian newspapers, in the provincial centers where the reporting staff are based. Some of them, like the *Chaminuka News,* are reportedly proving very popular with the local people. The question, however, is whether they will remain publishing long after the donor funds have dried up. It is likely that the Zimbabwe Mass Media Trust, the government parastatal that administers the funds, may opt to fold them up when there are no more foreign funds flowing in.

Before the current crop of sponsored rural newspapers, Zimbabwe had more self-reliant rural newspapers such as *Mrewa News,* which have disappeared as a result of lack of encouragement from the government. These were cheaply produced mimeographed news sheets, which were published by the local people themselves with limited support from outside. In contrast, the present rural newspapers are produced on desktop publishing computers and printed in the central town of Gweru on the latest printing machines.

CONCLUSION

As with other aspects of human life in Africa, the media are also a complex institution faced with many problems and challenges, as was shown in this chapter. Although the media on this continent have already developed a great deal since the first papers were printed and the first radio broadcasts were heard, there still lies a rather troublesome way ahead.

Only recently have many countries gained their independence, and still in many independent countries, democracy is not practiced as it should be. Many countries' journalists and media practitioners are still intimidated by government officials, and also in many cases government still controls the media in one way or another.

Fortunately, this situation is slowly starting to change. In many countries, the last few years saw the emergence of independent newspapers and other publications, as well as independent radio and television stations. African governments will have to accept in the future that the public has a right to be informed and that the airwaves are public property and not the sole domain of authoritarian political leaders. If governments in Africa start to see the media as partners rather than enemies, the continent of Africa will at last be able to become a full partner in the global village, sending and receiving news to and from the rest of the world in an unbiased and professional manner.

Clearly, the picture drawn of Africa is a rather negative one, with Africans seeing themselves as victims of a colonial history. As indicated in this chapter, there is a lot of truth in this view, but the reality in Africa after independence showed that Africans have also been their own victims. Africans therefore have to take responsibility to find self-driven solutions for the situation they find themselves in (Ndebele 1994). One impressive example that has been set is that of the Republic of Korea. Within one generation's life span, from 1962 to 1988, the country's GNP increased from $2.3 billion to $169 billion. This remarkable achievement on the economic front is a shining example of what countries in the developing world can achieve. The opportunities for Africa glimmer on the horizon.

BIBLIOGRAPHY

Abiolo, K. O. *The Military Impediment to Democracy in Africa.* Unpublished paper read at the 43rd International Press Institute Annual General Assembly, Cape Town, South Africa, February 1994.

Abuoga, J. B., and A. A. Mutere. *The History of the Press in Kenya.* Nairobi: The African Council on Communication Education, 1988.

Ansah, P., C. Fall, B. C. Kouleu, and P. Mwaura. *Rural Journalism in Africa.* Paris: UNESCO, 1981.

Anyaoku, E. *The Challenge of Africa.* Unpublished paper read at the International Press Institute 43rd Annual General Meeting, Cape Town, South Africa, 14 February 1994.

Boafo, S. T. K. "Sub-Saharan Systems." *Journal of Communication* 35, no. 2 (1985): 196-198.

Brice, K. "Muzzling the Media." *Africa Report* 37 (July-August 1992): 49-51.

Broadcasting Monitoring Project. *6 months of the new SABC. Annual Report, December 1993.* Johannesburg, South Africa: Broadcasting Monitoring Project, 1993.

Burger, I. S. W. "The SABC as a National Broadcaster." *Ecquid Novi* 8, no. 2 (1987): 127-139.

Butscher, M. *Publish and Be Caught. (A report on Five West African Countries).* Unpublished paper read at the 43rd International Press Institute Annual General Assembly, Cape Town, South Africa, February 1994.

Cancel, R. "Broadcasting Oral Traditions: The 'Logic' of Narrative Variants—the Problem of 'Message'." *African Studies Review* 29, no. 1 (1986): 60-70.

The Citizen, 30 December 1993, 12.

Committee to Protect Journalists. *South Africa and Zimbabwe: The Freest Press in Africa?* New York: Committee to protect journalists, March 1983.

"Danie Schutte Waarsku Onwettige Uitsaaiers." *Beeld,* 26 January 1994, 2.

De Beer, A. S. *The Censorship of Terror: a South African Case Study.* Unpublished paper read at the International Communication Division, Association for Education in Journalism and Mass Communication, Annual Convention, Boston, 7-9 August 1991.

———. "The Role of the Media in Building a Nation for a Unified South Africa." *Plural Societies* 22, nos. 1, 2 (1992): 214-237.

———. "Censorship of Terror and the Struggle for Freedom: A South African Case Study." *Journal of Communication Inquiry* 17, no. 2 (1993): 36-51.

———. *Some Trends in the South African Mass Media.* Discussion: Transnet Breakfast Seminar Session, Esselenpark, South Africa, 25 February 1994.

De Beer, A. S., and E. F. Steyn. *Towards Defining News in the South African Context: The Media as Generator or Mediator of Conflict.* Paper read at the 12th Biannual Convention of the World Communication Association (WCA) in cooperation with the Southern African Communication Association (Sacomm), Human Sciences Research Council Building, Pretoria, July 1993a.

———. "The National Party and the Media: a Special Kind of Symbiosis." In *Media Debates of the 1990s.* Edited by P. E. Louw, 204-227. Bellville, France: Anthropos, 1993b.

De Beer, E. "Ander Stasies Dreig Hulle sal ook Uitsaai." *Beeld,* 26 January 1994, 2.

De Klerk, W. J. "Die Probleem Tussen Regering en Pers." *Ecquid Novi* 1, no. 2 (1980): 81-83.

De Villiers, C. "Radio. Chameleon of the Ether." In *Mass Media for the 90s. The South African Handbook of Mass Communication.* Edited by A. S. de Beer, 123-146. Pretoria: Van Schaik, 1993.

Dexter, G. L. "Africa's Shadow Voices." *Africa Report* 31, no. 5 (1986): 84-86.

Diederichs, P. "Newspapers. The Fourth Estate—a Cornerstone of Democracy." In *Mass Media for the 90s. The South African Handbook of Mass Communication.* Edited by A. S. de Beer, 69-98. Pretoria, South Africa, Van Schaik, 1993.

Dodson, D. C. *Research in African Literatures* 18, no. 1 (1987): 99-100.

Domatob, J. K. "Appropriate Media Technology in Black Africa." In *Mass Media and the African Society.* Edited by J. Domatob, A. Jika, and I. Nwosu. Nairobi: African Council on Communication Education, 1987.

Downer, M. "Clandestine Radio in African Revolutionary Movements: A Study of the Eritrean Struggle for Self-Determination." *Journal of Communication Inquiry* 17, no. 2 (1993): 93-104.

"Editorial." *The New York Times,* 4 January 1994.

Egbon, M. "Western Nigeria Television Service: Oldest in Tropical Africa." *Journalism Quarterly* 60, no. 2 (1983): 329-334.

Eksteen, J. A. "Sleutelrol vir SAUK in 'nuwe' Suid-Afrika." *Ecquid Novi* 5, no. 2 (1984): 113-121.

Fair, J. E. "War, Famine, and Poverty: Race in the Construction of Africa's Media Image." *Journal of Communication Inquiry* 17, no. 2 (1993): 5-22.

Fair, J. O. "The Role of the African Media in Patron–Client Relationship: A Preliminary Look." *Ecquid Novi* 8, no. 2 (1987): 103-126.

Family Mirror, April 1992a.

Family Mirror, May 1992b.

Faringer, G. L. *Press Freedom in Africa.* New York: Praeger, 1991.

Fellowship of Christian Communicators in South Africa. *Minutes of the Annual General Meeting.* Pretoria, South Africa, 16 October 1993.

Ferdon, D., and B. T. Harle. "The 1985 Media Controls Have Improved American News Coverage About South Africa." *Ecquid Novi* 10, nos. 1, 2 (1989): 220-226.

Fiofori, F. O. "The New World Information Order and International Communication." *Africa Today* 32, nos. 1, 2 (1985): 108-110.

Fitzgerald, M. A. "In Defense of the Fourth Estate." *Africa Report* 32, no. 2 (1987): 24-26.

———. "The News Hole: Reporting Africa." *Africa Report* 34, no. 4 (1989): 59-61.

Foote, J. S., and H. Amin. "Global TV News in Developing Countries: CNN's Expansion to Egypt." *Ecquid Novi* 14, no. 2, (1993): 153-178.

Gevisser, M. "Not the End of the World News." *Leadership* 12, no. 3 (1993): 49-53.

Giffard, C. A. "Closing the gap. The New World Information Order." *Africa Report* 32, no. 2 (1987), 61-64.

Gray, J. "MPLA Muzzles Angola's Media." *Sunday Times* 27 February 1994, 13.

Gurirab, T. B. *The Quest for Democracy: Which Way Forward for Africa?* Unpublished paper read at the International Press Institute 43rd Annual General Assembly, Cape Town, South Africa, 14 February 1994.

Hachten, W. A. *The Growth of Media in the Third World. African Failures, Asian Successes.* Ames: Iowa State University Press, 1993.

Hachten, W. A., and B. Beil. "Bad News or No News? Covering Africa 1965-1982." *Journalism Quarterly* 62, (1985): 626-630.

Hall, B. L., and T. Dodds. *Voices for Development: The Tanzanian Radio Study Campaigns. Radio for Education and Development: Case Studies.* World Bank Staff Working Paper, vol. 266, 260-299. Washington, D.C.: World Bank Staff, 1977.

Heath, C. W. "Private Sector Participation in Public Service Broadcasting: The Case of Kenya." *Journal of Communication* 38, no. 3 (1988): 96-107.

Heuva, W. "Resistance in Print: The Nationalist Press during the Namibian Liberation Struggle." *Ecquid Novi* 14, no. 1 (1993): 94-103.

Hooyberg, V. "Mass Media in Africa. From Distant Drums to Satellite." In *Mass Media for the 90s. The South African Handbook of Mass Communication.* Edited by A. S. de Beer, 29-47. Pretoria: Van Schaik, 1993.

Imanyara, G. "Africa Through Blinkers." *Africa Report* 35, no. 4 (1990): 17-18.

Index on Censorship. London: Writers and Scholars International, 1992.

Index on Censorship. London: Writers and Scholars International, 1993.

International Press Institute Report. 42, no. 12 (1993).

International Centre against Censorship. "Freedom of Expression in Malawi: More Change Needed." *Censorship News,* 3 February 1994, 1-22.

Kasoma, F. P. *The Press in Zambia.* Lusaka, Zambia: Multimedia Publications, 1986.

———. *The State of the Media in the SADCC Countries: Overview of the Media in Angola, Botswana, Lesotho, Mozambique, Swaziland, Tanzania, Zambia and Zimbabwe.* Nordic/SADCC Media Seminar Proceedings, 17-33. Harare, Zimbabwe, 16-19 September. Tampere, Finland: University of Tampere, 1988.

———. *Communication Policies in Botswana, Lesotho and Swaziland.* Tampere, Finland: University of Tampere, 1992a.

———. *Press Freedom and the African Charter on Human and People's Rights.* Unpublished paper read at the special seminar on The African Charter and its Impact on Communication Policy and Practice, African Council for Communication Education (ACCE) and the International Association for Mass Communication Research (IAMCR), 8th ACCE Biennial Conference, Cairo, Egypt, 16-23 October 1992b.

———. *The Rural Newspaper.* Nairobi: African Council for Communication Education, 1994.

Keane, J. *The Media and Democracy.* Cambridge, Mass.: Policy Press, 1991.

King, A. Unpublished paper read at the International Press Institute 43rd Annual General Assembly, Cape Town, South Africa, February 1994.

Lungu, G. F. "The Church, Labour and the Press in Zambia: The Role of Critical Observers in a One-Party State." *African Affairs* 85, no. 340 (1986): 385-410.

Maja-Pearce, A. "The Press in Central and Southern Africa." (1986): *Index on Censorship* 21, no. 4 (1992): 42-73.

Makama, T. "The Swaziland Broadcasting Service." In *Making Broadcasting Useful: The African Experience. The Development of Radio and Television in Africa in the 1980s.* Edited by G. Wedell, 210-213. Manchester, England: University Press, 1986.

"Malawi: Press Comes in from the Cold." *Southern African Chronicle,* 10 November 1993, 8.

Mandela, N. "The Media and Democracy." *Ecquid Novi* 12 no. 2 (1991): 172-176.

McClurgh, J. "The Afrikaans Press: From Lapdog to Watchdog?" *Ecquid Novi* 8, no. 1 (1987): 53-62.

Martin, L. J. "Africa." In *Global Journalism.* Edited by John C. Merrill, 155-204. New York: Longman, 1991.

Martin, R. "Africana. Building Independent Mass Media in Africa." *The Journal of Modern African Studies* 30, no. 2 (1992): 331-340.

Mbindyo, J. *The Study of Rural Press in Kenya.* Mimeograph available from the School of Journalism, University of Nairobi, 1985.

Mersham, G. M. "Television. A Fascinating Window on an Unfolding World." In *Mass Media for the 90s. The South African Handbook of Mass Communication.* Edited by A. S. de Beer, 173-197. Pretoria, South Africa: Van Schaik, 1993.

Molapo, J., and T. Ntsani. "The Organization and Management of Broadcasting in Lesotho." In *Making Broadcasting Useful: The African Experience. The Development of Radio and Television in Africa in the 1980s.* Edited by G. Wedell, 192–197. Manchester, England: University Press, 1986.

Momoh, P. T. "The Press and Nation-Building." *Africa Report* 32, no. 2 (1987): 54–57.

Moshiro, G. "The Role of Radio Tanzania Dar es Salaam in Mobilizing the Masses: A Critique." *Africa Media Review* 4, no. 3 (1990): 18–35.

Muller, P. "Suid-Afrika: Die Afrikaner en sy Pers." *Ecquid Novi* 5, no. 1 (1984): 62–68.

Mwaffisi, S. "Development Journalism: How Prepared Are Tanzanian Journalists?" *Africa Media Review* 5, no. 2 (1991): 85–93.

Mwakawago, D. "Radio as a Tool for Development." In *Making Broadcasting Useful: the African Experience. The Development of Radio and Television in Africa in the 1980s.* Edited by G. Wedell, 81–90. Manchester, England: University Press, 1986.

Mytton, G. *Mass Communication in Africa.* London: Edward Arnold, 1983.

Nation Printers and Publishers. *State of the Media in Kenya.* Nairobi: Nation Printers and Publishers, 1994.

National Mirror, 26 December 1993.

National Mirror, 16 January 1994.

Ndebele, N. *Vision of the Future Africa: Political Aspects.* Unpublished paper read at the 43rd International Press Institute Annual General Assembly, Cape Town, South Africa, 16 February 1994.

Nordenstreng, K., and S. T. K. Boafo. *Promotion of Textbooks for the Training of Journalists in Anglophone Africa.* Final report of an IPDC project. Paris: International Association for Mass Communication Research, Occasional Papers, 1989.

Ochola, F. W. *Aspects of Mass Communication and Journalism Research in Africa.* Nairobi: Africa Book Services, 1983.

Ogboajah, F. O., Editor. *Mass Communication, Culture and Society in West Africa.* Oxford: Hans Zell, 1985.

Okoth-Owiro, A. "Law and the Mass Media in Kenya." *Africa Media Review* 4, no. 1 (1990): 15–26.

Olusa, S. "Programme Building on Limited Budgets." In *Making Broadcasting Useful: the African Experience. The Development of Radio and Television in Africa in the 1980s.* Edited by G. Wedell, 3–16. Manchester, England: University Press, 1986.

Oniororo, N. *The Nigerian Press Freedom Situation.* Unpublished paper read at the 43rd International Press Institute Annual General Assembly, Cape Town, South Africa, February 1994.

Palmer, R. "Africa in the Media." *African Affairs* 86, no. 343 (1987): 241–247.

Paterson, C. "Western Television News from the Frontline States." *Ecquid Novi* 12, no. 2 (1991): 133–151.

Paterson, C. "Television News from the Frontline States." In *Africa's Media Image.* Edited by B. G. Hawk. London: Praeger, 1992.

Pratt, C. B., and J. B. Manheim. Communication research and developmental policy: agenda dynamics in an African setting. *Journal of Communication* 38, no. 3 (1988): 75–89.

Puri, S. "Malawi. Good-Bye Banda, Hello Freedom?" *IPI Report* 42, no. 8 (1993): 11–13.

Qwelane, J. *Living with Intimidation and Violence.* Unpublished paper read at the 43rd International Press Institute Annual General Meeting, Cape Town, South Africa, February 1994.

Rademeyer, R. "PMO en Radio Pretoria Draai Weer in Hof." *Beeld,* 28 January 1994, 4.

Rama, K., and E. Louw. "Community Radio: People's Voice or Activist Dream?" In *South African Media Policy. Debates of the 1990s.* Edited by P. E. Louw, 71–78. Bellville, France: Anthropos, 1993.

Reynolds, P., and P. Jenkins. "Press Can Now Play Rightful Role." *Sowetan,* 4 November 1990, 16.

Roodt, Z. "Career and Training Opportunities. Embarking on a Spellbinding Journey." In *Mass Media for the 90s. The South African Handbook of Mass Communication.* Edited by A. S. de Beer, 369-390. Pretoria, South Africa: Van Schaik, 1993.

Roser, C., and L. Brown. "African Newspaper Editors and the New World Information Order." *Journalism Quarterly* 63, (1986): 114-121.

Schipper, M. "Kenya: An Injury to all Mankind." *Index on Censorship* 21, no. 6 (1992): 30.

Shamuyarira, N. M. "Foreword." In *Reporting Africa. A Manual for Reporters in Africa.* Edited by D. Rowlands and H. Lewin, vii-x. Harare: Mardon Printers, 1985.

Shelby, B. "The Measure of Freedom." *Africa Report* 5, no. 1 (1993): 60-63.

Smith, L. "Muzzling the Media." *Africa Report* 32, no. 2 (1987): 58-60.

Snijders, M. *Training African Journalists.* Unpublished paper read at the 43rd International Press Institute Annual General Assembly, Cape Town, South Africa, 16 February 1994.

The Sun, 17 January 1994.

Svarre, K. L. *Training African Journalists.* Unpublished paper read at the 43rd International Press Institute Annual General Assembly, Cape Town, South Africa, 16 February 1994.

Thloloe, J. *Living with Intimidation and Violence.* Unpublished paper read at the 43rd International Press Institute Annual General Assembly, Cape Town, South Africa, February 1994.

Tomaselli, K. G., and P. E. Louw. "The South African Progressive Press 1986-1988." *Ecquid Novi* 10, nos. 1, 2 (1989): 70-94.

Udoakah, N. "Press freedom, the West and Africa." *Africa* 154 (June 1994): 35.

Uganda Confidential, 14 February 1992a.

Uganda Confidential, 15 March 1992b.

UNESCO. *Broadcasting for Development in Zambia. Vol. 2. Interim Report.* Paris: UNESCO, 1989.

UNESCO. *Final Report.* Seminar on Promoting an Independent and Pluralistic African Press. Hotel Safari, Windhoek, Namibia 29 April to 3 May 1991. Paris: UNESCO, 1991.

Vosloo, T. "The Press as Watchdog of Corruption." *Ecquid Novi* 10, nos. 1, 2 (1989): 198-203.

Weekly Express, 17 January 1994.

"Western Democracy Is Losing Ground All Over Africa." *The Citizen* 12, no. 30 (1993): 12.

Williams, M. *International Affairs* 63, no. 3 (1987): 527-528.

Winship, T. *Training African Journalists.* Unpublished paper read at the 43rd International Press Institute Annual General Assembly, Cape Town, South Africa, 16 February 1994.

The World Almanac. 1990. Mahwah, N.J.: Funk and Wagnall's Corp.

Youm, K. H. Review of *Press Freedom in Africa* by G. L. Faringer. *Journalism Quarterly* 69, (1992): 483-484.

Yushkiavitshus, H. Unpublished, untitled paper read at the International Press Institute, 43rd Annual General Assembly, Cape Town, South Africa, 16 February 1994.

Zaffiro, J. J. "Regional Pressure and the Erosion of Media Freedom in an African Democracy: the Case of Botswana." *Journal of Communication* 38, no. 3 (1992): 108-120.

———. "Media Policy Development in Botswana: Patterns of Change and Continuity." *Ecquid Novi* 13, no. 2 (1992): 125-141.

Ziegler, D., and M. K. Asante. *Thunder and Silence. The Mass Media in Africa.* Trenton, N.J.: Africa World Press, 1992.

chapter 13

Asia and the Pacific

Anju Grover Chaudhary and Anne Cooper Chen

"The press always takes on the form and coloration of the social and political structures within which it operates," wrote Siebert, Peterson, and Schramm in 1956 (p. 1). To understand the mass media of Asia, where three-fifths of the world's people live, we must look briefly at the social and political life of the region. Asia is defined in this book as the nations and dependent territories that stretch from Afghanistan east to Japan and south to Australia and New Zealand, but excluding the former Soviet Union. About 15 percent of the population is urban, but because the region is so populous, that small percentage represents many millions in real terms.

As Table 13.1 shows, the countries in the region vary widely in terms of virtually any index one cares to mention. No other region shows such diverse population figures. Asia includes China, with over 1.1 billion people, and India, with nearly 883 million—the two most populous nations on the earth. By 2100, India is expected to move into first place with 1.63 billion people, making China the second largest nation with 1.57 billion.

By contrast, certain independent states in the South Pacific have fewer people than Toledo, Ohio: Kiribati, for example, has about 64,000 inhabitants; Tonga, about 109,000; and Vanuatu, about 135,000. Tiny Nauru, with 8,400 people, has little in the way of mass media. Thus, because of space limitations in this chapter, the following discussion will concentrate on nations with more than 500,000 people and a media system that can accurately be described as "mass."

But contrasts in population figures in themselves do not tell us much about the quality of life. The statistics commonly used to compare countries should be used with caution, but each can contribute to our understanding of the context in which mass media operate. A single measure of literacy does not tell us whether differences exist between men and women. However, we can learn from them that in all the countries of South Asia, and in Papua New Guinea, less than half the population over age 15 can read and write.

TABLE 13.1 Comparative indices for 26 Asian nations and Hong Kong

	Print Media				Electronic Media		
	Population (millions)	Adult Literacy (%)	No. of Daily Newspapers	Gov. Control of Content	Radios in Use (in thousands)	TVs in Use (in thousands)	Gov. Control of Content
South Asia							
Afghanistan	16.9	29.4	14	Strong	1,670	130	Strong
Bangladesh	111.4	35.3	72	Moderate	4,650	500	Moderate
Bhutan	0.7	18.0	1	Strong	NA	NA	Strong
India	882.6	48.2	1978	Weak	65,000	7,000	Moderate
Nepal	19.9	25.6	28	Moderate	625	30	Strong
Pakistan	121.7	34.8	183	Moderate	10,200	1,527	Strong
Sri Lanka	17.6	88.4	21	Moderate	3,300	550	Moderate
Southeast Asia							
Burma (Myanmar)	42.5	80.6	7	Strong	3,300	70	Strong
Cambodia (est.)	9.1	NA	NA	Strong	860	65	Strong
Indonesia	184.5	78.4	60	Moderate	26,000	8,000	Strong
Laos	4.4	84.0	3	Strong	500	20	Strong
Malaysia	18.7	73.0	47	Strong	8,300	2,500	Strong
Philippines	63.7	89.7	29	Moderate	7,560	2,500	Moderate
Singapore	2.8	86.1	8	Moderate	822	1,000	Strong
Thailand	56.3	93.0	40	Strong	10,000	6,000	Strong
Vietnam	69.2	90.0	5	Strong	860	65	Strong

(continued)

TABLE 13.1 (continued)

	Print Media				Electronic Media		
	Population (millions)	Adult Literacy (%)	No. of Daily Newspapers	Gov. Control of Content	Radios in Use (in thousands)	TVs in Use (in thousands)	Gov. Control of Content
East Asia							
China	1165.8	73.3	78	Strong	206,000	30,000	Strong
Hong Kong	5.7	88.1	NA	Weak	3,700	1,500	Moderate
Japan	24.4	100.0	158	Weak	11,000	75,000	Weak
Mongolia	2.3	90.0	2	Moderate	280	80	Moderate
North Korea	22.4	90.0	11	Moderate	2,500	300	Strong
South Korea	44.3	96.3	39	Moderate	42,570	8,800	Strong
Taiwan	20.8	92.0	77	Moderate	NA	NA	Moderate
Pacific							
Australia	17.8	100.0	68	Weak	21,000	8,000	Weak
Fiji (est.)	0.8	86.0	6	Strong	430	11	Strong
New Zealand	3.4	100.0	35	Weak	3,100	1,250	Weak
Papua New Guinea	3.9	52.0	2	Weak	260	44	Weak

NA = not available

SOURCES: *The Far East and Australasia 1993*, 24th Edition (London: Europe Publications Ltd., 1993); *International Marketing Data and Statistics 1993*, 17th Edition (Great Britain: Euromonitor, 1993); *UNESCO Statistical Yearbook, 1992* (Paris: UNESCO, 1992); Freedom House, *Freedom in the World, '92–'93* (New York: Freedom House, 1993); various government agencies.

The often-used statistic to measure economic development, gross national product (GNP) per capita, has limitations because of what it doesn't tell about the non-monetary components of daily life. Infant mortality per 1,000 live births is commonly used to judge physical well-being and health care, but it does not tell us, for example, about the treatment of the elderly. According to the United Nations (UN) International Children's Fund, Asia includes four countries with the lowest number of children who die before their first birthday—Japan, Hong Kong, Singapore, and Australia—and four countries with the highest number—Afghanistan, Cambodia, Bhutan, and Nepal.

Even more telling is the "human suffering index," a composite figure that includes infant mortality and literacy among its 10 components. According to the Population Crisis Committee's human suffering index, the people of eight Asian nations live under extremely poor conditions; on the other hand, four nations (Japan, Singapore, Australia, and New Zealand) can boast of minimal suffering (Figure 13.1). Other regions of the world, notably Africa, suffer more extreme hardships overall, but no other region exhibits the marked contrasts that Asia does.

HISTORICAL HIGHLIGHTS

Invented in China, paper has been dated, using surviving specimens, back to 49 BC. The use of ink (for making marks with brushes) started even earlier, at least as far back as 1300 BC. Writing, in the form of graphs on pottery, has been dated back to about 5000 BC. The Chinese began using woodblock printing extensively in the 900s AD, while Koreans perfected metal movable type in the early 1400s. Thus, print media have existed in Asia longer than anywhere else in the world.

Although classical Chinese united people in Japan, Korea, Vietnam, and other countries in Southeast Asia, only elites mastered it. Even in China itself, a mere 1 or 2 percent could read and write the language in 100 BC, and only about 5 percent as late as 1800. But with a population of about 300 million in 1800, China had about 15 million potential readers.

Beginning in the Ming Dynasty (1368–1644), competing publishers issued court-news periodicals for sale to literate officials and merchants. Printed from hand-carved blocks, these gazettes lasted into the 1800s. More popular illustrated newspapers carrying sensationalized news appeared occasionally before 1800 (Bishop 1989, p. 42).

Westerners—including colonial authorities, missionaries, and trading companies—started the first regularly published, modern periodicals. In 1616, the Dutch East India Company in Indonesia issued a newsletter called *Memoires des Nouvelles.* The first general interest publication, the Dutch-language *Bataviasche Nouvelles,* appeared in 1744; edited by a Dutch official in Indonesia, it lasted only two years. During the remainder of the century, various Dutch journals appeared and disappeared.

In 1780 in India, an Englishman, James Hicky, started a two-sheet weekly called the *Bengal Gazette.* Also known as *Hicky's Gazette,* the paper exposed the private lives of East India Company officials and Governor-General Warren Hastings and his wife. In 1782, Hicky was sued for libel and imprisoned in poverty.

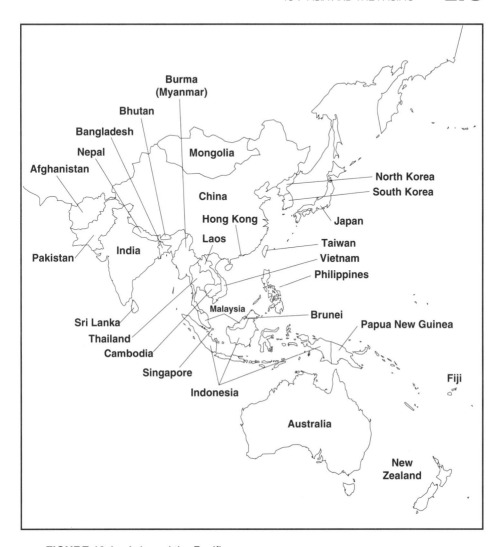

FIGURE 13.1   Asia and the Pacific

The Press in the Nineteenth Century

Papers in indigenous languages appeared later than those in colonists' languages. A British missionary began a monthly magazine in vernacular Chinese in 1815. The first newspapers in Afghanistan, Burma, and Korea were also in the native language.

An American missionary established the pioneering *Bangkok Recorder* in Thailand in 1844. Other missionaries active in publishing set up a printing press, which had been "reinvented" by Gutenberg and exported back to Asia, in the important port of Malacca (now Melaka, Malaysia).

The first Indian paper owned by an Indian was the English-language *Bengal Gazette,* established by Gangadhar Bhattacharjee in Calcutta in 1816. Raja Ram Mohan Roy, one of India's greatest champions of political and press freedom, published the country's first non-English language paper, *Mirat-ul-Akhbar,* in 1821. Sometimes called the "father of modern India," he wrote a noted memorial for the repeal of the press ordinance of 1823.

In South and Southeast Asia, a number of existing publications have nineteenth-century roots. Both Singapore's *Straits Times* and Malaysia's *New Straits Times* share common parentage in the original *Straits Times,* founded in 1834 and a daily since 1858. *The Times of India,* the country's oldest English-language daily, was established in 1838 as a commercial biweekly and converted into a daily in 1851. Other long-established Indian papers include the *Amrita Bazar Patrika,* a Bengali-language daily in Calcutta (1868); the *Statesman,* an independent liberal English-language daily (1875); and the *Hindu,* an English-language daily in Madras (1878).

As in India, the press in Sri Lanka has strong British roots. The colonial authorities started the *Government Gazette* for foreign residents in 1802. The first newspaper in a conventional sense was the *Colombo Journal* (1832), while the first in Sihnalese was the weekly *Lakminapahana* (1862).

Both the *China Mail* in Hong Kong (1845) and the *North China Herald* in Shanghai (1850, the precursor of the renowned *North China Daily News*) were published in English for foreign residents. Other non-Chinese publications—in Portuguese, French, German, Italian, Japanese, and Russian—likewise sprang up to serve the expatriate population in China's port cities.

Hong Kong's first modern Chinese-language newspaper, *Chung-wai Hsin-pao* ("Sino-foreign News"), got its start in 1860 because a group of Chinese rented a font of metal Chinese characters from the English-language *Hong Kong Daily Press* office, which used the font for job printing.

In 1864, noted journalist Wang Tao, who had fled China and settled in the British crown colony, became the editor of the Chinese-language *Hong Kong News.* Using vernacular Chinese, Wang "became an influential reformer and investigative reporter, exposing corruption and giving advice" (Bishop 1989, p. 45).

In Japan, the first vernacular newspaper started in 1868. At first, the press toed the government line, but by the summer of 1875, reformist demands of Japanese who had studied abroad were finding their way into the press. Both the *Asahi Shimbun* ("Rising Sun Newspaper") and *Yomiuri Shimbun* ("Read and Sell Newspaper") were established during this era, in the 1870s. The third of Japan's Big Three, the *Mainichi Shimbun* ("Daily Newspaper"), is the successor to a paper established in 1870s as well. In the Philippines, journals specializing in commerce, agriculture, and industry appeared earlier than general-interest periodicals. The monthly *Registro Mercantil de Manila* debuted in 1824, while the bilingual (Spanish–English) *Precios Corrientes de Manila* was established in 1839.

The press of the Pacific is generally young, without nineteenth-century roots. Exceptions are the *Fiji Times* (1869) and four of Australia's dailies: the *Sydney Morning Herald* (1831), the *Melbourne Herald* (1840), the *Age of Melbourne* (1854), and the *Daily Telegraph of Sydney* (1879).

The Press in the Early Twentieth Century

In South Asia, the story of the press is intertwined with independence movements. The press in Pakistan is a direct descendant of the Muslim League press of pre-independence India, founded primarily to advocate for a separate Muslim state on the Indian subcontinent. By 1925, the Muslim press had grown in size and circulation and comprised about 220 newspapers in nine languages, including Urdu (the first Urdu journal had been founded in 1836), English, and Bengali.

Muhammad Ali Jinnah, who assisted in founding the first Muslim news agency in the 1930s, greatly helped the Muslim national cause. He was involved in establishing a number of publications, including *Dawn,* the official organ of the Muslim League, still one of the most powerful dailies in Pakistan.

Until 1947, when India achieved its independence from the British, the spirit of nationalism stimulated the growth of the press. Social and political reforms and nationalism were considered the press's three main objectives. Mahatma Gandhi, India's most widely known leader in the struggle for freedom, was a journalist for 60 years. He used the press to propagate his ideas and views as editor of four weekly newspapers: *Indian Opinion, Young India, Navajivan,* and *Harijan.* Through these publications, he spread his ideas of freedom and nonviolence through India and to Indians in South Africa as well.

Jawahar Lal Nehru, the first prime minister of India, advocated complete freedom of the press. "I would rather have a completely free press, all the dangers involved in the wrong use of that freedom, than a suppressed or regulated press," he said ("Gandhi" 1989, p. 13).

Another towering political figure who made use of mass media during a period of revolution was Dr. Sun Yat-sen of China. When the *China National Gazette* of Shanghai was suppressed in 1903, it merely changed its name and registered under foreign ownership. Probably the best paper of the period was the *Eastern Times of Shanghai* (1904).

During the early years of the century, the press of Japan was engaged in circulation battles rather than battles for independence. It adopted some of the worst features of British and American yellow journalism and was well read but often unreliable. During the 1930s, the military forced a restructuring of the press, both to conserve supplies and make the press easier to control. The 1,200 dailies and 7,700 nondailies were reduced to 55 dailies and weeklies by 1943.

The story of postwar press development and the entire history of broadcasting are covered in the regional discussions in this chapter.

MEDIA OVERVIEW

Table 13.1 shows that contrasts prevail as well in the indices related to mass media. Newspaper circulation per 1,000 population averages 64 in Asia, far below the "saturation" figure of 200 (one paper for every five people). Indeed, five nations—Kiribati, Nauru, Samoa, Tonga, and Vanuatu—and a number of territories in Oceania as of the early 1980s had no daily newspapers at all. Against the bleak statistical picture for print media in Asia, we should consider that the United States and France ranked below Singapore and that Italy and Spain ranked below Fiji in circulation per 1,000 people.

In the realm of electronic media, the Asia/Pacific region had 10 radios and 2.5 television receivers per 100 people in 1985, both figures exceeding the UNESCO criteria of five radios and two TV sets. According to UNESCO, by 1985 all Asian countries except Bangladesh, Bhutan, and Nepal had reached the standard for radios (*Statistical Yearbook 1986*). The average figure of 2.5 TV sets brings to mind the child who drowned in a river whose average depth was 10 inches. The Asian "media haves" contrast no more strikingly with the "media have-nots" than when we look at TV set distribution.

Yet despite Asia's diversity, we can isolate patterns that apply to parts of Asia, and even to the entire region. South Asia and parts of the rest of the region, for example, share the Hindu–Buddhist tradition. East and Southeast Asia share the Chinese language. Although in Malaysia and Indonesia, Chinese does not dominate as a language, many media use Chinese; even in Japan, Chinese ideographs are used, despite the dissimilarity of spoken Japanese and Chinese.

According to Tran Van Dinh (1989), mass communication in modern Asia has been shaped by three factors:

1. Western domination, motivated originally by Europeans' desire to reach India for trading purposes, but resulting in transplanted technology, media institutions and popular culture
2. The modernization of Japan, whose use of an Eastern ethics, Western science strategy stands as a model that still influences developing Asian nations in the 1980s
3. Independence, resulting in regional rather than colonial alignments for communication systems and individual solutions regarding the role and form of national mass media

One tangible legacy of Western domination, the strong English-language press of Asia, started out as an extension of British rule. It remains strong in former British colonies—India, Pakistan, Malaysia, Ceylon, and Burma—but would not have survived so long or sprung up in places outside Britain's sphere had it not answered local needs. The United States established the language in the Philippines, while missionary influence and the presence of troops after World War II led to the establishment of other English-language media.

English now functions as a lingua franca in multilingual countries and an international language to serve tourists and business people. Moreover, its alphabetic script presents few typesetting problems and takes up less space than most Asian languages, which saves on newsprint. Older papers have been joined by the *International Herald Tribune* and the *Wall Street Journal*'s Asia edition to provide same-day access to international news.

PRINT MEDIA

According to Merrill (1990), three of the world's 20 top newspapers can be found in the Asia/Pacific region: the *Asahi Shimbun* (Japan) and the *Age* and *Sydney Morning Herald* (Australia).

South Asia

Among the oldest and freest in South Asia, the press in India is also one of the most influential in the developing world. Its growth has been phenomenal. At the time of independence from British rule in 1947, only 200 newspapers were being published in the country. Today, 47 years later, in 1994, approximately 25,000 newspapers and magazines are published in 92 languages and dialects with a combined circulation of about 65 million copies. Of these 2,100, are dailies, and the rest weeklies, biweeklies, monthlies, quarterlies, semiannuals, and annuals. The distribution of print media in India is largely an urban phenomenon, with about 80 percent of circulation confined to cities where only 20 percent of the country's population lives. About 30 percent of newspapers are published in the four major cities of Delhi, Bombay, Calcutta, and Madras.

Despite the literacy rate of around 52 percent according to the 1991 census, the English-language press plays an influential role in the country's political milieu. Mostly owned by large business concerns, they reach the educated elite throughout the country as well as abroad and are looked on by the government as a barometer of public thinking. Five newspapers rank as elite papers: the *Times of India*, the *Statesman*, the *Hindustan Times*, the *Indian Express*, and the *Hindu*. The English-language dailies are serious in content and tone and are widely known for their comprehensive national and international coverage as well as independent views.

In the last two decades, there has been a remarkable growth of Indian-language newspapers. For example, the circulation of dailies increased by 140 percent in 12 years—from 9.3 million copies a day in 1976 to 22.6 million in 1988 (Jeffrey 1993, p. 2004)—which was due to improved literacy rate, improved economy and technology, as well as increased political awareness among people.

The Hindi-language press leads both in number and circulation. Between 1988 and 1992, the number of Hindi dailies belonging to the Audit Bureau of Circulations (1993) rose by almost 50 percent—from 33 to 49—and the circulation of dailies in Hindi grew by 35 percent—from 2.6 million a day to more than 3.2 million a day. *Punjab Kesari* is the largest selling Hindi daily, with a circulation of 563,000 copies. Several new Hindi dailies have been started recently, of which the most notable is *Rashtriya Sahara*, started in August 1992 from New Delhi.

Overall, the newspaper industry in India is becoming increasingly competitive. *The Times of India*, for example, recently underwent a change in both format and content. Its publishers believe that the newspapers of the future are "more viewsy than newsy," so they incorporated magazine journalism. Aggressive marketing and coverage of exclusive, highly personalized reports are keeping the regional newspaper *Malayala Manorama* ahead of others. Tabloids are becoming extremely popular for train commuters in Bombay. According to Harindra Dave, editor-in-chief of the Gujarati tabloids *Pravasi* and *Janmabhoomi,* "a boom has come (in tabloids) like the stock-market boom" (Rattanani 1992, p. 124). Among the new tabloids jostling for a readership are *Hamara Mahanagar, Dopahar, Sanjh Jansatta, Sanjh Loksatta,* and *Alpa Mahanagar.* In Delhi, *The Pioneer* has made a niche for itself as the alternate paper by focusing on subjects such as gender, media, health, law, and the arts.

The regional language press constitutes the bulk of mainstream journalism in India and has a much higher readership than the English-language press. It played an active role in the struggle for Indian independence and still remains the most sought-after vehicle to reach the increasingly literate non-Anglophone provincial population. According to the latest report of the Registrar of Newspapers in India, regional language newspapers constitute more than half of the country's newspapers and periodicals. *Malayala Manorama,* a Malayalam paper published from three centers, is the largest selling daily newspaper. The Urdu-language daily *Pratap,* Kerala's daily *Mathribhumi,* and the Oriya daily *Samaj* are the other prominent regional-language newspapers.

Among periodicals, the Malayalam language *Manorama,* published in the state of Kerala is the largest, followed by *Mangalam,* also a weekly published in Kerala. The third largest is *Kumudam,* a Tamil language weekly of Madras.

The newsmagazines carrying investigative stories have become especially widespread over the last decade. One of the most influential is *India Today* (circulation 900,000), a political news fortnightly published from New Delhi. *Sunday* and *India Week* are the other two serious and quality opinion news weeklies that provide insights into the political and social reality of the country. All these newsmagazines, generally modeled after *Time* and *Newsweek,* are ranked along with any respected daily newspaper in terms of influencing public opinion. But in the past few years, with the exception of *India Today,* readership of other periodicals is going down. Even the most well-known and one of the largest circulated magazines, the *Illustrated Weekly of India,* a pictorial news weekly, founded in 1880, folded in 1993. However, the competition is sharpening in specialized fields. Two areas of new interest are in the fields of business magazines and technology. *Business Today, Business World,* the *Economic Times,* and *Technocrat,* launched fairly recently, are doing well in terms of circulations.

Magazines in other major Indian languages are becoming increasingly influential in molding public opinion. Special interest magazines, particularly film magazines and women's magazines, have become a booming industry in India, catering to the needs of a dramatically emerging middle class. All top film magazines, including *Cine Blitz, Filmfare, Movie,* and *Star and Style,* have undergone radical facelifts in the last two years to appeal to a much wider audience. The most widely read women's magazines include *Femina* and *Society* in English and *Manorama* and *Mahila* in Hindi.

When Pakistan appeared on the map of the world on August 14, 1947, there were only two English dailies and two Urdu dailies published from Lahore. Soon after independence, the English daily *Dawn,* and two Urdu dailies, *Jang* and *Anjam*—all of which were appearing from Delhi, shifted to Pakistan. It took six years for the number of dailies to reach 55, but by 1992 (the latest year for which figures are available), a total of 1,587 newspapers and journals were published, including 133 dailies, 346 weeklies, and 597 monthlies.

Among the major national Urdu language dailies are *Jang* (largest circulation daily), *Nawa-i-Waqt, Mashriq* (government owned), and *Hurriyat.* The major English-language dailies are *Dawn,* the *Muslim,* the *Nation,* and the *Pakistan Times.* The *Pakistan Times* is a government newspaper, published by the National Press Trust, a nonprofit organization, set up in 1964 by businessmen but now owned by the government. Other newspapers and periodicals are owned either by private individual proprietors or joint stock companies or by trusts. The major private groups owning newspaper chains are Pakistan Herald Publications, Jang Group, Nawa-i-Waqt Limited, and Milat Group.

The English-language papers are mostly read by the elite class, whereas Urdu papers are read by the elite as well as the masses. Most educated people subscribe to at least two papers—one in English and one in Urdu to get a taste of the conservative as well as liberal viewpoints. The English dailies are mostly conservative, whereas the Urdu dailies are more aggressive in expressing viewpoints.

A majority of newspapers are full of political news and essays and hardly carry any cultural and entertainment news. One unique feature of Pakistani press is the publication of statements from political leaders. Approximately 70 percent of the news is based on statements made by political leaders. Another characteristic of Pakistani press is its religious orientation. Practically all newspapers in the country have an insert on religion on every Friday. Several newspapers specialize in business news also. *Dawn,* the English-language daily, issues a weekly four-page economic and business review along with its regular edition. The English daily *Business Recorder* and the Urdu daily *Business Report* also have large circulations.

A comprehensive coverage of the country's development activities is also on the rise. Several newspapers have added special pages containing development news. The overall quality of newspapers in Pakistan has improved considerably in recent years. Interpretative reporting and columns—a rare phenomenon in the early years of Pakistan—have been introduced in almost all major newspapers.

Weekly newsmagazines are also widely read in Pakistan. *Akhbar-e-Jehan* ("News of the World"), a weekly newsmagazine, owned by *Jung* group of publications, has the largest circulation. Other major weekly news magazines are *Takbeer* and *Zindagi.* Two major English-language weeklies are *Mag* and *Herald.*

The Pakistani periodicals dealing with literary and cultural subjects, religion, sports, films, women, science, medicine, health, trade, tourism, and so on are also quite popular.

In the smaller South Asian nations—Sri Lanka, Bangladesh, Nepal and Bhutan—prospects for the press have brightened. In Sri Lanka, there has been a tremendous growth of newspapers and other publications over the last two decades, especially since 1977, when President J.R. Jayawardene considerably relaxed the press controls imposed by previous regimes. In 1979 alone, the circulations of Sri Lanka's newspapers increased by more than 30 percent. With the relaxation of press controls by President D. B. Wijetunga, who assumed presidency on May 1, 1993, the circulation of Sri Lankan newspapers is expected to rise even further.

The newspaper industry in Sri Lanka is dominated by two major publishing houses, each of which publishes daily and weekly newspapers and several magazines in English, Tamil, and Sinhala (the official language). The Associated Newspapers of Ceylon Ltd., one of South Asia's best established newspapers publishers, owns the prestigious English language daily, *Ceylon Daily News,* which received an award for Media Excellence in 1984 from the International Press Institute. In addition, it owns the largest Sinhala-language daily, *Dinamina* (140,000 circulation) and the largest Sunday Sinhala paper, *Silumina* (254,000 circulation). It also publishes the largest English-language Sunday paper, *Sunday Observer,* and several other weekly newsmagazines and general interest magazines in all three languages. A second major publishing house is the Upali Newspapers Ltd., which also publishes daily Newspapers in English and Sinhalese. *The Island* (English) and *Divaina* (Sinhalese) are two of its major daily newspapers. In addition, the Communist party of Sri Lanka also publishes one daily, *Atta* ("Truth").

Some of the well-known general interest periodicals are *Ferguson's Ceylon Directory, Reader's Relish, Outlook, Public Opinion* in English, *Ceylon Government Gazette* in English and Tamil, and *Sinhala* and *Subasetha* in Sinhalese. In addition, some children's and women's magazines have become quite popular. *Mihira* and *Priyavi* are two of the popular children's magazines in Sinhalese, and *Sri* and *Tharuni* are the well-circulated women's magazines in the Sihnalese language.

The Bangladesh press has also grown considerably since martial law ended there in 1979. Today, 146 daily newspapers are published in the country. *Ittefaq* ("Unity") is the largest circulation daily published in Bengali language, and *Inquilab* ("Revolution") is the second largest. Other well-known Bengali daily newspapers are *Sangbad* ("News"), *Khabur* ("News"), *Dainik Bangla* ("Daily Bangla"), *Jana Kantha,* and *Azad* ("Freedom").

The largest and most influential English-language daily is the *Bangladesh Observer.* The other well-known English language papers are *Bangladesh Times,* the *New Nation, Daily Star, Daily Telegraph, Morning Sun, Financial Express,* and the *Daily Life.*

Weekly newspapers are quite popular in Bangladesh. Presently, there are approximately 242 weeklies and 132 monthlies besides several fortnightlies and quarterlies. *Holiday* is the largest circulated newsweekly in English, and *Bichitra* ("Unusual") is the largest circulated Bengali newsweekly. *Dhaka Courier* and *Weekly Friday* are also quite popular. Some of the well-known general interest periodicals are *Bangladesh Illustrated Weekly, Kishore Bangla* (children's magazine), *Chitrali* (cinema), *Fashal* (agriculture), *The Commercial Bulletin* (commerce), and *Shachitra Bangladesh* (Bangladesh Pictorial Youth Group).

Nepal was isolated from the mainstream of world events for a century (1846–1950) under the Rana regime. Only after 1950 did newspapers come into existence in a real sense. By 1990 there were a total of 476 publications, including 63 dailies, 364 weeklies, and several other semiweeklies and fortnightlies.

The oldest and the major Nepalese-language newspaper is *Gorkhapatra* (35,000 circulation), owned by the Gorkhapatra Corporation, an autonomous newspaper organization managed by a Board of Directors, consisting of members nominated by the government. Other Nepalese-language newspapers include *Awaj, Dainik Nepal, Hamra Desh,* and *Jana Jivan.*

Among the major English-language newspapers, *The Rising Nepal,* the oldest daily established in 1961, is a semiofficial newspaper, also owned by the Gorkhapatra Corporation. Other English-language dailies include *Commoner, Daily News,* the *Motherland,* and *New Herald.* Two new newspapers—*Kantipur* in Nepali and *Kathmandu Post* in English—were started in 1993 by Goenka Publishers, a private organization of Indian group of publishers, registered in Nepal. The news weeklies *Jagaran, Spotlight,* and a host of political mouthpieces, bulletins, and literary magazines are also quite popular. In addition, several magazines on tourism and culture, such as *Nepal Traveller* and *Explore Nepal* are quite popular. *Himal,* a new magazine on environment, is also widely read.

Bhutan, with less than 1 million population, can now boast of publishing its own national newspaper. *Kuensel* ("The Enlightener"), the country's only newspaper, was sanctioned by the government in 1986 to operate as a weekly. Before 1986 it was a small government newsletter. The newspaper is printed in English, Nepali, and Dzongkha, the official language of Bhutan. Circulation is about 8,500 in English, 2,850 in Dzongkha, and 630 in Nepali. The 12-page tabloid consists of national and international news and features, sports, public notices, and a letters page. It also contains photographs, comics, and a crossword puzzle. Besides the newspaper, there are two general interest periodicals in Bhutan—*Kuenphen Digest* and *Kuenphen Tribune*—both of which are published in English.

In Afghanistan, the Afghan Resistance Group, known as the *Mujahideen,* came into power on April 28, 1992 and established a free Islamic regime in the country by Afghans. On June 28, 1992, Hal-o-Aqd (Grand Assembly) Council was convened, and Professor Burhanuddin Rabbani, the first elected President of the Islamic State of Afghanistan, formed the coalition government of all resistance parties on the basis of Jalalabad Agreement, which states that the affairs of the country will be run by laws made before the communist coup of 1978. Newspapers are no longer bound to relay communist propaganda and reflect Sovietization.

The *Kabul Times* is the English-language official daily newspaper. *Anis* and *Hewad* are the two other official newspapers in Dari and Pashtu languages. Besides the official newspapers, some independent newspapers are also published in Kabul. Some of the well-known publications are *Mujahid* and *AFGHANews,* both published fortnightly in Dari and Pashtu by Jami'at Islami party. Another weekly independent newspaper, *Hafta Nama Kabul* was started in 1993. This paper, in Dari and Pashtu, is quite free and even publishes cartoons criticizing the government. Besides the newspapers, *Zhwandon* (Life) and *Awaz* are the two well-known general interest periodicals, both published in Dari and Pashtu. *Afghanistan,* published in French and English and *Aryana,* published in Dari and Pashtu, are the two well-known quarterly periodicals on history and culture.

Southeast Asia

Just as World War II affected most print media in Asia, so the Vietnam War had a cataclysmic effect on parts of Southeast Asia. In the early 1970s, South Vietnam had more than 40 dailies, published in Vietnamese, Chinese, English, and French. After the fall of Saigon in April 1975, a press crackdown left only government, party, and army-controlled media. Many journalists who had served in the Thieu regime were arrested immediately, while in the next decade, others who were not conforming to policy were rounded up.

Then in 1987, party general secretary Nguyen Van Linh told journalists that they should be "chasing away darkness," but without "smearing the regime." However, after a period of sanctioning mild muckraking, the government in 1989 cracked down again by imposing a new press law. The country's six dailies all are based in either Hanoi or Ho Chi Minh City (Saigon). The ban on foreign periodicals will likely ease, now that diplomatic relations with the United States have been restored (1994).

The press in Cambodia and Laos, which had never been important, virtually shut down in 1975. In Laos, ever since private publishing ceased in 1975, only two government dailies have operated. In Cambodia, change began brewing in September 1989 when Vietnam pulled out its forces after more than 10 years of occupation. The National Assembly, elected in May 1993, is expected to include free press guarantees when it writes a new constitution. In the meantime, the situation is fluid and changing. A formerly underground paper can now legally publish, but its editor was shot and wounded when he did so. English-language journalism has come to Phnom Penh in the form of the newly established *Cambodia Times*.

Myanmar (Burma), a one-party socialist state, has lived in not-so-splendid isolation since a 1962 coup by General Ne Win. The only Western media that Pico Iyer (1989) found for sale in 1985 at Rangoon newsstands were old copies of *Good Housekeeping* and *Reader's Digest*.

The military remains in power, despite a 1990 election victory by opposition forces, whose leader, Aung San Suu Kyi, remains under house arrest. All media are government owned. In 1993, the Information Ministry closed two dailies and started three new ones: *Kyehmane* (the Mirror), *Myanmur Lh Lin*, and the latter's English version, *New Light of Myanmar*. An underground press flourishes in parts of the country.

Burma's neighbor, Thailand, has a free-wheeling private press that practices some self-censorship. In this constitutional monarchy, nothing negative is ever written about the royal family. Almost everyone else, however, is fair game. Politicians and wealthy businessmen use bribes and favors more than restrictive laws to influence stories, which can range from colorful to sensational to downright libelous. The color extends to form as well as content. Thailand's growing economy has brought enormous advertising revenues to newspapers, which can now afford to print many (or even all) of their pages in color.

Thailand has scores of daily, weekly, and monthly publications in Thai, Chinese, and English. The prestigious daily *Matichon* has had to add lighter content to compete with the hugely profitable *Thai Rath* (the largest daily, about 1 million circulation) and the *Daily News*. These and other Thai-language papers are criticized as having too little foreign and hard news, along with too much gossip, sports, and entertainment news. The two English dailies, the *Bangkok Post* and the *Nation*, have more reliable, less scurrilous content.

South of Thailand, Malaysia has tame, development-oriented press unlike Thailand's, except that one subject is taboo. In Malaysia's case, it is forbidden to publish anything that might adversely affect national cohesion in this complex society, whose ethnic makeup is Malay (44 percent), Chinese (36 percent), Indian (10 percent), and other groups. Newspapers in various languages reflect this diversity; some papers away from Kuala Lumpur combine several languages in one publication.

The largest publishing house, the *New Straits Times Group,* produces the nation's largest English-language daily, the progovernment *New Straits Times.* The group also includes *Berita Harian,* a Malay-language daily. The other English daily, the *Star,* used to oppose the government; however, after being banned in 1987, it returned subdued and chastened, having lost many of its reporters to other professions.

In the mid-1980s, the circulation of Malay newspapers surpassed that of those in English. *Berita Harian* has a slightly higher circulation than *Utusan Malayu.* Both use Roman script, while the *Utusan Malay* used Arabic. The smaller Tamil-language press is based in Kuala Lumpur. More titles exist in Chinese than Malay or English, partly because merchants in Sabah and Sarawak, on the island of Borneo, sponsor many local papers. The lively Chinese press has considerable freedom because authorities do not attend much to outlying periodicals and because the Chinese engage in commerce rather than politics.

Malaysia and the city-state of Singapore agreed to break politically in 1965. Singapore occupies an island of only 244 square miles on the tip of the Malay peninsula. It has the same ethnic groups as Malaysia, but in different proportions Chinese (77 percent), Malays (15 percent), and Indians (6 percent). However, by mutual agreement, Malaysian and Singporean newspapers are not distributed in each other's territory.

Thus, the daily newspapers being published in Singapore in the 1990s served a varied readership. Because of a bilingual educational system, many residents read both English and Chinese publications. (Indeed, former Prime Minister Lee Kuan Yew encourages the use of English as an integrative force and an aid in international commerce.) Dailies are also published in Tamil and Malay. The number of dailies has fallen since 1980, mainly because of government action to shut them down. The *Eastern Star, Singapore Herald, New Nation,* and *Singapore Monitor* have all ceased publication.

One company, Singapore Press Holdings, dominates the newspaper scene in the city-state. Its flagship publication, the *Straits Times,* has a circulation of about 280,000. Founded in 1845 by Robert Carr Woods, when Singapore had a population of only 40,000, the *Straits Times* served the commercial interests in the seaport. During the Japanese occupation, many staff members were interned.

Today, this former "great daily"—indeed, all the press in Singapore—has been tamed by Lee Kuan Yew, who ruled Singapore from 1959 to 1990. Few can argue that Lee's strict social control measures and guided economic policies have brought material well-being, with Singapore enjoying a per capita Gross Domestic Product in 1991 of $13,900. Indeed, Lee believes that press controls have aided economic development, whereas the Western-style free press in India and the Philippines has fostered unrest and economic problems.

In addition to the *Straits Times,* the Singapore Press Holdings company publishes all other newspapers except Tamil Murasu: *Berita Minggu,* the *Business Times,* and

Berita Harian (all dailies); the *Sunday Times;* and three Chinese newspapers, *Shin Min Daily News, Lianhe Zaobao,* and *Wanbao.*

As if to compensate for frequent closings, new papers spring up frequently. In 1988 the *New Paper,* modeled on *USA Today,* began publishing with an appeal to young readers. It promised to avoid politics and offer fun-to-read stories. As if all this were not enough for the city-state's 2.7 million people, some 3,700 publications, including the Asian *Wall Street Journal* and *Time* magazine, are imported into the island—but not without certain travails (see the section on government–press relations).

In Indonesia, despite the multiplicity of ethnic groups, a variety of languages, and geographical and cultural barriers, the Indonesian press has grown considerably both in quantity and quality in recent years. The country now has 50 daily newspapers. One of the most respected and largest dailies is *Kompas,* published in Jakarta with over 500,000 circulation. *Kompas* was started as a Catholic newspaper in 1967 but later left its religious orientation. Because of its serious style and coverage of international events, it appeals to the elitist class of Indonesia. Two other large-circulation Jakarta dailies are *Pos Kota* (500,000 circulation) and *Suara Pembaruan* (300,000 circulation). Other influential Jakarta papers, smaller in circulation, are *Media Indonesia,* an outspoken paper, cultivating a nongovernmental editorial policy; *Sinar Harapan,* a Protestant paper; *Berita Buana,* a sensational paper known for "circus-type" graphics; *Berita Yudha* ("War News"), the top-selling army newspaper; *Bisnis Indonesia,* a financial daily; *Meredka* ("Independence"), a nationalistic paper, formed during the struggle for independence in 1945; and *Suara Karya,* the official paper.

The *Indonesian Times,* the *Jakarta Post,* and the *Indonesian Observer* are the three most widely read English-language papers of Jakarta. The first two are government spokespapers with unwavering seriousness, while the *Observer* claims to give Indonesia an international perspective. The English-language newspapers are widely read by government officials, diplomats, the military, and the elite strata of Jakarta and other major cities. The sole Chinese-language paper, *Harian Indonesia,* is also read widely by the Bahasa community.

Outside Jakarta, some of the influential dailies are published in West Java, Yogyakarta, North Sumatra, Central Java, East Java, and Bali.

In addition to daily newspapers, Indonesia has several weekly papers that serve provincial and rural areas. In 1979, in its third five-year development, the Indonesian government introduced a rural press program, popularly called Koran Masuk Desa (KMD), "Newspapers for Villages." These newspapers, written in simple language, were designed to help the rural Indonesians become an educated society. In line with the KMD program, the Indonesian Press Council in 1980 limited daily newspapers to 12 pages and to 30 percent advertising content to enable the weeklies to obtain more newsprint and advertising. The government also provides a three-and-one-half-cent-per-copy subsidy for the first 5,000 copies of the village editions for the first year of publication. These weekly newspapers generally consist of four pages and usually appear in the local language of the region.

The total number of newspapers entering the villages has increased considerably in recent years. In 1991–1992, it increased to 153,600 copies per day, although nationally, the total copies decreased from 6 million copies in 1990–1991 to 5.74 million copies in 1991–1992. Business groups, recognizing a boom market, have started investing money in the regional press. Moreover, the government also protects the rural press from big-city competition by providing subsidies.

Indonesian newsmagazines are well-known for publishing provocative editorials and columns. The most influential among news magazines are *Topik, Prospek,* and *Indonesia Magazine.* Magazines dealing with fashion, women, men, health, hygiene, and tourism are also quite popular.

In the Philippines, before the declaration of martial law in 1972, newspapers flourished as well as exercised their freedom and went so far as to call the president one of the richest, most corrupt leaders in Southeast Asia. With the declaration of martial law, all media establishments were confiscated or closed, with the exception of the *Daily Express* and Kanlaon Broadcasting's radio and television stations, owned by the family and friends of Ferdinand Marcos. In the final years of Marcos' rule, only four daily newspapers were publishing in Manila. However, within two years of Marcos's fall, 30 daily newspapers were published in Manila. Today, under the free press policy of President Fidel Ramos, newspapers are again proliferating. About 28 dailies and several weeklies are presently published in Manila, while approximately 150 papers, mainly weeklies, are published in the provinces.

The *Manila Bulletin,* with an estimated circulation of 250,000, is the nation's largest and most respected serious paper, supporting the Philippines in its nation-building efforts. *The Philippine Daily Inquirer,* founded in 1985, criticized the Marcos regime and became a very powerful opposition paper. With an estimated daily circulation of 150,000, it is the second largest paper in the Philippines. *The Philippine Star,* founded in 1986 by Maximo V. Solven, is the nation's third largest paper. Among the other important Manila daily papers are the *Manila Chronicle,* the *Manilla Standard,* the *Manila Times, Malaya,* the *Philippines Journal* and, the *People's Journal.* The business dailies, *Business World* and *Business Star,* are also quite popular. In addition, the Chinese language dailies, *Chinese Commercial News, United Daily News,* and *World News,* have large circulations. Several regional dailies are published from Metro Manila. They include *Baguio, Midland Courier, Monday Post, Mindano Star, Mindano Daily Mirror, Sun Star,* and *Davao Star.* Moreover, two tabloids, *Tempo* and *Balita,* feature a mix of English and Tagalog, often referred to as "Taglish."

The bulk of the daily newspapers are owned by wealthy business entrepreneurs. Recently, large businesses have been buying interests in the newspapers. And there are already signs that these business owners use the media to promote their own interests. However, not all the papers in the country are owned by families and businesses. Some journalists also own newspapers. The *Philippine Daily Inquirer, Malaya,* and *Business World* are mainly owned by journalists, and the popular tabloids *People's Journal* and *People Tonight* are owned by Philippine Journalists Inc. There are no government-owned newspapers. Yet the newspapers tend to practice self-censorship, and journalists are inclined to be protective of the government in power. Page one news in virtually all of the dailies consists of the president's official statements and actions; and editorials lack any solid stands on politics.

Several general interest and special interest magazines are also quite popular in the Philippines. A number of newspapers have Sunday supplement magazines. These include *Panorama, Sunday Enquirer, Sunday Times, Sunday Malaya, Star Week,* and *Journal Weekend.* Among fashion magazines, *She* and *Style;* among women's magazines, *Woman's Home-Companion, Women's Journal, Women Today,* and *Mod* are widely read; among showbiz, *Glitter, Gossip, Jingle, Movie Flash, Movie Star,* and *Kislapar* are quite popular. In addition, *The Philippines Free Press,* a magazine on social and political issues, is quite popular. However, despite the popularity of the magazines, the Philippines has no newsmagazines of any significance.

East Asia

In May 1989, the mass media of the People's Republic of China made news in non-Chinese mass media all over the world for their coverage of the Tiananmen uprising. Beijing journalists carried aloft banners that said, "Don't believe us—we print lies"and wrote front-page stories sympathetic to the hunger strikers. But after June 4, the official media made a complete about-face, praising soldiers as "model heroes" and condemning the protesters. In a purge that reached even into the journalism schools, supporters of the protest were arrested, discharged, sent to rural areas or put on "study" leave. The *World Economics Herald, Economics Weekly,* and other newspapers were shut down. At the *People's Daily,* where 500 journalists had to write self-criticisms, the military's propaganda director took over as editor. Authorities are still sensitive to foreign reports on the anniversaries of the Tienanmen massacre; a Japanese journalist was beaten in 1992, while others were detained or had materials seized.

To understand the mass media of the world's most populous nation, Robert Bishop (1989) points out that one must understand the forces that shape that media. China, with a physical size slightly larger than that of the United States, remains to this day a nation of villagers. The 80 percent of Chinese who live in rural areas, many of them isolated as a result of geographical barriers, have limited access to mass media. There, the extended family "forms a closed, face-to-face, wheel-like system of communication, strongly resistant to outside influences" (Bishop 1989, p. 9).

Regionalism meant that local dialects developed, a serious barrier to nonprint mass communication. At the same time, print media faced the problem of a low rate of literacy, which in turn resulted from the time required to master several thousand written characters. Both the typesetting problems associated with the writing system and delivery problems have hindered print penetration of the countryside. Thus, when we speak of media in China, we are really talking about two Chinas: the cities, especially the port cities, and the rural villages.

The first large-scale mass media audience survey in China took place in 1982 in Beijing. Everett Rogers and his colleagues (1985) discovered that a majority of those surveyed read two or more dailies each week in this city of nearly 6 million. The local Beijing newspapers had the most readers, with 72 percent of those surveyed reading the *Beijing Evening News* and 71 percent reading the *Beijing Daily.* Sizable audiences also existed for the national *People's Daily* (48 percent) and the *Reference News* (40 percent).

In the early 1990s, China had about 1,700 newspapers. The flagship *People's Daily,* founded in 1948, is printed in 20 Chinese cities besides Beijing and in Hong Kong and

Tokyo. About 1,000 staff members produce the paper, which typically runs eight pages, seven days a week. About 3 million copies are distributed.

As an organ of the Central Committee of the Chinese Communist party, the *People's Daily* (along with the central broadcasting station and *Xinhua*) set the line for all other publications; National, provincial, municipal, and district papers all practice self-censorship, looking to the *People's Daily* (Remin Ribao) for guidance. As an antidote to this top–down communication, the letters section (which receives 2,000–3,000 letters a day) used to let readers express complaints, but the practice changed after June 1989.

For the major publications in China, readers number many more people than subscribers for several reasons. Members of units (for example, rural work teams, factory teams, or offices) that subscribe to a paper all have access to it, while passersby can read papers posted on "newspaper walls." Sometimes study groups meet to read and discuss the news.

The *Reference News* (*Cankao Xiaoxi*) mentioned above belongs to a special class of publications called "internal." Originally created to keep party officials informed about overseas news, now just about anyone can subscribe to this Xinhua publication. A second level of restricted publication is *Reference Material* (*Cankao Ziliao*), a twice-daily foreign news digest for middle- to high-ranking party officials, running 100 pages in the morning and 50 pages in the afternoon.

In 1981, an English-language newspaper that carries advertising, *China Daily*, began publication. Now, thanks to satellite transmission, the eight-page broadsheet can reach North America and Europe the same day as the home editions. Its format and style do not have an American look, reflecting the start-up assistance of Australian and British journalists. It did not cover the prodemocracy movement before June 4 with the same passion as did the *People's Daily*.

Important local papers include the *Liberation Daily* in Shanghai, which espouses Deng Xiaoping's liberal economic views. The *Shenzen Special Zone Daily* publishes in Guangdong Province, right across the border from Hong Kong. After the 1989 crackdown in Mainland China, massive public protest demonstrations were held in Hong Kong, and the pace of outmigration increased. The uncertainty about the post-1997 years, when Hong Kong will be returned to China, extends to the press as well as to individuals' lives. Hong Kong has the freest Chinese-language papers in Asia, but their future remains uncertain. Already the press seems more cautious, unwilling to offend the powers-that-be on the mainland.

In the early 1990s, Hong Kong's 5.7 million people supported more than 600 newspapers and magazines in Chinese and English. According to a 1988 survey, the journalists who work for these newspapers and for other media are young (84 percent aged 35 and under), single (66 percent), and on the job less than five years (60 percent). About half the journalists are female. Low pay, heavy workloads, and pessimism about 1997 make journalism unattractive as a lifelong career.

Joseph Man Chan and Chin-Chuan Lee (1988) divide the present-day press into four groups. The ultraleftist group includes *Ta Kung Pao* and *Wen Wei Pao*, both supervised by Xinhua's Hong Kong branch; they give Hong Kongers the official Beijing viewpoint. The centrist group includes advertising-supported papers not linked to any political party, including *Ming Pao, Sing Pao*, and the racy *Oriental Daily News*

(1.5 million circulation). The ultrarightist group includes the *Hong Kong Times,* established in 1949 as the Kuomintang party withdrew to Taiwan.

The mainstream group includes the conservative, influential and very profitable *South China Morning Post;* it has about four times the circulation of the other English-language daily, the *Hong Kong Standard.* The *Standard* and its stable mates, the *Sing Tao Daily News* and the *Sing Tao Evening News,* are published by Sian "Sally" Aw.

Hong Kong's free media environment has attracted international publishers *Asiaweek* and the *Far Eastern Economic Review.* Both the *Asian Wall Street Journal* and the *International Herald Tribune* have offices and printing plants in Hong Kong, from where copies circulate throughout the region.

In Taiwan, significant changes occurred in 1987 when martial law was ended and the 1950s-era restrictions on print media were lifted. Under martial law, the *China Times* and *Central Daily News* (organ of the Kuomintang party)—had more than 80 percent of the nation's daily newspaper circulation and more than 70 percent of newspaper advertising.

After the print media restrictions were lifted, the private *United Daily News* (owned by the Wangs, a mainland family) rose up to challenge the *China Times* (owned by the Yu family, who are more favorably disposed to Taiwanese independence). Together, these daily giants account for about half of all newspapers sold. The United Daily News Group also publishes Taiwan's first business daily, a life-style daily, and four overseas newspapers. In 1988, it launched a new daily, the *United Evening News.*

With the restrictions in force, newspapers had to have licenses to publish and could only print 12 pages. Now, buoyed by healthy advertising revenues, the two giants print as many as 60 pages on weekends, in color, with computerized typesetting equipment; one system lets typists set 125 Chinese characters per minute.

Since martial law ended, newspapers have increased from 31 titles to about 160. Similarly, hundreds of new magazines have appeared, ranging from *PC World* to *Career Woman Fashion.* Some of these publications are in English, including two dailies—the *China Post* and *China News*—that predate the lifting of restrictions. The new Chinese-language *Liberty Times* already has a circulation of 200,000.

Striking parallels exist between Taiwan and South Korea, although we should not forget important differences, such as the role of religious (Christian) media in South Korea. In 1987, both broke from an authoritarian, controlled press system after achieving dazzling economic success. In both, advertising dollars buoy a now-uncensored, ever-expanding publication industry. Martial law under Chun Doo-hwan brought with it the repressive Basic Press Act and the biggest press purge in the history of the nation; 172 publications were closed, and 683 journalists dismissed.

A dissident Korean poet called 1985 the "most nightmarish" year in Korean cultural history when authorities shut down two magazines. The Ministry of Culture and Information (MOCI) issued daily instructions to the press about what it could not say; censors monitored every newsroom. Following student protests in spring 1987, Roh Tae-woo won the presidency that November in Korea's first free election. In late 1987, a new constitution was put in place and a new press law enacted. Changes began happening.

In 1984, South Korea had 25 daily newspapers, including 6 with a nationwide circulation of more than 700,000 each. By the early 1990s, 71 dailies and thousands of new periodicals were being published. The largest and most prestigious papers, *Dong-A Ilbo* and *Chosun Ilbo,* both founded in 1920, maintain many foreign bureaus. The other two major dailies, the *Joong-ang Ilbo* and *Hankok Ilbo,* have circulations of 1.5 million. The two English-language dailies are the *Korea Times* and the government-owned *Korea Herald.*

Despite legal freedom, the press club system and custom of *chonji* (gifts to journalists) make for a cozy rather than adverserial relation between journalists and those in power. Sometimes journalists even demand *chonji.* In March 1989, several reporters were arrested for extorting about $40,000 from factory owners whose illegal pollution practices they promised not to expose. Going against this grain, the *Hankyoreh Shinmun* (established 1988) forbids the acceptance of *chonji.* Popular with young readers, this new daily attacks both the Korean establishment and the United States while sympathizing with North Korea.

Compared to South Korea, the press of North Korea lacks variety, veracity, and vitality. Foreign publications are carefully excluded, although elites can get a digest of world press reports. A major task of the media is to enhance the personality cult of the present leader, Kim Jong Il son of Kim Il Sung, who died in 1994; one six-page issue of the party paper *Rodong Sinum* (circulation 1 million) referred to the two men more than 200 times.

Another mission is to denounce South Korea as a country ruled by a "puppet clique" of U.S. imperialists. In one disinformation campaign, newspapers said the United States had exported AIDS-contaminated blood to South Korea to run some tests.

If China draws international power from the sheer size of its population, Japan, the other potent force in Asia, draws power from its economic well-being (GNP per capita is $25,430). Daily newspaper circulation of 580 copies per 1,000 people, the highest in the world, means that the average family of four gets more than two papers—in practice, probably one national and one local daily.

Various explanations have been given for the high figure, such as Japan's homogeneous population, large middle class, high-density urbanization, heavily used public transportation, and high literacy—all of which characterize other countries with lower readership. The answer may lie in the broad-based content of the newspapers, which has something for everyone—from comics to fact-laden news stories. All of these factors are coupled with a phenomenal circulation system whereby each adult contractor (students are too busy studying) distributes an average of 250 copies in two hours. About 93 percent of households get a home-delivered paper. Many of the papers sold at newsstands are "sports" (really sports, entertainment, and soft-core pornography) dailies.

Of the nation's 158 dailies, the Tokyo Big Three—the *Asahi, Yomiuri,* and *Mainichi*—account for 43 percent of daily newspaper circulation. Add in the *Nihon Keizai Shimbun* and *Sankei Shimbun* (both business/economics papers), likewise published in Tokyo, and those five account for more than half of total circulation. The *Yomiuri* had a 1992 circulation of 9.7 million; the *Asahi,* 8.2 million; and the *Mainichi,* 4 million (morning editions only).

Why are the Big Five all based in Tokyo? As the political and economic capital of Japan, the city generates more news than any other region. Second, organizations of all types in Tokyo place bulk subscription orders. Third, more than 10 percent of the population lives in the Tokyo–Yokohama metropolis (the world's largest), representing well over 10 percent of purchasing power.

The *Asahi Shimbun* ("Rising Sun Newspaper"), founded in 1879 in Osaka, and the *Yomiuri Shimbun* ("Read and Sell Newspaper"), founded in 1874, are two of the oldest papers in Asia. All of the Big Five—except perhaps the *Sankei*—have similar viewpoints on major issues. As profitable companies with mass readerships, the papers see no need to rock the boat.

All the Big Five dailies have numerous media and nonmedia holdings, ranging from English-language dailies to baseball teams. (The "sister papers" of the Big Three join the *Japan Times* to provide a choice of four English-language daily publications.) The papers from early on have sponsored projects and events, from art exhibits to Antarctic explorations, to the first airplane flight in Japan, making them an integral part of national life—and trying to attract readers in the process.

Yet all is not rosy in the Japanese print media picture. Readers spend fewer minutes with newspapers, even as trust in reporting has somewhat declined. Further, whereas newspapers used to stand out as the mass medium, since about 1970, television has emerged as an equal force. In 1975, television displaced newspapers as the leading advertising medium.

Newspapers carry comics, but the phenomenal cartoon appetite of the Japanese has created its own industry. About two-thirds of all magazines are *manga* (books or magazines using a cartoon-panel format). The most popular *manga* publication, *Shonen Jump,* has a weekly circulation of about 4 million.

During the 1960s, according to Chugo Koito, college students carried around left-leaning magazines. During the 1970s teenagers turned to *manga,* which college students and adults now have taken up. *Manga* run the gamut from science fiction/fantasy to how-to manuals, pornography, and economics. Beyond *manga,* Japanese have thousands of monthly and weekly magazines to read. Unlike newspapers, they are sold in stores, not by subscription. Like newspapers, a handful of Tokyo-based companies dominate the market.

Pacific

Pacific Australia appropriately belongs in a chapter on Asia, since in recent years, half of all its immigrants have been Asian, although Asians still make up only 5 percent of the country's population. (Under 2 percent are aborigines.) Before Asians began arriving in the 1970s, waves of immigrants poured in from Europe and the Middle East, such that "white Australia" has now become multicultural Australia. Australia, China, and the United States all have about the same geographical size, making Australia, with only 16 million people, still roomy enough for more newcomers.

Australia's private press now includes a publication for almost every language group. But in the past, journalists looked to Britain for its models, so the older prestige press has a British feel. Started in 1831, the *Sydney Morning Herald* prides itself on its watchdog-of-the-government role. It stands as one of those great dailies that have great popular as well as elite appeal, boasting a circulation of around 400,000 in a city of 3.5 million.

The *Herald* is published by a holding company, the Fairfax group, which also publishes the *Australian Financial Review* and the *Melbourne Age.* The *Age*, the most serious Australian newspaper, has a strong following among the nation's elite. For almost 150 years, the Fairfax family controlled its namesake group. Then in 1990, the benign proprietors lost their empire to a rougher, tougher Canadian, Conrad Black. Black, who had previously acquired Rupert Murdoch's *Daily Telegraph,* instituted staff cuts and replaced several editors.

Other groups, whose broad activities include book publishing, newsprint production, magazine publication, and broadcasting, combine with Fairfax to dominate the Australian press scene. The Melbourne-based *Herald* and *Weekly Times* group publishes, besides its namesake newspapers, the popular and unrestrained *Sun News-Pictorial.* Australian Consolidated Press publishes some of the nation's most popular magazines.

Located 1,000 miles east of Australia, New Zealand's population of 3.3 million is 12 percent Maori, but Maoris represent only 1 percent of journalists and say they do not get adequate coverage. Women likewise complain about their press.

As of late 1985, typewriters and pencils were the norm, with not a single VDT in the nation's newsrooms. Of the country's 33 dailies, most have local monopolies. The largest daily, the *New Zealand Herald,* is published in Auckland. Wellington has two dailies, the morning *Dominion* and the *Evening Post,* as does the southern city of Christchurch, with its morning press and its evening *Christchurch Star.* Because of historical and geographic factors, New Zealand has much less influence on the mass media of the Pacific than does Australia.

Papua-New Guinea, located north of Australia in the Pacific, has a larger population than New Zealand but a much less developed press. Like its economic, military, and technical spheres, the press of Papua-New Guinea partially depends on Australia. The *Melbourne Herald* and *Weekly Times* group owns the English-language *Post-Courier.* The island nation's own publishing group, the Word Publishing Co., is owned by five Christian churches. It publishes nondaily periodicals in English and Pidgin.

After a military leader staged a coup in 1987, Fiji's private press was subjected to censorship. Now, with civilian control restored, Suva is regaining its place as the publishing center of the Pacific Islands; the long-established *Fiji Times* competes with the newer *Daily Post,* established in 1987.

Elsewhere in the Pacific, weeklies characterize the press scene, with English the dominant language. (Exceptions are *Tahiti* and *New Caledonia,* which produce daily newspapers in French.) In some locations, such as tiny Pitcairn Island, only a small monthly is published. Common problems of the island societies include geographic isolation, small populations, and the vestiges of top–down colonial structures. Many of the periodicals are new, having been established within the last 30 years.

In late 1989, Peter Lomas, editor of the magazine *Islands Business* (p. 5), listed the top three English-language newspapers in the South Pacific as the *Times of Papua New Guinea,* the *Papua New Guinea Post-Courier* and the *Samoa News* of American Samoa. The best of the northern islands papers, in his view, are the *Pacific Daily News* (Guam), the *Marshall Islands Journal,* and the *Marianas Variety.* All six are free of government control.

ELECTRONIC MEDIA

Both radio and television broadcasting began in some parts of Asia soon after being established in the West. The Philippines, an early adopter, had radio service in the 1920s and television by 1953; Thailand, another pioneer, established radio in 1931 and television in 1954. By the mid-1960s, 18 Asian countries had television, while by the 1990s, only certain Pacific islands lacked TV service. Asian/Pacific countries with high penetrations of videocassette recorders include Japan, Taiwan, Australia, Singapore, and Malaysia, as well as Hong Kong. Wired Asia thus represents a potential gold mine for Hong Kong-based STAR TV (Satellite Television Asian Region), which sends out one channel in Mandarin and five in English: MTV, British Broadcasting Corporation (BBC) World Service, Prime Sports, and Star Plus (entertainment). STAR TV's footprint reaches as far as the Middle East, giving it a potential audience of half the world's population—albeit the segment that understands either English or Mandarin. Seeing STAR TV's dizzying profit potential, Rupert Murdoch's News Corporation bought a controlling interest in July 1993. Revenues come from advertisers in many countries who want to reach STAR TV's audience of about 2 million. By the time you read this, six pay-TV channels also may be available. As satellite dishes get smaller, countries that want to restrict what their citizens receive will have less ability to do so.

Asiavision, which began visual news exchanges experimentally in March 1983, grew out of UNESCO-sponsored symposia. According to Flournoy, the participants feel that news of Asia "gets short shrift" on the global news services (1985, p. 5).

The "free-to-offer, free-to-choose" daily news exchange operates via coordinating centers in Japan and Malaysia. Based on interest in the proposed offerings, each center sends out 10- to 15-minute individualized visual packages of items that other members have produced. By the mid-1980s, Asiavision's two zones approached the volume in news items of Western visual services.

South Asia

Radio remains the principal broadcast medium throughout most of South Asia, and in some places where illiteracy is widespread, it is more important than newspapers. It is particularly well suited to the communication needs of nations where there is a multiplicity of languages and cultures and where the mountainous terrain (including Afghanistan and Nepal) is a formidable obstacle to the use of television. The development of inexpensive battery-operated transistor sets has greatly increased the size of radio audiences everywhere. Some governments have made radio programs more available to rural masses by establishing community listening centers. In India, for example, a scheme of community radio sets was introduced in 1954. Under the rural forum, information on all aspects of rural development is communicated to the villages.

All India Radio (AIR) is one of the largest radio systems in Asia with 170 stations broadcasting for a total of more than 700 hours a day. The programs, which are radiated from 190 transmiters, cover 95.7 percent of the population spread over 85 percent area of the country. No other medium in the country has a comparable capacity to reach such a gigantic mass of people. With the recently established FM transmitters and satellite radio network, it is possible to take radio signals anywhere in the country. FM channels have opened up new avenues for listeners and potential for advertising. FM has caught on faster than anyone expected, especially in big cities like Bombay, Delhi, and Madras. According to music legend Louis Banks, "We have a mini revolution. The radio is back and a rage on, thanks to FM opening up" (Agarwal and Rattanani 1993, p. 177).

The government is now leasing out time to private organizations. In 1993, a news channel—*Times FM*—opened up and has cornered the bulk of the FM slots in Delhi, Bombay, and Madras. It is getting so many requests for its "Dial-In" program that it has already made it a daily feature.

Radio broadcasting began in India in 1927 with two privately owned transmitters in Bombay and Calcutta. In 1930, broadcasting operations were taken by the government, where they remain today. AIR is supported mainly by license fees. It also obtains revenue from sales of program journals and related publications; and since 1967, it has been operating as a commercial service.

AIR maintains three distinct services for its domestic and foreign audience. It is now broadcasting 285 bulletins for a duration of over 38 hours in domestic, external, and regional services. The domestic service has three main components: the news service, the Vividh Bharati Service, and the general cultural service. The news organization of AIR is one of the biggest of its kind in Asia; it broadcasts 273 bulletins daily for a duration over 36 hours in more than 92 languages and dialects. The Vividh Bharati Service broadcasts popular music, film and nonfilm music including folk and patriotic songs and Western music. The foreign service of AIR, the External Services Division, broadcasts daily programs for 75 hours in 23 foreign languages for listeners in 54 countries. It recently set up a 12-hour daily service for Sri Lanka. The External Services Division has assumed the role of a cultural ambassador in projecting and promoting the Indian image abroad. The programs are also designed to serve as a link with the people of Indian origin living or settled abroad. In the regional services, 132 bulletins are broadcast daily in about 72 languages and dialects for a duration of nearly 17 hours.

In addition, AIR regularly broadcasts programs on family planning, health, hygiene, nutrition, vocational training, farming, industries, and various other aspects of rural life. AIR also provides programs for special audiences, which include women and children, students, youth, and senior citizens.

Television in India was introduced on September 15, 1959 with a $20,000 UNESCO aid as a one-hour, twice-a-week experimental service to provide social education to the urban slum dwellers in New Delhi. It was reorganized in 1965 and began its regular service. In April 1976, television was separated from AIR and formed into an independent unit, Doordarshan (Distant Vision), under the Ministry of Information and Broadcasting.

In its efforts to act as a catalyst for social change, Doordarshan television offers a variety of information, cultural, entertainment, educational, and scientific programs. After more than 30 years of its operation, Doordarshan has now grown into a giant network. There are 30 million television sets in India, and television today reaches 88 percent of the urban population and 30 percent of the rural population. On February

3, 1990, AIR launched a new program, *"News Sameeksha,"* comprising listeners' comments on its views and current affairs programs. This program, first of its kind, throws open news bulletins and various current affairs programs of AIR for criticism, comments, and suggestions.

Satellite and microwave facilities have further helped in the spreading of the TV network programs all around the country. In 1975, a one-year Satellite Instructional Television Experiment (SITE) was launched, in which more than 2,300 villages experienced television. SITE is often described as one of the biggest communication experiments ever undertaken. Currently, India's national multipurpose Satellite (INSAT-IB) is being used for telecommunication, meteorology, and radio as well as television. INSAT-2B went into geostationary orbit in July 1993.

Television turned commercial from January 1, 1976 with the initial introduction of advertising spots. Currently, in addition to the spots, series of sponsored programs are being telecast. It started its color transmission in August 1982 and its first multichannel transmission in 1984. In 1987, it started its teletext service in "Picture Mode," which enables the viewers to obtain information on normal receiver without the aid of a decoder.

In 1993, Doordarshan launched five new satellite channels: metro, business, sports, entertainment, and enrichment, which includes developmental stories, and so on. Besides Doordarshan, private organizations have launched additional television channels via satellite such as MTV, Zee TV, and Skyvision TV. MTV specializes in modern Western music. Zee TV offers entertainment and within the next two years plans to offer 20 more channels and also to specialize in news programs. Skyvision TV, launched by the Electronics Corporation of India in February 1993, gives all the satellite programs at the flick of a remote-control switch. It has 47 programmable channels and can receive anything beamed on C band (satellite reception) or ordinary VHF or UHF (Doordarshan). The ultramodern set also has facilities to accommodate the 60 channels expected over Indian skies by 1998. In addition, access to BBC and Cable News Network (CNN) has made the globalization of television a reality.

Radio Pakistan has been broadcasting programs for the information, education, and entertainment of listeners since it came into existence on August 14, 1947. In Pakistan's multilingual, largely rural society, radio is an extremely powerful communication vehicle that transmits programs in 21 languages. In cities, three of every four households have radios, and in villages, two of three households have radio sets.

The Central News Organization of Radio Pakistan puts out 80 news bulletins daily in the Home Service, External Services, and World Service to keep the listeners abreast of latest news. The External Services broadcast in 15 foreign languages for 18 hours a day to 64 countries. Its main object is to project Pakistan's views and policies on important national and international matters including developmental activities and to promote goodwill between Pakistan and other countries.

Music, drama, and features constitute about 45 percent of the total broadcast of Radio Pakistan. The next highest category is that of religious broadcasts (16 percent). Religious programs are broadcast at least twice a day, in which recitations from the Koran are followed by talks and discussions to relate Koran teachings to problems of everyday life.

In addition to propagating the Muslim faith and reflecting the official views and policies of the government, Radio Pakistan is used extensively as an educational tool. In 1960 Pakistan started radio broadcasts for schools with five different regional languages. In 1974 a distance learning educational institution known as the Institute of Educational Technology was established; it uses radio broadcasts for its distance education program. Moreover, each station broadcasts university/college magazine programs that are geared toward guiding the youth in becoming patriotic and responsible citizens of Pakistan.

The radio is also considered an effective medium for farm broadcasting. Introduced on an experimental basis in 1966, farm programs have become an integral part of Radio Pakistan. They are broadcast by all 16 stations twice a day. Over 60 percent of the farmers depend on Radio Pakistan for agricultural information and guidance. Eighty percent of Pakistan's population lives in villages, and radio plays a tremendous role as an instrument of change, education, and information.

Pakistan's television reaches more than 82 percent of the total population. Its five production centers provide more than 7 hours of transmission daily to over 10 million viewers. Like India, Pakistan also uses television to promote adult literacy. The coverage now extends to about 86.33 percent of the total population, with an average viewership of about eight persons per set. PTV has devised seven major educational programs covering adult functional literacy and formal school/college education. In addition, various programs are produced and televised on religion, culture, and politics that depict Islamic values and national development and support the policies of the government. In addition to PTV, another TV channel, People's Television Network (PTN), started its telecasts from Islamabad and Karachi in 1990.

Both radio and television are state owned and supported by license fees, government subsidies, and advertising. Radio broadcasting is handled by the Broadcasting Corporation of Pakistan, a statutory corporation under the direct control of the Ministry of Information and Broadcasting. Television is administered through the Pakistan Television Corporation Ltd., a public limited company whose shares are held by the government.

Radio in Bangladesh, as in Pakistan and India, is also a government operation, supported by license fees, government subsidies, and advertising. The daily combined broadcasts of all nine stations of Radio Bangladesh total 92 hours. In 1990, there were 406,000 licensed radio receivers in use.

Bangladesh TV (BTV) started in 1965. After the independence of Bangladesh in 1971, a big TV complex was set up at Rampura, in the suburb of Dacca. It transmits programs through 11 relay stations and broadcasts more than 52 hours of programs every week. The daily transmission time is generally more than six hours on one channel. Seventy-one percent of the programs are locally produced, and the remaining 29 percent are imported. In 1990, there were 482,000 television receivers in use.

The present democratic government under Begum Khaleda Zia believes in the global free flow of information and has recently taken an epoch-making decision of allowing the use of dish antenna to receive foreign television programs via satellites. Most dish owners could pick up several channels like Star Channel from Hong Kong, BBC World Service, Prime Sports, MTV and Zee TV from India, as well as national channels from Pakistan and Burma. With the same object in view, Bangladesh Television started relaying CNN International and BBC programs in 1992 for six days a week except on Fridays. On Fridays, special religious programs and cultural programs for children are transmitted. In October 1992, Prime Minister Khaleda Zia announced plans to begin a second channel for the use of Open University.

In Sri Lanka, where radio listening is extremely popular, broadcasting is handled by the Sri Lanka Broadcasting Corporation, a public corporation under the Ministry of Information, financed by license fees and advertising revenues. Radio programs consist of news, music, and cultural programs and are broadcast in six languages: Sinhalese, English, Hindi, Urdu, Tamil, and Arabic. Experimental TV began in 1979 as a private venture and was sold to the government later that year. This Independent Television Network (ITN) broadcasts news and cultural programs for six hours daily in English, Tamil, and Sinhalese. In addition to ITN, there are three other television networks. Rupavahine, another government network, also broadcasts for six hours daily and nine hours on Saturdays. MTV, an independent network TV, was started in 1992 by the Maharaja Organization in Sri Lanka, and Telshan was started on April 22, 1993 by Telshan Network Pvt. Ltd., owned by Sri Lankan TV pioneer, Shan Wickremesinghe, who obtained the license to operate ITN and establish TV in Sri Lanka in 1979. Telshan provides countrywide transmissions of local and foreign programs on four channels. For the first time in Sri Lanka, Telshan Network has introduced stereo and dual-language transmissions of the same program in Sinhala, Tamil, and English. These television programs can also be simultaneously received on radio. TNL also plans to dub Japanese programs in English and Sinhala for telecasting here and to export Sri Lankan programs dubbed in English to Japan.

In Nepal, because the Nepalese people were kept in total darkness until 1950 during the Rana regime, even radio sets were not available in the country. Radio Nepal came into existence in 1952, but it was not until the government sanctioned a National Communications Plan in 1971 that the radio developed in a modern sense. With technical assistance from Great Britain, the United States, Japan, and Australia, Radio Nepal has made considerable progress in recent years. The studio building of Radio Nepal, constructed with U.S. assistance, consists of six studios and is fitted with the latest equipment, provided by the United Kingdom. In 1987–1988, relay stations were established in Eastern Nepal and in Western Nepal.

Radio is used extensively for educational purposes and for educating the rural masses in agricultural, public health, and family planning programs. Radio news is broadcast in English, Nepali, Newari, Hindi, and Maithili.

Television in Nepal began in 1982, and the age of satellite communications in the Himalayan Kingdom was ushered in in October 1982 with the installation of the Satellite Earth Station. The regular transmission of color television began in 1985. According to UNESCO, in 1989, there were 625,000 radio receivers and 30,000 television receivers in use.

There are several television channels in Nepal: Star Plus, MTV, BBC, and Zee TV. In addition, the Nepalese are sports fans. There is a separate sports channel: Prime Sports. In 1992, media mogul Neer Shah introduced the Shangri-La Channel, a Nepali-language direct satellite broadcast channel, which is soon expected to become a major distance learning resource for the country.

Bhutan Broadcasting Service started as Radio NYAB (National Youth Association of Bhutan) in 1973. It broadcasts local, national, and international news as well as developmental issues and music everyday in four languages: English, Nepali, Dzongkha, and Sharchop (Eastern Bhutanese). At present, there are 36 radio stations—34 for international communications and two for external stations serving the Bhutanese diplomatic missions in India and Bangladesh. A daily FM program was started in 1987. In 1989, 23,000 radio receivers were in use.

In Bhutan, there is no television. The country is presently investing nearly $6 million on their own satellite.

In Afghanistan, Kabul Radio and Kabul Television broadcast programs in Dari and Pashtu. According to the Jalalabad Agreement of 1992, radio and television are run by the government, and no individual or party is allowed to have its own radio or television. As a result of the new government, the radio and television programs have become more open than before. Women newscasters have started appearing on the screen of Kabul television, and both radio and television have started allowing more entertainment programs such as dramas and songs. One year after the establishment of the Islamic government, a cinema house in Kabul has started showing movies. However, a censorship board has been established to make sure the films do not contradict Islamic values and traditional norms of Afghan society. Both radio and television did a good job in keeping the people informed about the developments during the meetings of Hal-o-Aqd Council and the first anniversary of the Islamic Revolution.

Southeast Asia

Myanmar (Burma), Cambodia, Laos, and Vietnam all have state-run, strictly controlled systems. Radio Myanmar programs music extensively, with its spoken messages reinforcing the ideological content of the press. Television came to the country in 1980, but as of the mid-1980s, TV-Myanmar was on the air only from 7:30 to 9:30 PM. Television came to Vietnam in 1966, introduced by the U.S. government in the midst of the war. Three entities now exist: Central Television, the State Committee for Radio and Television, and the Voice of Vietnam.

Laos takes advantage of signals from Thailand. Almost all Thai operators have official status, such as branches of the military, public universities, and the royal household, but private entrepreneurs often handle the actual program scheduling, then share profits (Thai television carries advertisements) with the operators. About 90 percent of Bangkok homes have TV sets.

Content includes both Thai and foreign syndicated material, much of the latter from the United States. Tan and Suarchavarat (1988) found that frequent viewing of U.S. programs influenced Thai students to have stereotypes of Americans as pleasure-loving, athletic, individualistic, and sensual. The independent producers previously concentrated on entertainment but now have begun news analyses, newsmagazines, and (influenced by CNN) on-site, probing reporting. Even government censorship cannot always control the influence of foreign news. In 1992, bootleggers made videotapes of the BBC's coverage of antigovernment demonstrations in Bangkok and circulated them, despite an official ban on critical reporting.

During the Vietnam war years, the United States helped Thailand build a radio system—now encompassing 300 national and local stations—that reached previously isolated rural areas. Before 1993, official radio stations airing government news programs coexisted with unofficial clandestine stations. (For example, from 1962 to 1981, the illegal Communist party of Thailand broadcast from various locations within and outside of Thailand.) Now, under a policy of privatization, entrepreneurs are setting up new national and regional stations.

In Malaysia, the Ministry of Information keeps tight control over broadcasting. Radio-Television Malaysia (RTM), established in 1963, runs two TV channels, receiving revenue from licenses and from commercials. The government party, UMNO, owns most of the shares in a third TV channel. RTM operates out of a modern $19 million facility in Kuala Lumpur.

As the economy expands, advertising revenue is growing, but ads for many products (tobacco, alcohol, blue jeans) are forbidden, as are scenes of sex and violence. Entertainment content, including imports (about half of all programming), must reflect Malaysian values. News programs portray the government positively; CNN is not available.

Microwave links tie in regional production centers and transmitters in every part of the country, including Sabah and Sarawak. Both radio and television broadcast in Bahasa Malaysia (the national language), English, Chinese, and Tamil.

Malaysian television can be received in Singapore. Domestically, Singapore Broadcasting Corp. (SBC) broadcasts in Malay, English, Chinese (Mandarin and a number of dialects), and Tamil. SBC, a unit under the Ministry of Culture, will eventually be broken up and sold. But privatization will not mean the end of censorship, even on pay-TV services. As in Malaysia, sex, violence, homosexuality, and drug use will be forbidden topics. Public affairs programs stress racial tolerance and national unity.

Because Indonesia is made up of isolated islands scattered across thousands of miles and has a low literacy rate, radio is the nation's only true "mass" medium. The state-owned Radio Republik Indonesia (RRI) is the largest network in the country. It was founded on September 11, 1945, within days of declaration of independence.

In 1992, RRI had 49 broadcasting stations consisting of five "Nusantara" relay stations. There are also 27 RRI stations in each of the 27 provinces, 17 stations in the districts, and 133 regional broadcastings managed by the local administrations. The national service broadcasts an average of 69 hours altogether every day.

A smaller, government radio network, known as Voice of Indonesia, broadcasts 12 hours daily in Indonesian, English, German, French, Spanish, Arabic, Chinese, Thai, Malay, and Japanese. In addition to the government stations, a number of privately owned commercial stations play mostly popular music.

The current policy of RRI is directed to the improvement of broadcast quality, particularly to improve the quality of the Groups of the Rural Broadcasting listeners, which constitute a part of the Groups of Listeners, Viewers, and Readers (KLOMPENCAPIR). KLOMENCAPIR plays an important part in the overall information strategy of the nation to create an equal and balanced flow of information. In addition, it is also designed for educating the rural media audience. RRI promotes government and political values.

Televisi Republik Indonesia (TVRI), the state-owned television service was begun on August 24, 1962 with the cooperation of the Japanese government in preparation for the Fourth Asian Games. Thirty-two percent of the budget comes from the 15 percent of time devoted to advertisements; 65 percent from license fees; and the remainder from a government subsidy. By 1993, there were 10 television broadcasting stations in major towns and 240 transmitters in various provinces, which enabled the population at the border areas and remote places to watch the television national programs. In addition, the government has made available 10 mobile production units in 10 provinces to expand its TV broadcasting network.

TVRI national broadcasting service programs are on the air for an average of 10 hours daily, and regional services broadcast an average of 2 hours daily. With programs from regional stations and mobile units, TVRI has been able to produce almost all of its programs in-house.

National television programs can now be viewed in all the capital towns of Indonesia's 27 provinces as well as in almost all district capitals. The official network follows policies laid down by the Ministry of Information and makes every effort toward building a unified society. Therefore, programs that might offend any religious or ethnic groups are avoided.

In November 1988, a new private-owned special television network, Rajawali Citra Televisi Indonesia (RCTI), was started in Jakarta. Its programs consist of 55 percent entertainment, 20 percent education and culture, 10 percent news and government programs, and 15 percent commercials. It must broadcast the government newscast from TVRI. RCTI reaches only the wealthy viewers, because it requires an expensive decoder. It relies mostly on advertisements for its revenue. Two other television stations started broadcasting in 1990 and 1991. A privately owned television Surya Citra Televisi (SCTV) began to broadcast in August 1990; and PT Cipta Televisi Pendidikan Indonesia (TPI) started its educational programs in January 1991. The program is produced by the Department of Education and Culture and promotes the school programs of both intra- and extracurriculum.

Indonesia has its own domestic communications satellite system, Palapa, which was launched in 1976. As a result, television is received in the most isolated villages. The Palapa satellite has united Indonesia through one communication and information system and has enabled the cultures of smaller minority groups to be telecast nationally. The satellite is also being used for the Packet Switched Public Data Network, which is connected to international data centers in Europe, Japan, and the United States. Indonesia is the first country in the world to use a domestic satellite for such a network.

The Philippine broadcasting media had enjoyed the same freedoms as the press before the martial law. With the declaration of martial law in 1972, a number of radio and television studios were sealed, and several others were placed under military control. During that time, editorials, opinion, and commentary were forbidden over the air, and all radio and television stations were required to "broadcast accurate, objective, straight news reports of the government to meet the dangers and threats that occasioned the proclamation of martial law, and the efforts to achieve a 'new society'."

Currently, with the "free access" policy of the new government, radio stations and television channels are multiplying. Radio is the most important medium in rural

Philippines and reaches 89 percent of the population. Approximately 270 radio stations broadcast music, serials, mysteries, soap operas, and contest shows to the people throughout the country. Radio talk shows are increasingly becoming quite popular and influential. Most radio stations are owned and controlled by powerful wealthy families. The Catholic Church also exerts tremendous influence over the Philippines' population through its group, Radio Veritas, which runs 45 radio stations throughout the Philippines islands. Radio Veritas's programming is aired in about 35 different dialects. There are five privately owned television networks and one public network. Only one channel is owned by the government. Among the privately owned networks, Channel 2 (ABS), owned by the wealthy Lopez family, has the largest audience. It shows some local entertainment programs, some American programs, and has adopted the style of some American news/talk shows. For example, *Inside Story,* modeled after *60 Minutes,* exposes malfeasance. The public network—People's Television (PTV), Channel 4—which broadcasts approximately 96 hours per week, stresses national development and Philippine culture and history.

East Asia

Japan's Nihon Hoso Kyokai (NHK) radio service, unabashedly modeled on the BBC when it was established in 1926, became a military propaganda tool during World War II. After the war, in 1950, the Occupation forces approved the licensing of private, commercial radio stations, giving Japan the mixed system it has today. NHK's radio coverage now far exceeds that of commercial broadcasters.

Television began in 1953 after the Occupation ended. The autonomy of NHK derives partly from its ability to set and collect its own fees, although the legislature does review fee proposals. Moreover, NHK has complete freedom in programming; the government can neither include nor exclude content.

According to Sydney Head, "Japan has a rich artistic heritage that lends itself readily to television"(1985, p. 22). A typical viewer in the Kanto (Tokyo metropolitan) area has a choice of two NHK channels (educational and entertainment); five commercial channels (Nihon TV, TBS, Fuji TV, TV Asahi, and TV Tokyo); UHF channels with in-school programs and local news; two NHK satellite channels (requiring purchase of a small dish); and Wowow, a pay-TV channel.

For overseas coverage, Japan's electronic media make frequent use of satellites and have numerous overseas correspondents. (Japan has a larger corps of correspondents in the United States than any other country.) However, Cooper-Chen (1994) found NNK's news reporting to be the least international of five countries studied.

In entertainment TV programming, Japan exports animated cartoons and imports major movies; however, it has virtually stopped importing regular series, meaning that it must shoulder its production burden alone (about 150 hours a week for most stations). Considering only one genre, the quiz show, viewers have a choice of 32 domestically produced weekly programs that differ markedly from game or quiz shows anywhere else in the world.

As for the future, virtual TV saturation (one set per 1.8 people) means NHK cannot expect increased revenues from new customers. Nor can TV advertisers expect much more attention to their messages, since the average Japanese already watches four hours a day. Indeed, domestic channels may see falling audience shares as STAR TV enters on the heels of expected legal liberalizations regarding international broadcasting.

If Japan's uniquely non-Western television culture impresses an outsider as sophisticated, modern, and highly developed, China gives a visitor the chance to witness historical change in the making. The USSR was just helping China start its state-run television system in 1958 when the two countries had a falling out; the Soviet advisors went home, leaving radio as the prime means of instant communication through the Mao years.

Radio uses a three-layer system: (1) the national Central People's Broadcasting Station (in China, the English word "broadcasting" refers to radio, not television); (2) about 100 regional, provincial, and municipal networks; and (3) grass-roots stations that send national programs and local announcements by wires to loudspeakers in communes, marketplaces, fields, and homes. During the Cultural Revolution, loudspeakers blared everywhere, but in the 1980s, government policy favored over-the-air stations. With the wired layer included, radio reaches about 95 percent of China's people.

Radio Beijing sends shortwave broadcasts out from China. Ever since the 1989 Tienanmen massacre, radio programs coming into China have been discredited and jammed: the Voice of America, BBC, and Broadcasting Corporation of China (beamed from Taiwan). In January 1994, despite Chinese opposition, the U.S. Senate approved a new service, Radio Free Asia, to send objective news to China and certain other nations.

Since 1976, the year Mao died and the cultural revolution ended, television in China has developed exponentially. Now its estimated 600 million viewers form the largest TV audience in the world. China has about one TV set for every eight people— a much higher penetration than its telephones (about one for every 89 people).

Because of China's size and terrain, Chinese Central Television (CCTV) has turned to satellites to increase the reach of Channels 1 and 2, which now serve all 29 provinces, including Tibet and Xinjiang. (Channel 3 can be seen only in Beijing.) CCTV produces three news programs a day and much of its own sports and entertainment fare.

The first U.S. series, "The Man from Atlantis," which was chosen for its bargain price rather than ideological content, aired in 1979. In choosing a color system, however, China chose not to follow the U.S. model (National Television Standards Committee, or NTSC), which had also been adopted in Japan, the Philippines, and South Korea. Instead, it opted for the German PAL system ("Phase Alternate Line").

Residents of Hong Kong can receive signals from China in addition to their four privately owned commercial channels, new Wharf Cable channel, and one government educational channel (RTHK). The Cantonese Jade Channel now has the lion's share of viewership, while the British colony's two legally mandated English channels are losing money. TV advertisements must take up no more than 10 percent of programming time. Commercial radio, which began in 1959, must likewise limit the time devoted to ads.

Although only 400 miles square, Hong Kong serves as a major radio and television production center for overseas Chinese language media from Taiwan to California. Its TV exports emphasize kung fu and other action fare, while its Cantonese-language radio programs range from storytellers to serial dramas. The Hong Kong-based STAR TV (see preceding discussion) has a backup facility in Thailand in case Chinese authorities try to shut the service down after July 1, 1997.

Taiwan's three government-affiliated, commercial TV networks offer both modern-dress and costume-opera dramatic series, as well as game shows, variety shows, news, and public affairs. Government regulations require 70 percent of programming to be domestic.

With the end of martial law in 1987, restrictions on television eased somewhat. Taiwanese can now legally purchase satellite dishes for receiving signals from Japan in Japanese, a language that many young Taiwanese study and that all Taiwanese who went to school before 1945 can understand. (Japan ruled Taiwan as a colony from 1898 to 1945.) While cable regulations are being worked out, pirate cable operators feed programs—including pornography—cheaply and illegally to small subscriber groups.

Financing and ownership of the three TV networks involve a complex arrangement among government, military, party (the Kuomintang), private, and overseas interests. Radio ownership shows a similar mixed pattern. The KMT does fully control two overseas radio services, the Voice of Free China, and a second service aimed specifically at the mainland. The English-language radio station formerly operated for U.S. forces was converted into a service for foreign residents after the United States broke diplomatic relations with the island.

The penetration of television in South Korea stands at nearly 100 percent. The government owns 51 percent of both the Korean Broadcasting System (KBS) and the Munwa Broadcasting Co. (MBS), but the Seoul Broadcasting Corp. (established in 1989 and suffering from poorer reception quality) is 100 percent privately owned.

Government regulations require TV blackouts at night, midnight to 6 AM and during weekdays (10 AM to 5:30 PM). Content can be only 20 percent foreign—none of it, however, from Japan. STAR TV and CNN viewing is permitted without restriction; a glance at any Seoul apartment building shows a generous crop of satellite dishes sprouting from balconies. The American Forces Korean Network (AFKN) runs six stations, which reach the entire Korean population, with no Korean official interference. AFKN, which began its TV service in 1957, broadcasts nothing but U.S. programs.

During the 1988 Olympic games, the media played a role in already-strained U.S.-Korean relations. After NBC repeatedly played footage of a Korean trainer assaulting an American boxing referee, the Korean media heavily covered the arrest of two U.S. swimmers who stole a ceremonial mask. Despite these incidents, the Olympics bore witness worldwide to the sophistication and maturity of Korean telecommunications.

South Korea has more than 200 TV sets per 1,000 people, while North Korea has only 12. Both entities, which are still officially in a state of war, send radio broadcasts to each other. In fact, North Korea's external service in eight languages rivals the BBC's. But little South Korean content gets through to the North, since all radios have fixed dials to receive domestic programs only.

The Pacific

Geography practically ordained that Australia would, from broadcasting's earliest days, have a mixed system. The concentration of two-thirds of Australia's 17.5 million people in the southeastern coastal region made commercial broadcasting, which started in 1924, attractive in that region. However, only a publicly supported system was feasible in the thinly populated outback. Today, Australia has about as many private as government stations.

The nation has a healthy entertainment TV production industry that exports to the worldwide English-language market. For example, the organization founded by Australian Reg Grundy, which produces 50 hours of television a week, has sold 263 episodes of the series "Neighbors" to STAR TV.

The Australian Broadcasting Corp. (ABC), established in 1932, has much in common with the BBC. Its board guards ABC's independence from government interference, although the ABC relies on Parliament to transfer over the license-fee funds collected from the public. Between 1986 and 1991, ABC lost more than 20 percent of its funding but increased its production output. It even sponsors symphony orchestras in all six Australian states.

In the 1960s, the ABC began losing audience numbers to the commercial broadcasters. Then two dramatic changes transformed broadcasting on the island continent. First, immigrant groups and Aborigines who felt unconnected to Australia's European roots began lobbying for multicultural media. Using an access station set up in 1976, these groups started radio programs in 26 languages. In 1980, the government set up the multicultural Special Broadcasting (television) Service.

Second, with the launching of Aussat in 1985, homes and institutions could now receive television, radio, and phone service via low-cost satellite ground stations. Aussat also provides television service to Fiji and Papua-New Guinea and assists telephone service in New Zealand. New Zealand depends even more on broadcasting than Australia to unite, inform, and entertain its small, scattered, agricultural population. The country even has a minister of broadcasting in the ruling cabinet.

New Zealand adopted the BBC model in 1932 but preserved the government monopoly many years longer than did the mother country. Because of competition from offshore pirate radio stations in the 1960s, the New Zealand Broadcasting Corp. (NZBC) finally began licensing private radio stations.

NZBC waited until 1960 to begin two television networks and until 1984 to approve an independent, nongovernment TV network. The two government networks, however, run commercials on certain days of the week, relying on advertisements for 85 percent of their budgets. TV-2, which emphasizes entertainment fare, has in the past run many American situation comedies but now tries to emphasize local production.

Radio came to the Pacific Islands in 1935, when service started in Fiji. However, more than half of the services are much more recent, dating from after 1960. They show the influence of nearby Australia and distant colonial powers, with American influence strong in Micronesia and American Samoa and British (BBC) influence in Fiji. In the 1970s, local staffs for the most part replaced the expatriates who managed many media enterprises in the islands.

Despite problems with funding, government interference, low salaries, inadequate training, outdated equipment, and multiple languages, radio serves as the only timely link between many islands and the rest of the world. Even those that lack a daily newspaper have a radio system; Nauru, for example, the smallest republic in the world, has one 200-watt AM station to serve its 8,000 citizens. Papua-New Guinea, which has the

Pacific's most extensive system, inherited a service that Australia began in 1946; it broadcasts in 33 languages.

Guam joined the television age in the mid-1950s; other early adopters, in the 1960s, include New Caledonia, Tahiti, and American Samoa. Except for funding problems, virtually all Pacific nations and dependencies could link into INTELSAT, even if lack of facilities and staff limited local productions. While television has been established in several island states, videocassette systems continue to thrive throughout the region. A cassette circulation network poses a creative alternative to television in places that cannot or choose not to go the TV route.

NEWS SERVICES

The existence of myriad news agencies in Asia holds both hope for better information availability and the specter of managed news flows. The various patterns found in Asia include the presence of a government agency only, government and private agencies operating side by side, private agency or agencies only, private agencies subject to indirect government control, and regional cooperation of various kinds.

The Asian News Network, created in 1981, answered a need for an exchange of development and other regional news. However, it is still dwarfed by the regional services of the Big Four international services. Likewise, Asiavision complemented but in no way replaced the international news film and videotape services of Visnews and WTN (World Television News).

Worldwide, 56 percent of countries (a total of 90) have a government news agency, whereas 50 years ago, only 28 countries had one. Freedom House found that for 1987, 89 percent of the world's nations with the lowest civil liberties rating operated a government news agency. The pattern holds for Asia, but even more strikingly.

Only six Asian countries have no national government news agency: Australia, Bhutan, Fiji, Taiwan, Japan, and New Zealand. Of these, Australia, Japan, and New Zealand have the highest civil liberties ranking (1); indeed, in all of Asia, only these three have attained that rank.

The national agencies in Asia range from those that act solely as gatekeepers (e.g., the Korean Central News Agency of North Korea, which controls domestic consumption of news from regional and international sources) to those that do active local reporting to those that rival the Big Four international agencies in the scope of their overseas staffs. Kyodo News Service of Japan approaches true world agency status, but Xinhua (the New China News Agency) and the Press Trust of India have an impressive reach as well. Kyodo is free of government control, while Xinhua is the state-owned agency of the People's Republic of China.

Depthnews, a development news service, established in 1969, caters to clients throughout the Asian region and serves as a voice for Asian development journalism. It provides a service distinctly different from Western news services. *Depthnews* stands for development, economics and population themes. Depthnews emphasizes coverage of women, environmental concerns, and regional science and health issues as well as areas of economic, social, and political interest in Asia. A 1989 survey shows that Depthnews's emphasis on development topics is favorably received by its clients, and many see it as a force for advancing South–South communication and understanding.

South Asia

Among South Asian countries, India has a diverse national news agency system, including four major agencies and several other specialized agencies. The most widely known is the privately owned Press Trust of India (PTI), which has been called the backbone of daily journalism in the country. It was established in 1947 and operates as a nonprofit company. In addition to providing services to the newspapers and periodicals, it provides a TV screen news in capsule form round-the-clock to hotels, airports, ministries, and public sector undertakings. In 1986, PTI launched its TV operations under the banner of PTI-TV, and in 1987, it started a photographic service on a nationwide scale. PTI has news bureaus in London and New York and has correspondents in 30 world capitals. It has news exchange agreements with 100 countries. PTI is a leading participant in the Pool of News Agencies of the nonaligned countries and the Organization of Asian News Agencies (OANA). From March 1985 until July 1988, PTI was the president of OANA. PTI's main rival, United News of India (UNI), established in 1961, has news bureaus and correspondents in 25 world capitals. UNI also has a photographic service of its own and supplies news clips and features to the television station. It is now one of the largest news agencies in Asia, with over 100 news bureaus in India and abroad. In July 1986, a television wing of the news agency was started, providing news features, clips, and documentaries for Indian television.

The other two news agencies, The Hindustan Samachar and Samachar Bharati, are multilingual.

In Pakistan, there are two major news agencies, The Associated Press of Pakistan (APP) and the Pakistan Press International (PPI). APP, founded in 1947, supplies national and international news to newspapers, radio, and TV stations, government departments, and other commercial subscribers. Pakistan Press Association (PPA) was established in 1956 as a private joint stock company. Both APP and PPI have bureaus in major cities of Pakistan and exchange agreements with major news agencies of the world.

Bangladesh has three news agencies: Bangladesh Sangbad Sangstha (BSS), a news service in English, owned by the Government; United News of Bangladesh (UNB), a computerized news service with latest equipment established in 1988; and Development Features Agency.

Sri Lanka has two news agencies, Press Trust of Ceylon and Sandesa News Agency.

Nepal's news agency, The Rashtriya Samachar Samiti (RSS) was founded in 1962 in Kathmandu. It has correspondents in all 75 districts and exchange agreements with AP, Agence France-Presse, and Sinhua News Agency of People's Republic of China.

Bhutan has no news agency.

Afghanistan's Bakhtar News Agency (BNA) transmits news to many countries including those in Asia, Europe, the Middle East, Africa, and the neighboring social-ist countries.

Southeast Asia

With UNESCO's encouragement, a number of countries established national news agencies in the 1970s. As of 1987, Burma, Cambodia, Laos, Indonesia, Malaysia, the Philippines, Singapore, and Vietnam all had government news agencies. Cambodia's pro-Vietnamese news agency, SPK, employs more than 100 reporters, making it that nation's largest single news operation. Thailand's Thai News Agency is an exception in its freedom from direct government control.

One of the largest, Bernama of Malaysia, was established in 1968 under the Min-istry of Information. It derives most of its income from government subscribers, in-cluding the state-controlled radio and television services. Like many third-world agen-cies, it shares news directly with a number of other national agencies and indirectly by belonging to the Non-Aligned News Agency Pool. Bernama does not act as the sole media gatekeeper for information coming into Malaysia, since the international agen-cies can sell directly to customers.

Indonesia has three national news services. Antara, meaning "between" in Bahasa Indonesian, is the major agency. Founded in 1937 to distribute news about the inde-pendence movement with a nationalist interpretation, Antara became an official agency in 1962 and is governed through a council composed of representatives from gov-ernment and the private sector. The oldest surviving and the biggest Indonesian news service, Antara provides news, feature and photographic services to newspapers, radio stations, foreign embassies, and commercial institutions. In addition to bureaus in all 27 provinces of Indonesia, it has bureaus or correspondents in several major cities of the world and exchange agreements with several major agencies of the world. It is also an active member of the confederation of ASEAN journalists, Non-Aligned News Pool and Organization of Asian News Agencies (OANA).

Two other major news agencies besides Antara are the Pusab Pemberitaan Angkatan Bersendjata (PAB) and the Independent Kantorberita Nasional Indonesia (KNI). PAN, formed in 1965, handles primarily army news but is in the business of gen-eral news reporting as well. KNI, formed in 1966 by 11 Djakarta newspapers, is an in-dependent service free of government or political ties. In 1970, KNI started an Eng-lish "KNI Daily Bulletin," specializing on economic issues, for its foreign readers. KNI has bureaus or correspondents throughout Indonesia.

In the Philippines, with the restoration of press freedom in 1987, the government-owned Philippine News Agency has been discontinued.

East Asia

North Korea, South Korea, and Mongolia all have government news agencies, but they are dwarfed in scope by Xinhua. Xinhua, which celebrated its fiftieth anniversary in 1981, has more than 300 employees in 80 overseas bureaus; correspondents are classified as diplomats and enjoy diplomatic immunity. With a total staff of more than 5,000, it transmits about 50,000 words daily to the Chinese media and about 60,000 words overseas in six languages. Furthermore, it monitors all incoming news and culls from that flow the 10-million circulation Reference News.

In Hong Kong, Xinhua's role goes far beyond that of a news agency, according to Chan and Lee (1988), with only 30 of its 500 staff members working in the news division. Instead of having a news agency structure, Xinhua's divisions were changed in 1983 to coincide with those of the Hong Kong government. As Beijing's surrogate presence in Hong Kong, Xinhua organizes and supervises the committees that are designing Hong Kong's post-1997 future.

Kyodo, a private cooperative agency formed in 1945, has bureaus in some 40 countries. For its large domestic clientele, it produces more than 200,000 Japanese characters a day, while for overseas clients, it sends out about 40,000 words a day in English; the English service has recently responded to increased demands for news about Japanese sports.

Jiji Press, a business-oriented private agency, also was born in 1945. Like Kyodo, it produces domestic Japanese and overseas English files but also sends out about 12,000 words a day in Chinese.

Pacific

The nongovernmental New Zealand Press Association and (especially) the Australian Associated Press (AAP) serve not only their home countries' media but Pacific communities as well. From its headquarters in Sydney, the AAP supplies both Fiji and Papua-New Guinea with a file that it culls from major agencies and its own members' news output.

GOVERNMENT–MEDIA RELATIONS

Every year since 1972, Freedom House has looked at political rights and civil liberties in all of the world's nations and dependent territories, paying close attention to the degree of government control over print and broadcast media. According to the 1992 ratings of the Freedom House (1993), worldwide, 25 percent of countries have generally free broadcast and print media, but in Asia only 15 percent of countries do (Japan, Australia, New Zealand and Papua-New Guinea). Table 13.1 shows the status of print and broadcast freedom in relation to other media factors. Generally speaking, the laws of Asian countries contain sweeping powers for controlling media.

In 1987, Merrill (1988) interviewed 58 information/press officers posted in the United States regarding nations' inclinations to control the press. Of the 10 Asian nations studied, China ranked with those having the most severe controls, or a Control Inclination Index (CII) score of 24. Australia and Japan had the lowest (freest) scores, 11 (compared to the United States with 8). The other nations are India, 12; Philippines, 14; Bangladesh, Indonesia, and South Korea, all 18; Malaysia, 20; and Pakistan, 19 (Merrill 1988).

Control mechanisms on the press include annual licensing of publications, exorbitant security deposits, confiscation, cutting allowable circulation, control of newsprint and official advertising, and outright closure. Journalists themselves can be punished under sedition, libel, security or martial law provisions.

South Asia

In most of South Asia, governments try to restrain the press by promoting a "guidance" concept to be used in conjunction with national development aims. Media must cooperate, according to the "guidance" concept, by stressing positive, development-oriented news and by supporting government policies and plans of national development. The guidance comes in the form of supplying news releases and actual stories to the media, providing public speeches by officials on the desired role of the press in a developing society, and telephone calls from government officials offering advice. In Pakistan, Bangladesh, Sri Lanka, Nepal, and sometimes even in India, telephone guidelines are provided by the government in power. Official speeches in practically all South Asian countries are published verbatim on front pages. For fear of displeasing the government, journalists most often practice self-restraint and avoid investigative reporting. For years now, Tamil journalists in Sri Lanka have been keeping quiet about terrorism, willingly censoring their own stories.

Besides promoting a guidance concept, most governments use direct censorship, suspend offending newspapers, and arrest journalists who do not conform to the official policy. Direct censorship is prevalent in Sri Lanka, Pakistan, Bangladesh, Nepal, and Afghanistan.

In Sri Lanka, direct censorship is permitted under the antiterrorism law and parliamentary privileges can be invoked to shield parliamentary discussion. As a result of direct censorship, Sri Lanka's mainstream publications do not contest the government's viewpoint directly or probe its activities deeply. On a recent Tamil ethnic problem, much of the press fully backed the government's military campaign, presenting it as a justified, patriotic war. However, under the new President, D. B. Wijetunga, press controls have been relaxed considerably.

The Bangladeshi government closed two Bengali-language daily newspapers in February 1988 on the grounds that they had published "objectionable news" and that they had attempted to undermine the sovereignty and independence of the country. However, the Press Institute of Bangladesh and Bangladesh Press Council have the power to make observations against any authority and to consider complaints.

In Pakistan, there was no mention or glimpse of opposition figures in the media for years. Under the leadership of Prime Minister Benazir Bhutto, in a dramatic reversal of years of blackout on the activities of the Pakistan People's Party, the opposition politicians now get a share of airtime.

Nepal functions under the guidelines of the Press and Publications Act, which prohibits publication of material detrimental to the national interest, peace, law and order, and the power of the king. In 1990, major political changes took place as a result of a successful People's Movement. The partyless Panchayat System was abolished, and a multiparty democracy with the king as a constitutional head restored. The new constitution, promulgated on November 9, 1990, guarantees full fundamental rights including human rights.

In Afghanistan, after the coup in 1978, all private printing houses were forbidden to operate. Newspapers could not publish anything that would tend to disobey government laws or that discloses state secrets or defames the Islam religion. According to the Jalalabad Agreement of 1992, the affairs of the country will be run by laws made before the coup of 1978. Newspapers are no longer bound to relay communist propaganda and reflect Sovietization. However, contradiction of Islamic values is still not tolerated. For example, a censorship board of films was established in 1993 to make sure the films do not contradict Islamic values and traditional norms of Afghan society.

Suspension of newspapers and harassment and arrest of journalists occur when officials or anybody in a position of power and influence do not like what is written about them. Though India's press is among the freest in Asia and there is no direct censorship, the Indian government has not hesitated at times to use its enormous powers over the press. In June 1989, the *Indian Post* of Bombay, an independent newspaper known for its investigative reporting, was tarnished overnight when its editor, Vinod Mehta, was asked to resign by its owner because the paper had published critical reports involving some power brokers close to the Prime Minister. More recently, on February 19, 1994, Bal Thackeray, leader of the political party Shiv Sena, asked a journalist of *The Daily Citizen* of Aurangabad to leave the press conference, and later that day the journalist and nine others were beaten by Shiv Sena activists. The press in India, however, is still holding its own despite pressure. The resignation of the *Post's* editor, for example, generated much concern with the journalistic community in India. Several journalists issued a statement warning that the resignation of the editor "disturbingly reveals the perils to press freedom in the country today" ("Editors" 1989, p. 1). A storm of protest has broken in the press over the attack of journalists by Shiv Sena activists. Journalist trade unions and editors of small and big newspapers, including national dailies such as *The Times of India* and *The Indian Express,* have announced a ban on covering the activities of the Shiv Sena Party, pending an apology by Thackeray.

In 1990, an 84-year-old editor of a Hindi daily in the state of Bihar was dragged from his house to a police lock-up, where he was physically assaulted because he had written an editorial over an instance of alleged police brutality. According to the Indian Federation of Working Journalists, more than 50 such attacks were reported in 1988 from almost every state. Media analyst and former *Times of India* editor, M.V. Desai, however, sees otherwise: "These attacks also go to show that the press is doing its job in exposing misuses of authority in institutions answerable to society" (Basu 1989, p. 12). Bangladeshi writer Taslima Nasrin faces death threats from extreme right-wing groups in her country for her book *Lajja (Shame)*, a novel focusing on the plight of the minority Hindu community in Bangladesh.

The press in India and Sri Lanka has recently also been the target of rebel groups, who have sought to intimidate and assassinate journalists and disrupt newspaper distribution. Because of the Hindu–Sikh communal strife and strife in Kashmir, journalists and others associated with the press in India are risking their lives to keep the flag of a free press flying. In May 1989, three persons were killed by terrorists when the *Hind Samachar* group of publications ignored the warnings of terrorist organizations to shut down their widely circulated papers in Punjab. In Kashmir, for example, a militant outfit sometimes goes beyond burning an editor's house or a newspaper office. The editor of *Al-Sofa,* a Kashmiri newspaper, was killed in 1991. In Sri Lanka, the Tamil militant groups have from time to time used both threats and violence against journalists writing articles that the rebels found displeasing. In January 1988, Tamil rebels bombed the home of the editor of *Divaina,* the largest circulation Sinhalese daily, and later tried to cripple the operation of Associated Newspapers of Ceylon Ltd., the country's leading publishing house. The newspaper distribution systems have also been attacked by rebels time and again in Sri Lanka.

Liberty of the press must constantly be fought for in most South Asian countries where the governments allocate newsprint, distribute advertising, stipulate registration rules, and operate the broadcast media.

In India, Pakistan, Bangladesh, Sri Lanka and Nepal, governments control newsprint and advertising quotas. In India, quality newsprint must be imported through State Trading Corporation, a government agency, because domestic producers are unable to meet even a quarter of the annual requirement. In 1990, the government announced a 30 percent increase in the price of newsprint. As a result, several newspapers folded, and others are becoming more and more dependent on government advertisements for their survival. The newspapers see the rising cost of newsprint as an attempt to punish the newspapers for their role in exposing corruption at the highest level. In Pakistan, newsprint controls and government advertisements account for about 70 percent of advertising revenue.

Although the new government of Prime Minister Benazir Bhutto has announced new guarantees of press freedom, journalists still feel that the press cannot be really free until the state monopoly on newsprint allocation is lifted. In Nepal, government is the country's largest advertiser. Hence, advertisements are placed lavishly with only government newspapers. Corporate influence in journalism has also become quite pronounced. Owners have invested a lot of money in publishing houses and expect favors from them in return. Sometimes an editor is totally bypassed. Messages are sent directly to the news desk, and the editor sees the news item in the following day's paper. In India, for example, the freedom of the professional editor is increasingly being negated by the proprietors themselves.

Because the broadcast media in the entire region of South Asia are owned and operated by the government, the broadcasts are usually replete with official news and views. In India, during the regime of late Prime Minister Indira Gandhi, media coverage of All India Radio was government oriented to such an extent that some critics labeled it as "All Indira Radio"; under the leadership of Rajiv Gandhi, critics called it "All India Rajiv." Government-controlled broadcasting in Sri Lanka presents a narrow range of views. The success of Sri Lanka's radio is usually measured in terms of how convincingly it presents the government policies and projects to the people.

Southeast Asia

In Burma, Cambodia, Laos, and Vietnam, where mass media is run by and constitutes an arm of the government, one can discuss press philosophies more readily than relations between media and government. Freedom House considers all four of these countries to have highly controlled print and broadcast systems. The other countries in the region, as Table 13.1 shows, have at least some degree of freedom—except Malaysia.

Malaysia's highly publicized run-ins with the *Asian Wall Street Journal* (which the government accused of having an "anti-Malaysia bias" in its investigative reporting) resulted in a three-month publishing ban imposed on the paper in 1986 and the expulsion of two reporters. "We gave them a publishing permit, but why haven't they said anything good about us?" asked an official. In addition, under provisions of the Official Secrets Act, a reporter for the domestic *New Straits Times* was fined $4,000 in 1985, followed by the fining of a reporter for the *Far Eastern Economic Review* in 1986.

In Thailand, according to *Asia Magazine,* "the right to publish is a right wholly defined by the government, as is the right to revoke the right to publish" (Asia Magazine Staff 1987, p. 42). As one newspaper editor told the magazine, "It's not right that we can be shut down by an unhappy man whose emotions may have gotten the better of his judgement." Indeed, in 1987, the sensational Thai-language daily *Khaosod* was ordered closed. However, that had been the first closure in some time and was not seen as a precursor of a major press curb. (After a month, *Khaosod* resumed publication under a different name.)

In Singapore, critics claim that the threat of government action has effectively tamed the press. Some local journalists have been arrested, but recently foreign publications have been more frequent targets. In 1986, *Time* and the *Asian Wall Street Journal* had the number of allowable copies cut—*Time*'s, from 18,000 to 2,000, and the *Asian Wall Street Journal*'s, from 5,000 to 400.

The Indonesian Press Law, enacted in 1966 and amended in 1982, bars censorship. However, it requires a balance between the freedom of the press and the responsibility of the press and under the guise of the "responsibility of the media," stipulates that the press should not publish materials that violate the national ideology (Pancasila). Four vital and sensitive issues that are considered to be in violation of the national ideology are *Suku* (ethnic group) issues; *Agagma* (religious) issues; *Ras* (racial) problems; and *Antar-golongan* (intergroup) conflicts or issues. These four issues, known as SARA (consisting of the first letters of the four points) are practically taboo, because any mention of such issues could flare up a given situation leading to chaos and political instability. Indonesian journalists who want to stay in the profession recognize the limitations on their freedom and are careful to avoid reporting anything that could be construed as dissent. The law also requires a license to publish. The government has the authority to cancel the license at any time.

The government is as sensitive about the foreign press as it is about its own. A supplement to the Press Act of 1966, enacted in 1972, regulates the foreign press and journalists in Indonesia. Foreign publications have to obtain government permission to circulate. All foreign publications are screened carefully, and those that harm or endanger the society or are considered to be contrary to the national ideology (*Pancasila*) are banned. Foreign journalists writing about such sensitive issues are barred from entry into the country. Barbara Crossette of *The New York Times* was ousted and later barred entry in 1987 for writing a piece that displeased President Suharto. Earlier, Australian journalist David Jenkins had written a piece in *The Sydney Morning Herald* that likened Suharto to ousted Philippine President Marcos. The story described how Suharto had built a $2 billion business empire fashioned out of banking, manufacturing, steel, shipping, real estate, and so on. The Indonesian government not only barred Jenkins but barred all Australian journalists, banned the Australian newspaper, and even refused entry to Australian tourists.

Broadcasting is also strictly censored. All programs are screened so that no offense may be caused to any religious or ethnic groups and must conform to the SARA doctrine. Private radio stations are prohibited from broadcasting their own newscasts and are expected to broadcast programs that would advance Indonesia's development. Private radio stations have to renew their licenses every year. Hence, they reflect the government's policy.

In the Philippines, during the last years of the Marcos regime, an alternative press played a tremendous role in the People Power Movement that helped unseat Marcos. *The Philippine Daily Inquirer,* founded in 1985, for example, was highly critical of Marcos and his wife. It printed on its masthead, "Honest News, Fearless News." Although journalists claimed to report the news honestly and express fearless views in the aftermath of Marcos regime, 27 journalists were assassinated or ambushed during Mrs. Aquino's presidency. In 1987, Mrs. Aquino sued the *Philippine Star* and its columnist Mr. Luis Beltran for reporting that the president hid under her bed while the firing was going on during the August 28, 1987 coup attempt. Although the *Star* apologized the next day on the front page of the newspaper, Mrs. Aquino filed a criminal libel suit. This incident certainly had a chilling effect on the Philippine media. Mrs. Aquino introduced a National Emergency Act, which gives the president the power to control any privately owned company (including media companies) serving the public interest if it is crucial to national security. Moreover, Mrs. Aquino required the journalists to obtain accreditation to gain access to government offices and documents.

Perhaps because of the aftereffects of Marcos's dictatorship, newspapers in Philippines still hesitate to displease the government; hence, they tend to practice self-censorship. Editorial criticism is often muted in a majority of newspapers, or whenever there is criticism, it is manipulated along the lines of "constructive criticism." Moreover, newspapers tend to be supportive of the developmental efforts of the country. The *Manila Times,* for example, calls itself "The Exponent of Philippine Progress," and the *Manila Bulletin* carries on its front-page the national flag with the inscription "Rally to the Flag!"

East Asia

China, North Korea, and Mongolia follow the Marxist–Leninist concept of total integration between the press and government. In Taiwan and South Korea, as in other parts of Asia, the press has until recently followed the concept of guidance, which means extensive use of government news releases, avoidance of investigative reporting and downplaying opposition elements. Telephone calls from and speeches by officials clarify what is expected.

However, by 1987, most print media in South Korea could publish without restraint. In 1988, two journalists who had been previously purged established the nation's first major independent newspaper; half of its staff had likewise been purged.

In Taiwan, as the 1986 municipal election approached, action against opposition publications increased. Censorship incidents against opposition magazines increased from 33 in 1984 to 302 in 1986. By early 1987, only three of 15 opposition magazines were still publishing. Between 1984 and early 1987, six opposition journalists were jailed for libel. The situation in the postmartial law years (after 1987) is still fluid but shows signs of increased freedom.

The 1946 constitution of Japan guarantees freedom of expression unconditionally, unlike the previous constitution, which added the insidious phrase "within the limits of the law." The self-censorship that still occurs in Japan derives partly from the rigid official censorship that prevailed until the end of the Occupation; the imperial family, for example, is treated with kid gloves. Furthermore, the newspapers' huge circulations tend to dampen initiative, because editors fear that outspoken writing might antagonize large numbers of readers.

As in most democratic states, Japanese citizens may sue the mass media for libel after publication, but relatively few do so. According to Kyu Ho Youm, the "low rights consciousness of Japanese as individuals" (1990, p. 1110) and a respect for the media as important social institutions discourage such suits. Indeed, the Japanese courts have tended to expand rather than contract protected expression over the past 30 years.

Pacific

Australia's and New Zealand's print media are among the freest in the world, but New Zealand's tough libel law requires provable truth as a defense in defamation cases. More state control exists over broadcast media. For example, the Australian Broadcasting Tribunal can regulate program content and advertising and has set a maximum standard of 30 percent for foreign-produced TV programs (to encourage indigenous productions). New Zealand's customs agents censor objectionable videocassettes at points of entry.

Elsewhere in the Pacific, media suppression does not reach the magnitude seen on the Asian continent. In Papua-New Guinea, for example, critical viewpoints are allowed on the government-controlled radio system.

CONCEPTS OF MEDIA FREEDOM

Over the years, media scholars have devised several theoretical frameworks to divide the world's diverse media into distinct groups or theories. The Hutchins Commission's Report (1947) made the first such attempt in defining the social responsibilities of the mass media. Siebert, Peterson, and Schramm (1956, 1963) were commissioned to a follow-up study of media social responsibility. They divided the world's media into four theories—authoritarian, communist, libertarian, and social responsibility—on the premise that media is either controlled by government (authoritarian and communist) or is independent of government (libertarian and social responsibility). Hachten (1987, 1992) later updated the basic Four Theories and provided Five Concepts: authoritarianism, communism, revolutionary, development, and Western. Martin and Chaudhary (1983) classified media systems into three political worlds: Western, communist, and third world. Herbert Altschull (1984) described the world's media systems along the same lines. Stevenson (1994) in his latest book, *Global Communication in the Twenty-First Century,* finds Hachten's five concepts of the press to be the most current and useful in dividing up global media systems. However, to discuss the concepts of media freedom in Asia, the following grouping of theories is considered useful here: authoritarian, modified libertarian, and communism. The authoritarian media systems are still the most prevalent type of media systems in a number of Asian countries. The development model can also be classified as an offshoot of the authoritarian concept. Stevenson (1994, p. 227) states that the authoritarian concept is likely to gain strength as countries move from communist and development media systems. The modified libertarian concept—which is a combination of libertarian, social responsibility, and Western theories—is highly relevant for democratic countries in Asia whose media acts as a watchdog on government. The communist concept of media, although discarded in Central and Eastern Europe as a result of the collapse of communism, is still in use in the few remaining communist countries.

Authoritarian Concept

Since the invention of the Gutenberg press, authoritarian media systems have been the most common. Hachten (1981, 1992) defines this concept as constant direct or implied control from above, with consensus and standardization as a goal and dissent an "annoying nuisance" (1981, p. 17). As long as the press (broadcast media are more likely to be under direct government control) operates within mutually understood boundaries, the government does not intervene. However, to portray the press as a would-be adversary just barely reined in would be inaccurate.

Singapore's government and tamed press both see the media as a partner with government in development. One official explained his distaste for James Bond-style journalists who attack national leaders at will, while the progovernment *Straits Times* agreed; it warned Westerners in an editorial not to apply the American ideal of press freedom to a multiethnic society such as Singapore. Similarly, a Malaysian official warned against applying Western-style individual liberties in a non-Western context. In Taiwan, a government spokesman called the Taiwanese approach "management" rather than control.

The "partnership" arrangement means that the mass media does not broach certain subjects. In Taiwan, for example, three topics have long been taboo: Taiwanese independence (the idea of two Chinas, which grants de facto legitimacy to the mainland); communism or mainland China (if treated favorably); and the private lives of political leaders. In Malaysia, one must not write about racial disharmony. In Thailand, one must not show disrespect for the royal family.

Indonesia has the trappings of a parliamentary democracy, but in practice it is ruled by a strongman backed by a single dominant party. In March 1993, 71-year-old President Suharto was elected to his sixth five-year-term of office.

While corruption is widespread among those in positions of power, rarely do Indonesian journalists investigate wrongdoing or expose it. Although the press is private, the government closely monitors and controls it, which has led to a rather tame news media. There is not a great deal of diversity of opinion reflected in the press. Indonesian journalists do not have the same vision of themselves that Western journalists have. They do not see themselves as watchdogs of the state or crusaders for social causes or justice; instead, they view themselves as part of the overall power structure in Indonesia. Journalists are expected to report on the country in a positive way; self-censorship is defined as "social responsibility."

Even though the Constitution guarantees freedom of speech and anyone is allowed to publish a newspaper, access is not quite so available as it sounds. Government control, self-censorship, and deference to institutions have drained the Indonesian press of its zest.

Modified Libertarian Concept

In Japan, too, self-censorship reigns in discussion of the imperial family. When Emperor Hirohito died in January 1989 after 62 years of rule, Japanese television showed scenes of Japanese military action from the 1930s and 1940s. However, the programs did not show footage of the "Rape of Nanking" (called in Japan "the Nanking incident") or discuss in any depth the occupation of Korea. The emperor was portrayed as peace-loving but manipulated, with no alternative explanations offered.

Investigative journalism has never been the strong suit of Japan's mass media. Accuracy and insight mark the material that the media produce, but much that goes on does not appear. Many people knew about the Lockheed matter, for example, but no one broke the story until a former prime minister referred to it in a speech. Then teams of reporters went to work.

Journalism professor Hideo Takeichi says that the characteristics of Japanese corporate life apply just as much to corporations that happen to be newspapers. Once an employee passes the entry gate, the newspaper assumes he will work there all his life. Much like bureaucrats, journalists work their way up the promotion ladder, following majority opinion and directives from above rather than risk antagonizing lifelong colleagues. Because few freelance journalists exist in Japan, an outcast reporter literally has nowhere to go.

A blend of Eastern practices and Western libertarian trappings also marks the press of India. Except during the Emergency Rule imposed by the late Prime Minister Indira Gandhi in 1975, when direct censorship dampened journalistic ardor, the press in India has been one of the freest in Asia. "For 28 years there were no real constraints on the press till the Emergency came," said Kuldip Nayar a former editor of the *Statesman* and the *Indian Express* (Basu 1989, p. 12). With the lifting of Emergency Rule, Indian press reverted to what is generally considered a free-press philosophy in the Western tradition. Even though the government has never

quite accepted the concept of the adversial relationship of the press and authority (former Prime Minister, Rajiv Gandhi, for example, believed that the fostering
of an adversary relationship between the press and the government is not always
conducive to good governance), the press in India does play a significant watchdog role. Newspapers and newsmagazines are constantly engaged in aggressive,
yet responsible journalism in exposing corruption, malfeasance, and nepotism on
the part of the authorities in power. Investigative journalists have been quite outspoken in revealing the financial scandals of politicians, including the Prime Minister. Newspapers across the country, for example, published Hershad Mehta's
charge that he paid money to Prime Minister Rao to help him contest the by-elec-
tion to the Parliament. Almost all leading papers have been critical of the government in power. Most papers write strong editorials criticizing the acts of government. *The Statesman* has an "Insight" investigating team. So has Bombay's *Free
Press Journal. The Economic Times* and a host of other newspapers have a
similar "Insight" page as well. One media magazine, *Critique: A Review of Indian
Journalism,* begun in 1991, carries investigative gut issues. Its editor, Alok Ti-
wari, states:

> Isn't it audacious on our part to become a watchdog on the fourth estate?
> What gives us the right to do so? The answer is that our authority is no more,
> and no less, than that enjoyed by the mainstream media to comment on pub-
> lic affairs—the right of every Indian to speak freely on matters important to
> the well-being of the country. (quoted in Singh, N. 1992d, p. 13)

Not long ago, journalists, editors, and publishers of various newspapers were engaged in a nationwide protest against the Defamation Bill of 1988, which resulted in
the successful withdrawal of the Bill from the Parliament by the Indian government.
The Bill had been introduced into the lower house of Parliament without any prior
consultation of the press. It was widely perceived as an effort to intimidate the press
into submission. The withdrawal of the Defamation Bill is a perfect example of victory for press freedom. Moreover, the Press Council of India safeguards freedom of
the press. Being a statutory body, the Council has sufficient scope to act independently
of government pressures.

In the Philippines also, the traditional concept of the role of the press is based on
libertarian philosophy. Dramatic changes in press philosophy have occurred over the
past two decades as a result of the political changes. Before the declaration of martial
law in 1972, the Republic of the Philippines experienced the most libertarian press in
Asia. After martial law, the press was completely under authoritarian control. Under
the present leadership, the press claims to be free once again. According to the Constitution of the Republic of the Philippines, ratified in 1987, "No law shall be passed
abridging the freedom of speech, of expression, or of the press, or the right of the people peaceably to assemble and petition the government for redress of grievances." The
Constitution also provides for access to government meetings and records, but the government limits ownership and management of mass media to Philippine citizens, prohibits media monopolies, and regulates advertising.

Communist

According to Hachten (1987), the communist concept holds that a free press, divisive by its very nature, gets in the way of the key job of nation building; by contrast, state-owned media can pursue in unison their tasks of agitating, propagandizing, and organizing. News is any information that serves the state.

From the early days of Mao Tse-tung's revolution, communicating through media has been crucial. The Maoist "thought determines action" dictum means that people must receive correct information so they will think and in turn act correctly. Mao incorporated all channels in this task—from traditional *tatsupao* ("big character posters") to national newspapers—but did not pay as much attention as he might have to television.

According to Godwin Chu (1978), the mass media provide do's (such as profiles of model workers) and don'ts (bad news from overseas), while omitting ideas that contradict party policies or bad news that might depress the spirit of the people. In July 1976, an earthquake in Tangshan, China, killed an estimated 800,000 people, but the print media did not carry any news of the disaster until August. Casualty statistics, which listed the death toll as 242,000, were not released until 1979.

Because television developed in the post-Mao era, it followed a different pattern from that of the press. Advertising has appeared on the air since 1979. The news, free of harangues and stories long on ideology, draws high viewership. According to Rivenburgh (1988), television functions less for political consolidation and more as an entertainment medium.

However, when cataclysmic bad news occurs, time lags occur while party officials decide how to portray the incidents. For example, viewers did not see anything about the 1987 Tibet uprising until three days after it started. Monumental but brief changes occurred in May 1989, including a televised session when prodemocracy student leaders were shown lecturing Premier Li Peng. But by June, the patterns of the past had returned. An army documentary showed how "hooligans" had attacked soldiers, while the news showed "criminals" who admitted their guilt. On June 24, the dismissal of party General Secretary Zhao Ziyang was aired.

MEDIA ECONOMICS AND SPECIAL PROBLEMS

The mass media in Asia derive revenues from subscriptions, user fees (in the case of cable television), advertising (private and/or government), government or institutional subsidies, and allied enterprises. Where a healthy advertising base exists, mass media can turn huge profits; in 1984–1985, for example, New Zealand's major papers reported profits ranging from 34 to 72 percent. In China, state-controlled media now run ads from private firms.

By the 1980s, concentrated ownership characterized much of the Asian press. The Singapore-based *Straits Times Press,* for example, has bought into media in more than 10 countries. In Japan, the Big Three (*Asahi, Mainichi,* and *Yomiuri*) have myriad editions that blanket the nation. Sing Tao Ltd. of Hong Kong, in addition to a stable of publications worldwide, now has expanded into real estate and pharmaceuticals.

No one has extended his reach beyond the Asia/Pacific area as dramatically as Australian Rupert Murdoch. Ironically, however, his first Asian purchase (Hong Kong's *South China Morning Post*) did not occur until 1988. Murdoch's News Corporation Ltd., which has newspapers in Fiji and Papua-New Guinea, expanded outside Australia in 1968, moved into Britain, and later the United States. In 1987, when he bought the *Herald* and *Weekly Times* group of Australia, his corporation became the world's largest publisher of English-language newspapers.

Like English, the Chinese language has spread throughout the world, such that Chinese publications exist from Manila to New York and Taiwan to Vancouver. To confront common problems, Sian "Sally" Aw founded the International Chinese-language Press Institute in Hong Kong.

Other issues now confronting Asian media include the difficulty of serving rural (often illiterate) populations, the fear that imported film and TV fare may smother local cultures, and apprehension about the effects of television (especially on young people).

In countries less developed than Japan and Singapore, the profitability and accessibility of an urban base have accentuated a tendency for newspapers to serve city dwellers. The gradual penetration of television into rural areas does not overcome the need for print media and literacy.

Global marketing of television has resulted in a one-way flow of programming, most of it entertainment fare from the United States. Pricing structures mean that nations can import programming for a fraction of production costs, thus expanding their broadcasting hours. For example, in 1985–1986, a half-hour episode from the United States costs $600–850 in Hong Kong or $500–600 in India, whereas in Japan it would run $6,000–7,000.

Does imported programming have adverse effects? It does discourage local production, but the more subtle effects on attitudes are harder to measure. Some nations, such as Australia, have put limits on the amount of imported programming that can be shown domestically.

Does television itself, even domestic programming, have detrimental effects? The case of Japan may shed some light on this crucial question. As Table 13.1 shows, Japan has the highest figure for TV penetration in Asia. Yet at the same time, Japan has the highest ratio of newspaper readers, with 584 copies per 1,000 people—in other words, newspapers and TVs are about equally available. Compare that picture with the United States, which has only 244 newspapers per 1,000 people. Our easy arguments about TVs displacing the reading habit just don't seem to hold up.

JOURNALISM EDUCATION AND TRAINING

Many journalists in Asia and the Pacific still get their training on the job. Despite this tradition, Asia has more institutes and academic programs in communications than any other region in the world except North America. About half of these follow the U.S.

pattern, offering a degree in communications or journalism that combines academic study with practical experience.

The first schools began in the 1920s and 1930s, but real expansion in training for mass media jobs did not occur until after World War II. The pioneer programs include three departments of journalism in China—at St. John's University, Shanghai (1920); Yenching University, Beijing (1924); and Fudan University, Shanghai (1929)—the Department of Journalism in the Faculty of Letters at Jochi (Sophia) University, a Jesuit institution in Tokyo (1932); a bachelor of arts in communications at a branch of Far Eastern University in Manila (1934); and a program at Chengchi University, founded in China (1935) but now located in Taiwan.

Because of the growth of such programs, especially in the 1970s, fewer practitioners and teachers will need to go overseas to study in the future. The following descriptions highlight a few examples, but many other notable programs exist.

South Asia

One of the best training institutions in South Asia is the Indian Institute of Mass Communication, which was set up in New Delhi in 1965 as a center for advanced study and research in mass communication. The Institute conducts teaching and training programs, organizes seminars, and contributes to the creation of an information infrastructure suitable for India and other developing countries. The Institute's Diploma Course in New Agency Journalism, which is open to third-world countries, is highly sought after by middle-level working journalists from Africa, Asia, and Latin America. The institute also provides its expertise and consultancy services to other institutions in the country as well as other developing countries of the world. More recently, the Indian Institute of Mass Communication has started offering short courses, workshops, and seminars in broadcast journalism. In November 1992, it offered seminars on satellite and cable television in collaboration with the Friedrich Ebert Foundation of Germany.

The tradition of journalism education and training in India began in 1941 with the establishment of a department of journalism at Punjab University in Lahore (now Pakistan), which was transferred to Delhi in 1947, and finally to Chandigarh in 1962. Madras University also established its journalism department in 1947, followed by the universities of Calcutta, Mysore, Nagpur, and Osmania in the 1950s. In the 1960s and 1970s, many universities throughout the country started offering programs in journalism and mass communication.

Today, there are more than 50 universities and 20 private coaching institutions, besides 20 agricultural universities that annually train approximately 1,000 students in various specialized areas, including print journalism, broadcast journalism, and films. Yet the vast infrastructure of national education from schools to universities built up so far is not enough to cope with the needs of a populous country. Realizing that mass communication is an essential catalyst for national development and social change, the University Grants Commission undertook to set up centers for education and training in Mass Communication in six universities of the country. The Centre for Mass Communication Research, established at Jamia Millia Islamia University in Delhi in 1983, is the first such center, and has a wide range of sophisticated and modern audio, video, and film equipment for its studios. The university offers a two-year master's degree in mass communication involving theoretical and practical instruction in radio, audiovisual, television, and film production. Two universities, Makhanlal Chaturvedi Hindi Journalism University in Bhopal and the Telugu University at Hyderabad, have full-fledged courses in Indian-Language journalism, while several other universities have bilingual courses or optional papers in Indian-language journalism. In some universities, departments of journalism offer language courses in several languages.

Some newspapers, including the *Times of India,* the *Hindustan Times,* the *Hindu, United News of India, Fenadu,* and *Manorama* have their own in-service training programs in English and Indian languages. The All India Radio also trains its own employees at its staff training school in New Delhi. For training in the art of filmmaking, the Film and TV Institute of India at Poona is the largest of its kind in Asia. Established by the Ministry of Information and Broadcasting in 1961, the Institute offers courses in film direction, motion picture, photography, sound recording, film editing, and television production.

Journalism education at the university level in Pakistan also dates back to 1941, when a one-year diploma in journalism was offered at the University of Punjab at Lahore. Later, Karachi University and other universities began diploma and degree programs in journalism and mass communication. The University Grants Commission has recently recommended that all universities in Pakistan offering programs in journalism should upgrade their two-year master's journalism courses to a four-year course in mass communication leading to the degree of master's of science in mass communications. In the field of broadcast journalism, the Pakistan Broadcasting Academy conducts in-service courses for the professional training of producers, news editors, and broadcast engineers. In addition, major newspapers provide on-the-job training to journalists.

In Bangladesh, Dacca University offers diplomas in journalism. The Bangladesh Press Institute, run by the government, also provides journalistic training. A majority of journalists, however, receive in-service training at the newspapers. In addition, three London-based organizations—Commonwealth Journalist Association, Commonwealth Press Union, and Thompson Foundation—offer scholarships to journalists for training in London as well as organize courses for them in Dacca.

The University of Sri Lanka and Kabul University in Afghanistan have also established journalism programs for the training of their journalists.

In Nepal, Tribhuvan University has recently started some courses in journalism. Most journalists get their training in India. The Ministry of Communication organizes seminars and symposiums for journalists. All journalists have to obtain a permit to work from the Ministry of Communication. All newspapers have to register with them.

However, these specialized courses in journalism and mass communication in a majority of South Asian countries are academically oriented and do not provide sufficient practical training. A majority of journalism and mass communication programs in universities lack resources needed for purchasing equipment, training material, or offering practical experience for students. Very few universities have their own radio, television, or film studios or even possess basic facilities for producing a student newspaper. The Indian Institute of Mass Communication is perhaps the only center in South Asia that is well equipped and offers training in all the media. The institute has a laboratory press and highly developed audiovisual facilities, which cater to the training and publication needs of the center. The institute publishes a quarterly research journal, *Communicator* in English and *Sanchar Madhyam* in Hindi, besides other publications. As the concept of development journalism is gaining a much wider meaning in developing countries, the institute has started emphasizing the study and practice of communication relevant to developmental needs and resources.

Most other universities in India as well as Pakistan, Bangladesh, Nepal, Sri Lanka, and Afghanistan do not appear to adopt an integrated approach to mass communication. Moreover, a majority of universities are inadequately financed and therefore lack a trained staff to prepare the students adequately to enter the media profession. In several countries, there is a shortage of local university teachers with an academic background in mass communication. As a result, the universities resort to part-time teachers who are often less committed to the profession than full-time teachers. This reflects a lack of concern with research activities. Scholarly research in communication is almost nonexistent in most universities. There is a grave shortage of suitable textbooks written from the local or national perspectives of individual countries. As a result, most students depend on American and British textbooks and reference books.

Despite these pitfalls, South Asian countries have advanced more than others in mass communication education. Mass media owners are now beginning to recognize the importance of formal training and to employ more graduates in journalism and communication.

Southeast Asia

Malaysia exemplifies the tremendous growth that can occur in a short time when a society decides to pursue mass media education wholeheartedly. The nation's first courses were offered in 1971 at the University Sains Malaysia. The next year, the School of Mass Communication at the MARA Institute of Technology was established; it now ranks as the largest such school in Malaysia. By the late 1980s, 800 students were enrolled at programs in five universities and colleges.

With support from the Friedrich Ebert Foundation, the government of Singapore created the Asian Mass Communication and Research and Information Center (AMIC). This regional mass media center sponsors research, offers training, and holds conferences.

In Indonesia, professional journalists have now started to replace some of the former politicians and experienced journalists who learned their trade mostly through association with the independence movements. In late 1950s and early 1960s, several universities started offering the equivalent of master's degree in *publicistiks* (mass communication). The earliest program was started in 1948 at the Gadjah Mada University in Jokjakarta as the Department of Information. Thereafter, several universities started offering five-year programs leading to a master's degree, such as Indonesia University, Pajajaran University, Diponegoro University, and Hasanuddin University. In addition, many bright journalists are sent abroad for study at American journalism schools.

Many private institutions also train journalists. The Perguruan Tinggi Publisistik offers a master's degree. The Newspaper Publishers' Association and the Surabaya Journalism Academy also offer courses in journalism and mass communication.

Larger media organizations offer in-house training for journalists. In 1990, Dr. Soetomo Press Institute started offering training for professional journalists. The Institute, which is partially funded by the Asia Foundation and the U.S. Agency for International Development, also offers short seminars and has a library and a publication of its own.

To meet the needs of specialists and skills in multimedia, The Multi Media Training Center (MMTC) of Yogyakarta started conducting diploma programs in 1992. The MMTC is now running a College for Radio and TV, which will be expanded into a College of Film and Video and a College of Printing and Publication.

Several private institutions also train journalists. For example, the Newspaper Publishers' Association offers a five-year program leading to a master's degree. The Indonesian Institute for Press Training and Consultancy and the Surabaya Journalism Academy also offer extensive courses. The most notable is probably the Perguruan Tinggi Publisistik, which is both a private teaching institution, giving instruction up to the master's degree level, as well as an institute for mass communication research. In addition, several organizations offer short courses and seminars to working journalists. For instance, the Indonesian Journalists' Association, in cooperation with the government, offers one- to two-week courses and seminars on special subjects to working journalists. The Ministry of Information offers training to its own personnel through the Academy of Information. TVRI also operates a training center for its employees, known as Pusat Latihan TVRI. Another organization, Pendidikan Periklanan Jakarta, offers short courses in advertising and public relations.

Yet, many working journalists have little or no college education or any special education. Marsden Epworth, who recently worked as a journalist in Indonesia for two years, observed: "If they (journalists) can read and write, if they can get a security clearance, and if they can tell what news bolsters the regime and what news does not, they've got a job" (1988, p. 42).

In the Philippines, at least one of every three colleges or universities offers training in journalism. Postgraduate degrees in journalism and mass communication are offered at the University of the Philippines, University of Santo Tomas (Manila), and Silliman University with focus on population communication, development communication, and community press, respectively. The University of Philippines Institute of Mass Communication offers a joint doctoral program with U.S. universities.

The Asian Institute of Journalism in Manila offers a graduate course in media management and a master's degree in journalism in addition to short-term seminars and workshops for practicing journalists. Moreover, the Institute, in cooperation with the Communication Foundation of Asia, is also promoting the writing and publishing of communication books by Asians. A journal of communication research was also founded recently.

The Philippine Press Institute, another organization, frequently holds a series of training sessions for reporters and editors around the country. In addition, Nieman fellowships are available to Philippine journalists to study abroad.

East Asia

Japanese mass media tend to follow recruitment patterns similar to other Japanese corporations, with the most prestigious institutions hiring (for lifetime jobs) students from the most prestigious universities. The newspapers or broadcasting firms then handle their own training. For example, NHK pursues both training and research, as does the Japan Newspaper Publishers and Editors Association.

Korea, on the other hand, has followed the U.S. model. Since the mid-1970s, it has established a network of 20 programs at four-year colleges, in addition to 10 master's and 8 doctoral programs. According to Jin Wan Oh, foreign influence on journalism education is "tremendous," resulting in a field "equipped with Japanese technology, armored with American theory, and reinforced by philosophy from Germany" (1985, p. 22). But by the late 1980s, the picture was changing, as Korean-educated "second-generation" faculty began to teach in South Korean schools.

In China, a lecture series on journalism began in 1918, but little development in education occurred until after World War II. In the 1950s, Soviet influence pervaded but later retreated from mass media education. By the mid-1980s, 26 universities had journalism departments, but at that time only about 6 percent of journalists had specialized degrees. In fact, less than half had any college training. With more than 1,200 mass media outlets, China will need an estimated 90,000 journalists by the year 2,000.

Five important journalism schools in China today are at Fudan University, whose prestigious program incorporated the department at St. John's University; People's University, Beijing (1950), which incorporated the department at Yenching; the Beijing Broadcast College (1959); Xiamen University (1981), located in a coastal city on the Taiwan Straits; and Jinan University, Guangzhou, which trains overseas Chinese to work at newspapers outside China. In addition, the Chinese Academy of Social Sciences, Beijing (1979), carries out mass media research and trains graduate students.

Pacific

In the late 1980s, Australian universities had no full professorships in mass media studies. The nation's 15 degree-granting programs were scattered over 18 universities and 50 colleges and institutions, with little uniformity in academic content. Much mass media research goes on in the social sciences and other departments rather than in journalism schools.

In New Zealand, by tradition, new employees joined newspapers out of high school and received on-the-job training. Now a number of training programs exist, but they are specialized short courses for high school graduates lasting less than a year.

PROSPECTS FOR THE FUTURE

The 1989 prodemocracy uprising in China dramatized the information-gathering potential of citizens armed with technology. In the aftermath of the uprising, facsimile machines were used to bypass government controls, carrying newspaper stories into China about events within China. Photocopying machines then multiplied the contraband stories so that they could be distributed widely. In China and elsewhere, camcorders in the hands of citizens have permitted amateurs to record scenes that authorities claim never happened or would have slipped quietly into history without being officially mentioned.

The vehemence of the June 1989 crackdown could mean that Chinese citizens may not gain the right of free expression for another 15–20 years. More immediately, the force with which the Chinese government brought the media into line raised questions about the media in Hong Kong, which will revert to China in 1997. Self-restraint has been evident since 1984, some journalists say.

By contrast, a pattern of expanded rights seems on the horizon for other countries. A free, well-developed media system does not need to precede or even accompany economic development. Taiwan, South Korea, and Singapore, with their partly free media and booming economies, have taught the world this lesson. They may yet teach the world that civil liberties—including free, developed, and diverse media—can follow as well as precede economic development, presenting a model quite different from that of the West.

According to most journalists in Asia, progress toward press freedoms is becoming a reality. Jakob Oetama, editor-in-chief of *Kompas,* an Indonesian newspaper, told the Freedom Forum delegation, "Before the focus of newspapers was political. . . . Today, it is more broad, looking at all societal aspects" (Freedom Forum 1993, p. 14). The Indian press is freer today than it has been ever before, according to S. Nihal Singh, a media columnist for *Sunday* magazine. "The new constraints," he states, "arise out of particular parties' attempts to create a climate of fear and intimidation, with the authorities looking the other way" (1993c, p. 6).

Asia and the Pacific, like the rest of the world, partake in global culture. For better or worse, technology is changing the ways Asia uses the electronic media. During the next few years, there will be an explosion of new television receivers and new channels. As Pico Iyer notes in *Video Night in Kathmandu,* the "most remarkable anomalies in the global village today are surely those created by willy-nilly collisions and collusions between East and West" (1989, p. 10). Iyer found bands in Burma (Myanmar) playing the Doors' song "L.A. Woman" to perfection, a million people in Beijing rushing to see *First Blood* within ten days of its opening, and a copy of the second volume of *Best Disco '84* for sale in Tibet.

Iyer questions the assumption that the West is corrupting the East, "both because corruption often says most about those who detect it and because the developing world may often have good reason to assent in its own transformation" (1989, p. 13).

We hope that our discussion has underscored the difference between modernization and Westernization and has helped readers appreciate the strength and variety of Asia's cultures and the depth of its media's roots.

BIBLIOGRAPHY

Abbas, Razia. "Radio and Distance Learning in Pakistan." *Media Asia* 14, no. 1 (1987): 13-14.

Agarwal, Amit, and Lekha Rattanani. "FM Channel: Reviving the Radio Age." *India Today,* 30 September 1993, 177.

Altschull, J. Herbert. *Agents of Power: The Role of the News Media in Human Affairs.* Urbana: University of Illinois Press, 1963.

————. *Agents of Power: The Role of the News Media in Human Affairs.* New York: Longman, 1984.

Asia Magazine Staff. "The Press in Asia." *Asia Magazine,* 14 June 1987, 10-19, and 28 June 1987, 42-46.

Audit Bureau of Circulations. *A Preliminary List of Circulations Certified for the Six Monthly Audit Period Ended 31st December 1992.* New Delhi, 1993.

Bain, David Haward. "Letter from Manila: How the Press Helped to Dump a Despot." *Columbia Journalism Review* (May/June 1986): 27-36.

Bangladesh Basic Information and Media Guide. Bangladesh: Ministry of Information, 1993.

Basu, Tarun. "Papers Hold Their Own Despite Attacks." *India Abroad,* 25 August 1989, 12.

"Bhutan: Between Two Worlds." *India Today,* 15 September 1989, 134-137.

Bishop, Robert. *Qi Lai! Mobilizing One Billion Chinese: The Chinese Communication System.* Ames: Iowa State University Press, 1989.

Boyle, Kevin, Editor. "Article 19." In *World Report 1988.* New York: Times Books, 1988.

Chan, Joseph Man, and Chin-Chuan Lee. "Shifting Journalistic Paradigms: Editorial Stance and Political Transition in Hong Kong." Unpublished paper read at the AEJMC convention, Portland, Ore., 1988.

Chu, Codwin. *Radical Change through Communication in Mao's China.* Honolulu: University of Hawaii Press, 1978.

Chu, Leonard. "Changing Faces of China's TV." *The Asian Messenger* (Winter/Spring, 1980-1981).

"Circulation of Indian Press Touches New High." *India News,* August 1989.

Cohen, Margot. "Letter from the Philippines." *Columbia Journalism Review* (November/December 1987), 46-48.

Cooper, Anne. "Televised International News in Five Countries." *International Communication Bulletin* 24, nos. 1, 2 (1989): 4-8.

Cooper-Chen, Anne. *Games in the Global Village: A 50-Nation Study of Entertainment Television.* Bowling Green, Ohio: The Popular Press, 1994.

Dahlan, M. Alwi. "The Palapa Project and Rural Development in Indonesia." *Media Asia* 14, no. 1 (1987): 28-29, 32-36.

Dinh, Tran Van. "Asia: 20th Century." *International Encyclopedia of Communications,* 143-146. New York: Oxford University Press, 1989.

Domingo, Ben. "Rural Press Development in the Philippines, 1976-1986." *Media Asia* 14, no. 2 (1987): 81-88.

"Editors Decry 'Pressure' on 'Post'.", *Times of India,* 10 June 1989, 1.

Epworth, Marsden. "Indonesian Journalism." *Columbia Journalism Review* (September/October 1988): 41-45.

Far East and Australasia 1993. 24th Edition. London: Europa Publications Ltd., 1993.

Flournoy, Donald. *Asiavision: A Satellite News Exchange.* Paper read at the National Association of Educational Broadcasters convention, Las Vegas, 1985.

Freedom Forum. *Voices from the East.* Arlington, Va.: Freedom Forum, 1993.

Freedom House. *Freedom in the World, '92-'93.* New York: Freedom House, 1993.

"Gandhi to Gandhi: Views on Press." *India Abroad,* 25 August 1989, 13.

Gangadhar, V. "For a Few Dollars More: Newspapers Are Happy to Dance to the Corporate Tune." *Sunday,* 22-28 November 1992, 84-85.

Gastil, Raymond. *Freedom in the World: Political Rights and Civil Liberties, 1987-88.* New York: Freedom House, 1988.

Gaunt, Philip. "Improving Cooperatiion for Communication Training." *Gazette* 51 (1993): 35-51.

Ghorpade, Shailendra. "Retrospect and Prospect: The Information Environment and Policy in India." *Gazette* 38 (1986): 5-28.

Gupta, V. S. "Rural Press Development in India: Status, Factors Affecting Its Growth and Future Prospects." *Media Asia* 14, no. 2 (1987): 67-72.

Hachten, William. *The World News Prism.* Ames: Iowa State University Press, 1981.

——. *The World News Prism.* 2nd Edition. Ames: Iowa State University Press, 1987.

——. *The World News Prism.* 3rd Edition. Ames: Iowa State University Press, 1992.

Head, Sydney. *World Broadcasting Systems.* Belmont, Calif.: Wadsworth, 1985.

Hopkins, Mark. "Watching China Change." *Columbia Journalism Review* (September/October 1989): 35-40.

Howkins, John. *Mass Communication in China.* New York: Longman, 1972.

Hutchins Commission. *A Free and Responsible Press.* Chicago: University of Chicago Press, 1947.

India 1992: A Reference Annual. New Delhi: Ministry of Information and Broadcasting, Government of India, 1993.

Indonesia 1989: An Official Handbook. Republic of Indonesia: Department of Information, 1989.

International Encyclopedia of Communications. New York: Oxford University Press, 1989.

International Marketing Data and Statistics 1993. 17th Edition. Great Britain: Euromonitor, 1993.

Irani, Cushrow. "India: To Toe the Line, Or Not to Toe the Line." *IPI Report* (August 1989): 8.

Iyer, Pico. *Video Night in Kathmandu.* New York: Vintage, 1989.

Jeffrey, Robin. "Indian-Language Newspapers and Why They Grow." *Economic and Political Weekly,* 18 September 1993, 2004-2011.

Kamath, Madhav, V. "Sex: Handle with Care." *Probe* (October 1989): 73-76.

Kang, Jong Geun, and Michael Morgan. "Culture Clash: Impact of U.S. Television in Korea." *Journalism Quarterly* 65, no. 2 (1988): 431-438.

Kennedy, George. "Newspapers in New Zealand." *Presstime,* May 1986, 23-25.

Koito, Chugo. "The Newspaper and Its Rivals in Japan." In *Journalism Theory.* Tokyo: Sophia University (no date).

Lansipuro, Yrjo. "Asiavision News Exchange." Unpublished paper read at the Seminar on the Communication Revolution in Asia, New Delhi, 1986.

Li, Xiaohong. "Peking Review's Coverage of the 1976 Tangshan Earthquake in China." Unpublished paper read at the AEJMC Convention, Washington, D.C., July 1989.

Lent, John A. "Mass Communication in Asia and the Pacific: Recent Trends and Developments." *Media Asia* 16, no. 1 (1989): 16-24.

——. "Press Freedom in Asia: The Quiet, But Completed, Revolution." *Gazette* 24 (1978): 41-60.

——. "To and from the Grave: Press Freedom in South Asia." *Gazette* 33 (1984): 17-36.

Lomas, Peter. "How Good Is Your Local Paper?" *Islands Business,* October 1989, 5.

Lull, James, Editor. *World Families Watch Television.* Newbury Park, Calif.: Sage, 1988.

Mankekar, D. R. *Media and the Third World.* New Delhi: Indian Institute of Mass Communication, 1979.

Martin, L. John, and Anju Grover Chaudhary. *Comparative Mass Media Systems.* New York: Longman Inc., 1983.

Massey, Ruth. "Publishing in Bhutan." *Presstime* (November 1987): 12-14.

McKay, Floyd J. "Development Journalism in an Asian Setting: A Study of Depthnews." *Gazette* 51 (1993): 237-251.

Merrill, John. "Inclination of Nations to Control Press and Attitudes on Professionalization." *Journalism Quarterly* 65, no. 4 (1988): 839-845.

———. "Global Elite: A Newspaper Community of Reason." *Gannett Center Journal* (fall 1990): 93-101.

Merrill, John, and Harold Fisher. *The World's Great Dailies.* New York: Hastings House, 1980.

Ministry of Information and Broadcasting. *Annual Report 1992-93.* New Delhi: Allied Publishers Pvt. Ltd., 1993.

———. *Mass Media in India 1992.* New Delhi: Publications Division, Ministry of Information and Broadcasting, 1993.

Morgan, Frank. "Listen to the Pacific View: Needs and Demands of Professional Media Education and Training in the Pacific." *Australian Journalism Review* 13, nos. 1, 2 (1991): 126-136.

Nepal's Mass Media. Nepal: HMC Press Singhadurbar Kathmandu, 1988.

Oh, Jin Wan. "Foreign Influence on Korean Journalism Education." *Journal of the Korean Society for Journalism and Communication Studies* 20 (1985): 19-33.

Pakistan 1991: An Official Handbook. Lahove: Government of Pakistan, 1992.

Prabhu, A. N. "Media and Rural Development." *Mainstream* (11 September 1993): 16-18.

Qadri, Ismail. "Paradise Lost." *Index on Censorship* 17, no. 9 (1988): 7, 41.

Rai, L. Deosa. "Nepal's Communication Policy Then and Now." *Media Asia* 14, no. 3 (1987): 149, 152-153.

Ramanathan, Sankaran, and Katherine Frith. "Mass Comm Education Young and Growing in Malaysia." *Journalism Educator* 42, no. 4 (1988): 10-12.

Rampal, Kuldip R. "Adversary vs. Developmental Journalism: Indian Mass Media at the Crossroads." *Gazette* 34 (1984): 3-20.

Rattanani, Lekha. "Tabloid Tussle: A Deluge of Eveningers Hits the Stands." *India Today,* 15 April 1992, 124.

Rawanake, Chitra. "Roundtable." *Media Asia* 14, no. 3 (1987): 150-151.

Ray, Shantanu. "The Heart of Mainstream Journalism: Growing Regional Language Press No Longer a 'Poor Cousin'." *India Abroad,* 25 August 1989, p. 4.

Rivenburgh, Nancy. *China: The Television Revolution.* Unpublished paper read at at the AEJMC convention, Portland, July 1988.

Rogers, Everett, Xiaoyan Zhao, Zhongdang Pan, and Milton Chen. "The Beijing Audience Study." *Communication Research* 12, no. 2 (1985): 179-208.

Saelan, Ahmad. "Rural Press Development in Indonesia: A Case Study of Pikiran Rakyat." *Media Asia* 14, no. 2 (1987): 76-80.

Sankhdher, N. *Press, Politics and Public Opinion in India.* New Delhi: Deep Publications, 1984.

Schramm, Wilbur, and Erwin Atwood. *Circulation of News in the Third World: A Study of Asia.* Hong Kong: Press of the Chinese University of Hong Kong, 1981.

Shamsuddin, M. "Constraints on the Pakistan Press." *Media Asia* 14, no. 3 (1987): 166-173.

Siebert, Fred, Theodore Peterson, and Wilbur Schramm. *Four Theories of the Press.* Urbana: University of Illinois Press, 1956.

———. *Four Theories of the Press.* 2nd Edition. Urbana: University of Illinois Press, 1963.

Sinaga, Janner. "The Pancasila Press System." Republic of Indonesia: Department of Information, 1987.

Singh, Nihal S. "The Alternate Paper." *Sunday,* 26 July to 1 August 1992a, 6.

———. "Codes of Conduct: According to the Likes of Bal Thackeray." *Sunday,* 25 April to 1 May 1993a, 6.

————. "Do or Die: The Media in the Kashmir Valley Have to Toe the Militants' Line." *Sunday,* 26 September to 2 October 1993b, 6.

————. "Looking Ahead: Indian News Magazines Have to Keep Pace with Changing Times." *Sunday,* 19-25 April 1992b, 11.

————. "A Pressing Matter: The Need for a Self-Policy Organization for Journalists." *Sunday,* 29 November to December 1992c, 7.

————. "Roving Eye: At Last, A Magazine to Watch over the Fourth Estate." *Sunday,* 9-15 February 1992d, 13.

————. "Setting the Agenda: The Indian Press Needs to Set Its Own Priorities Right First." *Sunday,* 18-24 July 1993c, 6.

————. "Soul Searching Time." *India Today,* 15 May 1989, 167.

————. "The Unseen Battle." *India Today,* 15 August 1989, 118.

————. "Views, Not News: Doordarshan's Bulletins Are Nothing but Government Hand-Outs." *Sunday,* 4-10 July 1993d, 6.

————. "Wages of a Free Press." *India Today,* 15 August 1989, 118.

Sinba, Arbink K. "Communication and Rural Development: The Indian Scene." *Gazette* 38 (1986): 59-70.

Soley, Lawrence, and Sheila O'Brien. "Clandestine Broadcasting in the Southeast Asian Peninsula." *International Communication Bulletin* 22, nos. 1, 2 (1987): 13-20.

Statistical Yearbook 1986. UNESCO, 1987.

Statistical Yearbook 1992. UNESCO, 1993.

Stein, M. L. "The Press in Philippines." *Editor and Publisher,* 18 August 1987, 12-13.

Stevenson, Robert. "An Atlas of Foreign News." *Research Review Monograph No. 3.* Chapel Hill: School of Journalism, University of North Carolina, 1984.

————. *Communication, Development and the Third World.* New York: Longman, 1988.

————. *Global Communication in the Twenty-First Century.* New York: Longman, 1994.

"Tabloid Tussle." *India Today,* 15 April 1992, 124.

Tan, Alexis, and Kultida Suarchavarat. "American TV and Social Stereotypes of Americans in Thailand." *Journalism Quarterly* 63 (Fall 1988): 648-654.

Thomas, Pradip N. "Broadcasting and the State in India: Towards Relevant Alternatives." *Gazette* 51 (1993): 19-33.

Vanden Heuvel, Jon, and Everette Dennis. *The Unfolding Lotus: East Asia's Changing Media.* New York: Freedom Forum Media Studies Center, 1994.

"Will the Press Survive?" *The Illustrated Weekly of India,* 25 September to 1 October, 1993, 10-13.

World Press Encyclopedia. New York: Facts on File, Inc., 1982.

"World Press Freedom Review." *IPI Report* (December 1988): 23-24.

Youm, Kyu Ho. "Libel Law and the Press in Japan." *Journalism Quarterly* 67 (1990): 1103-1112.

————. "Press Freedom in 'Democratic' South Korea: Moving from Authoritarian to Libertarian?" *Gazette* 43, (1989): 53-71.

Zhang, Jingming, and Jianan Peng. "Chinese Journalism Education: Slow Progress since 1918." *Journalism Educator* 41 (Spring 1986): 11-18.

chapter **14**

Latin America and the Caribbean

Gonzalo Soruco and Leonardo Ferreira

INTRODUCTION

Traditionally, studies of Latin American and Caribbean journalism have tended to be descriptive, emphasizing radio and TV sets ownership and newspaper circulation. For that type of analysis, the reader is referred to Aliski (1981) and Salwen and Garrison (1991).

This chapter parts with that tradition. To write about the present state of journalism in some 30 Latin American and Caribbean countries and do it justice is a difficult, if not impossible, task. We focus, instead, on issues that bind Latin American and Caribbean journalism today and will do so in the future. We also thought it prudent to introduce the reader to the history of Latin American and Caribbean journalism and to the institutions that have shaped it for the past 400 years.

Like its sister institutions, the region's press did not develop in a vacuum. It was influenced and shaped by various forces, domestic and foreign. To understand their problems today, one must come to grips with circumstances that shaped them yesterday. Most works we read on the topic lack such an approach.

Today, Latin America and the Caribbean (Figure 14.1) face several challenges as they prepare to enter the twenty-first century. The region's economic growth and development continue to be uneven, sometimes stagnant, and the promise of "privatization" remains unfulfilled. The North American Free Trade Agreement (NAFTA), which some day may include the markets of Caribbean Common Market (CARICOM) and Latin America, is a distant dream for businessmen and politicians. Narcotraffic and the militarization of the "drug war" burden several nations and pose serious problems to freedom of the press. Democracy remains unsteady on its feet after returning to Argentina, Bolivia, Brazil, Chile, Ecuador, Nicaragua, Panama, and other countries during the 1980s. For journalists of Latin America and the Caribbean, these are issues of great importance.

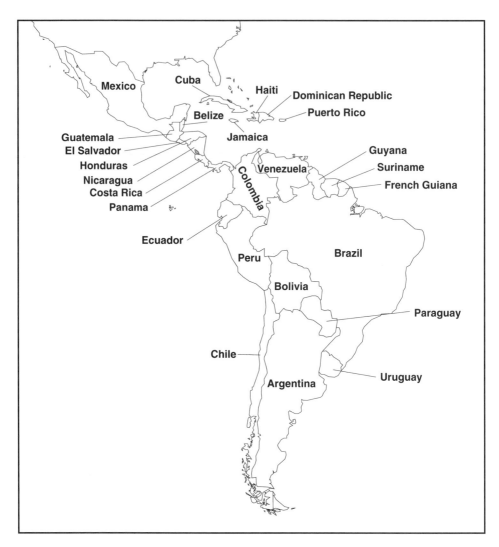

FIGURE 14.1 Latin America and the Caribbean

HISTORY OF THE REGION'S PRESS

To understand the press in Latin America and the Caribbean, first one must understand the people it serves, the institutions that rule it, and the territories it covers. The task is complicated because contrary to common belief, the region is not monolithic, evenly underdeveloped, or all tropical. Latin America is a mosaic of peoples, institutions, topographies, and economic development.

Its people are as varied as they are complex. Emphasizing the racial, social, and economic differences among Colombians, Fluharty describes the modern Colombian as follows:

> To begin with, each region was settled by different "nations" of Spaniards. They each found new environments in the New World, just as they had come from different ones in the Old. Particular interests, economic and racial, frequently brought them into conflict. The seacoast opposed the capital; the province, the city; the highlander, the plains dweller. Still today, there is great difference between the Bogotano and the Costeño; between the citizen of Cundinamarca and the man from Antioquia. (1957, p. 23)

Fluharty could be describing the modern Bolivian, Peruvian, Mexican, Venezuelan, or Trinitarian. Latin American and Caribbean societies are that complex. Meeting the information needs of these societies has challenged journalists since the birth of the press in Latin America some 400 years ago.

Not surprisingly, the region's administrative systems are equally as complex. To this day, Latin American institutions retain much of their centralist traits inherited from Imperial Spain. Those institutions favored the crown rather than the colonies. Today, they favor the capital over the peripheral cities, the well-to-do over the poor, the elites rather than the masses.

The Spanish Empire used a two-tier system of administration. The king and his council of advisers formed the top level. The monarch's decision was final. The vast empire was managed by viceroys, *audiencias,* captains general, and *adelantados* appointed by the king. These formed the second level of administration and reported directly to the crown. With the exception of the *audiencias,* whose function was largely judicial, the appointees held supreme political authority over their territory. As the conquest of Latin America got underway, this model of territorial administration was transplanted to the conquered lands.

Predictably, the system benefited Spain at the expense of the colonies and their inhabitants. A classic dependency system, it encouraged commercial trade and communications between each colonial territory and the crown while discouraging it among the colonies. Following a divide and conquer policy, the king dispensed favors to some territories and denied them to others. Strict control of the territories allowed further control over expression. The crown's rigid prior restraint laws, such as the *abuso de imprenta* (abuse of the printing press) could be, and was, applied at will in one territory or another.

The Latin American Print Press

In 1541, roughly one century before the *Mayflower*'s arrival in New England, Juan Pablos, by authority of Don Antonio de Mendoza, Viceroy of New Spain, published a page believed to be the first printed news of the continent: "Relación del espantable terremoto que . . . ha acontecido en las Indias en una ciudad llamada Guatemala" (Account of the frightening earthquake that has taken place in the Indies in a city called Guatemala). Ironically, Latin American journalism was born publishing bad news about the continent. It is also important to note that before the arrival of the Spaniards, Maya, Aztec, and Inca civilizations had developed means of disseminating the news, which included oral as well as written communication.

Newspapers operating periodically and for public circulation appeared in the late 1500s. Published also by authority, the colonial papers were a product of the status quo, publishing information on official, administrative, commercial, and religious matters. Some publications carried news. Several of these "newspapers" appeared in Lima and in Mexico City. *Hojas de Noticias* and *Relaciones* were published in 1594 and 1619 in Lima. *Nuevas de Castilla,* a Spanish newspaper was reprinted in Lima in 1624. *La Gazeta de Mexico* was published in Mexico City in 1722. The *Gaceta de Lima* appeared in 1743 and lasted until 1767. Lima's first daily, *Diario de Lima,* appeared in 1791 and lasted three years.

In some ways, the development of the press in Latin America paralleled those of North America and Europe. In 1931, Walter Lippmann distinguished several stages in the development of the press. First, he suggested, publication is a monopoly of the government. Later, it becomes the privilege of recognized parties within the state. As society matures, its newspapers become politically independent of government and party "by enlisting the commercially profitable support of a large body of readers" (p. 433).

In the Spanish colonies, the print press began with a lengthy period of leaflets and other works of religious character during the sixteenth and seventeenth centuries. It was followed by the appearance of official gazettes that published news mostly from Spain and Europe in the 1700s. In the early nineteenth century, the revolutionary newspapers were born. Their objective was to promote the cause of independence from Spain. Examples of these are Hidalgo's *El Despertador Americano* (1810) in New Spain (Mexico), Nariño's *La Bagatela* (1811), and Bolívar's *Correo del Orinoco* (1818) in the New Granada (Colombia). Such publications were not welcomed by the Spanish authorities, and when possible they were silenced. In 1794, for example, Antonio Nariño was condemned to 20 years' imprisonment in Africa for printing the 17 articles of the French Declaration of the Rights of Man and the Citizen.

Finally, after a little over two-and-a-half centuries since the importation of the first printing press to the Spanish colonies, allegedly by Mexico's Franciscan Bishop Fray Juan de Zumárraga (c. 1539), the Americas proclaimed their independence and established a free press in several capitals. In Buenos Aires, for example, the Assembly of 1813 promulgated the end of the Spanish inquisition and slavery and the beginning of a new nation with freedom of the press.

The extent to which the Latin American press developed in parallel fashion in so many places and almost at the same time makes it difficult to write a concise history of it. Unlike the colonial and revolutionary press of the United States, which was largely centered around Boston and Philadelphia, that of Latin America was scattered along the entire continent. The vast territory, the diverse information needs and interests of the colonists, the political and strategic importance of the various provincial capitals to the Spanish crown, from Mexico City to Buenos Aires, and the crown's own desire to control the colonies resulted in an uneven development of the press in Latin America. Thus, while some capitals had relatively sophisticated press systems, others lacked them altogether. Similarly, Spanish laws proscribing publication were applied arbitrarily, often unevenly.

Peruvian historian José Tamayo Herrera (1985, p. 150) writes that the first printing press arrived in Peru in 1580, brought by the Italian printer Antonio Ricardo. Ricardo could not start "printing right away" because of a "royal prohibition that barred the printing of books in Lima and the rest of Peru" (which at that time would have included today's Bolivia). After obtaining the proper permission, and "royal signatures," Ricardo published a flyer in 1583 entitled *Pragmática De Los Diez Días Del Año* and his first book, *Doctrina Cristiana y Catecismo Para La Instrucción De Los Indios,* a catechism that appeared in 1584, which the historian considers the first book published in South America.

Argentine historian Luis Trenty Rocamora (1948) writes that the printing press arrived accidentally in Buenos Aires in 1742. It was found among the goods that Monsignor Andrés de Vergara y Uribe, appointed Bishop to Santa Cruz de La Sierra (today Bolivia's second largest city), was taking to his new residence when he suddenly became ill and died. "This domestic print" writes the author "was the first in Buenos Aires" (p. 158). It is not clear how, when, or if that press was ever used.

A regular printing press began to operate in Buenos Aires in 1780. Its operation was granted to one José de Silva y Aguiar with a ten-year contract stipulating that he could keep 30 percent of the proceeds from it and that the rest would be given to the local orphanage. The shop where the press operated was named Taller De Los Niños Expósitos (The Orphans' Shop). It printed religious books, prayers, obituaries, and official proclamations.

Further incentive for the development of the press in the Spanish colonies was the turmoil that shook Europe in the aftermath of the French revolution, the rise of Napoleon, and the "renting" of the Spanish crown. Of great concern to the Spanish colonists was the apparent ineptitude of King Carlos IV of Spain. The King, whose affinity for dissipation was legendary, had entrusted the reins of the Spanish empire to Manuel Godoy, a young soldier whom he had elevated to the highest ranks and who was rumored to be the queen's lover. Godoy unwisely attempted to save the French monarchy from the revolutionaries and restore Louis XVI to the throne. He failed, and the French armies invaded Spain.

Eager to isolate England from Europe and close all its ports to her commerce, Napoleon intervened in Spain and Portugal. The result was war between Spain and England and the fleeing of the Portuguese royal family to Brazil. The British defeated the Spanish at Trafalgar in 1805, crippling Spanish sea power. In a show of power, the British invaded Buenos Aires in 1806. In 1807 Carlos IV arrested his son Fernando and charged him with conspiring to kill Godoy. A year later, they reconciled, and Carlos abdicated in favor of his son. Taking advantage of the kings' unpopularity, Napoleon forced them to yield the throne to his own brother Joseph.

The turmoil divided Spanish loyalties. Some favored the old King, others favored Godoy, others were loyal to Fernando. Some preferred Napoleon's brother Joseph. Presently, the unrest reached the Spanish colonies. The circumstances generated an independence movement among the colonists. Some of its leaders, such as Francisco de Miranda, Símon Bolívar, and Antonio Nariño, whose European education had introduced them to the liberal philosophies of Rousseau, Burke, and Franklin, disliked the choices offered by the old empire and advocated independence.

To control the quantity and quality of information while keeping the colonists informed about the developments in Europe, colonial administrators set up printing presses in their provinces. In 1804, *El Telégrafo Mercantil* appeared in Buenos Aires and lasted for a over a year. In 1808 a printing press was founded in Brazil.

One of the best examples of the gazette period of the press in Latin America is that of Venezuela. The Province of Caracas, established in the early 1600s, did not have a regular press until 1808. Two North Americans from Philadelphia, Matthew Gallagher and James Lamb, assembled a printing press in Caracas and published the *Gazeta de Caracas*. Its first issue appeared on Monday, October 24, 1808. Its publication was welcomed by the colonists, who hungered for information about the developments in Europe. Like the rest of the *gazetas* (or *gacetas*) published in other provincial capitals, the *Gazeta de Caracas* had an international inclination.

The administrator of the province, Juan de Casas, Captain General of Caracas, praised the publication of the *Gazeta* as an important tool for informing the restless colonists about the developments taking place in Spain and to rally their support for King Carlos IV and his son. The record is not clear on whether the *Gazeta* was an independent entrepreneurial venture of the two North Americans or a strategic move by the captain general to control information in the province. Whatever the arrangement, de Casas maintained a strict control on the contents of the publication.

The *Gazeta de Caracas* appeared twice weekly at the subscription rate of eight pesos per year until 1810, when Simon Bolivar and a group of patriots ousted the captain general and declared the independence of Venezuela. During its brief history as a monopoly of the government, the *Gazeta*'s publishers did not test the legal bounds that governed its publication. They did not attempt to publish it without the proper "official inspection." They never asked for a definition of what was "offensive" to the Catholic Church or the government. And they did not request for a definition of what "good customs" were. In this, the Latin American colonists were markedly different from their neighbors to the north. Acquiescence to the "laws of god and man" and to the "good customs" of the people were the rule, rather than the exception. This rule would dominate the Latin American press long after independence. The notion of free expression subject to the "good customs" of the people would be interpreted later by governments and journalists as a doctrine that respected freedom of the press, provided it exercised social responsibility.

The bulk of the *Gazeta*'s news was private and official correspondence forwarded to the printers by the captain general himself. At times, he clearly intended to control the information the colonists received regarding developments in the Spanish main and to give them as much propaganda against Napoleon as possible. Despite his loyalist fervor, Juan de Casas never picked up the pen to appeal for support of his king. Only one issue, that of 2 December 1808, carries a personal note from the captain general. In it, Juan de Casas asks the colonists for funds which would "arm, dress, and feed the armies that were being gathered in England against Napoleon."

The *Gazeta*'s adherence to the government line news proved to be counterproductive to de Casas. Vessels arriving from the old continent brought news that conflicted with the publication's. Confused by the news, the colonists began to distrust the captain general and doubt the *Gazeta*'s credibility. Taking advantage of the anarchy, a group of patriots expressed openly their desire to separate from Spain. The captain general reacted strongly against the separatists and jailed them. Early in 1810, old and disappointed with the developments in his homeland, de Casas retired, naming Vicente Emparán as his successor.

Under Emparán, the *Gazeta* continued publishing the government line. In a significant departure from the old regime, Emparán took the pen on several occasions to express his views. These did not differ greatly from de Casas's. Utterly confused and frustrated, the colonists turned to the patriots.

That the *Gazeta* would be so submissive to the captain general's demands is not surprising. Being foreigners in a land about to explode into a revolutionary war, Gallagher and Lamb opted to do as they were told. Domestic printers would not have acted differently. Spanish rules governing expression were strict, and the punishment for breaking them was harsh. Venezuela, like the rest of the Spanish colonies, lacked a liberal tradition. The European philosophy of the divine right of kings ruled in the mainland and in the colonies. Spain did not witness a Petition of Right, which in 1628 forced Charles I of England to cease the billeting of troops, trial by matial law, arbitrary imprisonment, and taxation without the consent of parliament. It did not face the challenges to contemporary thinking on freedom of expression, such as Milton's *Aeropagitica* did in England. It lacked philosophers and thinkers like John Locke calling for a limited, liberal state.

Venezuelans and their colonial counterparts in the rest of the continent also lacked a communication and transportation structure. The empire's mercantilist practice openly discouraged trade among its colonies. Thus, the office of postmaster, which was instrumental in establishing newspapers and gazettes in the English colonies, did not exist in Latin America.

On the morning of April 19, 1810, a group of patriots ousted Captain General Vicente Emparán and declared the independence of Venezuela. Their first move was to take control of the *Gazeta* and close its operations temporarily. When it reappeared on April 27, some changes were apparent. It published news from the provinces, from other capitals, and reprinted news from European and American newspapers.

On 5 July 1811, Venezuela adopted its first constitution. Article One of the new law proclaimed that the supreme power was to be divided into three equal and independent bodies, one Legislative, one Executive, and one Judicial. Regarding freedom of the press, Article 181 stated: "[T]he right of manifesting all ideas by means of the press shall be free; but any person who may exercise the same shall be answerable to the laws, if he attacks and disturbs with his opinions the public tranquility, the faith, Christian morality, or the property, honor, and good opinion of any citizen." This philosophy became the foundation for most of the laws on freedom of expression in Latin America.

Between 1810 and 1850, the press in Latin America entered into what Lippmann (1931) calls the "party press stage." As the revolutionary armies gained strength and the colonial territories gained their independence from Spain, the need to inform the citizenry intensified. Gazettes and local newspapers flourished. After independence, with the formation of political parties, the "patriot" newspapers became political organs. A few commercial newspapers, such as Lima's *El Comercio,* also began to make an appearance.

During the mid-to-late 1800s, in many countries the party press fused with the commercial press, and their distinctions became blurred. In a few countries, the distinction remains unclear to this day. At the turn of the century in Colombia, for example, *El Tiempo, El Espectador,* and the *Diario de Colombia* were owned by eminent politicians. Their news and editorials were highly partisan. Only recently, some of Latin America's major newspapers have acquired a more commercial flavor.

The laws that governed the gazettes and party papers, have not changed much. The issues facing the Latin American press today, on the other hand, are complex. They demand dialogue, argumentation, and above all free expression. There are issues that the press must cover, analyze, and report. Governments, which sometimes include the United States, institutions, and interest groups often oppose that freedom.

CONTEMPORARY ISSUES AND THE PRESS IN LATIN AMERICA

Recent developments in various Latin American nations have created a new climate for the press. The return of democracy to Argentina, Brazil, Chile, and others has brought greater freedom for journalists but also greater responsibilities. Violence and narcotraffic, believed to have an asymmetrical relationship, have forced journalists to review issues of fairness, libel, and self-censorship. The rapid adoption of communication technologies, such as communications satellites, is changing the nature, composition, and direction of news, with which the presses of Latin America seem unable to cope. The increasing presence of U.S. military and so-called police agencies in the region has created additional burdens to journalists who are critical of U.S. actions. On more than one occasion, Latin American journalists have been pressured by the local U.S. embassy to censor articles critical of Uncle Sam. Finally, academic programs generously financed by the U.S. Government and purportedly designed to improve Latin American journalism are increasingly polarizing the press with their dubious objectives, methods, and techniques. The rest of the chapter analyzes some of these issues in detail.

The Press and the Return of Democracy

The return of democracy to Argentina, Brazil, Bolivia, Chile, Nicaragua, Panama, and Paraguay has had mixed results for the region's presses. It has expanded the bounds of freedom of expression, to be sure. But it has not increased tolerance for diverse ideas. The Inter-American Press Association reports that 114 journalists have been murdered in Latin America in the past five years. In addition, 38 journalists were kidnapped, another 700 were assaulted, more than 100 (54 in Cuba alone) were arrested, and almost an equal number were arraigned during the same period. The same report cites 146 attacks on the media.

On the other hand, democracy has brought new challenges to journalists. Copying from the developed nations, the new leaders of Latin America have learned to manipulate public opinion through the use of news management, public relations, pseudo-events, and opinion polls. In fact, the pistol-packing *caudillo* of yesterday has been replaced with a Harvard-educated technocrat whose image is carefully shaped by media experts. He is more likely to be interested in the results of the latest focus groups than in techniques of crowd control.

Untrained in statistics and relatively ignorant of today's sophisticated media strategies, Latin American journalists are at the mercy of the government and special interests groups. They are easy prey to marketing experts and their statistics.

Chile and Argentina are particularly good case studies. In both countries, the media are credited with bringing about political change. Media analysts believe, for example, that in 1988, a media campaign, carefully orchestrated by the opposition, brought down the dictatorship of General Augusto Pinochet in Chile. Catchy television commercials, carefully placed public announcements, and craftily arranged pseudo-events, analysts argue, convinced the Chilean people to vote no to eight more years of the dictatorship. Others are less certain of the power of the media. "Social, political and economic conditions were most influential," argues Hirmas, "the media campaign simply reminded viewers of prevailing conditions" (1993, p. 82).

Similarly, shrewd use of television is said to have affected the outcome of the 1989 presidential election in Argentina. As in neighboring Chile, Argentine political parties used "modern campaign techniques," such as strategic planning, public opinion polls, motivational research, and direct as well as indirect advertising messages. Cafiero in 1987 and Menem in 1989 are said to have triumphed mainly because their opposition was largely influenced by U.S. campaign practices. Although the winners used "modern techniques," writes Zuleta-Puceiro (1993), their campaigns were more judicious in their uses of the tube and avoided U.S.-style aggressive and "dirty" political strategies.

Whatever the effects of the media on the political outcome in Chile, Argentina, Bolivia, and Peru (which also engaged in "modern campaign techniques" with devastating consequences for the candidates who used them), journalists were limited to reporting the events. Untrained in the artifices and tactics of public relations experts, journalists often became pawns of the political parties and their U.S. advisers. Unschooled in statistics and opinion polling, they simply reported the numbers given to them by the politicians and their experts.

Admittedly, inadequate training in social research is a problem among journalists everywhere. But in Latin America, the problem goes beyond training. Reliable statistics are scarce, and data bases, where available, are incomplete. Government structures that could obtain and store basic information, such as demographics, employment, and production statistics, are poorly staffed and underfunded. During the "massive" June 9 earthquake of 1994 (8.2 on the Richter scale) that struck northern Bolivia, for example, the seismographs of La Paz and Cochabamba were inoperable because of a lack of parts. Journalists were forced to obtain their statistics from abroad.

Privatization and the Press

Democracy has also brought pragmatic capitalism to Latin America. Media are treated increasingly as good investment ventures by local and foreign entrepreneurs. Not surprisingly, investment in Latin American media is at an all-time high. Newspapers, magazines, radio, and television stations are investing large sums of money in the latest technologies from the developed countries. Computers, switchers, transmitters, cameras, and software are being adopted at an accelerated pace.

Democracy and the newly acquired freedom of expression, however, have forced an introspective look at freedom of expression and what it means to the press in Latin America. Urged from abroad, media owners talk of the internationalization of the First Amendment. Others feel Uncle Sam's devilish trident prodding at the presses of Latin America once again.

Recently, intercultural communication scholars meeting in California emphasized the inadequacy of the label "American" in international contexts. Indeed, millions of native Brazilians, Argentineans, Mexicans, and other Latin Americans will argue that they are as much or even more Americans than the average U.S. citizen, historically known for his or her more recent arrival to the continent and distinctive European characteristics.

Musing on the same topic during an interview in *Playboy,* Gabriel García-Márquez, Nobel Prize winner and former member of UNESCO's MacBride Commission for the study of world communication problems, suggested that the United States is "a country without a name" ("Interview" 1983). Strictly speaking, he said, there is certain logic in the title "United Mexican States," "United States of Brazil," or even "United States of Colombia," but "United States of America"? America is an entire continent. Thus, not surprisingly, the use of this term in inter-American relations is often erroneous and misleading, if not "imperialistic and insulting" (Lustig and Koester 1993, p. 17). Given U.S. history of political, economic, and military aggression toward Latin America, it is very appropriate, nevertheless.

After World War II, pondering over the deadly results of Axis powers, U.S. government officials and businessmen began to consider the importance of spreading First Amendment values and a free-market media philosophy worldwide, fighting against communism and state-controlled systems.

The idea was to turn Article 19 of the Universal Declaration of Human Rights, adopted in 1948 by the United Nations (UN) General Assembly, into a global First Amendment mandate. For example, the United States has applied this principle in its war of words with Cuba. Radio and TV Marti, observes Gallimore (1992, p 160), have been authorized and funded by the U.S. Congress because of both the First Amendment right to communicate and the free flow of information philosophy.

Many Latin American reporters, especially those connected with the print press, have also echoed the transnationalization of the First Amendment, suggesting that it may be a solid mechanism against undue government interference of the press. But, is this really possible, or even desirable? After all, who could be opposed to the spirit and potential benefits of a legal text as committed to individual freedom of expression as the First Amendment? Yet, in practice, pushing its implementation as if we were dealing with a media-based Manifest Destiny is utopian and arbitrary. It underestimates the history of the press in the rest of the continent.

Historically, unlike in the United States, where communications are primarily a commercial activity, social structures in most, if not all countries of Latin America and the Caribbean, were not erected on free-market, competitive, and individualistic principles. And although commercialization has greatly permeated the mass media through-out the Americas, few countries would renounce the notion that information is above all a service to the public.

Consequently, unlike that of the United States, constitutional laws in Latin America usually prescribe a free but responsible press, giving state authorities powers to regulate and guarantee its legitimate exercise. Hence, if the U.S. federal media system is institutionally arranged to be suspicious of the government, the Latin American countries have been structurally designed to trust the state as defender of the public good. Indeed, in Roman law societies, the state is a primary actor rather than an spectator, including press matters, which are not essentially different from other fundamental prerogatives.

It is commonly recognized that there is no absolute freedom of expression either in Latin America or in the United States. In the case of Latin America, however, there is a greater propensity for the state to intervene. Whereas in the United States, the evil is the monopolistic practice disrupting the natural order of the marketplace, in Latin America it is any form of dictatorship abusing power and breaking the public trust or the democratic institutions.

Juridically, if the Anglo-American press is individual based, market driven, and ethically rather than legally responsible, the Latin American press is social centered, service oriented, and legally rather than morally accountable. Thus, in this context, the First Amendment clearly contradicts the regulatory spirit of almost every Latin American constitution.

Although the idea of the First Amendment's transnationalization has regained strength because of the sweeping wave of privatization worldwide, there has been little material advancement in that direction in Latin America. For instance, Mexico and Argentina, echoing the liberalization of the United States, deregulated the use of satellite dishes in the early 1980s to facilitate the reception of foreign news and entertainment. As an Argentine professor once asked: "how could a country stop the proliferation of these antennas when there are systems (CNN, Noticias NBC, TELEVISA's Eco, Noticias Telemundo, etc.) in the international market?"

Even, so most Latin American governments, including the leaders of privatization, Argentina, Chile, and to a lesser extent Mexico, believe that an unconditional deregulation of the media is a double-edged sword when transnational companies manage to control the marketplace. Not surprisingly, the North American Free Trade Agreement (NAFTA) is a mixed bag for communications because national laws protecting media services will remain in effect. Indeed, NAFTA "will have no immediate benefits on the services side" of this crucial industry, simply because individual signatories would retain significant prerogatives as far as domestic regulations are concerned (Mantua 1993, pp. 22, 24).

Generally, media owners throughout the continent reject regulation—even on economic grounds—as a threat to freedom of the press. Conversely, workers and popular classes see deregulation as a strategy for handing over national sovereignty to foreign interests.

As in the mid-1960s, transnational television is now a major item in this continent, particularly for U.S. corporations. In the past, there were NBC's Cadena Panamericana, CBS's Cadena de las Américas, and the ABC/Worldvision Group interested in inter-

American networks. Today, in competition with cable and satellite services, they are coming back to take on the old dream of international channels operated from Miami, New York, Atlanta, or Los Angeles.

Because of the friendlier environment of privatization and the end of the cold war, several U.S. television ventures have announced their entry into the Latin American space, including Turner's CNN International and TNT-Latin America, since January 1991; ABC/Capital Cities' ESPN, since March 1989; HBO-Olé and Cinemax-Olé of Time/Warner/Omnivision, since September 1990; Tele-Uno, a World-Vision/Spelling/Blockbuster-Video consortium, since March 1993; the USA Network of Universal and Paramount/Viacom Pictures, since September 1993; Noticias NBC, since April 1993; Fox-Latin America, since August 1993; and MTV-Latin America of Viacom International, since October 1993. Not to be left behind, Mexico's giant TELEVISA and its Eco/Galavisión have also entered the market (since 1989), UNIVISION channels in association with Venezuela's VENEVISION, since 1992; plus UNIVISION's competition, the U.S.-based Noticias TELEMUNDO, since 1994 in association with Reuters Television/BBC. The attraction? The roughly 70 million TV households of Latin America, a potential audience equivalent to 80 percent of the U.S. market.

How is Latin America likely to respond to this avalanche of foreign programs from space to this "invasion," as they call it in the good sense (freedom of choice) and bad sense of the word (cultural alienation)?

The Caribbean: Big Concerns

Both English-speaking and non-English-speaking Caribbean nations are equally preoccupied with the ongoing process of acculturation blamed on foreign broadcasts and other alien media products. Indeed, in terms of public policy, issues of literacy and education, cultural sovereignty and identity, as well as development and integration often take precedent over entertainment, competition, and privatization affairs.

Following a New World Communication Order philosophy, most Caribbean states think that news and information should be at the service of development, public access, and participation. "If competition within the mass media is not designed to give the poor new and open channels of expression, privatization and liberalization reforms are worthless," said a regional report on the state of the media, sponsored by the Caribbean Community and the Institute of Mass Communication Research (CARIMAC) (Brown 1987, p. 8).

Historically, the Caribbean (except for the Dominican Republic) has been slow to adopt new media technologies. This was especially the case during colonial times when print presses and newspapers arrived late. In modern times, satellite dishes are more widespread in the region than in many other parts of the continent. In fact, few would have imagined the Caribbean turned into "the only area of the world where satellites dominate telecommunications," where nations such as Belize, independent since 1981, became space signal receivers even before regular television was locally available (Lent 1990, p. 284). Little has been written on this and other distinctive Caribbean media experiences.

A historical note of the region mentions the international printing arrangements made by Benjamin Franklin in Antigua to launch the *Antigua Gazette* (1748), which, according to Lent, may well represent "one of the first instances of media imperialism" by the United States in the Americas (1990, p. 3). Later, as the twentieth century unfolded, colonial controls of the British, French, Dutch, and North Americans (many still in place), and intrusions in the political and media structures of the region (e.g. U.S. military and/or CIA interventions in Cuba [1961], the Dominican Republic [1965], Grenada [1983], and Haiti [1991]), contributed to further erode the image of a peace-loving and democratic developed world.

Throughout the cold war (which has not ended in the Caribbean), reporters of all ideologies continue to be persecuted, tortured, and killed in the name of socialism or democracy. In Cuba, for instance, freedom of the press has been a luxury for those falling on the side of the revolution. Dissenters have been regularly intimidated, incarcerated, or put into exile. Cuban mass media are in crisis and in a state of alert. Shortages since the fall of the Soviet Union have forced Cuban authorities to reduce the number of dailies, editions, and hours of operation in various broadcast and print media stations, for example; *Juventud Rebelde* has become a weekly newspaper.

Similarly, in Haiti, although for the opposite reason, dissenters are murdered or vanished for trying to defend a democratically elected socialist government. Certainly, Haiti's history of the print and broadcast press could easily win the gold medal as far as official repression, censorship, and abuse are concerned.

Today, media professionals in the Caribbean are increasingly frustrated because of insurmountable problems, including the excessive government (broadcasting) and private (print press) media ownership, run by increasingly smaller elites; the lack of public access and the exaggerated partisanship and politicization of communications; the negligible amount of regulation regarding libel, obscenity, and privacy issues as well as new media technology operations; and finally, low salaries, poor professional standards, lack of training facilities, and weak infrastructure, which continue to overwhelm media professions.

Recently, a symposium sponsored by the Caribbean Association of National Telecommunication Organizations (CANTO) in conjunction with the Trinidad Express Newspapers, identified as major challenges for the future the protection of freedom of the press from government abuses, the need for media deconcentration, appropriate technology, integration, and literacy programs in most countries, and the necessity to curve the negative impact of U.S. media flows, protecting the Caribbean cultures from any further Americanization. Plans include co-production, exchange, and distribution of cultural, development, and entertainment television programs region-wide, under the coordination of the Caribbean Broadcasting Union and the support of UNESCO. These steps resemble those taken by the Caribbean News Agency (CANA) since 1976 in terms of sharing nongovernment information. There is also the hope of strengthening telecommunications, including a Caribbean satellite (CARISAT), improving flows of news and information, as well as extending services of education, health, and agriculture.

Central America: Giving Peace a Chance

Central America has also been haunted by years of poverty, war, foreign interference, and violations of basic human rights. Today, as Perez stated during a postwar symposium organized by the Salvadorean Association of Journalists, "the media's primary task is to support the reconstruction of the democratic process, showing respect for every ideology in an atmosphere of harmony, solidarity and pluralism. If there is something to end right away it is that hideous practice of sectarianism" (1991, p. 101).

After so many years of violence, terrorism, distortions of fundamental values, and a subculture of war with profound hatreds and resentments, it is extremely difficult to rediscover democracy, a luxury almost nonexistent in most of the region. In fact, even before the escalation of the conflict, the reality of print and broadcast journalism had been one of selective violence, self-censorship, official constraints, corruption, and intimidation.

In El Salvador, says Castro, "it has never been possible to really dissent from government authorities and the armed forces because this kind of journalism would be regarded as a mortal enemy of the state and its national security" (1991, p. 22). Similarly, in the former "Popular Nicaragua," the Sandinista rule and its Marxist–Leninist conception of the press (i.e., as an extension of the state) regarded dissenters such as Chamorro's daily *La Prensa* as enemies of the revolutionary process.

To be fair, not even the Western industrialized world has been totally free from sedition laws and regulations in modern times (the red scare and the McCarthy eras were both dark periods for U.S. newsmen). Journalists throughout the globe, especially in the print press, have ample reasons for mistrusting the state every day.

At one point, important social achievements were made using the mass media for development purposes in Cuba and Nicaragua. Literacy, distant formal education, health, cultural diffusion, and agricultural campaigns had positive results there as well as in some third-world revolutionary systems. Still, such creativity and dynamism were rarely reflected in newsrooms or public affairs broadcasts, since, ultimately, the overriding principle of the Sandinista's communication policy was the mass media as collective propagandists, educators, and organizers.

Undoubtedly, the champion of stability and democracy in this conflicting region has been Costa Rica. According to the Costa Rican editor of San Jose's *La Nación,* Eduardo Ulibarri (1988), the Latin American newspapers could be divided into three main periods: the traditional literary and proselytizing journalism of the old times (up to World War I); the modern "objective" journalism of the Great Depression and World War II, copying North American patterns and including descriptive, ideological, and sensational formats; and the newest contextual, investigative, or interpretative reporting emerging in the early 1970s. Buenos Aires' *La Opinión,* Mexico City's *Uno Más Uno,* and the Venezuelan *Diario de Caracas* are among the few dedicated "to print not mere news but information accompanied by antecedents and necessary explanations" (p. 97).

In Costa Rica, as in many other countries, some of most common problems cited by radio, television, and newspaper professionals are the various local and outside government pressures, the economic weakness of numerous media organizations, the low educational level of the audience, the poor salaries, and the deficient practical and humanistic preparation of those working for the mass media.

Overall, Central America—as well as the Caribbean—has been the target of repeated foreign intrusions and manipulations in detriment to the entire civil society. In 1989, the region was invaded again by U.S. intelligence and military operations during the Noriega crisis, just as it occurred in Guatemala and Nicaragua in 1954 and Honduras and El Salvador throughout the 1980s. Actually, radio broadcasting was inaugurated in 1931 by the Marines in Nicaragua, backing the Somoza dictatorship and fighting against insurgent guerrillas—much the same way that Panama became the first Latin American country with an interactive satellite antenna in 1968 because of the Canal Zone.

During the last 20 years of conflict, observed Contreras, a Salvadoran editor and local correspondent for the German DPA news wire services, established radio, television, and newspaper entities in Central America (with the probable exception of Costa Rica) "have been primarily devoted to lucrative more than information pursuits" (1991, p. 67), the type of press traditionally committed to conservative, plutocratic, and militaristic interests and ideas.

On several occasions, from Panama to Guatemala, Catholic priests, human rights workers, and international correspondents have been the only ones reporting on massacres and abuses that took place during the "culture of terror." With the end of the cold war (at least, in most parts of the world), the Central American press is looking for a new, independent, and self-defined beginning.

NARCOTRAFFIC AND THE PRESS

The rise of narcotrafficking during the decade of the 1980s, with its awesome economic leverage, callous disregard for life, and increasing penetration of local and foreign governments, has raised a new specter for the press of Latin America. What, when, and how much to publish about the drug traffic has meant life or death decisions for journalists, editors, and publishers. Journalists in Mexico, Colombia, and Peru have been killed by narcotraffickers for reporting on their trade. At times, reporting on this subject has brought about a confrontation with the government, a prospect that most editors do not relish.

Narcotraffic presents a double-edged sword to the cocaine-producing countries, and it puts the press in an awkward position. The drug is illegal and preys on society, but it is also a source of precious foreign exchange. Criticism of one must be balanced against the importance of the other.

The specter of narcotraffic is particularly real for Bolivian, Colombian, Panamanian, and Peruvian journalists. Bolivia and Peru, for example, produce the vast majority of coca leaf, which is the raw material used in the production of cocaine. These countries manufacture most of the world's coca paste as well. The proceeds from cocaine represent a substantial proportion of these countries' national economy. Lacking a solid industrial base that can earn them foreign exchange, these countries depend on the "coca revenues" for their financial stability.

Colombia's role in the manufacturing and distribution of the final product is also well-known. Tightly organized and disciplined, Colombian drug dealers have been very successful in their business. Ruled by a group of families, known as the drug barons, the Colombian drug traffickers have become the symbol of good and evil among local populations. Some barons have been known to share bits of their wealth with the poor, like Robin Hood. They have also been ruthless with their enemies, particularly journalists critical of their illegal trade.

As for Panama, it is well-known that this country serves as the distribution point for most of the illegal drugs shipped to the United States and Europe. This was one of the reasons given by the United States for its invasion and occupation in December of 1979 that ended with the unprecedented apprehension and arraignment of its leader, "strongman" Manuel Noriega. Panama's role in the trans-shipment of the drug, however, is only one part of the equation. More important, perhaps, for the narcotraffickers is Panama's role in "laundering" the proceeds from drug sales.

Covering and investigating this aspect of the drug trade is particularly difficult. Access laws are vague and give journalists little freedom to pursue the truth. Privacy and libel laws work on the side of the narcotraffickers and against journalists.

Understandably, the governments of Latin America look at the drug traffic with grave concern. They see it as a scourge that threatens every institution of the democratic state. They fear that its economic power, which enables narcotraffickers to purchase anything and anybody that makes business easier—aircraft, weapons, institutions, and people—may become impossible to stop. Thus, the war on drugs has taken the unmistakable hue of a real war. Indeed, the U.S. government has been a strong supporter of the military option to eradicate cocaine paste laboratories and coca plants that fall outside agreed production parameters. Weapons, ammunition, military equipment, and military advisers from the United States have poured in great numbers on the four republics to help stem the production and distribution of drugs.

Yet, victory in this war is far from certain. Corruption, poor organization, and unclear objectives among the various organizations fighting the narcotraffickers are just some of the problems these governments face. The symbiosis between the Maoist-inspired "Sendero Luminoso" and the drug dealers in Peru made for un uphill struggle in that country. Colombia itself witnessed some connection between narcotraffickers and antigovernment guerrillas.

Not surprisingly, the war against narcotrafficking in Latin America has produced an atmosphere of intimidation and fear. It is, after all, a war. And times of war never favor a free press. Justice Holmes's test of "clear and present danger," as applied in the famous U.S. cases of Schenck and Abrams is absent from Latin American jurisprudence. Nevertheless, most of these nations recognize the concept and apply it readily when they feel press restrictions are necessary. Sometimes they do it directly, sometimes indirectly. In either case, it has a chilling effect on journalists.

The nature of the drug traffic itself, with its rags-to-riches stories, pay-offs of government officials, cover-ups, even murder, have put journalist on thin ice. Corrupt government officials have used a number of legal maneuvers to silence exposing articles. Fear of defamation suits also can be an effective censor. Access to information, which is not guaranteed by most governments—not even the U.S. government—can hamper journalists' efforts. On the other hand, fear of death at the hands of narcotraffickers is, undoubtedly, the most effective means of muzzling the press in Latin America.

Despite the powerful incentives to look the other way in the war against the narco-traffic, Latin American journalists have waged their own brave battle to keep their readers informed. They have reported on their own governments' corruption, on the narco-traffickers crimes, and on the effects of the use of drugs at home as well as abroad. True to tradition, Latin American journalists have made every attempt to fulfill the role of the press.

"THE G-3": THE MASS MEDIA IN MEXICO, COLOMBIA, AND VENEZUELA

Not only the history of the Cuban, Haitian, and Dominican Republic media have a lot in common with one another and with the English-speaking Caribbean communications; Central America is also very much a part of the Caribbean economy, political context, and media dynamics. Yet, more determinant has been the influence of the so-called "Group of Three" (G-3), Mexico, Colombia, and Venezuela, in the Caribbean Basin and the rest of the continent.

In fact, major Latin American exponents of the big press (both newspapers and broadcast organizations) are based in Mexico City, Bogota, and Caracas, including *El Excélsior* and TELEVISA (Mexico), *El Tiempo* and *El Espectador* (Colombia), and *El Nacional* and VENEVISION (Venezuela). *El Excélsior,* for instance, founded on March 8, 1917 right after the revolution (1910–1917), was born as a Mexican version of the *New York Times,* emerging as the symbol of an industrialized and commercial press. Its strongest competition at the time, Mexico City's *El Universal,* was also one the first Latin American newspapers publishing a supplement in English.

Between 1940 and 1960, however, *El Excélsior* was criticized for its conservative reporting and lack of independence. This was the beginning of the decline of the big presses' reputation, credibility, and moral power in Mexico. Indeed, as years went by, the famous daily became more and more a speaker of the state, the hegemonic party, and the ruling classes.

In time, not only *El Excélsior* but many other capital and provincial newspapers fell into the tedious practice of easy and conciliatory reporting, greater circulation ambitions, and optimal relations with government and industry officials, leaving behind its duty to criticize the administration and the private sector as a true Fourth Estate. Not surprisingly, a newspaper such as Monterrey's *El Norte,* with a simpler writing, attractive format, aggressive competition, and a willingness to denounce corruption and the status quo is winning respect from the public.

In the broadcast industry, a progovernment conglomerate named TELEVISA also took center stage early on, incorporating 212 affiliated TV stations, or approximately half the national total. In fact, Silverstein points out

In Mexico there is almost no escaping the reach of TELEVISA. Switch on the television and you're likely to tune in to one of TELEVISA's three national networks. Go to a bullfight in Mexico City, and you'll be sitting in Plaza de Toros—owned by Emilio Azcárraga, the Grupo TELEVISA's founder and one of the richest man in Latin America. Flip the radio on and you may very well capture one of TELEVISA's ten stations. (1993, p. 25)

Furthermore, Azcárraga owns the largest cable operator in Mexico City, Cablevision, with roughly 150,000 subscribers, in addition to 110 magazine titles, film and recording industries, two of Mexico's first division soccer teams, and the nation's largest soccer stadium.

Relationships between TELEVISA and the PRI (Mexico's ruling party for the last 65 years) have been very close and mutually beneficial. "In return for soft journalism," adds Silverstein, "TELEVISA, like other media in Mexico, pays off taxes by supplying the government with free advertising, thereby tying the government to the company"; then, with 95 percent of all Mexican homes tuned to TELEVISA on a given day, "it is no surprise that the opposition parties complain about access to the media" (1993, p. 25).

Optimal presidential contacts, have won the network—one of the top five of the world, along with Brazil O'Globo and the three U.S. chains—substantial leverage with the Ministry of Communications.

On January 15, 1986, Mexico's SCT (Transportation and Communications Secretary), proclaimed:

[That] the successful launching of Morelos's couple of satellites, have inaugurate[d] a new era in the development of telecommunications in this country. In effect, Morelos and its dishes . . . constitute[d] the fundamental part of Mexico's modern national telecommunications system, offering, in addition to new services of high quality and reliability, a total coverage of our national territory. (García-Moreno 1988, p. 1023)

TELEVISA was very much behind the project, pushing for the integration and commercial advantages of via-satellite communications in the mass media. In fact, in December 1992, the Azcárraga family bought 50 percent of the U.S.-based Alpha Lyracom/Pan American Satellite Corporation (PANAMSAT), a $200 million investment backing the scheduled launching of three more satellites, covering Latin America in its entirety. As experts commented: "satellites are revolutionizing the Latin American television industry, for one popular show, Sábado Gigante, now appears in eighteen countries and advertisers realize that an audience of [eventually] 300 million people can be reached" ("Good Morning" 1991, p. 14).

Typically, third-world countries place much hope on modern mass media technologies, seeking to impart disease prevention, family planning, peace and security, medical and nutrition, as well as housing, agriculture, and environmental campaigns, favoring disadvantage populations. Regrettably, social aims are always publicized, rarely implemented, and seldom accomplished.

Even so, in August 1989, a First Meeting of Latin American and Caribbean Ministers of Culture held in Brasilia discussed the old subject of education, satellite technology news, and audiovisual programs. Subsequent meetings in Mexico (1990) and

Cuba (1991), with delegations from 24 countries and various international organizations (the Organization of American States, UNESCO, and the Inter-American Development Bank, among others) decided to explore the possibility of moving cultural goods through existing telecommunication media networks.

A committee of experts has set up a working group to study the feasibility of a television channel, approving unanimously a "Letter on Latin American and Caribbean Unity and Cultural Integration," intended to pursue regional television projects and a public service and cooperative media spirit across the Americas. Television programs such as the Convenio Andres Bello's *Expedición Andina,* which has co-produced 189 episodes on cultural, children, and environmental issues, and 252 additional radio and TV programs transmitted in the Andean region (including the series *Cielos de América* on educational and scientific activities), have been recommended as a working model (Inter-American Development Bank 1992).

To critical reporters, scholars, and intellectuals, the priority not only in Mexico but in the rest of Latin America is to revindicate popular cultures and traditions. This should be done, not in the narrow sense of more museums, media products, ballet companies, or opera concerts, but in terms of mediations involving urban settings, cultural industries, and the three major agents of every society: "the state, the private initiative, and the social movements." As Martín-Barbero (1991) noted, during the First International Seminar of Cultural Journalism in Colombia, the professional ideology of our communicators represented in the compulsive interest for the latest and the spectacular clashes head on with the needs and cultural lives of our peoples.

The main themes in today's Mexican journalism are social and technological modernization, professional ethics, regionalization, pluralism or democracy, and access or participation. To be sure, there is a difference between the modern Mexico as portrayed in the big press of the Distrito Federal (the capital), and the indigenous Mexico depicted in the regional newspapers of Oaxaca or Chiapas, so vividly demonstrated by the Zapatista revolt.

Similarly, in Venezuela and Colombia, participation, privatization, and transnationalization are major items in the communications policy agenda. "The serious lack of communication and the need for authentic channels of popular expression," says O'Sullivan-Ryan, "are forcing vast popular sectors everywhere in Venezuela to create alternative newspapers, radio stations, popular theaters, etc." (1989, p. 12). In Caracas, for instance, two community newspapers, *El Pastoreño* and *El Hatillano,* have won considerable local support because of their commitment to popular causes and their promotion of social change.

The inspiration of this type of channel of communication are Bolivia's legendary Radios Mineras (Mining radio stations). In fact, Bolivia may be the only third-world country where unionized workers built their own autonomous broadcast stations. Unfortunately, after 50 years of operation, they are dying for lack of funds. Of the 24 radio stations transmitting full- time in 1960, only 5 continue to operate today and do so on a part-time basis.

But, beyond reflecting diversity and pluralism, the proliferation of alternative communications in the Americas is the symptom of a vertical and increasingly monopolized established media. In Venezuela, for example, television was introduced by dictator

Marcos Pérez-Jiménez on November 22, 1952, moved by modernization and political propaganda purposes. Within the next ten years, television and radio were almost an exclusively commercial phenomenon, though the rhetoric of public broadcasting services and cultural-oriented programming was never withdrawn. There are no commercial cultural stations in Venezuela, and the so-called TV Nacional counts on barely sufficient money to pay its payroll and produce extremely mediocre programming.

Similarly, Colombia's dictator Gustavo Rojas Pinilla inaugurated television on June 13, 1954 with the proceeds of a coffee bonanza. Within a decade, television was in the hands of a small group of select families and their commercial empires. After the generals came the media entrepreneurs with private and commercial networks heavily dependent on advertising. In fact, during the 1960s and 1970s, Colombia had a domestic cartel called the "pool," controlling the television market through a strategic cooperation of the three biggest television programmers: CARACOL, RTI, and PUNCH, which, at the time, had in the Consuelo de Montejo's Teletigre (a local channel in Bogota, in association with the ABC/World Vision Group) its strongest competitor.

The Rojas dictatorship and its broadcast legislation defined telecommunications, including broadcasting, as a public service to be provided directly by the state, a service the government could yield to the private sector in a temporary fashion for their commercial exploitation. Ultimately, however, the exception became the rule. The Pinilla dictatorship used the notion of public service to censor broadcast news and other programming. Censorship has indeed been a recurrent phenomenon in the history of both the print and broadcast journalism in Latin America, restricting political information in the most outrageous circumstances. For example, during Colombia's 1970 presidential elections, the government banned all radio reports on partial polls. The next morning, the official candidate was announced president, even though, a few hours before he was clearly trailing the opposition.

Radio, the most widely available medium of Latin America and the Caribbean, began in Colombia in 1929, after years of a radio telegraphy monopoly set up and run by the Marconi Wireless Telegraph Company. As in other parts of the continent, broadcast radio is the only source of information and entertainment and sometimes the only means of contact with civilization for Colombia's poorest households.

Emerging broadcast stations imported from the United States, not only technology, but also its spirit of mercantilism, organizational structure, and programming formats. Not infrequently, radio businessmen simply identified their local stations with trade names in English, such as the Colombia Broadcasting or the Colombian Radio and Electric Corporation, after RCA.

Interestingly, the tragic death in Medellin of Argentinean singer Carlos Gardel marked the initiation of an innovative genre of radio programming in Colombia: news. This type of program would later become one of the most profitable and widely accepted formats by the national audience, with networks creating all-news radio stations throughout the country.

Still, newspaper and broadcast news have been frequently criticized for their political biases, lack of independence, and presentation of information through the filter of political bipartisanship. In 1980, Yamid Amat, the best known radio news director in Colombia, said in a television forum that radio news was subject to strong political pressures, although in a less politicized fashion than TV news. He observed that "television is in Colombia the medium where news is more distorted because programs [have been] distributed with a clear political criterion." Referring to television news, Luis Carlos Galan, a presidential candidate assassinated by the Medellin Cartel, once stated that news programs were gifts given not only to traditional parties but to particular political leaders and their friends.

In the end, Colombian broadcasting organizations, like most others in Latin America, were largely based on U.S. patterns of free enterprise, minimum government interference, and commercial revenue, even though the government tried to monopolize radio as it did with other communication services, such as the mail in 1913, telecommunications in 1960, and television between 1954 and 1957.

Unlike many Latin American countries, Colombia did have a relevant educational broadcast development program in Radio Sutatenza. It began in 1947 when Monsignor Jose Joaquin Salcedo, at that time curate at Sutatenza (a village with 80 percent illiteracy, located 90 miles from Bogota), organized a shortwave rural radio school for adult education. The initiative, also known as Acción Cultural Popular (ACPO), was supported by UNESCO in 1951, after Monsignor Salcedo explained the idea to the UN in 1948.

Sutatenza's central objectives were to motivate peasants into reaching higher levels of individual, community, and productivity developments, promoting human progress at various physical, intellectual, and spiritual levels. Over time, ACPO produced a large number of high-quality entertainment and news programs, keeping the station competitive with commercial radio stations. Unfortunately, Radio Sutatenza was commercialized in 1988 and sold soon after to a major private network. At one point, ACPO published the largest rural newspaper of Colombia, *El Campesino,* with an approximate weekly circulation of 70,000. Similar educational radio programs were initiated in Venezuela (ACUDE) and Honduras (AVANCE), following Sutatenza's design, using radio broadcasts, tapes, records, and audiovisuals, in conjunction with newspapers, texts, and other printed materials for low-income rural families. Nevertheless, notes Pareja (1984), Radio Sutatenza arrived in Colombia at a time when the government badly needed to pacify the country affected by unprecedented "violencia" (1948–1957) that took thousands of victims. Not surprisingly, he says, the station adopted conservative Catholic stands in a conservative period, giving peasants a vision of themselves and of the world unconnected to social conflicts and the manipulations of the ruling elite.

In addition, Radio Sutatenza received significant economic assistance from the U.S. Agency for International Development (USAID), as well as programming from both the United States Information Service (USIS) and the Voice of America (VOA). In time, ACPO's Símon Bolívar Foundation, with offices in New York, became an instrumental fund raiser, obtaining donations from entities such as American Express, Chase Manhattan International, Pepsico, Rockefeller Brothers, General Mills, H.J. Heinz Co., and the Xerox foundation, among others.

After Sutatenza, the United States became enthusiastic with the idea of a Latin American satellite for education, a project called CAVISAT (Via-Satellite Audiovisual Center), launched in Santiago, Chile, in 1969. Within one month of this announcement, during the Sixth Meeting of the Interamerican Cultural Council, Bolivia, Colombia, Chile, Ecuador, Peru, and Venezuela expressed big reservations about the plan, pledging to pursue their own common goals in education, culture, science, and technology. Shortly thereafter, as signatories to the Convenio Andrés Bello, these same countries officially rejected CAVISAT as an affront to the cultural sovereignty of independent states in Latin America.

From the beginning, direct broadcast satellites (DBSs) were regarded as a technological, political, and cultural threat. An Argentine paper wrote in the early 1970s that DBS activities shall be carried out "on the basis of respect for national sovereignty and fundamental rights of states, of the family, and of the individual" (Powell 1985, p. 153). Indeed, whereas the Chileans advocated a DBS regulatory framework "in harmony with the inalienable right of states protect[ing] their social traditions and cultural identity," Colombians and Ecuadorians emphasized the need for adequate arrangements with the receiving state implying, as an Ecuadorian representative stated in COPUOS (the UN Outer Space Committee), "the reaffirmation of both prior consultation and prior agreement between the country having satellite facilities as a broadcaster, and the country found in a dependent situation as a receiver" (Powell 1985, pp. 165, 185, 187).

On November 1972, Argentina, Brazil, and Mexico urged Latin America at the UN General Assembly to vote for international agreements regulating the use of direct via-satellite television transmissions. One-hundred and two delegations, including every attending Latin American state except Somoza's Nicaragua (one of seven abstentions), voted against the U.S. free-flow philosophy when using DBS technology for television.

Nevertheless, starting with the Caribbean and its massive use of satellite dishes (TVROs), state monopolies began to feel the pressure of a voracious consumer appetite for video, cable, telephone, and other telecommunications. *Boom, explosion, fascination,* and other terms have been used to describe what Latin America is experiencing today, a remarkable growth of cross-border communications. Observed John Hewitt, president of the Satellite Broadcasting and Communications Association of America, "There is a big boom on the way in satellite delivery of services to Latin America, [and] what [we've] seen up to now is just a spark" (Ellison 1993, p. 1-K).

More than 1 million Mexicans own parabolic antennae, and 1.5 million families subscribe to pay-TV services; unfortunately for U.S.-based programmers, more than 1 million households also have illegal decoders in Mexico. Furthermore, there are approximately 800,000 antennas in Brazil, with families buying dishes at a rate of up to 30,000 per month; at this pace, 6 million Brazilian households would be connected to satellite TV within the next few years—"more than the rest of the Latin American market combined" (Ellison 1993, 3-K).

Latin American governments have a long and disappointing experience, however, with these free-market booms. In August 1989, for instance, the Brazilian Ministry of Communication rejected a letter by the U.S. embassy's commercial attaché, in which the U.S. government expected both Hughes Aircraft/McDonnell Douglas and NASA to be chosen as contractors in Brasilsat's second-generation bidding process. The missive was taken as undue foreign interference in internal Brazilian telecommunication affairs.

Likewise, the Andean Pact countries have complained of U.S. interference in sovereign regional decisions. During the adoption of color television, the American embassy contacted various government offices and tried to influence countries' decisions regarding the NTSC standard. In Colombia, the Department of Commerce circulated through the U.S. embassy a document criticizing both Germany's PAL and France's SECAM. According to U.S. officials in Bogota, the European systems were deficient and inconvenient, as these would represent a de facto isolation preventing Colombia from buying NTSC programming in Spanish or from receiving direct-satellite transmissions from North America unless expensive converters were used. In the end, the Colombian rationale was almost identical to that stated in the U.S. memorandum. In only 45 days, the North American standard was chosen, and the following year all five Andean republics were NTSC states.

As in the color-TV episode, Andean officials have repeatedly complained about undue foreign intrusion in the Andean satellite system. During a special board meeting following the advanced publication of the Andean Cóndor network in ITU, delegates confirmed having heard adverse comments against the regional satellite project. They were attributed to the customary political maneuvering of multinationals and foreign agencies trying to discredit third-world integration efforts like the Andean Pact.

Indeed, as a Peruvian delegate stated, "every time a new integration initiative emerges, foreign multinationals orchestrate a campaign to undermine it." Unfortunately, recommended another board member, in light of these "ill-intentioned rumors," there is little developing countries can do other than silently keep working on their respective projects (Asociación de Empresas Estatales 1985, p. 5).

On the other hand, as in the Caribbean, Colombia is also preoccupied with the amount of violent and sexually-oriented programming available in international and local broadcasts. Yet, recently, the Colombian Supreme Court ruled, based on a new right of *tutela* (protecting fundamental individual rights—Articles 20, 23, 73, and 86 of the 1991 Constitution), that it is difficult to come up with any legal or practical relief for the excessive violence seen in television via microwave or satellite signals. A topic that surfaced a few years ago during the First Pan American Space Conference in San José, Costa Rica, is that telecommunication satellites are being used to relay "a growing number of TV programs with violent or pornographic content (particularly in transborder transmissions from the USA)." "In all instances," said a host delegate, "developing countries have little choice or say as they have no control over the satellites or their uses" (Ospina 1990, p. 46).

BIBLIOGRAPHY

Academia Nacional de História. *Gazeta de Caracas,* vol. 1. Paris: Establissment H. Dupuy et Cie, 1939.
Aliski, Marvin. *Latin American Journalism.* Ames, Iowa: Iowa State University Press, 1981.
Argudín, Yolanda. *Historia del Periodismo en Mexico.* Mexico, D.F.: Panorama Editorial, S.A., 1987.
Asociacion de Empresas Estales de Telecomunicaciones de Acuerdo Subregional Andino. *Informe Sobre los Avances del Proyect Sistema Andino de Telecomunicaciones por Satélite, XVII.* Cusco, Peru: ASETA, 1985.

Bagley, B. Bruce Myths of Militarization: The Role of the Military in the War on Drugs in the Americas. Unpublished paper read at the conference on The United States and Latin America: Redifining U.S. Purposes in the Post Cold War Era, Austin, Tex., March 1991.

Beltran, Luis Ramiro, and Elizabeth Fox de Cardona. *Comunicación Dominada*. Mexico, D.F.: Editorial Nueva Imágen, 1980.

Borge, Thomas. "Marginal Notes on the Propaganda of the FSLN." In *Communicating in Popular Nicaragua*. Edited by Armand Mattelart. New York: International General, 1986.

Brown, Aggrey, and Roderick Sanatan. *Talking with Whom? A Report on the State of the Media in the Caribbean*. Kingston, Jamaica: CARIMAC/CARICOM/University of the West Indies, 1987.

Cacua-Prada, Antonio. *Historia del Periodismo Colombiano*. Bogota Colombia: Ediciones Sua, Ltd., 1983.

Castro, Enrique S. "El Periodismo Salvadoreno antes de la Guerra." In *El Papel de los Medio de Comunicación en el Proceso de Reconciliacion Post-Belica*. Edited by Asociacion de Periodistas de El Salvador (APES), 20–21. San Salvador, El Salvador: Centro de Investigaciones Tecnologicas y Cientificas, 1991.

Contreras, Jorge Armando. "Los Medios de Comunicación durante el Conflicto Bélico en El Salvador." In *El Papel de los Medios de Comunicación en el Proceso de Reconciliación Post-Bélica*. Edited by Asociación de Periodistas de El Salvador (APES). San Salvador: APES/Centro de Investigaciones Tecnológicas y Científicas, 1991.

Corona, Carmen. *Coloquio Nacional de Periodistas*. Mexico, D.F.: Publicaciones Mexicanas, S.C.L., 1990.

Demac, Donna, and Aggrey Brown. "Future Regional Satellite Systems: The Case of the Caribbean." In *Satellites International*. Edited by J. N. Pelton and John Howkins. New York: Stockton Press, 1987.

Diaz-Rangel, Eleazar. *La Información Internacional en la América Latina*. Caracas, Venezuela Monteavila Editores, 1991.

Ellison, Katheryn. "Dish Antennas Spead like Rain Forrest in Latin America." *The Miami Herald*, 1993: 1-K–3-K.

Ferreira, Leonardo, and Joseph Straubhaar. "Radio and the New Colombia." *Journal of Popular Culture* (Summer 1988).

Fluharty, Vernon L. *Dance of the Millions: Military Rule and the Social Revolution in Colombia, 1930-1956*. Pittsburgh: University of Pittsburgh Press, 1957.

Frederick, Howard. "The Radio War Against Nicaragua." *Studies in Latin American Popular Culture* 6 (1987): 217–234.

Gallimore, Tim. "Radio and Television Broadcasting to Cuba: U.S. Communication Policy and the Quest for an International First Amendment." *Proceedings Ninth Annual Intercultural and International Communication Conference,* Miami, Florida, May 1992: 159–162.

García-Canclini, Nestor. "La Experiencia Mexicana," *Gaceta* [Santa Fe de Bogota] (October/November, 1989): 42–46.

García-Moreno, Victor, "Los Satélites y el Derecho International." *Boletín Mexicano de Derecho Comparado* 21, no. 62 part 2 (May/August 1988).

"Good Morning, Latin America." *América Económica* no. 52 (July 1991): 10–14.

Grases, Pedro. *Materiales Para La Historia del Periodismo en Venezuela*. Caracas, Venezuela: Ediciones Escuelas de Periodismo, 1950.

Hirmas, Maria E. "The Chilean Case: Television in the 1988 Plebiscite." In *Television, Politics and the Transition to Democracy in Latin America*. Edited by T.E. Skidmore, 82–96. Baltimore: Johns Hopkins University Press, 1993.

Inter-American Development Bank. *The Latin American Integration Process in 1988/1989/1990*. Buenos Aires: IDB/INTAL, 1992.

Inter American Press Association. *Press Freedom in the Americas.* Miami, Fla.: IAPA, 1994.

Interesting Documents Relating to the United Provinces of Venezuela. London: Longman, 1812.

"Interview: Gabriel García-Márquez." *Playboy Magazine.* February 1983: 65–77, 172–178.

Katz, Elihu, and George Wedell. *Broadcasting in the Third World.* Cambridge, Mass.: Harvard University Press, 1977.

Lent, John A. *Bibliography of Cuban Mass Communications.* Westport, Conn.: Greenwood Press, 1992.

———. *Mass Communications in the Caribbean.* Ames: Iowa State University, 1990.

Lins da Silva, Carlos Eduardo. "La Influencia Norteamericana en el Periodismo Brasileño," *Diálogos,* 4 June 1989.

Lippman, Walter. "Two Revolutions in the American Press." *Yale Review* 20 (1931): 433–441.

Lustig, Myron W., and Jolene Koester. *Intercultural Competence.* New York: HarperCollins College Publishers, 1993.

Malamud-Goti, J. *Smoke and Mirrors: The Paradox of the Drug Wars.* Boulder, Colo.: Westview Press, 1992.

Manuta, Lou. "NAFTA: Stairway to Heaven or Temple of Doom?" *Satellite Communications* (October 1993).

Marsland, William, and Amy Marsland. *Venezuela Through Its History.* New York: Thomas Crowell Co., 1954.

Martín-Barbero, Jesus. "Un Periodismo para el Debate Cultura." In *Periodismo y Cultura.* Edited by Colcultura. Bogota, Colombia: Tercer Mundo Editores, 1991.

Ogan, Christine, and Ramona Rush. "Development News in CANA and INTERLINK." In *Media in Latin America and the Caribbean: Domestic and International, Perspectives.* Edited by W.C. Soderlund and S.H. Surlin. Windsor, Ontario: Ontario Cooperative Program in Latin American and Caribbean Studies, 1985.

O'Sullivan-Ryan, Jeremiah. *Alternativas Comunicacionales en Venezuela.* Caracas: Escuela de Comunicación Social/Universidad Católica Andrés Bello, 1989.

Ospina, S. "Report of the First Pan American Space Conference." *Journal of Space Law* 18, no. 1 (1990).

Oviedo, Carlos. *Prensa y Subversión.* Lima, Peru: Mass Communicación SRL, 1989.

Palacio, Ernesto. *Historia de La Argentina, 1515–1983.* Buenos Aires, Argentina: Abeledo-Perrot, 1988.

Pareja, Reynaldo. *Historia de la Radio en Colombia: 1929–1980.* Bogota, Colombia: Servicio Colombiano de Communicación Social, 1984.

Pasquali, Antonio. *El Orden Reina: Escritos Sobre Comunicaciónes.* Caracas, Venezuela: Monteavila Editores, 1991.

Perez, Luis Mario. "El Periodismo Después del Conflicto." In *El Papel de los Medios de Comunicación en el Proceso de Reconciliación Post-Bélica.* Edited by Asociación de Periodistas de El Salvador (APES) San Salvador: Centro de Investigaciones Tecnológicas y Científicas, 1991.

Powell, Jon T. *International Broadcasting by Satellite.* Westport, Conn.: Quorum Books, 1985.

Robertson, William S. *History of the Latin American Nations.* New York: Appleton and Company, 1926.

Ruiz, Maria del Carmen. *La Prensa: Pasado y Presente de Mexico.* Mexico, D.F.: Universidad Nacional Autónoma de México, 1987.

Salwen, Michael, and Bruce Garrison. *Latin American Journalism.* Hillsdale, N.J.: Lawrence Erlbaum, 1991.

Silverstein, Jeffrey. "Foreign Challenge to TELEVISA?" *International Business Chronicle* 3, no. 28 (13 December 1993).

Tamayo Herrera, José. *Nuevo Compendio de Historia del Perú.* Lima: Editorial Lumen, 1985.

Trenty Rocamora, Luis. *La Cultura en Buenos Aires Hasta 1810.* Buenos Aires, Argentina: Universidad de Buenos Aires, 1948.

Ulibarri, Eduardo. *Periodismo para Nuestro Tiempo.* San Jose, Costa Rica: Libro Libre, 1988.

Zenarrusa, Oswaldo. "La Libertad Actual de Recepción de Emisiones Procedentes de Satélites en el Sistema Legal Argentino." In *Revista Jurídica Argentina La Ley.* Buenos Aires, Argentina: 1987.

Zule-Puceiro, Enrique. "The Argentine Case: Television in the 1989 Presidential Campaign." In *Television, Politics and the Transition to Democracy in Latin America.* Edited by T.E. Skidmore. Baltimore: The Johns Hopkins Press, 1993.

chapter 15

North America

Herbert Strentz and Vernon Keel

$\mathbf{A}$ Canadian judge issued an order in the summer of 1993 prohibiting news coverage of a celebrated murder trial and banning American journalists from his courtroom. This served as a stark reminder to observers on both sides of the border that the media in these two friendly nations, despite their many similarities, are different and that they operate within two separate judicial systems. Canadian law (like British law) decidedly is more concerned with rights to a fair trial than with freedom of expression, while U.S. law protects the latter, making unconstitutional such sweeping edicts as the one issued by the Canadian judge.

This "border battle with Canadian law," as one U.S. media periodical called it, was the most recent in a long series of controversies that has spanned the current century and has affected the flow of information, entertainment, and culture across this North American dividing line (Figure 15.1).

Print media of books and magazines and, to a lesser extent, newspapers have freely crossed the border from the beginning. However, the real cultural concerns began with the advent of radio, whose signals respect no national boundaries, and resulted in creation of the Aird Commission in 1928. This was the first of many Canadian royal commissions and governmental committees formed to deal with issues related to national unity, cultural identity, and foreign, mostly American, cultural influence through the media of mass communication. These concerns have resulted in various national communication policies, regulations, and controls which, in turn, have influenced the structure and performance of the Canadian media, resulting in a media system that is unique and different from the one in the United States.

For example, no area of mass communication has been affected more by federal government regulation and control than the broadcasting industry. While this is true in both countries, federal broadcast policy in Canada has gone beyond licensing and efforts to ensure that broadcast stations serve the "public interest, convenience, and

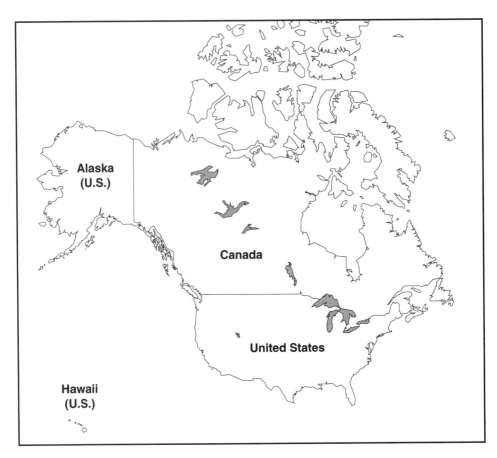

FIGURE 15.1 North America

necessity," which is the primary basis for broadcast regulation in the United States. In Canada, broadcast policy has also responded to concerns about national unity, resulting in government ownership of part of the broadcasting industry, as well as fear of cultural domination through the U.S. media, which has resulted in content requirements designed to limit foreign programming and promote Canadian identity.

This has not been the case in the United States where, when the federal government has become involved in media regulation affecting Canada, it has been mainly in the form of "mirror" legislation responding to the establishment of Canadian rules affecting foreign media and Canadian advertisers.

In fact, two separate and distinct systems of mass communication operate in the United States and in Canada. (Some would argue that there are actually three, including the French-language media system, operating mainly in Quebec, which grew out of different historical, political, and cultural circumstances and which has been influenced more by French models and traditions.) The American and Canadian media systems are as different in some ways as they are similar in others, and this is not readily apparent when one compares the newsstands, bookstores, movie theaters, or radio and television broadcasts in both countries.

In addition to content similarities and availability of certain media on both sides of the border, the two media systems face many of the same problems and experience many of the same trends. For example, concerns about concentration of ownership, the growing number of single-newspaper cities, government regulation, media violence, and the uncertainty of new communication technologies are discussed on both sides of the border.

Despite these many similarities, some more apparent than others, vast differences exist. That is why the Canadian and U.S. media systems are discussed in two separate sections rather than together, as was the case in the first two editions of this book. These two North American media systems grew out of different geographical, historical, political, and cultural realities and have been shaped by different events and circumstances. Or as Ferguson put it, "The similarities of geography, democracy, and economy are many, but divergent philosophies, values, policies, and organizing principles exist materially and symbolically across an invisible continental divide" (1993, p. 53). The result is a media system in Canada that is more tolerant of government involvement and more dependent on government support. It is also a system that has developed in response to American proximity and presence, to the influence of American media and to the constant bombardment of the printed word, of movies, radio, television, and ideas in general from the United States. The American media system, on the other hand, developed on its own in response to changing social and economic situations and without concern about developments beyond national borders. While Canada and Canadians have considered the American media as a cultural and economic threat, American media owners have considered Canada as an economic opportunity.

A key question, though, as we approach the millennium, is how the convergence of communication technologies and developments like the information superhighway will affect these media systems, their audiences, and the regulatory infrastructures on both sides of the border.

Canada

THE CONTEXTS

Historical

Communication scholar Harold Innis, himself a product of the Canadian experience, suggested that to understand a society, it is essential to understand the dimensions of time and space. More specifically, to understand Canadian concerns about communication and development of the media industry, it is necessary to consider Canada's unique history and geography.

In terms of geography, Canadians are a "border people" with the average citizen living about 100 miles from the U.S. border. Three-fourths of the population lives within 200 miles of the United States, and about two-thirds live in the densely pop-ulated industrial border region from Windsor, Ontario, to Quebec City, which includes the major metropolitan areas of Montreal and Toronto. Canadian unity is further com-plicated by the fact that Canada is a nation of regions. Because the geological conti-nuities of North America run north and south across the border, Canadians often find that they have more in common with neighboring regions in the United States than with other regions of the country.

Canada has sought physical solutions to these physical barriers to national unity. The result has been complex, well-developed communications and transportations sys-tems that have helped tie this vast, regional nation together, causing one writer to com-ment that "The political concept of 'Canada' was a race between communications and geography in which communications won" (Beattie 1967, p. 668).

The political reality of the Canadian nation emerged over the years amid a diffi-cult and continuing struggle for national unity. On one hand, the country's size, unique population distribution, and proximity to the United States have made it dif-ficult to tie the various, distinct regions together. On another hand, a long history of accommodation between Canada's two founding peoples—the English and the French—has failed to bring about a satisfactory answer to the old question of how the two can survive together. Similarly, regionalism, historical influences from England and France, and contemporary cultural influence from the United States have made it difficult for a distinct cultural identity to emerge in Canada. All of these vast and powerful influences have shaped the nature and structure of the Canadian media system.

Wilfred Kesterton (1967), one of the foremost historians of Canadian journalism, has divided the history and development of journalism in Canada into four time periods: (1) The Transplant (1752-1807); (2) Thickening Growth (1807-1858); (3) The Western Transplant and Spreading Growth (1858-1900); and (4) The Mutation (1900-1967). Added to that original list is the fifth time period: (5) The Modern (1967 to present).

Period 1. The Transplant (1752–1807).   During the first period, Canadian jour-nalism got its start as a "transplant" of American journalism, which strongly influenced its development. As Kesterton explains, "British North American pioneer newspapers did not begin as a seed growth. They came as a transplant from the New England colonies." The first newspaper in Canada was the *Halifax Gazette,* which began pub-lishing March 23, 1752, under the editorship of John Bushell, who was originally from Boston. It was published in the first printing office in Halifax, which had been es-tablished by Bartholomew Green, Jr., whose father was the first printer of America's first newspaper, the *Boston News Letter.* While the younger Green did not live to see the first issue of the *Gazette* in print, he was nonetheless responsible for publishing the first true newspaper in Canada. Quebec's first pioneer paper was the bilingual *Quebec Gazette,* established in 1764 in Quebec City by two Philadelphia printers. The *Quebec Gazette* survives today as part of the weekly *Quebec Chronicle-Telegraph,* which disputes the claim of the Hartford Courant to be North America's oldest sur-viving newspaper. During this period, newspapers were started in all six of the original provinces, while magazines made only a token beginning in several of the provinces. The *Nova Scotia Magazine and Comprehensive Review of Literature, Politics and News* was the first British North American periodical, which lasted less than three years.

Period 2. Thickening Growth (1807–1858). During the second period, the journalism foliage thickened in the six provinces where the first transplants had been made. The increase in newspapers was from 20 in 1813 to 291 in 1857. Almost all of this growth was in the six eastern provinces. War with the United States in 1813 killed some papers and caused others to suspend publication. A new type of editor emerged during this period to change the nature of the newspaper and the newspaper business. By relying more on earnings from printing advertisements and selling subscriptions, newspapers became less dependent on government patronage and more critical of irresponsible government. The struggle between newspapers and the government began with passage of the Constitutional Act of 1791 and ended with the Rebellions Losses Act of 1849. During that time, the libel trial of Joseph Howe provided major precedent for press freedom when he was found guilty and then acquitted of sedition charges. Libertarian press theory began to replace the authoritarian model of the first press period, and newspapers became more active and critical in their reporting of government. The first iron printing press arrived in 1832, and newspaper formats began to change from their original dull and gray appearance to more lively pages with bold-face headlines and advertising. More magazines were established during this period than the first but survival was still a struggle.

Period 3. The Western Transplant and Spreading Growth (1858–1900). This press period involved newspapers being transplanted to the Western and Prairie provinces, but this time they were transplants from Eastern Canada, not the United States. The first was the *Victoria Gazette and Anglo-American* and then the French-language *Le Courrier de la Nouvelle Calédonie,* both established in 1858 in British Columbia. Next was the first Alberta newspaper, the *Edmonton Bulletin,* which began publication in 1880. During this period, the number of Canadian newspapers increased from 291 to 1,266 in 1900. Newspaper development accompanied migration caused in the west by the lure of gold and in the prairie provinces by the rush of settlers in the late 1800s. The westward reach of the railroad also helped encourage settlement in Manitoba and Saskatchewan. The magnetic telegraph and later the telephone aided the flow of news from west to east, and in 1859 the Canadian Press Association was organized to further improve news coverage throughout Canada. The introduction of the rotary press in 1888 (*Vancouver News-Advertiser*) helped newspapers develop mass audiences that would increase revenue support from advertising and reduce newspapers' reliance on financial support from political parties. Newspaper appearance changed slowly during this period, although some newspapers began using illustrations. Daily newspapers became more common during this period, with the number increasing from 23 in 1864 to 121 in 1900. Magazines, however, continued to struggle, with few surviving into the 20th Century.

Period 4. The Mutation (1900–1967).   Growth of newspapers during the fourth press period was, for the most part, confined to British Columbia, the prairies, and the Canadian north. It was similar to the "thickening" growth that took place during the second period in the six eastern provinces. External forces that affected media development included significant increases in the population, urbanization, immigration, the depression, and technological change. The number of daily newspapers continued to increase and peaked at 138 in 1913. While the number of dailies declined, total circulation outpaced the rate of population of growth. The trends toward consolidation, centralization, and the single-newspaper city began during this period. By 1966, 63 publishers owned 110 dailies, of which seven publishers controlled 54. The three major groups were Free Press Publications, Southam Company, and Thompson Company. Technological developments that included faster and more sophisticated printing presses, teletypes, scan-a-gravers, teletypesetters, and even computers were accompanied by more lively appearing but more depersonalized and standardized newspapers. Radio entered the scene in the early part of the century when the Marconi Wireless Telegraph Company obtained the first license specifically granted for sound broadcasting in Canada. Television followed several decades later. Three federal broadcasting acts (1932, 1936, 1958) resulted in the creation of the Board of Broadcast Governors, the broadcast regulatory agency, and the Canadian Broadcasting Corporation (CBC). In 1961, private television stations formed their own network, Canadian Television (CTV), which linked stations in 80 cities. The Canadian magazine industry continued to struggle, mainly because of the aggressive competition of foreign, mainly American, publications. When the Royal Commission on Publications (the O'Leary Commission) was established in 1960, three of four magazines read in Canada were from the United States, and over 40 percent of the magazines sold on Canadian newsstands were controlled by two American companies (*Time* magazine and *Reader's Digest*).

Period 5. The Modern (1967 to present).   The trends toward consolidation, centralization, and group ownership of newspapers continued into the present period. In 1980, a Royal Commission on Newspapers, headed by Tom Kent, was appointed after the August 27, 1980, closing of the Ottawa *Journal* (a Thomson newspaper) and the Winnipeg *Tribune* (a Southam newspaper), leaving each newspaper group without competition in the other city. The number of daily newspapers has held constant at about 110, with only nine cities having competing dailies (Montreal has four). The Broadcasting Act of 1968 established what is now the Canadian Radio-Television and Telecommunications Commission (CRTC), which replaced the Board of Broadcast Governors. The result has been the establishment of a "mixed" system of public and private broadcasting regulated by one commission. That same year, Canadian ownership of the broadcasting industry in Canada was protected when the government acted to ensure that in any broadcasting company, 80 percent of the voting shares had to be Canadian and that all such companies had to have Canadians as directors and chairmen. Also in 1968, the CRTC moved to tighten "Canadian content" regulations for television and for the first time established a minimum requirement for radio. The results have been to ensure a certain level of Canadian programming on both public and private stations, a move designed to bolster the television production industry and performing talent. Access to cable television in Canada grew dramatically during this period. Of the 92 percent of Canadian homes that had access to cable services in 1991, four of five were subscribers. Other technological developments involving computers, satellites, fiber optics, and interactive television continue to change the Canadian communication landscape. In addition to the Kent Commission on Newspapers, the Davey Committee on the Mass Media (1971) and the Caplan-Sauvageau Task Force on Broadcasting Policy (1986) were formed during this period to examine issues related to the media in Canada.

Legal

Until the early 1980s, the constitution for Canada was embodied in the British North America Act (the Constitution Act) of 1867, which could only be amended by the British Parliament. The preamble to the Act provided that Canada was to have a constitution "similar in principle" to that of the United Kingdom. While the Federal Parliament in Canada passed a 1960 law containing a bill of rights, which provided for freedom of speech and the press, it was a regular statute that was not part of the Constitution and could be applied only to federal laws. However, when the British Parliament passed the Canada Act in 1982, Canada was given control of its own constitution that included a Charter of Rights and Freedoms. Section 2(b) includes "freedom of thought, belief, opinion and expression, including freedom of the press and other media of communication" among the fundamental freedoms guaranteed to everyone in Canadian society.

The Charter begins, however, with a qualifier in Section 1 that guarantees these freedoms "subject only to such reasonable limits prescribed by law as can be demonstrably justified in a free and democratic society." According to Martin and Stuart in their 1991 *Sourcebook of Canadian Media Law,* this substantially expanded the scope of judicial review in Canada by requiring courts to determine, among other things, the extent to which limits on fundamental freedoms can be justified. Before that, the courts dealt mainly with questions of jurisdiction between the provinces and the federal government.

Martin and Stuart also offer a useful distinction between the right to gather information and the right to pass it on and to express opinions about it. Concerning the right to gather information, two federal laws went into effect on July 1, 1983. The Privacy Act is designed to protect citizens from invasions of personal privacy. The Access to Information Act provides a right of access to government records "in accordance with the principles that government information should be available to the public." It is similar to the U.S. Freedom of Information Act, except that it does not apply to federal cabinet ministers, an exemption that limits its value to Canadian journalists. In all, it has 5 mandatory and 12 discretionary exemptions and is limited to citizens and to declared permanent residents of Canada. The act also provides for an information commissioner to receive and investigate complaints from users. The vast majority of complaints filed have to do with undue delay in responding to requests for information. In addition to the federal act, various provinces have passed similar laws dealing with access to provincial government information.

Alongside these efforts to improve access to government information is a long tradition of secrecy inherited from the British parliamentary system. The 1939 Official Secrets Act, which has its roots back in the nineteenth century, deals with espionage but can also be applied to anyone who releases or receives secret information classified by the government. It has been used twice against journalists. A 1978 prosecution of a newspaper reporter was unsuccessful, and charges in 1989 against a television reporter were eventually dismissed. The Emergencies Act, formerly the War Measures Act, provides the government considerable powers during a national emergency, including the suspension of civil liberties. The most recent application of this law was during the 1970 October Crisis in Quebec.

Another area where information can be controlled relates to news coverage of crimes and criminal trials, which is more restrictive in Canada than in the United States. Media cannot, for example, release information about a prior criminal record or other information that might interfere with defendant rights to a fair trial. Also, the Young Offenders Act passed in 1985 prohibits revealing the identity of juveniles charged with or convicted of a crime. A troublesome area relates to publications scandalizing the court or its members through undue criticism, although a 1987 Ontario Court of Appeals decision offered some clarification by overturning a lawyer's conviction on grounds that the contempt rule against him violated his rights under Section 2(b) of the Charter of Rights and Freedoms.

Punishment for misdeeds after publication or broadcast comes under libel or defamation law, mainly through civil litigation. The media defenses of truth, fair comment, and privilege are similar to those in U.S. libel law, except that Canada has not developed a similar "public law of libel" applying to suits by public officials. In the area of obscenity law, the Supreme Court in 1992 ruled that the obscenity provisions in the Criminal Code do not violate the guarantee of freedom of expression in the Charter of Rights and Freedoms.

Political

The most direct relationship between the media and government is in the day-to-day coverage of government institutions, politicians, and the political process, including elections. At the federal level, this is carried out by the Ottawa Press Gallery and includes coverage of the often-feisty daily Question Period in the House of Commons. According to Peter Desbarats (1990), former federal reporter and now a journalism educator, the nature of the Ottawa Press Gallery has changed over the years, mainly in terms of the growing number of journalists and also because of the emergence of television (cameras were installed in the House of Commons in 1977) and the introduction of public opinion polling. Coverage of government at the provincial level is similar in many ways to coverage of the federal government in Ottawa.

Federal election coverage is defined largely by an extensive Canada Elections Act, which, among its many provisions, limits the length of campaigns to approximately eight weeks, limits the amount of campaign spending allowed, determines the period during the campaign when candidates may advertise, requires the networks to provide free time to political parties, and restricts the release of election results until voting is completed across the nation.

Contemporary Issues

Canada faces many of the same difficult and complicated issues related to the rapidly changing media and communication industry as do the United States and many other Western nations. These issues include concerns about individual privacy, violence and the media, the social effects of advertising, concentration of ownership, government regulation, limits on freedom of expression, especially those related to the communication media, and the uncertainties related to the growth and development of new communication technologies.

For the most part, though, these issues for Canadians are linked to two important areas. One is constitutional, and the other is technological. Canada's constitution, including the Charter of Rights and Freedoms, has been in place for only a decade and a half. Before the Canada Act, 1982, when British Parliament gave Canada ownership of its own constitution, the operating constitution was "similar in principle" to that of the United Kingdom, and the courts had little to do with interpretation and more to do with resolving questions of jurisdiction between provinces and the federal government. Now the courts, mainly the Supreme Court, are faced with developing a body of Canadian constitutional law that will define, among other things, the limits and scope of fundamental freedoms such as "freedom of thought, belief, opinion and expression, including freedom of the press and other media of communication." These decisions will define the nature of the important relationships between the media and government and the media and society.

The second area deals precisely with these "other media of communication." The convergence of communication technologies, including microcomputers, voice, video, and data, is resulting in new forms of media and in new configurations within the communications industry. This presents a particular challenge for Canada, which has spent the better part of this century developing policy to protect and develop the Canadian media and cultural industries and to foster national unity and cultural identity. It must now deal with threats from the so-called "information superhighway" and from new technologies such as direct-to-home (DTH) satellite services, dubbed by some as "Deathstars." These new technologies make possible the transmission of messages in many new and varied forms that do not respect national boundaries and are not easily made responsive to national regulation.

In *Split Screen* (1993), communication consultant David Ellis deals with issues related to the development of Deathstar satellites, video compression, multimedia computers, the spread of CD-ROMs, the encroachment of cable into telephone services and telephone into cable services, and the changing relationship between TV set and TV viewers. He argues that "broadcasting can no longer be regulated and subsidized in isolation from other communications media, and that the regulator must start to take account of new social issues such as fair and equitable access to networks for both video suppliers and end-users" (p. xviii). This will provide special challenges to the regulatory process and may well involve constitutional issues related to the fundamental rights of individuals and the media.

THE PRINT MEDIA

While time spent watching television, listening to music, and going to movies occupies much of the leisure time of most Canadians, a 1991 survey found that the average adult spent 4.4 hours of the previous week reading books, 3.6 hours reading newspaper, and 2.1 hours reading magazines. However, while newspapers are Canadian owned, foreign books continue to dominate the Canadian market, and Canada has a major trade deficit in magazines and other periodicals. While the federal government has taken action to protect the periodical industry and recently announced plans to spend $140 million over five years to strengthen the book publishing industry, a new 7 percent Goods and Services Tax and an economic recession continue to have a negative effect on Canadian book and periodical sales.

Newspapers

The total number of daily newspapers has held fairly constant in recent years, but circulation continues to decline. The 109 papers have a combined total circulation of 5.16 million, down from 5.47 million for the 110 dailies that existed in 1989. Eleven are published in French and the other 98 are English language newspapers. Groups own 94 of the dailies in Canada, accounting for over 80 percent of the total circulation. Nearly 60 percent of that circulation is controlled by three newspaper groups: Southam, 27 percent; Thomson, 20 percent; and Toronto Sun Publishing, 11 percent. The number of Sunday papers, a relatively recent phenomenon in Canada, increased to 30, although the Saturday paper is still the largest and contains various inserts, color comics, and specialty sections commonly found in Sunday papers in the United States.

The largest circulation newspaper in Canada is the *Toronto Star,* with a daily circulation of nearly 495,000. This newspaper has a long and colorful history that includes two periods separated roughly by the 1950s. Early in the century it earned the distinction of "the last home of razzle-dazzle journalism," but in 1961 was ranked among the prestige newspapers of the world.

The largest circulation French language newspaper is *Le Journal de Montréal,* which was started in 1964 during a strike at *La Presse* and which is characterized by its more sensational coverage of news. With a daily circulation of 282,000, *Le Journal* is owned by Quebecor, which also owns a similar tabloid, *Le Journal de Québec* (nearly 100,000 circulation daily), and other daily and weekly newspapers, magazines, and printing plants.

Another successful tabloid newspaper is the *Toronto Sun,* which was started in 1971 by former employees of the *Toronto Telegram* when it ceased publication that year. The paper began with a circulation of about 60,000 and now boasts 253,000 daily and 446,000 on Sunday. It and other *Sun* newspapers in Calgary, Edmonton, and

Ottawa are owned by The Toronto Sun Publishing Company, which is owned by Maclean Hunter Ltd., another large communications company in Canada.

Two of the more respected newspapers in Canada are owned by the Thomson Corporation of Toronto, Canada's largest communications company and third largest in the world. *The Globe and Mail,* which has been called "the jewel in the crown of Canadian newpapers," is the only truly national newspaper in Canada and has long been recognized as one of Canada's leading newspapers of record. Its daily circulation of 323,000 includes a national edition that is transmitted by satellite to printing plants across the nation. The *Winnipeg Free Press* is another Thomson newspaper that has a distinguished past and a reputation as the prestige paper of the prairie provinces. Its circulation is about 152,000 daily.

Southam Inc. of Toronto, another media conglomerate, owns 15 newspapers that account for approximately 38 percent of the total daily circulation Canada. Among its properties are two similar-sized papers, *The Ottawa Citizen* and the *The Gazette* in Montreal. The *Citizen* is the leading newspaper in the nation's capital with a daily circulation of about 173,000. The *Gazette,* the only English-language daily in Montreal, has a daily circulation of close to 160,000.

Two other Montreal daily newspapers include *La Presse* and *Le Devoir.* With a daily circulation of 187,000, *La Presse,* which began publishing in 1884, is the leading French-language newspaper in Canada. It is owned by the Trans-Canada Newspapers group. *Le Devoir,* which was established in 1910, is one of the most unique daily newspapers in North America. With a daily circulation of only 24,000, it has long been regarded as one of the most influential dailies in Canada because of its appeal to the intellectual elite of French Canada.

The number of community newspapers continues to grow, and their share of national advertising revenues has increased to over 7 percent. According to the Canadian Community Newspapers Association, there are more than a thousand community papers with a weekly circulation of over 5 million, which is more than twice what their total circulation was in 1980. In addition, Canada has over 131 ethnic newspapers serving the many ethnic groups that make up Canada's cultural mosaic, as well as nearly 100 specialized newspapers, armed forces newspapers, supplements, and free-distribution "shoppers" that consist primarily of advertising.

Magazines

Development of the Canadian magazine industry has been influenced over the past 30 years by direct American competition and federal government intervention. When the Royal Commission on Publications (The O'Leary Commission) was established in 1960, three of four magazines read in Canada were from the United States. Over 40 percent of the magazines sold on Canadian newsstands were controlled by two American companies, *Time* magazine and *Reader's Digest,* which had established Canadian editions in 1943. Subsequent legislation in the form of an income tax bill disallowed as income tax deductions the cost of advertising aimed at the Canadian market and placed in non-Canadian newspapers or periodicals. However, when the law went into effect in 1966, it specifically exempted *Time* and *Reader's Digest,* which, as one writer put it, "locked the two biggest wolves in with the sheep." This exemption was removed when the law was amended in 1975, but not until after *Saturday Night,* the national magazine that was started in 1887 as *Toronto Saturday Night,* declared bankruptcy and discontinued publication the year before. As a result of the 1975 amendment to the tax law, *Time* magazine dropped its Canadian edition, and *Reader's Digest* sold its shares to Canadians to become Reader's Digest Association (Canada) Ltd., or RDACL. Within a year, the Magazine Association of Canada reported that Canadian magazines had increased their advertising revenues by 34 percent.

These and other regulatory and legislative measures have helped foster and support growth of a Canadian-owned magazine industry. In the first part of this decade, nearly 1,100 publishers produced about 1,500 Canadian periodicals. About 60 percent were published in English, 22 percent in French, 15 percent were bilingual, and the rest were in other languages. Over 70 percent were consumer periodicals, about 15 percent were business, and the rest were of religious, farm, or scholarly interest. The annual circulation is about 520 million copies with revenues estimated at nearly $885 million. Advertising sales generate about two-thirds of this total, subscription sales account for 21 percent, and the rest is from single-copy sales and other sources. While the federal government has provided legislative and other support to the Canadian magazine industry, in 1989 it began phasing out Canada Post's periodical subsidy, causing postal rates to jump more than 50 percent. In addition, the new 7 percent Goods and Services Tax and an economic recession have put further stress on both Canadian book and periodical sales. In addition to the few national and more general interest magazines—such as the largest, *Maclean's,* with a circulation of over 600,000, *Châtelaine,* which has separate French and English editions (both are published by Maclean Hunter), and *Saturday Night,* which resumed publication in 1975—growth of the magazine industry in Canada, as in the United States, is characterized by the trend toward specialized publications.

THE ELECTRONIC MEDIA

No area of the Canadian media industry has been influenced more by federal government regulation and control than broadcasting. While this is also true in the United States and other Western nations, federal broadcast policy in Canada has gone beyond licensing and beyond efforts to ensure that broadcasting serves the public interest. Canadian broadcast policy has also responded to concerns about national unity, resulting in government ownership of part of the broadcasting industry, as well as to fear of cultural domination through the U.S. media, which has resulted in content requirements designed to limit foreign programming and promote Canadian identity.

The first of many royal commissions, government committees, and special task forces was established in 1928 in response to what has been a major and continuing concern about American domination of the air waves and to related threats to Canadian unity and cultural identity. The Aird Commission was charged to examine the broadcasting situation and make recommendations to the government concerning future administration, management, control, and financing of radio. During the more than six decades that have followed, numerous government reports, hundreds of committee recommendations, and several revisions of the federal broadcast act have shaped the unique structure of the Canadian broadcasting industry.

The result has been a mixed system, with one part owned by the Canadian people and largely supported out of public funds and with the other sector composed of individually owned radio and television stations licensed by the federal government. The system is further mixed in that both the public and private sectors of the broadcast industry include French and English stations, and that the public system, the Canadian Broadcasting Corporation (CBC), is funded by the federal government and also earns revenue from commercial advertising sales.

In addition to influencing the structure of the broadcast industry in Canada, federal government involvement has also sought to affect the content of Canadian broadcasting. In 1958 the Board of Broadcast Governors, which was later replaced by the CRTC, tried to limit the number of foreign programs carried by Canadian television stations. Private stations outnumbered CBC stations, and the expanding number of commercial stations increased the importing of foreign programs, mainly from U.S. networks and film sources. The BBG made the requirement that at least 55 percent of any television station's programs should be Canadian in origin. However, the rule was interpreted so loosely that most private stations failed to meet this requirement, especially in prime time.

In 1968 the CRTC moved to tighten the content regulations for television, and for the first time established a minimum requirement for radio. Television content regulations passed by the CRTC in 1970 went into effect in 1972 and required that 60 percent of all television material broadcast on Canadian stations be Canadian, not just overall, but prime time as well. This was later relaxed not only for the private television stations but for CBC stations as well when the content quotas were said to apply only to the hours of 6 PM to midnight. Further, while CBC stations had to broadcast at least 60 percent Canadian content during that time period, private stations had to broadcast only 50 percent Canadian content during those hours. These percentages are now determined on an annual average, making it possible to concentrate on less expensive Canadian content in the summer months when audiences are small and concentrate on American produced programming in the prime season.

Nearly 90 percent of the programming on CBC television now consists of Canadian content in prime time, and about 70 percent is Canadian produced, though not necessarily by the CBC. The remainder is imported mostly from the United States, England, France, and Belgium. The Canadian Broadcast Program Development Fund was established in 1983 to encourage the production and broadcast of quality television programs by private producers in Canada. Administered by Telefilm Canada, a Crown Corporation established in the 1960s to support the television and feature film industry, the fund has provided over $500 million to help support the production of over 900 projects with total budgets of more than $1,500 million.

The 1991 Broadcasting Act reaffirmed the general principles of earlier legislation that the broadcasting system must be Canadian, must offer services in both English and French that are widely available through the nation, and must provide a wide range of programming that informs, enlightens, and entertains. It also acknowledged that French-language and English-language broadcasting operate under different circumstances to meet different needs.

Radio

Canadian broadcasting officially dates back to 1919 when the Marconi Wireless Telegraph Company obtained the first license specifically granted for sound broadcasting in Canada. The Canadian Broadcasting Corporation (CBC) was created in 1936 to provide a national radio service. Today, CBC Radio is available in English and French to nearly 99 percent of all Canadian households. It owns and operates 65 radio stations and 615 rebroadcasters and low-power relay transmitters. CBC programming is also carried by 19 private affiliates and 28 rebroadcast transmitters. Regional and network programming are available in AM mono and FM stereo and include classical and popular music, drama and commentary, news and public affairs, analysis, weather, and sports. CBC also includes Radio Canada International, a shortwave radio service broadcasting in seven languages that is financed by External Affairs and International Trade Canada. Its showcase news and public affairs magazine programs, the daily "As It Happens" and the weekly "Sunday Morning", set new standards for public broadcasting.

In addition to the CBC, Canada has nearly 500 privately owned radio stations broadcasting in many and varied music and other formats to serve various segments of the Canadian radio audience. Annual revenues for privately owned radio broadcasting operations exceed $760 million.

Television

The Canadian Broadcasting Corporation introduced television to Canada in 1952 and now operates several national services: English and French (Radio Canada) television networks; CBC North, which provides radio and television programming to the nation's northern regions in English, French, and seven native languages; and Newsworld, a 24-hour satellite-to-cable English-language news service supported completely by cable subscriptions and revenues from commercial advertising. CBC is also a shareholder with seven other Canadian partners in the Canadian branch of TV5, the international French-language consortium. Unlike CBC radio, which carries no commercials, CBC TV earns over $377 million from advertising and other revenues. This represents about a fourth of the corporation's total revenues, with the largest portion coming directly from government appropriations.

The private English-language Canadian Television Network, CTV, began operating in 1961. Other nonpublic television operations include Global Television in Ontario, Le Réseau de Télévision Quatre Saisons in Quebec, the TVA network in Quebec and the Atlantic Provinces, the Atlantic Satellite Network providing regional satellite-to-cable service, and other independent stations in the larger markets. Total annual revenues for privately owned television stations are about $1,460 million, although private television as an industry lost money for the first time in 1991.

Four provinces operate their own educational television networks. These include Radio-Québec; TVOntario, which also began a French-language network in 1987; Access Alberta; and the Knowledge Network in British Columbia.

Cable

Canada is a wired nation. Of the 92 percent of Canadian homes with access to cable services, four of five are currently subscribers. Nearly 1,800 cable television systems currently operate in Canada, although three groups dominate the industry: Rogers Telecommunications Ltd., Télévision Vidéótron Ltée., and Maclean Hunter Ltd. Combined annual revenues for all cable companies totals $1.6 billion.

Cable television is regulated by the CRTC, although Quebec and other provinces originally claimed it to be a provincial authority. The CRTC is also involved in establishing a rate structure for cable, as well as setting regulations on the services that cable firms must provide. The initial rules required cable systems to give priority to Canadian advertisers and sources of programming, to provide community channels for local self-expression, and to carry American channels only when all relevant Canadian channels were already on line. These rules, designed to protect Canadian advertisers and broadcasters, were rendered ineffective with the introduction of the cable converter that increased the number of channels considerably, making plenty of room for American signals.

MOVIES AND FILM

The federal government became involved in the film business in 1939 when it established the National Film Board of Canada. Under its revised mandate in 1950, the NFB has the responsibility to produce and distribute films designed to interpret Canada to Canadians and to other nations. The second largest producer of Canadian films (CBC is first), the National Film Board has been a pioneer and pacesetter in the production of film documentaries. Telefilm Canada, a Crown Corporation established in the 1960s to support the television and feature film industry, manages the Canadian Broadcast Program Development Fund to encourage the production and broadcast of quality television programs, the Feature Film Fund to help support production of feature films, and the Feature Film Distribution Fund to support Canadian distribution companies. Most recent figures show that the federal government annually spends more than $225 million to support the National Film Board and Telefilm Canada.

NEWS SERVICES

During its 75th anniversary year in 1992, the Canadian Press, the major news service in Canada, was threatened by major budget shortfalls and the establishment of three satellite news networks involving member newspapers. When its board of directors refused for the first time in four decades to approve a rate increase, the news cooperative was left with an $882,000 shortfall in its editorial budget. The financial situation was made even worse through circulation membership losses since member newspaper fees or assessments are based on total weekly circulation.

More troubling, perhaps, was the establishment of three satellite news networks. Southam *Star* Network was established when the 17-member Southam Newspaper Group and the Toronto *Star,* Canada's largest newspaper, agreed to exchange domestic and international news, features and sports. A week later, the *Globe and Mail* in Toronto and the *Wall Street Journal* in New York agreed to begin exchanging news. After that, the Thomson News Service announced an expansion that would allow all 37 Thomson newspapers to share stories electronically.

During the same year, the Canadian Press announced two developments to better serve member newspapers and help cut costs. Introduction of NewsStream would increase the rate of transmission of news and other reports from 80 words per minute to 1,200 words per minute. This move was designed not to increase the amount of material available to members but to move it faster and eliminate bottlenecks. NewsStream would also make it possible for copy to be edited and sent directly to newspapers from originating bureaus rather than sending it through a second editing process in Toronto. Another change in 1992 was to drop the Agence France-Presse (AFP) wire from the international service, a move that affected only the French-language Broadcast News members. The large French-language Canadian dailies subscribe directly to AFP for its full report.

The Canadian Press, organized as a member cooperative like the Associated Press in the United States, was officially established in 1917 as the Canadian Press Limited, a merger of regional components of the nation's daily newspapers (the Central Provinces, the Western Associated Press, and Eastern Press Association). A reincorporation in 1923 included the new name of the Canadian Press. It operates bureaus in major world centers and has arrangements to receive international news from the Associated Press, Reuters, and AFP. While it was established to serve member newspapers, it also provides news to Canadian broadcast stations through Broadcast News Ltd. for private broadcasters and Press News Ltd. for the CBC and other outlets.

ADVERTISING

In the introduction to this chapter, we briefly noted that federal regulation of advertising has been used as a weapon in the border battle with the United States to protect the Canadian magazine and broadcast industries from competition from across the border. The Canadian Income Tax Act disallows Canadian business deductions for the cost of advertising in foreign magazines and on foreign broadcast stations serving Canadian markets while allowing this deduction for Canadian advertisers who advertise in Canadian media.

Governments at all levels in Canada are involved in regulations that affect media advertising, resulting in a mix of federal and provincial rules and regulations alongside attempts at self-regulation by the Canadian Advertising Foundation in Toronto and the Advertising Standards Council (ASC). In addition to receiving complaints from the public and from industry groups concerning the conduct of advertisers, ASC also generates and maintains codes of standards and reviews in advance of distribution certain types of advertising, like that directed to children or for feminine personal products. The Supreme Court of Canada became involved in 1990 when it ruled that a rule by the Royal College of Dental Surgeons of Ontario prohibiting advertising was a violation of freedom of expression guaranteed in the Charter of Rights and Freedoms.

In recent years, social concerns about advertising in Canada have paralleled those in the United States and involve issues such as the effects of commercial advertising on children; tobacco and alcohol advertising; the effects of gender, ethnic, and age portrayals in advertising; advocacy and comparative advertising; political advertising; and sexually explicit messages in media advertisements. On the federal level, the Tobacco Products Control Act of 1989 prohibits advertising tobacco products in newspapers and magazines and on radio and television and requires graduated reduction of such advertising on billboards, outdoor ads, and retail signs with complete compliance by 1993. Advertising of alcoholic beverages is regulated at the provincial level with every province except Prince Edward Island permitting such advertising in mass media, although there are variations on types of products and types of media. The CRTC "preclears" commercials for alcoholic beverage advertising on radio and television.

Mass media advertising in Canada dates back to the first occurrence of a newspaper advertisement in the *Halifax Gazette* in 1752. It developed considerably during the nineteenth century during industrialization, mass production, and the emergence of mass circulation newspapers and magazines. The first advertising agency was founded in 1889, when Anson McKim, known as the father of Canadian advertising agencies, opened A. McKim and Company in Montreal. The introduction of radio and television during the twentieth century continued to transform the nature of the industry, as are recent developments in communication technology including videocassette recorders, cable television, pay TV, and the remote control that makes it possible for television audiences to avoid commercials while "grazing" the cable spectrum.

Today, advertising accounts for most of the more than $10 billion in revenues for broadcasting, newspapers and magazines, directories, and outdoor advertising in Canada (compared to just over $4 billion in 1980). The figure would be even higher if all direct mail, point-of-purchase, circulars, theater, and other forms of specialized advertising were included.

Daily and weekly newspapers with advertising revenues of almost $3 billion still enjoy the largest share of net advertising revenues, although that share has dropped to under 30 percent in recent years. Television has held steady at about 16 percent, while radio has dropped to just over 8 percent. Magazines have increased slightly to just over 16 percent, as have outdoor advertisers, who now enjoy about 8 percent of net advertising revenues.

Television dominates in national advertising sales, with over three-fourths of its sales for national and network sales. The percentages are reversed for radio, with local advertising making up about three-fourths of all airtime sales. Newspapers, as well, generate most of their advertising revenue from local sales (almost 80 percent for daily newspapers and over 90 percent for weeklies).

EDUCATION AND TRAINING FOR JOURNALISTS

While the original approach to journalism education in Canada was modeled after programs at major universities in the United States, particularly Columbia University in New York City, its development over the past nearly half-century has been uniquely Canadian. The result is nine university programs, located mainly in Ontario and Quebec, which vary considerably one from the other but continue to maintain a particular focus on journalism as opposed to journalism and mass communication, as is the case for most American programs.

The development of university programs in journalism in Canada took place during two time periods. The first was immediately following World War II, when programs were established in Ontario at the University of Western Ontario in London, Ottawa's Carleton College (now Carleton University), and Toronto's Ryerson Institute of Technology (now Ryerson Polytechnical Institute). Both the Western program, which was established in 1946, and the program at Carleton, established a year later, were modeled largely after the graduate school of journalism at Columbia University. The Ryerson program was established in 1949 as a separate program within the Graphic Arts Department.

The second phase was in the 1970s and 1980s when journalism programs were established at Concordia University in Montreal in 1975, the University of King's College at Dalhousie University in Halifax, Nova Scotia, in 1978, the University of Regina in Saskatchewan in 1979, and the University of Moncton in New Brunswick in the 1980s. In 1974, Western replaced its undergraduate program with a 12-month graduate program, similar to the graduate program at Columbia University.

During the same period, the first journalism programs at French universities were established at Université Laval in Quebec City in 1968 and at the Université du Québec à Montréal (UQAM) in the 1970s. The program at the Université de Montréal was started in the 1980s through the university's Faculty of Continuing Education. In addition to these university programs in journalism, a large number of community colleges across Canada offer specializations in journalism, broadcasting, and related areas.

According to Peter Desbarats (1990), dean of the Graduate School of Journalism at the University of Western Ontario, the absence of any system of national accreditation, like the one in the United States, has permitted a healthy diversity of approaches to education in journalism at Canadian universities. Nevertheless, all of the Canadian programs have largely maintained a primary commitment to journalism education, unlike the journalism and mass communication programs south of the border in which enrollments in advertising, public relations, and radio-television are as large as or larger than those in journalism. Carleton University is the only journalism program in Canada to offer a substantial program in mass communication, making it more like programs in the United States, although its emphasis continues to be on the preparation of students for careers in journalism. It is headquarters for the Centre for Investigative Journalism, which has chapters across Canada.

While university programs of continuing education or professional development for working journalists have been slow to develop in Canada, Western has, for many years, offered a two-week annual program for journalists in law and economics. Ryerson offers a National Training Seminar for Copy Editors, and most of the other journalism programs are now involved, in one way or another, in offering professional development programs for journalists, as are most of the major print and broadcast professional associations and organizations.

Even though journalism education is relatively new in Canadian universities, its impact through placement of graduates in the media industry is significant. Dean Peter Desbarats at Western estimates that about half of the positions in major news organization are held by graduates of Canadian journalism programs with the proportion continuing to grow.

United States

THE CONTEXTS

Historical

The press, as it exists, is not, as our moralists sometimes seem to assume, the willful product of any little group of living men. On the contrary, it is the outcome of an historic process in which many individuals participated without foreseeing what the ultimate product of their labors was to be. (Park 1923, p. 273)

The words of 20-20 hindsight are "of course" and "obviously." The words of foresight often are "no way" or some variant of "you've got to be kidding."

When one looks back on the fabric of the history of American journalism, the garment fashioned by the Franklins, Greeleys, Hearsts, Sarnoffs, and others is seamless. When one looks ahead, however, the threads are twisted or unraveling, impossible to make sense of.

True to sociologist Robert Park's observations, there are pressures on the news media today that will be far clearer to writers in the mid-twenty-first century than they are today—as we wonder about the effects of violence depicted on television, about the impacts of the apparent mergers between telephone companies and cable television giants, about the efforts of the print media to adjust to fragmented audiences, and about the increasing visual orientation of those audiences.

Because the movers and shakers could not always bend the media or society to their will does not mean that there was no logic or rationale to the nature of how the news media developed. At least to our own satisfaction, we can impose a logic or rationale on the outcomes of this process.

For practical purposes, a survey of American journalism history can begin naturally enough in colonial Boston, a center of population and commerce. Postmasters were the primary traffickers in information of the day, and Boston postmaster John Campbell founded the *Boston Newsletter*, first published on April 24, 1704, and considered to be the first continuously published American newspaper. He kept his paper even when he was no longer postmaster. William Brooker, Campbell's successor, started his own paper, too, the *Boston Gazette.* James Franklin, a printer for Brooker, started his paper, the *New England Courant,* when a new postmaster moved the *Gazette* from Franklin's shop. Franklin's paper, published without permission of the governor and royal council, is said to mark the end of government licensing of the press in the colonies. He later started a newspaper in Rhode Island, and his younger brother Ben grew up to develop one of the first newspaper chains in the nation, to write one of the best read advice columns ever published and is credited, too, with having started one of the nation's first magazines.

Perhaps the most successful and wealthiest of the young nation's printer/journalists was Isaiah Thomas, who wrote a classic history of the development of the American press, and whose *Massachusetts Spy* serves as bridge between the press of the colonies and the press of a young nation. The press of that nation was highly political and fiercely partisan—so much so that historians characterize the political and journalistic battles between Thomas Jefferson's Republicans and Alexander Hamilton's Federalists as "The Dark Ages of Partisan Journalism." Historian Frank Luther Mott (1962) noted "Few papers were ably edited; they reflected the crassness of the American society of the times. Scurrility, assaults, corruption, blatancy were commonplace. Journalism had grown too fast" (p. 215).

The politicization of the press continued into the patronage and political spoils system of the Andrew Jackson administration. Such a state of journalism yielded, however, to the development of the Penny Press and the emergence of a mass audience that made financial and commercial gain more appealing to editors than the struggles of partisan journalism.

The modern media have their roots in the *New York Sun* of Ben Day, the *New York Herald* of James Gordon Bennett Sr. and Jr.—who made the novel discovery that people are interested in reading about police news—Horace Greeley of the *New York Tribune,* and others. The creed of the penny press of the 1830s and 1840s matches up well against what the print and broadcast media do today. The philosophy of the penny press was that the common people should have a realistic view of society, that abuses should be exposed, that the first duty of the press is news, not political support, and that local and human interest news is important.

The philosophical foundation laid by the penny press was augmented by technological developments of the later nineteenth century. By the dawn of the twentieth century, the American newspaper had the relatively high-speed rotary press, the linotype, the typewriter, and the telephone. For most practical purposes, the news reporter of the 1890s would have had little trouble recognizing and working in most newsrooms of the 1950s and early 1960s—a condition that suggests why a rush of technological changes have both traumatized and excited the journalists of the 1980s and 1990s.

Not until the 1920s did the broadcast media begin to arise, not until the 1930s was government regulation well in place, and not until the 1940s and the 1950s did the print media begin to fully realize—rather than only fear—the impact the broadcasters would have. In later decades, the broadcast media would have fears of their own.

In the early 1920s, Atlantic Telephone & Telegraph Company built what was to become WNBC in New York City; Westinghouse, the current owner of the NBC network, had stations in Boston, Chicago, New York, and Philadelphia; General Electric built WGY in Schenectady, New York. Those three companies also created RCA, the Radio Corporation of American, in 1919, but AT&T withdrew from the consortium in a few years.

Under the leadership of David Sarnoff, RCA led to the creation of NBC in 1926, and NBC developed two networks. The Red was the forerunner of today's NBC, and the Blue became ABC in 1945 after a 1943 sale mandated by the Federal Communications Commission. CBS has its roots in 1927 in an alliance of the United Independent Broadcasters and the Columbia Phonograph Broadcasting System, Inc.

At the same time, the government regulatory system for telecommunications was taking shape under the direction of the then Secretary of Commerce Herbert Hoover.

The Radio Act of 1927 created the Federal Radio Commission (FRC), which had to bring some measure of control to the broadcast stations, public services, and emergency services seeking space on the electromagnetic spectrum. The FRC issued licenses, allocated broadcast frequencies, and controlled station transmitting power.

The Communications Act of 1934 replaced the FRC with the current Federal Communications Commission, a seven-member board appointed by the President and confirmed by the Senate to help ensure that electronic communication is operated in the public interest.

Newspapers did not equate their interests with those of the public. In an early newspaper–radio war—eventually won by the broadcasters by the end of the 1930s— newspapers tried to treat radio station program listings as paid advertising and also sought to restrict what news the Associated Press, United Press, and International News Service could provide to radio stations.

But that proved folly, particularly with the onset of World War II, when Edward R. Murrow and his radio news colleagues at CBS began to set the standard by which all broadcast journalism would be measured, even into the 21st Century. Murrow, William Shirer, and others reported live from London and other European capitals as the world began to come to grips with what Adolph Hitler and Nazi Germany meant to the course of world history.

The FCC gave permission to 18 television stations to begin commercial broadcasting on July 1, 1941, but further development was delayed by the onset of the nation's direct involvement in World War II.

The immediate post-war years seemed stable enough. Publishing tycoon Henry R. Luce had already written and published in *Life* in 1941 an essay, "The American Century," in which he envisioned—as did most Americans—a saner post-war world taking its cues and leadership from the United States.

As might have been expected, television continued from where it had left off before the war, developing faster and faster. The first regularly scheduled network newscasts began in 1948 with Douglas Edwards on CBS-TV and John Cameron Swayze on NBC. Those were only 15-minute newscasts, but more inroads on print media status and revenue were made in what came to be called the "Golden Age" of television in the 1950s as dramas, variety shows, movies, and even test patterns enthralled the American audience in its infant years of television viewing.

But here the seamless garment of historical interpretation begins to unravel a bit. And one can at best sort out a few landmarks that shaped the U.S. media systems as they moved toward the end of the twentieth century into the twenty-first:

- The power of television to capture and focus the nation's attention was evident in Edward R. Murrow's coverage credited with bringing about the end of the climate of fear and suspicion engendered by U.S. Senator Joseph R. McCarthy of Wisconsin. Congress recognized the power of the medium, too, when the U.S. Senate brought organized crime into a national spotlight in hearings directed by Senator Estes Kefauver of Tennessee. The assassination of President John F. Kennedy and televised events related to it remain a nightmare for millions of American viewers. The TV industry was credited with or blamed for bringing the Vietnam War into the living rooms of American citizens and, perhaps, generating opposition to the war, although it is argued that media coverage reflected public disenchantment rather than caused it.

- Growing public disenchantment with government, with the press, and with other political and social institutions grew from being a matter of curiosity to a matter of concern. While the news media may have gloried in their coverage of the Vietnam War, Watergate, the Iran-Contra scandal, and other evidences of government misconduct, there was a backlash. The public became increasingly suspicious of all institutions, and the news media struggled to bear up under increasing introspection and internal criticism as journalism reviews and media critics often concluded that the media were more a part of the problem than a part of the solution. Even the hallowed concept of "objective reporting" was vilified by those within journalism who contended that the news media often covered up more than they disclosed.

- New media were merging, and older media were redefining themselves. Transmission of television signals by cable and satellite developed almost overnight. The computer and communications industries underwent more rapid and dramatic changes in months than the established medium of newspapers underwent in decades or generations. The mass circulation magazine in a no-contest bout yielded to special interest magazines. Newspapers began to redesign and refashion themselves as circulation fell behind population growth. Cable News Network (CNN), moved from being a somewhat shoestring afterthought of cable entrepreneurs to being the premier news medium in coverage of the Gulf War in 1991.

Further developments of U.S. media are explored in the following sections on newspapers, magazines, and broadcast journalism.

Legal

Congress shall make no law respecting an establishment of religion or pro-hibiting the free exercise thereof; or abridging the freedom of speech or of the press, or the right of the people peaceably to assemble, and to petition the Government for a redress of grievances. (The First Amendment to the U.S. Constitution)

The legal context of American journalism is at least as old as the Magna Carta in 1215, which symbolized that the king was not above the law, and at least as young as such twentieth century U.S. Supreme Court decisions as *Near v. Minnesota* in 1931, *New York Times v. Sullivan* in 1964, and the Pentagon Papers Case, *New York Times v. U.S.* in 1971. *Near* and the Pentagon Papers cases provide a bulwark against government's prior restraint of expression; *Sullivan* reaffirmed the concept of a marketplace of ideas as central to a democracy.

In *Near,* the Court ruled that the State of Minnesota could not silence a roughhouse newspaper for its virulent, anti-Semitic nature. In *Times v. Sullivan,* the Court preached a sermon of democracy, of the great experiment of self-government launched by Jefferson and James Madison. Seven years later, the U.S. Supreme Court ruled that the government did not make a convincing enough case in its bid to gag the *New York Times* and other newspapers from printing the Pentagon Papers, the supposedly secret history of the nation's involvement in Vietnam.

Further, in *Sullivan,* the Court recognized "a profound national commitment to the principles that debate on public issues should be uninhibited, robust and wide open" and that citizens not only have a right to criticize government but have a duty to do so. "It is as much his [the citizen's] duty to criticize as it is the official's duty to administer," Justice William Brennan wrote.

The interplay of the freedom of the press and the freedom of citizens throughout the *Sullivan* decision is instructive. The Supreme Court has not distinguished in any significant way between a freedom of speech and a freedom of the press. Rather, the Court recognizes the First Amendment as protecting a freedom of expression, thus extending protections to symbolic speech, such as the wearing of an arm band or the burning of a flag.

Nor has the court really distinguished between a freedom of expression protecting an individual against government and a freedom protecting a newspaper or broadcast station against government. Theoretically, individuals can assert that they have as much constitutional protection as the *New York Times* and even more constitutional protection than ABC, CBS, or NBC news because the broadcast media are regulated by government through the FCC.

In addition, U.S. courts say the news media have no greater constitutional rights of access to information or to public or private facilities than do individual citizens.

Plainly, in practice, journalists can reach a wider audience much faster than any individual citizen; public officials also are more likely to respond to a network newscaster than they are to a private citizen, even though the network journalist is subject to some government regulation.

The individual journalist and the institutional press do enjoy some legal protection against government not available to every citizen. Chief among these is protection against automatically having to testify in court or in other judicial processes. If a citizen is subpoenaed to testify, the citizen must testify or face contempt of court proceedings. If journalists are subpoenaed to testify as to what a news source told them or what they know about a person involved in a legal proceeding, they can invoke some First Amendment protection made available by the courts and by state legislatures. That protection does not mean that journalists never have to testify; it does mean that before testimony can be compelled, the government must show that the information sought is vital to a case and is not available from any other source.

Political

In many respects, the political context of the press is inseparable from its historical and legal context, particularly given the end to be served by the First Amendment—an informed electorate capable of self-government. But, somewhat separably, a narrower political context is twofold: One part is, of course, the role of the press as a Fourth Estate of government, consistent with Joseph Pulitzer's belief that the highest mission of the press is to render public service. The second part of the political context is a self-serving one in which the institution of the press seeks favors or assistance through the political process.

At its best, the mission of the press to render public service is illustrated by activities that range from informing citizens about the intricacies of international diplomacy, to telling them about proposals for a bond issue to build a new elementary school in the district. More questionable is the role of the press in seeking to shape political developments. Many of the nation's misadventures in Asia and in Vietnam, for example, are attributed to the politics of Henry Luce, as reflected in his publications, including *Time* magazine.

As for the media seeking political favors, some of those include legislation that serves a general public need—legislation to increase access to government records and government meetings, for example. Other legislation may be peculiar to the nature of the news media—legislation to exempt newspaper carriers from child labor laws that would prohibit delivery of morning newspapers.

But tougher political battles are under way now within and among the news media, and the outcome of those battles will shape the nature of the news media in the twenty-first century.

- In 1982, the federal courts broke up AT&T, the world's largest corporation. The tremors from that continued in the halls of Congress and state legislatures and in courts as newspapers and the broadcast industry sought to prevent the seven Regional Bell Operating Companies (RBOCs) from developing entertainment or information programs in the regions they served. Gradually, however, the AT&T offspring are freeing themselves from court restrictions of the 1980s, and the traditional news media have moved to negotiating with the significant new players in the mass communication industry.

- The onset of fiber optics, the flowering of satellite technology, and other technological changes have forced a reckoning with new terms describing the mass media scene—words such as *interactive,* media *convergence,* and *infrastructure.* The prospects for cooperation between the print media and the telephone companies, for example, have already been preceded by a merger of Time, Inc. and Warner, a cable company, and by proposed mergers of RBOCs and other major cable companies whose combined resources are at least in the tens of billions of dollars.

- In the 1970s, the federal government made the U.S. Post Office into a quasi-private agency, the U.S. Postal Service, which was to try to pay its own way. The philosophical nature of that change—that government would not be primarily responsible for ensuring pathways for communication among the citizens—was not fully realized. Now, 20 years later, government is talking about a new information superhighway—something that could resemble reconfiguration of the postal service into an electronic, computerized message system, linking citizens and public and private agencies throughout the nation and across the globe. But the political questions of control and cost are not yet fully appreciated, let alone addressed.

- Debate over the Fairness Doctrine symbolizes how technological winds cause changes in news media politics and philosophy. For almost 40 years in the second half of the century, the Fairness Doctrine mandated that the broadcast media must provide their audiences with information about important societal issues and also must present two or more sides of such issues. While that demand would be unconstitutional if proposed for the print media, the broadcast media—as a government-regulated institution—had to follow the Fairness Doctrine. In 1987, the Federal Communications Commission itself found the Fairness Doctrine either unnecessary or unconstitutional, or both, because the development of cable and other technologies meant that broadcasting opportunities no longer were scarce or limited. But certain to continue is the issue of whether and under what conditions government can mandate access to communication channels and dictate program content.

CONTEMPORARY ISSUES

"The truth, slowly emerging, is that human society cannot improve, cannot function properly, may not even be able to survive, if the media do not do their job well" (Christians et al. 1993, p. vi).

Contemporary journalism issues, including many of those listed in this book, revolve around an age-old question: Which is the more important, the individual or society? Is that society best which maximizes individual freedom, or does the individual have value only in terms of maximizing contributions to society?

Much of journalism and First Amendment rhetoric seeks to have it both ways, contending that the society benefits the most when individual freedom is expanded and well-defended. But that view of the Enlightenment is challenged in contemporary journalism by, among others, advocates of what is called "social responsibility" theory. They wonder whether today's journalism plays a larger role in solving or creating social problems.

Does a journalistic ethic of focusing on news of the unusual or of conflict fit as well in a fragmented society as it did in what was presumed to be a homogenous community?

Is the "marketplace of ideas" concept an unworkable myth in a news media marketplace controlled by large and impersonal corporations?

Is the level of public discourse and rational debate aided in any way by news coverage that is characterized by 10-second "sound bites," glib quotes, and political debates that are scored—by media insistence—almost like boxing matches?

As early as 1947, the likely answers to such questions caused the Commission on Freedom of the Press to issue a call for a news media that put greater emphasis on social responsibility than on individual freedom of expression.

The Commission, consisting of nonmedia scholars and philosophers, asked essentially whether negative freedom—freedom from restraints—was enough to serve society well. In subsequent years, scholars in media ethics have emphasized positive freedom—the use of freedom to accomplish something, to serve society.

THE PRINT MEDIA

Newspapers

In the past 30 years, the newspaper industry in the United States has undergone more change, conducted more studies, worried more about its readers and how to relate to them, and sought more women and minority group members than it had in its previous 250 years as a national industry. And that understates the point, partly because there was so little change in the previous 100 or so years, and partly because there has been so much change in the 1970s, 1980s, and 1990s.

The industry also has become more profitable as annual returns of 18 to 20 percent profits are one result of the growth of group ownership and of communications companies. Such properties are traded on the public stock exchanges, rather than held by private families as they were for much of the twentieth century. The larger companies and their holdings include those listed in Table 15.1.

TABLE 15.1 Newspaper ownership and circulation among larger newspaper groups

	Number of Dailies	Circulation	Sunday Editions	Circulation (in Millions)
Gannett Co. Inc.	81	5.88	66	6.0
Knight-Ridder Inc.	28	3.7	24	5.2
Newhouse Newspapers	26	3.0	21	3.9
Dow Jones & Co. Inc.	23	2.4	14	0.5
Thompson Newspapers	120	2.1	78	1.9

In the early to mid-1990s, more general numbers continue to look something like this:

There are about 1,570 daily newspapers in the nation. About 40 percent of them are published in the morning, and about 60 percent in the afternoon. About 890 of the newspapers have Sunday editions. In recent decades, scores of newspapers, perhaps hundreds, have changed publication from evening to morning to better compete with television and to face fewer traffic problems as the newspapers are circulated in metropolitan areas. In 1975, for example, there were 339 daily morning newspapers; 20 years later, there are close to 600.

The total number of daily newspapers has never been lower in this century; there were 100 more dailies just 10 years ago. The number of Sunday newspapers, however, has never been higher. There are about 100 more Sunday newspapers than there were 10 years ago. The total daily circulation of daily newspapers has been in the low 60 millions since 1965, not keeping pace with population growth. The Sunday circulation over the past 25 years, however, has increased from a total of about 48 million to 62.5 million.

Often, people think that a newspaper with circulation under 50,000 is a small newspaper. Perhaps so, but almost 85 percent of the nation's dailies have circulations below 50,000. Forty to 45 have circulations over 250,000, and these typically include those papers considered to be the best in the nation—among other reasons because of their size and resources, because they serve capitals of commerce and politics, and because they help set the national agenda. The five largest in the nation by average daily circulation usually are the following:

- The *Wall Street Journal,* about 1.8 million. The *Journal* is highly regarded because of its status as the premier newspaper of the financial communities. But readers are also rewarded by outstanding news coverage and feature writing on nonbusiness topics. Dow Jones & Company, Inc., owns the *Journal* and a score of other daily newspapers.

- *USA Today,* about 1.5 million. *USA Today* is the flagship newspaper of Gannett Co. Inc., also owner of such well-regarded papers as the Louisville *Courier-Journal* and the *Des Moines Register. USA Today's* graphics, design, and shorter stories typify the newspaper industry's efforts to attract and keep readers in a visual age. The paper has not been a profitable one, however. In fact, it reported its first and only profitable year so far in 1993. Its losses have been offset by other Gannett properties.

- The *New York Times,* about 1.1 million. The *New York Times* is the nation's newspaper of record, the one U.S. newspaper certain to be included in any list of the world's best newspapers. It was founded by Henry Raymond in the 1850s and served as an early organizer and supporter of the Republican Party and the candidacy of Abraham Lincoln. In decline in the early 1890s, the paper was rescued from bankruptcy by Adolph Ochs in 1896. The New York Times Co. owns 24 daily newspapers, several magazines, and broadcast properties.

- The *Los Angeles Times,* about 1.1 million. The *Los Angeles Times* emerged in the latter third of the twentieth century as perhaps the finest paper west of the

Mississippi River, or perhaps west of the Hudson, after decades of being viewed as the handmaiden of the Republican party in California under the partisan publisher Norman Chandler.

- The *Washington Post,* 800,000. The *Post* is inseparable in most people's minds from "Watergate," the one-word summary of the paper's investigative reporting that led to the resignation of President Richard Nixon in August 1974. More important to the paper's status is the fact that it is read daily by the movers and shakers in the capital of the world's most powerful nation. Its publisher, Katharine Graham, stood among the most visible publishers in the nation, and reporter-columnist David Broder among the most respected of the nation's working press. The Washington Post Co. also owns *Newsweek* magazine and broadcast and cable properties.

Weekly Newspapers

For news closest to home, millions of readers turn to their weekly newspapers. In the early 1990s, the number of weeklies was fairly stable, at about 7,400 to 7,500, with the average circulation about 7,500 copies. From the mid-1960s to the mid-1990s, the total circulation of weekly newspapers in the nation increased from about 21 million to more than 55 million. The start of that period marked the onset of two trends that shaped the weekly newspaper field: (1) the change from letterpress to offset printing production and (2) the development of central printing plants in which one plant would print, and perhaps own, several weekly newspapers in one region of a state. In that regard, many smaller communities, too, lost a locally owned press.

The weekly newspaper industry finds much of its political and economic strengths in state newspaper associations. Leaders of those associations faced new challenges in the mid-1990s, working with an RBOC to assess how deregulation of the RBOCs at the federal and state levels would affect the community press with regard to both advertising revenue and information services.

Magazines

The magazine industry is among the most resilient of the nation's journalistic outlets. Like all other media, its demise has been prophesied from time to time because of societal changes. Magazines seem to have more "Golden Ages" than their media competitors, however, perhaps because the industry is less monolithic, adapts quicker to change, and also has a "survival of the fittest" atmosphere in which from 100 to several hundred new magazines are started each year, of which about 80 percent fail within five years. In the mid-1990s, there were about 12,000 regularly published magazines in the nation—not counting hundreds of publications on irregular schedules, serving various interest groups and narrow audiences of at best scores of people.

For some historians, an early Golden Age of magazines was the muckraking era of the early 1900s, when writers like Ida M. Tarbell, Lincoln Steffens, and Ray Stannard Baker exposed the evils of government and business in such mass circulation magazines as *McClure's, Cosmopolitan, Everybody's, Colliers,* and even *Ladies' Home Journal.*

For others, another Golden Age or Ages are the years bracketing World War II, with the onset of the picture magazine, with *Life* and *Look* leading the way, and the age of photojournalism. Magazines, like some newspapers, were developing and serving a visually oriented audience before the onset of television in the 1950s. But that onset, and the time it took advertisers as well as journalists to adjust to the strengths and weaknesses of the new medium, took its toll on magazines in what some characterize as a depression era of the 1950s and early 1960s.

But another so-called Golden Age was in the wings in the late 1970s and the 1980s. The industry, having once called the tune with regard to visual communication, also either presaged or reacted quickly to the onset of the fragmented audience— a time that, in retrospect, may come to mark the end of an era that emphasized mass communication.

The trends are not without trauma or loss as such giants as *Life, Look, Collier's, Saturday Evening Post,* and others either vanish or are diminished.

Mass circulation magazines remain, of course. In 1993, the top 10 magazines in paid circulation were *Modern Maturity,* the publication of the American Association of Retired Persons, 22.4 million; *Reader's Digest,* 16.3 million domestically; *TV Guide,* 14.6 million; *National Geographic,* 9.5 million; *Better Homes & Gardens,* 7.6 million; *The Cable Guide,* 5.3 million; *Ladies' Home Journal,* 5.1 million; *Family Circle,* 5 million; *Good Housekeeping,* 5 million; and *McCall's,* 4.6 million.

The second edition of *Global Journalism* listed various categories of magazines to illustrate the diversity of the industry and the sizable audiences that may still accompany such specialized appeals. For example:

Newsweeklies: *Time,* 4.3 million; *Newsweek,* 3.3 million; *U.S. News & World Report,* 2.4 million.

Women's magazines: At least four of these are in the top ten, followed by number 11, *Woman's Day,* 4.5 million, and *Redbook,* number 16, at 3.4 million.

Fashion magazines: Among them *Cosmopolitan,* 2.7 million; *Glamour,* 2.1 million; *Vogue,* 1.2 million; *GQ,* 735,000.

Business Magazines: *Money,* 2.2 million; *Business Week,* 900,000; *Fortune* and *Forbes,* at about 770,000 each.

City and regional magazines: *Southern Living,* 2.4 million; *Sunset,* 1.4 million.

For comparative purposes, here are the circulations of several other popular magazines: *Sports Illustrated,* 3.6 million; *People* and *Playboy,* about 3.4 million each; *Field & Stream,* 2 million; *Rolling Stone,* 1.2 million, *Weight Watchers,* 1 million, and *PC Magazine,* 1 million.

THE ELECTRONIC MEDIA

Three otherwise unrelated events in 1992 and 1993 will provide fodder for future analysts of United States journalism as they consider what watershed developments signaled new eras in the nation's media.

- Print media reporters and columnists found themselves on the outside, looking and listening in as talk shows—talk shows of all things!—were considered significant in the election of President Bill Clinton in 1992. An appearance with Larry King was coveted more than editorial endorsements from the nation's influential newspapers. The talk shows and broadcast appearances were also central to the third-party candidacy of H. Ross Perot.
- The nation's largest cable television company, TCI (Tele-Communications Inc.), and Bell Atlantic Corp.—one of the seven RBOCs—announced plans for a merger worth about $26 billion. The communications Goliath resulting from such a merger would own wires into 59 of the nation's top 100 markets along with perhaps unmatched programming resources.
- Heretofore upstart Fox Network outbid CBS for the television rights to the games of the National Football Conference of the National Football League, with the bid exceeding $1 billion.

Each of the developments illustrates the high stakes in the communications industry and the new alliances that will shape the nature of the media in the twenty-first century. And each suggests that the influence of the broadcast media will not be lessened.

Radio

Radio is the most familiar, the most personal, of the U.S. media. It accompanies the listener in the car, in the office, in the bedroom, in the bathroom, in an airplane, on the beach—literally, almost everywhere. There are an estimated 558 million radio sets in the nation, more than two for each single citizen. About 356 million radio receivers, 64 percent, are in some 94.4 million homes of the radio audience.

On more than half a billion radios, listeners can tune into more than 11,000 stations: about 5,000 commercial AM stations, 4,750 commercial FM stations—which began developing in the 1960s—and 1,570 public or noncommercial stations. FM stations draw about 70 percent of the radio audience.

Stations in Arbitron's MSA markets serve audiences as large as New York City with a population of more than 14 million people over the age of 12 to one as small as 263rd in market size, Minot, North Dakota, with 45,600.

There are different opinions as to what the first radio station was. KDKA of Pittsburgh often is cited because it signed on air on November 2, 1920, to broadcast news of President Harding's election. But the *Detroit News* had an experimental station on the air in August of that year, and its WWJ was licensed in October 1921. A Westinghouse engineer, Dr. Frank Conrad, did some experimental broadcasting in October 1919. Emery and Emery (1992) note that Charles David Herrold opened a broadcasting school in 1909 in San Jose, California, and he and his wife, Sybil, had a regularly scheduled, weekly news and music program. Their station eventually became KCBS in San Francisco.

The 1930s and the 1940s were part of the "Golden Age" of radio, offering network entertainment programming, soap operas, adventure serials, news, and coverage of sports events. But media analysts suggest radio may have been hit the hardest by the coming of television and that it took at least two decades after the early 1950s for the radio industry to find a new niche—one in which the medium changed from seeking a mass audience to seeking specialized audiences by offering narrow formats in music and news, supplemented by network programming. Of the 46 different types of formats defined by the radio industry, more stations program "Country" than any other.

Television

Of the various media, ownership of a television station most commonly is characterized as "having a license to print money."

More than 1,100 commercial licenses are granted by the FCC. There are about 560 commercial very high-frequency (VHF) TV stations in the nation. VHF stations broadcast over channels 2–13. There are about 590 commercial ultra-high-frequency (UHF) stations on channels 14–82. Viewers can also choose from among some 125 noncommercial VHFs and 237 noncommercial UHFs. More than 400 commercial stations operate as independents, not affiliated with any of the three major networks.

While television is not as pervasive as radio, it certainly penetrates more U.S. households than the print media do, and it consumes more time, too. Television sets are found in 98 percent of all U.S. residences, and 65 percent of those homes and apartments have more than one set. In almost all of the TV homes, perhaps more than 98 percent, there is a color TV. Not only that, but about 80 percent are equipped with video cassette recorders, and more than 60 percent are linked with a cable system. Research by the A.C. Nielson Company suggests that the TV is on, and probably being viewed, seven hours a day in the typical U.S. home.

Of the 209 ADI (Area of Dominant Influence) markets where viewership was surveyed in 1992–1993 by the Arbitron rating service, the largest was New York City, with 6.8 million television households; the smallest, Alpena, Michigan, with 15,600 households.

The amount of attention paid and influence ascribed to television make the medium a frequent target of accusations about the harmful impacts of TV on U.S. society. Consequently, the industry is subject to considerable government regulation of broadcast content, especially regarding advertising and concerns about the effects of TV on children. Television suffers more critical abuse than do other media for catering to the lowest common denominator of the audience in quest of high ratings and lucrative advertising. Local television news typically is criticized for insipid "happy talk," for shallow or nonexistent coverage of public affairs and for focus on fires, accidents, and crime because of the visual impact such coverage often provides. But such news programs are profit centers for local television stations.

One answer to such programming concerns has been the development of public and noncommerical television stations, with public or governmental control present in individual stations or limited networks rather than owning and operating almost all of the broadcasting services, as is the case in some countries. Not all noncommercial stations are "public," however. Many are low-powered television stations, serving limited areas or limited audiences with religious, ethnic, or similarly specialized programming. There also are about 95 college, university, or school-owned television stations.

KUHT in Houston was the first educational TV station to go on the air; that was in 1953. In 1955, the first statewide educational TV network was established in Alabama. Seven years later, federal legislation provided funds to the Department of Health, Education, and Welfare to provide matching grants to build educational stations; a 1967 law extended the support to radio stations.

The federally funded Public Broadcasting System and the Corporation for Public Broadcasting also support the noncommercial and educational stations, as do many private foundations and, occasionally, commercial sponsors, who do so with only name recognition and no advertising time.

Despite the continuing concerns over the quality of television program, the top-ranked programs over the years have been such highly thought of productions as "60 Minutes," the CBS news show, and well-crafted comedies, mysteries, and other entertainment and adventure programming.

Cable

A truism in the development of U.S. journalism may be that the younger a medium or service is the more change it has undergone—testimony to the rapidity of change in the media. Cable TV is a good example of this.

Developed as community antenna television (CATV), a way to improve television reception in hilly areas of the nation, cable systems have developed into major players in television access and programming. Conceived as a way to bring television to a relative handful of communities that could not receive direct, over-the-air signals, cable television now reaches into more than 60 percent of American homes and all of the major television markets.

While cable technology may have to compete with satellite transmissions direct to homes, the merger of Warner cable with Time, Inc.—and similar mergers in the embryonic stage in 1994—suggests that the cable companies will adjust to changes in technology as newspapers, magazines, radio, and now television have done before them.

News Services

The Associated Press (AP) is the dominant news service in the United States. The news and features that the AP provides to newspapers and broadcast stations often are supplemented by those media with information from smaller news and features syndicates, such as those provided by the *Los Angeles Times, Washington Post, New York Times,* and from chains such as Gannett and Knight Ridder.

United Press International (UPI) no longer is a strong competitor and, judging from commentary in trade journals, may not survive the 1990s. UPI was formed in 1958 by a merger of two of the AP's competitors—United Press, founded by the Scripps Newspapers, and International News Service, founded by the Hearst Newspapers.

The AP is a membership cooperative; while newspapers and broadcast stations pay for the information they receive from the AP, they also are members of the AP, co-owners with other media around the world, who, as part of the membership, agree that information they gather can be shared with others. The AP has its roots in news coverage of the Mexican-American war in 1848 and the use of the telegraph to transmit news to New York papers. The AP grew out of the New York Associated Press.

Its creation led, in considerable degree, to the ethic of objective news reporting because a wire service seeking to provide news to as many customers as possible need to be sure that the news reports are free of political or partisan bias.

The AP serves more than 1,700 daily and weekly newspapers in the United States, and about 6,000 radio and television stations receive AP news reports. Internationally, the wire service has 8,500 customers in 110 countries.

ADVERTISING

The idiom about "biting the hand that feeds you" is an apt one to describe the attitude toward advertising in American culture. Surely, advertising pays most of the bills for the information and entertainment that Americans consume; surely, advertising provides a good measure of the independence that American journalists enjoy—what people pay to get a newspaper, subscription or circulation revenue, amounts to about 10 percent of the revenue of most papers. Almost all of the rest comes from advertising.

Surely, advertising provides information that many American consumers need and value just as much, if not more, than they do scores of sporting events or even outcomes of many elections. Surely, the nature of a free enterprise, capitalist economy mandates a creative and responsible advertising industry—an industry that most agree does a good job on self-regulation when it comes to deceptive or misleading ads.

Nevertheless, the advertising industry is under assault daily for misdeeds and effects that include distorting American values, encouraging destructive behavior—such as cigarette smoking and alcohol consumption—influencing the content of the news media, and reducing, if not eliminating, the quality of broadcast programming to increase audience size. Because of such concerns, commercial speech—speech that proposes a commercial transaction—has limited First Amendment protection. Misleading and deceptive commercial speech is illegal. (Misleading and deceptive political speech generally is not). And government can regulate the content of accurate commercial speech about legal products if that regulation addresses a significant public interest and would advance that public interest a least restrictive way.

What drives all these pluses and minuses, of course, is money. In 1994, annual advertising revenue for the late-night talk shows of David Letterman and Jay Leno exceeded $100 million for each of their shows. A 30-second television spot for the professional football Super Bowl likely will cost more than $1 million by the middle or late 1990s; it was $900,000 for 1994.

Some facts and figures from the bigger picture:

Media advertising in 1992 topped $131 billion dollars. Daily newspapers accounted for about $30 billion or (23 percent of the total), television about $29 billion (22 percent), radio $8.7 billion (6.6 percent), and magazines about $7 billion (5.2 percent). Direct mail at $25 billion (19 percent) and the Yellow Pages at about $9.3 billion (7 percent) round out the major purveyors of advertising.

These figures include classified advertising, which constitutes about one-third of newspaper advertising revenue. In nonclassified advertising, television leads the field by far in revenue.

To keep its market shares, the news media must adjust to sophisticated marketing techniques. Historically, advertisements in the news and entertainment media have been aimed at an amorphous mass audience—speaking to millions of people to reach the hundreds or thousands who are interested in listening. Computer-driven information systems now allow advertisers to target their ads to specific audiences, married women, 25 to 35, with household incomes in excess of $25,000, for example. With the development of data bases that can sort out such specialized markets, advertisers have less value for a newspaper that can guarantee delivery of an advertisement to each of its, say, 100,000 subscribers. If an advertiser's market is primarily the women mentioned, much of the advertising dollar may be considered wasted if it is spent on delivering the message to thousands of people not in that market. Increasingly, advertisers want assurance that their messages are being sent to target audiences and even that their messages are being received.

Reflecting these concerns, the National Newspaper Association of America reported that in 1993, 81 percent of daily newspapers had programs in which they delivered advertisements to nonsubscribers, 40 percent of them had increased their ability to target advertisers' messages, and 25 percent more planned to increase target marketing. Three-fourths of the papers had developed a nonsubscriber data base; almost all already had a subscriber data base.

Newspaper and broadcast discussions about advertising revenues, even in the face of optimistic projections, are marked by concerns about how the deregulation of telephone companies might allow them to expand beyond the Yellow Pages and compete more aggressively for the advertising dollar that the traditional media have routinely assumed was theirs.

DIVERSITY

"In San Jose [California] bearers of the Vietnamese surname Nguyen [pronounced Win] outnumber the Joneses in the telephone directory fourteen columns to eight" (Christians et al. 1993).

Perhaps no element of U.S. journalism has either grown as much or become more visible in between editions of *Global Journalism* as has the presence of a thriving minority or ethnic media.

Long-time standard bearers continue to be recognized—*Jet* and *Ebony* magazines with circulations of 2 million and 1 million and newspapers such as the Chicago *Daily Defender* (31,000 daily) and the *New York Amsterdam News,* (31,000 weekly).

Hispanic newspapers and broadcast programming are found across the nation, not only in the southwest or southeast. While it is obvious that the *Miami Herald* would have Spanish-language editions, it is also becoming apparent that there is demand for such reporting elsewhere. A weekly in Iowa, The *Perry Chief,* has reports in Spanish to serve its Hispanic community, and the *Des Moines Register* coverage of the flood of 1993 included news reports in Spanish and Vietnamese.

Media directories list ethnic newspapers printed in 42 languages, from A (Albanian) to Y (Yugoslavian) if not A to Z. Of those, 63 are Hispanic, 42 Jewish, 13 Polish, 10 Lithuanian, and 10 Japanese. Directories, too, list some 200 black newspapers and some 70 black magazines; some 200 Hispanic publications, more than 100 Jewish publications, and several hundred serving a wide range of other religious communities.

Themes and trends of the growing diversity of U.S. journalism include at least the following:

- Diversity within diversity: The black, Hispanic, Vietnamese, and other communities are not monolithic. The nature of publications and broadcast stations serving minority groups defies stereotypes and reflects dynamic and diverse audiences. A quick sampling of black magazines, for example, finds not only *Jet* and *Ebony,* but *YSB* (a teen magazine for Young Brothers and Sisters), *Heart & Soul* (health issues), *American Visions* (arts and literature), and *The Best of Rap* and *R&B,* among dozens of others.

- Wealth within diversity: The growth of diverse media reflects relative gains in minority incomes, much as the development of a working class in the 1830s, the emergence of the middle class in the post–Civil War years, and the waves of immigrants in the early 1900s provided markets and audiences for the news media of their day. Improvements in the economic status of minority groups can both lure attention from the long-established media as well as found and support new minority media.

- Diversity within the "mainstream": Ideally, if more women and minority are hired as journalists, the nation's media ranks will more closely reflect the nature of U.S. society, and media content will better reflect the interests and aspirations of all citizens. In 1960, women constituted about 20 percent of the 325,000 persons employed by newspapers; in 1992, they made up about 45 percent of the 453,000 employees. Minority group members make up about 11 percent of the newsroom employees in the nation's newspapers and about 18 percent of total newspaper employment. A 1993 survey by the American Society of Newspaper Editors (ASNE) reported that 24 percent of all first-time newsroom hires were minority group members as were 39 percent of newsroom interns ("Newsroom Minorities" 1993). Information from the Radio Television News Director Association (RTNDA) indicates that women make up about a third of TV news staffs, and minorities make up about 17 percent. In radio news, minorities made up about 12 percent of the news staffs. Newspaper employment of women and minorities has been increasing bit by bit over the years; broadcast employment, however, has been about the same for more than a decade.

• People within diversity: The history of the minority media, like the history of the established media, is a history of people—of John Russwurm and the Rev. Samuel Cornish who founded *Freedom's Journal,* in 1827; of Frederick Douglass, whose friends in England raised money to buy his freedom and help him found the *North Star* in 1847; of Samuel Ringgold Ward, a son of slave parents, who fled the South to found the *True American* and the *Impartial Citizen* in Syracuse, New York, in the late 1840s, and the *Provincial Freeman* in Canada in the 1850s; of Ida B. Wells-Barnett, the first prominent black woman editor who campaigned against lynching as editor of the Memphis, Tennessee, *Free Speech* and, who until her death in 1931, continued civil rights efforts on behalf of blacks and women in the *New York Age* and Chicago's *Conservator;* of Bob Maynard, perhaps the most highly regarded black editor of the latter part of the twentieth century, the publisher and editor of the *Oakland Tribune,* who died of cancer in 1993.

EDUCATION AND TRAINING FOR JOURNALISTS

At the undergraduate level, about 415 colleges and universities award degrees in the field of journalism and mass communication. Of those schools, about a fourth, 95, satisfy the accreditation standards of the Accrediting Council on Education in Journalism and Mass Communication (AEJMC) AEJMC has a dozen accrediting standards on such things as curriculum, placement, faculty, and affirmative action, which a journalism program must address to receive accreditation.

The roots of such educational programs are many. Confederate General Robert E. Lee helped start journalism education in post-Civil War America. Better journalism, he thought, would facilitate nonviolent solutions to social and political problems. Consequently, one of the earliest journalism programs was at what became Washington and Lee University in Lexington, Virginia. Other roots of journalism education are in the Columbia University Graduate School of Journalism, founded in 1912 with support from Joseph Pulitzer, and in the University of Missouri School of Journalism, established four years before Columbia.

Some 133,000 undergraduates were enrolled in journalism/mass communication undergraduate programs in the early 1990s, almost 10,000 in master's degree programs and a thousand in doctoral programs. At the undergraduate level, the students are spread fairly evenly across a number of majors with each of these claiming 12 to 14 percent of the total enrollment: advertising, newspaper reporting and editing, public relations, and radio-television. Broadcast News had about 11 percent of the majors, and general journalism 10 percent. Contrary to conventional wisdom, growth in journalism education enrollments preceded the Watergate chapter in journalism history, and growth after Watergate came in such areas as advertising and public relations, not in news reporting.

In addition to preparing many students for careers in mass communication, as a rule, journalism education programs are the only place in U.S. secondary or higher education where students find heavy emphasis on good writing and First Amendment issues—curricular areas central to an informed and active democracy.

Continuing education opportunities for American journalists range from such outstanding programs as Nieman Fellows at Harvard and grants for study at Stanford University to workshops and seminars sponsored by the ASNE, RTNDA, the Associated Press Managing Editors, and the newspaper and broadcast associations in each state. Highly regarded programs also are offered by the American Press Institute in Reston, Virginia, the Freedom Forum at Vanderbilt University and in Arlington, Virginia, and the Poynter Institute in St. Petersburg, Florida, linked with the *St. Petersburg Times* (358,000), another of the nation's outstanding newspapers.

THE NORTH AMERICAN FUTURE?

This chapter began by arguing against the notion of a "North American media system," suggesting instead that two systems have emerged in response to different historical, legal, political, and cultural developments in Canada and the United States. The chapter ends by suggesting that this may indeed be the case, but not for long.

The very title of this text, *Global Journalism*—originally intended to describe the nature of varied journalism practices around the world—in future editions may describe the varied participants in a global information system. If regions around the world cannot resist the unifying pressures of many new technologies, multinational corporations, transborder information flow, the economic realities of the media world, and so on, it seems unlikely that friendly, symbiotic nations like the United States and Canada can long withstand those pressures either.

Indeed, some research suggests that in the early 1990s, Canada and the United States were the only two information societies in the world (Dordick 1993). (Japan fell short because it did not satisfy one of the researchers' criteria—that an information society should have at least half of its college-age population enrolled in higher education.)

Such joint-status suggests that Canada and the United States continue to travel similar roads in economic and technological development. And the "road" analogy may be an apt one. For just as south-bound highways and railroad tracks out of Canada and north-bound ones out of the United States do not abruptly end at the border, neither will the telephone lines and the fiber optic networks.

The existence and development of two separate media systems can, to some degree, help ensure the maintenance of a Canadian identity. But the separate systems will become more interdependent. Market and technological developments will ensure that outcome. The telephone companies will be major players in the mass media and information systems.

As recently as the 1970s, one could distinguish rather easily between print and broadcast media and between those two and public utilities, such as the telephone companies. But those lines have been blurred by the information age and by technology that sends newspaper material over cable television, has cable television companies merging with telephone companies, has telephone companies interested in producing television programs, and has television supplanting newspapers as the major source of news for many citizens. What seems likely is that what historically have been called media systems will remain to a considerable degree, serving many of their longtime constituencies. But information networks will continue to develop as North Americans begin to realize what terms such as *interactive media* and *convergence of media* mean to their daily lives. Increasing ease of interpersonal communication and related commerce across international boundaries and related commerce will ensure a new North American media/information system.

BIBLIOGRAPHY

Barnouw, Erik. *A History of Broadcasting in the United States. Vol. 1. A Tower of Babel (to 1933)*. New York: Oxford University Press, 1966.
———. *A History of Broadcasting in the United States. Vol. 2. The Golden Web (1933-53)*. New York: Oxford University Press, 1968.
———. *A History of Broadcasting in the United States. Vol. 3. The Image Empire (from 1953)*. New York: Oxford University Press, 1970.
Beasley, Maurine, and Sheila Silver. *Women in Media: a Documentary Source Book*. Washington, D.C.: Women's Institute for Freedom of Press, 1977.
Beattie, Earl, "In Canada's Centennial Year, U.S. Mass Media Influence Probed."*Journalism Quarterly* 44, no. 4 (winter 1967): 667-672.
Broadcasting Yearbook 1993. Washington, D.C.: R.R. Bowker, 1993.
Brown, Shelley, "CP Under Siege." *Content* (January/February 1992): 16-19.
Canada: A Portrait. Ottawa: Minister of Supply and Services, 1992.
Canada, Communications Division. *Canada Year Book 1994*. Ottawa: Statistics Canada, 1993.
Chafee, Zechariah, Jr. *Government and Mass Communication*. Chicago: University of Chicago Press, 1947.
Christians, Clifford G., John P. Ferre, and P. Mark Fackler. *Good News, Social Ethics & the Press*. New York: Oxford University Press, 1993.
Commission on Freedom of the Press. *A Free and Responsible Press*. Chicago: University of Chicago Press, 1947.
Dennis, Everette E., and William L. Rivers. *Other Voices: The New Journalism in America*. San Francisco: Canfield, 1974.
Desbarats, Peter. *Guide to Canadian News Media*. Toronto: Harcourt Brace Jovanovich, Canada, 1990.
Dordick, Herbert S., and Georgette Wang. *The Information Society: A Retrospective View*. Newbury Park, Calif.: Sage Publications, 1993.
Douglass, Frederick. *My Bondage and My Freedom*. Chicago: Johnson Publishing, 1970.
Editor and Publisher International Yearbook, 1993. New York, 1993.
Ellis, David. *Split Screen*. Toronto: Friends of Canadian Broadcasting, 1993.
Emery, Michael, and Edwin Emery. *The Press and America: An Interpretive History of the Mass Media*. 7th Edition. Englewood Cliffs, N.J.: Prentice-Hall, 1992.
Ferguson, Marjorie. "Invisible Divides: Communication and Identity in Canada and the U.S."*Journal of Communication* 43, no. 2 (1993): 42-57.
Franklin, Benjamin. *The Autobiography of Benjamin Franklin*. Edited by Leonard W. Labaree.

New Haven, Conn.: Yale University Press, 1964.

Gans, Herbert J. *Deciding What's News: A Study of CBS Evening News, NBC Nightly News, Newsweek and Time.* New York: Vintage, 1979.

Halberstam, David. *The Powers that Be.* New York: Knopf, 1979.

Head, Sydney W., and Christopher Sterling. *Broadcasting in America.* 5th Edition. Boston: Houghton Mifflin, 1987.

Holmes, Helen, and David Taras. *Seeing Ourselves: Media Power and Policy in Canada.* Toronto: Harcourt Brace Jovanovich, Canada, 1992.

Innis, Harold A. *The Bias of Communication.* Toronto: University of Toronto Press, 1951.

Jonas, Hans. *The Imperative of Responsibility: In Search of an Ethics for the Technological Age.* Chicago: University of Chicago Press, 1984.

Kesterton, W.H. *A History of Journalism in Canada.* Toronto: McClelland and Stewart, 1967.

Leonard, Thomas C. *The Power of the Press: The Birth of American Political Reporting.* New York: Oxford University Press, 1986.

Levy, Leonard W. *Emergence of a Free Press.* New York: Oxford University Press, 1985.

Luce, Henry R. "The American Century." *Life,* 17 February 1941, 61–65.

Martin, Robert, and G. Stuart Adam. *A Sourcebook of Canadian Media Law.* Rev. Ed. Ottawa: Carleton University Press, 1991.

Marzolf, Marion. *Up from the Footnote: A History of Women Journalists.* New York: Hastings House, 1977.

Merrill, John C. *The Dialectic in Journalism: Toward a Responsible Use of Press Freedom.* Baton Rouge: Louisiana State University Press, 1989.

Miller, Sally M., Editor. *The Ethnic Press in the United States: A Historical Analysis and Handbook.* Westport, Conn.: Greenwood Press, 1987.

Mott, Frank Luther. *American Journalism: A History, 1690–1960.* New York: Macmillan, 1962.

Murphy, James E., and Sharon M. Murphy. *Let My People Know: American Indian Journalism 1828–1978.* Norman: University of Oklahoma Press, 1981.

National Newspaper Association. Personal Interview.

Near v. Minnesota, 281 U.S. 697 (1931).

"Newsroom Minorities Top 10 Percent, ASNE 1993 Survey Shows." News release from ASNE, American Society of Newspaper Editors. Reston, Va., 30 March 1993.

New York Times Co. v. Sullivan, 376 U.S. 254 (1964).

New York Times Co. v. United States, 713 U.S. 403 (1971).

Park, Robert. "The Natural History of the Newspaper." *American Journal of Sociology* 39, no. 3 (1923).

Peterson, Theodore. *Magazines in the Twentieth Century.* Urbana: University of Illinois Press, 1964.

Pollard, James E. *The Presidents and the Press.* New York: Macmillan, 1947.

Raboy, Marc. *Les Média Québécois: Presse, Radio, Télévision, Câblodistribution.* Boucherville, Québec: Gaetan Morin Éditeur, 1992.

Romanow, Walter I., and Walter C. Soderlund. *Media Canada.* Mississauga, Ontario: Copp Clark Pitman, 1992.

Rotzell, Kim B., James E. Haefner, and Charles H. Sandage. *Advertising in Contemporary Society.* Columbus, Ohio: Grid, 1976.

Schudson, Michael. *Advertising: The Uneasy Persuasion.* New York: Basic Books, 1984.

Siebert, Fredrick Seaton. *Freedom of the Press in England, 1476–1776.* Urbana: University of Illinois Press, 1952.

Siebert, Fred S., Theodore Peterson, and Wilbur Schramm. *Four Theories of the Press.* Urbana: University of Illinois Press, 1956.

Singer, Benjamin D. *Communications in Canadian Society.* Scarborough, Ontario: Nelson Canada, 1991.

Smith, Anthony. *Goodbye Gutenberg: The Newspaper Revolution of the 1980s.* New York: Oxford University Press, 1980.

Smith, Jeffery A. *Printers and Press Freedom: The Ideology of Early American Journalism.* New York: Oxford University Press, 1988.

Steffens, Lincoln. *The Autobiography of Lincoln Steffens.* New York: Harcourt Brace Jovanovich, 1931.

Stephens, Mitchell. *History of News from the Drum to the Satellite.* New York: Viking, 1988.

Stone, I.F. *In a Time of Torment.* New York: Vintage, 1964.

Swanberg, W.A. *Citizen Hearst.* New York: Scribner's, 1961.

———. *Luce and His Empire.* New York: Scribner's, 1972.

———. *Pulitzer.* New York: Scribner's, 1967.

Taras, David. *The Newsmakers: The Media's Influence on Canadian Politics.* Scarborough, Ontario: Nelson Canada, 1990.

Thomas, Isaiah. *History of Printing in America,* vols. 1, 2. Worcester, Mass.: Isaiah Thomas, Jr. (first printing), 1810; Albany, N.Y.: Joel Munsell, 1874.

Thomas, Lowell. *Good Evening Everybody.* New York: Morrow, 1976.

Weaver, David A., and G. Cleveland Wilhoit. *The American Journalist: A Portrait of U.S. News People and Their Work.* Bloomington: Indiana University Press, 1986.

Wells-Barnett, Ida B. *Crusade for Justice.* Chicago: University of Chicago Press, 1970.

Wolseley, Ronald E. *The Black Press, U.S.A.* Ames: Iowa State University Press, 1990.

About the Contributors

Bob J. Carrell (Global Advertising and Public Relations) is a professor emeritus of the University of Oklahoma, where for 12 years he was director of the School of Journalism and Mass Communication. Since retirement from OU, he has been a visiting professor at The University of Texas Pan America's School of Business and at Texas Women's University in the Mass Communications Program. Carrell was a Fulbright lecturer in India attached to the journalism faculty at Osmania University. He has conducted workshops in India, Singapore, and South Africa. Carrell is the co-author (with Doug Newsom) of *Public Relations Writing* and the author of an advertising principles workbook. He also works as a communications consultant. Before going into education, Carrell spent 8 years with newspapers, mostly in advertising sales and management. Carrell's doctoral degree in mass communication is from the University of Illinois, and his bachelors and master's degrees are from East Texas State University.

Anju Grover Chaudhary (Asia and the Pacific) is an Associate Professor in the Department of Journalism at Howard University, Washington, D.C., where she teaches courses in comparative journalism and news reporting and writing. She has been a freelance writer and editor, was an editorial assistant of *Design* magazine in India, and worked at the *Washington Star* as a copy editor. Chaudhary is the co-editor of *Comparative Mass Media Systems* and author of several articles that have appeared in *Journalism Quarterly, Gazette, World Communication, Media Asia,* and *International Philosophical Quarterly,* among other journals. She holds a doctorate in Public Communications from the University of Maryland and holds two masters degrees, in journalism and in history. She is a member of the society of Professional Journalists and the Association for Education in Journalism and is listed in *International Who's Who in Education* and the *Outstanding College Students of America.*

Anne Cooper Chen (Asia and the Pacific), Associate Professor in the E.W. Scripps School of Journalism at Ohio University, heads the school's Foreign Correspondence Internship Program. She earned a bachelor of arts in English from Vassar College, a master's in Japanese studies from the University of Michigan, a master's in mass communication from Virginia Commonwealth University, and a doctorate from the University of North Carolina at Chapel Hill. During more than a decade of professional experience, Cooper Chen has worked for the *Asahi Evening News,* an English-language daily in Tokyo; for a Japanese book publisher; and for several publications in the United States. She is coauthor of *Idols, Victims, Pioneers: Virginia's Women from 1607* and has been listed in *Outstanding Young Women of America* and *Who's Who in American Women.* In the 1970s, she received several writing awards from Sigma Delta Chi and the National Federation of Press Women.

Arnold S. de Beer (Sub-Saharan Africa), who has a master's from Rand Afrikaans, a master's in journalism from Baylor, and a doctorate from Potchesfstroom, is Professor and Head of the Department of Communication, as well as Director of the Institute for Commercial Research at Potchefstroom University, South Africa. He is the founder-editor of *Ecquid Novi,* the South African research journal for journalism, and serves on the editorial boards of *Communication* and *Communicare.* He has published nationally and internationally (e.g., on media policy and news analysis, professionalism and journalism, and the mass media in South Africa) and has on several occasions read papers and lectured in Europe, Asia, and in the United States. He co-authored a number of books and is editor of the standard handbook, *Mass Media for the 90's, the South African Handbook of Mass Communication* (1993). He is a member of the executive committee of the SABC Board and the executive committee of the South African Press Council. He is a Fellow of the South African Academy of Arts and Sciences and is a former President of the South African Communication Association. Formerly a journalist (*Die Transvaler* and *Die Burger*), and editor *of Ensiklopedie van die Wereld,* he freelanced for the SABC's *Monitor* program in Europe, the United States, Asia, and the Middle East.

Leonardo Ferreira (Latin America and the Caribbean) is an Assistant Professor in the School of Communication, University of Miami. Ferreira is a professor specializing in mass media policy and international communications, particularly in U.S.–Latin American issues. His publications in both English and Spanish have dealt with electronic media systems and regulatory structures in the Americas. He has also recently served as a communication consultant for UNICEF and has assisted several private regional organizations in broadcast, common carrier, and copyright law. While at Michigan State University, he received an Excellence-in-Teaching Award. Ferreira received his doctorate in jurisprudence from Universidad Nacional de Colombia. He holds a master's and doctorate from Michigan State University.

Tim Gallimore (Barriers to Media Development) is assistant professor in the School of Journalism at the University of Missouri-Columbia, where he teaches courses in international communication, freedom of information, and news writing. He earned a doctorate in mass communications from Indiana University. Gallimore conducts research and writes on international communication, communication policy, and First Amendment theory. Several recent journal articles and chapters have been published in *Gazette, Media Development,* and *In the Camera's Eye: News Coverage of Terrorist Events.* He has lectured and conducted training workshops for journalists in Eastern Europe and Africa under the Fulbright-Hays and U.S. Information Agency programs. He is a member of the Commission on the Status of Minorities and the Association for Education in Journalism and Mass Communication.

Paul Grosswiler (Continuing Media Controversies) is an assistant professor of journalism and mass communication at the University of Maine in Orono. His research interests include the political economy of mass communication and cross-cultural mass communication. He has conducted media research in Tanzania. Grosswiler teaches courses in international mass communication, history of mass communication, alternative mass communication, editorial and opinion writing, news reporting, and editing. He received his doctorate and master's in journalism from the University of Missouri and his bachelor of arts from Antioch College.

Owen V. Johnson (East Central and Southeastern Europe, Russia, and the Newly Independent States) is director of the Indiana University Russian and East European Institute and a member of the faculty of the School of Journalism. He is the author of *Slovakia 1918-1938: Education and the Making of a Nation.* His articles have appeared in *Journalism Quarterly, Journalism History, Studies in East European Social History,* and in other journals and books. His professional journalism has been published in the *Christian Science Monitor* and broadcast on National Public Radio's "All Things Considered." He has served as president of the Slovak Studies Association, editor of *Czech Marks* (the newsletter of the Czechoslovak History Conference), and head of the History Division of the Association for Education in Journalism and Mass Communication. He is a recipient of the Stanley Pech Award for outstanding scholarship on Czechoslovak history.

Francis P. Kasoma (Sub-Saharan Africa), has a bachelors from Zambia, a master's from Oregon, a licentiate in social sciences from Tampere, and is Associate Professor and Head of the Department of Mass Communication, University of Zambia, Zambia. He is author of the following books: *The Press in Zambia, Communication Policies in Zambia,* and *Communication Policies in Botswana, Lesotho and Swaziland.* He was a journalist for the *Times of Zambia* (1969-1977) and for the *Tanzania Standard.* His special interest areas include media ethics (for which he has edited a forthcoming book: *Journalism Ethics in Africa*), media law, and development communication. Kasoma was President of the African Council for Communication Education, 1986-1988.

Vernon Keel (North America) is professor and founding director of the Elliott School of Communication at Wichita State University. Before that, he was chair of journalism and later director of the School of Communication at the University of North Dakota, where he served as chair of the Canadian Studies Coordinating Program. He holds a doctorate in mass communication from the University of Minnesota. He has served as head of the International Communication Division of the Association for Education in Journalism and Mass Communication and as president of the Association of Schools of Journalism and Mass Communications.

Dean Kruckeberg (International Journalism Ethics) is coordinator of the public relations degree program and associate professor in the Department of Communication Studies at the University of Northern Iowa, Cedar Falls. He has taught at the University of Minnesota St. Paul, at the University of Iowa, and at Northwest Missouri State University. He has also had over a decade of professional experience in journalism and public relations. Kruckeberg is a fellow of the Public Relations Society of America and is Midwest District Chair of that professional association. He is former National Faculty Advisor to the Public Relations Student Society of America and former advisor to *Forum,* the national newspaper of the PRSSA and is former head of the Public Relations Division of the Association for Education in Journalism and Mass Communication. He is coauthor of the book *Public Relations and Community: A Reconstructed Theory* and of several book chapters, articles, and papers dealing with international public relations and international public relations ethics. He holds master's in journalism from Northern Illinois University and a doctorate in mass communications from the University of Iowa.

Edmund B. Lambeth (Global Media Philosphies), a former president of the Association of Schools of Journalism and Mass Communication, is professor and chair of the International Committee at the University of Missouri School of Journalism. A former Washington correspondent, Nieman Fellow, and Congressional Fellow, he originated and since 1984 has directed the National Workshop on the Teaching of Ethics in Journalism. He has lectured and consulted on journalism in Brazil, the Czech Republic, Hong Kong, the Netherlands, Slovakia, Spain, and Taiwan. The author of *Committed Journalism* (Indiana University Press, 2nd Ed.), his articles have appeared in numerous scholarly and professional journals.

Aralynn Abare McMane (Western Europe) is a maitre de conferenc associe at the Centre de Formation des Journalistes journalism school in Paris with which she has been associated since 1987. She founded the Paris Reporting Project, a study-abroad program, while an assistant professor at the University of South Carolina. After several years at U.S. newspapers, she worked in Western Europe as an editor at the International Herald Tribune and in Central Europe as an editing and technology consultant. She has published on comparative journalistic values in scholarly journals in both the United States and Europe, where she continues her research on new communications technologies. Her doctorate is from Indiana University.

Eronini R. Megwa (Sub-Saharan Africa) has a bachelors from the University of Nigeria, a master's of science from Iowa State, a doctorate from Missouri-Columbia, and is Senior Lecturer and Head, Department of Journalism, Peninsula Technikon, Bellville, South Africa. Megwa taught mass communication at Howard University (1987–1991); University of Maryland (part-time, 1988–1990), Bowie State University (part-time, 1990–1991), and at the University of Swaziland (1991–1993), where he served as co-ordinator of Communication Studies. His recent publications include "Communication and Rural Development in Swaziland" in *Africa Media Review* and "Media Image and Development: Political and Economic Implications of U.S. Media Coverage of Africa" in *Development and Democratization* (edited by K.E. Bauzon). He served as reporter, editor, producer, newscaster, and acting head of the Current Affairs department for the Nigerian Television Authority, Channel 6 Aba (1978–1981).

John C. Merrill (editor) is Professor Emeritus at the School of Journalism University of Missouri-Columbia, where he has taught for twenty years. He still teaches graduate seminars at Missouri. He is the author and editor of more than twenty books. *A Handbook of the Foreign Press* in 1959 was the first textbook in English that compared the press systems of the world. Since then he has written six other books in international communication. He has taught at several universities in the United States and abroad and has conducted workshops and given lectures in some 80 countries. Most recently he was a distinguished visiting professor (1994) at the American University in Cairo. He holds two master's degrees (in journalism and in philosophy), and a doctorate in mass communications from the University of Iowa (1961).

Douglas Ann Newsom (Global Advertising and Public Relations) is a professor in Texas Christian University's Department of Journalism, where she has been teaching since 1969. Before that she was a full-time public relations practitioner and has continued working in the field. She has been a Fulbright lecturer in India, where she taught at Osmania University and conducted public relations workshops across the country for the Public Relations Society of India. Newsom has also conducted public relations workshops in Singapore, South Africa, and Bulgaria. She is the past head of the Public Relations Society of America's College of Fellows and has been president of the Association for Education in Journalism and Mass Communication. Newsom also is the co-author of three textbooks: *Media Writing* (with the late James Wollert), *This Is PR* (with Alan Scott and Judy VanSlyke Turk) and *Public Relations Writing* (with Bob Carrell). All four of her degrees, two bachelors, a master's and doctorate, are from The University of Texas at Austin.

Christine Ogan (Middle East and North Africa) is associate professor of journalism at Indiana University, where she teaches classes in international communication, communication and national development, communication technologies, reporting, and media management. She has lived and worked in Turkey and traveled in the Middle East. She has taught at North Carolina Central University; Hacettepe University and Ankara Koleji, both in Ankara, Turkey; and Ithaca College. Ogan conducts research and writes about the role of new technologies in the development process and has published several recent articles on international video in *Media Development, Journal of Broadcasting and Electronic Media, Journal of Communication,* and *Telecommunications Policy.* She is also the author of a chapter in the 1989 book *The VCR Age,* edited by Mark Levy, and a contributor to the last edition of Merrill's *Global Journalism.* She has served as head of the International Division of the Association for

Education in Journalism and Mass Communication and is presently vice head of the Intercultural/Development Communication Division of the International Communication Association. She holds a doctorate in mass communication research from the University of North Carolina at Chapel Hill.

Kuldip R. Rampal (The Collection and Flow of World News) is professor of mass communication at Central Missouri State University in Warrensburg. His research on development communication, press regulation, media ethics, international broadcasting, and international press has appeared in a variety of books and journals. He has traveled to five continents in connection with his research work. In recognition of his publications on Confucianism and press and political liberalization in Taiwan, the government of the Republic of China awarded him the 1993 International Communication Award. He is co-authoring a reference book on Afro mass media worldwide. Rampal was a visiting professor at the National University of Singapore during 1992–1993, where he also served as a part-time assistant news editor at the *Straits Times*. He holds a doctorate in journalism from the University of Missouri School of Journalism and a master's in journalism from Boston University. A native of India, he worked as a political correspondent for the *Indian Express* before coming to the United States.

M. Kent Sidel (Western Europe) is director of Electronic and Print Journalism at the University of South Carolina. He has served as a broadcast media consultant for the United States Information Agency in the Caribbean and Europe and has worked with the Agency for International Development on media projects. He was a Fulbright recipient in 1981. He has published on the transition of media systems and the evolution of media law in developing countries. His doctorate is from Northwestern University.

Gonzalo Soruco (Latin America and the Caribbean) is assistant professor of advertising and public relations at the University of Miami's School of Communication, where he teaches advertising principles, advertising research, and public opinion. His research has focused on minorities and the media, research methodology and minorities, public opinion, and the media in Latin America. Soruco earned his master's and doctorate from Indiana University.

Lowndes F. (Rick) Stephens (Media Systems: Overview) is associate dean for graduate students and research, College of Journalism and Mass Communications, University of South Carolina, where he was named one of the university's outstanding teachers in 1988. Stephens, who has served as head of two divisions (International, and Mass Communication and Society) of the Association for Education in Journalism and Mass Communication, has traveled extensively in Europe and Asia. His research— supported by the Rockefeller and Gannett foundations, the American Newspaper Publishers Association, the U.S. Office of Education, and the U.S. Department of Defense— has appeared in more than a dozen scholarly journals and in the *New York Times* and other major newspapers. He recently codirected a Gannett-sponsored News Media and Terrorism Project with Robert Picard of Emerson College. He appears in *Who's Who in America* and the *Directory of American Scholars*.

Robert L. Stevenson (Freedom of the Press Around the World) is William Rand Kenan Jr. Professor of Journalism and Mass Communication at the University of North Carolina at Chapel Hill. He has been a Fulbright Senior Scholar in Germany and assistant director of the American Journalism Center in Budapest. His books include *Global Communication in the 21st Century* (Longman, 1994), *Communication, Development, and The Third World* (Longman, 1988), and *Foreign News and the New World Information Order* (edited with Donald L. Shaw, Iowa State University Press, 1984).

Elanie Steyn (Sub-Saharan Africa) is a researcher and graduate student in the Institute for Communication Research, Potchefstroom University, Potchefstroom, South Africa. She is assistant editor of *Ecquid Novi.* She coauthored a chapter in *South African Media Policy-Debates of the 1990's,* edited by P. Eric Louw. She was a member of the South African team for an international research project involving 27 countries on the media coverage of the 1992 Olympic Games in Barcelona, and coauthor of a research paper on the same topic, "South African Media Coverage of the 1992 Olympic Games: Coming in from the Cold," read at the International Division, Association for Education in Journalism and Mass Communication in Kansas City, in 1993. She was coauthor of a paper, "Towards Defining News in the South Africa Context: The Media as Generator or Mediator of Conflict," read at the World Communication Association, Pretoria, 1993.

Herbert Strentz (North America) is a professor and director of graduate studies in the School of Journalism and Mass Communication at Drake University in Des Moines, Iowa. He teaches undergraduate courses in mass communication law and graduate seminars in information policy and in social responsibility. He also serves as executive secretary of the Iowa Freedom of Information Council and is on the board of the National FOI Coalition. He received his doctorate from Northwestern University, his master's from Syracuse University and his bachelor of arts from Fresno State College. He worked for several years as a newspaper and wire service reporter.

Index